Asset Management

FINANCIAL MANAGEMENT ASSOCIATION

Survey and Synthesis Series

Asset Pricing and Portfolio Choice Theory
Kerry E. Back

Beyond Greed and Fear: Understanding Behavioral Finance and the Psychology of Investing
Hersh Shefrin

Beyond the Random Walk: A Guide to Stock Market Anomalies and Low-Risk Investing
Vijay Singal

Debt Management: A Practitioner's Guide
John D. Finnerty and Douglas R. Emery

Dividend Policy: Its Impact on Firm Value
Ronald C. Lease, Kose John, Avner Kalay, Uri Loewenstein, and Oded H. Sarig

Efficient Asset Management: A Practical Guide to Stock Portfolio Optimization and Asset Allocation, 2nd Edition
Richard O. Michaud and Robert O. Michaud

Last Rights: Liquidating a Company
Dr. Ben S. Branch, Hugh M. Ray, Robin Russell

Managing Pension and Retirement Plans: A Guide for Employers, Administrators, and Other Fiduciaries
August J. Baker, Dennis E. Logue, and Jack S. Rader

Managing Pension Plans: A Comprehensive Guide to Improving Plan Performance
Dennis E. Logue and Jack S. Rader

Mortgage Valuation Models: Embedded Options, Risk, and Uncertainty
Andrew Davidson and Alex Levin

Real Estate Investment Trusts: Structure, Performance, and Investment Opportunities
Su Han Chan, John Erickson, and Ko Wang

Real Options: Managing Strategic Investment in an Uncertain World
Martha Amram and Nalin Kulatilaka

Real Options in Theory and Practice
Graeme Guthrie

Slapped by the Invisible Hand: The Panic of 2007
Gary B. Gorton

Survey Research in Corporate Finance: Bridging the Gap between Theory and Practice
H. Kent Baker, J. Clay Singleton, and E. Theodore Veit

The Financial Crisis of Our Time
Robert W. Kolb

The Search for Value: Measuring the Company's Cost of Capital
Michael C. Ehrhardt

Too Much Is Not Enough: Incentives in Executive Compensation
Robert W. Kolb

Trading and Exchanges: Market Microstructure for Practitioners
Larry Harris

Truth in Lending: Theory, History, and a Way Forward
Thomas A. Durkin and Gregory Elliehausen

Value Based Management with Corporate Social Responsibility, 2nd Edition
John D. Martin, J. William Petty, and James S. Wallace

Valuing the Closely Held Firm
Michael S. Long and Thomas A. Bryant

Working Capital Management
Lorenzo Preve and Virginia Sarria-Allende

Asset Management

A Systematic Approach to Factor Investing

ANDREW ANG

OXFORD
UNIVERSITY PRESS

OXFORD
UNIVERSITY PRESS

Oxford University Press is a department of the University of Oxford.
It furthers the University's objective of excellence in research, scholarship,
and education by publishing worldwide.

Oxford New York
Auckland Cape Town Dar es Salaam Hong Kong Karachi
Kuala Lumpur Madrid Melbourne Mexico City Nairobi
New Delhi Shanghai Taipei Toronto

With offices in
Argentina Austria Brazil Chile Czech Republic France Greece
Guatemala Hungary Italy Japan Poland Portugal Singapore
South Korea Switzerland Thailand Turkey Ukraine Vietnam

Oxford is a registered trade mark of Oxford University Press
in the UK and certain other countries.

Published in the United States of America by
Oxford University Press
198 Madison Avenue, New York, NY 10016

Library of Congress Cataloging-in-Publication Data
Ang, Andrew.
  Asset management : a systematic approach to factor investing / Andrew Ang.
    p.   cm. — (Financial Management Association survey and synthesis series)
  Includes bibliographical references and index.
  ISBN 978–0–19–995932–7 (alk. paper)
1. Asset-backed financing. 2. Capital assets pricing model. 3. Investments. I. Title.
  HG4028.A84A54 2014
  332.601—dc23
                                        2013042000

9 8 7 6 5 4

Printed in the United States of America on acid-free paper

To Jihong

CONTENTS

PREFACE

ASSET MANAGEMENT

The two most important words in investing are *bad times*.

That notion—that bad times are paramount—is the guiding principle of this book, and it is based on more than a half century of financial theory. I offer a systematic approach to the age-old problem of where do you put your money? My experience as a finance professor and an advisor to sovereign wealth funds, asset management firms, and other firms in the finance industry has led me to see that the narrow approach focusing only on asset classes (usually with mean-variance optimizers) is too crude, misses the economics of why assets earn returns, and is ultimately too costly to serve investors adequately. I focus instead on "factor risks," the sets of hard times that span asset classes, which must be the focus of our attention if we are to weather market turmoil and receive the rewards that come with doing so.

The essential problem is that asset owners—from a modest household to sovereign wealth funds entrusted with the savings of a nation—generally feel the pain of bad times much more acutely than they do the elation of good times. Different investors each have their own set of bad times defined by their liabilities, income streams, constraints and beliefs, and how they perceive and react to different kinds of risks. Bad times are more than just periods when your wealth has taken a hit: you can still be rich and encounter bad times if your consumption drops below what you are used to, or if your competitor generates a higher return than your portfolio. As investors move through their life cycles and as they dynamically invest over long horizons, their set of bad times can change. Optimal portfolio allocation involves taking into account an investor's bad times, and accepting the risks of these bad times in exchange for the compensation of factor premiums, which aren't available without taking risk. Holding diversified portfolios lessens the impact of bad times because there is a possibility that some assets will have high returns when the bad times hit. This describes Part I of the book.

In Part II, I show asset owners can earn risk premiums through exposure to factor risks. Periods of slowing economic growth, high or accelerating inflation, and
skyrocketing volatility are bad times for most people. Other factors are tradeable
investment styles like value-growth investing, momentum investing, and overweighting illiquid assets. Assets are bundles of factors, each of which defines a
set of bad times for the average investor. Over the long run, investors exposed to
factors earn high returns. But there is risk. There are superior returns to factors,
on average, because during bad times they can underperform—sometimes dramatically. Factor premiums also result from the behavior of investors that is not
arbitraged away.

Comparing an investor's set of bad times with those of an average investor
allows her to assess whether she can reap factor premiums that will pay off in
the long run. If she can withstand bad times better than the average investor,
then she can embrace risks that most investors can shy away from. These factors
will lose money during bad times, but make up for it the rest of the time with
attractive rewards. Factor investing is about comparing how an investor feels and
acts during his bad times with how the average investor feels and acts. Different
investors will have optimal allocations of factor risks depending on how well they
can tolerate losses during their bad times. Just as eating right requires us to look
through food labels to underlying nutrients, factor investing requires us to look
through asset class labels to underlying factor risks.

Finally in Part III, I discuss how asset owners can add as few bad times as
possible when they delegate the management of their portfolios. The worst relationships between asset owners and managers cause the asset owner to endure
many more bad times; what is best for the fund manager is generally not in the
interests of the asset owner. Appropriate governance structures and contracts can
minimize the bad times resulting from agency conflicts. I show that for the most
common investment vehicles—mutual funds, hedge funds, and private equity—
fund managers have talent, but little of it enriches asset owners, on average, and
this result is in line with financial theory. Hedge funds and private equity are
not asset classes; both are simply bundles of well-known factor risks wrapped in
opaque contracts. Hedge funds are especially exposed to volatility risk, and private
equity is largely public equity with a dose of leverage.

The three main themes of this book, then, are:

Part I: Asset owners need to be cognizant of their bad times.
Part II: Factors carry premiums to reward the losses during bad times. Factors
          matter, not asset class labels.
Part III: Watch that your manager does not load you with another set of bad
          times.

Asset management is actually about defining the bad times of investors, managing the bad times when investment factors do badly, and mitigating the bad

times brought by delegated agents. Asset allocation, the practice of choosing appropriate asset classes and investments, is actually factor management.

The viewpoint of this book is that of the asset owner. I discuss banks, insurance companies, and other financial enterprises, but I see them as intermediaries to the largest owners of assets: nations, through sovereign wealth funds, collective owners like pension funds, endowments, and foundations, down to individuals and families. All the topics are presented from the asset owners' perspective.

This book is opinionated. There are active, and important, debates on many of the topics in this book. I expect many will disagree with me on some points, and this is as it should be. The greatest compliment you can give me is to become a better investor as the result of reactions elicited by my analysis.

I've written the book for a wide audience. Even if you don't understand all of the mathematics, I emphasize intuition and application. Since I teach in a business school, and cases are an important way of putting lessons in context, I've started each chapter with a real-life setting. The book is anchored by the case studies I've written.

I recommend that if you are a trustee, director, or similar individual charged with safe-keeping funds on behalf of others, and you want to avoid mathematical and statistical analysis, then you should read chapter 1: Asset Owners; chapter 14: Factor Investing; and chapters 16 through 18 on Mutual Funds and Other 40-Act Funds, Hedge Funds, and Private Equity, respectively. Many trustees are grappling with how to manage commodity investments and illiquid assets, and although both chapter 11: "Real" Assets and chapter 13: Illiquid Assets contain some equations, most of the material should be accessible to investors without a technical background.

If you manage funds for a living—either as an asset owner or as a delegated fund manager for an asset owner—then I encourage you to add chapter 2: Preferences. My pet peeve is that we rely too much on mean-variance optimization in asset management, and this chapter emphasizes the variety of different preferences held by investors. I do look at the mean-variance paradigm in chapter 3: Mean-Variance Investing, but do it with a twist to cover socially responsible investing and "risk parity," a method of allocating to asset classes based on volatilities that is becoming popular. Then read chapter 4: Investing for the Long Run, which covers dynamic portfolio choice and chapter 10: Alpha (and the Low Risk Anomaly), which is probably what you're trying to find in your asset management job. The low risk anomaly is a special interest of mine. Look through chapters 6 to 9, which discuss the nuts and bolts of factor risk: Factor Theory, Factors, Equities, and Bonds, respectively. The last two asset classes I consider to be investable factors in their own right.

Individuals will find chapter 5: Life-Cycle Investing and chapter 12: Tax-Efficient Investing relevant. In the former, I show how to optimally save during our working lives to fund retirement. The latter deals with allocating assets to minimize the amount we pay to Uncle Sam. It turns out that taxes affect asset prices and are a factor, too.

I believe all asset owners must pay special attention to their relationships with delegated managers, which I discuss in chapter 15: Delegated Investing. Dysfunctional principal-agent relationships are as big a problem for asset owners as finding an appropriate investment (actually factor!) strategy. In fact, governance and investment strategy go hand-in-hand. I discuss mutual funds, hedge funds, and private equity in chapters 16 to 18, respectively, in the light of factor risk exposures and agency problems.

Students of asset management will find this book different because it is not strictly a textbook, although it applies concepts that many finance courses cover. It should be more interesting, hopefully, because the theory is related directly to specific individuals, funds, or companies, and because I don't pretend to be objective. I use the book in MBA courses on basic investments and a more advanced class on asset management, but supplement it with class slides (with more math than there is in the book), plenty of problem sets, case studies, and guest speakers (the last two being the best parts). The book contains too much material for a one-semester course, so if you're a professor, pick and choose which chapters are most relevant; each will have some lecture notes available upon request. Each chapter is designed to be self-contained, but has references to relevant discussions in other chapters.

Academics should find this book of interest because I cover much of the recent literature. An important aim of the book is to distill the relevant parts of academic theory to improve the practice of asset management. I can't mention all the papers written on these subjects, so the selective references skew towards older, seminal works as well as more recent ones; references in between are relatively sparse. I apologize to academic colleagues whom I've left out.

I heartily endorse disclosures as an important tool to align the interests of asset owners and delegated managers, so here are mine. I have received consulting fees or honorariums from the following firms and institutions mentioned in this book: Bank of America Merrill Lynch, Canada Pension Plan Investment Board (CPPIB), Commonfund, European Central Bank (ECB), Federal Reserve Bank of New York (FRBNY), Federal Reserve Board of Governors, Fidelity Investments, Folketrygdfondet, The Hamilton Project at Brookings Institution, Harvard University (Kennedy School), International Monetary Fund (IMF), Martingale Asset Management, Morgan Stanley, Norwegian Ministry of Finance, Norges Bank, and the World Bank. I have received consulting fees or honorariums from other firms in the financial industry, including asset management firms, central banks, commercial and investment banks, and hedge funds.

The website for materials accompanying this book may be found at www.oup.com/us/assetmanagement.

THE ASSET OWNER

CHAPTER 1

Asset Owners

Chapter Summary

All asset owners—from the very largest sovereign wealth funds (SWFs) to the smallest individual investors—share common issues in investing: meeting their liabilities, deciding where to invest and how much risk to take on, and overseeing the intermediaries managing their portfolios.

1. Timor-Leste

The Democratic Republic of Timor-Leste is a small country of a million people in Southeast Asia.[1] It lies northwest of Australia and occupies the eastern half of Timor Island along with an enclave in the western part of the island. The rest of the island belongs to Indonesia.

In the sixteenth century, the area that is now Timor-Leste was colonized by the Portuguese, who introduced Catholicism, which remains the dominant religion, and coffee, which is the mainstay of Timor-Leste's low-productivity agricultural economy. During World War II, the Australians and Dutch landed in Timor-Leste to fight the Japanese. World War II devastated the country, and recovery under reinstated Portuguese rule was slow.

When Portugal began to withdraw from its overseas colonies, civil war broke out in Timor-Leste. The Revolutionary Front for an Independent East Timor (Fretilin) declared independence in November 1975. Fearful of a Marxist state on its doorstep, and with the support of Western governments amid the Cold War, Indonesia invaded less than a month later, and in July 1976, declared Timor-Leste its twenty-seventh province.

Indonesia's occupation was brutal. An estimated 200,000 Timorese lost their lives to fighting, disease, or famine. In 1996, the Nobel Peace Prize was awarded to two Timorese leaders, Bishop Carlos Filipe Ximenes Belo and José Ramos-Horta, drawing attention to Indonesia's human rights abuses. After Indonesia's

---

[1] Figures in this section come from the *Economist*, IMF, World Bank, and United Nations.

President Suharto was forced to resign in 1998, his successor held a referendum in Timor-Leste on independence.[2] Four out of five Timorese voted in favor and on May 20, 2002, Timor-Leste became independent.

Timor-Leste is poor. Its annual GDP per capita is less than $900, and four out of ten residents live in poverty. Half the adults can't read. Unemployment reaches up to 20% in rural areas and 40% among urban youth. There are few paved roads outside the capital, Dili, and many roads become unusable during the rainy season. There is no national electricity grid and even in Dili, power can be uneven and unreliable. Most of the population lives off subsistence agriculture; slash-and-burn farming methods have contributed to soil erosion and deforestation. The country does not have its own banking system or currency and instead uses U.S. dollars.

At the same time, Timor-Leste is rich. In 2004, ConocoPhillips began production of oil and gas from the nation's reserves in the Timor Sea, and in 2005, the government established the Petroleum Fund. At the end of 2012 it contained $11.8 billion.

Why did the government of Timor-Leste set up the Petroleum Fund instead of immediately spending the windfall on medical care, education, housing, roads, utilities, and other basic necessities?

We'll answer that question in the pages to come. For now what's important is that the Petroleum Fund of Timor-Leste is a SWF, which makes the nation of Timor-Leste an asset owner. This chapter describes the main characteristics of different asset owners—from nations down to individuals. I consider SWFs, pension funds, endowments and foundations, and individuals and families. I do not describe banks, insurance companies, asset management firms, or similar financial institutions, which I treat as *intermediaries* for these owners of assets. (Part III of the book deals with delegated portfolio management.) The line, however, between asset owner and intermediary is blurry; SWFs and pension funds ultimately serve the owners of the funds, which include individuals, but are managed as separate entities.

2. Sovereign Wealth Funds

SWFs are big gorillas—both because the giant SWFs have some of the largest pools of assets under management (AUM) and also because they represent the largest number of underlying owners, the citizens of their countries.[3]

---

[2] Australia—where I grew up—was the only Western country to officially (and shamefully) recognize Indonesian rule. In 1999, the United Nations sent peacekeeping forces to Timor-Leste to stabilize the country after the Indonesians left. These forces were spearheaded by Australia, and the last Australian Defense Force personnel left in 2013. Australia remains the largest provider of foreign aid to Timor-Leste. Australians commonly refer to Timor-Leste as East Timor.

[3] Some of this section is taken from Ang (2012a).

SWFs are special for me because of my association with Norway, whose SWF is among the world's largest; at the end of 2012, it managed $685 billion, sixty times more than the Timor-Leste's Petroleum Fund. (Yet in economic terms Timor-Leste's is the giant because Norway's fund is "only" equal to a year's GDP, while Timor-Leste's is ten times that nation's annual output.) I have advised the Norwegian SWF since 2005, and my consulting work for the Norwegians on strategic asset allocation has influenced my research and teaching. I am extremely grateful to Norway for inspiring me—the work on factor investing, especially, has shaped some of the arguments of this book. Through Norway, I have had the privilege of meeting people representing governments and large fund managers from Europe, the Middle East, Asia, Australia, New Zealand, and of course, the United States.

2.1. THE GROWTH OF SOVEREIGN WEALTH

SWFs are part of overall sovereign reserves, which include central bank reserves, commodity savings or stabilization funds, national pension reserves, government holding management companies, and state-owned enterprises. A working definition of a SWF is an investment fund controlled by a government and invested at least partly in foreign assets.[4] At its most basic level, a SWF is a vehicle for moving a country's savings from the present to the future. SWFs have been created by many types of governments—from democratic to autocratic—and are managed in a variety of structures, from independent crown corporations to operations within central banks.

The United States has several SWFs, all at the state level.[5] The largest and oldest in the United States is the Alaska Permanent Fund, which was established under the state's constitution in 1976 and is funded by mineral lease rentals. It had grown to $42 billion as of August 31, 2012. Each year, all residents of Alaska receive a dividend, which in 2012 was $878. The newest SWF in the United States is the North Dakota Legacy Fund, which receives 30% of the state's taxes on oil and gas and was established in 2011. This fund is projected to rapidly grow alongside the shale oil boom. Then there are the New Mexico Severance Tax Permanent Fund (1973), the Wyoming Permanent Mineral Trust Fund (1974), and the Alabama Trust Fund (1985).

While SWFs are a heterogeneous group of investors, their distinguishing characteristic is government ownership, which makes the management of a SWF different from the management of private sector financial institutions. The biggest SWFs are colossal. Norway has more than half a trillion dollars in assets. China Investment Corporation (CIC) and the State Administration of Foreign

---

[4] The term "sovereign wealth fund" was coined by Rozanov (2005). A legal framework is provided by Gelpern (2011).

[5] States are sovereigns too, see chapter 12.

Exchange (SAFE), both Chinese, and the Saudi Arabian Monetary Authority (SAMA) are about equally large. Other comparably sized funds include the Abu Dhabi Investment Authority (ADIA) and the Government of Singapore Investment Corporation (GIC), but their size has only been estimated because these funds do not report their AUM. So there is an enormous amount of money in SWFs—estimates put the figure at upwards of $5 trillion and growing.

The line between SWFs, reserves, and national pension funds is blurry, but we do know that all these funds have dramatically increased since 2000. Figure 1.1 graphs world foreign exchange reserves as compiled by the IMF (the Currency Composition of Official Exchange Reserves, or COFER). These are voluntary reports and don't coincide with the monies in SWFs, but there is some overlap. In fact, some countries, like China and Korea, have created a SWF (or two) by hewing them out of foreign exchange reserves. Figure 1.1 shows a dramatic growth in reserves from less than $2 trillion in the 1990s to more than $10 trillion in 2012. The AUM of SWFs (which we do not directly observe) would mirror this trend. The COFER numbers hugely underreport foreign reserves because China, which holds more than $3 trillion in reserves, does not report to the IMF.[6] Although some developed countries, like Norway, are accruing large amounts of foreign assets in SWFs, the rise in sovereign wealth has been concentrated in emerging markets.

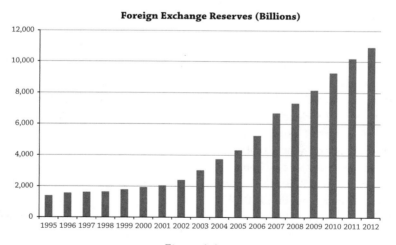

Foreign Exchange Reserves (Billions)

Figure 1.1

---

[6] China is one of the few countries not to disclose the portfolio composition of its foreign currency reserves. Experts estimate, though, that it is the largest holder of U.S. Treasuries. The breakdown of reserves within SAFE, which is responsible for investing most of China's foreign exchange reserves, is convoluted. See Hu (2010).

The rise of SWFs over the past fifteen years reflects two broader, related geopolitical trends:

1. The redistribution of wealth from the Western world (especially the United States and Europe) toward emerging countries, especially those in the East.

    It is not that the West has become poorer—it is that developing markets have rapidly become much richer. Partly this is due to surging commodity prices: oil prices skyrocketed from around $20 per barrel in the late 1990s to a high of $147 in July 2008. Countries like Timor-Leste wished to save some of these commodity revenues in SWFs. The United States has also been running trade deficits, and emerging markets have been putting some of their corresponding trade surpluses into SWFs.
2. An increasing role of governments in managing sovereign wealth.

    The financial crisis highlighted this for developed countries, but other governments—particularly in Asia—have played much more active roles in managing their economy and setting industrial policy than has the United States. Relevant policies include managing exchange rates, nurturing export-oriented industries, and setting import tariffs. Several governments, including Australia, Singapore, and Korea, have deliberately run budget surpluses and channeled these into SWFs.

2.2. OPTIMAL SOVEREIGN WEALTH

Perhaps the number one reason sovereign wealth has been rapidly increasing is simply that *the United States told emerging market countries to save more*.

The 1980s was *La Decada Perdida* for Latin America. The largest economies all went bankrupt: Brazil, Argentina, Mexico, and Venezuela. During 1997 and 1998, Thailand, Indonesia, Malaysia, the Philippines, and Korea were hit by plunging stock markets and currency collapses. In 1998, Russia defaulted on its debt.

In an influential 1999 article in *Foreign Affairs*, Martin Feldstein, former Chairman of the White House Council of Economic Advisors and a noted economist at Harvard University, wrote that "emerging market countries must protect themselves through increased liquidity" against episodes like the 1980s Latin American debt crisis and the 1997–1998 Asian crisis:

> Liquidity is the key to financial self-help. A country that has substantial international liquidity—large foreign currency reserves and a ready source of foreign currency loans—is less likely to be the object of a currency attack. Substantial liquidity also enables a country already under a speculative siege to defend itself better and make more orderly financial adjustments.

Feldstein also said that emerging markets could not rely on the IMF or other international organizations; emerging markets must save on their own. They did just as he instructed and beefed up their sovereign savings during the 2000s.

In the argot of economists, SWF savings are needed for *precautionary* reasons and are a form of *self-insurance*.[7] But perhaps the AUM in SWFs are too high; Lee (2004) reports reserves of 17% of GDP, on average, for emerging market countries. Just as miserly Ebenezer Scrooge initially misses out on the joys of Christmas in Charles Dickens' novel *A Christmas Carol*, excessive saving by a country reduces consumption. Countries could use this capital more productively elsewhere in the economy, and offer better social insurance, health, or education programs (making life more enjoyable for Scrooge's poor clerk, Bob Cratchit, and his disabled son, Tiny Tim). The optimal level of sovereign savings is a balancing act between the opportunity costs of consumption and investment, and the value of self-insurance.

2.3. DUTCH DISEASE

Timor-Leste created its SWF not out of precautionary savings motives; it was to avoid the *Dutch disease*.

The Dutch disease (or *resource curse*) was a term first used by the *Economist* in 1977 for the shrinking of the manufacturing sector in the Netherlands after natural gas was discovered in the previous decade. The same effect occurred in Britain in the 1970s when oil was found under the North Sea. Once a country finds natural resources, manufacturing and other traded sectors decline while real exchange rates appreciate, causing the country's traded sectors to be less competitive. Resource bonanzas also increase corruption and wasteful government spending.[8]

Nigeria is perhaps the worst example of the Dutch disease.[9] Oil prices rose dramatically from the 1960s to the 2000s, but Nigeria has always been among the twenty poorest countries in the world. Between 1970 and 2000, the proportion of the population surviving on less than $1 per day increased from 25% to 70%. A series of military dictatorships have plundered the oil money.

---

[7] In Jeanne and Rancière's (2006) language, the SWF can sustain demand in times of "sudden stops." Heller (1966) is the first to develop the precautionary savings story for sovereign reserves. The Greenspan–Guidotti rule, which is named after a former chairman of the Federal Reserve Board and a former deputy minister of finance of Argentina, recommends a country hold reserves equal to its short-term external debt. An alternative, *new mercantilist* explanation for the rise of sovereign wealth is Dooley, Folkerts-Landau, and Garber (2005). They argue that the increased sovereign wealth arises as a product of some countries wanting to fix exchange rates. Related work on international savings (or equivalent dis-savings by some countries) is by Gourinchas and Rey (2007).

[8] See van der Ploeg (2011). A model of the Dutch disease, and the use of a SWF to counter it, is Collier et al. (2010).

[9] As recounted here by Sala-i-Martin and Subramanian (2003).

Norway discovered oil in 1969.[10] It experienced many symptoms of the Dutch disease in the 1970s and 1980s. When oil prices fell in the mid-1980s, the economy entered a period of prolonged subdued growth. To facilitate a more sustainable fiscal policy and diversify the nation's assets away from oil, it created a SWF in 1990, which was originally called the Oil Fund. The government changed the fund's name in 2006 to the Government Pension Fund—Global (want to bet it was named by a committee?), even though it has nothing directly to do with pensions. By placing money into the fund, the government shields the economy from fluctuating oil prices, and the country can sustainably increase consumption as resources are depleted.

Timor-Leste created its SWF so that its new riches would not overwhelm its small economy and wipe out everything not related to oil and gas. In winning the petroleum jackpot on its doorstep, would Timor-Leste go the way of Nigeria, or could it cure the Dutch disease and find a brighter future?

Timor-Leste got plenty of advice from the Norwegians and other international experts; Tørres Trovik (thank you Tørres for introducing me to the Norwegian SWF) serves on the advisory board of the Petroleum Fund.[11] Timor-Leste faces more challenges than just the Dutch disease: in many poor countries, serendipitous wealth from oil tends to go poof! and disappear into politicians' (and many others') pockets. The Peterson Institute for International Economics, a research group based in Washington DC, ranks Timor-Leste's SWF the third best based on structure, governance, transparency, and accountability.[12] Only Norway and New Zealand rank higher.

2.4. INTEGRATION INTO GOVERNMENT POLICY

Timor-Leste has used its SWF as part of an overall policy of economic development, like Botswana, Chile, Korea, and others. The Petroleum Fund Law defines the *estimated sustainable income* (ESI) as 3% of Timor-Leste's total petroleum wealth, which is defined as the current Petroleum Fund's assets plus the net present value of future petroleum receipts. That is, the ESI is 3% of total petroleum wealth—financial wealth in the fund plus oil and gas wealth still to be pumped from the reserves. Given the paucity of other industries in Timor-Leste, total petroleum wealth is essentially the entire worth of Timor-Leste. The ESI serves to guide government spending from the oil wealth, but it is a flexible rule.

[10] For more details, see "The Norwegian Government Pension Fund: The Divestiture of Wal-Mart Stores Inc.," Columbia CaseWorks, ID#080301.

[11] The IMF has recommended resource-rich countries put windfalls into SWFs since 2000. See Davis et al. (2001).

[12] See Truman (2010).

Norway is similar in that it also specifies a flexible spending rule, in this case 4% of the value of the fund. Chapter 5 will show that Timor-Leste is actually closer to economic theory, which advocates setting a payout rule based on *total* wealth, rather than just *financial* wealth. Both countries, however, have well-defined rules for how the funds should be tapped, through which the monies are gradually drawn down.

Constant (proportional) spending rules are not the only way to draw money from a SWF. The precautionary motive for a SWF is to hold adequate reserves to meet unexpected large, negative shocks to a country's economy. SWFs designed to be drawn upon during such bad times are sometimes called *reserve* or *stabilization funds*, and they are special cases of SWFs. Chile's first SWF (it now has two) is designed to store copper revenues during good times, and be drawn down during bad times. It was originally called the Copper Stabilization Fund. But during bad times some governments draw on SWFs that are not specifically designated as reserve or stabilization funds. When oil prices fell below $10 per barrel in the 1990s, the Saudi government transferred money from SAMA to finance Keynesian-style stimulus spending. The Saudi government also tapped SAMA during the 2008 financial crisis. Transfers from the Kuwait Investment Authority (KIA) allowed Kuwait to rebuild its economy after the 1990 Gulf War, which is the only time that Kuwait's SWF has been drawn upon.

Spending rules—either proportional payouts each year like Timor-Leste, or contingent payouts during bad times for Chile or Kuwait—are liabilities of SWFs. When SWFs provide funds to governments during downturns, sufficient liquid reserves need to be on hand. A few SWFs have never had payouts—yet. Singapore's GIC, for example, has never been tapped.[13] But if the reason that GIC exists is a precautionary one, then it would likely be drawn down in the worst possible circumstances—outbreaks of conflict, natural disasters, or economic calamities. And few types of assets retain their value at such times, especially during war. Therefore the investments of the SWF should reflect the fund's purpose and the way that monies are to be disbursed.

One criticism of Timor-Leste is that the government has been consistently withdrawing more from the Petroleum Fund than the ESI level: the government spent 3.8% in 2009, 4.8% in 2010, and 4.3% in 2011.[14] According to the Asian Development Bank, most of the recent economic growth in Timor-Leste has been

---

[13] Norway has a second, much smaller SWF, The Government Pension Fund–Norway (also called Folketrygdfondet), which invests primarily in Norway and in other Nordic countries. There is no payout from the fund, or planned new injections of capital, so Folketrygdfondet is essentially a closed-end fund (see chapter 16).

[14] IRIN, "Is Timor-Leste's Plan for Oil Fund Investments a Risk Worth Taking?" *Guardian*, Oct. 24, 2011.

achieved from high levels of government spending, which is dependent on the Petroleum Fund.[15]

Timor-Leste is still finding the balance between spending on infrastructure and avoiding the Dutch disease. I met the Finance Minister, Emilia Pires, and other Timorese delegates in Sydney. She is an unassuming woman of quiet determination and is the first Timorese to graduate from an Australian University. Like many civil servants, she studied abroad when her country was in turmoil, and returned to rebuild it. "Right now," Pires says, "if you don't invest in the people, what future have we got? There's not enough schooling, or quality of schooling. We are suffering from dengue, malaria, you name it. Should we take more? Of course, logically we have to; otherwise where is the future generation? For me, it's just irrational to think otherwise."[16] It is amazing that the country can have this conversation while respecting the overall purpose of the SWF and not spend everything immediately. Timor-Leste has money to spend precisely because it carefully set up its SWF to ensure legitimacy.

2.5. AGENCY ISSUES

A SWF can only exist in the long run if it has public support. Legitimacy does not mean preservation of capital, but preserving capital may play a part in conferring legitimacy on the management of the SWF—especially at a SWF's inception. Timor-Leste, as befits a new country finding its way, has so far managed the Petroleum Fund conservatively. At the start, it invested almost all of it in United States and other reserve currency bonds, but Timor-Leste is moving into riskier assets. In October 2010, the government allowed 4% of the fund to be invested in global equities. In 2012, the fund's equity mandate was increased to a maximum of 20%. In slowly enlarging its portfolio to include riskier assets, it is following its bigger cousin Norway. Now known for its sophistication, Norway started out 100% bonds, and then, only after long public debate, moved its portfolio first 40% and then 60% into equities (1998 and 2007, respectively), and only in 2011 made its first real estate investments (with a modest 5% limit). The Norwegian SWF moved into riskier assets only after it established trust with its citizens and proved it could successfully steward the funds.

To its credit, Timor-Leste recognized it did not have expertise to manage a SWF. But rather than just outsource the job, Timor-Leste made sure its own citizens were getting trained—the fund sends its own portfolio managers to the money centers in Europe and America to trade alongside some of its appointed external managers. Singapore and Korea have also partly managed their SWFs with an eye

[15] Asian Development Bank, Asian Development Outlook 2010: Democratic Republic of Timor-Leste.

[16] Quoted by Wright, C., "East Timor: The World's Most Important Sovereign Wealth Fund?" *Euromoney*, September 2008.

to increasing financial expertise for their overall economies. The worst outcome for Timor-Leste would be just to place its billions with external managers without understanding or learning how these assets are managed. Eventually they should do it all themselves and use their new expertise to develop their own financial system.

For Norway and Timor-Leste, transparency is crucial in maintaining the legitimacy of their SWFs. Transparency per se, however, is neither a necessary nor sufficient condition for countries to establish stable, robust self-restraint mechanisms so that they do not immediately spend their cash. Kuwait and Singapore, for example, operate highly successful SWFs that have long histories (Kuwait's was the very first one created, in 1953), and broad public support. Both are opaque; they report neither their total assets nor portfolio holdings. In fact, Kuwait's SWF makes it clear on its web page that it is against the law to disclose information concerning KIA's assets and other information about the fund.[17] Part of Kuwait's and Singapore's success is that although information is not released to the general public, detailed information is released regularly to certain authorities. There is accountability, if not public accountability, and fund managers are held responsible for their actions.

Large sums of money are very tempting for politicians to spend willy-nilly (especially on themselves). Having a clear outline of how the SWF is integrated into the overall government and economic strategy minimizes this risk. Russia established a SWF in 2004 funded by oil revenues and raided a significant amount of the capital to plug budget deficits in 2009 and 2010, to shore up unfunded state pension systems, and to pay for domestic infrastructure—none of which were contemplated when the SWF was created. Ireland depleted its SWF, the National Pensions Reserve Fund, by bailing out troubled Irish banks. While Ireland needed all the cash it could get during its meltdown, shoring up dodgy banks was not in the fund's original economic framework and was a terrible investment for pensioners.

So far, Timor-Leste has fared far better than Russia and Ireland in this regard, even though Timor-Leste is much more politically unstable. In April and May 2006, Prime Minister Mari Alkatiri fired six hundred soldiers who had gone on strike over what they regarded as poor pay, working conditions, and discrimination. Violence quickly spread and more than 100,000 people had to flee. President Ramos-Horta survived an assassination attempt in February 2008 organized by the leader of the rebel forces. The opposition Fretilin Party continues to argue that the Ramos-Horta government is illegitimate. Throughout, only the question of deviating from the ESI was debated; the integrity and management of the Petroleum Fund remained unsullied.

[17] http://www.kia.gov.kw/En/About_KIA/Tansparency/Pages/default.aspx.

3. Pension Funds

The largest pension funds are managed at the sovereign level. In fact, national pension funds can be considered SWFs, although the line is blurry. Australia's and New Zealand's SWFs are explicitly designed to meet future national pension liabilities, and they embrace the SWF moniker. On the other hand, Canada Pension Plan takes great pains to explain why it should not be called a SWF.[18]

There are four types of pension savings:

1. National pension plans like Social Security;
2. Private *defined benefit plans*, where future certain, or pre-determined, benefits are promised to beneficiaries by companies;
3. Private *defined contribution plans*, where payments into the plan are predefined, but the future benefits are not fixed; and
4. Funds privately managed by individuals—in the United States, these include IRA, Keogh, and 401(k) plans, which have advantageous tax treatments but strict contribution limits (see chapter 12).

Economists often refer to *pillars* or *tiers* of support when talking about the design of pension systems.[19] Social Security is a first pillar and is designed to provide minimal support for most citizens. The second pillar, consisting of work-related pensions, includes (2) and (3), which capture the bulk of retirement savings in the United States. The third pillar is private voluntary savings, which is (4), but it also includes non-tax advantaged savings used in retirement. And finally there is now a fourth pillar: if retirement savings are inadequate, (great-) grandma may have no choice but to go back to work.

3.1. DEFINED BENEFIT VERSUS DEFINED CONTRIBUTION

In defined benefit plans, the employer pays a retirement benefit based on worker age, years of employment, and current and past wages. Hence, the benefit is "defined." A typical payout at retirement is something like "benefit factor × highest average pay over a three-year period × number of years of service," where the benefit factor might increase with age. For example, the benefit factor is equal to 2.0% for a teacher retiring at age fifty-five under the California Public Employees' Retirement System (CalPERS), the largest pension plan in the United States. The benefit factor increases to 2.5% for a teacher sixty-three or older. Since the employee is assured a predictable amount at retirement, the employer (mostly) bears the investment risk.

---

[18] See www.cppib.ca/files/PDF/SWFBkgr_Dec10_2007.pdf.

[19] This terminology comes from the influential World Bank 1994 report, Averting the Old Age Crisis.

In defined contribution plans, by contrast, the employer contributes a fixed amount. Hence, the contribution is "defined." The retirement account works like a glorified bank balance and is invested in a variety of asset classes like stocks, bonds, or real estate. Investment choices are made by the employee, but the employer usually chooses the types of funds available.[20] Since returns fluctuate over time, and individuals bear the investment risk, and since some employees put in more of their own money than do others, the amount available at retirement is not fixed.

The biggest development in pensions over the last thirty years is that defined benefit plans are increasingly scarce. "Defined benefit plans are going the way of the dodo," says Olivia Mitchell, a pension and retirement expert at the Wharton School.[21] They are still the mainstay type of plan for government workers, but many corporations have frozen their old defined benefit plans and do not permit new entrants. Companies have also converted defined benefit plans to defined contribution ones.[22]

There are huge sums sitting in pension funds. Total pension assets represent over 70% of GDP in the United States. Pensions are even more important in other countries, including Australia and the Netherlands, where they represent over 90% and 135% of GDP respectively.[23]

Figure 1.2, Panel A graphs the total value of private pension fund AUM in the United States (all data in Figure 1.2 are from the Flow of Funds). At the end of 2012, there were $6.6 trillion of private pension fund assets. Pension assets have been growing at 8.2% a year, but Panel A shows strong dips during the 2000s due to the dot-com bust and the 2008 financial crisis, when pension AUM shrank by 29%. The large declines in AUM occurred because pension funds have enthusiastically embraced risk and their increased holdings of equities and other risky assets did poorly during these periods.

Panel B of Figure 1.2 shows that the proportion of private pension fund money in non-fixed income assets rose from less than 20% in the early 1950s to exceed 70% in 2012. Most of this diversification was into U.S. equities in the 1960s, with international and emerging market equities added in the 1970s and 1980s. Since the mid-1990s, and especially over the 2000s, pension funds have scrambled to add *alternative assets*—notably hedge funds and private equity, although chapters 17 and 18, respectively, will show that these are not asset classes and

---

[20] This limited universe is often not in the best interest of the employee, see chapter 3.

[21] Quoted in "Defined Contribution Plans: Over to You," *Economist*, April 9, 2011.

[22] Defined benefit plans technically include *cash balance* plans, which are plans where the employers prefund contributions. From the point of view of the employee, cash balance plans look like defined contribution plans—they receive statements with their own balances, which they can withdraw when they leave the firm or retire—even though these balances are notional; the funds are pooled and managed centrally. Munnell and Soto (2007) and Rauh, Stefanescu, and Zeldes (2012) study defined benefit pension freezes and conversions to defined contribution plans.

[23] See OECD, Pension Markets in Focus, September 2012, Issue 9.

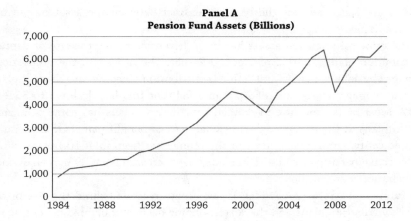

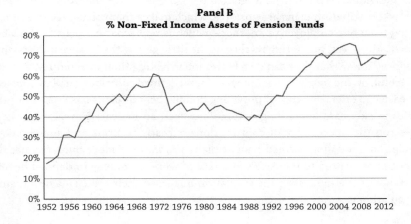

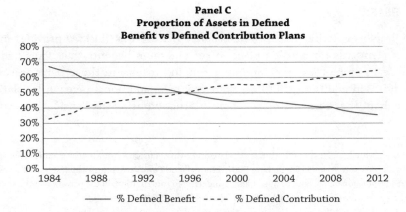

Figure 1.2

instead are just labels for the type of contract between the asset owner and intermediaries.

The growth in pension assets has been driven mainly by the rise of defined contribution plans. Panel C of Figure 1.2 splits the AUM into the proportions managed by defined benefit and defined contribution plans. Defined benefit plans used to manage nearly 70% of AUM in 1984, but this has declined to 35% in 2012. Most of the increase in defined contribution plans has come from new 401(k) plans at the expense of traditional defined benefit plans. Of this rise in defined contribution plans, most of the money has been in 401(k) plans. Since 1984, active participants in 401(k) plans have increased from 29% of all defined contribution plans to about 90%.[24]

Munnell and Soto (2007) identify two main reasons behind the rise of defined contribution plans and the corresponding decline of defined benefit plans. First, individuals wanted to do it on their own (*increased demand* from employees). Defined contribution plans are portable, which makes them attractive to workers flitting from one employer to another—which is now what happens in the labor market. Moreover, marketing pitched at the little guy by the finance industry has convinced many that they can do a better job investing their own money.[25]

Second, on the *supply side,* employers found defined contribution plans cheaper and easier to offer. The cost of providing defined benefit plans has risen since the 1980s: workers are living longer, there has been an increase in real wages over time, and the uncertainty of contributions is costly to firms and shareholders. Regulation governing defined benefit plans has become more burdensome; the government wanted to increase the safety of workers' money in defined benefit plans, but at the same time the regulation increased their cost. This new regime of regulation is . . .

3.2. ERISA

The Employee Retirement Income Security Act of 1974 (ERISA) provides minimum standards for pension plans: it set minimum benefits that plans had to provide to employees, and minimum funding to ensure those benefits could be paid.[26] In addition to ERISA, there has been additional pension legislation throughout the years, the most recent incarnation being the Pension Protection

---

[24] See Munnell, A. H., and P. Perun, An Update on Private Pensions, Initiative on Financial Security, the Aspen Institute, Issue Brief October 2007. Munnell and Perun also report the fraction of workers covered by pension plans, both defined benefit and defined contribution, in the private sector has been trending downward over time from 51% in 1979 to 46% in 2004.

[25] A scathing, but thoughtful, review of the personal finance industry is Olen (2012).

[26] ERISA is one of the most complex sets of legislation affecting business. Title I protects rights of beneficiaries. Title II concerns taxation issues. Title III mandates the role of actuaries in certifying pension liabilities and asset values. Title IV creates the Pension Benefit Guaranty Corporation.

Act (PPA) of 2006. The term "ERISA" is used to refer to all laws concerning pension regulation, including legislation subsequent to the original act. ERISA only regulates pension plans after companies create them; it does not mandate that companies form them.

ERISA's primary purpose is to protect the fund beneficiaries. ERISA specifies that companies with a defined benefit plan set aside sufficient money to meet its liabilities. Under the PPA, the target is that 100% of liabilities (to be made precise shortly) should be met, and if the plan is *underfunded*, the company must make additional contributions to close the gap over seven years.[27] For "at-risk" or "critical" plans, which are well under water, there are additional penalties and contributions to be made. (Of course, the funding issue is irrelevant for defined contribution plans.) These contributions are costly: money put into corporate pension plans means less money for the firm to invest and lower payouts for shareholders.[28] Pension expenses have large effects on share prices: AT&T's pension fund went from a $17 billion surplus in 2007 to a nearly $4 billion dollar deficit in 2008, and this played a major role in the decline of AT&T's equity over this period.[29]

ERISA came about due to a number of high-profile bankruptcies, particularly in the automotive sector, during the late 1950s and 1960s. The head of the United Auto Workers Union at the time, Walter Reuther, pressed federal policymakers for a mechanism to protect worker pensions similar to the Federal Deposit Insurance Corporation (FDIC), which protects depositors in banks.[30] Since mandating 100% funding does not guarantee that funds will always meet their liabilities because of investment risk, ERISA specifies a safety net to protect beneficiaries of failed pension plans. This safety net is the Pension Benefit Guaranty Corporation (*PBGC*).

PBGC

The PBGC takes over pension plans of bankrupt companies and can also take over pension funds of companies that have not yet declared bankruptcy but are in financial distress. The PBGC receives the pension plan assets and becomes an unsecured creditor for the unfunded benefits. Beneficiaries of failed pension plans administered by the PBGC receive their pensions, up to an annual maximum, which in 2012 was $55,841. This covers most workers' pensions: for the 16%

---

[27] In addition, FAS 158, implemented in 2006, requires plan sponsors to "flow through" pension fund deficits into their financial statements. In 2008 and 2010, Congress passed "funding relief" laws to temporarily relax some of the tighter funding requirements imposed by the PPA. Prior to the PPA, sponsors were required to generally fund only 90%, and sometimes only 80%, of pension liabilities and to make up smaller fractions of shortfalls over much longer periods.

[28] See Rauh (2006).

[29] See Ang, Chen, and Sundaresan (2013).

[30] For further history, see Schieber (2012).

of workers who lose benefits when the PBGC takes over their plans, the average benefit reduction is 28%.[31]

In return for this guarantee, pension plans pay premiums to the PBGC, which in 2012 were $9 per member for multiemployer plans and $35 per member for fully funded single-employer plans. Underfunded plans pay more. As is so often the case when governments provide insurance, PBGC premiums are way below the true cost of the coverage. The Congressional Budget Office estimates that premiums should be increased by more than six times to cover the shortfall from projected future claims, and this does not even include underfunding on the existing claims covered by the PBGC.[32]

PBGC protection is a *put option* for employers: when things are going really badly, you let the government pick up the tab.[33] The PBGC floor leads to an *incentive problem*: the pension fund manager can take *excessive risk* and the firm has an incentive to *underfund* because taxpayers ultimately bear the pension risk. If the bets work out, that's wonderful—the company gets a *contribution holiday* and in some cases can even extract money from the pension plan.[34] If things turn out disastrously, you let the PBGC mop up the mess. Many companies, like United Airlines and American Airlines, entered bankruptcy partly to shed their pension liabilities. These didn't disappear—the taxpayer picked up the tab.

3.3. PENSION UNDERFUNDING

The big drop in asset prices during 2008–2009 was not kind to pension funds. Milliman, a pension consulting firm, tracks the one hundred largest defined benefit plans sponsored by American public companies. Figure 1.3 plots the funding status of the Milliman 100 from 1999–2011.[35] The health of these plans has suffered twice in the last decade, mostly due to steep declines in asset values (see also Figure 1.2). In fiscal year 2011, the Milliman 100 companies had a record funding deficit of $327 billion, corresponding to a funding ratio of 79%. The funding ratios in 2007 were positive, at 105%, and despite equity markets recovering post-2009, pension funds did not fully bounce back—partly because pension liabilities grew faster than recovering asset values.

---

[31] See the 2008 report, PBGC's Guarantee Limits—An Update, published by the PBGC.

[32] See Congressional Budget Office, The Risk Exposure of the Pension Benefit Guaranty Corporation, 2005. For a summary of academic work, see Brown (2008).

[33] This is first noted by Sharpe (1976) and Treynor (1977). Sharpe and Treynor play large roles in developing the CAPM, the first model of factor risk (see chapter 6). Pennacchi and Lewis (1994) compute explicit values for the PBGC put option guaranty.

[34] Section 4980 of the Internal Revenue Code makes it extremely costly for a company to simply close an overfunded pension plan and collect the value of the pension fund in excess of its liabilities (or surplus) by imposing an excise tax of 50%.

[35] Data from the Milliman 2012 Pension Funding Study.

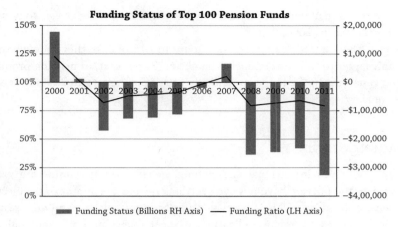

Figure 1.3

Underfunding of public pension plans is much, much worse than their corporate counterparts. Finance professors Robert Novy-Marx and Joshua Rauh estimate the underfunding problem of states and municipalities in a series of papers.[36] As of June 2009, states had accrued $5.7 trillion of retirement liabilities to their workers, yet assets in state pension plans totaled less than $2 trillion. This is a black hole of over $3 trillion, which is more than three times larger than the total outstanding publicly traded debt issued by states. Things are even worse for municipalities. Examining the largest pension plans of major cities and counties, Novy-Marx and Rauh estimate a total unfunded obligation of $7,000 per household.

Social Security, the pillar one U.S. retirement scheme, is itself underfunded. The Social Security Administration estimates that the fund will be empty in 2033, after which payroll taxes will cover only 75% of its promised obligations. The additional money required to pay all scheduled benefits is $8.6 trillion.[37] This is equivalent to 80% of total U.S. Treasury debt ($11 trillion at year-end 2012). Pension promises can be extremely expensive, especially when payouts are linked to inflation, as they are with Social Security. MetLife estimates that an annuity

---

[36] See Novy-Marx (2009, 2011a, 2011b). In certain circumstances, Bohn (2011) shows that underfunding a public pension plan can be optimal—but he assumes that there will always be municipal revenue available (at some time in the future) to meet the pension obligations.

[37] Numbers from the 2012 Annual Report of the Board of Trustees of the Federal Old-Age and Survivors Insurance and Federal Disability Insurance Trust Funds. My colleague Stephen Zeldes at Columbia Business School argues that the shortfall is less if market values of Social Security liabilities would be used (see Geanakoplos and Zeldes (2011)), but there is still a shortfall. The calculation depends crucially on the correlation of labor income with equity returns, a topic that we cover in chapter 5. Note also that Social Security liabilities do not have the "full faith and credit" backing of the U.S. government and are officially not a U.S. government liability.

paying out the maximum Social Security benefit for a couple at age sixty-sixty would cost almost $1.2 million.[38]

So even though U.S. pension assets amount to 70% of GDP, they should be considerably larger to fully meet pension liabilities. Either that, or pension promises are too generous. In the long run, one way or another, assets and liabilities have to be equal.

3.4. AGENCY ISSUES

The agency issues in national and defined benefit pension funds are grave. Economists and lawyers have not even settled on what the appropriate objective of a pension fund is.[39] This is because several parties have a claim on a private pension fund's assets, or have obligations to meet a pension fund's shortfall, and their claims often conflict. The parties include (i) beneficiaries who are current employees of the firm, (ii) retired beneficiaries who no longer work for the firm, (iii) the sponsoring firm, and (iv) the government—through the PBGC, taxpayers have a stake in all company pension plans, and the government also grants tax benefits to pension savings. Furthermore, the sharing rules are *path dependent* and *asymmetric*. If the pension fund performs well, the company may be pressured to improve benefits, which only increases its liabilities. Thus, the claims of beneficiaries increase in good times. In contrast, the cost to taxpayers through the PBGC increases during bad times.

Liability-Driven Investment

How should pension money be managed? The obvious thing would be to manage the fund to meet its liabilities. Martin Leibowitz, then an analyst at Salomon Brothers, introduced this liability-driven investment (*LDI*) framework in 1986.[40] Under LDI, the pension fund manager should manage *surplus*, which is the difference between the pension fund's asset values and liabilities, and maximize surplus returns for a given level of risk.[41] The *risk aversion* incorporated in this

---

[38] As reported in "Falling Short," *Economist*, April 9, 2011.

[39] Technically, the economics literature has not settled on an appropriate *preference* specification (see chapter 2) of the pension fund. Love, Smith, and Wilcox (2011) deal with workers, the firm, and the PBGC. But they do not pit retired workers against current employees. Firms have great power, but not complete control, over defined pension plans. Both corporations and beneficiaries share, in different circumstances, the surplus (or deficit) of the pension plan. See Bulow and Scholes (1983), Bodie (1990a), Gold (2005), and Scherer (2005).

[40] Leibowitz, M. L., 1986, Liability Returns: A New Perspective on Asset Allocation, Salomon Brothers. See also Sharpe and Tint (1990).

[41] Technically this is mean-variance utility (see chapter 4) over surplus. I extend this framework in Ang, Chen, and Sundaresan (2013) to incorporate downside risk.

optimization could reflect a reluctance to take risk on the part of beneficiaries, the firm, or both.[42]

This is easier said than done. Several liability measures are computed by actuaries; the two most common are the Accumulated Benefit Obligation (ABO) and the Projected Benefit Obligation (PBO). The ABO is the value of the benefits currently earned by employees and retirees. This is the contractual liability if the firm shut down immediately. Healthy firms, however, are going concerns, and so the PBO also counts the future expected salaries of current employees. (Thus the PBO is larger than the ABO.) But even the PBO is incomplete: firms generally grow over time, and the PBO does not count the future benefits of new hires. ERISA's measure of liabilities is the ABO. The true economic liability valuation probably exceeds even the PBO.

Public pension plan liabilities are hugely underestimated because the valuation methods assume that the pensions are very risky, while in reality state pension benefits are close to risk free.[43] The pension benefits should therefore be valued, like safe government bonds, using low discount rates, rather than with the high discount rates implied by risky equities. To see the problem with using high discount rates, consider a couple with a mortgage.[44] This is a liability, and its value does not change whether they hold equities or bonds in their retirement accounts. Yet in public pension plans, their actuarial liabilities magically become smaller if they hold more equities in their 401(k). This is pure fiction in economic terms, of course, because the mortgage liability is not affected by the rate the couple earns in their 401(k) plan.

It also matters whether the ABO or the PBO is used.[45] If the fund's liabilities are measured by the ABO, then the best *liability-hedging* portfolio is a portfolio of bonds with the same cash flows or *duration* (the average time the liability outflows come due). This implies the optimal asset allocation for a pension fund

---

[42] ERISA Section 404(a)(1) specifies that investment fiduciaries must perform their duties solely in the interest of participants and for the exclusive purpose of providing participants with retirement benefits. This is part of the *prudent man* investment standards set by ERISA. Thus, under ERISA, the surplus utility function cannot represent the utility function of the fund manager.

[43] In many states, pension liabilities are guaranteed under state constitutions. New York State, for example, gives state pension liabilities the same seniority as general obligation debt. (See "Who Watches the Watchman? New York State Common Retirement Fund," Columbia CaseWorks ID#110307.) Thus, pension liabilities are close to risk free and should be discounted using discount rates resembling risk-free (Treasury or municipal) bond yields. Under accounting standards (GASB 25) and actuarial standards (ASOP 27), the discount rate is much higher, and is the expected long-term return on assets. This effectively considers public pension liabilities to be extremely risky. It also violates a fundamental principle in economics that the value of any stream of payments should be independent of the way that it is financed, which is the Miller and Modigliani (1958) principle. (Merton Miller and Franco Modigliani were awarded Nobel Prizes in 1990 and 1985, respectively.) See also Novy-Marx and Rauh (2009, 2011).

[44] This argument is in Ang and Green (2011).

[45] See Black (1989) for more details on these arguments.

should be primarily bonds. But if the fund's liabilities are the PBO, then stocks might be a more appropriate inflation hedge in the long run because wage growth, like economic growth in general, is correlated with stock returns (see chapter 7). ERISA has caused many large plans to *de-risk* partly because it emphasizes the ABO. Milliman reports that the one hundred largest pension plans have reduced their equity allocation from 80% in 2005 to below 40% in 2011.[46] The ideal, from the beneficiaries' point of view, is to match the *factor* exposures of the assets and liabilities, so that the promised pensions can be met in most economic environments.

Management

Pension funds share many of the management problems of SWFs—even though pension funds in the private sector should theoretically be able to find competent people, fire incompetent people, and build optimal management structures.

The pay and skill of people working for pension funds resembles a pyramid. At the top of the pyramid, the board gets paid the least, and some board members often have little or no investment knowledge. Public pension plan boards, especially, can be dominated by politicians or union members with little financial expertise. In the middle of the pyramid sit the pension fund managers. Their pay often increases with the AUM they are responsible for, rather than the actual value they generate. The bottom of the pyramid is where most of the money is paid out in compensation—particularly to external managers in the form of fees.

The biggest decisions that affect the pension fund's portfolio resemble an inverse pyramid. The most important decision for the fund is how much risk to take and which factor risk premiums to collect.[47] This is a decision made by the board members—usually the least compensated and least informed parties involved. At the bottom of the pyramid, the highest paid fund managers trying to find elusive alpha (outperformance relative to a benchmark, see chapter 10) generate returns that have the smallest impact on the fund. They get paid the most, yet what they do matters least.

Public pension plans, and many private ones as well, are too often inefficient bureaucracies. They are hampered in what they can pay; the talent and expertise are on the wrong side, making them inviting prey for the predators of Wall Street. Building an organization of skilled investment professionals is hard. Compensation does matter. But most important is the creation of management structures that emphasize responsibility and accountability, where employees are measured against sufficiently rigorous benchmarks, and there are consequences for failing to meet those benchmarks. Some organizations have countered bureaucracy by creating independent management organizations. Canada Pension

---

[46] General Motors is a case study in de-risking. See "GM Asset Management and Martingale's Low Volatility Strategy," Columbia CaseWorks ID #110315.

[47] See chapters 14 and 15.

Plan is managed by an independent crown corporation that can set its own salaries and hire whomever it likes. It is designed to be as far removed as possible from meddling politicians.[48] Norway's SWF is managed by a separate division of its central bank, a structure that allows it to operate somewhat independently of the rest of the institution.

Intergenerational Equity

National pension plans and defined benefit plans ensure retirement security by having different generations pay and receive different benefits. Social security pensions paid to one generation must be financed by generations following them, and private defined pension plans must be paid by a paternalistic company making contributions over time.

In a sustainable pension plan, the sum of all generational accounts must be zero: a benefit enjoyed by one generation must be paid for by another generation. Blake (2006) reports that there is large inequality across generations in the Social Security system. The generation born in the 1920s and 1930s is "the most favored generation in history according to the generational accounts" and the least favored generation is the cohort of the youngest workers today.

Some form of intergenerational inequality is actually optimal. *Intergenerational risk sharing* allows Social Security to absorb a shock that can be catastrophic for one generation—like those who were in the peak earnings years when the Great Depression struck—and diversifies it across a series of generations.[49] In defined benefit plans, employers help smooth risk across cohorts of workers. The amount of inequality in many pension systems today is very large and disadvantages younger workers; the old have stolen from the young.

The decline in the *dependency* (or *support*) *ratio*, which is the ratio of current workers to retirees, makes this problem worse. As people live longer, more retirees are being supported by fewer workers. The dependency ratio shrank from 5.3 in 1970 to 4.6 in 2010 and is projected to hit 2.6 in 2050.[50] The large retiree population in General Motors contributed to its bankruptcy: before bankruptcy it was supporting 2.5 retirees for every active worker, and retirees accounted for 70% of its health costs.[51]

Norway, like many developed countries, has an aging population and needs to save to meet increasing retiree costs. Between 2010 and 2060, the number of

---

[48] See "Factor Investing: The Reference Portfolio and Canada Pension Plan Investment Board," Columbia CaseWorks ID#120302.

[49] Intergenerational accounting was introduced by Auerbach, Gokhale, and Kotlikoff (1991) and uses the concept of successive *overlapping generations*, with each generation following a life-cycle model (see chapter 5). Paul Samuelson (1958) and Peter Diamond (1965) developed overlapping generations models, which can be used to measure generational inequity.

[50] As reported in "Falling Short," *Economist*, April 9, 2011.

[51] Hakim, D., and J. W. Peters, "For GM Retirees, A Growing Sense of Unease," *New York Times*, June 30, 2005.

people aged sixty-seven and above is expected to double, increasing government expenditures by 12% of GDP.[52] Perhaps Norway is right in putting the words "pension" in the name of its SWF, the "Norwegian Pension Fund—Global," because it stresses the current generation's responsibility to save for the future.

4. Foundations and Endowments

Like the SWFs of Timor-Leste and Norway, foundations and endowments generally set (flexible) spending rules based on some proportion of AUM. Private foundations are required to pay out at least 5% of AUM every year, a figure established by the Tax Reform Act of 1969. Although the law frames this as a minimum, in practice many foundations simply pay out 5% regardless of other considerations.[53]

University endowments are not subject to the 5% minimum, but endowments spend at about that rate anyway and only slowly vary through time.[54] Why should Congress mandate a minimum payout for foundations but not endowments? The only plausible justification that I find in the literature is that *private* foundations are less accountable than *public* charities, which include universities.[55] Private foundations are often set up by a single donor, family, or corporation. Once the principal donor has died, foundations are accountable to few stakeholders, and this lack of oversight often leads to their doing little "charitable" work. Even when the donor is alive, some private foundations are set up to control wealth, exempt from tax, even while the wealth is being (gradually) disbursed. The reports of Rep. Wright Patman, a Texas Democrat in the early 1960s, detailed some of these abuses and influenced legislation passed in 1969.[56] These *governance* problems are less of a concern at colleges and universities, which must answer to students, faculty, staff, alumni, and donors, and also must comply with a host of federal guidelines associated with receiving federal money.

---

[52] Reported by the OECD Economic Survey of Norway, 2010.

[53] See Deep and Frumkin (2006). Strictly speaking, foundations are free to spend below 5%, but then the foundation's assets are subject to an excise tax of 30%.

[54] The average spending rate for endowments was 4.2% in 2012 according to NACUBO. The Uniform Prudent Management of Institutional Funds Act (UPMIFA) has been adopted in forty-seven states and requires that the spending take into consideration "the duration and preservation of the endowment fund" and "general economic conditions." UPMIFA specifies that a spending rate of more than 7% is a "rebuttable presumption of imprudence." See comments by Conti-Brown (2010) on why this does not constitute a fixed payout ceiling.

[55] Most of this is in the law literature. See Troyer (2000), Cowan (2008), Conti-Brown (2010), and Wolf (2011).

[56] See Troyer (2000).

4.1. RESTRICTED VERSUS UNRESTRICTED FUNDS

Unlike SWF and pension funds, the world of endowments and foundations prominently features *restricted* funds. Harvard has the largest university endowment, at $30.7 billion as of June 30, 2012. But only 17% is unrestricted. The remainder has temporary restrictions (64%), or is permanently restricted (19%). If these restrictions are not adhered to, donors may sue for return of their money—as the Robertson family did in accusing Princeton of mismanaging their gift.

Originally intended to educate students at Princeton's Woodrow Wilson School for careers in government, the Robertson family, heirs to a fortune from the A&P supermarket chain, donated $35 million in 1961. But the family was dismayed to learn, years later, that the funds were being used to teach students going into all sorts of careers except government ("advanced study, the teaching profession, college administration, private business, journalism, law, medicine, and music"). Thanks to Princeton's talented investment managers, the money grew to roughly $900 million. Princeton settled in December 2008, right before trial, and the terms required Princeton to pay all of the Robertson Foundation's substantial legal fees ($40 million), and give the Robertson family $50 million to launch a new foundation to carry out the original intent of the gift.[57]

Most endowment money is restricted. Table 1.4 breaks down the $408 billion in university and college wealth reported to the National Association of College and University Business Officers (NACUBO) and Commonfund in 2011. Of the total endowment, only $15.4 billion (4%) is *unrestricted*. *True endowment*,

Table 1.4

Components of Total Endowment in 2011 (Billions) NACUBO		
	Billions	*Percent*
True Endowment	188.11	46
Donor-restricted	172.67	42
Unrestricted	15.44	4
Term Endowment	16.88	4
Quasi-Endowment	92.44	23
Funds Held in Trust by Others	16.46	4
Other	94.24	23
Total Endowment	408.13	100

[57] Recounted by Conti-Brown (2008) and "Princeton and Robertson Family Settle Titanic Donor-Intent Lawsuit," *Chronicle of Higher Education*, Dec. 10, 2008.

which consists of unrestricted and restricted endowment, represents 46% of total endowment. *Term endowment*, which is about the same size as unrestricted endowment, represents nonperpetual funds. *Quasi-endowment* constitutes 23% of total endowment and does not come from gifts, but from other sources of university income like operating surpluses. Quasi-endowment is unrestricted, but it cannot be spent until a board reclassifies it as true endowment.

The most interesting part of total endowment is the "other" category. This is a large category representing $94.2 billion, or almost one quarter, of total endowment wealth. It includes artwork, farmland, patents, trademarks, and royalties. The last three result from commercial application of research projects and are now large sources of revenue for universities. The "Axel patents," for example, generated close to $800 million in revenue for my home institution, Columbia University, and the inventors. The Axel patents, now expired, showed how foreign DNA could be inserted into a cell to produce certain proteins. They are named after Richard Axel, a professor of neuroscience who won the Nobel Prize in Physiology or Medicine in 2004 for work (quite unrelated to the Axel patents) on how the brain interprets smell.

4.2. UNIVERSITIES ARE INVESTING PIONEERS

The leading university endowments have long been investing pioneers. During the 1920s and 1930s, despite the Great Depression, universities shifted toward equities.[58] We remember John Maynard Keynes as one of the greatest economists of the twentieth century, but lesser known is that he was also an endowment manager. Keynes managed the endowment of King's College, Cambridge, and was one of the pioneers of the trend to move into equities.[59] These greater equity allocations proved hugely beneficial in the long run, but at the time many questioned the sanity of endowment managers. It turned out that the Great Depression was the perfect time to buy equities, as prices were low and expected returns were high—but buying when everyone was selling took guts.

During the 1980s the leading universities—Harvard, Princeton, and Yale (HPY)—started to shift into alternative assets, especially more illiquid asset classes. Yale, led by David Swensen, moved first: by reducing its public equity allocation from 60% in 1980 to 20% by the mid-1990s. Its allocation to private equity, meanwhile, shot up from below 5% to above 20%.[60] Swensen's (2009) thesis, called the *endowment model*, was that long-lived investors had an edge in

---

[58] See Goetzmann, Griswold, and Tseng (2010).

[59] As described by Chambers and Dimson (2012).

[60] Numbers from Goetzmann and Oster (2012, Figures 2 and 3). See also Lerner, Schoar, and Wong (2008).

illiquid asset investing if they could ferret out talented managers who had skill.[61] Princeton followed close behind, and then Harvard joined the party.

In the 1990s, Yale again led the way by investing in hedge funds. Yale held no hedge funds in 1990, and by the end of the decade held over 20% of its portfolio in these *marketable alternatives*. Princeton followed suit, moving into hedge funds in 1995. Harvard again was the last of the three to move, doing so in 1998.

Panel A of Figure 1.5 graphs the allocation to alternative assets by endowments according to NACUBO from 2002 to 2012. Like lemmings, most endowments have enthusiastically followed HPY in allocating to private equity, hedge funds, and other alternative assets. In 2012, over half of all U.S. endowment assets were invested in alternative asset classes.

Most of these endowments, however, did not generate the superior returns enjoyed by HPY. Panel B of Figure 1.5 shows endowment returns computed by NACUBO. The large allocations to alternatives did not save endowments during the 2008 and 2009 financial crisis, when returns were –3.0% and –18.7%, respectively. Returns in 2012 were a dismal 0.3%. The illiquidity of the endowment model portfolios also proved to be a big problem when many universities, like Harvard, desperately needed cash during this time.[62] Endowments would have been better off just holding the standard mix of 60% equities and 40% bonds. Since 2001, endowment returns averaged 4.6% compared to 5.4% in the 60/40 portfolio (consisting of the S&P 500 and U.S. Treasuries). The volatility of the 60/40 portfolio was also lower, at 10.2%, compared to the endowment return volatility of 11.3%.

4.3. KEEPING UP WITH THE JONES

William Goetzmann (my sometime co-author) and Sharon Oster, professors at Yale School of Management, argue that the rush to alternatives triggered by HPY resulted from "a form of arm's race in which universities focus on ensuring adequate resources for tomorrow's battlefield."

Universities compete vigorously.[63] Of course, they try to outdo each other in sports. But they also try to outdo each other in the classroom and laboratory. They bid for the same students and try to hire the same professors. Goetzmann and Oster argue that as HPY moved to alternatives, competitive pressures forced other universities to follow suit. Endowment managers are also benchmarked against each other. This herding causes them to mimic each other. This *keeping up with*

---

[61] Chapter 13 shows that the superior returns generated by these endowments were not due to the illiquid assets being illiquid, but to the skillfulness of the endowment managers in picking the right managers.

[62] See "Liquidating Harvard," Columbia CaseWorks ID #100312. Chapter 13 deals with investing in illiquid assets.

[63] A major paper documenting this is by Epple, Romano, and Sieg (2006).

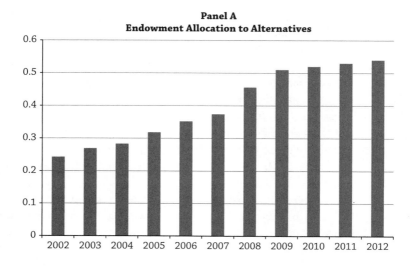

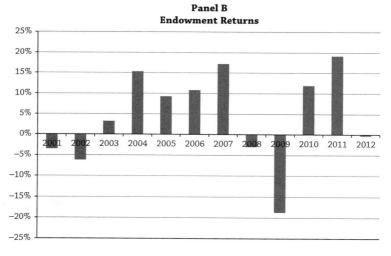

Figure 1.5

the Joneses (see chapter 2) leads endowments to hold the same sort of portfolios. Not surprisingly, most of them have followed the Yale Pied Piper in loading up on illiquid alternatives.

5. Individuals and Families

The rich really are different.

Cornelius Vanderbilt (1794–1877), known as the "Commodore," was born rich, created even more wealth, and amassed a fortune of more than $100 billion in today's dollars, enough to make him the richest person in the world by a comfortable margin. Even today "Vanderbilt" has the connotation of rolling-in-dough, filthy rich. His heirs lived the high life, squandering their inherited wealth on yachts, enormous estates, grand parties, and whatever took their fancy. In two generations, they had burned through all of it. According to a scion of the Vanderbilt family, several descendants died penniless, and "when 120 of the Commodore's descendants gathered at Vanderbilt University in 1973 for their first family reunion, there was not a millionaire among them."[64]

Generally speaking, the rich are divided into those with *ultra-high net worth*, which means $10 million to $30 million, and those of merely *high net worth*, who range from around $1 million to $10 million. (To put this into perspective, the median annual income and net worth of U.S. households are $46,000 and $77,000, respectively, according to the 2010 Survey of Consumer Finances.) The absolutely filthy rich sometimes form *family offices*, which manage family assets much like endowments. Some family offices serve multiple families and even manage non-family money. In fact, the richest family offices manage much more than the top endowments, and they provide boutique concierge services to family members (like helping to get Junior admitted to a fancy private school and organizing a last-minute jaunt to the Caribbean).

Capgemini and RBC Wealth Management estimate that high-net worth individuals controlled $42 trillion in assets in 2012.[65] For comparison, the total market capitalization of stocks listed on the NYSE was around $14 trillion. The ultra-high net worth and high net worth markets are also growing fast. Approximately half of the wealth resides in the United States and Europe, but Asia is furiously churning out millionaires at the fastest rate. Banks and other intermediaries are eyeing these enormous sums through their *private wealth management* divisions, but they face competition from stand-alone asset management firms.[66] At Columbia Business School, I have taught several students who later started or joined new low-cost firms that help individuals invest on their own.

5.1. FAMILY DYNAMICS

The biggest risk for family or individual wealth is what happened to the Vanderbilts: your descendants waste it. Wealthy families and SWFs are actually alike in many ways: the principal aim is to avoid spending all of the money now and instead make it last through future generations. To accomplish this, both need to create robust governance structures to ensure that they can spend slowly. In general, families are terrible at preserving wealth: 70% of family money dissipates in two generations, much like what happened to the Vanderbilts.[67]

---

[64] From Vanderbilt (1989).

[65] Capgemini and RBC Wealth Management, World Wealth Report 2012.

[66] See "Private Pursuits," *Economist*, May 19, 2012.

[67] Research reported by Sullivan, M., "Lost Inheritance," *WSJ Money*, Spring 2013. The common saying, "From shirtsleeves to shirtsleeves in three generations," is, on average, correct.

Several issues in wealthy families cause their riches to disappear:

1. Families fight

    Tolstoy is spot on when he says that "all happy families are alike; each unhappy family is unhappy in its own way." Bickering family members can't decide on how a *family firm* will manage the business or on the appropriate investment style for the family office. In the worst case, millions are spent on deadweight legal fees as the parties wrangle in court. The wealthy need to pay attention to *succession planning*, and grooming their children in handling wealth, shepherding it, and managing it. Investing the nest eggs of high net worth individuals is as much about psychology as finance.[68]

2. Nepotism

    Just because the family is wealthy doesn't mean that a family member should manage its assets. Families are better off using professional management—in their firms, their foundations, and in managing their fortunes. A family member could be, but probably is not, the best person for the job. Pérez-González (2006) and Bennedsen et al. (2007) show convincingly that favoring family members hurts the performance of family firms; outside CEOs generally perform much better than next-generation family CEOs inheriting the mantle. Yet families are reluctant to hire outsiders. Even the founding CEOs tend to hang on too long as their skills atrophy or become irrelevant to a changing firm. Not surprisingly, stock prices tend to jump when a corporate founder dies.[69]

3. Lack of diversification

    It can be counterintuitive for rich individuals to realize that preserving wealth involves holding well-diversified portfolios that have exposure to different factor risk premiums. They created their wealth by doing just the opposite: holding highly concentrated positions in a single business. Athletes, models, and to a lesser extent actors, dancers, and musicians are similar to SWFs in that they generate their wealth relatively suddenly and then have to plan carefully so that the money will last.[70] Timor-Leste's Petroleum Fund diversifies away from oil and gas wealth to other assets. Diversification reduces risk and improves returns, as shown in chapter 3.

---

[68] See "Stay the Course? Portfolio Advice in the Face of Large Losses," Columbia CaseWorks, ID #110309. Economics has a literature on the governance of family firms. See the summary written by my colleague Daniel Wolfenzon at Columbia Business School, Bennedsen, Pérez-González, and Wolfenzon (2010).

[69] This is shown in a famous paper by Johnson et al. (1985).

[70] It is a myth that most lottery winners blow through all their winnings. While this certainly happens to some of them, most winners do not engage in lavish spending sprees, as Kaplan (1987) and Larsson (2011) report. Kaplan also finds "winners were well-adjusted, secure and generally happy from the experience." (Surprise, surprise.)

4. Slouching

The wealthy also suffer from the Dutch disease. Inheriting wealth that you didn't earn by your own hands makes you lazy. Why bother creating new sources of income? Timor-Leste and Norway created SWFs so that their economies nurture other income streams; wealthy families need to create structures to ensure their children do as well.

5. Spending too much

Of course, if you spend more than you bring in, your assets decline. Payout rules based on the size of the assets, like those used by Timor-Leste and endowments, mitigate this by automatically reducing payouts when investment performance is bad. This hurts when people get used to a certain level of spending (economists capture this effect with *habit utility*). Chapter 5 discusses how to set payout rules when you want consumption not to fall.

5.2. THE REST OF US

The net worth of the household sector in the United States was $66.1 trillion at December 2012. This wealth is highly skewed: the richest 1% own 35%, the richest 5% own 62%, and the richest 10% own 75%.[71] The richest 1% includes the ultra-rich whom we discussed before, but also include many who would call themselves (upper) middle class. This skewness has become more pronounced over time; the poor are getting (relatively) poorer and the rich are getting (relatively) richer.[72] The top 1% took home 9% of total income in 1976, and 20% in 2011. We are back to the same levels of inequality the United States experienced during and before the 1930s.[73]

The middle class has the same main concern as the other asset owners discussed up to now: to save more today so that tomorrow we can eat (retirement) or that our children can eat (bequests), even though we also need to worry about eating today. We must be especially mindful of the fees paid to intermediaries because the fees represent foregone consumption: since we are not rolling in dough, consumption matters more for us than the rich. (Technically, since we are poorer we have higher *marginal utilities* of consumption, see chapter 2.)

There are several additional considerations the rich don't have to worry about (or that the rich worry about less):

1. Labor income

The biggest asset is not financial; it is human capital. We should invest according to our total wealth, which is the sum of financial and human capital wealth. Timor-Leste recognizes this as it explicitly counts its oil wealth still in the Timor Sea in its EIS. As we age, our balance sheets resemble those

---

[71] Numbers from Wolff (2010).

[72] See Cagetti and De Nardi (2008) and Kopczuk, Saez, and Song (2010).

[73] Numbers from Alvaredo et al. (2013).

of resource-rich countries with SWFs: over time, wealth is transferred from human capital to financial wealth, just as Timor-Leste transfers wealth from under the sea to its Petroleum Fund. When human capital is exhausted (the oil is gone), we consume from retirement savings (or the SWF). This *life-cycle* profile affects how we need to save; the composition of our financial portfolios changes as we age (see chapter 5). The fact that we can lose our labor income over our working years, hopefully just temporarily, leads us to hold portfolios that cushion the fall when we lose our jobs.

2. Leverage

   Borrowing enables us to smooth consumption, but leverage leads to increased risk. Housing, the largest asset position for individuals, is typically highly levered and also highly illiquid. Leverage is a short position in bonds, and so the middle class is highly exposed to *interest rate risk* (or *duration risk*). Illiquidity risk also carries its own consideration (see chapter 13).

3. Health care

   A bad health shock can be disastrous. The government, through Medicare and Medicaid, provides some support for health care, but it is highly incomplete. We can buy health and disability insurance to hedge some of this risk, but we cannot completely remove the effects of these *idiosyncratic shocks*.[74] The presence of such *background risk* leads us to be effectively more risk averse than would be the case if we were guaranteed perfect health at all times.

And what about the poor? Studies show that financial education actually makes little difference for the poor: what's the point of good financial knowledge if you don't have any money to invest in the first place?[75] Addressing the (in)adequacy of savings for our poor and even middle class involve national-level savings systems to deal with bad bouts of unemployment, health-care shocks, and for retirement. There have been many proposals to reform our national pension system and many involve an increased role for government.[76] This takes us back where we started—to the management of SWFs.

6. Timor-Leste Redux

According to the IMF, Timor-Leste is "the most oil-dependent economy in the world."[77] The government obtains 95% of its revenue from oil and gas, and the

---

[74] This is the notion of Kimball (1990), where any unexpected, uninsurable risk raises the demand for safe assets.

[75] Lusardi, Michaud, and Mitchell (2013) show that if you are poor enough, it is optimal to remain financially illiterate over your whole life.

[76] One that is surprisingly contentious is by Teresa Ghilarducci (2008), who recommends introducing compulsory savings levies managed by Social Security.

[77] IMF Executive Board Concludes 2010 Article IV Consultation with the Democratic Republic of Timor-Leste, IMF Public Information Notice No. 11/31, March 8, 2011.

undeveloped state of the rest of its economy means that currently Timor-Leste has little else.

The Petroleum Fund is a tool to enable the use of Timor-Leste's oil and gas wealth for the benefit of both current and future generations and prevents the Timorese from spending everything today. The petroleum wealth is many times the current size of the country's economy. Timor-Leste's SWF shields the economy from the fluctuations of oil and gas prices, so that the greatest resource of any country—human capital—ultimately develops.

Like flies attracted to rotting flesh, large amounts of money elicit the worst tendencies of politicians and intermediaries. The Petroleum Fund has $12 billion now—and there will be even more to come with reserves still to be tapped in the Timor Sea. Timor-Leste needs to do more than just monitor its delegated managers; it needs to develop deep external partnerships so that it can ultimately transfer knowledge of asset management back to the Timorese.

Timor-Leste does not want to imitate Libya, which lost $4 billion from 2009 to 2013, $1 billion of it on derivatives. Troublingly, the fund's manager, Societe Generale, could not even explain how the money was lost.[78] This is on top of an episode in 2008 when Libya entrusted $1.3 billion to Goldman Sachs, which lost 98% of it in nine equity trades and one currency trade.[79] Nauru is another sad story.[80] The small island nation established trusts in the 1960s to accumulate wealth from phosphate mining. Gross mismanagement and overspending shrank the fund from a peak of $1 billion in 1991 to less than a tenth that size a decade later. Nauru now barely functions as a nation; the country is insolvent and three-quarters of its GDP is from external financial aid.

Preserving legitimacy of the SWF involves maintaining professionalism in its management. As Alfredo Pires, the Timor-Leste Secretary of State for Natural Resources, says, "It comes back to people and the leadership."[81] Perhaps Angola, which started its SWF in 2012 with $5 billion, should heed the empirical evidence on sub-par performance resulting from favoritism in families. Angola's SWF is run by José Filomeno de Sousa dos Santos, the thirty-five-year old son of the president who has ruled Angola since 1979. The sole fund manager is a Swiss asset manager, Quantum Global, with fewer than a dozen clients. Quantum Global's founder is a partner with dos Santos in an Angolan bank.[82]

[78] Quoted by Scheffer, B., "Libya Wealth Fund Seeking SocGen Explanation on $1 Billion Loss," Bloomberg, March 12, 2013.

[79] Coker, M., and L. Rappoport, "Libya's Goldman Dalliance Ends in Losses, Acrimony," *Wall Street Journal*, May 31, 2011.

[80] Recounted by Cox (2009).

[81] Quoted by Wright, C., "East Timor: The World's Most Important Sovereign Wealth Fund?" *Euromoney*, September 2008.

[82] See McGroarty, P., "Angolan Wealth Fund Is Family Affair," *Wall Street Journal*, Feb. 26, 2013.

In the worst case, large sums in SWFs are an invitation to graft. Their management can be nepotistic and incompetent. In the best case, proper management of SWFs can protect a country from the distortion and corruption that accompanies natural resource windfalls and play an important role in the economic development of a country. With any luck, that is how things will work out in Timor-Leste.

CHAPTER 2

Preferences

Chapter Summary

Investors generally dislike the risk of losses during bad times. Optimal portfolio choice trades off these risks with the potential of returns. While mean-variance utility treats gains and losses symmetrically, other models of preferences allow investors to seek safety first, to weight the pain of losses more heavily than the benefit of gains, and to have their utility depend on their past consumption (habit) and the returns or actions of other investors.

1. Picking Up Nickels and Dimes in Front of a Steamroller

Short volatility strategies are like the sly fox in the tale of the little gingerbread man. Just as the fox hoodwinked the tasty gingerbread man to ride on his back to cross a river, the steady and high profits generated by short volatility strategies during stable times often lure investors into complacency. Many investors pile into short volatility strategies after they have seen stable profits for many years. Then, when volatility spikes during market crashes, short volatility strategies suddenly turn around and give investors a nasty bite. Most of the profits earned during normal times are given back at a quick snap.

Figure 2.1 graphs the cumulated wealth of $1 invested in a short volatility strategy at the end of March 1989 to December 2011.[1] Volatility strategies are implemented in derivatives markets using options, variance swaps, and even derivatives on derivatives such as options on swaps. (Merrill Lynch's index is produced by trading variance swaps.) Volatility traders also buy and sell securities with embedded options such as convertible notes and bonds.

The returns graphed in Figure 2.1 are for an investor who has sold volatility—this investor collects a premium during normal times for selling volatility protection. On the other side, the people paying the premiums have purchased

---

[1] Monthly returns on the volatility strategy are given by the MLHFEV1 index produced by Merrill Lynch.

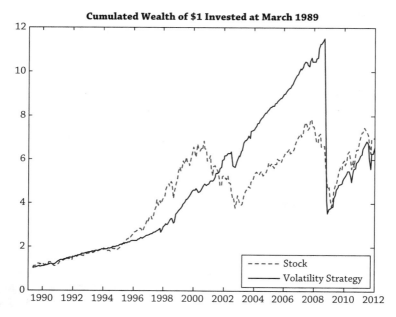

Figure 2.1

protection against increases in volatility. When volatility jumps, investors with short volatility positions suffer losses. These losses represent gains to those who have bought volatility protection. The seller's position is similar to that of a fire insurance company: the insurer collects premiums when there is no fire. When a fire breaks out, the insurance company experiences a loss, which is the payout to the policyholder. (In this chapter I will always refer to volatility strategy profits from the point of view of the investor selling volatility insurance.)

The losses from short volatility strategies can be horrendous. In Figure 2.1, there are some blips in the cumulated wealth in the volatility strategy like the 1998 emerging markets crisis, the recession and turbulence following the 9/11 attacks of 2001 and even a little wobble during the beginning of the subprime crisis in 2007. But overall returns marched steadily upward—until late 2008, when the global financial crisis caused volatility to skyrocket and stocks around the world crashed. From September to December of 2008, the volatility strategy lost more than 70%. Then in 2009, when policymakers stabilized the financial markets, the volatility strategy's profitability recovered. For comparison, Figure 2.1 also overlays the cumulated wealth of $1 invested in the S&P 500. Stock returns have exhibited more swings than the volatility strategy and from 2000 to 2010, stock returns ended the first decade of the twenty-first century flat (the *Lost Decade*). They rode a rollercoaster getting there though, dipping down through the early 2000s recession, climbing upward during the mid-2000s and then also screamed downward, but not to the same extent as the volatility strategy, during the financial crisis.

How much should we allocate to volatility strategies? Given that there are pronounced (left-hand) tail risks, what sort of investor should pick up the small nickels and dimes in front a roaring steamroller?

2. Choices

Economists want agents (people, firms, or institutions) to have as many choices as possible and to guide agents to make optimal choices.[2] These choices reflect asset owners' preferences. Preferences are ultimately a collection of trade-offs: how do I balance a set of risks against a set of rewards? Trade-offs apply at a point in time, as in the choice between holding boring T-bills or picking up nickels in front of the oncoming steamroller in the volatility strategy. Trade-offs also occur across time, as in deciding how much to save today for retirement in the future. Preferences are unique to each asset owner, and ethics and morals (and sometimes lack thereof) can be important factors. Each asset owner has different goals, plans, and lifestyle choices. Psychological and family or institutional dynamics also play a role, and choices are influenced as well by the decisions of peers and other social factors.

We represent preferences by *utility*, an index numerically describing preferences in the sense that decisions that are made by ranking or maximizing utilities fully coincide with the asset owner's underlying preferences. (Economists call utility values "*utils*.") Utility is about choice, and we build a *utility function* to measure how satisfied an agent is by making choices.

Good choices in the context of optimal asset management policy start with the ancient Greek maxim "know thyself." Specifically, we build advice that depends upon how you feel during bad times. To capture this notion quantitatively, we define how the asset owner perceives risk and how she responds to it.

2.1. RISK

In his book, *Against the Gods: The Remarkable Story of Risk*, Peter Bernstein (1998) chronicles our astonishing progress in measuring risk through the development of statistics and probability from the invention of Arabic numerals to

---

[2] My colleague Sheena Iyengar (2010) at Columbia Business School shows that in some contexts, too much choice ends up being detrimental to consumers in making choices. I do not go down this route. Framing and other psychological contexts matter in adhering to optimal portfolio choice strategies as I discuss in section 2.6.

today's (cloud) computers.[3] We model all risk and rewards through these statistical methods. Our notion of risk today is extremely broad—it is not just the likelihood of a set of returns. We think of risk today in terms of probability functions encompassing many different kinds of events (or even parallel universes, if you are a theoretical physicist).[4] We even think of risk as the probability of sets of probabilities changing over time, as I explain below.

Risk in financial economics is inherently a subjective concept. We do not have controlled laboratory conditions in finance and must estimate the distribution of asset returns. The procedures used to estimate probabilities and the model that is behind the estimation impart subjectivity. Nevertheless, we refer to direct estimates of the behavior of returns from data as being *real world measures* or *objective measures*. In contrast, *subjective measures* are probabilities that an asset owner believes in and that differ from real-world probabilities. A coin flip, for example, has a 50% objective probability of landing heads, but an investor might believe the coin is biased and assign a subjective probability of 60% to the coin coming up heads. Probabilities of returns are harder to estimate than probabilities of coin flips because there are an infinite number of return outcomes ranging from losing all your money (a return of –100%) to becoming a bazillionaire (a return of nearly infinity), and everything in between. (If you invest with leverage, your return may even be lower than –100%.)

In Panel A of Figure 2.2, I estimate objective probabilities for the volatility strategy at the monthly frequency from April 1989 to December 2011. The top half presents a histogram of returns and the bottom half graphs the strategy's *probability density function* (or *probability distribution function*, or just *pdf*). In both graphs, the *x*-axis lists the returns (what can happen), and the *y*-axis lists the probabilities of the return outcomes (how often they happen). The huge occasional loss that occurs in volatility investing, which happened during 2008–2009, imparts a very long left-hand tail to its probability distribution. The very long left-hand tail is the statistical representation of picking up the nickels and dimes right before the steamroller crushes you.

The estimated probability density function of the volatility strategy has a much thinner body and longer tail than a fitted normal distribution. We call these distributions *leptokurtic*, which is Greek for "thin hump," since they have much more slender distributions at the center than a normal distribution. When your distribution has a more slender body, it also has longer tails than a normal distribution. Figure 2.2, Panel B, repeats the same exercise for the S&P 500 for comparison. Equity returns over this time period are also leptokurtic, but much less so than the volatility strategy. While there is a noticeable left-hand tail for equities, the normal distribution is not a bad approximation. (While it is a much closer

---

[3] The 2008–2009 financial crisis shows that we remain far from mastering systemic risk.

[4] This is measure theory. Even the foundation of Brownian motion, which we use in option pricing and dynamic portfolio choice (see chapter 4), rests on probabilities specified over function spaces (called "functionals").

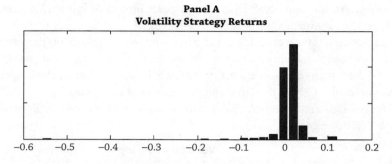

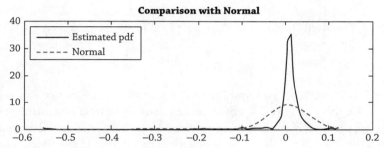

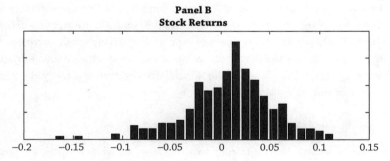

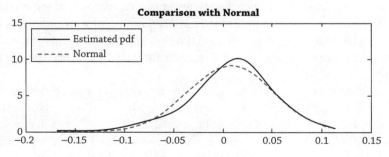

Figure 2.2

approximation for equity returns, an enormous literature formally rejects that equity returns are normally distributed.)

We summarize the probability density function by *moments*. Moments measure the shape of the probability density function, like where it is centered (*mean*), how disperse the returns can be (*variance* or *standard deviation*, which is the square root of the variance), how far the left-hand or right-hand tails extend (*skewness*), and how fat the tails are (*kurtosis*). The first four moments for the volatility strategy and S&P 500 are:

	Volatility Strategy	Equities
Mean	9.9%	9.7%
Standard Deviation	15.2%	15.1%
Skewness	–8.3	–0.6
Kurtosis	104.4	4.0

The volatility strategy and equities have approximately the same mean, around 10%. We see this in Figure 2.1 where the cumulated wealth of both strategies results in approximately the same ending value.[5] While the standard deviation (or volatility—and I will use these two terms interchangeably) of the short volatility strategy and equities are similar at 15%, the long-left tail of the volatility strategy gives it very large negative skewness, of –8.3, and a humungous kurtosis of 104. The S&P 500 has small skewness of –0.6 and relatively small kurtosis of 4.0. In comparison, the normal distribution has a skewness of zero and kurtosis of 3.0. Hence, in Figure 2.2, Panel B, the normal distribution is a fairly close match for the distribution of equity returns.

2.2. RISK AVERSION

While the probability distribution of wealth shows us what returns are possible and how often, investors do not directly use these returns in making decisions. Instead, returns are used as inputs into a *utility function*, which defines how a return outcome is felt as a bad time or good time by the investor. Simply put, utilities convey the notion of "how you feel." The utility function defines bad times for the investor.

Let us define the utility as a function of wealth, W, so that bad times are times when we are poor. (Technically we write $U(W)$, where utility, U, is a function of wealth, W.) The investor's utility is not final wealth itself—the utility transforms wealth into an investor's subjective value of wealth. Figure 2.3 plots three commonly used utility functions as a function of wealth: exponential, logarithmic, and constant relative risk aversion (CRRA), which is also called *power utility*.

[5] The correlation of the returns of the volatility strategy and equities is 0.51. This chapter only considers portfolio choice between single risky assets and a risk-free asset. Portfolio choice over multiple risky assets is considered in chapter 3.

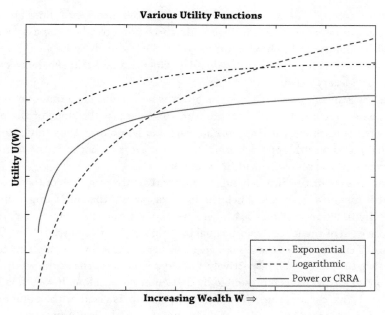

Various Utility Functions

Legend:
- – ·– ·– Exponential
- – – – – Logarithmic
- —— Power or CRRA

Figure 2.3

I have purposely left the units off the x- and y-axes. These utility functions are *ordinal*, so that the actual numerical value of utility has no meaning. The numbers merely denote ranks: we can replace the utility function U by $a + bU$ for any positive constants a and b without changing the preference ordering. (That is, utility orderings are unchanged by *affine transformations*.)

All of the utility functions in Figure 2.3 increase with wealth, which realistically reflects the fact that asset owners are generally greedy. Furthermore, utility functions are all *concave* over wealth. Concavity is a measure of how much investors value an extra \$1 of wealth. When investors are poor, we sit close to the y-axis in Figure 2.3, and the slopes of all the curves are very steep. When you only have \$1, you really value going from \$1 to \$2. When wealth is high, the utility curves flatten out: when you already have \$10 million, there is little to be gained from going from \$10,000,000 to \$10,000,001 in wealth. The utility curves exhibit *diminishing marginal utility* in wealth. This is an appealing property of concave utility functions.

The slope of the utility function (the changing marginal utility as wealth increases) is how we measure just how bad or good the investor feels. Utilities that decrease very fast as wealth decreases correspond to investors for whom losses really hurt. Asset owners who have utilities that are very flat as wealth increases don't care much for increasing their wealth when wealth is already very high. *Bad times are times of high marginal utility.* Bad times are when the utility curve is very steep: at these points the asset owner really, really wants another \$1 ("Brother can you spare a dime?") as the extra $1 makes a big difference. Good times are when marginal utility is low, which in Figure 2.3 correspond to when the asset owner is wealthy and the utility function is very flat. She's already so happy ("Plenty of sunshine heading my way, zipa-dee-doo-dah, zip-a-dee-ay") that she doesn't value that extra $1 very much.

The investor's *degree of risk aversion* governs how painful bad times are for the asset owner. Technically, risk aversion controls how fast the slope of the utility function increases as wealth approaches zero and how slowly the utility function flattens out as wealth approaches infinity. Risk aversion controls the degree of concavity in the asset owner's utility function.

Everyone wants the bird in hand. An alternative interpretation of risk aversion is that it measures just how much the investor prefers the sure thing. Consider the utility function in Figure 2.4. There are two outcomes: X (low) and Y (high). Suppose each of them occurs with equal probability. The two vertical lines drawn at X and Y correspond to the asset owner's utility at these low and high outcomes of wealth, $U(X)$ and $U(Y)$, respectively. Consider what happens at the wealth outcome $\frac{1}{2}X + \frac{1}{2}Y$, which is represented by the center vertical line. If wealth is equal to $\frac{1}{2}X + \frac{1}{2}Y$ for certain, then the asset owner's utility is given by the point on her utility curve denoted by $U(\frac{1}{2}X + \frac{1}{2}Y)$. This point is marked with the star.

Now consider the straight, diagonal line connecting $U(X)$ and $U(Y)$. If future wealth is X with probability $\frac{1}{2}$ and Y with probability $\frac{1}{2}$, then the expected utility

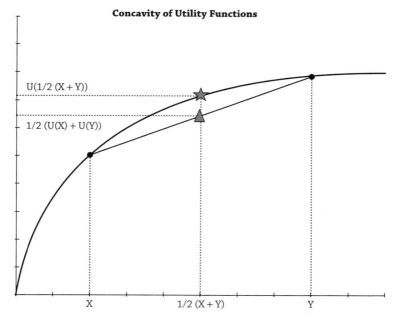

Figure 2.4

$\frac{1}{2}U(X) + \frac{1}{2}U(Y)$ lies on the diagonal line connecting $U(X)$ and $U(Y)$ and is shown by the triangle. Utility is higher for the certain outcome than for the random amount:[6]

$$U\left(\frac{1}{2}X + \frac{1}{2}Y\right) \geq \frac{1}{2}U(X) + \frac{1}{2}U(Y).$$

The greater the difference between the star and the circle in Figure 2.4, the more risk averse the investor. Put another way, the more risk averse the asset owner becomes, the more she wants the sure thing. The more concave the utility function, the more risk averse the investor.

In the special case that the investor is *risk seeking*, the utility function becomes convex rather than concave. If an investor is *risk neutral* the utility function is linear. These cases are rare; most investors are risk averse.

2.3. HOW RISK AVERSE ARE YOU?

Risk aversion can change as wealth changes, and for most individuals risk aversion decreases as wealth increases—individuals generally take on more risk as they become more financially secure. For this reason, I will talk about (relative) risk aversion, where risk aversion is measured relative to wealth, and for short hand I will drop the word "relative" from now on.[7]

CRRA utility takes the following form:

$$U(W) = \frac{W^{1-\gamma}}{1-\gamma}, \tag{2.1}$$

where g is the asset owner's risk aversion coefficient. CRRA utility is widely used in portfolio choice theory. A very attractive property of CRRA utility is that it leads to portfolio weights that do not depend on wealth: it doesn't matter whether one is managing \$10 million or \$100 million—the technology of asset management is exactly the same—and this is the beauty of the scalability of the wealth management industry, at least for the fund manager. (This property is called *wealth homogeneity*). Under CRRA utility, risk aversion is the same for all levels of wealth—so the advantage for this utility function is also an inherent disadvantage, because investors are generally more risk averse over losses than over gains (see section 4). But it is convenient that we can summarize all behavior with just one risk aversion parameter. With this caveat in mind, what risk aversion levels do investors have?

---

[6] Or $U(E[X]) \geq E[U(X)]$, which is a consequence of Jensen's inequality for the concave function.

[7] Formally, there is the absolute risk aversion coefficient introduced by Arrow (1971) and Pratt (1964) defined as $-U''(W)/U'(W)$ and the relative risk aversion coefficient defined as $-WU''(W)/U'(W)$. Note these definitions of risk aversions are invariant to affine transformations just as utility ordering is itself invariant to affine transformations. Levy's (1994) subjects exhibited decreasing absolute risk aversion as they become wealthier and approximately CRRA.

This question is pretty meaningless for most people. I don't describe myself using CRRA utility in equation (2.1) and rattle off a risk aversion parameter (but yes, some of my academic colleagues can). We can, however, estimate risk aversion levels indirectly. Suppose I gave you the following lottery:

where you can win $1,000 with 50% probability or win $500 with 50% probability. That is, you will get $500 for sure, but you have the possibility of winning $1,000. How much would you pay for this opportunity? The real-life counterparts to this lottery are financial advisors' questionnaires that try to infer clients' risk aversion.[8]

We can map what an investor would pay against the investor's degree of risk aversion, γ. (We compute this through a *certainty equivalent*, and we detail this concept further when we discuss mean-variance utility below.) The following table allows us to read off risk aversion levels as a function of the amount you would pay to enter the gamble:

Risk Aversion γ	Amount You Would Pay
0	750
0.5	729
1	707
2	667
3	632
4	606
5	586
10	540
15	525
20	519
50	507

An individual not willing to risk anything—you get $500 for sure—is infinitely risk averse. An individual willing to pay the fair value of the gamble, which is $750, is risk neutral and has a risk aversion of $\gamma = 0$. If an investor is willing to risk more than the fair value, then she is risk seeking.

Most individuals have risk aversions between 1 and 10; it's very rare to have a risk aversion greater than 10. That is, most people would be willing to pay

---

[8] Some of these are covered, along with other techniques to elicit clients' risk aversions, in "Stay the Course," Columbia CaseWorks, ID#110309. See also Grable and Lytton (1999).

between \$540 and \$707 to enter this lottery. These estimates come from a very large body of experimental and survey evidence. Some of the papers in the literature are quite creative. Andrew Metrick (1995) studied participants on the game show Jeopardy. The stakes on this show are high, and there is tremendous pressure because only the winning player gets to return. (Jeopardy participants are also really smart, so you can't say that they don't know what they're doing!) Metrick finds that risk aversion levels are low and near risk-neutrality. More recent estimates are provided by Aarbu and Schroyen (2009), who surveyed Norwegians and found risk aversion estimates around four. Kimball, Sahm, and Shapiro (2008) also perform surveys and their estimates are higher, at around eight. Note that these are surveys, however, rather than real financial choices. At Columbia Business School, Paravisini, Rappoport, and Ravini (2010) examined actual financial decisions made by investors in an online person-to-person lending platform deciding who gets funding, and how much. They estimated investors have risk aversions around three.

2.4. EXPECTED UTILITY

Expected utility combines probabilities of outcomes (how often do these events occur?) with how investors feel about these outcomes (are they a bad time for me?):

$$U = E[U(W)] = \sum_s p_s U(W_s). \tag{2.2}$$

In equation (2.2), the subscript s denotes outcome s happening, so expected utility multiplies the probability of it happening, p_s, with the utility of the event in that state, $U(W_s)$. Technically, we say that expected utility involves *separable* transformations on probabilities and outcomes. The probabilities measure how often bad times occur, and the transformations of outcomes capture how an investor feels about these bad times.

Expected utility traces back to the 1700s to the mathematicians Gabriel Cramer and Daniel Bernoulli, but its use as a decision-making tool exploded after John von Neumann and Oskar Morgenstern formalized expected utility in *The Theory of Games and Economic Behavior* in 1944. Von Neumann was one of the greatest mathematicians of modern times, and he also made seminal contributions in physics and computer science. He and the economist Morgenstern created a new field of economics—game theory—which studied how agents interact strategically, as in the famous Prisoner's Dilemma game. Von Neumann and Morgenstern initially developed expected utility to apply to games of chance; expected utility theory was just an accompaniment to the overall theory of games. The stock market is a game of chance—but unlike poker, stock market probabilities are ultimately unknown. In an important extension, Savage (1954) showed that expected utility still applied when the probabilities were subjective and derived from agents' actions, rather than being taken as given. Thus, the probabilities in equation (2.2) can be objective or subjective.[9]

To make choices, the asset owner *maximizes expected utility*. The problem is formally stated as:

$$\max_{\theta} E[U(W)], \tag{2.3}$$

where θ are choice (or control) variables. Some examples of choice variables include asset allocation decisions (portfolio weights), spending/savings plans, and production plans for a firm, and so on. The maximization problem in equation (2.3) is often solved subject to constraints. For an asset owner, these constraints often involve constraints on the *investment universe, position constraints* like *leverage constraints*, no *short-sale constraints*, or the inability to hold certain sectors or asset classes, and, when the asset allocation problem is being done over time, there may be constraints that depend on an investor's past asset positions (like *turnover constraints*).

A very special class of the expected utility framework is the set of *rational* expected utility models. Traditionally, these were derived to satisfy certain axioms (like the independence axiom, which states roughly that if I prefer x to y, then I also prefer the possibility of getting x to the possibility of getting y when x and y are mixed with the same lottery; violation of this maxim led to the loss aversion utility that I describe in section 4 of this chapter). Not surprisingly many of these axioms are violated in reality.[10] Rejecting the whole class of expected utility as a decision-making tool solely on this restrictive set of rational expected utility models is misguided; expected utility remains a useful tool to guide asset owners' decisions—even when these investors have behavioral tendencies, as most investors do in the real world. In fact, the broad class of expected utility nests behavioral models, as I describe below.

2.5. WHAT CHOICE THEORY IS NOT ABOUT

How agents make decisions, and giving them advice to make good decisions, is not about

1. Wealth

    Greater wealth gives asset owners more choices. But wealth per se is not the objective. Figure 2.1 illustrates that how we get to a given level of wealth— through slow and steady increases or by extreme ups and downs—can matter

---

[9] See Schoemaker (1982) for a summary on the expected utility model and its variants.

[10] An excellent book that offers insight into investors' behavioral tendencies is Kahneman's (2011) *Thinking Fast and Slow*.

just as much as our ultimate net worth. The entire concept of a utility function captures the notion that investors do not value each dollar of wealth one for one.

2. Happiness

Happiness is an important emotion, and maximizing happiness could be a criterion for making a decision. Happiness is also correlated with wealth in empirical studies.[11] One popular interpretation of an asset owner maximizing utility by taking a series of actions is that she achieves bliss (or as close to it as possible) by choosing a particular portfolio. This is not strictly correct. The asset owner balances risk and return and dislikes certain risks, such as the risk of large and ruinous losses, more than others, such as the risk of small fluctuations. The preferences of the asset owner capture both risk and return, which pure happiness-seeking does not.

3. Rationality versus behavioral approaches

A healthy debate rages between finance academics over whether high returns for a particular style of investing (value stocks, e.g., have higher returns on average than growth stocks, see chapter 7) are due to rational or behavioral stories. This is less relevant for the asset owner, who should treat the rational and behavioral frameworks as ways to make optimal decisions. Most people do not have rational expected utility. But that does not mean that certain rational expected utility models are not useful in making decisions.

2.6. THE NORMATIVE VERSUS POSITIVE DEBATE

An important distinction is between normative economics (what is the best portfolio to hold?) versus positive economics (what do people actually hold?). The normative versus positive debate is ultimately philosophical, but the asset owner needs to spend some time thinking about this issue.

The normative approach starts with characterizing the asset owner. This approach assumes you "know thyself" and can describe the set of bad times and how you feel about those bad times. Combined with estimating the probability of bad times, expected utility provides a way for us to set an optimal allocation policy. This advice is what you should do. This is normative economics.

But what if the investor does not follow this "optimal" advice? We could conclude that our theory is not describing what the investor is actually doing. For a better description of how the investor is acting, perhaps we should revisit the utility function, or go back and reestimate the probabilities perceived by the investor. We can now find the actual utility function the investor has, rather than

---

[11] Although wealthier people are happier than poorer people within countries, Easterlin (1974) found rich countries are not happier, on the whole, than poorer countries. There was no change in happiness over time, even though there have been tremendous increases in GDP per capita. Stevenson and Wolfers (2008) have disputed some of these findings.

the utility function that we originally assumed. Since our investor failed to act in the way we prescribed, let's better characterize how the investor perceives risk. This is positive economics.

I concentrate on normative asset management. That is, I give prescriptive advice for what asset owners should do. It turns out that most people and institutions do not, unfortunately, invest the way optimal theory tells them. For example, the theory that we develop advocates:

– Diversifying widely
  But many individuals hold concentrated positions in their employers' stock. Many also suffer from home bias and thus fail to invest overseas. (We take up these issues in the next chapter.)
– Rebalancing
  But many asset owners fail to rebalance, since it involves buying assets that have lost value. Why, they wonder, should I buy a loser? (see chapter 4).
– Dis-saving after retirement
  Many individuals actually continue to save when they enter retirement instead of dis-saving as predicted by lifecycle models (see chapter 5). Annuities are also predicted to be very good investments for retirees, but sadly few hold annuities.
– Using factors, not asset class labels, in investing
  Putting a label on a type of financial intermediary does not make them new investment classes. Putting "private" in front of "equity," for instance, does not create an asset class called "private equity." Calling a collection of funds "absolute return strategies" does not make them so. Few investors delve into the underlying factor drivers of their portfolio returns (see chapter 14).
– Recognizing that your asset manager is not your friend
  Agency issues permeate the asset management industry. People often do not give asset managers the proper incentives or monitor them correctly (see chapter 15).

Many investors fail to follow normative advice because of behavioral tendencies, poor governance, or the inability to be time consistent. Couching normative recommendations in ways that mitigate these effects is a newly developing science that takes into account the way people respond to framing and incentives.[12] We will discuss many of these issues in the chapters to come. Meanwhile, bear in mind that the best normative frameworks take into account the behavioral or institutional settings that hinder asset owners from following sound advice, especially advice given in traditional ways. Good normative structures also take into account the possibility that the asset owner will fail and give advice specifically for these contingencies.

---

[12] See Thaler and Sunstein (2009), among others.

2.7. NON-MONETARY CONSIDERATIONS

Choices reflect our underlying personalities—who we are, our ethics, the culture of our institutions, and our core beliefs. These considerations should enter our utility framework as well. In my exposition, utility functions represent how investors quantitatively measure bad times. Violations of core principles are some of the worst times—moral and social indignation can also be translated to extremely low utility values (states where marginal utility is extremely high).

For some institutions, stakeholders expect asset management to be conducted in a certain way to support the institution. The Norwegian sovereign wealth fund, CalPERS, CalSTRS, and other prominent large funds refuse to hold tobacco stocks. Norway goes further and automatically excludes all companies making cluster munitions and nuclear weapons from its portfolio. It has divested from companies for human rights violations (Wal-Mart), destroying the environment (Rio Tinto and Freeport McMoRan), and other violations of ethical norms (Potash Corporation of Saskatchewan). Many of these decisions have generated substantial attention in the press.[13]

For Norway's sovereign wealth fund, ethical investing reflects the preferences of the asset owner—the Norwegian people. Doing this confers legitimacy on the funds in the eyes of the stakeholders. In many other funds, the asset management style choice also reflects stakeholder preferences. In the extreme case, risking the existence of an institution by failing to manage assets in a certain way actually brings on the worst bad time possible—annihilation.

Utility is a representation of how asset owners make choices. We use utility to (normatively) derive asset management policies. Thus, if an asset owner needs to make choices that reflect non-monetary considerations, asset management should reflect those choices, subject to whether our optimal policies reflect normative or positive considerations. The most important thing is to take a stand on who we are.

2.8. SUMMARY

Expected utility is a tool for asset owners to quantitatively assess how they feel about bad times. Risk is captured by the (potentially subjective) probabilities of bad times occurring, and utility functions allow an investor to perceive how they feel about outcomes during these bad times. The more risk averse the asset owner, the more these bad times hurt and the more the asset owner prefers sure things.

While the simplest expected utility models capture bad times by the probabilities and marginal utilities of low wealth outcomes, utilities are a shorthand to represent the underlying preferences of the asset owner. Low wealth isn't the only

---

[13] See "The Norwegian Government Pension Fund: The Divestiture of Wal-Mart Stores Inc.," Columbia CaseWorks, ID#080301.

definition of bad times. Preferences are also affected by ethics, psychological tendencies, peer decisions, and other social factors. We return to some of these utility
functions in section 4.

3. Mean-Variance Utility

With mean-variance utility, asset owners care only about means (which they like),
and variances (which they dislike). Mean-variance utility defines bad times as low
means and high variances.

Mean-variance utility is given by:

$$U = E(r_p) - \frac{\gamma}{2}\text{var}(r_p), \qquad (2.4)$$

where r_p is the return of the investor's portfolio and g is her coefficient of risk
aversion.

Mean-variance utility is closely related to CRRA utility (see equation (2.1)).
In fact, we can consider expected utility using CRRA utility and mean-variance
to be approximately the same, and we will do so for many purposes in this book.[14]
Thus, the γ in equation (2.4) has the same interpretation as the risk aversion in
section 2.3, and we expect most investors' γs to lie between 1 and 10. The parameter of $\frac{1}{2}$ in equation (2.4) is simply a scaling parameter; it is of no consequence
and can be ignored.

Mean-variance utility is the workhorse utility of the investment industry.
It was introduced by Harry Markowitz in his pathbreaking work in 1952, but
Markowitz did not fully rationalize using mean-variance utility in an expected
utility framework until 1979 in a paper co-authored with Haim Levy. Levy and
Markowitz approximate any expected utility function by a mean-variance utility
function:

$$E[U(1 + r_p)] \approx U(1 + E(r_p)) + \frac{1}{2}U''(1 + E(r_p))\,\text{var}(r_p), \qquad (2.5)$$

where $U''(\bullet)$ denotes the second derivative of the utility function. Utility functions are concave, so their second derivatives are negative and the second term in
equation (2.5) is negative. Hence, equation (2.5) shows that an investor maximizing expected utility is approximately the same as an investor maximizing mean
for a given level of variance, and thus equation (2.5) takes the same form as
mean-variance utility in equation (2.4).

---

[14] The portfolio choices made with CRRA utility and mean-variance utility are very close and
will converge to each other under certain conditions, like employing (log) normal distributions and
sampling intervals that tend to zero.

The intuition behind the Levy–Markowitz approximation in equation (2.5) of mean-variance utility to any expected utility function is that the two most important effects are where the returns are centered (the mean) and how disperse they are (the variance). There is a trade-off between these two effects, which is captured by the investor's risk aversion. This is precisely the mean-variance utility setup of equation (2.4). Mean-variance utility is ubiquitous in the investment industry (much less so, thankfully, in academia). It has been relentlessly criticized, quite rightly, but mean-variance techniques nonetheless bring us a great deal of intuition that extends to more complex situations. And the two most important things are indeed means and variances. Often other things also matter—and unfortunately mean-variance utility does not allow us to capture anything other than the mean and variance.

Mean-variance utility does not assume returns are normal. Often people confuse using mean-variance utility with assuming normally distributed returns. This error comes about because, with normal distributions, there are only two parameters—the mean and the variance, and these completely describe the normal distribution (they are called *sufficient statistics*). Since with normal distributions only means and variances matter, mean-variance utility is perfect. Levy and Markowitz showed that using mean-variance utility is often a good approximation with non-normal returns. But sometimes the approximation can be lousy. Let's go back to Figure 2.1 showing the cumulated wealth of the volatility strategy and the S&P 500. Both end up with approximately the same return, and they have approximately the same mean (around 10%) and the same standard deviation (around 15%). But investing in the volatility strategy is like picking up the nickels and dimes before an oncoming steamroller—the skewness is –8 and kurtosis is 104. The S&P 500 is much closer to a normal distribution. Using only the mean and variance would imply that both the volatility strategy and the S&P 500 would be approximately the same. But clearly the volatility strategy and the S&P 500 are not the same. Would you want to use the mean and variance exclusively?

Having said that, we'll stick with using means and variances for now and return to more realistic utility functions in section 4.

3.1. INDIFFERENCE CURVES

We represent mean-variance utility pictorially by *indifference curves*. One particular indifference curve represents one particular level of utility. Figure 2.5 plots three different indifference curve for different utility levels for an asset owner with a risk aversion of $\gamma = 3$. We plot these in mean-standard deviation space on the y-axis and x-axis, respectively. Along one particular indifference curve, an investor is indifferent to all the mean-volatility combinations. For example, on the indifference curve with the triangles in Figure 2.5, which corresponds to a utility of $U = 0.15$, the asset owner does not care which mean-volatility combination that she picks; all of them result in the same number of utils. Investors seek the

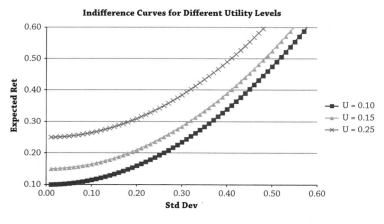

Figure 2.5

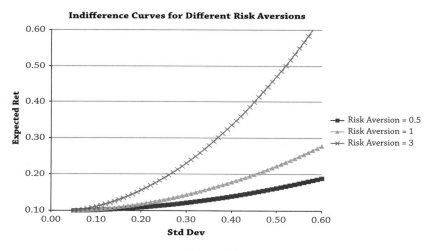

Figure 2.6

highest possible utility. Higher indifference curves lie to the left. Higher indifference curves have higher means and lower volatilities, which correspond to higher utility from equation (2.4). While Figure 2.5 plots just three indifference curves, there is in fact an infinite family of indifference curves for every investor. These indifference curves lie parallel to each other.[15]

In section 2.3, we interpreted the shape of a utility function as being summarized by the risk aversion coefficient. The same intuition applies to indifference curves. The more risk averse an investor, the steeper the slope of his indifference curves. In Figure 2.6, I plot indifference curves for three levels of risk aversion. For

[15] They are parabolas because equation (2.4) is quadratic in σ_p.

the risk aversion of $\gamma = 3$, the indifference curve has the steepest slope. If we increase risk (standard deviation), this investor needs to be compensated the most so the indifference curve shoots sharply upward as risk increases. In contrast, the investor with $\gamma = 0.5$ is relatively risk tolerant: this investor does not need to be compensated as much with high expected returns when risk is increased. Thus, her indifference curves are relatively flat. It is important to note that an investor has one risk aversion parameter and a family of indifference curves (as drawn in Figure 2.5). Figure 2.6 compares indifference curves for different investors.

3.2. CERTAINTY EQUIVALENT

The utility certainty equivalent is the sure amount of wealth, or the risk-free return, that makes the investor feel the same as holding a risky asset position.[16] The certainty equivalent is the compensation the investor requires that would make him relinquish a risky asset.

For mean-variance utility, the indifference curve provides a convenient way to compute the certainty equivalent. An investor has the same utility along all combinations of risk and return on an indifference curve, by definition. The intersection at the y-axis of an indifference curve represents an asset with a positive return and no volatility—a risk-free asset. Thus, we can trace the indifference curve going through a risky asset position to the y-axis intercept to find the certainty equivalent.

Figure 2.7 plots the mean and standard deviation of the volatility strategy, which is marked with the square, and the indifference curve that goes through the volatility strategy for a $\gamma = 3$ investor. The certainty equivalent of the volatility strategy is 6.45%. This means that if the investor could not invest \$1 in the volatility strategy, the investor would need to be compensated 6.45 cents on that \$1; the volatility strategy is equivalent to a risk-free return of 6.45%. The certainty equivalent is also called *willingness to pay*. An asset owner would be willing to pay 6.45 cents per dollar of wealth (risk-free) to be able to have the same utility as investing in the volatility strategy (which is risky).

Mean-variance utility ignores the large negative skew of the volatility strategy in computing this certainty equivalent. The mean and standard deviation of the volatility strategy are almost the same as the stock market, so this would be approximately the same certainty equivalent of the S&P 500 as well.

When we compute the certainty equivalent with mean-variance utility, we make use of the fact that the mean-variance utility function in equation (2.4) has economic meaning stated in terms of its level. In equation (2.4), the utility level itself is the certainty equivalent value. That is, mean-variance utility exhibits

---

[16] Formally the certainty equivalent is the amount C satisfying $U(C) = E[U(X)]$ for the risky lottery X.

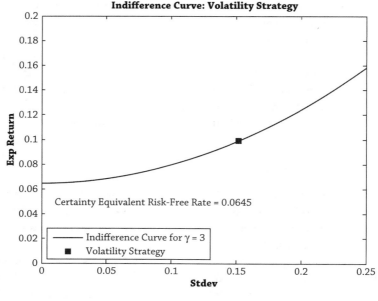

Figure 2.7

cardinality as opposed to the formulation of expected utility in section 2, which was only ordinal.

Certainty equivalent values are extremely useful in portfolio choice. We will use them, for example, to gauge the cost of not diversifying (see chapter 3), to compute the cost of holding illiquid asset positions and to use certainty equivalents to estimate illiquidity premiums (see chapter 13), and to estimate how much compensation an investor would require in exchange for foregoing the right to withdraw capital from a hedge fund during a lock-up period (see chapter 17).

3.3. THE RISK AVERSION OF A TYPICAL PENSION FUND

A typical pension fund holds 40% in fixed income and 60% in more risky assets, a category that includes equities, property, and alternative assets such as hedge funds and private equity. What risk aversion level does this asset mix imply?

Figure 2.8, Panel A, graphs all possible combinations of risk (standard deviation) and return that can be achieved by holding equities and bonds. I use U.S. data from January 1926 to December 2011 from Ibbotson as my proxies for fixed income and riskier assets. The square and circle plot the volatility and mean of stocks and bonds, respectively. The curve linking the two represents all portfolio positions holding both stocks and bonds between 0% and 100%.

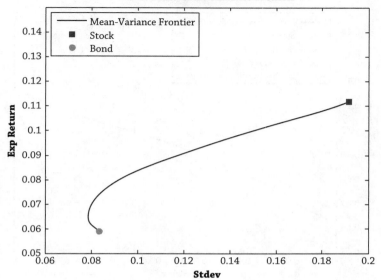

Panel A
Stock-Bond Mean-Variance Frontier

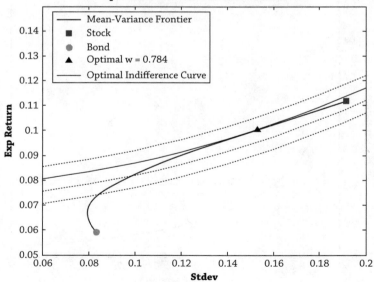

Panel B
Optimal Asset Choice for Risk Aversion = 2

Figure 2.8

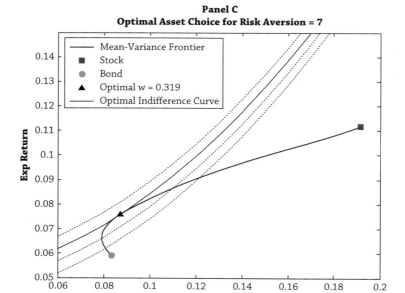

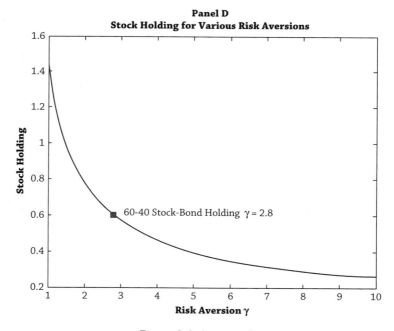

Figure 2.8 (continued)

It is called the *mean-variance frontier*. (The next chapter will delve deeper into the economics of mean-variance frontiers for multiple assets.) In this example, the mean-variance frontier represents all the possible risk-return combinations that we can obtain by holding stock and bond positions (without employing leverage).[17]

Bonds lie on an *inefficient* part of the mean-variance frontier. By holding some equities, we move in a clockwise direction and strictly increase the portfolio's expected return while lowering the portfolio's volatility. Thus, we would never hold a portfolio of 100% bonds. Equity diversifies a bond portfolio because equities have a low correlation with bonds; the correlation of equities with bonds in this sample is just 11%. Thus, the investor optimally will hold some equities because equities have a chance of paying off when bonds do poorly. But how much equity should the asset owner hold?

The optimal portfolio holdings depend on the asset owner's degree of risk aversion. Panel B of Figure 2.8 overlays indifference curves for an investor with risk aversion $\gamma = 2$. She wishes to maximize her utility:

$$\max_{w} E(r_p) - \frac{\gamma}{2}\text{var}(r_p), \tag{2.6}$$

where we choose the optimal portfolio combination w. For this problem, specifying a weight in one asset (equities) automatically determines the weight in the other asset (bonds) as the weights sum to one. Panel B of Figure 2.8 visually depicts the optimization problem in equation (2.6). Maximizing utility is equivalent to finding the highest possible indifference curve.

The highest indifference curve is tangent to the mean-variance frontier in Panel B at the triangle. At this point, the asset owner holds 78% in equities. There are higher indifference curves graphed, but these indifference curves do not intersect the mean-variance frontier—these indifference curves are *infeasible*. We have to lie on the mean-variance frontier as these represent the only set of portfolios that can be obtained by holding positions in equities and bonds. Thus, the triangle is the highest utility that can be obtained.

---

[17] For two assets, the mean-variance frontier is traced by taking all combinations of the two assets A and B. Denoting the mean and volatility of asset A by $E(r_A)$ and σ_A, respectively, the mean and volatility of asset B by $E(r_B)$ and σ_B, respectively, and the correlation between the returns of asset A and asset B by ρ, the portfolio mean and volatility for the mean-variance frontier for two assets are given By

$$E(r_p) = wE(r_A) + (1-w)E(r_B)$$

$$\sigma_p = \sqrt{w^2\sigma_A^2 + (1-w)^2\sigma_B^2 + 2w(1-w)\rho\sigma_A\sigma_B} \ ,$$

where we vary the portfolio weight w held in asset A. The charts in Figure 2.8 restrict w to lie between 0 and 1.

In Panel C of Figure 2.8, I show indifference curves for a more risk-averse investor with a risk aversion level of $\gamma = 7$. (Note that these indifference curves are steeper than the ones in Panel B.) The tangency point is marked in the triangle and is closer to the 100% bonds point on the mean-variance frontier. For the $\gamma = 7$ asset owner, a 32% equities position is optimal.

So what risk aversion level corresponds to a 60% equities position? Panel D of Figure 2.8 plots the equities weight as a function of risk aversion. A 60%/40% equities–bond position corresponds to a risk aversion level of $\gamma = 2.8$. Thus, typical pension funds—like most individual investors—are moderately risk averse. This method of backing out risk aversion from portfolios that are observed is called *revealed preference*.

3.4. THE MARKET'S RISK AVERSION

The *capital allocation line* (CAL) describes portfolios that can be chosen when there is one risky asset, say equities, and a risk-free asset. For now, interpret the latter as U.S. T-bills, even though these have a tiny bit of (sovereign) risk (see chapter 14), which we will ignore for the time being. We assume that a period is known— say, a quarter—so that we know what the risk-free rate is. We denote the risk-free rate by r_f and the expected return and standard deviation of the risky asset as $E(r)$ and σ, respectively.

The CAL is described in portfolio mean-standard deviation space $(E(r_p), \sigma_p)$ by the following line:

$$E(r_p) = r_f + \frac{E(r) - r_f}{\sigma}\sigma_p. \tag{2.7}$$

The CAL traces out all the possible portfolios of a risk-free asset and a risky asset. Figure 2.9 plots the CAL for a risk-free rate of $r_f = 1\%$ and U.S. equities using Ibbotson data over January 1926 to December 2011. U.S. equities are marked in the square.

The slope of the CAL is the Sharpe ratio, named after William Sharpe, one of the founders of the capital asset pricing model and winner of the 1990 Nobel Prize:

$$\text{Sharpe Ratio} = \frac{E(r) - r_f}{\sigma}. \tag{2.8}$$

In Figure 2.9, the Sharpe ratio for U.S. equities was 0.53, using the average equity return over the sample and a 1% risk-free rate.[18] The Sharpe ratio is actually a zero-cost trading strategy: in the context of Figure 2.9, it is long equities and short T-bills, divided by the risk of equities. It is the reward (mean excess return)

---

[18] Note that "risk-free" rates move around in data. The empirical Sharpe ratio using T-bills as the risk-free asset is $0.0766/0.1918 = 0.40$.

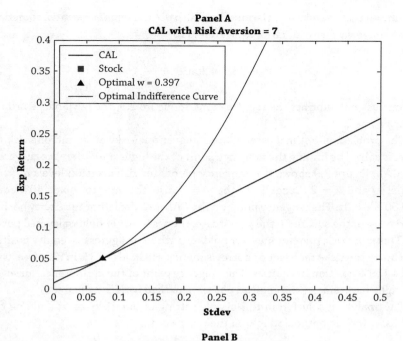

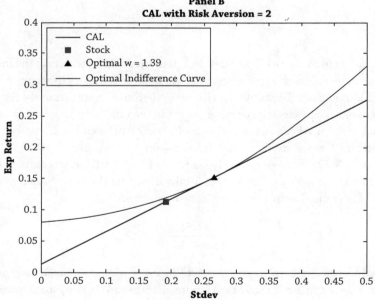

Figure 2.9

per unit of risk (standard deviation). I will also use the *raw Sharpe ratio*, sometimes called the reward-to-risk ratio, which refers to

$$\text{Raw Sharpe Ratio} = \frac{E(r)}{\sigma}, \tag{2.9}$$

which does not subtract the risk-free rate. In Figure 2.9, the raw Sharpe ratio for equities was 0.58.

The problem of optimal asset allocation over one risky asset and one risk-free asset is solved by finding the tangency point of the highest indifference curve with the CAL. Figure 2.9 shows two tangency points for risk aversion levels of $\gamma = 7$ (Panel A) and $\gamma = 2$ (Panel B). In the $\gamma = 7$ case, the investor holds 40% equity and 60% T-bills. The tangency point on the CAL is to the left of the equity position marked with the square. In the $\gamma = 2$ case, the asset owner holds a levered portfolio. This more risk-tolerant investor holds a much more aggressive equity position. He shorts the risk-free asset or borrows money. He holds –39% in risk-free assets and a 139% position in equities. The tangency point of the indifference curve is to the right-hand side of the equities position marked with the square.

The analytical solution in this simple setting of one risky asset and one risk-free asset for the optimal weight in the risky asset, w^*, is

$$w^* = \frac{1}{\gamma} \frac{E(r) - r_f}{\sigma^2}, \tag{2.10}$$

and $1 - w^*$ held in the risk-free asset. In equation (2.10), note that as the investor becomes more risk averse ($\gamma \to \infty$), the risky asset weight goes to zero and the investor holds entirely T-bills. As the risky asset becomes more attractive ($E(r) - r_f$ increases or σ decreases) the optimal weight in the risky asset also increases.

What is the market's risk aversion coefficient? At the end of December 2011, the combined stock market capitalizations on the NYSE and NASDAQ were $11.8 and $3.8 trillion, respectively—a total of $15.6 trillion in equities. At the same date there were $1.5 trillion in T-bills issued by the U.S. Treasury. Taking only T-bills as the risk-free asset, we have a weight of

$$w^* = \frac{15.6}{15.6 + 1.5} = 91.2\%$$

invested in equities by a "representative" investor who is assumed to represent the U.S. equity and T-bill markets. (I ignore all the non-U.S. risky markets and the risky fixed income markets for the purposes of this question.) Rearranging the optimal weight in equation (2.10) at a risk-free rate of 1% and using the equity premium and equity volatility over January 1926 to December 2011, we have

$$\gamma = \frac{1}{w^*} \frac{E(r) - r_f}{\sigma^2} = \frac{1}{0.9123} \frac{0.1019}{(0.1915)^2} = 3.0,$$

and thus the typical participant in the equity market has a modest degree of risk aversion.

The mean-variance solution in equation (2.10) turns out to be the same as CRRA utility (see equation (2.1)) if returns are log-normally distributed. This is one sense that mean-variance and CRRA are equivalent.

4. Realistic Utility Functions

There are several shortcomings of mean-variance utility:

1. The variance treats the upside and downside the same (relative to the mean).
   However, asset owners generally exhibit asymmetric risk aversion, feeling losses more powerfully than any equivalent gain.
2. Only the first two moments matter.
   People prefer positive skewness, like the chance of a big lottery payoff, and dislike negative skewness, like the barreling steamroller crushing you as you pick up nickels and dimes.
3. Subjective probabilities matter.
   The way that people perceive probabilities differs from the actual distribution of returns. In particular, people tend to overestimate the probability of disasters.
4. Bad times other than low means and high variances matter.
   Bad times aren't just times of low wealth. Mean-variance utility rather simplistically portrays bad times as consisting only of low means and high variances. But being rich or poor in absolute terms might not matter so much as whether you are rich or poor relative to your neighbor or whether you are rich or poor now relative to whether you were rich or poor in the past. That is, your utility could be relative.

There are many richer models of utility that incorporate all these considerations. Some of these models fit into the expected utility framework of the previous sections, so all of the previous intuition and economic machinery apply. In economics, there are many utility functions that realistically describe how people behave. In the asset management industry, unfortunately, only one utility model dominates—by a long shot, it's the restrictive mean-variance utility model. It would be nice if we had a commercial optimizer where one could toggle between various utility functions, especially those incorporating downside risk aversion. It would be even better if an application could map a series of bad times, and how the risk of these bad times is perceived by an investor, to different classes of utility functions. Sadly, there are no such asset allocation applications that I know of at the time of writing that can do this. And yet all the economic theory and optimization techniques are already published.

What follows are some examples of asset allocation in the context of the volatility strategy graphed in Figure 2.1, where the risk in the left-hand tail is especially pronounced and a risk-free asset pays 1%.

4.1. SAFETY FIRST

In the safety first utility framework, investors do exactly what the name suggests—they seek safety first. Roy's (1952) utility is very simple: it is just zero or one depending on whether a portfolio return is greater or less than a pre-determined level. If it is less than this level, a disaster results. If the return is greater than this level, the disaster is averted. Safety first minimizes the chance of a disaster; it is ideal for agents for whom meeting a liability is crucial. Not surprisingly, since safety first takes care of the downside first, asset allocation in the safety-first approach is very straightforward: you conservatively hold safe assets up until the pre-determined level is satisfied, and then you take on as much risk as you can after the safety level is met.

A related approach, formulated by Manski (1988) and Rostek (2010), is quantile utility maximization. In this approach, agents care about the worst outcomes that can happen with a given probability. Probability cutoffs of a probability density function are called quantiles. Quantiles are intuitive measures of investor pessimism. An asset owner might look at the worst outcome that can occur in 90% of all situations, for example. In this case, the relevant outcome is what happens at the 0.1 quantile (which is the first decile).[19] Another asset owner might look at the worst outcome that might happen 50% of the time, which is what happens at the 0.5 quantile (which is the median). In Manski-Rostek's utility, the quantile is a parameter choice, like risk aversion, and it is a measure of the investor's attitude to downside risk. Because the quantile parameter choice is an alternative measure of investors' downside risk aversion, the asset allocation from this framework is similar to loss aversion, which we now discuss.

4.2. LOSS AVERSION OR PROSPECT THEORY

Developed in a landmark paper by Kahneman and Tversky in 1979, loss aversion was originally created as an alternative to pure, rational expected utility. It is, however, a variant of expected utility, broadly defined, because it involves measuring risk by separable functions of (subjective) probabilities and utility functions of returns. Daniel Kahneman won the 2002 Nobel Prize for his work combining psychology and economics, especially for his work on prospect theory. His long-time collaborator, Amos Tversky, unfortunately did not live long enough to be awarded

---

[19] Value-at-risk that is so commonly used in risk management is a quantile measure. People usually pick the 0.01 or 0.05 quantiles.

the same honor. Kahneman and Tversky formulated prospect theory based on how people actually make decisions (it was a positive theory).[20]

There are two parts to prospect theory:

1. Loss aversion utility

   Investors find the pain of losses to be greater than the joy from gains. Loss aversion utility allows the investor to have different slopes (marginal utilities) for gains and losses.
2. Probability transformations

   Kahneman and Tversky move beyond probabilities—even subjective probabilities. They transform probabilities to *decision weights*, which do not necessarily obey probability laws. They do not, for example, have to sum to one like probabilities. Decision weights allow investors to potentially severely overweight low probability events—including both disasters and winning the lottery.

We can write prospect theory as a form of expected utility similar to equation (2.1):

$$U = \sum_s w(p_s)U(W_s), \qquad (2.11)$$

for a probability weight function $w(\bullet)$ and a loss aversion function $U(\bullet)$, which operate over different states s, which occur with probability p_s.

Let's focus on loss aversion utility. Figure 2.10 graphs a typical loss aversion utility function. Utility is defined relative to a reference point, which is the origin on the graph. The reference point can be zero (absolute return), or it could be a risk-free rate (sure return) or a risky asset return (benchmark return). Gains are defined as positive values on the x-axis relative to the origin, and losses are defined as negative values. The utility function has a kink at the origin, so there is asymmetry in how investors treat gains and losses. The utility function over gains is concave, so investors are risk averse over gains. The shape of the utility function for losses is *convex*, which captures the fact that people are *risk seeking over losses*—that is, they are willing to accept some risk to avert a certain loss. The utility function for losses is also steeper than the utility function over gains. Thus, investors are more sensitive to losses than to gains.

The fact that investors are risk seeking over losses is borne out in many experiments that involve choosing between bets like:

A: Losing $1,000 with probability of 0.5.
B: Losing $500 for sure.

---

[20] For a summary of applications of prospect theory and other behavioral theories to finance, see Barberis and Thaler (2003).

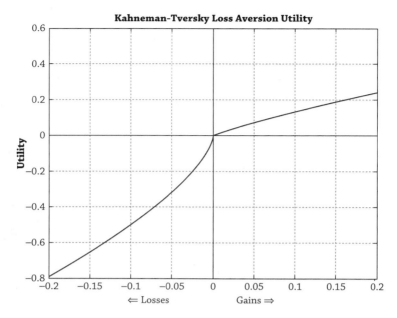

Figure 2.10

People overwhelmingly choose A over B. They are willing to take on some risk to avoid a sure loss.

How investors respond to losses relative to gains is governed by the coefficient of *loss aversion*, which we denote by the parameter λ. Experimental evidence points to estimates of λ around two, so losses are penalized about as twice as much as what gains add in investors' utilities. Tversky and Kahneman's (1992) estimate of λ is 2.25.

In Figure 2.11, I plot portfolio weights for optimal investment in the volatility strategy. The graph is produced starting for a regular CRRA investor holding 100% in the volatility strategy. The CRRA investor is a special case of the loss averse investor with no risk asymmetry and $\lambda = 1$. This investor has a risk aversion of $\gamma = 1.68$.[21] Now we start overweighting losses relative to gains, and we use a reference point of the risk-free rate of $r_f = 1\%$. As the asset owner places greater weight on downside outcomes, he lowers the weight in the volatility strategy. At $\lambda = 2$, he holds approximately only 20% in the volatility strategy and then when he weights downside outcomes more than 2.2 times the weight given gains,

---

[21] For comparison, a mean-variance investor with a risk aversion of $\gamma = 3.86$ would hold 100% in the volatility strategy. In this case, mean-variance is not such a good approximation to CRRA—as expected because of the very long left-hand tail of the volatility strategy. Note that that the CRRA investor needs to be more risk tolerant (lower γ) because CRRA utility takes into account the higher moments (see equation (2.1)), whereas mean-variance utility does not.

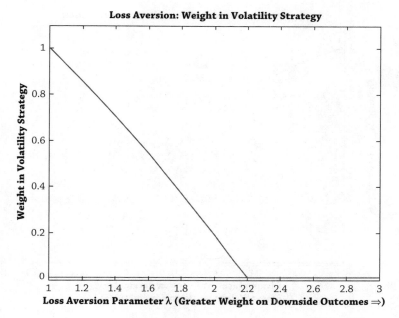

Figure 2.11

he foregoes the volatility strategy entirely and chooses a portfolio consisting wholly of risk-free assets.

4.3. DISAPPOINTMENT AVERSION

Disappointment aversion is the rational cousin to loss aversion. Like loss aversion, the asset owner cares more about downside versus upside outcomes. It is "rational" because it is axiomatically derived (originally by Gul in 1991) and thus it is appealing for those who like the rigor of formal decision theory. This does bring benefits—the disappointment utility function is mathematically well defined and so always admits a solution (while Kahneman-Tversky's specification sometimes sends optimal portfolio weights to unbounded positions), it can be extended to dynamic contexts in a consistent fashion (see chapter 4), and it also gives economic meaning to concepts like reference points that are quite arbitrary in classical loss aversion theory.[22]

The upside outcomes in disappointment aversion are called "elating" and the downside outcomes, "disappointing." This is just relabeling; investors overweight losses relative to gains, just like in loss aversion utility. What is different to loss

---

[22] See Ang, Bekaert, and Liu (2005) for an asset allocation application of disappointment aversion utility. Disappointment aversion is generalized by Routledge and Zin (2010) so that the reference point is not restricted to be the certainty equivalent.

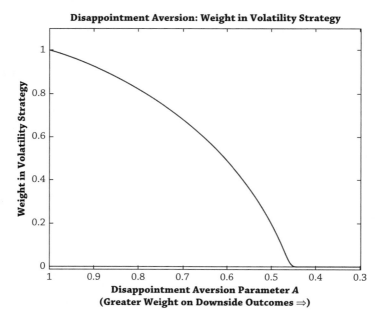

Figure 2.12

aversion is that the reference point is *endogenous,* and equal to the certainty equivalent (see section 3.2).

The disappointment aversion parameter, A, is the equivalent of the loss aversion parameter, λ, in disappointment aversion utility. In Figure 2.12, I plot the optimal weight in the volatility strategy as a function of A. Disappointment aversion nests CRRA as a special case, so I start with a 100% investment in the volatility strategy, which corresponds to a risk aversion of $\gamma = 1.68$ (similar to the loss aversion plot in Figure 2.11). The disappointment utility investor weights disappointing outcomes more than elating outcomes by $1/A$, so values of A smaller than 1 indicate the investor is averse to downside risk. Figure 2.12 shows that as we decrease A (or we become more downside risk averse), she lowers the weight of her portfolio allocated to the volatility strategy. At a disappointment aversion level of $A = 0.45$, she holds entirely risk-free assets. This corresponds to her weighting disappointing outcomes approximately twice as much as elating outcomes. This is quite similar to the loss aversion weight of λ being approximately 2 where the loss aversion investor has also completely divested from the volatility strategy.

4.4. HABIT UTILITY

Habit utility falls into a class of utility functions that define bad times not just by wealth outcomes, but also by an investor's environment. Specifically, it is not wealth (or more correctly how wealth is perceived by the investor) that matters; it is wealth relative to a reference point that is important. With habit utility, bad times are defined by an investor's wealth coming close to habit.[23]

Agents quickly get used to a particular level of consumption. When you're stuck at the back of the plane, you're just glad that you're travelling somewhere exotic; the hard seat, having your knees crammed into the tray table in front of you, and battling your neighbor over the armrest aren't that bothersome (in most cases). Then you get an upgrade to business class. Whoa, is it hard to go back! And then you get the lucky bonanza of a first-class upgrade on one of those spiffy international airlines whose pampered patrons enjoy seats that lie flat, plus unlimited champagne. Stepping back down to cattle class really hurts, even though by any objective standard you are better off—and certainly no worse off—than had you never escaped from coach.

The "habit" in habit utility can be interpreted as a "subsistence" level of re-quired wealth—perhaps literally subsistence consumption, but more generally it is the level required to live a certain lifestyle. As wealth comes close to habit, the investor acts in a much more risk-averse fashion. Thus, with habit utility, *risk aversion is endogenous*. There is an overall curvature of an agent's utility function, but local curvature is always changing.

Habit, too, evolves over time. Your income could skyrocket, so you really don't have to go back to economy class. Or your investment bank employer could blow up, and then you are stuck at the back of the plane. Habit can be external—driven by factors outside an investor's control, such as macro factors—or internal, where it depends on the past consumption and wealth of an individual.

Asset allocation with habit utility requires you to state your portfolio's returns in relation to your habit. In the case where you are close to habit, the asset owner's implied risk aversion will be very high—this is a bad time for her and she wants safe assets. But in good times when her wealth is far above habit, she will be risk tolerant and hold large amounts of equities. Habit investors are not good volatil-ity strategy investors—when volatility spikes, prices tend to crash, and these are times when their wealth creeps closer to their habits. The volatility strategy loss comes at a particularly bad time.

4.5. CATCHING UP WITH THE JONESES

Catching up with the Joneses utility defines bad times relative to other investors. It is not your performance in absolute terms that matters; what matters is your performance relative to your peers. We say that utilities exhibit *externalities*

---

[23] Some important papers in this large literature include Sundaresan (1989), Constantinides (1990), and Campbell and Cochrane (1999).

because they depend on both your own returns as well as those of your peers.[24] You want to "keep up with the Joneses." I call this family of utility functions *"relative utility"* because a person's utility is defined relative to the wealth or actions of others.

Catching up with the Joneses is a realistic utility function for individuals who don't want to feel left out when their golf club buddies are jumping on the hottest investment tips. The same individuals feel schadenfreude when their neighbors stumble. The syndrome is especially relevant for endowment managers, mutual fund managers, and others who are explicitly benchmarked against their peers. If the standard expected utility framework in section 2 involving wealth can be described in terms of greed, catching up with the Joneses is really about envy.

Another interpretation of having utility depend on the wealth or consumption of others is that relative utility reflects status. In asset management, status is associated with better performance, more wealth, or consuming more than one's peers.[25] Michael Lewis (1989) would refer to catching up with the Joneses preferences as "big swinging dick" utility, in the spirit of his book about Wall Street, *Liar's Poker.*

One of the consequences of catching up with the Joneses is that investors herd. Demarzo, Kaniel, and Kremer (2005) show that when one set of investors (the Joneses) in a local community takes a position in certain stocks, whether for a rational reason like hedging or even for irrational reasons, then other investors hold the same stocks to keep up with the Joneses. If portfolio managers are benchmarked to each other, they will want to hold the same stocks. Herding arises endogenously, even if there is no explicitly set benchmark, in catching up with the Joneses, because there is large risk for investors in deviating from the pack. The positive versus normative implications really bite with this utility formulation. Take the board of trustees of an endowment. Do you explain (ex post) the fact that you are going with the crowd because your endowment manager has used a catching-up-with-the-Joneses utility function (positive), or are you adopting a catching-up-the-Joneses utility function because you really are benchmarked against your other endowment peers, in which case the optimal asset allocation policy is to go with the pack (normative)?[26]

4.6. UNCERTAINTY AVERSION

We measure how often bad times occur with a probability density function (see section 2.1). But what if agents do not have a single probability distribution in

---

[24] These are also called interdependent preferences and consumption externalities in utilities, which were first introduced by Dusenberry (1952). Catching up with the Joneses utility was first formulated by Abel (1990) and Galí (1994). Note that whether you "catch up" or "keep up" with the Joneses is just a matter of timing and irrelevant for the purposes of this discussion.

[25] See Heffetz and Frank (2011).

[26] Goetzmann and Oster (2012) argue that universities vigorously compete with each other, resulting in herding in asset allocation policies.

mind but have beliefs about a whole family of possible probability distributions? For example, an emerging country has newly liberalized. There's no return history. If the country is stable, returns could be drawn from a "good" distribution. But if there are multiple coups, or if investors' capital is confiscated, returns would be drawn from a "bad" distribution. There could be all possible distributions in between. There is a distinction between a single probability distribution—the traditional measure of risk—and a range of possible distributions. We call the latter *Knightian uncertainty*, for Frank Knight (1921), after terminology introduced by Gilboa and Schmeidler (1989).

Under uncertainty aversion, investors' utility depends on both risk and uncertainty. The more precise information is available about the set of possible distributions that can occur, the higher the agent's utility. Agents have an *uncertainty aversion* parameter, just as they have a risk aversion parameter. Uncertainty aversion is also called *ambiguity aversion*, as the existence of multiple distributions is also known as ambiguity. Researchers also talk about *robust utility*, which is closely related and also deals with multiple sets of probability distributions.[27] With robust utility, agents exhibit a preference ("concern") for how robust their decisions are under different probability distributions. (My MBA students might call this a glorified version of sensitivity analysis.) It is also referred to as *maxmin utility* because uncertainty averse agents take the worst possible probability distribution of risk (min) and then maximize utility (max).

A comprehensive review of uncertainty aversion and portfolio choice was conducted by Guidolin and Rinaldi (2010). I have the following brief remarks:

1. Uncertainty aversion causes agents to effectively behave in a much more risk-averse fashion than just using plain old risk aversion. You will hold a much smaller weight in equities when you are uncertainty averse. In fact, if you dislike uncertainty enough, you won't hold any equities.[28]
2. Many of the tools in expected utility can be used—and, more important, the same intuition as in this chapter applies in many cases. There is an explicit connection even to mean-variance utility.[29] (Clearly, in a very simple case, expected utility is uncertainty aversion with only one probability distribution.)
3. There are data on agents' different probability beliefs—surveys! Some of the more recent papers in the literature nicely exploit these to show how the set of beliefs evolve over time and how they can be used to infer future asset prices.[30]

---

[27] The reference tome on robustness is Hansen and Sargent (2007).

[28] This was first shown by Dow and Werlang (1992). See also Garlappi, Uppal, and Wang (2007) and Bossaerts et al. (2010), among others.

[29] In Maenhout (2004), you can reinterpret the classical CRRA risk aversion coefficient as the sum of the CRRA risk aversion coefficient and the uncertainty risk aversion coefficient. See also Trojani and Vanini (2004).

[30] See Ulrich (2011).

4. Not everyone is ambiguity averse: Dimmock et al. (2013) show that over one-third of U.S. households are ambiguity seeking, but people who are more risk averse tend to be more uncertainty averse.

5. Picking Up Nickels and Dimes in Front of a Steamroller Redux

Utility functions are a way to measure bad times. Times of low wealth are bad times. Bad times can also be defined relative to an absolute level of safety, a reference point defining gains and losses (across which investors can exhibit different attitudes to risk across gains and losses), past wealth (habit) of an investor, or the relative performance of other investors. During bad times, marginal utility is very high, and the investor considers every spare dollar especially precious.

Mean-variance utility is very restrictive in that bad times are represented only by low portfolio returns and very disperse portfolio returns (low means, high variances). The workhorse utility model of the financial industry is mean-variance. The volatility strategy has a mean and variance very close to the S&P 500, but it has much more pronounced crash risk and fatter tails than the stock market. The volatility strategy's probability distribution function exhibits a very skewed left-hand tail (skewness of –8) and enormous kurtosis (over 100). Mean-variance would not be an appropriate framework to evaluate this strategy, except for those rare (perhaps non-existent) investors who only have preferences over means and variances. Investors exhibiting downside risk aversion would hold much less of this volatility strategy relative to a mean-variance (or approximately CRRA) investor. If deciding between the volatility strategy and a risk-free asset, downside risk averse investors who weight losses about twice as much as gains would optimally choose to forego the volatility strategy and invest only in T-bills.

CHAPTER 3

Mean-Variance Investing

Chapter Summary

Mean-variance investing is all about diversification. By exploiting the interaction of assets with each other, so one asset's gains can make up for another asset's losses, diversification allows investors to increase expected returns while reducing risks. In practice, mean-variance portfolios that constrain the mean, volatility, and correlation inputs to reduce sampling error have performed much better than unconstrained portfolios. These constrained special cases include equal-weighted, minimum variance, and risk parity portfolios.

1. Norway and Wal-Mart

On June 6, 2006, the Norwegian Ministry of Finance announced that the Norwegian sovereign wealth fund, officially called "The Norwegian Government Pension Fund—Global," had sold Wal-Mart Stores Inc. on the basis of "serious/systematic violations of human rights and labor rights."[1] As one of the largest funds in the world and a leader in ethical investing, Norway's decision to exclude Wal-Mart was immediately noticed. Benson Whitney, the U.S. ambassador to Norway, complained that the decision was arbitrarily based on unreliable research and unfairly singled out an American company. Wal-Mart disputed Norway's decision and sent two senior executives to plead its case before the Ministry of Finance.

Norway is one of the world's largest oil exporters. Norway first found oil in the North Sea in 1969 and quickly found that its resulting revenue was distorting its economy. During the 1970s and 1980s, Norway experienced many symptoms of the *Dutch disease* (see chapter 1), with growing oil revenues contributing to a less competitive and shrinking manufacturing sector. When oil prices slumped in the

---

[1] This is based on "The Norwegian Government Pension Fund: The Divestiture of Wal-Mart Stores Inc.," Columbia CaseWorks, ID#080301. The quote is from Ministry of Finance press release No. 44 in 2006.

mid-1980s, overreliance on oil revenue contributed to a period of slow economic growth. Sensibly, Norway decided to diversify.

Norway's "Government Petroleum Fund" was set up in 1990 to channel some of the oil revenue into a long-term savings mechanism. The fund served two purposes: (i) it diversified oil wealth into a broader portfolio of international securities, improving Norway's risk–return trade-off, and (ii) it inoculated Norway from the Dutch disease by quarantining wealth overseas, only gradually letting the oil money trickle into the economy. In January 2006, the fund was renamed "The Norwegian Government Pension—Global," although it had no explicit pension liabilities. The new title conveyed the fund's goal of managing its capital to meet long-term government obligations and to benefit future generations.

At first the fund was invested only in government bonds. In 1998 the investment universe was enlarged to allow a 40% allocation to equities, and that was raised to 60% in 2007. In 2010 the fund was permitted to invest up to 5% of assets in real estate, and Norway bought its first properties, in London and Paris, in 2011. While the asset universe of the fund had gradually broadened, since the fund's inception the "reluctant billionaires of Norway" have always sought to meaningfully invest their fortune in line with the country's social ethos.[2] Norway practiced socially responsible investing (SRI). In 2005, government regulation was passed making this formal. The regulation stated that:[3]

- The financial wealth must be managed so as to generate a sound return in the long term, which is contingent on sustainable development in the economic, environmental and social sense.
- The fund should not make investments that constitute an unacceptable risk that the fund may contribute to unethical acts or omissions, such as violations of human rights, gross corruption, or severe environmental damages.

The Ministry of Finance appointed an independent Council on Ethics, which issued recommendations on whether an investment constituted a violation of the fund's ethical guidelines. If there was unacceptable risk, the Council would recommend the exclusion of a company. The Council continuously monitored all companies in the fund's portfolio to uncover possible violations using publicly available information, media sources, national and international organizations, and independent experts.

In April 2005 the Council began examining alleged unethical activities by Wal-Mart. These included many reported violations of labor laws and human rights, including reports of child labor, serious violations of working hour regulations, paying wages below the legal minimum, hazardous working conditions, and unreasonable punishment. The Council found widespread gender discrimination.

[2] Mark Landler, "Norway Backs Its Ethics with Its Cash," *New York Times*, May 4, 2007.
[3] Section 8 of the Government Pension Fund Regulation No. 123, December 2005.

Wal-Mart stopped workers from forming unions. There were reports of children performing dangerous work and the use of illegal immigrant labor.

In September 2005, the Council sent a letter to Wal-Mart asking the company to comment on the alleged human rights violations. Wal-Mart acknowledged the letter but did not otherwise respond.

From January until March 2006, the Ministry conducted its own assessment. The Ministry found that exercising the fund's ownership rights through an activist approach would not be effective in influencing Wal-Mart's business practices. Divestment decisions were always considered the last resort, but in Wal-Mart's case the Ministry decided it was appropriate.

When the Ministry announced on June 6, 2006 that it had sold all its holdings in Wal-Mart, it quoted the report from the Council of Ethics:

> What makes this case special is the sum total of ethical norm violations, both in the company's own business operations and in the supplier chain. It appears to be a systematic and planned practice on the part of the company to hover at, or cross, the bounds of what are accepted norms for the work environment. Many of the violations are serious, most appear to be systematic, and altogether they form a picture of a company whose overall activity displays a lack of willingness to countervail violations of norms in its business operations.[4]

Excluding companies is not without cost: by shrinking its universe, Norway's investment opportunities were smaller, and it lost diversification benefits and lowered its best risk–return trade-off. As more companies were excluded, there were further losses in diversification benefits. In January 2010, Norway excluded all tobacco companies. What did these exclusions do to the fund's maximum attainable risk–return trade-off? How much did it cost Norway to be ethical?

In this chapter I cover mean-variance investing. This is by far the most common way to choose optimal portfolios. The main takeaway is that diversified portfolios should be selected because investors can reduce risk and increase returns. The underlying concept of diversification can be implemented in different ways, and many of the approaches popular at the time of writing, like risk parity and minimum variance portfolios, are special cases of unconstrained mean-variance portfolios. An advantage of mean-variance investing is that it allows diversification benefits (and losses) to be measured in a simple way. We will later use mean-variance investing concepts to estimate how much Norway is losing in choosing to be socially responsible—in other words, to answer the question, how much does it cost Norway to divest Wal-Mart?

---

[4] Press release, Ministry of Finance, June 6, 2006.

2. Mean-Variance Frontiers

Mean-variance frontiers depict the best set of portfolios that an investor can obtain (only considering means and volatilities, of course!). Let's start by considering a U.S. investor contemplating investing only in U.S. or Japanese equities.

2.1. UNITED STATES AND JAPAN

In the 1980s Japan seemed poised to take over the world. Figure 3.1 plots cumulated returns of U.S. and Japanese equities from January 1970 to December 2011 using MSCI data. (I also use these data for the other figures involving G5 countries in this chapter.) Japanese returns are plotted in the solid line and U.S. returns are shown in the dashed line. Japanese equities skyrocketed in the 1980s. Many books were written on Japan's stunning success, like Vogel's (1979) *Japan as Number One: Lessons for America*. Flush with cash, Japanese companies went on foreign buying binges. Japanese businesses bought marquee foreign companies: Universal Studios and Columbia Records were sold to Matsushita Electric and Sony, respectively. The Japanese also bought foreign trophy real estate. The Mitsubishi Estate Company of Tokyo purchased Rockefeller Center in 1989. In 1990 the famous Pebble Beach golf course was sold to a Japanese businessman, Minuro Isutani. Figure 3.1 shows that the United States did well during the 1980s too, but not nearly as well as booming Japan.

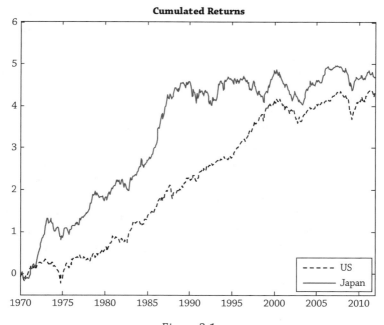

Figure 3.1

Then everything crashed. Isutani had bought Pebble Beach a year after the Nikkei had hit its peak in 1989, and he was later investigated for money laundering by the FBI.[5] Figure 3.1 shows that since 1990 Japanese stocks have been flat. But while Japan was languishing, the United States boomed. Even so, Japanese cumulated returns were higher at December 2011 than U.S. cumulated returns. Since 2000, Figure 3.1 shows that the United States and Japan have a greater tendency to move together. They jointly slowed during the early 2000s, experienced bull markets during the mid-2000s, and then crashed during the financial crisis of 2007–2008. Over the whole sample, however, Japan has moved very differently from the United States.

The average return and volatility for the United States in Figure 3.1 are 10.3% and 15.7%, respectively. The corresponding numbers for Japan are 11.1% and 21.7%, respectively. We plot these rewards (means) and risks (volatilities) in mean-standard deviation space in Figure 3.2. The United States is represented by the square, and Japan is represented by the circle. The x-axis is in standard deviation units, and the y-axis units are average returns.

The curve linking the United States and Japan in Figure 3.2 is the *mean-variance frontier*. Like the literature, I use the terms mean-variance frontier and mean-standard deviation frontier interchangeably as the two can be obtained simply by squaring, or taking a square root of, the x-axis depending on whether one

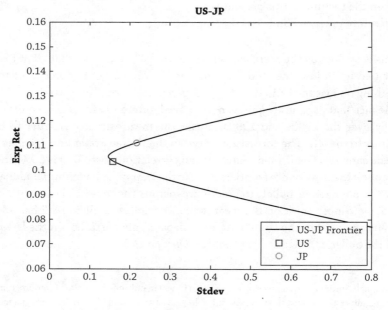

Figure 3.2

---

[5] "A Japanese Laundry Worth $1 Billion?" *Businessweek*, May 24, 1993.

uses volatility or variance units. The mean-variance frontier for the United States and Japan represents all combinations of the United States and Japan. Naturally, the square representing the United States is a 100% U.S. portfolio, and the circle representing Japan is a 100% Japanese portfolio. All the other positions on the mean-variance frontier represent portfolios containing different amounts of the United States and Japan.

The mean-variance frontier is a *parabola*, or a bullet. The top half of the mean-variance frontier is *efficient*: an investor cannot obtain a higher reward, or expected return, for a given level of risk measured by volatility. Investors will choose portfolios on the top, efficient part of the frontier. The United States sits on the underbelly of the bullet. You can achieve a higher expected return for the same volatility by moving onto the top half of the frontier. The United States is an *inefficient* portfolio. *No one should hold a 100% U.S. portfolio.*

2.2. DIVERSIFICATION

In the *Merchant of Venice*, Shakespeare tells us why we should diversify:

> . . . I thank my fortune for it,
> My ventures are not in one bottom trusted,
> Nor to one place; nor is my whole estate
> Upon the fortune of this present year:
> Therefore my merchandise makes me not sad.

This is spoken by the merchant Antonio, who diversifies so that all of his risk is not tied up in just one ship ("one bottom").[6] Similarly, we don't want to bet everything on just the United States or Japan in isolation ("one place").

The fact that Japanese equities have moved differently from U.S. equities, especially over the 1980s and 1990s, causes the mean-variance frontier to bulge outwards to the left. The correlation between the United States and Japan is 35% over the sample. (The United States–Japan correlation post-2000 is 59%, still far below one.) Mean-variance frontiers are like the Happy (or Laughing) Buddha: the fatter the stomach or bullet, the more prosperous the investor becomes. Notice that the left-most point on the mean-variance frontier in Figure 3.2 has a lower volatility than either the United States or Japan. This portfolio, on the left-most tip of the bullet, is called the *minimum variance portfolio*.

---

[6] Although Antonio owns many ships, his wealth is held in only one asset class—venture capital—and so is undiversified across asset classes and is illiquid. Antonio should diversify across factors (see chapter 14). Unable to raise cash to lend to his friend, he is forced to go to Shylock for a loan, which he is forced to pay with a "pound of flesh" when he defaults. I cover asset allocation with illiquid assets in chapter 13.

Starting from a 100% U.S. portfolio (the square in Figure 3.2), an investor can improve her risk–return trade-off by including Japanese equities. This moves her position from the United States (the square) to Japan (the circle) and the investor moves upward along the frontier in a clockwise direction. Portfolios to the right-hand side of the circle (the 100% Japan position) represent *levered* portfolios. Portfolios on the top half of the frontier past the circle are constructed by shorting the United States, like a –30% position, and then investing the short proceeds in a levered Japanese position, which would be 130% in this case. All the efficient portfolios lying on the top half of the frontier—those portfolios with the highest returns for a given level of risk—contain Japanese equities. The minimum variance portfolio, which is the left-most tip of the mean-variance bullet, also includes Japan.

The American investor can improve her risk–return trade-off by holding some of Japan because Japan provides *diversification benefits*. This is the fundamental concept in mean-variance investing, and it corresponds to the common adage "don't put all your eggs in one basket." The United States and Japan held together are better than the United States held alone. Owning both protects us from the catastrophe that one individual investment will be lost. The advantages of diversification imply that we cannot consider assets in isolation; we need to think about how assets behave together. This is the most important takeaway of this chapter.

Diversified, efficient portfolios of the United States and Japan have higher returns and lower risk than the 100% U.S. position. Why? When the investor combines the United States and Japan, the portfolio reduces risk because when one asset does poorly, another might do well. It's like buying insurance (except that the purchaser of insurance loses money, on average, whereas an investor practicing diversification makes more money, on average). When the United States does relatively poorly, like during the 1980s, Japan has a possibility of doing well. Some of the risk of the U.S. position is avoidable and can be offset by holding Japan as insurance.

What about the opposite? During the 1990s Japan was in the doldrums and the United States took off. Hindsight tells us that the U.S. investor would have been better off holding only the United States. Yes, he would—ex post. But forecasting is always hard. At the beginning of the 1990s, the investor would have been better off on an ex-ante basis by holding a portfolio of both the United States and Japan. What if the roles were reversed so that in the 1990s Japan did take over the world, and the U.S. swapped places with Japan? Holding Japan in 1990 diversified away some of this ex-ante risk.

The formal theory behind diversification was developed by Harry Markowitz (1952), who was awarded the Nobel Prize in 1990. The revolutionary capital asset pricing model (CAPM) is laid on the capstone of mean-variance investing, and we discuss that model in chapter 6. The CAPM pushes the diversification concept further and derives that an asset's risk premium is related to the (lack of) diversification benefits of that asset. This turns out to be the asset's beta.

Mathematically, diversification benefits are measured by covariances or correlations. Denoting r_p as the portfolio return, the variance of the portfolio return is given by

$$\text{var}(r_p) = w_{US}^2\text{var}(r_{US}) + w_{JP}^2\text{var}(r_{JP}) + 2w_{US}w_{JP}\text{cov}(r_{US}, r_{JP})$$
$$= w_{US}^2\text{var}(r_{US}) + w_{JP}^2\text{var}(r_{JP}) + 2w_{US}w_{JP}\rho_{US,JP}\sigma_{US}\sigma_{JP},$$

$$(3.1)$$

where r_{US} denotes U.S. returns, r_{JP} denotes Japanese returns, and w_{US} and w_{JP} are the portfolio weights held in the United States and Japan, respectively. The portfolio weights can be negative, but they sum to one, $w_{US} + w_{JP} = 1$, as the portfolio weights total 100%. (This constraint is called an *admissibility condition*.) The covariance, $\text{cov}(r_{US}, r_{JP})$, in the first line of equation (3.1) can be equivalently expressed as the product of correlation between the United States and Japan ($\rho_{US,JP}$), and the volatilities of the United States and Japan (σ_{US} and σ_{JP}, respectively), $\text{cov}(r_{US}, r_{JP}) = \rho_{US,JP}\sigma_{US}\sigma_{JP}$.

Large diversification benefits correspond to *low* correlations. Mathematically, the low correlation in equation (3.1) reduces the portfolio variance. Economically, the low correlation means that Japan is more likely to pay off when the United States does poorly and the insurance value of Japan increases. This allows the investor to lower her overall portfolio risk. The more Japan does not look like the United States, the greater the benefit of adding Japan to a portfolio of U.S. holdings. Mean-variance investors love adding investments that act differently from those that they currently hold. The more dissimilar, or the lower the correlation, the better.[7]

Figure 3.3 plots the United States and Japan mean-variance frontier for different correlation values. The solid line is the frontier with the 35.4% correlation in data. The dashed line is drawn with 0% correlation, and the dotted line drops the correlation to –50%. As the correlation decreases, the tip of the mean-variance frontier pushes to the left—the bullet becomes more pointed. The lower correlation allows the investor to reduce risk as Japan provides even more diversification.

2.3. G5 MEAN-VARIANCE FRONTIERS

In Figures 3.4 and 3.5 we add the United Kingdom, France, and Germany.

First consider Figure 3.4, which plots the mean-variance frontier for the G3: the United States, Japan, and the United Kingdom. The G3 frontier is shown in the solid line. For comparison, the old United States–Japan frontier is in the

---

[7] In this simple setting, there is only one period. In reality, correlations move over time and increase during bear markets. Ang and Bekaert (2002) show that international investments still offer significant diversification benefits under such circumstances. Christoffersen et al. (2013) report that correlations of international stock returns have increased over time but are still much lower in emerging markets than for developed ones. Investors also have access to frontier markets, which are the subset of the smallest, most illiquid, and least financially developed emerging markets.

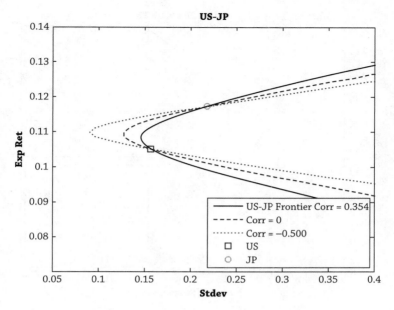

Figure 3.3

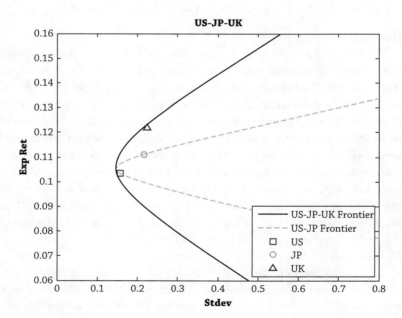

Figure 3.4

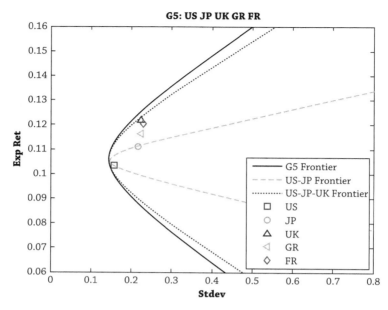

Figure 3.5

dashed line. Two things have happened in moving from the G2 (United States and Japan) to the G3 (United States, Japan, and the United Kingdom):

1. The frontier has expanded.

    The Happy Buddha becomes much happier adding the United Kingdom. The pronounced outward shift of the wings of the mean-variance bullet means that an investor can obtain a much higher return for a given standard deviation. (There is also a leftward shift of the frontier, but this is imperceptible in the graph.) Starting at any point on the United States–Japan frontier, we can move upwards on an imaginary vertical line and obtain higher returns for the same level of risk. Adding the United Kingdom to our portfolio provides further diversification benefits because now there is an additional country that could have high returns when the United States is in a bear market while before there was only Japan. There is also a chance that both the old United States and Japan positions would do badly; adding the United Kingdom gives the portfolio a chance to offset some or all of those losses.

2. All individual assets lie inside the frontier.

    Individual assets are *dominated*: diversified portfolios on the frontier do better than assets held individually. Now all countries would never be held individually. Diversification removes asset-specific risk and reduces the overall risk of the portfolio.

In Figure 3.5, we add Germany and France. The G5 mean-variance frontier is in the solid line, and it is the fattest: the United States–Japan and the United

States–Japan–United Kingdom frontiers lie inside the G5 frontier. There is still a benefit in adding Germany and France from the United States–Japan–United Kingdom, but it is not as big a benefit as adding the United Kingdom starting from the United States–Japan. That is, although Happy Buddha continues getting happier by adding countries, the rate at which he becomes happier decreases. There are *decreasing marginal diversification benefits* as we add assets. As we continue adding assets beyond the G5, the frontier will continue to expand but the added diversification benefits become smaller.

Figures 3.4 and 3.5 show that if we add an asset, the mean-variance frontier gets fatter. Conversely, if we remove an asset, the mean-variance frontier shrinks. Removing assets, as Norway did by divesting Wal-Mart, can only cause the maximum Sharpe ratio to (weakly) decrease. Thus, constraining the fund manager's portfolio by throwing out Norway has decreased investment opportunities and lowered the maximum achievable risk-return trade-off. We will later compute how the mean-variance frontier shrinks as we remove assets.

The mathematical statement of the problem in Figures 3.4 and 3.5 is:

$$\min_{\{w_i\}} \text{var}(r_p)$$
$$\text{subject to } E(r_p) = \mu^* \text{ and } \sum_i w_i = 1, \tag{3.2}$$

where the portfolio weight for asset i is w_i. We find the combination of portfolio weights, $\{w_i\}$, that minimizes the portfolio variance subject to two constraints. The first is that the expected return on the portfolio is equal to a target return, μ^*. The second is that the portfolio must be a valid portfolio, which is the admissibility condition that we have seen earlier. Students of operations research will recognize equation (3.2) as a *quadratic programming problem*, and what makes mean-variance investing powerful (but alas, misused; see below) is that there are very fast algorithms for solving these types of problems.

Figure 3.6 shows how this works pictorially. Choosing a target return of $\mu^* = 10\%$, we find the portfolio with the lowest volatility (or variance). We plot this with an X. Then we change the target return to $\mu^* = 12\%$. Again we find the portfolio with the lowest volatility and plot this with another X. The mean-variance frontier is drawn by changing the target return, μ^* and then linking all the Xs for each target return. Thus, the mean-variance frontier is a *locus* of points, where each point denotes the minimum variance achievable for each expected return.

2.4. CONSTRAINED MEAN-VARIANCE FRONTIERS

So far, we have constructed unconstrained mean-variance frontiers. But investors often face constraints on what types of portfolios that they can hold. One constraint faced by many investors is the inability to short. When there is a *no short-sales constraint*, all the portfolio weights have to be positive ($|w_i| \geq 0$), and we can add this constraint to the optimization problem in equation (3.2).

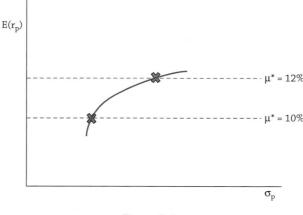

Figure 3.6

Adding short-sale constraints changes the mean-variance frontier, sometimes dramatically. Figure 3.7 contrasts the mean-variance frontier where no short-ing is permitted, in the solid line, with the unconstrained frontier, drawn in the dotted line. The constrained mean-variance frontier is much smaller than the un-constrained frontier and lies inside the unconstrained frontier. The constrained

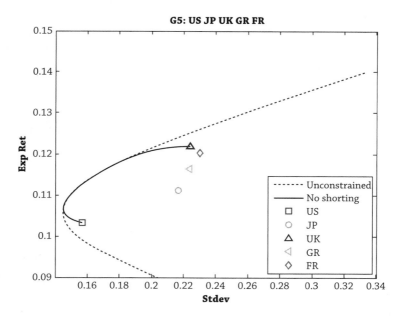

Figure 3.7

frontier is also not bullet shaped. Constraints inhibit what an investor can do and an investor can only be made (weakly) worse off. If an investor is lucky, the best risk–return trade-off is unaffected by adding constraints. We see this in Figure 3.7 in the region where the constrained and the unconstrained mean-variance frontiers lie on top of each other. But generally constraints cause an investor to achieve a worse risk–return trade-off. Nevertheless, even with constraints, the concept of diversification holds: the investor can reduce risk by holding a portfolio of assets rather than a single asset.

2.5. THE RISKS OF NOT DIVERSIFYING

Many people hold a lot of stock in their employer. Poterba (2003) reports that for large defined-contribution pension plans, the share of assets in own-company stock is around 40%. This comes usually, but not always, from discounted purchases and is designed by companies to encourage employee loyalty. For individuals, such concentrated portfolios can be disastrous—as employees of Enron (bankrupt in 2001), Lucent (which spiraled downward after it was spun off from AT&T in 1996 and was bought for a pittance by Alcatel in 2006), and Lehman Brothers (bankrupt in 2008) found out. Enron employees had over 60% of their retirement assets in company stock when Enron failed.[8] According to the Employee Benefits Research Institute, among 401(k) plan participants who had equity exposure in 2009, 12% had company stock as their only equity investment. For equity market participants in their sixties, 17% had equity exposure to equity markets only through their employers' stock.[9]

While the cost of not diversifying becomes painfully clear when your company goes bankrupt, mean-variance investing reveals that there is a loss even when your employer remains solvent. Individuals can generate a higher risk–return trade-off by moving to a diversified portfolio. Poterba (2003) computes the cost of not diversifying a retirement account relative to simply investing in the diversified S&P 500 portfolio. Assuming that half of an individual's assets are invested in company stock, the certainty equivalent cost (see chapter 3) of this concentrated position is about 80% of the value of investing in the diversified S&P 500 portfolio. This is a substantial reduction in utility for investors. An individual should regularly cash out company stock, especially if the stock is rising faster than other assets in his portfolio. As own-company stock rises relative to other assets, it represents even greater concentrated risk for that investor.[10] (Furthermore, your human capital itself is concentrated with that employer, see chapter 5.)

---

[8] See Barber and Odean (2011).

[9] See Van Derhei, J., S. Holden, and L. Alonso, 2010, 401(k) Plan Asset Allocation, Account Balances and Loan Activity in 2009, Employee Benefit Research Institute Issue Brief No. 350.

[10] Individual investors, unfortunately, tend to do exactly the opposite—individuals hold larger amounts in employer stocks, which have had the strongest return performance over the last ten years, as Benartzi (2001) shows.

The wealthy often fail to diversify enough. JP Morgan's 2004 white paper, "Beating the Odds: Improving the 15% Probability of Staying Wealthy," identified excessive concentration as the number-one reason the very wealthy lose their fortunes. The 15% probability in the study's title comes from the fact that in the first Forbes list of the richest four hundred people in America, fewer than 15% were still on the list a generation later. While the Forbes 400 tracks the mega-rich, the wealthy below them are also likely to lose their wealth. Kennickell (2011) reports that of the American households in the wealthiest 1% in 2007, approximately one-third fell out of the top 1% two years later.

Entrepreneurs and those generating wealth from a single business often find diversification counterintuitive.[11] After all, wasn't it concentrated positions that generated the wealth in the first place? This is the business that they know best, and their large investment in it may be illiquid and hard to diversify. But diversification removes company-specific risk that is outside the control of the manager. Over time, prime real estate ceases to be prime, and once-great companies fail because their products become obsolete. While some companies stumble due to regulatory risk, macro risk, technological change, and sovereign risk, other companies benefit. Diversification reduces these avoidable *idiosyncratic* risks. JP Morgan reports that of the five hundred companies in the S&P 500 index in 1990, only half remained in the index in 2000. Of the thirty titans comprising the original Dow Jones Industrial Average in 1896, only one remains: General Electric. This is testament to the need to diversify, diversify, and diversify if wealth is to be preserved.

Institutional investors also fail to sufficiently diversify. Jarrell and Dorkey (1993) recount the decline of the University of Rochester's endowment. In 1971, Rochester's endowment was $580 million, making it the fourth largest private university endowment in the country. In 1992, it ranked twentieth among private university endowments. What happened? From 1970 to 1992, the endowment earned only 7% compared to a typical 60%/40% equities–bonds portfolio return of 11%. Had Rochester simply invested in this benchmark portfolio, the endowment would have ranked tenth among private university endowments in 1992. By 2011, Rochester had dropped to thirtieth place.[12] A big reason for Rochester's underperformance was excessive concentration in local companies, especially Eastman Kodak, which filed for bankruptcy in 2012.

Boston University is another example. Over the 1980s and 1990s, Boston University invested heavily in Seragen Inc., then a privately held local biotech company. According to Lerner, Schoar, and Wang (2008), Boston University provided at least $107 million to Seragen from 1987 to 1997—a fortune considering the school's endowment in 1987 was $142 million. Seragen went public but

---

[11] See "Stay the Course? Portfolio Advice in the Face of Large Losses," Columbia CaseWorks, ID #110309.

[12] Counting only private university endowments using NACUBO data at 2011 fiscal year end.

suffered setbacks. In 1997, the University's stake was worth only $4 million. Seragen was eventually bought by Ligand Pharmaceuticals Inc. in 1998 for $30 million.

Norway's sovereign wealth fund, in contrast, was created precisely to reap the gains from diversification. Through its sovereign wealth fund, Norway swaps a highly concentrated asset—oil—into a diversified financial portfolio and thus improves its risk–return trade-off.

2.6. HOME BIAS

Mean-variance investing prescribes that investors should never hold a 100% U.S. portfolio. Many investors do not take advantage of the benefits of international diversification and instead hold only domestic assets. This is the *home bias* puzzle.[13]

One measure of home bias is the extent to which domestic investors' equity holdings differ from the world equity market portfolio. The world market is a diversified portfolio and, according to the CAPM, which adds equilibrium conditions to the mean-investing framework (see chapter 6), it is the optimal portfolio which investors should hold. (I show below, in section 5, that the market portfolio performs well in a horse race with other mean-variance diversified portfolios.) Ahearne, Griever, and Warnock (2004) contrast the 12% proportion of foreign equities in U.S. investors' portfolios with the approximate 50% share of foreign equities in the world market portfolio. Home bias is not just a U.S. phenomenon. Fidora, Fratzscher, and Thimann (2007) report the share of foreign assets in U.K. investors' portfolios is 30% compared to the non-U.K. weight of 92% in the world market portfolio. Japan is even more home biased, with domestic investors owning fewer than 10% foreign equities while the non-Japanese positions in the world market portfolio are greater than 90%.

What accounts for home bias?

1. Correlations vary over time

The diversification benefits of international investing depend on there being low correlations (or at least correlations that are not near one in absolute value). If correlations of international equity returns increase when there are global crashes—such as in 1987 (stock market crash), 1998 (emerging market crisis brought about by Russia's default), and the financial crisis over 2008–2009—then international diversification benefits may not be forthcoming when investors most desire them. Correlations of international stock markets do increase, and diversification benefits correspondingly decrease, during global bear markets. But Ang and Bekaert (2002) show that there

---

[13] See Karolyi and Stulz (2003) and Lewis (2011) for literature summaries.

are large benefits in international investments despite correlations changing through time.[14]

2. Exchange rate risk

   For a domestic investor, foreign equities bring exposure to international stock markets as well as foreign exchange rates.[15] Exchange rate movements are an additional source of risk, which may cause domestic investors to shun foreign assets. This explanation was rejected in an early study by Cooper and Kaplanis (1994). More recently, Fidora, Fratzscher, and Thimann (2007) show that exchange rate volatility can explain some, but far from all, of the home bias puzzle.

3. Transaction costs

   Transaction costs for investing abroad have fallen over the last thirty years, and the degree of home bias has also fallen over this time. Ahearne, Griever, and Warnock (2004) compute a home bias ratio, which is equal to one minus the ratio of the share of foreign equities held by U.S. residents to the share of foreign equities in the world portfolio. The home bias ratio is equal to zero when there is no home bias and equal to one when domestic investors are totally home biased. Ahearne, Griever, and Warnock show that the home bias ratio dropped from almost 1.0 in the early 1980s to below 0.8 in the early 2000s.

   We should, however, be skeptical of transaction costs explanations. The lucky U.S. investor does not need to invest directly in foreign markets— foreign companies have long listed their shares on U.S. exchanges through American Depositary Receipts (ADRs) where transaction costs are low.[16] And there are many financial intermediaries, like mutual funds, specializing in international assets, which U.S. investors can easily access. Viewed more broadly, transaction costs could also include the cost of becoming informed about the benefits of diversification. Both actual transaction costs and the costs of becoming financially literate are out of whack with the costs that economic models predict are necessary to match the pronounced home bias of investors. Glassman and Riddick (2001), for example, estimate that transactions costs need to be extraordinarily high—more than 12% per year—to explain observed home bias.

---

[14] See also Asness, Israelov, and Liew (2011). Chua, Lai, and Lewis (2010), among others, argue that international diversification benefits have decreased over time hand in hand with greater integration, but this is offset to some extent by the entrance of new international vehicles like emerging markets in the 1980s and frontier markets in the 2000s.

[15] Technically it is movements in real exchange rates that matter. If purchasing power parity (PPP) held, then there would be no real exchange rate risk (see Adler and Dumas (1983)). There is a very active literature on PPP. PPP certainly does not hold in the short run, and academics have not reached consensus on whether PPP holds in the long run (twenty- to one-hundred-year horizons). Taylor and Taylor (2004) present a summary.

[16] See Errunza, Hogan, and Hung (1999).

4. Asymmetric information

U.S. investors may be disadvantaged in foreign markets because foreigners know more about stocks in their local markets than U.S. investors do. Being less informed than foreigners, U.S. investors optimally choose to hold less foreign equity.[17] One implication of this story is that domestic investors should do better than foreigners in local markets.

The empirical evidence, however, is mixed. On the one hand, Shukla and van Inwegen (1995) find that in U.S. markets, domestic managers outperform foreigners. Coval and Moskowitz (2001) document "home bias at home," where U.S. mutual fund managers who stick to firms in their local region tend to perform better than their peers who invest all over the country. On the other hand, Grinblatt and Keloharju (2000), Seascholes (2000), and Karolyi (2002) all find the reverse: domestic residents and institutions underperform foreign investors in local markets.

5. Behavioral biases

Huberman (2001) argues that "people simply prefer to invest in the familiar." The lack of international diversification is then a result of people sticking to what they know. Morse and Shive (2011) assert that home bias is due to patriotism and find that countries whose residents are less patriotic exhibit less home bias.

The home bias puzzle literature is a good example of positive economics (see chapter 2). We still do not know, however, what prevents investors from taking up these opportunities. The concept of diversification from mean-variance investing is normative; sections 2.1 to 2.4 have demonstrated large benefits of international investing. Investors should seize the chance to diversify and improve their risk–return trade-offs. Your money should be like the testy adolescent who can't wait to leave home: invest abroad and reap the benefits.

2.7. IS DIVERSIFICATION REALLY A FREE LUNCH?

Diversification has been called the only "free lunch" in finance and seems too good to be true. If you hold (optimized) diversified portfolios, you can attain better risk–return trade-offs than holding individual assets. Is it really a free lunch?

Yes, if you only care about portfolio means and variances.

Mean-variance investing, by definition, only considers means and variances. Portfolio variances are indeed reduced by holding diversified portfolios of imperfectly correlated assets (see equation (3.1)). In this context, there is a free lunch.

---

[17] The first model along these lines was by Gehrig (1993). Recent models include Van Nieuwerburgh and Veldkamp (2009) where investors endogenously choose not to become informed about foreign equities in equilibrium.

But what if an investor cares about other things? In particular, what if the investor cares about downside risk and other higher moment measures of risk?

Variances always decrease when assets with nonperfect correlations are combined. This causes improvements in returns and reductions in risk in mean-variance space. But other measures of risk do not necessarily diminish when portfolios are formed. For example, a portfolio can be more negatively skewed and thus have greater downside risk than the downside risk of each individual asset.[18] Most investors care about many more risk measures than simply variance.

Diversification is not necessarily a free lunch when other measures of risk are considered. Nevertheless, from the viewpoint of characterizing the tails of asset returns, standard deviation (or variance) is the most important measure. Furthermore, optimal asset weights for a general utility function can be considered to be mean-variance weights to a first approximation, but we may have to change an investor's risk aversion in the approximation (see chapter 2).[19] While variance is the first-order risk effect, in some cases the deviations from the mean-variance approximation can be large. You still need to watch the downside.

In the opposite direction, diversification kills your chances of the big lottery payoff. If you are risk seeking and want to bet on a stock having a lucky break— and hope to become a billionaire from investing everything in the next Microsoft or Google—diversification is not for you. Since diversification reduces idiosyncratic risk, it also limits the extremely high payoffs that can occur from highly concentrated positions. The risk-averse investor likes this because it also limits the catastrophic losses that can result from failing to diversify. Just ask the employees of Enron and Lehman and the faculty and students at the University of Rochester and Boston University.

The overall message from mean-variance investing is that diversification is good. It minimizes risks that are avoidable and idiosyncratic. It views assets holistically, emphasizing how they interact with each other. By diversifying, investors improve their Sharpe ratios and can hold strictly better portfolios— portfolios that have higher returns per unit of risk or lower risk for a given target return—than assets held in isolation.

3. Mean-Variance Optimization

We've described the mean-variance frontier and know that the best investment opportunities lie along it. Which of these efficient portfolios on the mean-variance frontier should we pick?

---

[18] The technical jargon for this is that higher moment risk measures are not necessarily subadditive. See Artzner et al. (1999).

[19] Technically, you can Taylor expand a utility function so that the first term represents CRRA utility, which is approximately mean-variance utility.

That depends on each investor's risk aversion. We saw in the previous chapter that we can summarize mean-variance preferences by *indifference curves*. Maximizing mean-variance utility is equivalent to choosing the highest possible indifference curve. Indifference curves correspond to the individual maximizing mean-variance utility (see equation (2.4) in chapter 2 restated here):

$$\max_{\{w_i\}} E(r_p) - \frac{\gamma}{2}\mathrm{var}(r_p),$$

$$(3.3)$$

subject to any constraints.

The coefficient of risk aversion, g, is specific to each individual. The weights, $\{w_i\}$, correspond to the risky assets in the investor's universe. Investment in the risk-free asset, if it is available, constitutes the remaining investment (all the asset weights, including the risk-free asset position, sum to one).

3.1. WITHOUT A RISK-FREE ASSET

Figure 3.8 shows the solution method for the case without a risk-free asset.[20] The left graph in the top row shows the indifference curves. As covered in chapter 2, one particular indifference curve represents one level of utility. The investor has

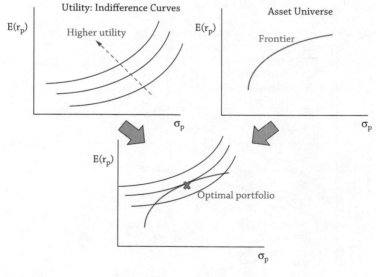

Figure 3.8

[20] The mathematical formulation of this problem corresponds to equation (3.3) with the constraint that the weights in risky assets sum to one or that the weight in the risk-free asset is equal to zero.

the same utility for all the portfolios on a given indifference curve. The investor moves to higher utility by moving to successively higher indifference curves. The right graph in the top row is the mean-variance frontier that we constructed from section 2. The frontier is a property of the asset universe, while the indifference curves are functions of the risk aversion of the investor.

We bring the indifference curves and the frontier together in the bottom row of Figure 3.8. We need to find the tangency point between the highest possible indifference curve and the mean-variance frontier. This is marked with the X. Indifference curves lying above this point represent higher utilities, but these are not attainable—we must lie on the frontier. Indifference curves lying below the X represent portfolios that are attainable as they intersect the frontier. We can, however, improve our utility by shifting to a higher indifference curve. The highest possible utility achievable is the tangency point X of the highest possible indifference curve and the frontier.

Let's go back to our G5 countries and take a mean-variance investor with a risk aversion coefficient of $\gamma = 3$. In Figure 3.9, I plot the constrained (no shorting) and unconstrained mean-variance frontiers constructed using U.S., Japanese, U.K., German, and French equities. The indifference curve corresponding to the maximum achievable utility is drawn and is tangent to the frontiers at the asterisk. At this point, both the constrained and unconstrained frontiers overlap. The optimal portfolio at the tangency point is given by:

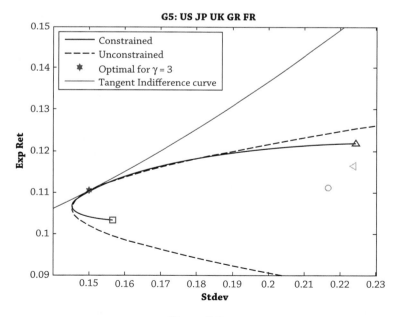

Figure 3.9

	U.S.	JP	U.K.	GR	FR
Optimal Portfolio	0.45	0.24	0.16	0.11	0.04

This portfolio is heavily weighted towards the United States and Japan with weights of 45% and 24%, respectively. Note that by construction, this portfolio consists only of risky assets, so the portfolio weights sum to one. (The weights in this example are also fairly close to the market capitalization weights of these countries.) With a risk-free rate of 1%, the Sharpe ratio corresponding to this optimal portfolio is 0.669.

3.2. WITH A RISK-FREE ASSET

The addition of a risk-free asset expands the investor's opportunities considerably. Since there is only one period, the risk-free asset has no variance. Think of T-bills as an example of a security with a risk-free return. (There is some small default risk in T-bills, which you should ignore for now; I cover sovereign default risk in chapter 14.)

When there is a risk-free asset, the investor proceeds in two steps:

1. Find the best risky asset portfolio.
      This is called the *mean-variance efficient* (MVE) portfolio, or tangency portfolio, and is the portfolio of risky assets that maximizes the Sharpe ratio.[21]
2. Mix the best risky asset portfolio with the risk-free asset.
      This changes the efficient set from the frontier into a wider range of opportunities. The efficient set becomes a *capital allocation line* (CAL), as I explain below.

The procedure of first finding the best risky asset portfolio (the MVE) and then mixing it with the risk-free asset is called two-fund separation. It was originally developed by James Tobin (1958), who won the Nobel Prize in 1981. Given the limited computing power at the time, it was a huge breakthrough in optimal portfolio choice.

Let's first find the best risky asset portfolio, or MVE. Assume the risk-free rate is 1%. Figure 3.10 plots our now familiar mean-variance frontier for the G5 and marks the MVE with an asterisk. The dashed diagonal line that goes through the MVE is the CAL. (We encountered the CAL in the previous chapter.) The CAL starts at the risk-free rate, which is 1% in Figure 3.10 and is tangent to the mean-variance frontier. The tangency point is the MVE. The CAL is obtained by

---

[21] I have personally found this terminology a little confusing because "mean-variance efficient" portfolio sounds similar to "minimum variance" portfolio. Unfortunately this terminology is engrained, and I will also use it here.

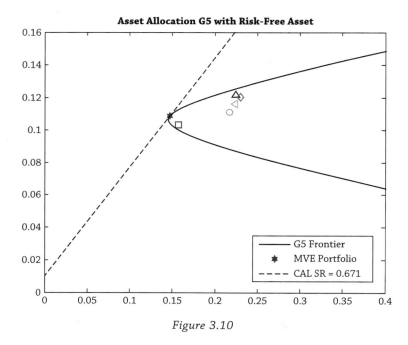

Figure 3.10

taking all combinations of the MVE with the 1% yielding risk-free asset. The MVE itself corresponds to a 100% position in only G5 equities and the intersection point of the CAL on the *y*-axis at 1% corresponds to a 100% risk-free position.

The slope of the CAL represents the portfolio's Sharpe ratio. Since the CAL is tangent at the MVE, it represents the maximum Sharpe ratio that can be obtained by the investor. A line that starts from the risk-free rate of 1% on the *y*-axis but with a larger angle, which tilts closer to the *y*-axis, cannot be implemented as it does not intersect the frontier. The frontier represents the set of best possible portfolios of G5 risky assets, and we must lie on the frontier. A line that starts from the risk-free rate of 1% on the *y*-axis but with a lesser angle than the CAL, which tilts closer to the *x*-axis, intersects the frontier. These are CALs that can be obtained in actual portfolios but do not represent the highest possible Sharpe ratio. The maximum Sharpe ratio is the tangency point, or MVE.

The MVE in Figure 3.10 has a Sharpe ratio of 0.671. It consists of:

	U.S.	JP	U.K.	GR	FR
MVE Portfolio	0.53	0.24	0.12	0.10	0.02

All the portfolios that lie on the CAL have the same Sharpe ratio, except for the 100% risk-free position that corresponds to the risk-free rate of 1% on the *y*-axis.

Now that we've found the best risky MVE portfolio, the investor mixes the risk-free asset with the MVE portfolio. This takes us off the mean-variance frontier.

Asset Allocation G5 with Risk-Free Asset

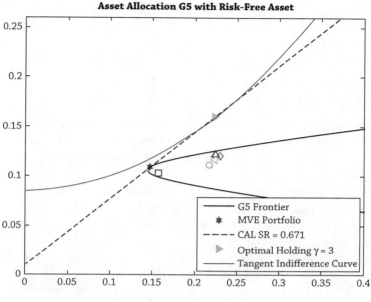

Figure 3.11

Finding the optimal combination of the MVE with the risk-free asset is equivalent to finding the point at which the highest possible indifference curve touches the CAL. The tangency point is the investor's optimal portfolio. In Figure 3.11, we graph the CAL and show the optimal holding in the triangle for an investor with a risk aversion of $\gamma = 3$. The indifference curve that is tangent to this point—which corresponds to the maximum utility for this investor—is also plotted.

In Figure 3.11, the tangency point of the highest indifference curve and the CAL lies to the right of the MVE. This means the investor shorts the risk-free asset, or borrows money at 1%, and has a levered position in the MVE. The optimal positions corresponding to the triangle, which is the tangency MVE point, are:

	U.S.	JP	U.K.	GR	FR	Risk-Free
MVE Portfolio	0.80	0.37	0.18	0.15	0.03	−0.52

The proportions of the risky assets relative to each other in this optimal portfolio are the same as the weights of the MVE. That is, the 0.53 MVE weight of the United States is the same as $0.80/(0.80 + 0.37 + 0.18 + 0.15 + 0.03)$. The optimal position for the $\gamma = 3$ investor has a Sharpe ratio of 0.671, which is the same as the CAL as it lies on the CAL.

How much has the investor gained in moving from our previous constrained setting in section 3.1 (no risk-free asset available) to the example with the risk-free asset included? The certainty equivalent of the tangency position with the short position in the risk-free rate is 0.085. The corresponding certainty equivalent restricting the investor to only risky asset positions obtained earlier is 0.077. Letting the investor have access to the (short) risk-free asset position represents a significant risk-free utility increase of eighty basis points.

3.3. NON-PARTICIPATION IN THE STOCK MARKET

Mean-variance investing predicts that with just equities and a risk-free asset, all investors should invest in the stock market except those who are infinitely risk averse. In reality, only half of investors put money in the stock market.[22] This is the *non-participation puzzle*.

Table 3.12 reports equity market participation rates by households in the United States calculated by Li (2009) using data from the Panel Study of Income Dynamics (PSID), a household survey conducted by the University of Michigan, and the Survey of Consumer Finances (SCF) conducted by the Federal Reserve Board. (Obviously you can't be poor if you have some savings, and researchers go further and exclude those with meager savings.)

In Table 3.12, the PSID and SCF stock holdings track each other closely and have hovered around 30%. The SCF also counts stocks included in pension plans and IRAs and when these retirement assets are included, the proportion of households holding stocks increases to around 50%. There has been a general increase in stock market participation when retirement assets are included from around 30% in the 1980s to 50% in 2005. Yet about half of U.S. households do not hold any equities. This is not just an American phenomenon; Laakso (2010) finds that stock market participation in Germany and France is well below 50% including both direct investments and those made indirectly through mutual funds and investment accounts. Italy, Greece, and Spain have stock participation rates at approximately 10% or less.

Several explanations have been proposed for the high non-participation in stocks markets. Among these are:

Table 3.12

Equity Market Participation Rates							
	1984	1989	1994	1999	2001	2003	2005
PSID	27%	31%	37%	28%	32%	29%	27%
SCF (excluding pensions and IRAs)	–	21%	23%	30%	32%	30%	29%
SCF (including pensions and IRAs)	–	32%	39%	50%	52%	51%	51%

[22] The first paper in this literature is Blume, Crockett, and Friend (1974). The non-participation puzzle rose to economists' attention with Mankiw and Zeldes (1991) as an explanation for the equity premium puzzle, which I discuss in chapter 8.

1. Investors do not have mean-variance utility.

   We covered many more realistic utility functions in chapter 2. Utility functions that can capture the greater risk aversion investors have to downside losses can dramatically lower optimal holdings of equities. Investors with disappointment utility, in particular, will optimally not participate in the stock market, as shown by Ang, Bekaert, and Liu (2005).

2. Participation costs.

   These costs include both the transaction costs of actually purchasing equities, but more broadly they include the expense of becoming financially educated and the "psychic" cost of overcoming fears of investing in the stock market. Consistent with a participation cost explanation, Table 3.12 shows that more people have invested in stocks as equities have become easier to trade since the 1980s with the arrival of online trading and easier access to mutual funds. According to Vissing-Jørgensen (2002), a cost of just $50 in year 2000 prices explains why half of non-stockholders do not hold equities. Conversely, Andersen and Nielsen (2010) conclude that participation costs cannot be an explanation. In their somewhat morbid paper, they examine households inheriting stocks due to sudden deaths. These households pay no participation costs to enter stock markets, yet most of these households simply sell the entire equity portfolio and move the proceeds into risk-free bonds.

3. Social factors.

   Several social factors are highly correlated with holding equities. Whether you invest in equities depends on whether your neighbor invests in equities and whether you are politically active. Non-equity holders may have less trust in markets than their peers. Investors' expectations of returns are highly dependent on whether they have been burned by previous forays into the stock market.[23] Provocatively, Grinblatt, Keloharju, and Linnainmaa (2012) find that the more intelligent the investor, the more he or she invests in stocks.

Whatever the reason, my advice is: Don't be a non-participant. Invest in the stock market. You'll reap the equity risk premium too (see chapter 8). But do so as part of a diversified portfolio.

4. Garbage In, Garbage Out

Mean-variance frontiers are highly sensitive to estimates of means, volatilities, and correlations. Very small changes to these inputs result in extremely

---

[23] See Hong, Kubik, and Stein (2004) for social interaction, Bonaparte and Kumar (2013) for political activism, Guiso, Sapienza, and Zingales (2008) for trust, and Malmendier and Nagel (2011) for investors being affected by past stock market returns.

different portfolios. These problems have caused mean-variance optimization to be widely derided. The lack of robustness of "optimized" mean-variance portfolios is certainly problematic, but it should not take away from the main message of mean-variance investing that diversified portfolios are better than individual assets. How to find an optimal portfolio mean-variance portfolio, however, is an important question given these difficulties.

4.1. SENSITIVITY TO INPUTS

Figure 3.13 showcases this problem. It plots the original mean-variance frontier estimated from January 1970 to December 2011 in the solid line. The mean of U.S. equity returns in this sample is 10.3%. Suppose we change the mean to 13.0%. This choice is well within two standard error bounds of the data estimate of the U.S. mean. The new mean-variance frontier is drawn in the dashed line. There is a large difference between the two.

The mean-variance frontier portfolios corresponding to a target return of 12% in the original case (U.S. mean is 10.3%) and the new case (U.S. mean is 13.0%) are:

	U.S. mean = 10.3%	U.S. mean = 13.0%
U.S.	−0.0946	0.4101
JP	0.2122	0.3941
U.K.	0.4768	0.0505
GR	0.1800	0.1956
FR	0.2257	−0.0502

Previously, we didn't have negative weights in the United States because we worked with the (constrained) optimal portfolio for a risk aversion of $\gamma = 3$. This corresponds to a target return of 11.0%. The portfolio on the frontier corresponding to a target return of 12% involves a short U.S. position of −9%. This small change in the target return and the resulting large change in the portfolio weights itself showcases the lack of robustness of mean-variance optimization.

Changing the U.S. mean to 13.0% has caused the U.S. position to change from −9% to 41%, the U.K. position to move from 48% to approximately 5%, and the French position to shrink from 23% to −5%. These are very large changes resulting from a small change in the U.S. mean. No wonder Michaud (1989) calls mean-variance portfolios "error maximizing portfolios."

4.2. WHAT TO DO?

Change Utility

My first recommendation is not to use mean-variance utility. Investors are fearful of other risks, they care about relative performance, like catching-up-with-the-Joneses or habit utility, and they dread losses much more than they cherish

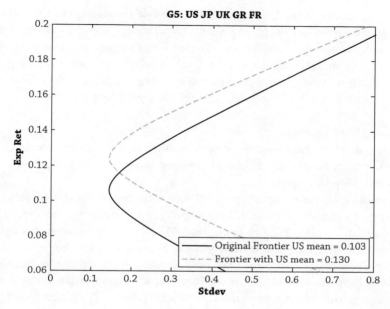

Figure 3.13

gains. (For more general utility functions, see chapter 2.) Unfortunately, we have
a dearth of commercial optimizers (none that I know about at the time of writing)
that can spit out optimal portfolios for more realistic utility functions, but there
are plenty of very fancy mean-variance optimizers. If you insist on (or are forced
to use) mean-variance utility. . . .

Use Constraints

Jagannathan and Ma (2003) show that imposing constraints helps a lot. Indeed,
raw mean-variance weights are so unstable that practitioners using mean-variance
optimization always impose constraints. Constraints help because they bring back
unconstrained portfolio weights to economically reasonable positions. Thus, they
can be interpreted as a type of *robust estimator* that *shrinks* unconstrained weights
back to reasonable values. We can do this more generally if we. . . .

Use Robust Statistics

Investors can significantly improve estimates of inputs by using robust statistical estimators. One class of estimators is *Bayesian shrinkage* methods.[24] These
estimators take care of outliers and extreme values that play havoc with traditional classical estimators. They shrink estimates back to a *prior*, or model, which
is based on intuition or economics. For example, the raw mean estimated in a

---

[24] Introduced by James and Stein (1961).

sample would not be used, but the raw mean would be adjusted to the mean implied by the CAPM (see chapter 6), a multifactor model, or some value computed from fundamental analysis. Covariances can also be shrunk back to a prior where each stock in an industry, say, has the same volatility and correlation—which is reasonable if we view each stock in a given industry as similar to the others.[25]

No statistical method, however, can help you if your data are lousy.

Don't Just Use Historical Data

Investors must use past data to estimate inputs for optimization problems. But many investors simply take historical averages on short, rolling samples. This is the worst thing you can do.

In drawing all of the mean-variance frontiers for the G5, or various subsets of countries, I used historical data. I plead guilty. I did, however, use a fairly long sample, from January 1970 to December 2011. Nevertheless, even this approximately forty-year sample is relatively short. You should view the figures in this chapter as what has transpired over the last forty years and not as pictures of what will happen in the future. As the investment companies like to say in small print, past performance is no guarantee of future returns. The inputs required for mean-variance investing—expected returns, volatilities, and correlations—are statements about what we think will happen in the future.

Using short data samples to produce estimates for mean-variance inputs is very dangerous. It leads to pro-cyclicality. When past returns have been high, current prices are high. But current prices are high because future returns tend to be low. While predictability in general is very weak, chapter 8 provides evidence that there is some. Thus, using a past data sample to estimate a mean produces a high estimate right when future returns are likely to be low. These problems are compounded when more recent data are weighted more heavily, which occurs in techniques like exponential smoothing.

An investor using a sample where returns are stable, like the mid-2000s right before the financial crisis, would produce volatility estimates that are low. But these times of low volatilities (and high prices) are actually periods when risk is high. Sir Andrew Crockett of the Bank of England says (with my italics):[26] "The received wisdom is that risk increases in the recessions and falls in booms. In contrast, it may be more helpful to think of risk as *increasing* during upswings, as financial imbalances build up, and *materializing* in recessions." The low estimates

---

[25] See Ledoit and Wolf (2003) and Wang (2005), among others. Strictly speaking, the mean-variance solution involves an inverse of a covariance matrix, so we should shrink the inverse covariance rather than the covariance. This is done by Kourtis, Dotsis, and Markellos (2009). Tu and Zhou (2011) show shrinkage methods can be used to combine naïve and sophisticated diversification strategies in the presence of estimation risk.

[26] "Marrying the Micro- and Macro-Prudential Dimensions of Financial Stability," speech at the Eleventh International Conference of Banking Supervisors, Sept. 20–21, 2000, http://www.bis.org/speeches/sp000921.htm.

of volatilities computed using short samples ending in 2007 totally missed the explosions in risks that materialized in the 2008–2009 financial crisis.

Use Economic Models

I believe that *asset allocation is fundamentally a valuation problem.* The main problem with using purely historical data, even with the profession's best econometric toolkit, is that it usually ignores economic value. Why would you buy more of something if it is too expensive?

Valuation requires an *economic framework.* Economic models could also be combined with statistical techniques. This is the approach of Black and Litterman (1991), which is popular because it delivers estimates of expected returns that are "reasonable" in many situations. Black and Litterman start with the fact that we observe market capitalizations, or market weights. The market is a mean-variance portfolio implied by the CAPM equilibrium theory (see chapter 6). Market weights, which reflect market prices, embody the market's expectations of future returns. Black and Litterman use a simple model—the CAPM—to reverse engineer the future expected returns (which are unobservable) from market capitalizations (which are observable). In addition, their method also allows investors to adjust these market-based weights to their own beliefs using a shrinkage estimator. I will use Black–Litterman in some examples below, in section 6.

An alternative framework for estimating inputs is to work down to the underlying determinants of value. In Part II of this book, I will build a case for thinking about the underlying factors that drive the risk and returns of assets. Understanding how the factors influence returns and finding which factor exposures are right for different investors in the long run enables us to construct more robust portfolios.

The concept of *factor investing* (see chapter 14), where we look through asset class labels to the underlying factor risks, is especially important in maximizing the benefits of diversification. Simply giving a group of investment vehicles a label, like "private equity" or "hedge funds," does not make them asset classes. The naïve approach to mean-variance investing treats these as separate asset classes and plugs them straight into a mean-variance optimizer. Factor investing recognizes that private equity and hedge funds have many of the same factor risks as traditional asset classes. Diversification benefits can be overstated, as many investors discovered in 2008 when risky asset classes came crashing down together, if investors do not look at the underlying factor risks.

Keep It Simple (Stupid)

The simple things always work best. The main principle of mean-variance investing is to hold diversified portfolios. There are many simple diversified portfolios, and they tend to work much better than the optimized portfolios computed in the full glory of mean-variance quadratic programming in equations (3.2) and (3.3).

Simple portfolios also provide strong benchmarks to measure the value-added of more complicated statistical and economic models.

The simplest strategy—an equally weighted portfolio—turns out to be one of the best performers, as we shall now see.

5. Special Mean-Variance Portfolios

In this section I run a horse race between several portfolio strategies, each of which is a special case of the full mean-variance strategy. Diversification is common to all the strategies, but they build a diversified portfolio in different ways. This leads to very different performance.

5.1. HORSERACE

I take four asset classes—U.S. government bonds (Barcap U.S. Treasury), U.S. corporate bonds (Barcap U.S. Credit), U.S. stocks (S&P 500), and international stocks (MSCI EAFE)—and track the performance of various portfolios from January 1978 to December 2011. The data are sampled monthly. The strategies implemented at time t are estimated using data over the past five years, $t-60$ to t. The first portfolios are formed at the end of January 1978 using data from January 1973 to January 1978. The portfolios are held for one month, and then new portfolios are formed at the end of the month. I use one-month T-bills as the risk-free rate. In constructing the portfolios, I restrict shorting down to -100% on each asset class.

Using short, rolling samples opens me up to the criticisms of the previous section. I do this deliberately because it highlights some of the pitfalls of (fairly) unconstrained mean-variance approaches. Consequently, it allows us to understand why some special cases of mean-variance perform well and others badly.

I run a horserace between:

Mean-Variance Weights where the weights are chosen to maximize the Sharpe ratio.

Market Weights, which are given by market capitalizations of each index.

Diversity Weights, which are (power) transformations of market weights recommended by Fernholz, Garvy, and Hannon (1998).

Equal Weights, or the $1/N$ rule, which simply holds one-quarter in each asset class. Duchin and Levy (2009) call this strategy the "Talmudic rule" since the Babylonian Talmud recommended this strategy approximately 1,500 years ago: "A man should always place his money, one third in land, a third in merchandise, and keep a third in hand."

Risk Parity is the strategy du jour and chooses asset weights proportional to the inverse of variance [*Risk Parity (Variance)*] or to the inverse of volatility [*Risk Parity (Volatility)*]. The term "risk parity" was originally coined by Edward Qian in 2005.[27] It has shot to prominence in the practitioner community because of the huge success of Bridgewater Associates, a large hedge fund with a corporate culture that has been likened to a cult.[28] Bridgewater launched the first investment product based on risk parity called the "All Weather" fund in 1996. In 2011 the founder of Bridgewater, Ray Dalio, earned $3.9 billion.[29] (I cover hedge funds in chapter 17). Bridgewater's success has inspired many copycats. The original implementations of risk parity were done on variances, but there are fans of weighting on volatilities.[30]

Minimum Variance is the portfolio on the left-most tip of the mean-variance frontier, which we've seen before.

Equal Risk Contributions form weights in each asset position such that they contribute equally to the total portfolio variance.[31]

Kelly (1956) **Rule** is a portfolio strategy that maximizes the expected log return. In the very long run, it will maximize wealth. (I explain more in chapter 4.)

Proportional to Sharpe Ratio is a strategy that holds larger positions in assets that have larger realized Sharpe ratios over the last five years.

Over this sample a 100% investment in U.S. equities had a Sharpe ratio of 0.35. This is dominated by all the diversified portfolios in the horserace, except for the most unconstrained mean-variance portfolio. This is consistent with the advice from the example in section 2 where no one should hold a 100% U.S. equity portfolio; diversification produces superior portfolios with lower risk and higher returns.

Table 3.14 reports the results of the horserace. Mean-variance weights perform horribly. The strategy produces a Sharpe ratio of just 0.07, and it is trounced by all the other strategies. Holding market weights does much better, with a Sharpe ratio of 0.41. This completely passive strategy outperforms the Equal Risk Contributions and the Proportional to Sharpe Ratio portfolios (with Sharpe ratios of 0.32 and 0.45, respectively). Diversity Weights tilt the portfolio toward the asset classes with smaller market caps, and this produces better results than market weights.

---

[27] Qian, E., 2005, Risk Parity Portfolios: Efficient Portfolios through True Diversification, PanAgora.

[28] Kevin Roose, "Pursuing Self-Interest in Harmony with the Laws of the Universe and Contributing to Evolution is Universally Rewarded," *New York Magazine*, Apr. 10, 2011.

[29] I cover hedge funds in chapter 17.

[30] Versions of risk parity where the weights are inversely proportional to volatility are advocated by Martellini (2008) and Choueifaty and Coignard (2008).

[31] See Qian (2006) and Maillard, Roncalli, and Teiletche (2010).

Table 3.14

Portfolio Strategies Across U.S. Government Bonds, U.S. Corporate Bonds, U.S. Stocks, International Stocks, 1978–2011

	Raw Return	Volatility	Sharpe Ratio	Comments
Mean-Variance Weights	6.06	11.59	0.07	Maximizes Sharpe ratio
Market Weights	10.25	12.08	0.41	
Diversity Weights	10.14	10.48	0.46	Uses a transformation of market weights
Equal Weights (1/4)	10.00	8.66	0.54	
Risk Parity (Variance)	8.76	5.86	0.59	Weights inversely proportional to variance
Risk Parity (Volatility)	9.39	6.27	0.65	Weights inversely proportional to volatility
Minimum Variance	7.96	5.12	0.52	
Equal Risk Contributions	7.68	7.45	0.32	Equal contribution to portfolio variance
Kelly Rule	7.97	4.98	0.54	Maximizes expected log return
Proportional to Sharpe Ratio	9.80	9.96	0.45	

Average Asset Weights

	U.S. Govt Bonds	U.S. Corp Bonds	U.S. Stocks	International Stocks
Mean-Variance Weights	0.74	−0.05	0.06	0.25
Market Weights	0.14	0.08	0.41	0.37
Diversity Weights	0.19	0.15	0.33	0.32
Equal Weights (1/4)	0.25	0.25	0.25	0.25

continued

Table 3.14 **(continued)**

	Average Asset Weights			
	U.S. Govt Bonds	U.S. Corp Bonds	U.S. Stocks	International Stocks
Risk Parity (Variance)	0.51	0.36	0.07	0.06
Risk Parity (Volatility)	0.97	−0.30	0.17	0.16
Minimum Variance	1.41	−0.51	0.07	0.03
Equal Risk Contributions	0.50	0.42	0.25	−0.17
Kelly Rule	1.18	−0.29	0.07	0.04
Proportional to Sharpe Ratio	0.24	0.21	0.21	0.35

The simple Equal Weight strategy does very well with a Sharpe ratio of 0.54. What a contrast with this strategy versus the complex mean-variance portfolio (with a Sharpe ratio of 0.07)! The Equal Weight strategy also outperforms the market portfolio (with a Sharpe ratio of 0.41). De Miguel, Garlappi, and Uppal (2009) find that the simple $1/N$ rule outperforms a large number of other implementations of mean-variance portfolios, including portfolios constructed using robust Bayesian estimators, portfolio constraints, and optimal combinations of portfolios which I covered in section 4.2. The $1/N$ portfolio also produces a higher Sharpe ratio than each individual asset class position. (U.S. bonds had the highest Sharpe ratio of 0.47 in the sample.)

Risk Parity does even better than $1/N$. The outperformance, however, of the plain-vanilla Risk Parity (Variance) versus Equal Weights is small. Risk Parity (Variance) has a Sharpe ratio of 0.59 compared to the 0.54 Sharpe ratio for Equal Weights. Risk Parity based on volatility does even better and has the highest out-of-sample Sharpe ratio of all the strategies considered, at 0.65. When risk parity strategies are implemented on more asset classes (or factor strategies, see chapter 7) in practice, historical Sharpe ratios for risk parity strategies have often exceeded one.

The outperformance of the Minimum Variance portfolio versus standard mean-variance weights and the market portfolio has been known for at least twenty years.[32] One reason that minimum variance portfolios outperform the market is that there is a tendency for low volatility assets to have higher returns

---

[32] At least since Haugen and Baker (1991).

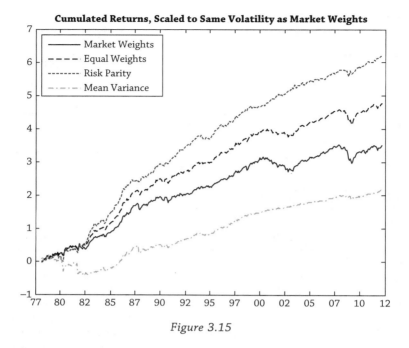

Cumulated Returns, Scaled to Same Volatility as Market Weights

Figure 3.15

than high volatility assets, which I cover in chapter 10, and the minimum variance portfolio overweights low volatility stocks. The last two strategies in Table 3.14 are the Kelly Rule and the Proportional to Sharpe Ratio strategies. Both also outperform the Mean-Variance Weights and the market portfolio in terms of Sharpe ratios. You would have been better off, however, using the simple $1/N$ strategies in both cases.

Figure 3.15 plots cumulated returns of the Market Weights, Equal Weights, Risk Parity (Variance), and Mean-Variance strategies. All these returns are scaled to have the same volatility as the passive market weight strategy. The dominance of the Equal Weights and Risk Parity strategies is obvious. In addition, Figure 3.15 shows that the Risk Parity strategy has the smallest drawdown movements of the four strategies.

5.2. WHY DOES UNRESTRICTED MEAN-VARIANCE PERFORM SO BADLY?

The optimal mean-variance portfolio is a complex function of estimated means, volatilities, and correlations of asset returns. There are many parameters to estimate. Optimized mean-variance portfolios can blow up when there are tiny errors in any of these inputs. In the horserace with four asset classes, there are just fourteen parameters to estimate and even with such a low number mean-variance does badly. With one hundred assets, there are 5,510 parameters to estimate.[33] For five thousand stocks (approximately the number of common stocks listed in U.S. markets) the number of parameters to estimate exceeds 12,000. The potential for errors is enormous.

Let's view what happens when we move from the optimal mean-variance strategy and turn off some of the inputs, so that we are relieved from estimating means, volatilities, correlations, or combinations of all three. Table 3.16 lists some special cases as the restrictions are imposed.

The minimum variance portfolio is a special case of full mean-variance that does not estimate means and in fact assumes that the means are all equal. Risk parity is a special case of mean-variance that does not estimate means or correlations; it implicitly assumes that all assets have the same mean and all assets are uncorrelated. The equally weighted portfolio has nothing to estimate. It is also a special case of mean-variance and assumes all assets are identical.

I have included market weights in Table 3.16. Like equal weights, there are no parameters to estimate using market weights. The important difference between equal weights and market weights is that the equal weighted portfolio is an *active strategy*. It requires trading every period to rebalance back to equal weights.

Table 3.16

	Assumptions on Means	Assumptions on Volatilities	Assumptions on Correlations	Comments
Optimal Mean-Variance	Unconstrained	Unconstrained	Unconstrained	Most complex
Minimum Variance	Equal	Unconstrained	Unconstrained	No need to estimate means
Risk Parity	Equal	Unconstrained	Equal to zero	No need to estimate means or correlations
Equally Weighted (1/N Portfolio)	Equal	Equal	Equal	Most simple and active, Nothing to estimate
Market Weight	–	–	–	Observable and passive, Nothing to estimate

[33] For N assets, you have N means and $N \times (N + 1)/2$ elements in the covariance matrix.

In contrast, the market portfolio is *passive* and requires no trading. The action of rebalancing in equal weights imparts this strategy with a *rebalancing premium*. Rebalancing also turns out to be the foundation of an optimal long-run investing strategy. I cover these topics in the next chapter.

As you go down Table 3.16 from full-blown mean-variance to equal weights or the market portfolio, you estimate fewer parameters, and thus there are fewer things that can go wrong with the mean-variance optimization. The extreme cases are the equal weight or market weight positions, which require no analysis of data (except looking at market capitalizations in the case of the market portfolio).

Long-run means are very tricky to estimate. Sampling at weekly or daily frequencies does not allow you to more accurately estimate means—only extending the sample allows you to pin down the mean more precisely.[34] For any asset like the S&P 500, the only way to gauge the long-run return is to look at the index level at the beginning and at the end of the sample and divide it by time. It doesn't matter how it got to that final level; all that matters is the ending index value. Hence, we can only be more certain of the mean return if we lengthen time. This makes forecasting returns very difficult.[35] The minimum variance portfolio outperforms mean-variance because we remove all the errors associated with means.

Volatilities are much more predictable than means. High-frequency sampling allows you to estimate variances more accurately even though it does nothing for improving estimates of means. Higher frequency data also allows you to produce better estimates of correlations. But correlations can switch signs while variances can only be positive. Thus, variances are easier to estimate than correlations. Poor estimates of correlations also have severe effects on optimized mean-variance portfolios; small changes in correlations can produce big swings in portfolio weights.[36] Risk parity turns off the noise associated with estimating correlations. (More advanced versions of risk parity do take into account some correlation estimates.) In the horserace, risk parity produced higher Sharpe ratios (0.59 and 0.65 using variances and volatilities, respectively) than the minimum variance portfolio (which had a Sharpe ratio of 0.52).

In summary, the special cases of mean-variance perform better than the full mean-variance procedure because fewer things can go wrong with estimates of the inputs.

5.3. IMPLICATIONS FOR ASSET OWNERS

I went from the full mean-variance case to the various special cases in Table 3.16 by adding restrictions. To practice mean-variance investing, the investor should start at the bottom of Table 3.16 and begin from market weights. If you

---

[34] This is shown in a seminal paper by Merton (1980).

[35] I cover this further in chapter 8.

[36] Green and Hollifield (1992) provide bounds on the average correlation between asset returns that are required for portfolios to be well balanced.

can't rebalance, hold the market. (The horserace results in Table 3.14 show that you will do pretty well and much better than mean-variance.)

If you can rebalance, move to the equal weight portfolio. You will do better than market weights in the long run. Equal weights may be hard to implement for very large investors because when trades are very large, investors move prices and incur substantial transaction costs. It turns out that any well-balanced, fixed-weight allocation works well. Jacobs, Müller, and Weber (2010) analyze more than 5,000 different portfolio construction methods and find that any simple fixed-weight allocation thrashes mean-variance portfolios.

Now if you can estimate variances or volatilities, you could think about risk parity. My horserace only estimated volatility by taking the realized volatility over a past rolling sample. Ideally we want estimates of future volatility. There are very good models for forecasting volatility based on generalized autoregressive conditional heteroskedasticity or stochastic volatility models, which I describe in chapter 8.

Suppose the hotshot econometrician you've just hired can also accurately estimate correlations and volatilities. Now you should consider relaxing the correlation restriction from risk parity. Finally, and hardest of all, is the case if you can accurately forecast means. If and only if you can do this, should you consider doing (fairly unconstrained) mean-variance optimization.

Common to all these portfolio strategies is the fact that they are diversified. This is the message you should take from this chapter. Diversification works. Computing optimal portfolios using full mean-variance techniques is treacherous, but simple diversification strategies do very well.

Warning on Risk Parity

The second panel of Table 3.14 reports the average weights in each asset class from the different strategies. Risk parity did very well, especially the risk parity strategy implemented with volatilities, because it overweighted bonds during the sample. Risk parity using variances held, on average, 51% in U.S. Treasuries and 36% in corporate bonds versus average market weights of 14% and 8%, respectively. There were even larger weights on bonds when risk parity is implemented weighting by volatilities rather than variances. Interest rates trended downward from the early 1980s all the way to the 2011, and bonds performed magnificently over this period (see chapter 9). This accounts for a large amount of the out-performance of risk parity over the sample.

Risk parity requires estimates of volatilities. Volatilities are statements of risk. Risk and prices, which embed future expected returns, are linked in equilibrium (see chapter 6). Howard Marks (2011), a hedge fund manager, says: "The value investor thinks of high risk and low prospective return as nothing but two sides of the same coin, both stemming primarily from high prices." Risk parity overweights assets that have low volatilities. Past volatilities tend to be low precisely when today's prices are high. Past low volatilities and high current prices, therefore, coincide with elevated risk today and in the future.[37] At the time of writing, Treasury bonds have record low yields, and so bond prices are very high. Risk-free U.S. Treasuries can be the riskiest investment simply because of high prices. And at a low enough price, risky equities can be the safest investments. Risk parity, poorly implemented, will be pro-cyclical because it ignores valuations, and its pro-cyclicality will manifest over decades because of the slow mean reversion of interest rates.

6. Norway and Wal-Mart Redux

Diversification involves holding many assets. In section 2 we saw that when we started with the United States and progressively added countries to get to the G5 (United States, Japan, United Kingdom, Germany, France), there were tremendous benefits from adding assets. Conversely, if we go backward and remove assets from the G5, we decrease the diversification benefits.

Norway is excluding Wal-Mart on the basis of alleged violations of human rights and other ethical considerations. Removing any asset makes an investor worse off, except when the investor is not holding that asset in the first place. When we are forced to divest an asset, what is the reduction in diversification benefits?

6.1. LOSS OF DIVERSIFICATION BENEFITS

When I teach my case study on Norway and its disinvestment of Wal-Mart in my MBA Asset Management class, I ask the students to compute the lost diversification benefits from throwing out Wal-Mart. We can do this using mean-variance investing concepts. I will not do the same exercise as I give my students, but I will go through an experiment that removes various sectors from a world portfolio. This is also relevant to Norway because as of January 2010, Norway no longer holds any tobacco stocks. Other prominent funds including CalPERS and CalSTRS are also tobacco-free.

I take the FTSE All World portfolio as at the end of June 2012, when it had thirty-nine sectors and 2,871 stocks. What happens if we eliminate tobacco? Let's use mean-variance concepts to quantify the loss of diversification benefits. In this exercise, I compute variances and correlations using a Bayesian shrinkage estimator operating on CAPM betas (see Ledoit and Wolf (2003)) and estimate expected

---

[37] A contrary opinion is Asness, Frazzini, and Pedersen (2012). They argue that investors are averse to leverage and this causes safe assets to have higher risk-adjusted returns than riskier assets. Risk parity allows some investors to exploit this risk premium.

returns using a variant of Black-Litterman (1991). I set the risk-free rate to be 2%. I compute mean-variance frontiers constraining the sector weights to be positive.

We start with all the sectors. Then, I'll remove tobacco. Next I'll remove the aerospace and defense sector. Norway has selectively divested some companies in this sector because it automatically excludes all companies involved in the manufacture of nuclear weapons and cluster munitions.[38] A final exclusion that I'll examine is banks. Sharia law prohibits the active use of derivatives and debt as profit-making activities. Thus, it is interesting to see what diversification costs are routinely incurred by some Sharia compliant funds.

As we move from the full universe to the restricted universe, we obtain the following minimum standard deviations and maximum Sharpe ratios:

	Minimum Volatility	Maximum Sharpe Ratio
All Sectors	0.1205	0.4853
No Tobacco	0.1210	0.4852
No Tobacco and Aerospace & Defense	0.1210	0.4852
No Tobacco, Aerospace & Defense, and Banks	0.1210	0.4843

The increase in the minimum volatility is tiny—from 12.05% to 12.10%. Similarly, the reduction in maximum Sharpe ratio is negligible, moving from 0.4853 for the full universe to 0.4852 when tobacco is removed and to 0.4843 when all three sectors are removed. Thus, the loss in diversification from removing one or a few sectors is extremely small. Figure 3.17 plots the (constrained) mean-variance frontiers for each set of sectors. They are indistinguishable on the graph. Norway is effectively losing nothing by selling Wal-Mart.[39] It is also effectively losing nothing by excluding tobacco.

It is important to note that in this example that I am computing the loss of ex-ante diversification benefits, as measured by the minimum variance portfolio or the maximum Sharpe ratio portfolio—concepts that are relevant for an investor selecting from the FTSE sectors. I am not considering tracking error relative to the full FTSE universe or ex-post differences in returns (which is relevant for an investor forced to track the FTSE index).

---

[38] As of June 2012, nineteen defense manufacturers had been excluded. A full list of Norway's current exclusions is at http://www.regjeringen.no/en/dep/fin/Selected-topics/the-government-pension-fund/responsible-investments/companies-excluded-from-the-investment-u.html?id=447122.

[39] This does not include the actual transaction costs of divestment. My case "The Norwegian Government Pension Fund: The Divestiture of Wal-Mart Stores Inc.," Columbia CaseWorks, ID#080301, also estimates these transaction costs.

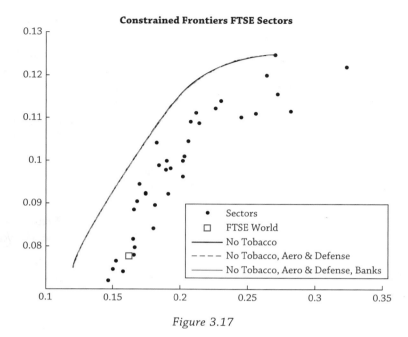

Figure 3.17

The extremely small costs of divestment are not due to the portfolios having zero holdings in the sectors that are being removed. In the full universe, the portfolio with the maximum Sharpe ratio contains 1.53% tobacco, 1.19% aerospace and defense, and 9.52% banks. Even removing an approximately 10% bank holding position has negligible cost in terms of diversification losses.

Diversification losses are so small because extra diversification benefits going from thirty-eight to thirty-nine sectors, or even thirty-six to thirty-nine sectors, are tiny (recall there are *decreasing marginal diversification benefits*). In section 2 when we added Germany and France to the G3 (United States, Japan, and United Kingdom), there was a much smaller shift in the frontier compared with moving from the United States–Japan to the G3 (see Figures 3.4 and 3.5). In our sector example the small marginal diversification benefits come about because there are few opportunities for that lost sector to pay off handsomely when the other thirty-eight sectors tank.

6.2. SOCIALLY RESPONSIBLE INVESTING

From the mean-variance investing point of view, SRI must always lose money because it reduces diversification benefits. Could it make money as an active management (alpha) strategy? Studies like Kempf and Osthoff (2007) find that stocks that rank highly on KLD measures have high returns. MSCI, an index provider, considers various social and environmental criteria in ranking companies in its

KLD indexes. While Norway has thrown Wal-Mart out, Wal-Mart gets high KLD ratings partly because it has taken many steps to reduce its carbon footprint. On the other hand, Geczy, Stambaugh, and Levin (2004) find that SRI mutual funds underperform their peers by thirty basis points per month. Harrison Hong, a Princeton academic and one of the leading scholars on SRI, shows in Hong and Kacperczyk (2009) that "sin" stocks like tobacco, firearms manufacturers, and gambling have higher risk-adjusted returns than comparable stocks.[40]

In his magnum opus written in 1936, Keynes says, "There is no clear evidence that the investment policy which is socially advantageous coincides with that which is most profitable." My reading of the SRI literature is that Keynes's remarks are equally applicable today.

I believe there is some scope for SRI in active management. There are some characteristics of firms that predict returns. Some of these effects are so pervasive that they are factors, as I discuss in chapter 7. Many of the firms that rank highly on SRI measures are likely to be more transparent, have good governance, senior managers who are less likely to steal, efficient inventory management, use few accounting gimmicks, and respond well to shareholder initiatives. These are all characteristics that we know are linked to firm performance. A simple example: limiting the rents managers can extract from shareholders allows shareholders to take home more. Gompers, Ishii, and Metrick (2003) create a governance index to rank companies from "dictatorships" to "republics." Companies that have many provisions to entrench management, anti-takeover provisions, and limit proxy votes, for example, would be defined as dictatorships. They find that republics— which are also likely to rank high on SRI criteria—have higher returns than dictatorships.[41]

If you are able to pick firms based on particular properties and characteristics and these are related to SRI, then you might be able to outperform. This method of SRI does not throw out companies; it actively selects companies on SRI criteria but does not limit the manager's investment opportunities by excluding companies.[42] Like all active strategies, it is hard to beat factor-based strategies (see chapter 14).

[40] Hong, Kubik, and Scheinkman (2012) argue against the hypothesis of "doing well by doing good" and argue exactly the opposite. They show that corporate social responsibility is costly for firms and firms only do good when they are not financially constrained. In this sense, corporate social responsibility is costly for firms.

[41] There is debate about whether this effect has persisted after the original Gompers, Ishii, and Metrick (2003) study and whether the effect is about risk or mispricing (see chapter 7). Cremers and Ferrell (2012) find stocks with weak shareholder rights have negative excess returns from 1978 to 2007 while Bebchuk, Cohen, and Wang (2013) argue the original Gompers, Ishii, and Metrick results disappear in the 2000s.

[42] A more aggressive form of doing this is shareholder activism. Shareholder activism by hedge funds adds significant value (see Brav et al. (2008)) even though the evidence for mutual funds and pension funds adding value for shareholders is decidedly mixed (see Gillan and Starks (2007)). Dimson, Karakas, and Li (2012) find that corporate social responsibility activist engagements generate excess returns.

SRI also serves an important role when it reflects the preferences of an asset owner. In Norway's case, practicing SRI gives the sovereign wealth fund legitimacy in the eyes of its owners—the Norwegian people.[43] SRI is the asset owners' choice, but the costs of imposing SRI constraints, or any other constraints, should be measured relative to the full investment set: how much are you giving up to be good?

The main message from mean-variance investing is to hold a diversified portfolio, which Norway does. Diversification benefits are a free lunch according to mean-variance investing. Doing SRI by exclusions is costly because it shrinks diversification benefits. But starting from a well-diversified portfolio (and some of the best-performing diversified portfolios are the most simple, like equal-weighted and market-weighted portfolios), the loss from excluding a few stocks is tiny. The cost of being socially responsible for Norway is negligible.

At the time of writing in 2013, Wal-Mart was still on Norway's excluded list.

---

[43] See Ang (2012a).

CHAPTER 4

Investing for the Long Run

Chapter Summary

The foundation of long-term investing is to rebalance to fixed asset positions, which are determined in a one-period portfolio choice problem where the asset weights reflect the investor's attitude toward risk. Rebalancing is a counter-cyclical strategy that buys low and sells high. It worked well even during the Great Depression of the 1930s and the Lost Decade of the 2000s. Rebalancing goes against investors' behavioral instincts and is also a short volatility strategy.

1. Stay the Course?

In April 2009, just after the worst of the financial crisis, Amy Harrison, an independent investment advisor, prepared to meet with her client, Amelia Daniel.[1] Harrison had been introduced to Daniel three years earlier. At that time, Daniel had just sold her medical information company, Daniel Health Systems, for $10 million cash. Daniel had also recently divorced. She felt that both the liquidity event and the end of a chapter in her personal life would allow her to start afresh on new, smaller ventures.

After their first meeting, Harrison drafted an investment policy statement (IPS) for Daniel that:

1. Described Daniel's understanding of risk and set her risk tolerance,
2. Identified Daniel's intermediate and long-term goals and her preferences and constraints,
3. Crafted a long-term investment plan,
4. Served as a reminder of guidelines to be used in achieving her goals, and
5. Defined the investment and monitoring process.

---

[1] This is based on the case "Stay the Course? Portfolio Advice in the Face of Large Losses," Columbia CaseWorks, ID #110309.

Harrison's first year of working with her new client had gone smoothly. It took some convincing, however, for Daniel to follow Harrison's advice. Like many entrepreneurs, Daniel had built up her wealth by holding a concentrated portfolio, essentially all in her own company. But Harrison's advice was rooted in diversification and optimal asset allocation based on reducing risk and maximizing return. Daniel had essentially no liabilities; her parents were well off, and she had no children and no plans for having any. She lived modestly, and her expenses were covered by the salary the acquiring company was paying her to stay on as a consultant. Given her entrepreneurial background, Daniel was comfortable taking risk and had a long-term investment focus. Thus, Harrison recommended that most of Daniel's portfolio be evenly split between a myopic (growth or market-oriented) investment portfolio and a long-term hedging demand (opportunistic) portfolio. The myopic portfolio consisted of liquid U.S. and international equities and high-yield bonds. The opportunistic portfolio consisted of some direct private equity investment in a friend's company (representing 10% of Daniel's total wealth), and investment vehicles (private equity funds and hedge funds) that allowed fund managers to time the market and take on factor risks unavailable in traditional index funds (see chapter 14).

Daniel's portfolio suffered terribly in 2008. Financial markets around the globe plummeted, and, like many investors, Daniel watched her portfolio take a beating. Equity returns were down 30% to 50% around the world in 2008. Daniel's portfolio lost 30%. Her direct private equity investment was wiped out. By April 2009, while the economy was in recession, there was a sense that the markets were no longer in free fall. Daniel was still very concerned about the state of her portfolio. Fortunately, she didn't need the wealth to support her standard of living. Nor did Daniel have immediate liquidity needs that required drawing down the capital in her investment portfolio. Daniel was still single but was now in a relationship. She felt there was some way to go before she would consider getting married. Although there were no plans in the immediate future to have children, she was worried that her greatly reduced portfolio would diminish the legacy that she could leave them if she had any. Daniel thought that her IPS and her asset allocation needed a "total overhaul."

Harrison knew this was going to be a difficult meeting. On the one hand, perhaps some of Daniel's attitude was an irrational overreaction to market conditions. On the other hand, perhaps Daniel had genuinely become more risk averse, and the advice that Harrison gave in 2007 was no longer valid. "People always think they have more risk tolerance when things are going well," as Harrison said. Should Daniel stay the course or revise her IPS and transition to a less risky portfolio?

In this chapter we discuss portfolio choice over long horizons and how an investor can *dynamically* change her portfolio in response to changing returns and investment opportunities. The theory behind *dynamic portfolio choice* was formulated initially by Paul Samuelson (1969), who won the Nobel Prize in 1970, and Robert Merton (1969, 1971). Merton won the Nobel Prize in 1997 with Myron Scholes, one of the creators of the Black–Scholes (1973) option pricing model, for the valuation of derivatives. As we'll see shortly, the solution to the dynamic portfolio choice problem is intimately related to derivative valuation, and both employ the same economic concepts and solution techniques.

2. The Dynamic Portfolio Choice Problem

An investor facing a dynamic portfolio choice problem has a long horizon, say ten years, and can change her portfolio weights every period. A period could be one year, which is common for retail investors meeting with their financial planners for an annual tune up, or one quarter, which is common for many institutional investors. For high-frequency traders, a period could even be even shorter than one minute. The portfolio weights can change each period in response to time-varying investment opportunities as the investor passes through economic recessions or expansions, in response to the horizon approaching (as she approaches retirement, say), and potentially in response to how her liabilities, income, and risk aversion change over time. In this section, we abstract from the last of these considerations and assume that she has no liabilities and no income and is (fortuitously) given a pile of money to invest. (We introduce liabilities in section 3 and consider income in chapter 5.) We also assume her risk aversion and utility function remain constant.

2.1. DYNAMIC TRADING STRATEGIES

At the beginning of each period t, the investor chooses a set of portfolio weights, x_t. Asset returns are realized at the end of the period $t+1$, and the portfolio weights chosen at time t, x_t, with the realized asset returns lead to the investor's wealth at the end of the period, W_{t+1}. The wealth dynamics follow

$$W_{t+1} = W_t(1 + r_{p,t+1}(x_t)), \qquad (4.1)$$

where wealth at the beginning of the period, W_t, is increased or decreased by the portfolio return from t to $t+1$, $r_{p,t+1}(x_t)$ and this is a function of the asset weights chosen at the beginning of the period, x_t.

I illustrate this in Figure 4.1 for a dynamic horizon problem over $T=5$ periods. At the beginning of each period the investor chooses portfolio weights, x_t. These weights, together with realized asset returns, produce her end of period wealth, W_{t+1}, following equation (4.1). The procedure is repeated every period. The sequence of weights over time, $\{x_t\}$, is called a *dynamic trading strategy*. It can

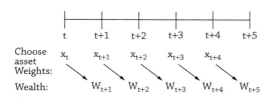

Figure 4.1

potentially change due to pre-determined variables, like investor constraints or liabilities changing, or due to time-varying investment returns, like booms versus busts.

The investor wishes to maximize the expected utility of end of period wealth at time T by choosing a dynamic series of portfolio weights:

$$\max_{\{x_t\}} E[U(W_T)], \qquad (4.2)$$

subject to constraints. Some examples of constraints are that an investor may not be able to short (this is a *positivity constraint* so $x_t \geq 0$), may not be able to lever (so the portfolio weight is bounded, $0 \leq x_t \leq 1$), or can only sell a certain portion of her portfolio each period (this is a *turnover constraint*). Although the portfolio weights $x_{t+\tau}$ are, of course, only implemented at time $t + \tau$, the complete set of weights $\{x_t\}$ from t to $T–1$ is chosen at time t, the beginning of the problem. The set of optimal weights can be quite complicated: they may not only vary through time as the horizon approaches, but they may vary by state. For example, x_t could take on two values at time t: hold 50% in equities if we are in a recession and 70% if we are in a bull market. The complete menu of portfolio strategies across time and states is determined at the start. Thus, the optimal dynamic trading strategy is completely known from the beginning, even though it changes through time: as asset returns change, the strategy optimally responds, and as utility and liabilities change, the strategy optimally responds.

For the remainder of this chapter, we work with constant relative risk aversion (CRRA) utility (see chapter 2):

$$E[U(W)] = E\left[\frac{W^{1-\gamma}}{1-\gamma}\right], \qquad (4.3)$$

where W is the investor's wealth at the end of the period and γ is her risk aversion coefficient. In what follows, I will omit the $1 - \gamma$ term in the denominator of equation (4.3) because maximizing $E[W^{1-\gamma}/(1-\gamma)]$ is exactly the same as maximizing $E[W^{1-\gamma}]$. CRRA is locally mean-variance so the risk aversion γ has the same meaning in mean-variance utility, U^{MV} (see chapter 3):

$$U^{MV} = E(r_p) - \frac{\gamma}{2}\text{var}(r_p), \qquad (4.4)$$

where r_p is the portfolio return. The unconstrained solution to both the CRRA utility and mean-variance utility problem with one risky asset and one risk-free asset paying r_f is: [2]

$$x^* = \frac{1}{\gamma} \frac{\mu - r_f}{\sigma^2}, \tag{4.5}$$

where the asset has expected return μ and volatility σ. The investor holds x^* in the risky asset and $(1 - x^*)$ in the risk-free asset. We developed this solution in detail in chapters 2 and 3. In this sense, CRRA and mean-variance utility are equivalent.

Since the optimal one-period weight is a mean-variance solution in equation (4.5), it nests as special cases many popular choices like equal weights, risk parity, market weights, and constant risk exposures considered in chapter 3. Thus, equation (4.5) does not necessarily mean a full-blown mean-variance solution—which we know does poorly. In the rest of the chapter, you can interpret the optimal one-period weight as any mean-variance optimal portfolio chosen by the investor in a single-period problem.

2.2. DYNAMIC PROGRAMMING

The dynamic portfolio choice problem is an *optimal control* problem. It is solved by *dynamic programming*—the same technique used to control nuclear power plants, send rockets to the moon, and value complicated derivative securities. (I admit, the last of these examples certainly feels much less impressive than the first two.) Portfolio choice turns out to be rocket science—literally. The reader not interested in the math behind representing long-run investing as a series of short-run investment problems can skip directly to section 2.3.

Long-horizon wealth is a product of one-period wealth:

$$W_{t+5} = W_t(1 + r_{p,t+1})(1 + r_{p,t+2}) \ldots (1 + r_{p,t+5}), \tag{4.6}$$

from equation (4.1), and we can apply CRRA utility (equation (4.3)) to each one-period wealth term. Apply CRRA expected utility to long-horizon wealth, we have a series of one-period CRRA utility problems:

$$E[U(W_{t+5})] = U(W_t)E\left[U(1 + r_{p,t+1})U(1 + r_{p,t+2}) \ldots U(1 + r_{p,t+5})\right]. \tag{4.7}$$

Since $U(W_t)$ appears outside the expectation in equation (4.7), it does not matter whether we start with \$1 or with \$1 million—the portfolio weights do not depend on the size of the initial wealth, which is the *wealth homogeneity* property

---

[2] Strictly speaking, the CRRA weight applies in continuous time or when the interval is very small. See Merton (1971).

(see chapter 2). Let's normalize W_t to be one so we don't have to worry about it. The portfolio returns, $r_{p,t+1}$, in equations (4.6) and (4.7) depend on the portfolio weights chosen at the beginning of the period, x_t, as equation (4.1) emphasizes. Thus, we can write equation (4.7) as

$$E[U(W_{t+5})] = U(W_t)E\left[U(1 + r_{p,t+1}(x_t))U(1 + r_{p,t+2}(x_{t+1}))\ldots U(1 + r_{p,t+5}(x_{t+4}))\right]$$
$$= E\left[U(1 + r_{p,t+1}(x_t))U(1 + r_{p,t+2}(x_{t+1}))\ldots U(1 + r_{p,t+5}(x_{t+4}))\right].$$
$$(4.8)$$

Figure 4.2 sketches an outline of the dynamic programming solution. Let's start at the end, at $t+4$ to $t+5$, where the investor chooses portfolio weights to maximize expected utility at the terminal horizon $T = t + 5$. This is Panel A of Figure 4.2. This is a static one-period problem, and, for CRRA utility without

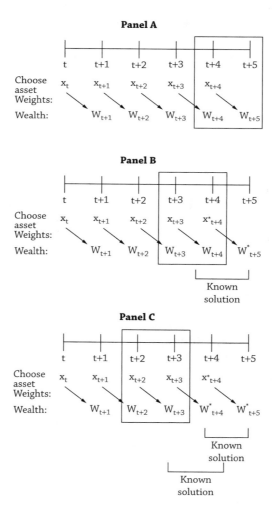

Figure 4.2

constraints, this is identical to the one-period mean-variance problem that we covered in chapter 3. The solution for a single risky asset with expected return μ and volatility σ, with a risk-free rate of r_f is given in equation (4.5), and we denote it by x_{t+4}^*, where the asterisk means that the portfolio weight is optimal. The investor holds x_{t+4}^* in equities and $(1 - x_{t+4}^*)$ in risk-free bonds. In principle, this portfolio weight can depend on what expected return and volatility are prevailing at $t+4$ (say, the economy is booming or in bust).

The maximum utility obtained at $t+4$ is:

$$V_{t+4} = E[U(1 + r_{p,t+5}^*)], \tag{4.9}$$

where the portfolio return from $t+4$ to $t+5$, $r_{p,t+5}^*$, is a function of the optimal portfolio weight chosen at $t+4$, x_{t+4}^*, so $r_{p,t+5}^* = r_{p,t+5}^*(x_{t+4}^*)$. The maximum utility V_{t+4} in equation (4.9) is called the *indirect utility*, and it potentially differs across economic conditions prevailing at time $t+4$.

Having solved the last period's problem, let us turn to the problem two periods before the end. At $t+3$, we need to solve both the portfolio weights at $t+3$ and $t+4$, which are x_{t+3} and x_{t+4}, respectively:

$$\begin{aligned} \max_{\{x_{t+3}, x_{t+4}\}} & \ U(W_{t+3})E[U(1 + r_{p,t+4}(x_{t+3}))U(1 + r_{p,t+5}(x_{t+4}))] \\ = \max_{\{x_{t+3}, x_{t+4}\}} & \ E[U(1 + r_{p,t+4}(x_{t+3}))U(1 + r_{p,t+5}(x_{t+4}))]. \end{aligned} \tag{4.10}$$

But, we already solved the last period problem and found the optimal portfolio weight at $t+4$, x_{t+4}^* for any outcome at $t+3$. This allows us to write the problem two periods before the end as the problem from $t+3$ to $t+4$, plus the problem with the known solution that we solved from $t+4$ to $t+5$:

$$\begin{aligned} \max_{\{x_{t+3}, x_{t+4}\}} & \ E[U(1 + r_{p,t+4}(x_{t+3}))U(1 + r_{p,t+5}(x_{t+4}))] \\ = \max_{x_{t+3}} & \ E[U(1 + r_{p,t+4}(x_{t+3}))U(1 + r_{p,t+5}(x_{t+4}^*))] \\ = \max_{x_{t+3}} & \ E[U(1 + r_{p,t+4}(x_{t+3}))V_{t+4}]. \end{aligned} \tag{4.11}$$

The first equality in equation (4.11) substitutes the last period's solution into the time $t+3$ problem. This now leaves just one portfolio weight at $t+3$, x_{t+3}, to solve. The second equality says that this problem is a standard single-period problem, except that it involves the indirect utility V_{t+4}, but we know everything about the indirect utility and the optimal strategies at $t+4$ from solving the last period's problem (equation (4.9)). We can solve the problem in equation (4.11) as a one-period problem, and we denote the optimal weight at $t+3$ as x_{t+3}^*. It has the same as the one-period solution in equation (4.5), except that we adjust equation (4.5) for the optimized strategies adopted at $t+4$ that are captured by the indirect utility, V_{t+4}. Panel B of Figure 4.2 shows this pictorially. Given the known solution at $t+4$, we use the optimal portfolio weight at $t+4$ to solve the portfolio weight at *t*+3. Equation (4.11) also shows the origin of the name "indirect utility" because the indirect utility from the previous problem, at *t*+4, enters the direct utility from the current problem, at *t*+3.

Solving the problem two periods before the end gives us the optimal *t*+3 portfolio weight, x^*_{t+3}. We compute the maximum utility at *t*+3, which is the indirect utility at *t*+3:

$$V_{t+3} = E[U(1 + r^*_{p,t+4}(x^*_{t+3}))V_{t+4}]. \qquad (4.12)$$

Panel C of Figure 4.2 shows the recursion applied once more to the *t*+2 problem having solved the *t*+3 and *t*+4 problems. Again, the *t*+2 optimization is a one-period problem. After solving the *t*+2 problem, we continue backward to *t*+1 and then finally to the beginning of the problem, time *t*. Dynamic programming turns the long-horizon problem into a series of one-period problems (following equation (4.11)). Dynamic programming is an extremely powerful technique, and Samuelson won the Nobel Prize in 1970 for introducing it into many areas of economics. Monetary policy (see chapter 9), capital investment by firms, taxation and fiscal policy, and option valuation are all examples of optimal control problems in economics that can be solved by dynamic programming. In continuous time, the value function is given by a solution to a partial differential equation called the Hamilton–Jacobi–Bellman equation. A more general form is called the Feynman–Kac theorem, widely used in thermodynamics. These are the same heavy-duty physics and mathematics concepts used in controlling airplanes and ballistic missiles. Portfolio choice is rocket science.

2.3. LONG-HORIZON INVESTING FALLACIES

The important lesson from the previous section on dynamic programming is not that you should hire a rocket scientist to do portfolio choice (although there are plenty of ex-rocket scientists working in this area), but that dynamic portfolio choice over long horizons is first and foremost about solving one-period portfolio choice problems. Viewing the dynamic programming solution of long-horizon portfolio choice this way demolishes two widely held misconceptions about long-horizon investing.

Buy and Hold Is Not Optimal

A long-horizon investor never buys and holds. The buy-and-hold problem is illustrated in Figure 4.3: the investor chooses portfolio weights at the beginning of the period and holds the assets without rebalancing over the entire long-horizon problem. The buy-and-hold problem treats the long-horizon problem as a single, static problem. Buy-and-hold problems are nested by the dynamic portfolios considered in the previous section; they are a special case where the investor's optimal choice is to do nothing. Buy and hold is dominated by the optimal dynamic

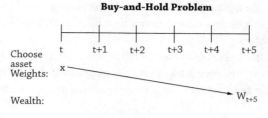

Figure 4.3

strategy that trades every period. Long-horizon investing is not to buy and hold; long-horizon investing is a continual process of buying and selling.

There is much confusion in practice about this issue. The World Economic Forum, for example, defined long-term investing as "investing with the expectation of holding an asset for an indefinite period of time by an investor with the capability to do so."[3] Long-horizon investors could, but in almost no circumstances will, buy and hold an asset forever. They dynamically buy and sell those assets over time.

The buy-and-hold confusion is also partly due to the popular sentiment generated by Jeremy Siegel's famous book, *Stocks for the Long Run*, first published in 1994. This book is often described as the "buy-and-hold bible."[4] Siegel makes a case for sticking to a long-run allocation to equities. If this allocation is constant, then it is maintained by a constant rebalancing rule. Investors increase their share of equities after equities have done poorly to maintain this long-run, constant share. Long-run investors never buy and hold; they constantly trade.

Long-Term Investing Is Short-Term Investing

Another popular misconception about long-term investing is that by having a long-term investment horizon, long-run investors are fundamentally different from myopic, short-term investors. Some, like Alfred Rappaport (2011), suggest that long-run investors should act totally differently from short-term investors. The dynamic programming solution shows this to be blatantly false. Dynamic programming solves the long-horizon portfolio choice problem as a series of short-term investment problems. That is, *long-run investors are first and foremost short-run investors*. They do everything that short-run investors do, and they can do more because they have the advantage of a long horizon. The effect of the long horizon enters through the indirect utility in each one-period optimization problem (see equation (4.11)). I am not suggesting that long-run investors should engage in "short termism," the myopic behavior that often befalls short-term corporate managers and short-term investors.[5] The dynamic programming solution

---

[3] World Economic Forum, 2011, The Future of Long-Term Investing, p. 13.

[4] As James K. Glassman of the *Washington Post* says of the second edition of Siegel's book.

[5] Jeremy Stein (1988) and other authors show that short-termism can arise as a rational response to incentives and leads to underinvestment and misvalued firms.

suggests that, to be a successful long-run investor, you should start off being a successful short-run investor. After doing this, take on all the advantages that the long horizon gives you.

I now discuss one important case where there is no difference between long-run investors and short-run investors. This case happens to be the most empirically relevant and is the foundation of any long-term investment strategy.

2.4. REBALANCING

Suppose that returns are not predictable, or the investment opportunity set is independent and identically distributed (i.i.d.). The i.i.d. assumption is very realistic. Asset returns are hard to predict, as chapter 8 will show. A good way to think about the i.i.d. assumption is that asset returns are like a series of coin flips, except coins can only land heads or tails, and returns can take on many different values. The coin flip is i.i.d. because the current probability of a head or tail does not depend on the series of head or tails realized in the past. The same is true for asset returns: when asset returns are i.i.d., in every period returns are drawn from the same distribution that is independent of returns drawn in previous periods. Under i.i.d. returns, assets are glorified coin flips.

With i.i.d. returns and a fixed risk-free rate, the dynamic portfolio problem becomes a series of identical one-period problems, as shown in Figure 4.4. If returns are not predictable, then the long-horizon portfolio weight is identical to the myopic portfolio weight. Put another way, with i.i.d. returns, there is no difference between long-horizon investing and short-horizon investing: all investors are short term, and it does not matter what the horizon is. We can write this as:

$$\text{Long-Run Weight (t)} = \text{Short-Run Weight (t)}. \qquad (4.13)$$

The short-run weight is the myopic portfolio weight in equation (4.5). It is stated in terms of CRRA utility, but more generally it is the portfolio weight of

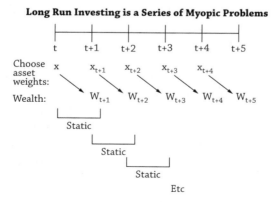

Figure 4.4

a one-period utility problem using most of the utility functions that we covered in chapter 2. All investors—whether they have short or long horizons—act like short-term investors in the i.i.d. world because returns are not predictable; the long-run investor faces a series of independent coin flips each period. The optimal strategy is to manage portfolio risk and return in each period, treating each period's asset allocation as a myopic investment problem. The optimal holding then is the myopic, short-run weight. The investor needs to rebalance back to this weight to avoid any one asset dominating in her portfolio for her given level of risk aversion.

If the optimal dynamic strategy is actually a myopic strategy, is the rebalancing strategy in Figure 4.4 different from a buy-and-hold strategy as shown in Figure 4.3? Absolutely. The dynamic problem is a series of one-period problems, and it involves *rebalancing* back to the same portfolio weight. The buy-and-hold problem involves doing nothing once the investor has bought at the beginning of the period. To rebalance back to the same weight, the investor has to trade each period.

Consider the simplest case of stocks and risk-free bonds. To maintain a fixed portfolio weight in stocks, an investor must invest *counter-cyclically*. If equity has done extremely well over the last period, equities now are above target and it is optimal to sell equity. Thus, the investor sells stocks when stocks have done well. Conversely, if equity loses money over the last period relative to other assets, equities have shrunk as a proportion of the total portfolio. The equity proportion is too low relative to optimal, and the investor buys equity. Thus, rebalancing buys assets that have gone down and sells assets that have gone up. This rebalancing is irrelevant to a myopic investor, because the myopic investor is not investing anymore after a single period. Rebalancing is the most basic and fundamental long-run investment strategy, and it is naturally counter-cyclical. An important consequence of optimal rebalancing is that long-run investors should actively divest from asset classes or even stocks that have done well and they should increase weights in asset classes or stocks that have low prices. Thus, rebalancing is a type of *value investing strategy* (see chapter 7): *long-run investors are at heart value investors*.

Rebalancing is optimal under i.i.d. returns, but it turns out to be advantageous when returns exhibit *mean reversion* or are predictable. If expected returns vary over time, prices are low because future expected returns are high—as our investor Daniel experienced during the 2008 financial crisis; prices of many risky assets plummeted, but their future expected returns from 2008 onwards were high. Rebalancing buys assets that have declined in price, which have high future expected returns. Conversely, rebalancing sells assets that have risen in price, which have low future expected returns.[6]

---

[6] I return to predictability in asset returns in chapter 8 and counter-cyclical factor investing in chapter 14.

2.5. REBALANCING IN PRACTICE

Rebalancing over 1926–1940

Figure 4.5 illustrates rebalancing from 1926 to 1940, which includes the Great Depression. The companion Figure 4.6 shows rebalancing over 1990 to 2011, which includes the financial crisis and the Great Recession. In each case I rebalance to a position of 60% U.S. equities and 40% U.S. Treasury bonds and use data from Ibbotson Associates. Rebalancing occurs at the end of every quarter.

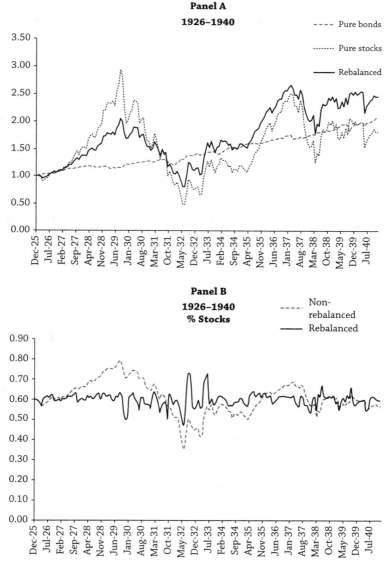

Figure 4.5

Figure 4.5 starts off with $1 at the beginning of January 1926. The dashed line represents a 100% bond position, which rises steadily. A 100% stock position is shown in the dotted line, and the stock wealth is relatively volatile. Stocks rise though the 1920s and reach a peak of $2.93 at the end of August 1929. Then the Great Depression hits with a vengeance. Stocks markets crash and remain depressed into the early 1930s. Stocks hit a minimum of $0.49 in May 1932. Stocks begin a slow climb upward from this point and end in December 1940 at $1.81, which is below the cumulated bond position of $2.08 at that time. The solid line in Figure 4.5, Panel A, shows the rebalanced 60%/40% position. It is much less volatile than the 100% stock position so, while it does not rise as much until 1929, it also does not lose as much during the early 1930s. The 60%/40% strategy ends at December 1940 at $2.46.

Rebalancing is beneficial during the early twentieth century because it counter-cyclically cuts back on equities as they were peaking in 1929 and adds equities when they were at their lowest point in the early 1930s. Panel B of Figure 4.5 shows the rebalanced strategy, which goes back to 60%/40% at the end of each quarter, versus a buy-and-hold strategy, which starts off at 60%/40% at the beginning of the sample and then fluctuates only according to how bond and stock returns vary. The rebalanced strategy, by design, hovers around the 60% equity proportion. There are some deviations because the strategy is not continuously rebalanced, but overall *the rebalanced strategy is less risky* because it does not allow equities to rise or fall to dangerously high or low levels. In terms of utility, the rebalanced strategy attains the optimal balance of stocks and bonds for the investor's risk aversion. But, as an added benefit, rebalancing is counter-cyclical. In contrast, the equity holding in the buy-and-hold strategy was very high in early 1929 (when stock prices are high and expected returns low), right before stocks crash in October 1929. The buy-and-hold equity weight was very low in 1932, right before stock prices pick up (stock prices are low, and expected returns are high).

Rebalancing over 1990–2011

Figure 4.6 does a similar exercise for the 1990–2011 period. In Panel A, we start with $1 invested at the beginning of January 1990. The bond position is shown in the dashed line. During 2008, bond prices suddenly spiked as there was a flight to quality when Lehman Brothers failed, but overall the series is relatively stable. The ending bond position at December 2011 is $7.12. The equity position in the dotted line shows two large peaks and declines: the bull market of the late 1990s followed by the bursting of the Internet bubble in the early 2000s and the rise in equity prices during the early to mid-2000s followed by the financial crisis in 2007 and 2008. The ending equity position at December 2011 is $6.10. Like Figure 4.5, the solid line shows returns of a rebalanced 60%/40% strategy where the rebalancing occurs at the end of every quarter. This dynamic strategy is less volatile, by holding fewer equities, than the 100% equity position, and ends up doing better at December 2011, at $7.41, than either than full stock or bond strategy.

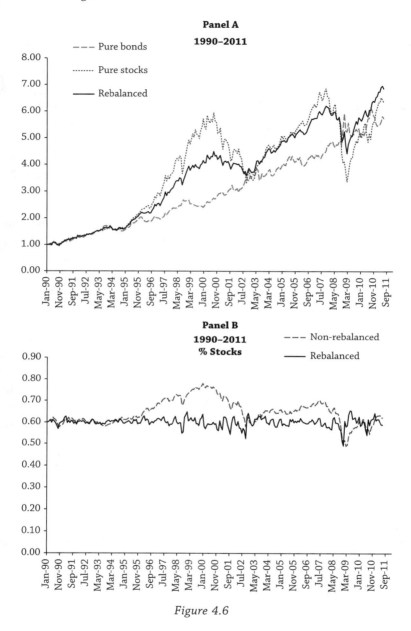

Figure 4.6

Panel B of Figure 4.6 shows the proportion invested in equities. The 60%/40% rebalanced strategy is optimal for the investor as it rebalances the equity position so that the risk of a single asset does not dominate. It also takes advantage of counter-cyclical investing. The buy-and-hold strategy shown in the dashed line loads up on equities, peaking at 2000, just as equities hit the post-bubble period. The equity proportion is also high right before the 2008 financial crisis. In contrast, the rebalanced strategy actively buys low-priced equities in late 2008 benefiting from the upward movement in prices (low prices, high expected returns) in 2009.

The standard 60%/40% strategy outperforms a 100% bond or 100% stock strategy over the 1926–1940 period (Figure 4.5) and over the 1990–2011 period (Figure 4.6). You should not take away that rebalancing will always outperform 100% asset positions—it won't. In small samples, anything can happen. But I show below that, under certain conditions, rebalancing will always outperform a buy-and-hold portfolio given sufficient time, resulting in a rebalancing premium. The main takeaway from the figures is to understand why rebalancing works for the investor: it cuts back on assets that do well so that they do not dominate in the portfolio. The investor rebalances so that the asset mix is optimal for her risk aversion every period. The 1926–1940 and 1990–2011 samples highlight an additional benefit of rebalancing: it is counter-cyclical, buying when prices are low and selling when prices are high.

Investment Policy Statement

Figures 4.5 and 4.6 may look impressive—but, in practice, rebalancing is hard. It involves buying assets that have lost value and selling those that have risen in price. This goes against human nature. Investors tend to be very reluctant to invest in assets that have experienced large losses. Investors are just as reluctant to relinquish positions that have done extremely well. How many investors can buy an asset because it has lost money? How many institutions can take capital away from traders because they have been successful and give it to their colleagues who have underperformed? The natural tendency of investors is to be *pro-cyclical*, whereas rebalancing is *counter-cyclical*.

Good financial advisors like Harrison, who is helping Daniel, play an important role in counteracting the pro-cyclical tendencies of individual investors. Maymin and Fisher (2011) argue that this is one of the areas where a financial advisor can add most value for a client. The IPS plays an important role in this process. Harrison as a financial advisor was right to insist on the IPS as the foundation of her advisor–client relationship with Daniel.

The IPS helps the investor to be *time consistent*: the investor has made decisions in written form, in consultation with the investment advisor, and in doing so lays out a game plan.[7] The IPS allows investors to stick to that game plan. Charles Ellis, an indefatigable advocate for the investor, says in *Investment Policy*, a book originally published in 1987 with its original concepts reiterated in many of his other books:[8]

---

[7] Kydland and Prescott wrote a famous paper in 1977 showing how to implement time-consistent monetary policy. It won them a Nobel Prize in 2004.

[8] Especially Ellis's *Winning the Loser's Game: Timeless Strategies for Successful Investing*, in its sixth edition in 2013.

The principal reason for articulating long-term investment policy explicitly and in writing is to enable the client and the portfolio manager to protect the portfolio from ad hoc revisions of sound long-term policy, and to help them hold to long-term policy when short-term exigencies are most distressing and the policy is most in doubt.

Medical directives, especially for the mentally ill, often take the form of Ulysses contracts, named for the wily Greek who, en route home from the Trojan War, commanded his crew to bind him to the mast of their ship so he could resist the Sirens' song.[9] The IPS is the Ulysses contract of an individual investor and helps him not to overreact. Shlomo Benartzi, a behavioral finance expert, is a keen advocate of using an IPS as a Ulysses strategy. He says, "Pre-commitment to a rational investment plan is important, because the intuitive impulse to act otherwise is strong."[10]

Ann Kaplan, a partner at Circle Wealth Management (and the donor of my chaired professorship), specializes in private wealth management. While the IPS is the capstone of her relationship with clients, she cautions that it takes effort to write, maintain, and reevaluate. "The challenge," she says, is to "translate the individual/family's multiple goals, changing cash flow needs and time horizons with the constraints of their current level of assets, tax status, investment biases, and psycho/social dynamics into a realistic and actionable investment policy."[11]

Take the challenge: having and hewing to an IPS is worth it.

Do Investors Rebalance?

Yes, but incompletely. Calvet, Campbell, and Sodini (2009) examine Swedish households. Data on Swedish asset holdings are very nearly complete because Swedes pay taxes on both income and wealth. Swedish households have a "surprisingly large propensity to rebalance," in the words of the authors. Wealthy, educated investors tend to hold more diversified portfolios and also tend to rebalance more actively. While there is active rebalancing, there is some inertia so that investors do not completely reverse the passive, buy-and-hold changes in their portfolios. In contrast, Brunnermeier and Nagel (2008) show that, for U.S. households, inertia is the dominant factor determining asset allocation rather than rebalancing. (Maybe Swedish households are smarter, on average, than American ones.) Households start with a fixed allocation and then the asset weights evolve as a function of realized gains and losses on the portfolio. Rebalancing does occur but sluggishly.

---

[9] Ulysses contracts have been used in medical treatments for mental disorders since the 1970s. Early references are Culver and Gert (1981) and Winston et al. (1982).

[10] Shlomo Benartzi, Behavioral Finance in Action, Allianz Global Investors white paper, 2011.

[11] Taken from Kaplan's Private Wealth Management presentation to my Asset Management class on Sept. 19, 2012.

Institutional investors often fail to rebalance. While many pension funds and foundations resorted to panic selling and abandoned rebalancing during 2008 and 2009, CalPERS stands out in its failure. CalPERS's equity portfolio shrank from over $100 billion in 2007 to $38 billion in 2009.[12] CalPERS did the opposite of counter-cyclical rebalancing: it invested pro-cyclically and sold equities right at their lowest point—precisely when expected returns were highest. While part of CalPERS's problems in failing to rebalance stemmed from inadequate risk management, particularly of liquidity risk, CalPERS also failed to buy stocks when they were cheap because of structural misalignments between board members and the delegated fund manager. These are *agency problems*, and I discuss them in chapter 15. CalPERS did have a *statement of investment policy*, the institutional version of an individual investor's IPS, but this did not help CalPERS to rebalance during the financial crisis. CalPERS either didn't believe or optimally use its IPS.

In contrast to CalPERS, the Norwegian sovereign wealth fund rebalanced during 2008 and 2009. It bought equities at low prices from those investors like CalPERS who sold at the wrong time. Norway had its own version of Ulysses bound to the mast: the Ministry of Finance and parliament decided on a rebalancing rule, rather than having committees make rebalancing decisions. Adopting a rule, which was automatically implemented by the fund manager (Norges Bank Investment Management), ensured that the rebalancing decisions were not left to a committee whose members could be swayed by panic, fear, or hubris.

Rebalancing Bands

There are some technical considerations in implementing a rebalancing strategy. The theory presented has rebalancing occurring at regular time intervals: in Figure 4.5 and 4.6, rebalancing is done quarterly.[13] But, in practice, if the equity portfolio weight is 61% at the end of a quarter, should the investor rebalance that small 1% back to a 60% target given transaction costs?

State-of-the-art rebalancing practices involve *contingent* rebalancing, rather than *calendar* rebalancing. Optimal rebalancing strategies trade off the utility losses of moving away from optimal weights versus the transaction costs from rebalancing. If the benefits of rebalancing outweigh the cost of doing so, then it is an optimal time to rebalance, and rebalancing becomes a contingent event.

Rebalancing bands are often used, set around optimal targets. The optimal rebalancing target may be 60% equities, for example, with bands set at 55% and 65%. A move outside the band triggers rebalancing. The bands are a function of transaction costs, liquidity, asset volatility, and minimum transaction sizes. When transaction costs are large or asset volatility is high, the bands are

---

[12] See "California Dreamin': The Mess at CalPERS," Columbia CaseWorks ID#120306.

[13] The original Merton (1969, 1971) theory is presented in continuous time so rebalancing happens at every instant.

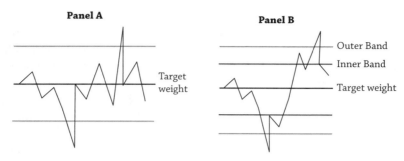

Figure 4.7

wider.[14] The first paper to derive optimal rebalancing bands was Constantinides (1979), and since then many variations have been developed.

The basic rebalancing model is shown in Panel A of Figure 4.7, where the horizontal axis indicates the evolution of an asset class weight. There is a single band around a target weight. If the asset weight lies within the band, the investor does not trade. As soon as the asset weight goes outside the bands, the investor rebalances to target. Other authors suggest rebalancing to the edge of the band. Whether you rebalance to the target or to the edge depends on whether the transaction costs are fixed exchange fees (rebalance to target) or proportional like brokerage fees and taxes (rebalance to the edge).[15]

Panel B of Figure 4.7 presents a more sophisticated rebalancing strategy with two bands surrounding the target weight. There is no trade if the portfolio lies within the outer band. But, if the portfolio breeches the outer band, then the investor rebalances back to the inner band. Institutional investors often use derivatives to synthetically rebalance, which in many cases have lower transaction costs than trading the physical securities.[16] In my opinion all of these technical considerations in rebalancing are precisely that—technical. The most important thing is to rebalance.

2.6. OPPORTUNISTIC STRATEGIES

We've shown that rebalancing is the foundation of any long-term strategy and applies under i.i.d. returns. In addition, if returns are predictable, then there are further benefits from a long-term horizon. I call these opportunistic strategies.

---

[14] The bands expand at an approximate rate of the cube root of the transaction costs. For example, for a 5% transaction cost, the bands are approximately $(0.05/0.001)^{1/3} \approx 3.7$ times larger than a 1% transaction cost. This is shown theoretically by Goodman and Ostrov (2010). Solutions for correlated multiple assets generally need to be obtained numerically; see Cai, Judd, and Xu (2013).

[15] See Pliska and Suzuki (2004).

[16] See Brown, Ozik, and Schotz (2007) on using derivatives in a rebalancing strategy. Gârleanu and Pedersen (2012) develop a model of dynamic trading with predictable returns and transaction costs.

When expected returns and volatilities change over time, the optimal short-run weight changes. In equation (4.5), we can put subscript *t*s on the means and standard deviations, μ_t and σ_t, respectively, of an asset indicating that these are conditional estimates at time *t* of expected returns and volatilities over *t* to *t*+1. The risk-free rate is likely to vary as well (note that the risk-free rate is known at the beginning of the period, so the risk-free rate from *t* to *t*+1 is denoted as $r_{f,t}$). The time-varying short-run weight in equation (4.5) now becomes

$$\text{Short-Run Weight (t)} = \frac{1}{\gamma} \frac{\mu_t - r_{f,t}}{\sigma_t^2}. \qquad (4.14)$$

Under time-varying, predictable returns, the optimal long-run strategy comprises the time-varying short-run strategy plus an opportunistic portfolio:

Long-Run Weight (t) = Short-Run Weight (t) + Opportunistic Weight (t).

(4.15)

The time-varying short-run weight is given in equation (4.14) and is called the *myopic portfolio*. The opportunistic weight is called the *hedging demand* by Merton, who chose the name because the hedging demand portfolio hedges against changes in the investment opportunity set. I prefer to think of it as how the long-run investor can opportunistically take advantage of time-varying returns.[17]

Tactical and Strategic Asset Allocation

Campbell and Viceira (2002) interpret the Merton–Samuelson portfolios in equation (4.15) as:

$$
\begin{aligned}
\text{Long-Run Weight (t)} =\ & \text{Long-Run Myopic Weight} \\
& + [\text{Short-Run Weight (t) - Long-Run Myopic(t)}] \\
& + \text{Opportunistic Weight (t)}
\end{aligned}
\qquad (4.16)
$$

where we split the short-run weight in equation (4.15) into two parts: the average, long-run myopic weight and a deviation from the constant rebalancing weight. We can interpret the first two terms in equation (4.16) as *long-run fixed weights* and *tactical asset allocation*, respectively. The overall long-run weight in equation (4.16) is sometimes called *strategic allocation*.

---

[17] Equation (4.15) was originally formulated by Samuelson (1969) and Merton (1969, 1971). The opportunistic weight, or hedging demand, for an investor with log utility (CRRA utility with $\gamma = 1$) is zero. Intuitively, a log investor maximizes log returns, and long-horizon log returns are simple sums of one-period returns. Since the portfolio weight is freely chosen each period, the sum is maximized by maximizing each individual term in the sum. That is, a log investor with a long horizon is always a short-run investor.

The first term in equation (4.16) is the average value of the short-run weight in equation (4.14):

$$\text{Long-Run Myopic Weight} = \frac{1}{\gamma} \frac{\bar{\mu} - \bar{r}_f}{\bar{\sigma}^2}, \tag{4.17}$$

where the mean and volatility of the asset are at steady state levels denoted by bars above each variable. This can be interpreted as the equivalent of the constant rebalancing weight in the i.i.d. case.

The short-run weight represents tactical asset allocation and is how a short-run investor responds to changing means and volatilities. Tactical asset allocation then comprises the constant rebalancing weight plus a temporary deviation from the rebalancing rule (the first two terms in equation (4.16)).

Strategic asset allocation is the long-run weight and is the sum of the long-run fixed weight, tactical asset allocation, and the opportunistic weight. It is the optimal strategy for a long-term investor.[18] As expected from the dynamic programming solution to long-term portfolio choice, long-run investors do everything that short-run investors do (tactical asset allocation), plus they can act opportunistically in a manner that their short-run cousins cannot. Thus, strategic asset allocation is the sum of all three terms in equation (4.16).

Characterizing Long-Run Opportunistic Portfolios
Computing the precise form of the long-run opportunistic portfolio can be difficult.[19] But insight can be obtained on opportunistic weights without wading through rocket science. There are two determinants of the opportunistic weight. The first is investor specific. Just like the myopic portfolio weight depends on the risk tolerance of an investor so does the opportunistic portfolio. But now the investor's horizon plays a role. Second, the opportunistic weights depend on asset-specific properties of how returns vary through time. The interaction between the investor's horizon and the time-varying asset return properties is crucial. This makes sense: an asset that has a low return today but will mean-revert gradually back over many years to a high level is unattractive to someone with a short horizon. Only a long-horizon investor can afford the luxury of waiting. Similarly, some assets or strategies can be very noisy in the short run, but over the long run volatility mean-reverts, and the risk premiums of these assets

---

[18] The term "strategic asset allocation" is much abused in the industry and is often used as an excuse not to rebalance to long-run asset weights. The term itself was introduced by Brennan, Schwartz, and Lagnado (1997).

[19] You might need to hire a rocket scientist after all to compute long-term portfolio weights. See Campbell and Viceira (2002), Brandt (2009), Avramov and Zhou (2010), and Wachter (2010) for literature summaries. The highly technical reader is encouraged to look at Duffie (2001). Cochrane (2013a) shows that you can avoid computing intertemporal hedging demands if you stick to long-term payoffs, but this does not necessarily help if the long-term payoffs are not directly traded.

manifest reliably only over long periods. Such strategies are also unattractive for short-run investors, but investors with long horizons can afford to invest in them.

Viewed broadly, the opportunistic portfolio for long-run investing also represents the ability of long-run investors to profit from periods of elevated risk aversion or short-term mispricing.[20] In rational asset pricing models, prices are low because the average investor's risk aversion is high and investors bid down prices to receive high expected returns. If a long-horizon investor's risk aversion remains constant, then he can take advantage of periods with low prices. In behavioral frameworks, prices can be low because of temporary periods of mispricing. These can also be exploited by a long-term investor who knows that prices will return to fair values over the long run.[21] While the simple rebalancing strategy is counter-cyclical and has a value tilt, some of the best opportunistic strategies are even more counter-cyclical and strongly value oriented. Crises and crashes are periods of opportunity for truly long-run investors. As Howard Marks (2011), a well-known value investor, explains with great clarity: "The key during a crisis is to be (a) insulated from the forces that require selling and (b) positioned to be a buyer instead." That's what rebalancing forces the investor to do.

There have been debates in the academic literature on how large these hedging demand, long-run opportunistic effects really are. In a major paper, Campbell and Viceira (1999) estimate hedging demands to be very large that are easily double the average total demand for stocks by short-run investors. In Campbell and Viceira's model, the portfolio weight in equities for a long-term investor would have varied from −50% to close to 400% from 1940 to the mid-1990s. However, Brandt (1999) and Ang and Bekaert (2002), which appeared around the same time as Campbell and Viceira's paper, estimate small hedging demands. The long-run opportunistic demands depend crucially on how predictable returns are and the model used to capture that predictability. In chapter 8, I show that the evidence for predictability is weak, so I recommend that both the tactical and opportunistic portfolio weights be small in practice. Opportunistic hedging demands become much smaller once investors have to learn about return predictability or when they take into account estimation error.[22]

A system of predictable equity returns that has been widely studied in the portfolio choice literature is the Stambaugh (1999) system, where stock returns are driven by a valuation ratio like the dividend or earnings yield. The valuation ratio is a convenient instrument to capture time-varying expected returns. As dividends yields drop (or equity prices rise), future expected returns increase. The

---

[20] See Ang and Kjær (2011).

[21] See chapter 7 for a discussion of rational and behavioral determinants of risk premiums.

[22] See Brandt et al. (2005) and Pástor and Stambaugh (2012a).

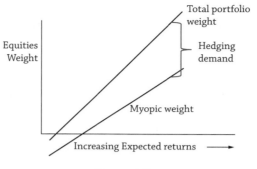

Figure 4.8

dividend yield itself also persistently varies over time.[23] Under the Stambaugh system, the long-term opportunistic portfolios are positive and increase with horizon.[24] This is shown in Figure 4.8 where the short-run, myopic weights and the total long-run weights increase as expected returns increase and investment opportunities become more attractive. Long-run investors actually are leveraged versions of short-run investors: if short-run investors want to buy when expected returns are high, long-run investors will buy more. Opportunistic investing allows long-term investors to exploit predictability even more than short-run investors do.[25]

The Norwegian sovereign wealth fund, following a constant rebalancing rule during 2008 and 2009, bought equities when prices were low and expected returns were high. Had the fund taken advantage of long-run, opportunistic strategies, it would have bought even more equities. Thus, the rebalancing rule functions as a conservative lower bound for "buying low and selling high." I advise you to concentrate on rebalancing first before focusing on opportunistic strategies. Simple rebalancing is itself counter-cyclical; long-run opportunistic investing in the Stambaugh model is much more aggressively counter-cyclical. If you cannot rebalance, which already involves buying assets that are falling in price (relative to other assets), then there is no way that you can implement opportunistic long-run investing. When returns follow the Stambaugh model, opportunistic long-run investing involves buying even more of the assets that have fallen in price than what simple rebalancing suggests. I also recommend that opportunistic portfolios should be modest: taking into account estimation error, combined

[23] Chapter 8 shows this is a good system to capture predictability. Although predictability is generally weak, the best predictor variables tend to be valuation ratios.

[24] This system is used by Campbell and Viceira (1999, 2002), for example, and is generalized by Pástor and Stambaugh (2009, 2012a).

[25] Opportunistic demands are not always positive, as Liu (2007) shows for different models of predictability.

with the overall very weak predictability in data (see chapter 8), any realistic application of Figure 4.8 considerably flattens both the time-varying short-run and opportunistic weights as a function of expected returns.

3. Rebalancing is Short Volatility

Rebalancing is an option strategy and, in particular, a *short volatility strategy*. (Option traders would call rebalancing a *negative gamma* strategy.) This is not well known, although at some level should not be surprising for the reader steeped in financial theory because the same method used in section 2 to solve long-horizon portfolio choice problems (dynamic programming) is used to value options (where it is called *backward induction*).[26] Showing how rebalancing is mechanically a short volatility strategy gives us deeper insights into what long-run investors are gaining and losing from rebalancing. Nothing is free after all, at least not in economic theory.

3.1. EXAMPLE

This example is highly stylized and simple but conveys enough to see rebalancing as a collection of options.

Suppose that a stock follows the *binomial tree* given in Figure 4.9, Panel A. Each period the stock can double, with probability 0.5, or halve starting from an initial value of $S = 1$. There are two periods, so there are three nodes in the tree. At maturity, there are three potential payoffs of the stock: $S_{uu} = 4$, $S_{ud} = S_{du} = 1$, and $S_{dd} = 0.25$, which have probabilities of 0.25, 0.5, and 0.25, respectively. In addition, the investor can hold a risk-free bond that pays 10% each period.

Let us first consider a buy-and-hold strategy that starts out with 60% equities and 40% in the risk-free asset. (We know buy and hold is not optimal for the long-run investor from section 2.) At the end of the first period, the wealth of this investor can increase or decrease to

$$W_u = 0.6 \times 2.0 + 0.4 \times 1.1 = 1.6400$$
$$\text{or } W_d = 0.6 \times 0.5 + 0.4 \times 1.1 = 0.7400, \tag{4.18}$$

which is shown by branching of the binomial tree in Figure 4.9, Panel B. In equation (4.18), the return on the stock is either $2 - 1 = 100\%$ if we go into the upper branch or $0.5 - 1 = -50\%$ if we go into the lower branch. In the upper node at time 1, the proportion of the buy-and-hold portfolio held in equities is $0.6 \times 2.0/1.64 = 73.17\%$ and the proportion of the portfolio in equities in the

---

[26] Perold and Sharpe (1988) and Cochrane (2007) discuss interpreting rebalancing as an option strategy.

Panel A
Stock Dynamics

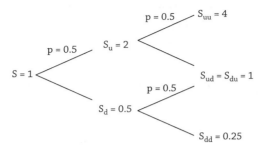

Panel B
Wealth of the Buy-and-Hold Strategy

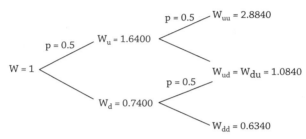

Panel C
Wealth of the Rebalanced Strategy

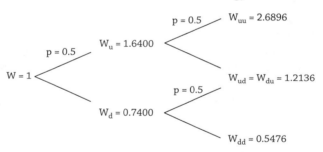

Panel D
Payoffs of Buy and Hold and Rebalanced

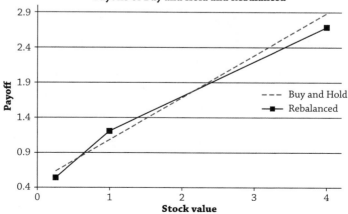

Figure 4.9

lower node is $0.6 \times 0.5/0.74 = 40.54\%$. For the last two nodes at time 2, the final wealth for the buy-and-hold strategy is

$$W_{uu} = 1.6400 \times (0.7317 \times 2.0 + 0.2683 \times 1.1) = 2.8840,$$
$$\text{or } W_{ud} = 1.6400 \times (0.7317 \times 0.5 + 0.2683 \times 1.1)$$
$$= 1.0840 = W_{du},$$
$$\text{which is the same as } W_{du} = 0.7400 \times (0.4054 \times 2.0 + 0.5946 \times 1.1)$$
$$= 1.0840 = W_{ud},$$
$$\text{or } W_{dd} = 0.7400 \times (0.4054 \times 0.5 + 0.5946 \times 1.1) = 0.6340.$$
$$(4.19)$$

This is shown in Figure 4.9, Panel B at the end of the binomial tree.

Now consider the optimal rebalanced strategy, which rebalances at time 1 back to 60% equities and 40% bonds. The end of period wealth at time 1 is exactly the same as equation (4.18). The final wealth at time 2 for the rebalanced strategy is

$$W_{uu} = 1.6400 \times (0.6 \times 2.0 + 0.4 \times 1.1) = 2.6896,$$
$$\text{or } W_{ud} = 1.6400 \times (0.6 \times 0.5 + 0.4 \times 1.1) = 1.2136 = W_{du},$$
$$\text{which is the same as } W_{du} = 0.7400 \times (0.6 \times 2.0 + 0.4 \times 1.1) = 1.2136 = W_{ud}$$
$$\text{or } W_{dd} = 0.7400 \times (0.6 \times 0.5 + 0.4 \times 1.1) = 0.5476.$$
$$(4.20)$$

This set of payoffs is shown in Panel C of Figure 4.9.

The last panel D of Figure 4.9 plots the payoffs of the buy-and-hold strategy (equation (4.19)) and the rebalanced strategy (equation (4.20)) as a function of the stock value at maturity time 2. The buy-and-hold, un-rebalanced strategy is shown in the dashed straight line. The gains and losses on the buy-and-hold position are linear, by construction, in the stock price. The payoffs of the rebalanced strategy, in contrast, are *concave* over the stock price. Rebalancing adds more wealth to the investor if the stock price returns to 1.0 at maturity (1.2136 for the rebalanced vs. 1.0840 for the buy and hold for $S_{ud} = S_{dd} = 1$). This is offset by the rebalancing strategy underperforming the buy-and-hold strategy when the ending stock values are low ($S_{dd} = 0.25$) or high ($S_{uu} = 4$).

This nonlinear pattern of the rebalancing strategy can be equivalently generated by short option positions. The strategy sells out-of-the-money call and put options and hence is short volatility.

Suppose there is a European call option with strike $3.6760 maturing at time 2. This call option has the following payoffs at time 2:

$$C_{uu} = \max(4.0000 - 3.6760, 0) = 0.3240,$$
$$\text{or } C_{ud} = \max(1.0000 - 3.6760, 0) = 0 = C_{du},$$
$$\text{or } C_{dd} = \max(0.2500 - 3.6760, 0) = 0$$
$$(4.21)$$

The value of this call option at time 0 is $0.0428.[27]

There is also a European put option with strike $0.4660 maturing at time 2. This put option is worth $0.0643 at time 0 and has the following payoffs at time 2:

$$P_{uu} = \max(0.4660 - 4.0000, 0) = 0,$$
$$\text{or } P_{ud} = \max(0.4660 - 4.0000, 0) = 0 = P_{du}, \qquad (4.22)$$
$$\text{or } P_{dd} = \max(0.4660 - 0.2500, 0) = 0.2160.$$

Now compare the following strategies:

	time 0		time 2	
Strategy		$S_{uu} = 4$	$S_{ud} = S_{du} = 1$	$S_{dd} = 0.5$
Sell Put	+0.0643	0	0	−0.2160
Sell Call	+0.0428	−0.3240	0	0
Buy Bonds	−0.1071	0.1296	0.1296	0.1296
Buy-and-Hold Strategy	1.0000	2.8840	1.0840	0.6340
Short Volatility + Bonds + Buy and Hold	1.0000	2.6896	1.2136	0.5476
Rebalanced Strategy	1.0000	2.6896	1.2136	0.5476

The table lists the values today in the column labeled "time 0" and the payouts of the various strategies at "time 2." The time 2 payouts are contingent on the stock values at time 2; hence, there are three columns representing the stock values $S_{uu} = 4$, $S_{ud} = S_{dd} = 1$, and $S_{dd} = 0.5$ at time 2.

Consider the first set of strategies. Selling a put today means money comes in (+ sign) with a put premium of $0.0643. If the stock price is low ($S_{dd} = 0.5$) at time 2, then the investor must pay out (− sign) an amount of $0.2160. Likewise, selling a call today means money comes in with a call premium of $0.0428. The investor must make a payout to the person buying the option of $0.3240 if the stock increases at time 2 ($S_{uu} = 4$). The investor also purchases $0.1071 of bonds at time 0. The purchase means a cash outflow, so there is a negative sign. At time 2, these bonds are worth $0.1071 \times (1.1)^2 = 0.1296$ at time 2. Finally, we have the payoffs of the buy-and-hold strategy starting with $1 invested at time 0. The payoffs of the strategy in each state of the world for the buy-and-hold strategy are listed in equation (4.19).

If we add the short call, the short put, the long bond position, and the buy-and-hold strategy, we get a value of $1 today at time 0, with identical payoffs to

---

[27] This can be valued using *risk-neutral pricing*. The call value at time 0 is $\frac{q^2 \times 0.324}{(1.1)^2} = 0.0428$, where q is the *risk-neutral probability* given by $q = \frac{1.1-0.5}{2-0.5} = 0.4$. For an introduction to risk-neutral option pricing, see Bodie, Kane, and Marcus (2011). The put value in equation (4.22) is worth $\frac{(1-q)^2 \times 0.216}{(1.1)^2} = 0.0643$ at time 0.

the rebalancing strategy at time 2 (which are listed in equation (4.20)). That is, a short volatility position that is financed by bonds together with the buy-and-hold strategy is identical to the rebalanced strategy. Hence, *rebalancing is a short volatility strategy.*

In Figure 4.9, Panel D, the buy-and-hold strategy is the completely *passive* straight line. The rebalancing strategy is an *active* strategy that transfers payoffs from the extreme low and high stock realizations (S_{uu} and S_{dd}) to the middle stock realization ($S_{ud} = S_{dd}$). Rebalancing does this by selling when stock prices are high and buying when stock prices are low. Short volatility positions do exactly the same. A call option can be dynamically replicated by a long stock position and a short bond position. This buys equity when stock prices rise and sells equity when stock prices falls. A short call option does the opposite: a short call position is the same as selling when equity prices rise and buying when they fall. Likewise, a short put is also dynamically replicated by selling equity when prices rise and buying when prices fall. These are exactly the same actions as rebalancing.

3.2. INTERPRETATION

What is the market value of rebalancing? In this two-period binomial example, the action of rebalancing relative to the buy-and-hold strategy can be replicated by selling a call, selling a put, and investing in bonds. This has value:

$$\text{Short Call} + \text{Short Put} + \text{Long Bonds} = 0.0643 + 0.0428 - 0.1071 = 0.$$

That is, the action of rebalancing is assigned a zero market value. *The market does not value rebalancing.*

The optimal rebalancing strategy is a *partial equilibrium* strategy. Not everyone can rebalance. For every institution like Norway buying equities during the darkest periods of the financial crisis, there were institutions like CalPERS who couldn't wait to shed their risky equity allocations. CalPERS's losses in failing to rebalance represent Norway's gains from successful rebalancing. Put simply, for every buyer, there must be a seller. In equilibrium, it is impossible for everyone to simultaneously sell or buy.[28] Rebalancing is not valued by the market. In fact, consistent with this fact, the average investor who holds the market portfolio does not rebalance: *the market itself is buy and hold!*[29]

[28] Because of this, Sharpe (2010) advocates long-horizon investors to use "adaptive" asset allocation strategies that just drift up and down with the market instead of actively rebalancing. These are dominated, strictly, by rebalancing with i.i.d. returns as shown in section 2. See also Perold and Sharpe (1988).

[29] In the CAPM and in multifactor models, which we cover in chapter 7, the average investor holds the market portfolio. The average investor does not rebalance. Individual investors can rebalance only if some investors do not. Investors following portfolio insurance strategies, created by Hayne Leland

The benefit to rebalancing is investor specific. Moving the payoffs from the extreme stock positions back to the center (as in Figure 4.9, Panel D) is optimal for the investor because it cuts back on risk. In our example, the 60% equity/40% bond portfolio turns out to be optimal for an investor with a $\gamma = 0.51$ degree of risk aversion. A certainty equivalent calculation (see chapter 2) reveals that he needs to be compensated 0.29 cents for each dollar of initial wealth for being forced to do the buy-and-hold strategy instead of optimally rebalancing.[30] The long-term investor values rebalancing because it reduces her risk and increases her utility. The market does not because there must be other investors who are not rebalancing to take the other side.

Because rebalancing is short volatility, it automatically earns the volatility risk premium. In our example, volatility is constant (the stock volatility is equal to 0.75), but in reality volatility varies over time. Volatility is a risk factor and earns a *negative risk premium*. An investor collects the volatility risk premium by selling options or by being short volatility. I discuss this further in chapter 7.

Viewing rebalancing as a short volatility strategy in moving the payoffs to the center, increasing the losses during extreme low markets, and underperforming the buy-and-hold strategy during extreme high markets makes clear that rebalancing profits from reversals. This is one reason that rebalancing performed well during 1926–1940 and 1990–2011 in Figure 4.5 and 4.6, respectively. When there are strong reversals from the steepest crashes, rebalancing works wonders. We experienced strong reversals after the Great Depression and more recently after the Great Recession and financial crisis in 2008–2009. Conversely, if reversals do not occur, such as in permanent bull or permanent bear markets, then rebalancing will underperform the buy-and-hold strategy.

The fact that rebalancing is equivalent to a short volatility strategy is equivalent to the statement, in the words of Antti Ilmanen, my fellow advisor to the Norwegian sovereign wealth fund, "rebalancing is short regime changes." Take the extreme case where a regime change occurs and permanently kills equity markets: rebalancing performs poorly because it adds equities as prices decline, and then equity prices are permanently lower. The opposite extreme case is a regime change

---

and Mark Rubinstein in 1976, which sell stocks as prices decrease—the opposite of rebalancing (see Rubinstein and Leland (1981)). Kimball et al. (2011) develop a model of equilibrium rebalancing. Chien, Cole, and Lustig's (2012) equilibrium model also has some investors who rebalance and others who do not.

[30] The optimal utility for rebalancing is $\frac{1}{1-\gamma} \left[(0.5)^2 \times (2.6896)^{1-\gamma} + 2 \times (0.5)^2 \times (1.2136)^{1-\gamma} + (0.5)^2 \times (0.5476)^{1-\gamma} \right] = 2.3303$ and the optimal utility for buy and hold is $\frac{1}{1-\gamma} \left[(0.5)^2 \times (2.8840)^{1-\gamma} + 2 \times (0.5)^2 \times (1.0840)^{1-\gamma} + (0.5)^2 \times (0.6340)^{1-\gamma} \right] = 2.3270$. The certainty equivalent compensation required by the investor to do buy-and-hold investing instead of optimal rebalancing is $\left(\frac{2.3303}{2.3270} \right)^{\frac{1}{1-\gamma}} - 1 = 0.29$ cents per dollar of initial wealth. Notice that these are the only calculations where we actually use the real-world 0.5 probability of an upward move in the tree. All the option valuations are done using risk-neutral probabilities.

so that stocks permanently go into a bull market. Rebalancing also underperforms a buy-and-hold strategy because rebalancing would have sold stocks that only keep going up.

Permanent regime changes sometimes occur, but they are rare.[31] I fully agree with Reinhart and Rogoff (2011) that people too often think, "This time is different." Two examples of true regime changes where "these times really were different" are the changing shape of the yield curve pre- and post-1933 and the pricing of out-of-the-money put options pre- and post-1987. Pre-1933 the yield curve was downward sloping, compared to its now (post-1933) normal upward-sloping shape. Academics think going off the gold standard plays a role in explaining the change (see Wood (1983)). Implied option volatilities were symmetric across strikes in the pre-1987 sample (called the *implied volatility smile*). After the 1987 crash, there has been significant negative skewness in implied volatilities (see Rubinstein (1994)), with option volatilities for low strikes much larger than option volatilities for high strikes. The implied volatility smile turned into an *implied volatility smirk*. The financial crisis in 2007 and 2008 was not a regime change. The European sovereign debt crisis since 2009 is also not a regime change. True permanent regime changes are rare.

The fact is that rebalancing is short volatility, and thus short regime changes, means that you must practice rebalancing on broad asset classes (or across factors, see chapter 14) that are extremely unlikely to undergo permanent regime change. Russian equities in 1900 were a large market and then totally disappeared, with investors receiving zero, less than two decades later. But global equities are still around more than a century later and are likely to be here for a long time, perhaps until capitalism disappears. Russian bonds also disappeared during the Russian Revolution, but global bonds did not. Global equities and global bonds have been and will continue to be with us for a long time. Rebalance with the tried and true.[32]

4. Liability Hedging

4.1. LIABILITY HEDGING PORTFOLIO

Few investors are without liabilities. Even investors lacking explicit liabilities (like Norway), at least over the short term, often have implicit liabilities through stewardship expectations of stakeholders. Liabilities can be fixed, like loan payments;

---

[31] Recurring regime changes, in contrast, are common. Examples include recessions versus expansions, bear markets versus bull markets, high volatility versus low volatility periods, and, more generally, bad times versus good times. Recurring regime changes are well described by regime-switching processes introduced into economics and finance by Hamilton (1989). See Ang and Timmermann (2012) for a summary.

[32] If asset returns follow *Markov processes*, then you want to rebalance over assets or strategies that are *recurrent*.

variable but steady, like pension costs; or contingent one-off payments, like a person's death benefit.

When liabilities are introduced, the optimal portfolio strategy has three components:

Long-Run Weight (t) = Liability Hedge (t)

$$+ \underbrace{\text{Short-Run Weight (t)} + \text{Opportunistic Weight (t)}}_{\text{Investment Portfolio (t)}}.$$

(4.23)

The investment portfolio is exactly the same as the nonliability case that we examined in sections 2 and 3: the optimal policy is to rebalance under i.i.d. returns and when returns are predictable, the optimal short-run portfolio changes over time, and the long-run investor has additional opportunistic strategies. The liability hedging portfolio is the portfolio that best ensures the investor can meet those liabilities. We solve for it by holding asset positions that produce the highest correlation with the liabilities.[33]

There are several special cases of optimal liability hedging portfolios:

1. Cash flow matching or immunization.

    This involves constructing a perfect match of liability outflows each period. You immunize each liability cash flow by holding bonds of appropriate maturities.

2. Duration matching.

    If liabilities can be summarized by a single interest rate factor, which is common for pension liabilities, then the liabilities can be offset by an asset portfolio with the same duration.[34]

3. Liability-driven investing.

    This aims to construct a portfolio of risky assets that best meets the liability obligations. It is also common in pension fund management and was introduced by Sharpe (1992). It is related to and often used synonymously with . . .

4. Asset–liability matching.

    This is a more general case than duration matching. In asset–liability matching, dimensions other than just duration are used to match liability characteristics with assets, including liquidity, sensitivity to factors besides only interest rates, and horizon.

The Merton–Samuelson advice of long-horizon asset allocation extended to liabilities is, first, to meet the liabilities and then to invest the excess wealth over the present value of liabilities in the same style as sections 2 and 3, using the myopic market portfolio and the opportunistic long-horizon portfolio.

---

[33] It was also introduced by the grandfather of portfolio choice theory, Merton, in 1993.

[34] Duration is exposure to the interest rate level factor, which is the most important factor in fixed income investments. See chapter 9.

For a long-horizon investor, U.S. Treasuries are usually neither a risk-free asset nor the optimal liability-hedging asset. If the investment horizon exceeds the longest available maturity of the risk-free bond, which is the case for some sovereign wealth funds and family offices, then investors do not have access to a risk-free asset. Furthermore, many investors have liabilities denominated in *real*, not *nominal*, terms. But even long-horizon real bonds are not the optimal liability-hedging asset if there are other factors. For pension plans, these include longevity risk, economic growth, and credit risk. Individual investors may face inflation risks, like for medical care and college tuition, that are not adequately reflected in general CPI inflation. The liability hedging portfolio emphasizes what types of assets (or more broadly what kinds of factors, see chapter 14) pay off to meet the worst times of the investor, in terms of when and how the liabilities come due. If liabilities increase when credit spreads narrow, for example, as they do for pension funds, then the liability-hedging portfolio must hold large quantities of assets that are sensitive to credit risk.

What if you can't meet the liabilities in the first place? Sadly, this condition applies to many investors today, especially public pension funds. CalPERS, for example, only had a funding ratio (the ratio of assets to actuarial liabilities) of 65% at June 30, 2010. Strictly speaking, the Merton–Samuelson asset allocation advice outlined in sections 2 and 3 applies only after the liabilities can be met, both in terms of the present value of the liabilities and after the liability-hedging portfolio has been constructed. If assets are not sufficient to meet current liabilities, then the investor must face the fact that default will happen in some states of the world. Portfolios can be constructed to minimize this probability, but avoiding insolvency requires a different optimization than the maximization of utility examined in equation (4.2). In certain cases, it may be optimal for the investor to engage in risk-seeking behavior if the assets are far enough below the value of the liabilities. It is the Hail Mary pass; you have nothing to lose, and you are likely to go bankrupt anyway.[35]

4.2. POPULAR INVESTMENT ADVICE

The three types of portfolios for long-term investors

1. Liability-hedging portfolio;
2. Short-run, or myopic, market portfolio; and
3. Long-run opportunistic, or long-term hedging demand, portfolio

---

[35] Ang, Chen, and Sundaresan (2013) demonstrate that this behavior is optimal in a liability-driven investment context with downside risk. Andonov, Bauer, and Cremers (2012) show that U.S. public pension funds, which have discount rates based on the earning rates of their assets, have incentives to take more risk. They show that funds that are more underfunded have invested proportionately more in risky assets.

that are derived in the Merton-Samuelson dynamic trading context accord well with the advice given by some financial advisors. A practitioner framework developed by Ashvin Chhabra (2005), who for a time managed the endowment of the Institute for Advanced Study in Princeton, suggests that an individual investor create three buckets:

1. Protective portfolio, which covers "personal" risk. The portfolio is designed to minimize downside risk and is a form of safety first (see chapter 2). The maxim is: "Do not jeopardize the standard of living."
2. Market portfolio, which is a balance of "risk and return to attain market-level performance from a broadly diversified portfolio" and is exposed to market risk.
3. Aspirational portfolio, which is designed to "take measured risk to achieve significant return enhancement." Aspirational risk is a property of an investor's utility function and is a desire to grow wealth opportunistically to reach the next desired wealth target.

This looks very much like the Merton–Samuelson advice. Chhabra's buckets correspond to the three Merton–Samuelson portfolios:

1. Protective portfolio = Liability-hedging portfolio;
2. Market portfolio = Short-run portfolio; and
3. Aspirational portfolio = Long-run opportunistic portfolio.

There are some small differences between Merton–Samuelson and Chhabra. Chhabra advocates mostly safe, fixed-income assets for the protective portfolio, while the concept of the Merton liability-hedging portfolio recognizes that U.S. Treasuries may not be safe and sometimes are extremely risky in terms of meeting liability commitments. But the overall concepts of Chhabra are similar to Merton and Samuelson's theory.

Thus, some financial planners have been advocating Merton–Samuelson dynamic portfolio choice theory even though they have not been exposed to the original Nobel Prize-winning papers written in the 1960s and 1970s. The difference is that the full (rocket science) glory of formal portfolio choice leads to quantitative solutions (equations can be numerically solved by rocket scientists to give portfolio weights when analytical solutions are not available), economic rigor, and some deep insights linking dynamic portfolio choice with option strategies to understand when and how long-run advice will do well or poorly.

5. Rebalancing Premium

Long-horizon investing is not complete without a final discussion of the *rebalancing premium*. This goes under a variety of names including the *diversification return, variance drain, growth-optimal investing, volatility pumping,* and the *Kelly criterion* or *Kelly rule,* named after John Kelly (1956), an engineer who worked at Bell Labs.[36] The term "diversification return" was introduced by Booth and Fama (1992) and is probably the best-known term in finance, whereas the Kelly rule and volatility pumping are better known in mathematics. I prefer not to use Booth and Fama's terminology because there is a difference between diversification in a single period and rebalancing, which earns a premium over time. Diversification gets you a benefit in one period, but this diversification benefit dies out if you do not rebalance.[37] The rebalancing premium only exists for a long-horizon investor, and he can collect it by rebalancing to constant weights every period. I use the term "rebalancing premium" to emphasize that the premium comes from rebalancing, not from diversification.

5.1. REBALANCING BEATS BUY-AND-HOLD OVER THE LONG RUN

Suppose that the price of each underlying asset is *stationary*; that is, the price of each asset tends to hover around a fixed range and never goes off to infinity. Holding 100% positions in each asset never gives you increasing wealth. But, a rebalanced portfolio does give you wealth that increases over the long run to infinity (wealth increases *exponentially fast*).[38] Furthermore, by rebalancing to a fixed constant weight each period, an investor can generate wealth that increases over time, and *any* such rebalancing strategy will eventually beat the best buy-and-hold portfolio. This seems like magic: Erb and Harvey (2006) call it "turning water into wine" and Evstigneev and Schenk-Hoppé (2002) call it going from "rags to riches."

Mathematically, this is not quite as impressive as Jesus' first miracle at the wedding at Cana. It arises as a consequence of compounding. We can see this in equation (4.7), where long-term wealth is a product of arithmetic returns, $(1 + r_t)(1 + r_{t+1})(1 + r_{t+2})\ldots$, rather than a sum of arithmetic returns, $(1 + r_t)(1 + r_{t+1})(1 + r_{t+2})\ldots \neq 1 + r_t + r_{t+1} + r_{t+2} +\ldots$. The compounding of products gives rise to many nonlinearities over time, which are called *Jensen's terms,*[39] and the effect of the nonlinear terms increases over time. The entire rebalancing premium is due to Jensen's terms, and in fact the whole diversification return and Kelly rule literature can be viewed as a paean to *Jensen's inequality.*

[36] For growth-optimal investing, see Latané (1959) and Messmore (1995) for the variance drain terminology. Luenberger (1997) introduced the term "volatility pumping." A nice collection of papers in the literature is MacLean, Thorp, and Ziemba (2011).

[37] See also Willenbrock (2011) who differentiates between diversification as being necessary to give you different weights over one period but not sufficient to earn the rebalancing premium over multiple periods.

[38] This is true also for modest transaction costs, as shown by Dempster, Evstigneev, and Schenk-Hoppé (2009).

[39] Named after the Danish mathematician Johan Jensen.

Jensen's terms arise because of the difference between *geometric* returns, which take into account the compounding over the long run, and *arithmetic* returns, which do not compound.[40] In a one-period setting, geometric and arithmetic returns are economically identical; they are simply different ways of reporting increases or decreases in wealth. Thus, there is no rebalancing premium for a short-run investor. Over multiple periods, the difference between geometric and arithmetic returns is a function of asset volatility, specifically approximately $\frac{1}{2}\sigma^2$, where σ is the volatility of arithmetic returns. The greater the volatility, the greater the rebalancing premium. As this manifests over time, only long-term investors can collect a rebalancing premium.

For U.S. stocks, the rebalancing premium a long-run investor can earn is approximately $\frac{1}{2}(0.2)^2 \approx 1\%$. Erb and Harvey (2006) estimate a rebalancing premium of around 3.5% in commodities. These are significant premiums for simple, automatic rebalancing. In his 2009 book, David Swensen, the superstar manager of Yale University's endowment, emphasizes that rebalancing plays an important role in his practice of investment management, especially in the daily rebalancing of Yale's liquid portfolio. He refers to a "rebalancing bonus" arising from maintaining a constant risk profile.

So, is rebalancing optimal not only because it reduces risk, but also because it provides a "free lunch" in the form of a rebalancing premium? Not so fast. In section 3, I showed that rebalancing has no value in the market by interpreting rebalancing as an option strategy. The rebalancing premium seems too good to be true—and in fact it is. Rebalancing is a short volatility strategy that does badly compared to buy and hold when asset prices permanently continue exploding to stratospheric levels or permanently implode to zero and disappear. Rebalancing is short a regime change. The crucial assumption behind the rebalancing premium is that the assets over which you rebalance continue to exist. If there are assets that experience total irreversible capital destruction, then rebalancing leads to buying more assets that eventually disappear—this is wealth destruction, not wealth creation. The rebalancing premium can only be collected for assets that will be around in the long run, so rebalance over very broad asset classes or strategies: global equities, global sovereign bonds, global corporate bonds, real estate, commodities, and so on, rather than individual stocks or even individual countries.

5.2. THE VERY LONG RUN

In the very long run, the portfolio that maximizes wealth is a rebalanced portfolio that holds constant asset weights that maximize the rebalancing premium. This

---

[40] The arithmetic return r represents $(1+r)$ at the end of the period. The same amount can be expressed as a geometric return, g, where $(1 + r) = \exp(g)$. The means of the arithmetic return and the geometric return are related by $E(r) \approx E(g) - \frac{1}{2}\sigma^2$, where σ is the volatility of r. This relation holds exactly for log-normal distributions. For more details, see the appendix.

strategy maximizes long-run growth and is called the Kelly rule. It is obtained by finding the portfolio that maximizes one-period log returns. Since this portfolio maximizes (very) long-run wealth, it is also called the *optimal growth portfolio*.

The Kelly optimal growth portfolio dominates all other portfolios with a sufficiently long time span.[41] So for the very long-run investor, should we hold the optimal growth portfolio if it maximizes very long-run wealth? No. This was settled by Samuelson in the 1970s, but the question is raised periodically by the unconvinced.[42] Samuelson wrote a cute paper in 1979, entirely written in words of one syllable, entitled "Why We Should Not Make Mean Log of Wealth Big though Years to Act Are Long," to answer this question. (Not surprisingly, limiting yourself to words of one syllable makes a paper quite hard to read.)

In a one-period model, you can maximize the portfolio growth rate by holding the portfolio that maximizes expected log returns. But do you have a log utility function? Probably not. You trade off risk and return differently than a log investor and are better off holding a portfolio optimized for your own risk aversion and utility function. Over the long run, you will outperform by following the Kelly rule. But, there is risk in doing so, and you might not be able to tolerate this risk. Furthermore, the long run in the Kelly rule could be very, very long. And as Keynes famously observed, in the long run, we are all dead.

In summary, follow the Merton–Samuelson advice and not the Kelly rule. Find your optimal one-period portfolio holdings over broad asset classes or strategies. Rebalance back to fixed weights. This is optimal with i.i.d. returns, and it will earn you a rebalancing premium. If you can forecast returns well, you also have a long-run opportunistic portfolio available.

6. Stay the Course? Redux

Daniel has suffered large losses and is feeling skittish about sticking to her long-term plan. But she is fortunate that she has no immediate liabilities and her income, which covers her expenses, is relatively safe. Yet the losses seem to have changed her tolerance for risk. She has told her financial planner, Harrison, that her IPS needed a "total overhaul" and she could not afford such big losses going forward.

According to the long-run investment advice from Merton and Samuelson, Harrison should advise Daniel to rebalance. Rebalancing to fixed weights (or exposures) is optimal when returns are not predictable. Even though returns are

---

[41] The formal mathematical statement is that there exists a number $M(W)$ that depends on current wealth W such that $\Pr(W_T \leq W)$ using the Kelly rule is strictly less than $\Pr(W_T \leq W)$ using any other portfolio for all $T > M(W)$. Thus as $T \to \infty$, the Kelly rule dominates any other rule.

[42] See Samuelson (1971) and Merton and Samuelson (1974).

predictable in reality, the amount of predictability is very small. This makes rebalancing the foundation of the long-run strategy. The small extent to which returns are predictable can be exploited by a long-run investor through an opportunistic portfolio. Daniel should stay the course and rebalance.

Rebalancing, however, goes against human nature because it is counter-cyclical. It is difficult for individuals to buy assets that have crashed and to sell assets that have soared. Part of Harrison's job as an investment advisor is to counteract these behavioral tendencies. The IPS can help by functioning as a pre-commitment device—a Ulysses contract—in preventing Daniel from overreacting and abandoning a good long-term plan.

But perhaps Daniel's risk aversion has truly changed. The classical assumptions, which we used in sections 2 to 4, are that risk preferences are stable and unaffected by economic experiences. This is not true in reality.[43] Malmendier and Nagel (2011) show that investors who experienced the searing losses of the Great Depression became permanently more risk averse and were far less willing to invest in stocks than younger investors who did not experience such large losses and economic hardships. They show further that after the recessions of the late 1970s and early 1980s, young investors who only experienced the market's low returns during these periods were more risk averse and held fewer equities and more bonds than older investors who had experienced the high returns of the stock market during the 1950s and 1960s. Thus, life experience does influence the extent to which investors are willing to take financial risks. But Malmendier and Nagel show that what changes after large losses is not so much investors' risk preferences but investors' expectations. People tend to lower their expectations about future returns as a response to searing losses rather than changing their utility functions.

If Daniel has truly become more risk averse, then rebalancing back to the old portfolio pre-2007 is no longer valid, and Daniel has to work with her financial advisor to come up with a new IPS. Changes should be made deliberately and carefully. The worst portfolio decisions often result from pure panic; many ad-hoc changes lead to pro-cyclical behavior. Otherwise, the dynamic portfolio choice advice is to stay the course. Rebalance.

---

[43] See Hertwig et al. (2004).

CHAPTER 5

Investing over the Life Cycle

Chapter Summary

Labor income is an asset, and for young investors the value of labor income usually dominates the rest of their financial holdings. An investor's mix of assets changes as her labor income evolves over her life cycle, and an investor whose labor income is bond-like should reduce his holdings of equities as retirement approaches. While economic theory suggests annuities are ideal for retirees, few hold them.

1. Employees' Retirement System of Rhode Island

The State of Rhode Island and Providence Plantations, or Rhode Island for short, is the smallest of America's fifty states.[1] Although often overshadowed by its larger neighbors, Massachusetts and Connecticut, people in Rhode Island (there are only slightly more than a million of them) have a reputation for wanting to do their own thing and doing it first. Rhode Island was the first of the thirteen colonies to declare independence from Great Britain on May 4, 1776—beating the other colonies by two months. When President Abraham Lincoln asked the Union states to send soldiers to fight in the Civil War, Rhode Island was the first to enthusiastically respond. And in 2011, Rhode Island became the first state to undertake a regime-changing reform of its public pension plan.

The Employees' Retirement System of Rhode Island (ERSRI) provides retirement, disability, and survivor benefits to public employees including state workers, school teachers, judges, and local uniformed personnel including police officers and firefighters. Like most public pension plans in the United States, it was grossly underfunded. In 2011, ERSRI had a funding ratio of 59% and held only $6.3 billion to meet liabilities of $10.8 billion. Each person in Rhode Island

---

[1] This is based on the case "Saving Public Pensions: Rhode Island Pension Reform," Columbia CaseWorks #120309.

would have needed to pay \$4,230 to meet the shortfall.[2] In addition, spending on pensions was crowding out other services. In 2002, 3 cents of each taxpayer dollar went to support pensions. This rose to 9 cents in 2009 and was projected to reach 20 cents in 2018.[3] State employee contributions, however, had remained flat at 8.75%, and teachers' contributions had also not changed from 9.5%.

An editorial in the *Providence Journal* summarized Rhode Island's problem:[4]

> Unless this unsustainable system is reformed, the state confronts a bleak future of brutally high taxes; deep cuts in government services and in assistance to our most needy and fragile citizens; the threatened loss of retirement security for our public employees; and the severe economic distress that will surely accompany these developments.

Rhode Island was not alone. Robert Novy-Marx and Joshua Rauh, finance professors at Rochester and Stanford, respectively, have shined a spotlight on the underfunding of our public pension plans. They estimate that by 2009, states had accrued \$5.7 trillion of liabilities to their workers while assets in these plans totaled less than \$2 trillion—a hole of \$3.7 trillion. By way of context, consider that the outstanding publicly traded debt issued by states is about \$1 trillion.[5]

Gina Raimondo, who took office as Rhode Island's treasurer in 2010, believed that fixing the state's pension system was essential to putting the state on a sound financial footing. Raimondo commissioned a report, *Truth in Numbers: The Security and Sustainability of Rhode Island's Retirement System*, which was released in June 2011. The report showed that the large pension deficits were due to five factors:[6]

1. Insufficient contributions;
2. Raising benefits from the 1960s through the 1980s without corresponding increases in contributions;

---

[2] Reported by Barkley, R., "The State of State Pension Plans: A Deep Dive into Shortfalls and Surpluses," Morningstar, Nov. 26, 2012.

[3] Raimondo, G., Truth in Numbers: The Security and Sustainability of Rhode Island's Retirement System, Rhode Island Office of the General Treasurer, June 2011.

[4] Editorial, "Stand Up for Rhode Island," *Providence Journal*, Nov. 17, 2011.

[5] See Novy-Marx and Rauh (2009, 2011a, 2011b) and Mitchell (2012).

[6] Glaeser and Ponzetto (2013) argue that public pension promises are high partly because they are "shrouded," meaning that they are hard for the taxpayer to understand. The study is worth reading if only for the detailed history of California, Pennsylvania, Massachusetts, and Ohio pensions. Public pensions are decentralized in the first two states and centralized in the latter two. Centralization appears to have reduced pension benefits by drawing state-level media attention to help taxpayers understand pension costs. Glaeser and Ponzetto also include a useful table describing the public pension plans in all fifty states.

3. Non-optimal plan design, in some cases allowing workers to get paid more in retirement than while working;
4. Greater life expectancy; and
5. Low investment returns, with Rhode Island's pension fund earning 2.3% from 2000 to 2010 while its projected return was 8.25% over the same period.

The pension deficits had accumulated over many years. "You're paying for the sins of the past," said Frank Karpinski, the Executive Director of ERSRI.[7] *Truth in Numbers* succeeded in drawing attention to the pension problem. It also framed the problem: no matter which side of the issue, everyone was talking from the same set of notes.

Together with Gov. Lincoln Chaffee, Raimondo put together a special commission that included representatives from labor unions, business, and academia. This Pension Advisory Group held public meetings across the state from June to September 2011 and allowed the public to share their views. Presentations at the meetings highlighted the seriousness of the problem. "At the end of the day, no one could criticize the process. It was long, it was thorough, it was open, and it was transparent," said Raimondo.[8]

Raimondo approached the process of pension reform by working backward. She first posed the question, "what does retirement security look like?" Targeting a *replacement rate* or ratio (the amount of income in retirement as a fraction of pre-retirement income) of 75% to 80%, Raimondo asked how the pension system should be designed to get there. In addition, she aimed to cut the unfunded liability in half immediately and to get to an 80% funded status in twenty years.

A key theme was *intergenerational fairness*. Under the current system, younger public employees were disadvantaged relative to older workers. Raimondo also wanted to design a plan in which risks were appropriately shared between the retirees and the state. She assured workers that reforms would not reduce accrued benefits.

"We are in the fight of our lives for the future of this state," said Raimondo.[9]

2. Labor Income

Labor income is a form of wealth. It is not traded (the Thirteenth Amendment abolished slavery), making it very different from the financial assets that we hold in our portfolios. Much of our lifelong allotment of human capital is determined at birth, but individuals can augment their human capital through education, while

[7] Quoted in Pew Center on the States, The Trillion Dollar Gap: Underfunded State Retirement Systems and the Road to Reform, 2012.

[8] Quoted in Burton, P., "Pension Reformer Honored," *The Bond Buyer*, Jan. 9, 2012.

[9] Quoted by Walsh, M. W., "The Little State with a Big Mess," *New York Times*, Oct. 22, 2011.

circumstances such as job loss or illness can reduce it. The riskiness of a person's labor income—its volatility and how it correlates with financial returns—affects her asset allocation.

We take account of human capital by treating it like an asset.[10] Suppose we denote the present value of an individual's wages as H (for human capital). Human capital is the discounted value of a person's lifelong earnings from work; it is the present value today that is equivalent to the wage profile of that individual. Human capital is risky because earnings from work can fluctuate—and in the most unfortunate case fall to and stay at zero.

We denote financial wealth as W. Total wealth is $H+W$, or, in other words, total wealth comprises both human capital and financial wealth.

2.1. ASSET ALLOCATION WITH NO LABOR INCOME

Consider an individual with no labor income and $1 million of financial assets. For simplicity, we'll assume that there are only equities, which have an expected return of $\mu = 10\%$ and a volatility of $\sigma = 15\%$, and risk-free T-bills paying $r_f = 2\%$. The investor has mean-variance utility, or equivalently has CRRA utility, with a risk aversion of $\gamma = 5$. (Chapters 2 and 3 cover utility functions and mean-variance investing, respectively.[11])

Our investor with only financial wealth holds $w^* = 62.5\%$ in equities, which is obtained from the mean-variance investing formula:

$$w^* = \frac{1}{\gamma} \frac{\mu - r_f}{\sigma^2} = \frac{1}{5} \frac{0.10 - 0.02}{(0.15)^2} = 62.5\% \tag{5.1}$$

(See equation (2.10) in chapter 2.) His asset allocation is then:

Hold $0.625 \times \$1$ million $= \$625,000$ in equities
$\underline{\$375,000 \text{ in T-bills}}$
$\$1$ million

2.2. ASSET ALLOCATION WITH RISK-FREE LABOR INCOME

Now contrast the asset allocation of an individual who has risk-free wages, like tenured professors at top universities (yes, I know, I'm lucky and very grateful) or federal judges. Her human capital is equivalent to her being endowed with risk-free assets. Let's assume her wage flow is equivalent to human capital today of

---

[10] This approach follows Merton (1990) and Bodie, Merton, and Samuelson (1992).

[11] In this example, we take risk aversion and the amount of human capital wealth (and total wealth) as given. In reality, risk aversion affects both the choice of financial assets and the choice and type of human capital—a highly risk-averse person is unlikely to pursue a career as a mountaineer, for example. See Ranish (2012) and section 3.6 on endogenous labor income.

$H = \$1$ million and she also has financial wealth of $W = \$1$ million. Her total wealth is thus $H+W = \$2$ million. Like our first investor, we'll assume her risk aversion is $\gamma = 5$.

The optimal holding of risky equities with risk-free labor income is:

$$w^* = \frac{1}{\gamma}\frac{\mu - r_f}{\sigma^2}\left(1 + \frac{H}{W}\right).$$ (5.2)

Note that when human capital is zero, $H = 0$, equation (5.2) is exactly the same as equation (5.1). Our investor with risk-free human capital tilts her portfolio toward stocks relative to an investor with only financial wealth. The proportion of equities held by the investor in this example is:

$$w^* = \frac{1}{\gamma}\frac{\mu - r_f}{\sigma^2}\left(1 + \frac{H}{W}\right) = \frac{1}{5}\frac{0.10 - 0.02}{(0.15)^2}\left(1 + \frac{1}{1}\right) = 125\%$$ (5.3)

The optimal holdings of our investor with labor income are:

Hold $1.25 \times \$1$ million $= \$1,250,000$ in equities
$\underline{- \$\ \ 250,000 \text{ in T-bills}}$
$\$1$ million

This is a much larger weight in equities than our first investor without labor income; the investor with risk-free labor income shorts the risk-free asset and holds a levered portfolio of 125% in equities. But it turns out that the combined portfolio has exactly the same 62.5% holdings in risky assets.

If we view the investor's *total wealth* portfolio, we have:

Endowed with $\$1,000,000$ in human capital
Hold $1.25 \times \$1$ million $= \$1,250,000$ in equities
$\underline{- \$250,000 \text{ in T-bills}}$
$\$2$ million

As a fraction of total wealth, her equity allocation is $1,250,000/2$ million $= 62.5\%$, which is the same as our first investor without labor income.

The presence of risk-free labor income allows the investor to take on more risk in her financial portfolio. In fact, equation (5.2) levers up the standard equity position (from equation (5.1)), and the leverage ratio is the ratio of human capital to financial wealth, H/W.

Asset allocation must be viewed in the broader context of total wealth, which sums both financial and human capital wealth. Risk-free labor income is equivalent to being endowed with risk-free bonds. Your financial portfolio has to hold more equities to balance out your risk-free human capital. In economists' jargon, the risk exposure in human capital wealth *crowds out* the risk-taking ability of our financial wealth.

2.3. ASSET ALLOCATION WITH RISKY LABOR INCOME

Let's take an investor who has risky labor income. We need to consider whether her labor income looks like a stock or a bond. If you are reading this book, you probably work in a field related to finance, so your labor income is probably positively correlated with equities. Most of my MBA students have human capital that is highly correlated with the stock market.

A positive correlation between labor income and equity returns reduces the optimal allocation to risky assets in an investor's financial portfolio. In this case, human capital is equivalent to already being endowed with equities. You wish to reduce your equity positions in your financial portfolio to offset your equity-like human capital. This undoes the equity risk added by your labor income. In short, when human capital acts like equities, you effectively already own equities and so you hold fewer equities in your financial portfolio.

What about those investors whose wages are negatively correlated with equity returns? These people actually earn more during stock market downturns. Some examples include bankruptcy attorneys, shrewd experts who can turn around poorly performing companies, and debt collectors. Human capital for these investors acts in the opposite way of equities, and so they have human capital that is anti-equities. If they are anti-equity in their human capital, they want to offset that by holding lots of equities in their financial portfolio. That is, their allocations to equity will be even more aggressively weighted toward equities than investors with risk-free labor income.

There are several important corollaries:

1. Investors with income that goes up and down with the stock market should hold more bonds (or other very low-risk assets) in their financial portfolios. These investors have equity-like human capital, so they need to take positions opposite to equities in their financial portfolios.
2. John Roberts, Antonin Scalia, Sonia Sotomayor, and all the other Justices of the Supreme Court should hold relatively aggressive positions in the stock market. Their incomes are like risk-free bonds, so their financial portfolios should take large, opposite positions in risky equities.
3. An investor should hold little or none of her employer's stock. Her labor income is already exposed to her employer's fortunes, and the last thing she should want is even more of the same risk in her savings. Her financial holdings should diversify away her employer's risk reflected in her labor income. (See chapter 3.)
4. If you work in the United States, your financial portfolio should actually hold more overseas stocks than domestic stocks. Your income already comes from a U.S. source, so you need to hold more non-U.S. securities in your financial portfolio.[12]

---

[12] See Baxter and Jermann (1997).

These are all *normative* statements, or statements about what investors should do (see chapter 2 for normative vs. positive economics). In reality, many do exactly the opposite. A few traders like to hold very risky assets in their personal portfolios, despite their labor income being highly dependent on the stock market. All too many investors hold outsized positions in their employers' stock, and they hold *home-biased* portfolios with little international exposure. These investors load up on the same risks in their financial portfolios as their human capital is exposed to and fail to diversify away some of their human capital risk (see also chapter 4).

2.4. LABOR INCOME RISK

Measuring labor income risk is tricky; we can't observe the value of human capital because it is not traded.

The first economist to treat human capital as an asset and put a value on it was Gary Becker (1964), who won the Nobel Prize in 1992. Becker showed that education is an investment in human capital, rather than just a luxury or consumption expenditure. He also showed that investment in human capital was integral to economic growth. A large literature in labor economics measures human capital returns by computing the benefits to investments in human capital: labor economists compute extra wages earned by those who have gone to graduate school over those who have gone to college, over those with only high school educations, and over those who did not attend high school. Not surprisingly, wages increase with investment in education going from less than a high school diploma (median earnings of \$471 per week in 2012 according to the Bureau of Labor Statistics) to bachelor degrees (\$1,066) to professional degrees (\$1,735). Interestingly, there is a drop to \$1,624 for PhDs. (Someone should have told me before I sweated over mine.) As is well known, women earn less than men, and blacks earn less than whites.

Human capital is the present value of all future wage flows. The return on human capital is often computed as the growth in wages.[13] Palacios-Huerta

---

[13] This is assumed by Shiller (1995), Jagannathan and Wang (1996), and Eiling (2013), among others. Denoting wages as L_t and the growth rate of wages as g_H, suppose wages follow the process:

$$L_t = (1 + g)L_{t-1} + \varepsilon_t,$$

where wages start at time 0 from the level L_0 and ε_t is an independent and identically distributed (i.i.d.) shock. If we discount the wage stream at the expected rate of return on human capital, r_H, then we can value the present value of wages as

$$H_t = \frac{L_t}{r_H - g},$$

and the growth in wages, g, is equal to the return on human capital, $H_t/H_{t-1} - 1$. Earlier work by Friedman (1957) and Hall (1978) discounted labor income at risk-free rates to compute human capital.

(2003) computes human capital returns for various professions and genders. He finds white males with one to five years of experience and a college degree have annual human capital returns of 14.2% versus 10.5% for those with some college but no degree. While college graduates have higher human capital returns, they are more volatile: the standard deviation of human capital returns for white male college graduates is 11.3% versus 4.7% for those with post-college education. Thus, the raw Sharpe ratio (which I define as the expected return [not excess] divided by volatility; see chapter 2) of white college males with one to five years of work experience is 14.2%/11.3% = 1.3, which is lower than the 2.2 raw Sharpe ratio of the same demographic group with post-college experience. In comparison, the S&P 500 has a raw Sharpe ratio of around 0.6. Education is a very good investment, on average.

In addition to the risk of your human capital varying over time, there is also large disparity in human capital across professions. Christiansen, Joensen, and Nielsen (2007) report the mean human capital return for doctors is over 25% with a standard deviation of 18%. Human capital returns for masters graduates in economics have a mean of 12% and a standard deviation of 16%. Christiansen, Joensen, and Nielsen find that some professions have significantly negative returns, like individuals with master degrees in education or music.

Wages can fall a lot during recessions.[14] Guvenen, Song, and Ozkan (2012) study the income dynamics of millions of individuals using Social Security Administration records. They find that during recessions, big upward movements of wages become very unlikely while severe drops in income become very likely. The middle part of the distribution tends to be fairly constant compared to the movement tails. The falls in income for the most wealthy—the top 1% (probably you, dear reader)—have the highest labor income risk. During the Great Recession in 2008–2009, the top 1% experienced enormous income losses, which were 21% worse, on average, than the losses of those in the ninetieth percentile.

Computing human capital returns using the growth in wages, however, actually understates the riskiness of human capital. Wages for individuals are like dividends for stocks. Stock prices can soar and plummet while their dividends remain fairly constant. Measuring stock returns by changes in dividends would produce very poor approximations to actual stock returns. In valuing stocks, we need to use *time-varying discount rates*. Likewise, the discount rates on human capital are not constant.[15] Human capital can be very risky.

---

[14] The major risk is that when you lose your job in a recession, your wage *permanently* falls. See Meghir and Pistaferri (2011) for a summary of permanent and temporary components in labor income.

[15] As shown by Heaton and Lucas (2000).

2.5. SUMMARY

Optimal asset allocation with labor income crucially depends on how risky your labor income is and how it correlates with equities. If your labor income is bond-like (lowly correlated with stock returns), treat it as such and hold more equities in your portfolio. Hold even more equities if your labor income acts the opposite way of equities. If your labor income is stock-like (highly correlated with stock returns), you will offset that equity risk by holding lots of bonds. Thus, paraphrasing Moshe Milevsky (2009), a pension finance expert at Canada's York University, *personal asset allocation depends on whether you are a stock or a bond.*

In summary, all else being equal:

Bond-like labor income => Hold more equities.
Stock-like labor income => Hold more bonds.

In real life, people seem to act as our theory predicts. Guiso, Jappelli, and Terlizzese (1996) and Vissing-Jørgensen (2002) show that individuals with very volatile wages tend not to hold equities, or, if they hold equities, they do so as a smaller share of their portfolio. Betermier et al. (2012) employ a data set that tracks 3% of the Swedish population and examine people changing jobs. As individuals move from jobs with less to more volatile wages, they reduce their exposure to risky assets. In their sample, the least volatile wages are earned by individuals working in the field of recycled metal waste and the most volatile wages are earned by those working in asset management (!). An individual moving from the former to the latter slashes her holdings of risky assets by 35%. Dimmock (2012) reports that universities with more volatile non-financial income (tuitions, fees, grants, donations, etc.) hold more fixed income and other low-risk securities. Very volatile nonfinancial income markedly reduces allocations to alternative assets, except for the most selective universities.

3. Life Cycle

Before we describe optimal asset allocation over the life cycle, let's review. . . .

3.1. FINANCIAL PLANNERS' ADVICE

Ubiquitous advice from financial professionals is to reduce your stock allocation as you age. A popular rule of thumb is *one hundred minus your age,* which says that the proportion of your portfolio invested in equities should equal the difference between your age and one hundred. There are many variants, but I will refer to any plan that reduces risky asset holdings as you approach retirement as the "one hundred minus your age rule."

Panel A of Table 5.1 lists the asset allocation for the Vanguard Target Retirement 2050 Fund. Such *target date funds* are designed to modify an investor's asset allocation as he approaches retirement—in this case, a date that falls between

Table 5.1

Asset Allocations over the Life Cycle			
Panel A: Vanguard Target Retirement 2050 Fund			
	Stocks	Bonds	Cash
25 Years before Retirement	90%	10%	0%
1 Year before Retirement	50%	50%	0%
In Retirement	30%	65%	5%
Panel B: Life-Cycle Allocations to Equities			
Age	100—Age Rule	Malkiel (1990)	Shiller (2005)	Federal Thrift
25	75%	70%	85%	85%
35	65%	60%	71%	75%
55	45%	50%	26%	50%

2048 and 2052. These are actually funds-of-funds and change the mix of under-lying funds over time. Investors pay fees both on the underlying funds and for the privilege of having their asset allocation automatically adjusted as they age. (These funds can be expensive!) According to Vanguard, an investor with twenty-five years to retirement should hold 90% equities and 10% bonds. This evolves over time until, a year before retirement, the mix is half and half (how the equity and bond mix changes as the individual ages is called the *glide path*). At retirement the investor further cuts equity holdings to 30%.

Panel B of Table 5.1 reports allocation to equities recommended by several sources: from the finance professor Burton Malkiel (1990), the economics pro-fessor Robert Shiller (2005), and from the "L Fund" of the federal Thrift Savings Plan, the retirement program for federal employees or members of the uniformed services (this is Uncle Sam's version of the 401(k), see chapter 1).[16] While the in-dividual equity proportions slightly differ, the overall pattern is that they all hold less equity with increasing age. The most aggressive decline is recommended by Shiller, who recommends moving from 85% equities at age twenty-five to 26% equities at age fifty-five.

3.2. EQUITIES ARE NOT LESS RISKY OVER THE LONG RUN

A common reason given for the one hundred minus your age rule is that stocks are less risky over the long run. This was made popular by adherents of Siegel

---

[16] These are taken from Social Security, Portfolio Theory, Life-Cycle Investing, and Retirement Income, Social Security Policy Brief 2007-02.

(1994). Saying that stocks are less risky over the long run is equivalent to saying that stock returns are *mean-reverting*. But the evidence for this is weak: chapter 8 shows that theory predicts and empirical evidence confirms that the amount of mean reversion in stock returns is very small.

Furthermore, if stock returns are predictable and mean-reverting, optimal asset allocation would *not* follow the one hundred minus your age rule. If stocks are mean-reverting, you want to load up on stocks when stock prices are low and expected returns are high (buy cheap), and you would reduce equity holdings when stock prices are high and expected returns are low (sell dear). Your portfolio composition would depend on the relative valuation of stocks and bonds; that is, your asset allocation would be sensitive to market conditions and your age. Luis Viceira, a finance professor at Harvard Business School, says: "It is logically inconsistent to count on reduced long-term risk while ignoring the variation in returns that produces it."[17]

Pástor and Stambaugh (2012a) argue that for an investor needing to forecast the variability of stock returns (*predictive variance*, for a statistician), the risk of stocks actually increases in the long run. They show that although there is weak mean reversion in equity returns, it is swamped by the uncertainty of current and future expected returns and the large estimation risk of parameters in an econometric model used to forecast returns. Mean-reverting returns do cause stocks' long run risk to decrease, but the other two components outweigh this effect, causing the riskiness of stocks to increase with horizon.

Protecting against Stock Underperformance in the Long Run

Zvi Bodie (1995), a pension finance expert at Boston University, demonstrates that stocks are not less risky over the long run by computing the cost of insuring against stocks underperforming bonds.

In Panel A of Figure 5.2, I graph the probability that stocks will outperform bonds as a function of horizon. All the panels in Figure 5.2 use U.S. stock and bond data from 1926 to 2012 from Ibbotson Associates.[18] The probability that stocks outperform bonds rises from 58% at a one-year horizon to 86% at a thirty-year horizon. This makes sense: stock returns have a mean of 11% versus 5.7% for bonds, so stocks will eventually dominate on average. But this is not a correct statement about risk.

Panel B of Figure 5.2 plots the cost of shortfall risk. Bodie shows that this insurance cost is a put option: it pays out when the cumulated amount in stocks is less

---

[17] From Viceira (2008). Viceira's papers and Campbell and Viceira (1999, 2001) are seminal references in dynamic portfolio allocation for individual investors. Viceira (2001) looks specifically at the case with labor income.

[18] The analysis assumes that stock returns are log-normally distributed and that the bond return is held constant and fixed at the mean log return of long-term government bonds. This is the Black–Scholes (1973) world.

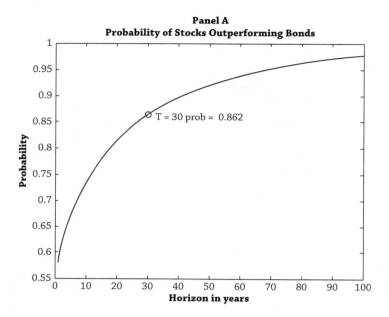

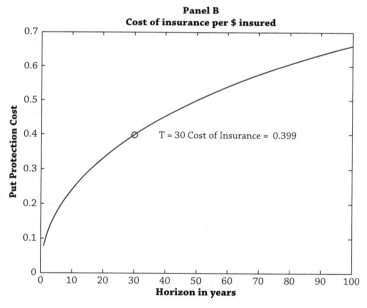

Figure 5.2

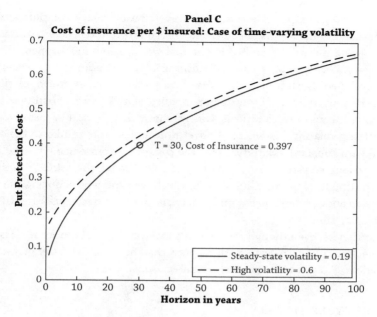

Figure 5.2 (continued)

than the cumulated value in bonds at the end of the period, and zero otherwise. If stocks are less risky in the long run, then the cost of this insurance should decrease over time. Panel B shows exactly the opposite: the cost of insuring against stocks underperforming bonds increases with horizon. For a thirty-year horizon, the insurance cost is 40 cents per dollar of initial investment in equities.

Bodie's analysis is clever because it doesn't matter whether stock returns are mean-reverting. One of the key insights of the Black–Scholes (1973) option pricing framework is that the expected return of stocks does not affect the value of the option.[19] Whatever the expected return of the stock, Bodie's cost of insurance in Panel B of Figure 5.2 shows that stocks are not less risky in the long run.

How can we reconcile Panel A of Figure 5.2, where the probability of stocks outperforming bonds increases over time, and Panel B, where the cost of insuring against shortfall risk also increases over time? The insurance cost in Panel B has two parts: the probability of stocks underperforming bonds and the loss contingent upon underperforming. When stocks underperform, they can really, really underperform. Investors who experienced the Great Depression or even more recently the financial crisis of 2007–2008 know that stock losses can be huge. In extreme cases you lose everything, as investors in Chinese or Russian equities learned in the early twentieth century.

---

[19] For a readable explanation sans differential equations, see Kritzman (2000).

Theoretically, it's possible that mean reversion of equity volatilities, rather than the conditional means of equity returns, could produce a downward-sloping cost of insurance over time. But in the real world, it doesn't happen. In Panel C of Figure 5.3, I compute shortfall costs using a model of time-varying volatility developed by Heston (1993). Heston's model specifies stock volatility as mean-reverting, and there is much more predictability in stock volatilities than in conditional means of stock returns. Panel C shows that the cost of insurance with time-varying volatility also increases over time and is quite similar to the cost in Panel B with constant volatility. I plot the cost of insurance using two volatility levels: the long-run steady state volatility of 19% through the 1926–2012 sample and a starting level of volatility of 60%, which we experienced during the Great Depression and the more recent financial crisis. In both cases, stocks are still risky over the long run.

Nevertheless, even though the conventional wisdom that stocks are less risky over the long run is incorrect, the advice that financial advisors give can be appropriate. To state this rigorously requires using . . .

3.3. LIFE-CYCLE MODELS

Individuals earn wages during their working lives, but this flow of income ceases when they retire. Thus, people have to save during their working lives so that they can support themselves during retirement. Economists use *life-cycle models* to study the consumption, savings, and investment decisions of people as they age. The first such model was developed by Franco Modigliani and his student Richard Brumberg. They wrote two papers, one published in 1954 and the other in 1980. Brumberg died early from heart disease, and Modigliani worked on the second paper again only when it was published in a volume of his collected papers.[20]

Life-cycle models contain at least two periods: an accumulation period in which individuals work and save and a decumulation period during which individuals draw down their savings and so dis-save. There are sometimes other periods, like early versus late retirement, being a young worker and then a middle-aged worker, and so. Individuals tailor their consumption, savings, and investment decisions to their needs at different ages, and pensions enable agents to *smooth consumption* over their life cycles.

Modigliani and Brumberg also created *overlapping generations* (OLG) economies where individuals each follow life-cycle models, and there are different cohorts or generations. In the setting of our simple two-period life-cycle model, there are two generations alive at each time. One generation is young and working, and their parents in the other generation are old and retired. In the next period, a new young generation is born and the previous young generation ages and becomes old. The previous old generation leaves the economy through death. In OLG

---

[20] As recounted by Deaton (2005).

models, pensions paid to one generation can be financed by the generations following them.[21] OLG models allow economists to measure *intergenerational inequality*: one of Raimondo's desires in reforming Rhode Island's pension plan was to reduce the subsidy paid by young workers to old workers and retirees. Modigliani won the Nobel Prize in 1985.

3.4. LIFE-CYCLE ASSET ALLOCATION

The key determinant of whether your stock allocation should shrink as you age is the correlation of human capital with equities. At a point in time, human capital is an asset, and if it is stock-like, we wish to hold a smaller equity allocation (and vice versa). The life-cycle approach takes into account how human capital changes through time.

Bond-Like Human Capital

A young person, at the start of his career, starts with relatively little financial wealth. Most of what he has is pluck, grit, and talent: human capital. If his human capital is bond-like, then his financial portfolio should offset that human capital bond position and be heavily weighted toward equities. We'll first take the extreme case and assume human capital is equivalent to risk-free bonds. Suppose that we can represent a young person's total wealth, $H+W$, comprising human capital and financial wealth by the following balance sheet:

Young Person

Human Capital (Bonds)	$ 800,000
Financial Wealth: Stocks	$ 200,000
Financial Wealth: Bonds	$ -
Total	$1,000,000
Equity Fraction of Total Wealth	20%
Equity Fraction of Financial Wealth	100%

Suppose the young person would like a target 20% equity holding over his whole portfolio, including human capital and financial wealth. Since his human capital is equivalent to bonds, this means that he holds only stocks—and no bonds—in his financial portfolio. We can represent this balance sheet by the pie

---

[21] See Kotlikoff (1988) for a survey. A deep insight generated by OLG models is that population and economic growth should drive savings. If there are more young than old people, the saving of the young outweighs the dissaving of the old, and there is positive net savings. If incomes are growing, the saving of the young will outweigh the dis-saving of the old.

Panel A
Young Person:
Bond-Like Human Capital

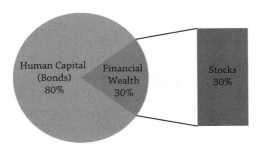

Panel B
Old Person:
Bond-Like Human Capital

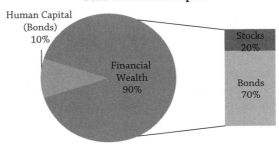

Figure 5.3

chart in Panel A of Figure 5.3. Although the young person holds 20% in equities as a fraction of total wealth, his equity allocation as a fraction of financial wealth is 100%. If human capital is bond-like, this young person should hold a large fraction of equities.

Now take this person when he is old and nearing retirement. We'll assume that his total wealth is the same, at $1 million, but most of it is now financial wealth; the investor has transferred his human capital to financial capital over his working career. His balance sheet is now:

Old Person

Human Capital (Bonds)	$ 100,000
Financial Wealth: Stocks	$ 200,000
Financial Wealth: Bonds	$ 700,000
Total	$1,000,000
Equity Fraction of Total Wealth	20%
Equity Fraction of Financial Wealth	22%

The old person still targets an overall 20% equity holding. To maintain this risk profile, he has replaced his bond-like human capital with actual bonds. His equity holding as a fraction of financial wealth is now $2/(2 + 7) = 22\%$. Thus, the old person has reduced his equity allocation in his financial portfolio compared to that of the young person. Panel B of Figure 5.3 is the pictorial representation.

So, if you're a Supreme Court Justice with risk-free labor income, you should reduce your equity holdings as you grow older. The standard financial planner advice is tailor made for you, as are the slew of target date funds offered by many asset management companies.

Stock-Like Human Capital

Let's consider the case of an investor whose human capital is stock-like. This investor targets an overall 80% proportion of equities in her portfolio (yes, she is more *risk seeking* than our first investor in this example). Suppose that her human capital and financial wealth sum to $1 million just as in our other example. When young, she will allocate heavily to bonds because her human capital is already equivalent to owning stocks. Here's a balance sheet:

Young Person

Human Capital (Stocks)	$ 800,000
Financial Wealth: Stocks	$ -
Financial Wealth: Bonds	$ 200,000
Total	$1,000,000
Equity Fraction of Total Wealth	80%
Equity Fraction of Financial Wealth	0%

Panel A

**Young Person:
Stock-Like Human Capital**

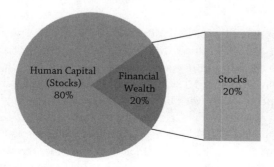

Figure 5.4

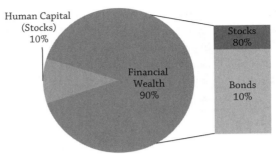

Panel B

Old Person:
Stock-Like Human Capital

Figure 5.4 (continued)

Figure 5.4, Panel A shows this balance sheet in a pie chart. Although the fraction of equity in her total wealth portfolio is 80%, her financial portfolio contains only bonds. Her stock-like human capital crowds out stocks in her financial portfolio. A more detailed analysis would derive these figures using the techniques of section 2. We're going to take these as given and focus on what happens when this person ages.

When this person is old, she needs to substitute stocks in her financial portfolio for the lost stock-like human capital. The balance sheet:

Old Person

Human Capital (Stocks)	$ 100,000
Financial Wealth: Stocks	$ 800,000
Financial Wealth: Bonds	$ 100,000
Total	$1,000,000
Equity Fraction of Total Wealth	80%
Equity Fraction of Financial Wealth	89%

The corresponding pie chart is in Panel B of Figure 5.4. The investor holds a large fraction of her financial portfolio, $8/(1 + 8) = 89\%$, in equities when old compared to the 0% position in equities when she was young. In both cases, her overall equity allocation is $8/10 = 80\%$ of combined human capital and financial wealth. Thus, a person with stock-like human capital tends to hold more equity as she ages.

So, a person with stock-like labor income, like a stockbroker, should do the exact opposite of the one hundred minus your age rule. It seems that for the average reader of this book working in asset management, with labor income highly correlated with the stock market, the traditional financial planner advice is inappropriate!

You are now going to object because you know a sixty-year-old stockbroker who lost his job in the Great Recession in 2008 and he held all his wealth in equities. He lost both his job and his wealth at one fell swoop and seemed to (unintentionally) follow the life-cycle investing advice. The life-cycle theory is a relative statement on how allocations change with time: for an individual whose labor income is stock-like, he should increase the allocation to equities as he ages to maintain a constant overall exposure for risk—the theory does not say that there should be a large allocation to equity when he is old. As section 2 shows, an individual would generally prefer to hold more bonds, all else equal, if her labor income is correlated with equities. Thus, according to life-cycle theory, the stockbroker might have optimally held mostly bonds, but his (hopefully very small) equity portion would have gradually increased as he approached retirement.

While these examples illustrate the main intuition of labor income across the life cycle—that human capital is an asset and our holdings of financial assets should adjust to counter-balance the bond-ness or stock-ness of human capital—actual life-cycle models used by economists add several features. We have abstracted from leverage constraints, how a person consumes, and changing liabilities. Many students today graduate with large debt—so they begin with negative net wealth. What is most lacking, however, is that we treated the young person's problem independently of the old person's problem. In a true life-cycle model, the young person preemptively takes into account the reduced labor income when she is old. Our next (stylized) example rectifies this but shows that the same intuition holds.

Sovereign Wealth Fund Example

Sovereign wealth funds (SWFs) are tantamount to a retirement plan for a nation. Any SWF set up to diversify from (and outlast) commodity wealth is like a retirement fund. Just as the correlation of human capital returns with asset returns drives asset allocation over an investor's life cycle, the correlation of commodity returns with asset returns should determine a SWF's asset allocation.

Consider the following simple model of a SWF.[22] There will be two periods: the first is when oil wealth is plentiful and the second when the resource has been mostly extracted. To simplify, we'll abstract from a spending rule (consumption) and just maximize the expected utility of terminal wealth. (Recall this is not the same as maximizing the amount of money because the utility function trades off risk and return; see chapter 2.) There are two financial assets: risk-free bonds,

---

[22] Some more formal models of SWF asset allocation are Scherer (2011) and Bodie and Brière (2013).

which we assume have an interest rate of zero, and equities. The SWF has CRRA utility (which is the academic version of mean-variance utility; see chapters 2 and 4) and decides on the amount of equities to hold in its portfolio in each period. These are given by α_1 and α_2, respectively:

$$\max_{\alpha_1, \alpha_2} E \left[\frac{W_2^{1-\gamma}}{1-\gamma} \right],$$ (5.4)

where γ is the nation's degree of risk aversion, which I set to 10. Equation (5.4) states that we want to maximize the country's expected utility, where the expression in the brackets is CRRA utility over terminal wealth, and we do that by finding the optimal period 1 and 2 portfolio weights. I constrain the portfolio weights to lie between 0 and 1 (so there can be no shorting).[23]

Oil is like labor income. The SWF can harvest oil of L_t at the beginning of each period, and fluctuating oil prices generating a return at the end of the period. Oil income reduces by 90% from period 1 to period 2, so $L_1 = 0.1 \times L_0$. Calibrating this model using data from 1983 to 2012, the correlation of oil returns with equities (S&P 500) is a low 4%. (This might seem surprising, and it turns out that commodities are also not very good inflation hedges, as chapter 11 discusses.)

Figure 5.5 graphs the asset allocations to equity as a function of L/W, the ratio of oil to financial wealth at the beginning of each period. Panel A shows the allocations to equities at the empirical correlation of 4%. In each period, the allocations to equity slope upward. As there is more oil, the SWF holds more equities because of diversification. Equities are lowly correlated with oil, so there is large scope for equities to pay off when oil does not, making equities increasingly attractive when oil reserves are large. Notice that the first period equity holdings are larger than the second period for a given L/W; the SWF reduces equities with time because oil is "bond-like," which in this case means oil is minimally correlated with equities. The SWF is endowed with a lot of bond-like securities at the first period, so holds more equities. In period 2, oil is mostly extracted, and so the SWF lowers the equity weight to counter the disappearing bond-like oil income.

In Panel B of Figure 5.5, I contrast the case where oil returns and S&P 500 returns are positively correlated at 0.3. In this case, the equity shares are decreasing in L/W and the period 0 and 1 weights flip. The SWF holds fewer equities for a given level of L/W in the second period because oil is now stock-like. In the first period, the SWF is endowed with a stock-like oil resource. After most of the oil is extracted, the SWF wishes to replace that stock-like exposure to maintain the same overall risk profile, so it increases equity holdings in the second period.

---

[23] For those who are technically adept: the case of power utility, i.i.d. log-normal returns for asset returns and labor income is not analytical. See Duffie et al. (1997) and Koo (1998). All interesting life-cycle models are solved numerically.

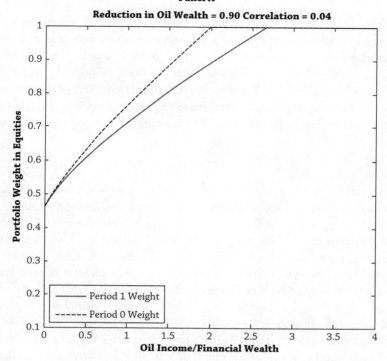

Panel A

Reduction in Oil Wealth = 0.90 Correlation = 0.04

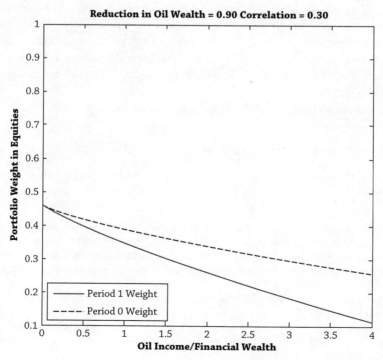

Panel B

Reduction in Oil Wealth = 0.90 Correlation = 0.30

Figure 5.5

This example also illustrates that looking only at the SWF's financial portfolio can result in the mistaken impression that risk aversion is changing. If the oil (or labor) income is bond-like, then reduced oil inflows imply that the SWF should reduce equities. An observer only looking at the financial portfolio might think the country has grown more risk averse. If oil income is stock-like, then the SWF increases equity holdings when oil inflows shrink. It may look as if the SWF has become more risk seeking, but all the SWF is doing is balancing oil risk across its life cycle.

Are You a Stock or a Bond?

A number of studies try to estimate the correlation between human capital returns and equities. At the overall level—a representative agent summing up the income of all workers in the United States or large subsets of workers—the correlation of human capital with stocks is low. Cocco, Gomes, and Maenhout (2005), for example, report that the correlation of labor income with stock returns is –2% for those with a college degree, 1% for those with only a high school education, and –1% for those not finishing high school. Thus for the average investor, human capital tends to be bond-like.[24] (Perhaps the one hundred minus your age rule is right after all, at least for the average person.)

The early life-cycle models relied on similar estimates.[25] Since they assumed the average worker had labor income that was bond-like with low correlations with equities, they predicted that young people should hold more equity than old people. They also predicted that young people should always hold some equities and poorer households would hold more equity than rich households. To understand the latter, bear in mind that, assuming they have the same risk profiles as rich households, the total wealth of poor families is dominated by human capital. Thus they would offset this bond-like capital by preferring equities in their financial portfolios.

It turns out all of these predictions are counterfactual.

3.5. WHAT PEOPLE ACTUALLY DO OVER THEIR LIFE CYCLES

There are three important facts of households' asset allocation over their life cycles:[26]

[24] See also Campbell et al. (2001). There is some variation, of course, in the estimates. Lustig and Van Nieuwerburgh (2008) are the exception in presenting a significantly negative correlation between labor income and stock returns. Bansal et al. (2011) estimate a large 35% correlation of labor income and equity returns. Neither paper uses direct estimates of labor income; they rely instead on asset prices to infer its behavior.

[25] These papers include Zeldes (1989), Heaton and Lucas (1997), Viceira (2001), and Cocco, Gomes, and Maenhout (2005).

[26] The first paper in this literature is Friend and Blume (1975). See also Heaton and Lucas (2000), Vissing-Jørgensen (2002), Ameriks and Zeldes (2004), and Calvet, Campbell, and Sodini (2006). Curcuru et al. (2004) is a literature summary.

1. About half of households do not hold any equity

    This is called the *stock non-participation puzzle*, and I discuss it further in chapter 3.
2. Older households hold bigger equity allocations than do young, working households.

    Another way to put this is that household equity shares are constant or even *increase* with age. Even at retirement, the equity fraction is very high. In retirement, households hang onto their equity holdings for as long as possible instead of moving as soon as they can to bonds and other low-risk assets.
3. The rich have larger equity weights than the poor.

There are also three stylized facts of households' consumption over their life cycles:[27]

1. Consumption is very smooth.

    Life-cycle models predict that when an individual's permanent income increases suddenly, the individual should consume more—after all, you've just enjoyed a windfall. But spending does not respond very fast to changes in income. This is called the *excess smoothness puzzle* in the literature.
2. At the same time, consumption is *excessively sensitive*.

    Although consumption doesn't move when projected income changes, consumption does react—and it reacts too much—to past changes in income.
3. Consumption is hump-shaped over the life cycle.

    The peak consumption years are in middle age. At retirement, consumption declines in line with lower labor income. Figure 5.6 shows consumption expenditures in different age brackets from 1984 to 2011 from the Consumption Expenditure Survey conducted by the Bureau of Labor Statistics. I have normalized the forty-five to fifty-four age bracket, where consumption peaks, at 100%. Note that the more recent retirees have started to consume more compared to those who retired in the 1980s.

It is an exciting time to be working in the life-cycle area. The newest models can explain these patterns by incorporating many realistic features: they take into account the inability to borrow (especially by the young), use utility functions that capture salient consumer behaviors, and model complex dynamics of labor income and asset returns.[28] These models can match the stylized facts of what people do

---

[27] This is a much larger literature than the life-cycle portfolio choice literature. The canonical references are Deaton (1991), Carroll (2001), and Gourinchas and Parker (2002). A literature summary is Attanasio and Weber (2010). Most of these papers, however, do not have portfolio choice decisions involving risky assets.

[28] For life-cycle models with financial constraints, see Rampini and Viswanathan (2013). Laibson, Repetto, and Tobacman (2012) and Pagel (2012) develop behavioral life-cycle models with hyperbolic

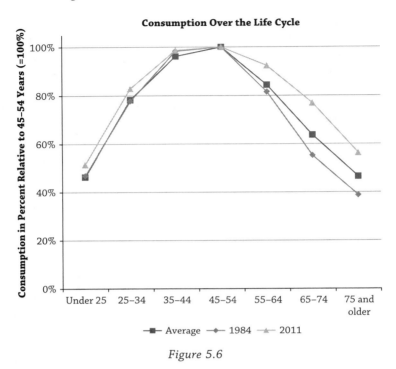

Consumption Over the Life Cycle

Figure 5.6

over their life cycles. In all of them, whether your labor income is stock-like or bond-like is a major determinant of your asset allocation over the life cycle.

Benzoni, Collin-Dufresne, and Goldstein (2007) and Lynch and Tan (2011) specify labor income processes that match the low correlation of labor income and stock returns for the average investor but allow more realistic dynamics where labor income and stock returns can co-move over business cycle and longer frequencies. This is intuitive: we expect labor income and stock returns to be correlated over long frequencies as both human capital and stock capital should benefit from growing economies. Anyone losing a job in the Great Recession also knows that labor income and stock returns can be highly correlated over certain short periods.

Benzoni, Collin-Dufresne, and Goldstein allow labor and stocks to move with each other in the long run (labor and stock returns are *cointegrated*). Because of this long-run comovement, the young person with a long horizon has stock-like human capital. The old person with a short horizon has bond-like human capital.

discounting utility and reference-dependent preferences, respectively. Peijnenburg (2011) uses ambiguity aversion in her life-cycle model. In addition to the papers in the main text, see also Gomes and Michaelides (2005).

Thus, the young optimally hold no equities (they actually want to short equities if they can), and equity portfolio shares increase with age.[29]

Lynch and Tan make the point that although the correlation of labor income and equities is close to zero *unconditionally*, it can mask pronounced *conditional* correlation over the business cycle. Put simply, while there isn't much correlation between labor income and equities overall, there is significant correlation when it really matters, like when stocks crash. In their estimates, conditional shocks to permanent components of labor income are 48% correlated with conditional stocks to stock returns even though the unconditional correlation between labor income and stock returns is just 2% in their sample. Since labor income is conditionally stock-like, the young optimally hold low equity portfolio weights.

3.6. OTHER CONSIDERATIONS

The surprising preference for more equities in old age is predicted by the life-cycle model if labor income is risky, like a stock. (I reiterate: this is the opposite of standard financial planner advice.) Other circumstances, however, may warrant reducing equities as retirement approaches. Perhaps the most important is . . .

Health-Care Risk

Health-care shocks can be truly debilitating. Health care is expensive and spending is concentrated in late life. Marshall, McGarry, and Skinner (2010) report that the median medical spending in the last year of an American's life exceeds $5,000, but for the top 5% it exceeds $50,000. Both the mean and variance of medical expenditure rise with age, especially in old age. Health-care shocks do not mean just a one-off medical expenditure. One serious medical problem is too often followed by others. De Nardi, French, and Jones (2010) unpack health-care spending into persistent and transitory components and show that the persistent components have autocorrelations of more than 90% per year.

Health-care risk is not just about being able to pay medical bills. Serious ill health means the loss of current income for a working family and the loss of future income as well. Substantial declines in wealth and future labor income follow bad health-care shocks.[30] Sickness often produces a downward spiral: ill health affects earnings, and lower earnings lead to poorer health.

Some health-care costs are borne by insurance and some by the government (Medicare and Medicaid). But a lot of health-care expenses in the United States are paid by individuals. Munnell et al. (2008) estimate the present value of out-of-pocket health-care costs from age sixty-five at $100,000 per person, excluding long-term care. Webb and Zhivan's (2010) estimates are even higher,

---

[29] They are actually slightly hump-shaped, with the old slightly decreasing their equity portfolio weights compared to the middle-aged.

[30] The large literature is summarized by Poterba, Venti, and Wise (2011).

at \$260,000 for a typical couple aged sixty-five. But there is large skew, and a 5% chance the couple will spend more than \$570,000. Many individuals also lack insurance—according to the Census Bureau, 21% of Americans earning between \$25,000 and \$49,000 per year do not have health insurance. Close to 20% of Americans between ages twenty-five and thirty-four do not have health insurance.[31]

Individuals can meet out-of-pocket health-care shocks and insure against the loss of income produced by poor health by holding safe assets. Health shocks are a form of *background risk*, which is the term given by economists to any risk on which individuals can't buy insurance.[32] Background risk raises *precautionary savings* and the demand for safe assets.[33] Empirical evidence is consistent with this: Rosen and Wu (2004) show that people in poorer health hold fewer stocks and other risky assets. Life-cycle models with health-care risk, like De Nardi, French, and Jones (2010) and Pang and Warshawsky (2010), demonstrate that it is optimal to increase holdings of risk-free assets as retirement approaches. In retirement, individuals should optimally continue to save to meet out-of-pocket health-care expenses, whereas standard life-cycle models predict that individuals should dis-save.

Changing Utility

It's well established that people tend to become more risk averse as they get older.[34] (Perhaps this explains why your father used to attend anti-establishment rallies when young and then later switched political affiliations.) By itself, this would favor the 100 minus your age rule because, as the investor ages, he becomes more risk averse and wishes to hold fewer equities.

Endogenous Labor Income

Investment in labor income is a choice variable; that is, labor income is (partly) endogenous. Earning an MBA, for example, improves one's future earnings, but you trade off the cost of being out of the work force and paying tuition in exchange for the benefit of higher pay when you graduate. Labor income can also be increased by working longer hours or switching occupations. Shocks to wealth can be partially offset by working harder.[35] A young person has great flexibility, but that declines with age.

---

[31] As reported by Rampini and Viswanathan (2013).

[32] See Kimball (1990).

[33] See Hubbard, Skinner, and Zeldes (1995) and Palumbo (1999). Yogo (2011) shows that spending on medical care can reduce some health-care background risk.

[34] A recent review is Paulsen et al. (2012).

[35] When there is a stock market crash, the investor could consume less, work harder, or both. This labor margin makes a person effectively less risk averse, as Swanson (2012) notes. Other authors developing life-cycle models with endogenous labor income choices include Farhi and Panageas (2007) and Gomes, Kotlikoff, and Viceira (2008).

On the one hand, the flexibility of a young person's human capital could argue for decreasing stocks with age. Youth has greater capacity to absorb risk—so when young you can hold more equities because you can afford the losses by absorbing them through the human capital dimension. The old person has less flexible human capital (you can't teach an old dog new tricks, supposedly), which limits the old person's ability to hold risky financial assets. On the other hand, if the flexibility of a young person's human capital is just a substitute for equities, then she will want to replace that dwindling capacity to take risk with equities as she grows older.

There are other complex and subtle interactions between labor income and capital markets. Higher wages can spur people to work harder (goofing off has a high opportunity cost). An offsetting effect is that earning a higher wage causes a person to become wealthier, and when you're really wealthy, you may really prefer to goof off.[36] Chai et al. (2011) show that the first effect dominates, so those with positive wage shocks early in life tend to work harder. These households consume more and build up relatively little financial wealth, but the savings that they do hold has a portfolio share in equities that decreases with age. The reason is that these households save through Social Security (which I comment on below) and because of high wage profiles, their Social Security benefits are higher at retirement.

3.7. SUMMARY

All else equal, the life-cycle theory predicts:

> Bond-like labor income => Reduce equities as you age.
> Stock-like labor income => Increase equities as you age.

Financial planner advice that you should reduce your equity holdings as you age (or the one hundred minus your age rule) is not appropriate for people whose labor income is positively correlated with equities. Life-cycle models predict that individuals with stock-like labor income should increase their equity holdings with age, as they wish to replace their decreasing stock-like human capital with the financial equivalent. This is what most households actually do. The need to meet health-care expenses, however, entails setting aside risk-free assets, and these risk-free positions should increase as the health-care risk rises over the life cycle.

Most financial planners and target date funds, which blindly follow versions of the one hundred minus your age rule, do not take into account how an individual's

---

[36] Economists label these income and substitution effects, and there is a positive relation between wages and labor supply. See Bodie, Detemple, and Rindisbacher (2009).

labor income co-moves with equities. Whether you should hold more or fewer equities as you approach retirement crucially depends on whether you are a stock or a bond.

4. Retirement

4.1. REPLACEMENT RATES

In reforming Rhode Island's pension plan, Raimondo started at the end and asked what would be optimal for an individual to do at retirement. Then, with a secure retirement in mind, she asked how a retirement plan should be designed to get there. Raimondo is not an economist (she graduated from Yale Law School), but she employed the same solution that an economist would have used. Economists solve life-cycle models by starting at the end of the problem, finding its solution, and then stepping back one period to solve the younger person's problem given the optimal solution of the older retiree. This procedure is called *dynamic programming* (see chapter 4).

In examining Rhode Island's pension plan, Raimondo's team found some cases where some individuals had replacement rates well above one. However, while most working Americans can rely on Social Security to establish a (minimal) base for their replacement income, over 50% of teachers and many public safety employees in Rhode Island's plan did not participate in Social Security.

Economists believe that the replacement rate, the amount of income in retirement as a fraction of pre-retirement income, should be less than 100% for most people. There are a number of justifications for this advice.[37] At retirement, households usually face lower tax rates. Social Security benefits, for example, are more lightly taxed than regular wages, or not taxed at all, in some states. Retirees sometimes downsize their housing (but many do not, see below), leading to lower property taxes. But most important, households do not need to save for retirement—they are now in retirement!

The World Bank, the Employee Benefit Research Institute, and other academic and policy institutions advocate a target replacement rate of 75% to 80%.[38] Scholz and Seshadri (2009) compute optimal replacement rates using a life-cycle model and find median optimal target rates of 75% for married couples and 55% for singles. There is, however, a large amount of dispersion as many other factors, like the number of dependent children, the level of income, and other household-specific considerations enter the computation.

Some people prefer other patterns of retirement income. Some prefer their income never to fall. In fact, for many institutions with their own life cycles, this is

---

[37] See Scholz and Seshadri (2009).

[38] The OECD estimates the average replacement rate is 60% across all OECD countries. See OECD, Pensions at a Glance 2011: Retirement-Income Systems in OECD and G20 Countries.

exactly the preferred "retirement" income pattern for a country with a SWF whose oil wells have run dry or a foundation whose benefactor has died. Surveys also indicate that most people prefer steady or rising real incomes, even in retirement: the declining consumption shares that we observe in data (see Figure 5.6) could be because people are forced to cut back consumption in retirement by a lack of money coming in and poor planning, not because they like replacement rates less than one.[39] Life-cycle models allow us to compute optimal pre-retirement savings and investment patterns for such investors by using special utility functions.

With *habit formation* utility, investors intensely feel the pain of being unable to live on in the style to which they've become accustomed. Countries and universities, for example, find it tough to cut spending below certain levels, and these levels (or habits) rise over time. Using habit formation in life-cycle models generates very smooth consumption patterns in late life.[40] The investor has to save a very large amount during her working life to finance this and continues to save after retirement (there is large wealth accumulation at all ages across the life cycle).

Ratchet Consumption

Dybvig (1995, 1999) develops a model of *ratcheting spending*, which should be attractive to investors wishing to maintain spending; it even allows spending to rise when investments have sufficiently appreciated.[41] To sustain their spending pattern, investors would set aside some of their portfolios in a risk-free asset. This risk-free portion can be thought of as an insurance policy guaranteeing future minimum spending, which is called the *liability-hedging portfolio*. The remainder of the funds is invested in a (levered) stock portfolio. When the risky portfolio has sufficiently appreciated, the investor ratchets up spending and can protect it by transferring some of the appreciated monies into the risk-free portfolio.

While Dybvig's framework is ideal for endowments, individuals, and even countries that do not wish to experience declines in their standards of living, current circumstances present two challenges in following ratcheting spending rules. First, interest rates now are very low (real rates are negative at the time of writing, see chapter 11), and the necessary minimum spending rates from Dybvig's model are very, very low. Second, a large liability hedging portfolio is held in bonds—and expected returns on bonds are very small at the moment and potentially negative. Nothing, unfortunately, comes for free.

---

[39] See Beshears et al. (2012).

[40] Fuhrer (2000) and Michaelides (2002) were the first to put habit utility in life-cycle models. See also Polkovnichenko (2007).

[41] Dybvig's (1995, 1999) ratchet consumption model is a dynamic generalization of constant proportion portfolio insurance. This was invented by UC Berkeley finance professors Hayne Leland and Mark Rubinstein, which they marketed through their firm LOR (Leland–O'Brien–Rubinstein). It was blamed for a large part of the 1987 stock market crash. See Bernstein (1992) for a history. Riedel (2009) generalizes Dybvig's original formulation, allowing for jumps and fat tailed processes.

By starting at the retirement problem and working backward, life-cycle models make clear that the true risk-free asset for retirees is not T-bills. Risk-free assets are securities that can lock-in increasing retiree spending in real terms.[42] The only way to do this is to hold a portfolio of real bonds (TIPS, see chapter 11) that completely *immunizes* a retiree's cash flow needs at retirement. Real bonds, however, have prices that are quite volatile and funding these retirement needs with real bonds can open up the investor to substantial investment risk as real rates change over time. Today's negative real yields mean that an individual, instead of counting on bond earnings to help achieve the savings goal, has to set aside even more money than will be needed later in retirement.

4.2. ARE WE SAVING ENOUGH?

Using life-cycle models, Skinner (2007) estimates how much we should save for a comfortable retirement. The numbers are startlingly high. Consider a forty-year old planning to retire at sixty-five, living to ninety-five, saving 7.5% of pre-tax earnings, and hoping income in retirement is just 30% of pre-retirement earnings. At age forty, this individual needs to have a wealth-to-income ratio of approximately 2, rising to 3 at age fifty and peaking at 5 when retirement occurs. This wealth does not include housing, and for non-homeowners the numbers are even larger at 4, 5, and 8 for ages forty, fifty, and sixty-five, respectively.

Most people are nowhere near these levels of savings.

Most households fail to save the amounts required by life-cycle models to ensure a comfortable retirement. Lusardi and Mitchell (2006) report that the early baby boomers had a median wealth-to-income ratio of just 2, far less than the optimal savings numbers calculated by Skinner (2007). Poterba, Venti, and Wise (2011a) report that half of households headed by someone sixty-five to sixty-nine had less than $52,000 in total net wealth in 2008, and 43% of such households could not scrounge up $25,000—which is often the minimum investment in annuities (see below). According to the Employee Benefit Research Institute in 2013, 57% of U.S. workers reported less than $25,000 in total savings excluding their homes, and 28%—a clear-eyed minority—were not confident they had enough money to retire comfortably.[43] An amazing 34% report that they had not saved anything for retirement!

The first-order problem is getting people to save. Consumption today is always more appealing than saving for tomorrow. Economists have modeled this type of behavior using a *hyperbolic discounting* function, which is the St. Augustine version

[42] See Bodie (1990b) and Campbell and Viceira (2001).

[43] The 2013 Retirement Confidence Survey: Perceived Saving Needs Outpace Reality for Many, Employee Benefit Research Institute, Issue Brief, March 2013, No. 384.

of utility ("Lord make me chaste, but not yet").[44] Fortunately, some economists have also exploited behavioral biases to entice people to save.

Thaler and Benartzi (2004) created the Save More Tomorrow program, described in Thaler and Sunstein's (2009) bestseller, *Nudge*. Thaler and Benartzi exploit human nature to get people to commit to saving future wage increases. People won't save out of today's funds, but they will save out of funds that they haven't yet received. When they receive those funds, they can't be bothered to change their original plans and inadvertently end up saving. Inertia is thus enlisted on behalf of thrift at no cost to current consumption. Thaler and Benartzi found savings rates increased from 3% to over 13% when employees committed to a program where they saved more tomorrow.

Conversely, Scholz, Seshadri and Khitatrakun (2006) provocatively argue that most households have adequately saved for retirement. There is, however, no mortality risk in their model for working people, no out-of-pocket health-care risk prior to retirement, and no risky assets. It's likely that taking into account these risks, households are not saving enough. Also, their study was completed before the Great Recession of 2008–2009, which decimated many households' balance sheets.

The lack of savings is also reflected in the underfunding of defined benefit pension plans. This is behind Rhode Island's travails and Raimondo's desire to reform its pension system. In these plans, employers save on behalf of workers, but employers have not been contributing enough. Or the benefits promised are too high. Or both. In the long run, there is an immutable *adding up constraint:* the money that we spend during retirement cannot exceed the savings (plus investment earnings) that we have set aside to fund retirement.

If we don't save enough, then we'll have to consume less during retirement. Skinner (2007) argues that we can consume less during retirement and still be happy. There is a lot more leisure during retirement. We may place great value on this unexpected richness of time, which can offset our lower consumption. Skinner had better be right, because most people are going to need to consume a lot less after they retire.

4.3. THE FOUR PERCENT RULE

The 4% *rule* was created by William Bengen (1994), a financial planner.[45] Bengen found that an investor holding 50% stocks and 50% bonds could make her portfolio last at least thirty years if she spent approximately 4% per year. In Bengen's original formulation, the investor started retirement by consuming 4% of her wealth at that time—so she starts with a nest egg of twenty-five times her desired

---

[44] See Laibson (1997).

[45] The rule has many variants, several due to follow-up work by Bengen. Milevksy and Huang (2011) develop versions with mortality risk, which Bengen (1994) omits.

retirement spending. Each year, she increases her spending in line with inflation. Although she started spending 4% of her wealth at her start of retirement, her *spending rate* fluctuates up and down depending on asset prices and inflation rates. For individuals retiring over 1926–1976, Bengen found that their wealth was sufficient to last for at least thirty-three years. Increasing the initial withdrawal rate to 6%, wealth would be often exhausted before twenty years, especially for those retiring during the 1960s and early 1970s.

The 4% rule is now generally known as a *fixed proportional spending rule*—spend a constant 4% of your wealth each year. Milevsky (2012) observes that "this 4% rule has taken on the status of a mythical beast in the retirement planning world. (You slay it, or it slays you.)" But the 4% rule is simple, easy to implement, and can be followed regardless of how much wealth an individual has accumulated. Consequently, the 4% rule is very popular. Many financial planners recommend rules similar to the 4% rule—if not 4%, then some other fixed fraction of wealth. It also helps that 4% is very close to the spending rates of endowments and foundations (see chapter 1) and is often used as a long-run average real interest rate (see chapter 11).

The main problem of the fixed 4% rule is that it forces retirees' consumption to go up and down with the market. That is, individuals are forced to spend more when markets are performing well and cut drastically back when markets crash. Most individuals do not like such volatility in their consumption plans—many of their outflows are fixed in dollar terms, not percentage of wealth terms.[46] Thus retirees tend to prefer regular fixed payments that remain approximately constant in real terms. There is also severe *longevity risk* with the 4% rule. The 4% rule is proportional to wealth, so if you live for a long time your wealth might dwindle to nearly nothing. And 4% of nothing is, well. . . .

Bengen never originally advocated a *fixed* rule of 4%. His was an *initial* spending rule, and he held spending fixed in real terms and adjusted the spending rate over time. The sure-fire way to ensure that your spending never falls, in nominal or real terms, is to follow Dybvig's ratchet rule. In Bengen's formulation, there is always risk that an investor will outlive his savings: even if in Bengen's original sample the retirement nest egg lasted for at least thirty years, pity the poor seniors who live past one hundred who will eventually have nothing.

Finance theory also says that the spending rate (consumption) should be determined simultaneously with the portfolio choice. If you're holding a risky portfolio, you probably want to spend less, and vice versa. This applies to both retirement and to how we save and consume getting to retirement. The 4% rule says nothing about optimal portfolio choice. The best financial planners do not use the 4% rule and instead craft a retirement plan that takes into account longevity risk, health

---

[46] Harvard University experienced some problems in meeting liabilities with its fixed spending rule from its endowment. See "Liquidating Harvard," Columbia CaseWorks ID #100312.

status, risk aversion, and all the other important considerations of a client—all the factors in an agent's life cycle.

4.4. ANNUITIES

Annuities should be a retiree's best friend. They provide steady payments, there is no risk of a retiree outliving his savings, and some versions index payments to inflation.

The beauty of annuities is that you receive other people's money. The best part is that they don't miss it because they are dead, so everyone is better off. This intuition was first shown in a seminal paper by Menahem Yaari (1965), an economist at Hebrew University. Yaari showed that an annuity is like an insurance policy with a negative price (in fact, annuities are reverse death insurance): those who die early subsidize the consumption of the lucky Methuselahs who die late. But everyone benefits because at the start you don't know if you're going to die early or late, and you can't consume once you die. Yaari demonstrated there were gigantic benefits of investing in annuities.

The original setting by Yaari was restrictive: he assumed the annuities were fairly priced, there were no fees or frictions, individuals didn't want to save anything to pass onto their heirs, and there were no uninsurable risks. Taking these into account reduces the attractiveness of annuities, but there are still large benefits. Yogo (2011) includes health shocks, bequest motives, and other considerations and shows that there are gains of more than 15% of household financial wealth if households were to purchase additional annuities (over those already embedded in Social Security).[47]

You never outlive your money with an annuity. The risk of an individual outliving her savings has been steadily increasing because lifespans have been getting longer. The Society of Actuaries reports that life spans have improved by around two years each decade for males, from 66.6 years in 1960 to 75.7 years in 2010, and around 1.5 years per decade for females, from 73.1 years in 1960 to 80.8 years in 2010.[48] "There is a general misunderstanding of what "average life expectancy" means, and when people are told that they will live to an age such as eighty or eighty-five, they don't realize that this means there is a 50% chance that they could live past that age," says an actuary. Many people don't even get the average right, with 41% underestimating their life expectancies by at least five years. The longevity risk is substantial: by age sixty-five, U.S. males in average health have a

[47] Davidoff, Brown, and Diamond (2005) also showed large benefits of annuitization even with health-care risk or when available annuity products could not exactly meet agents' desired consumption.

[48] Numbers and quotation are from McKeown, K., and E. Michalak, "Retirees Underestimate Life Expectancy, Risk Underfunding Retirement," Society of Actuaries press release, July 30, 2012. The full report is Society of Actuaries, 2011 Risks and Process of Retirement Survey.

40% chance of living beyond age eighty-five, and females have more than a 50% chance. For healthy people, these probabilities increase to 50% for males and 62% for females.

The beneficiaries of Rhode Island's pension plan do not face longevity risk because the state bears it for them. Increasing longevity substantially raises the cost of providing for pensions, and increasing lifespans are one reason behind the underfunding of Rhode Island's pension plan. Longevity risk also increases during recessions—people tend to die later during recessions—probably because the unemployed and underemployed have more time, exercise more, and spend more time with their families during recessions.[49] Defined benefit plan sponsors then face a double whammy during recessions as asset values fall and liabilities swell as a result of increased longevity and lower interest rates.

While annuities are in theory a great deal, they are not very popular, with fewer than 6% of households buying them.[50] This is termed the *annuitization puzzle* by Modigliani (1986). Why are people reluctant to buy annuities?[51]

Credit Risk

Once you buy an annuity, you are exposed to the credit risk of the insurance company that sold you the annuity. Unfortunately for consumers, many insurance companies are no longer staid and boring. In 2011, Liberty Life Insurance Co. was acquired by Athene Holding Ltd, a company funded by the private equity firm Apollo Global Management. Before its acquisition by Athene, Liberty Life held a "squeaky clean" portfolio of state government (muni) bonds and bonds issued by highly rated corporations. After its acquisition, Liberty Life's products were backed by securitized subprime mortgage products, time-share vacation homes, and a railroad in Kazakhstan. "All the upside would go to Athene if it worked out. And the downside would go to the annuity holders if it didn't," says a former bond

---

[49] Stevens et al. (2012) identify one more reason: in expansions it is easier for low-skilled health-care workers (especially those working at nursing homes and outpatient centers) to find other employment. During recessions, these workers return to their low-paid jobs in health care, and thus the standard of care rises during recessions.

[50] See Inkmann, Lopes, and Michaelides (2010). And those that buy annuities often do so non-optimally. Many purchase "period certain" annuities, which are the same as bonds as they pay a certain amount every year for a fixed number of years. Period certain annuities are not the life annuities that we consider in this section. Investors would be better off buying a regular bond and simultaneously buying a deferred annuity that starts making payments when the bond matures. See Scott, Watson, and Hu (2011).

[51] All of these considerations are shared by long-term care insurance products, except for some time many insurers actually underpriced long-term care insurance. See Brown and Finkelstein (2011). One important difference between annuity markets and long-term care insurance is that the presence of Social Security's means tests serves as an impediment (it is an implicit tax) on the private market providing long-term care insurance. See Pauly (1990) and Brown and Finkelstein (2007).

portfolio manager at Liberty Life.[52] This behavior has been repeated in insurance companies acquired by various private equity firms and investment banks, including Apollo, Goldman Sachs, Harbinger, and Guggenheim.

If an insurance company goes bust, the annuities are protected, but the protection is capped and the maximum protection differs across states. In my home state of New York, the cap is $500,000, which would be significantly below the value of annuities purchased by the average reader of this book. In California, the limit is $250,000. Consumers can minimize this risk by choosing highly rated insurance companies, but this doesn't guarantee a risk-free annuity. AIG was considered a safe name until it was downgraded in September 2008 and then would have spiraled into bankruptcy had it not been rescued by the federal government in what was at the time the largest bailout of a private company in U.S. history. Individuals can diversify this risk by buying annuities from several companies, but it's hard enough just to get a retiree to purchase one annuity. Partly, it's because . . .

They're Complicated

There are certain annuities, immediate annuities, deferred annuities, variable and indexed annuities, investment-linked annuities, joint and survivor annuities, fixed guarantees, contingent guarantees, annuities with floors or caps (or both), benefits that increase periodically at various high-water marks, sliding surrender scales, contingent protection, bundled life insurance, various degrees of inflation protection, annuities with and without (contingent) withdrawal penalties, and so on.[53] Annuities are really complicated.

"There is almost no investor capable of making an informed choice about this," says a director for the Consumer Federation of America.[54] The people selling annuities have terrible reputations, and some deserve them. "If you need to act in the customers' best interest," says a former SEC official, "you can't sell this crap."

The closest annuities to those in academic life-cycle models are "single premium immediate annuities," which investors buy at a single point in time with their retirement savings.[55] These investors then receive payments for the duration of their lives.

Bad Deals

Not only are these complicated products very far from the nice, clean products that academics treat in their life-cycle models, they can be much more expensive

---

[52] Quotation and details are from Mider, Z. R., "Apollo-to-Goldman Embracing Insurers Spurs State Concerns," Bloomberg, April 22, 2013.

[53] Obfuscation is in the interest of the general asset management industry, as Carlin and Manso (2011) show formally.

[54] Quotations from Olen (2012), who provides a blistering critique of this industry.

[55] The new generation of literature on annuities explores deferred and index annuities, like Milevsky (2005), Gong and Webb (2010), and Maurer et al. (2013).

than their actuarially fair values. Milevsky and Posner (2001) value the insurance guarantees in annuities and find these are worth between 0.01% and 0.10%, but the insurance industry charges 1.15%.[56] Mitchell et al. (1999) estimate the value of annuities offered by life insurance companies and find that it's 80 to 90 cents for each dollar. However, Mitchell et al. show that the difference between fair value and purchase price has shrunk over time.

Even if annuities are fairly priced for an average policyholder, they can be expensive for certain segments of the population. Brown, Mitchell, and Poterba (2002) report a male buying an annuity at age sixty-five would get 91 cents of value for every dollar put in, but a more general member of the public would be only getting 81 cents of value. This is because insurance companies selling annuities face . . .

Adverse Selection

Early in Jane Austen's *Sense and Sensibility*, Mrs. Dashwood convinces her husband not to help the family of our heroines (Elinor, Marianne, and Margaret), explaining: "People always live forever when there is an annuity to be paid them." Insurance companies take into account adverse selection when pricing annuities to avoid bankrupting themselves by paying people who "always live forever."

Perhaps there is a spiraling negative interaction of adverse selection with demand: adverse selection drives up the price of annuities, this leads to lower demand, which in turn leads to greater adverse selection, and so on. Chalmers and Reuter (2012b) rule out this explanation in a study of the Oregon Public Employees Retirement System. They do not find that participants in Oregon's pension plan buy more annuities when annuity prices fall, which must point to other investor-specific characteristics driving (lack of) annuity demand. Getting value for money is also not an issue in Oregon's system, as the lucky participants receive more than $1 in benefits in annuities for each $1 that they buy.

Framing

Consumers often view annuities as gambles. Benartzi, Previtero, and Thaler (2011) argue that consumers view annuities in an "investment" mindset, or *frame*, rather than in a "consumption" mindset. They come to an annuity decision with the question, "Will I live long enough for this investment to pay off?" The risk is that all the (usually considerable) money placed in the annuity, earned with blood, sweat, and tears, vanishes with early death. The investor benefits from guaranteeing his consumption each year (subject to credit risk) but does not view the annuity in terms of consumption benefits. Changing the frame can enhance demand.

---

[56] The basic benefit is that at least the original investment will be returned upon death. This is a put option with a strike price equal to the purchase price of the annuity. There are many variants, see They're Complicated.

Health-Care Risk, Again

Dylan Thomas doesn't take account of exponentially increasing health-care expenses in senescence when he says, "Old age should burn and rave at close of day; Rage, rage against the dying of the light." The upside of annuities is that they lock away a big chunk of capital to ensure regular payments. The downside is that this capital is not available to meet unexpected health-care shocks or the needs of your children (who have come back home to live with you).[57]

Annuities are initially priced by valuing the expected payments given the health of an individual at the time the annuity is purchased. But health varies over time and after a severe health shock, the value of annuities can decrease substantially. This loss happens exactly when an individual most needs resources to cushion the blow from reduced income. This makes annuities unattractive to hold, especially for investors facing large uncertainty about their health.[58]

Some annuity products, like variable annuities with guaranteed income benefits, allow policyholders to withdraw more than the regular amount (with penalties, of course) in emergencies. But understanding whether these are good deals is hard for most consumers (see They're Complicated, above).

They Already Have Some

Most Americans are entitled to receive Social Security—which is an inflation-indexed annuity. Inflation protection is extremely valuable for recipients but very expensive for the government. According to MetLife, an annuity paying out the maximum Social Security benefit for a couple at age sixty-six would cost almost $1.2 million.[59]

It is possible that Social Security meets the annuity needs of many Americans. Authors like Yogo (2011), however, report that it is still in the average consumer's best interests to purchase additional annuities over those in Social Security. I also bet that the desired retirement lifestyle of the average reader of this book would not be sustained by Social Security.

Social Security is itself underfunded; the Social Security Administration estimates that the fund will be empty in 2033. The additional money required to pay all scheduled benefits is equivalent to 80% of the amount of outstanding U.S. Treasury debt.[60] So it is not only private annuities that have credit risk.

---

[57] See Sinclair and Smetters (2004), De Nardi, French, and Jones (2010), and Pang and Warshawsky (2010).

[58] Reichling and Smetters (2013) show that the best hedge for most young individuals against time-varying mortality risk is actually life insurance, rather than annuities.

[59] As reported in "Falling Short," *Economist*, April 9, 2011.

[60] Numbers from The 2012 Annual Report of the Board of Trustees of the Federal Old-Age and Survivors Insurance and Federal Disability Insurance Trust Funds. Social Security liabilities do not have the "full faith and credit" backing of the U.S. government and are not counted as a government liability. The liabilities of Fannie Mae and Freddie Mac also didn't have an explicit guarantee, and now the federal government is the sole owner of both entities. Hamilton (2013) estimates the total of all

Bequests

Perhaps the dead do have utility functions. The very rich use trusts to ensure that their heirs follow certain rules as a condition of inheriting money, and donors tie up endowment money to universities and foundations with *restricted use* provisions (see chapter 1). Many individuals want to leave some kind of legacy to their children through bequests. Inkmann, Lopes, and Michaelides (2010) show the bequest motive is a particularly powerful incentive not to purchase annuities; many individuals would rather manage money themselves and bear the longevity risk so that they have something to pass onto their children.[61]

Encouraging Annuitization

Although few individuals purchase annuities, there is evidence that annuity participation rates increase with wealth, education, and life expectancy—the kind of factors that seem to determine whether investors are comfortable holding equities in the first place (see chapter 2).[62] These people are able to understand the benefits conferred by annuities, so there is scope for better financial education to expand the annuity market. Framing certainly can help. So too can the push by regulators to allow partial annuitization when retiring from defined benefit plans (allowing retirees to take combinations of annuities and lump sums).[63]

Some defined benefit plan sponsors are actively encouraging retirees to adopt annuities. United Technologies is automatically enrolling beneficiaries into a "secure income fund" that gives workers some upside, if stocks and bonds do well, but gives workers a minimum amount each year that is guaranteed for life.[64] The protection is bought periodically by United Technologies from insurance companies. (In finance terms, United Technologies' workers are receiving a straight annuity plus call options, or a deferred version of Dybvig's ratchet spending.) In Rhode Island's pension reform, Raimondo tried to keep cost-of-living adjustments (COLAs) in pension payments rather than eliminate them as other states have. Under her proposal, COLAs would be paid, but the amount depended on the funding status of the pension plan and was based on investment returns. In this way, the state would not bear all the inflation risk of the annuity payments.[65]

---

off-balance-sheet commitments by the federal government to be $70 trillion, which is six times the reported on-balance sheet liabilities.

[61] See also De Nardi, French, and Jones (2010) and Yogo (2011). Conversely, Hurd (1989) estimates bequests that are indistinguishable from zero.

[62] See Brown (2009), Inkmann, Lopes, and Michaelides (2010), and Beshears et al. (2012).

[63] See   www.treasury.gov/press-center/press-releases/Documents/020212%20Retirement%20 Security%20Factsheet.pdf.

[64] Bernard, T. S., "A 401(k) That Promises Never to Run Dry," *New York Times*, Nov. 14, 2012. Top-down proposals from regulators to mandate partial or full annuitization have not been greeted with favor by some parts of industry or the public; see Schieber (2012).

[65] The Wisconsin Retirement System is the only other public pension system that has a contingent COLA explicitly depending on investment returns. See Novy-Marx and Rauh (2012).

But these efforts can only go so far if the products themselves are deficient. Before the arrival of the market index fund in asset management, investors had no cheap way into a broad, diversified stock portfolio. They were stuck with expensive active management products, and active management on average underperforms the market (see chapter 16). The market index fund changed everything. Its introduction took immense effort by dedicated individuals, a large dollop of investor education, and the firms that pioneered it were relative outsiders to the asset management industry. And it almost didn't happen—the first attempt failed. Regime shifts are rarely engineered by companies profiting from the status quo.[66]

The annuity market is similarly ripe for innovation. There is currently no annuity product similar to the market index fund: an annuity that is dirt cheap, simple, can be sold in scale, avoids costly intermediaries, and is actually bought by investors rather than sold to them. There are more challenges here compared to the market index fund because insurance regulation varies by state, and adverse selection makes pricing tricky. But what a benefit this would be to investors!

4.5. ARE WE DIS-SAVING ENOUGH IN RETIREMENT?

For those lucky, or prescient enough, to enjoy a comfortable retirement, there is a final *retirement savings puzzle*: the elderly tend to dis-save much more slowly than predicted by simple life-cycle models. In fact, for those with relatively large retirement savings, Poterba, Venti, and Wise (2011b) show that retirement account balances continue to increase after individuals leave the workforce! Fewer than 20% of households withdraw prior to age 70.5, the age when households are forced by law to take minimum distributions, and when they do withdraw, the withdrawal rate is low. Even after age 70.5, the withdrawal rate tends to be below the rate of return earned on retirement assets. Not surprisingly, many people die with piles of savings.

The need to pay for medical care is one big reason. Another is the attachment to one's house, which is the largest investment for most individuals.[67] (Houses are highly illiquid assets with huge idiosyncratic risk, funded by a short position in bonds.) While the basic life-cycle model predicts that agents should reduce their housing when they retire, homeowners choose to stay in their homes for as long as possible and cannot easily borrow against them. This can be alleviated by reverse mortgages, but this market is still small and suffers from many of the same drawbacks as the annuity market. Housing wealth is not typically used to support

---

[66] See Christensen (1997).

[67] See Venti and Wise (2002). Nakajima and Telyukova (2012) show this behavior results from including housing in a life cycle model. Fischer and Stamos (2013) also develop a life-cycle model with housing.

consumption during retirement and is liquidated for the most part only following the death of a spouse or a forced move to a nursing home. Even in these cases, liquidated housing wealth is not used to support nonhousing consumption. The other reason saving continues in retirement is that individuals are looking beyond their own life cycle, to grant inheritances to their children and other relatives.

4.6. SUMMARY

The most important problem is to save now so that something will be available for retirement. Save, save, and save! While annuities meet most of retirees' needs—they remove longevity risk and provide guaranteed smooth payments during retirement—most people do not hold them. Current annuity markets are highly inefficient and hard for consumers to navigate; the flipside is that there is still large scope for innovation in annuity markets by new players.

5. Employees' Retirement System of Rhode Island Redux

On November 17, 2011, the pension regulation championed by Raimondo passed in the Rhode Island House and Senate, and the next day the Rhode Island Retirement Security Act of 2011 was signed into law by the governor. As a result, ERSRI's unfunded pension liability fell from $7.3 billion to $4.3 billion and the taxpayer contribution for 2012–2013 was cut to $300 million, from over $600 million. ERSRI's funding ratio was projected to rise steadily over the next few years. A senior director at Fitch Ratings said, "Fitch believes that Rhode Island's pension reform is the most comprehensive measure undertaken by any of the states in recent years."[68]

There were some reductions in benefits for state workers. The plan increased the retirement age to sixty-seven for employees with less than five years of service and to fifty-nine for employees with more than five years of service. The reform created a defined contribution plan that operated alongside the defined benefit plan, and contributions would be split between the defined benefit and defined contribution plans. The calculation of the COLA was subject to a 4% cap and a 0% floor and only applied to a retiree's first $25,000 of retirement income. The COLA would not be paid until the pension system had reached an 80% funding ratio and was calculated as the five-year average investment return less 5.5%. But as Raimondo promised, all benefits accrued prior to June 30, 2012 remained unchanged.

---

[68] Quote from Burton, P., "Reform in Rhode Island Could Start Trend," *The Bond Buyer*, Nov. 21, 2011.

The changes didn't please everyone. Unhappy pensioners and unions sued. After federal mediation, a settlement rolled back some of the original reforms: COLAs, for example, were no longer contingent just on investment returns but were based on half on returns and half on the inflation rate. COLAs could also be paid when the plan was less than 80% funded. The retirement age was scaled back to 65 from 67. Nevertheless, the settlement preserved 95% of the original savings.[69]

The full effects of the pension reform will take decades to manifest, just as it took decades for the pension fund to land in so much trouble. Raimondo tackled public pension reform by starting at the end, describing an optimal retirement income, and then seeking a path to that goal—in other words, by using the life-cycle approach to investing. ERSRI is not in the clear, but at least Rhode Island is on the right track.

---

[69] See Economist, "Little Rhody, Big Debts," Feb. 22, 2014.

PART

II

FACTOR RISK PREMIUMS

CHAPTER 6

Factor Theory

Chapter Summary

Assets earn risk premiums because they are exposed to underlying factor risks. The capital asset pricing model (CAPM), the first theory of factor risk, states that assets that crash when the market loses money are risky and therefore must reward their holders with high risk premiums. While the CAPM defines bad times as times of low market returns, multifactor models capture multiple definitions of bad times across many factors and states of nature.

1. The 2008–2009 Financial Crisis

During the financial crisis of 2008 and 2009, the price of most risky assets plunged. Table 6.1 shows that U.S. large cap equities returned –37%; international and emerging markets equities had even larger losses. The riskier fixed income securities, like corporate bonds, emerging market bonds, and high yield bonds, also fell, tumbling along with real estate. "Alternative" investments like hedge funds, which trumpeted their immunity to market disruptions, were no safe refuge: equity hedge funds and their fixed income counterparts fell approximately 20%. Commodities had losses exceeding 30%. The only assets to go up during 2008 were cash (U.S. Treasury bills) and safe-haven sovereign bonds, especially long-term U.S. Treasuries.

Why did so many asset classes crash all at once? And given that they did, was the concept of diversification dead?

In this chapter, we develop a theory of factor risk premiums. The factor risks constitute different flavors of *bad times* and the investors who bear these factor risks need to be compensated in equilibrium by earning factor risk premiums. Assets have risk premiums not because the assets themselves earn risk premiums; assets are bundles of factor risks, and it is the exposures to the underlying factor risks that earn risk premiums. These factor risks manifest during bad times such as the financial crisis in late 2008 and early 2009.

Table 6.1 **Returns of Asset Classes in 2008**

Cash	Three-month T-bill	1.3%
Core Bonds	Barcap Aggregate Index	5.2%
Global Bonds	Citigroup World Government	10.9%
TIPS	Citigroup US Inflation Linked	−1.2%
Emerging Market Bonds	JPM Emerging Markets Bond Index	−9.7%
US High Yield	Merrill Lynch High Yield Master	−26.3%
Large Cap Equity	S&P 500	−37.0%
Small Cap Equity	Russell 2000	−33.8%
International Equity	MSCI World ex US	−43.2%
Emerging Markets Equity	IFC Emerging Markets	−53.2%
Public Real Estate	NAREIT Equity REITS	−37.7%
Private Real Estate	NCREIF Property Index	−16.9%
Private Capital	Venture Economics (Venture and Buyouts)	−20.0%
Equity Hedge Funds	HFRI Equity Hedge Index	−20.6%
Fixed Income Hedge Funds	HFRI Fixed Income Index	−17.8%
Commodities	Dow Jones AIG Commodity Index	−35.7%

2. Factor Theory

Factors are to assets what nutrients are to food. Table 6.2 is from the Food and Nutrition Board, which is part of the Institute of Medicine of the National Academies, and lists recommended intakes of the five macronutrients—water, carbohydrates, protein, fiber, and fat—for an "average" male, female, and child. Carbohydrates can be obtained from food made from cereals and grains. Protein is obtained from meat and dairy products. Fiber is available from wheat and rice. Fat we can consume from animals but also certain plant foods such as peanuts. Each type of food is a bundle of nutrients. Many foods contain more than just one macronutrient: for example, rice contains both carbohydrates and fiber. Different individuals, whether sick or healthy, male or female, or young or old, have different macronutrient requirements. We eat food for the underlying nutrients; it is the nutrients that give sustenance.

Factor risks are the driving force behind assets' risk premiums. An important theory of factor risk is the CAPM, which we explore in the next section. The CAPM

Table 6.2 **Nutrients and Food**

Macronutrients				
	Male	*Female*	*Child*	*Examples of Food*
Water	3.7 L/day	2.7 L/day	1.7 L/day	
Carbohydrates	130 g/day	130 g/day	130 g/day	Bread, Beans, Potato Rice
Protein	56 g/day	46 g/day	19 g/day	Cheese, Milk, Fish, Soya bean
Fiber	38 g/day	25 g/day	25 g/day	Peas, Wheat, Rice
Fat	20−35% of calories		25−35% of calories	Oily fish, Peanuts, Animal fat

Source: Food and Nutritrion Board, National Academies, 2004.

states that there is only one factor driving all asset returns, which is the market return in excess of T-bills. All assets have different exposures to the market factor and the greater the exposure, the higher the risk premium. The market is an example of a tradeable, investment factor. Other examples include interest rates, value-growth investing, low volatility investing, and momentum portfolios. Factors can also be fundamental macro factors, like inflation and economic growth. Assets have different payoffs during high or low inflation periods or during economic recessions and expansions. We leave a complete exposition of the various types of factors to the next chapter. In this chapter, we describe the underlying theory of factor risk.

There are three similarities between food and assets:

1. Factors matter, not assets.

    If an individual could obtain boring, tasteless nutrients made in a laboratory, she would comfortably meet her nutrient requirements and lead a healthy life. (She would, however, deprive herself of gastronomic enjoyment.) The factors behind the assets matter, not the assets themselves. Investing right requires looking through asset class labels to understand the factor content, just as eating right requires looking through food labels to understand the nutrient content.

2. Assets are bundles of factors.

    Foods contain various combinations of nutrients. Certain foods are nutrients themselves—like water—or are close to containing only one type of nutrient, as in the case of rice for carbohydrates. But generally foods contain many nutrients. Similarly, some asset classes can be considered factors themselves—like equities and government fixed income securities—while other assets contain many different factors. Corporate bonds, hedge funds, and private equity contain different amounts of equity risk, volatility risk, interest rate risk, and default risk. Factor theory predicts these assets have risk premiums that reflect their underlying factor risks.

3. Different investors need different risk factors.

Just as different people have different nutrient needs, different investors have different optimal exposures to different sets of risk factors.

Volatility, as we shall see, is an important factor. Many assets and strategies lose money during times of high volatility, such as observed during the 2007–2008 financial crisis. Most investors dislike these times and would prefer to be protected against large increases in volatility. A few brave investors can afford to take the opposite position; these investors can weather losses during bad times to collect a volatility premium during normal times. They are paid risk premiums as compensation for taking losses—sometimes big losses, as in 2008–2009—during volatile times.

Another example is that investors have different desired exposure to economic growth. One investor may not like times of shrinking GDP growth because he is likely to become unemployed in such circumstances. Another investor—a bankruptcy lawyer, perhaps—can tolerate low GDP growth because his labor income increases during recessions. The point is that each investor has different preferences, or risk aversion coefficients, for each different source of factor risk.

There is one difference, however, between factors and nutrients. Nutrients are inherently good for you. Factor risks are bad. It is by enduring these bad experiences that we are rewarded with risk premiums. Each different factor defines a different set of bad times. They can be bad economic times—like periods of high inflation and low economic growth. They can be bad times for investments—periods when the aggregate market or certain investment strategies perform badly. Investors exposed to losses during bad times are compensated by risk premiums in good times. The factor theory of investing specifies different types of underlying factor risk, where each different factor represents a different set of bad times or experiences. We describe the theory of factor risk by starting with the most basic factor risk premium theory—the CAPM, which specifies just one factor: the market portfolio.

3. CAPM

The CAPM was revolutionary because it was the first cogent theory to recognize that the risk of an asset was not how that asset behaved in isolation but how that asset moved in relation to other assets and to the market as a whole. Before the CAPM, risk was often thought to be an asset's own volatility. The CAPM said this was irrelevant and that the relevant measure of risk was how the asset co-varied with the market portfolio—the beta of the asset. It turns out that asset volatility itself matters, as we shall see in chapter 7, but for the purpose of describing the CAPM and its incredible implications, we can ignore this for the time being.

The CAPM was formulated in the 1960s by Jack Treynor (1961), William Sharpe (1964), John Lintner (1965), and Jan Mossin (1966), building on the principle of diversification and mean-variance utility introduced by Harry Markowitz in 1952. For their work on CAPM and portfolio choice, Sharpe and Markowitz received the 1990 Nobel Prize in economics. (Merton Miller was awarded the Nobel Prize the same year for contributions to corporate finance.) Lintner and Mossin, unfortunately, had both died by then. Treynor, whose original manuscript was never published, has never received the recognition that he deserved.

I state upfront that the CAPM is well known to be a spectacular failure. It predicts that asset risk premiums depend only on the asset's beta and there is only one factor that matters, the market portfolio. Both of these predictions have been demolished in thousands of empirical studies. But, the failure has been glorious, opening new vistas of understanding for asset owners who must hunt for risk premiums and manage risk.

The basic intuition of the CAPM still holds true: that the factors underlying the assets determine asset risk premiums and that these risk premiums are compensation for investors' losses during bad times. Risk is a property not of an asset in isolation but how the assets move in relation to each other. Even though the CAPM is firmly rejected by data, it remains the workhorse model of finance: 75% of finance professors advocate using it, and 75% of CFOs employ it in actual capital budgeting decisions despite the fact that the CAPM does not hold.[1] It works approximately, and well enough for most applications, but it fails miserably in certain situations (as the next chapter will detail). Part of the tenacious hold of the CAPM is the way that it conveys intuition of how risk is rewarded.

What does the CAPM get right?

3.1. CAPM LESSON 1: DON'T HOLD AN INDIVIDUAL ASSET, HOLD THE FACTOR

The CAPM states that one factor exists and that factor is the market portfolio, where each stock is held in proportion to its market capitalization. This corresponds to a market index fund.[2] The factor can be optimally constructed by holding many assets so that nonfactor, or idiosyncratic risk, is diversified away. Asset owners are better off holding the factor—the market portfolio—than

---

[1] See Welch (2008) and Graham and Harvey (2001), respectively.

[2] Chapter 17 summarizes the history of index funds.

individual stocks. Individual stocks are exposed to the market factor, which carries the risk premium (it is the nutrient), but also have *idiosyncratic risk*, which is not rewarded by a risk premium (this is the part that carries no nutritional value). Investors can diversify away the idiosyncratic part and increase their returns by holding the market factor portfolio, rather than any other combination of individual stocks. The market portfolio represents *systematic risk,* and it is pervasive: all risky assets have risk premiums determined only by their exposure to the market portfolio. Market risk also affects all investors, except those who are infinitely risk averse and hold only risk-free assets.

The key to this result is diversification. The CAPM is based on investors having mean-variance utility and, as chapter 3 shows, the most important concept in mean-variance investing is diversification. Diversification ensures that, absent perfect correlation, when one asset performs badly, some other assets will perform well, and so gains can partly offset losses. Investors never want to hold assets in isolation; they improve their risk–return trade-off by diversifying and holding portfolios of many assets. This balance across many assets that are not perfectly correlated improves Sharpe ratios. Investors will diversify more and more until they hold the most diversified portfolio possible—the market portfolio. The market factor is the best, most-well diversified portfolio investors can hold under the CAPM.

The CAPM states that the market portfolio is held by every investor—a strong implication that is outright rejected in data. Nevertheless, it is useful to understand how we can leap from a diversified portfolio to the market being the only relevant factor.

Recall the mean-variance frontier with the capital allocation line (CAL) from chapter 3 (see Figure 3.10), which is reproduced in Figure 6.3. This is the solution to the mean-variance investing problem. Investors hold different amounts of the risk-free asset and the mean-variance efficient (MVE) portfolio depending on their risk aversion. Now here come the strong assumptions of the CAPM. Assume that the set of means, volatilities, and correlations are the same for all investors.

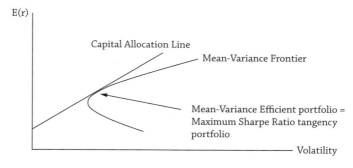

Figure 6.3

Then all investors hold the same MVE portfolio—just in different quantities depending on their own risk aversion. Since everyone holds the same MVE and this is the best portfolio that can be held by all investors, the MVE portfolio becomes the market factor in equilibrium.

Equilibrium

The equilibrium concept is extremely important. Equilibrium occurs when investor demand for assets is exactly equal to supply. The market is the factor in equilibrium because in CAPM land, everyone holds the MVE portfolio (except for those who are infinitely risk averse). If everyone's optimal risky portfolio (which is the MVE) assigns zero weight to a certain asset, say AA stock, then this cannot be an equilibrium. Someone must hold AA so that supply equals demand. If no one wants to hold AA, then AA must be overpriced and the expected return of AA is too low. The price of AA falls. The expected payoff of AA stays constant under CAPM assumptions, so that as the price of AA falls, the expected return of AA increases. AA's price falls until investors want to hold exactly the number of AA shares outstanding. Then, the expected return is such that supply is equal to demand in equilibrium. Since all investors hold the MVE portfolio, the MVE portfolio becomes the market portfolio, and the market consists of each asset in terms of market capitalization weights.

Equilibrium ensures that the factor—the market portfolio—will have a risk premium and that this risk premium will not disappear. The market factor is *systematic* and affects all assets. The market risk premium is a function of the underlying investors' risk aversions and utilities. That is, the risk premium of the market factor reflects the full setup of all people in the economy. The factors that we introduce later—tradeable factors like value-growth investing and volatility investing or macro factors like inflation and economic growth—will also carry risk premiums based on investor characteristics, the asset universe, and the production capabilities of the economy. They will disappear only if the economy totally changes. Equilibrium factor risk premiums will not disappear because clever hedge funds go and trade them—these types of investment strategies are not factors. Investors cannot arbitrage away the market factor and all other systematic factors.

3.2. CAPM LESSON 2: EACH INVESTOR HAS HIS OWN OPTIMAL EXPOSURE OF FACTOR RISK

In Figure 6.3, all investors will hold the market portfolio, just in different proportions. Pictorially, they have different proportions of the risk-free asset and the market portfolio and lie on different positions on the CAL line (see chapters 2 and 3). Thus, each individual investor has a different amount of factor exposure just as different individuals have different nutrient requirements.

3.3. CAPM LESSON 3: THE AVERAGE INVESTOR HOLDS THE MARKET

The market portfolio represents the average holdings across investors. The intersection of the CAL with the mean-variance frontier represents an investor who holds 100% in the MVE portfolio. This tangency point represents the average investor. The risk aversion corresponding to this 100% portfolio position is the risk aversion of the market.[3]

Note that as investors differ from the average investor, they will be exposed to more or less market factor risk depending on their own risk preferences. We will come back to this extensively in chapter 14 when we describe factor investing.

3.4. CAPM LESSON 4: THE FACTOR RISK PREMIUM HAS AN ECONOMIC STORY

The CAL in Figure 6.3 for a single investor is called the capital market line (CML) in equilibrium, since under the strong assumptions of the CAPM every investor has the same CML. (The MVE portfolio is the market factor portfolio.) The equation for the CML pins down the risk premium of the market:

$$E(r_m) - r_f = \bar{\gamma}\sigma_m^2, \tag{6.1}$$

where $E(r_m) - r_f$ is the market risk premium, or the expected return on the market in excess of the risk-free rate; $\bar{\gamma}$ is the risk aversion of the "average" investor; and σ_m is the volatility of the market portfolio. The CAPM derives the risk premium in terms of underlying agent preferences ($\bar{\gamma}$ is the average risk aversion across all investors, where the average is taken weighting each individual's degree of risk aversion in proportion to the wealth of that agent).

According to the CAPM in equation (6.1), as the market becomes more volatile, the expected return of the market increases and equity prices contemporaneously fall, all else equal. We experienced this in 2008 and 2009 when volatility skyrocketed and equity prices nosedived. Expected returns in this period on were very high (and realized returns were indeed high in 2009 and 2010). It is intuitive that the market risk premium in equation (6.1) is proportional to market variance because under the CAPM investors have mean-variance preferences: they dislike variances and like expected returns. The market portfolio is the portfolio that has the lowest volatility among all portfolios that share the same mean as the market, or the market has the highest reward-to-risk ratio (or Sharpe ratio). The market removes all idiosyncratic risk. This remaining risk has to be rewarded, and equation (6.1) states a precise equation for the risk premium of the market.

---

[3] Technically speaking, the market is the wealth-weighted average across all investors.

As the average investor becomes more risk averse to variance (so $\bar{\gamma}$ increases), the risk premium of the market also increases.

3.5. CAPM LESSON 5: RISK IS FACTOR EXPOSURE

The risk of an individual asset is measured in terms of the factor exposure of that asset. If a factor has a positive risk premium, then the higher the exposure to that factor, the higher the expected return of that asset.

The second pricing relationship from the CAPM is the traditional beta pricing relationship, which is formally called the security market line (SML). Denoting stock i's return as r_i and the risk-free return as r_f, the SML states that any stock's risk premium is proportional to the market risk premium:

$$
\begin{aligned}
E(r_i) - r_f &= \frac{\text{cov}(r_i, r_m)}{\text{var}(r_m)} \left(E(r_m) - r_f \right) \\
&= \beta_i \left(E(r_m) - r_f \right).
\end{aligned}
\tag{6.2}
$$

The risk premium on an individual stock, $E(r_i) - r_f$, is a function of that stock's beta, $\beta_i = \text{cov}(r_i, r_m)/\text{var}(r_m)$. The beta is a measure of how that stock co-moves with the market portfolio, and the higher the co-movement (the higher $\text{cov}(r_i, r_m)$), the higher the asset's beta.

I will not formally derive equation (6.2).[4] But it contains some nice intuition: mean-variance investing is all about diversification benefits. Beta—the CAPM's measure of risk—is a measure of *the lack of* diversification potential. Beta can be written as $\beta_i = \rho_{i,m}\sigma_i/\sigma_m$, where $\rho_{i,m}$ is the correlation between asset i's return and the market return, σ_i is the volatility of the return of asset i, and σ_m is the volatility of the market factor. Chapter 3 emphasized that the lower the correlation with a portfolio, the greater the diversification benefit with respect to that portfolio because the asset was more likely to have high returns when the portfolio did badly. Thus, *high* betas mean *low* diversification benefits.

If we start from a diversified portfolio, investors find assets with high betas—those assets that tend to go up when the market goes up, and vice versa—to be unattractive. These high beta assets act like the diversified portfolio the investor already holds, and so they require high expected returns to be held by investors. In contrast, assets that pay off when the market tanks are valuable. These assets have low betas. Low beta assets have tremendous diversification benefits and are very attractive to hold. Investors, therefore, do not need to be compensated very much for holding them. In fact, if the payoffs of these low beta assets are high enough when the market return is low, investors are willing to pay to hold these assets rather than be paid. That is, assets with low enough betas actually have

---

[4]A textbook MBA treatment is Bodie, Kane, and Marcus (2011). A more rigorous treatment is Cvitanić and Zapatero (2004).

negative expected returns. These assets are so attractive because they have large payoffs when the market is crashing. Gold, or sometimes government bonds, are often presented as examples of low (or negative) beta assets which tend to pay off when the stock market crashes. (Government bonds were one of the few asset classes to do well in the financial crisis in 2008. See also chapter 9 on fixed income.)

3.6. CAPM LESSON 6: ASSETS PAYING OFF IN BAD TIMES HAVE LOW RISK PREMIUMS

Another way to view the SML relationship in equation (6.2) is that the risk premium in the CAPM is a reward for how an asset pays off in bad times. Bad times are defined in terms of the factor, which is the market portfolio, so bad times correspond to low (or negative) market returns. If the asset has losses when the market has losses, the asset has a high beta. When the market has gains, the high beta asset also gains in value. Investors are, on average, risk averse so that the gains during good times do not cancel out the losses during bad times. Thus, high beta assets are risky and require high expected returns to be held in equilibrium by investors.

Conversely, if the asset pays off when the market has losses, the asset has a low beta. This asset is attractive and the expected return on the asset can be low—investors do not need much compensation to hold these attractive assets in equilibrium. More generally, if the payoff of an asset tends to be high in bad times, this is a valuable asset to hold and its risk premium is low. If the payoff of an asset tends to be low in bad times, this is a risky asset and its risk premium must be high.

In the CAPM, the bad returns are defined as low returns of the market portfolio. This is, of course, very restrictive: there are many more factors than just the market. In multifactor models, all the intuitions of CAPM Lessons 1 through 6 hold. Except that, with multiple factors, each factor defines its own set of bad times.

4. Multifactor Models

Multifactor models recognize that bad times can be defined more broadly than just bad returns on the market portfolio. The first multifactor model was the *arbitrage pricing theory* (APT), developed by Stephen Ross (1976). It uses the word "arbitrage" because the factors cannot be arbitraged or diversified away—just like the single market factor in the CAPM. In equilibrium, investors must be compensated for bearing these multiple sources of factor risk. While the CAPM captures the notion of bad times solely by means of low returns of the market portfolio, each factor in a multifactor model provides its own definition of bad times.

4.1. PRICING KERNELS

To capture the composite bad times over multiple factors, the new asset pricing approach uses the notion of a *pricing kernel*. This is also called a *stochastic discount factor* (SDF). We denote the SDF as m. The SDF is an index of bad times, and the bad times are indexed by many different factors and different states of nature. Since all the associated recent asset pricing theory uses this concept and terminology, it is worth spending a little time to see how this SDF approach is related to the traditional CAPM approach. There is some nice intuition that comes about from using the SDF, too. (For the less technically inclined, you are welcome to skip the next two subsections and start again at section 4.3.)

By capturing all bad times by a single variable m, we have an extremely powerful notation to capture multiple definitions of bad times with multiple variables. The CAPM is actually a special case where m is linear in the market return:[5]

$$m = a + b \times r_m, \tag{6.3}$$

for some constants a and b. (A pricing kernel that is linear in the market gives rise to a SML that with asset betas with respect to the market in equation (6.2).) With our "m" notation, we can specify multiple factors very easily by having the SDF depend on a vector of factors, $F = (f_1, f_2, \ldots, f_K)$:

$$m = a + b_1 f_1 + b_2 f_2 + \ldots + b_K f_K, \tag{6.4}$$

where each of the K factors themselves define different bad times.

Another advantage of using the pricing kernel m is that while the CAPM restricts m to be *linear*, the world is *nonlinear*. We want to build models that capture this nonlinearity.[6] Researchers have developed some complicated forms for m, and some of the workhorse models that we discuss in chapters 8 and 9 describing equities and fixed income are nonlinear.

---

[5] The constants a and b can be derived using equation (6.3) as

$$a = \frac{1}{1 + r_f} + \frac{\mu_m(\mu_m - r_f)}{(1 + r_f)\sigma_m^2},$$

$$b = -\frac{\mu_m - r_f}{(1 + r_f)\sigma_m^2},$$

where $\mu_m = E(r_m)$ and $\sigma_m^2 = \text{var}(r_m)$ are the mean and variance of the market returns, respectively. Note that the coefficient b multiplying m is negative: low values of the SDF correspond to bad times, which in the CAPM are given by low returns of the market.

[6] Related to this is that the requirement for the SDF is very weak: it requires only no arbitrage, as shown by Harrison and Kreps (1979). The CAPM, and other specific forms of m, on the other hand, require many additional onerous and often counterfactual assumptions.

4.2. PRICING KERNELS VERSUS DISCOUNT RATE MODELS

Here's how these pricing kernels work. In the traditional *discount rate* model of the CAPM, we find the price of asset i by discounting its payoff next period back to today:

$$P_i = E\left[\frac{\text{payoff}_i}{1 + E(r_i)}\right], \qquad (6.5)$$

where the discount rate is given by $E(r_i) = r_f + \beta_i \left(E(r_m) - r_f\right)$ according to the CAPM. Under the SDF model, we can equivalently write the price of the asset using m-notation:[7]

$$P_i = E\left[m \times \text{payoff}_i\right], \qquad (6.6)$$

and hence the name "stochastic discount factor," because we discount the payoffs using m in equation (6.6), just as we discount the payoff by the discount rate in the more traditional discount formula (6.5). The SDF is called a *pricing kernel*, borrowing the use of the word "kernel" from statistics, because one can estimate m in equation (6.6) using a kernel estimator. Since it is a kernel that prices all assets, it is a "pricing kernel." Students of probability and statistics will recognize that the price in equation (6.6) is an expectation taken with respect to the pricing kernel, so this gives rise to the SDF also being called the *state price density*.

We can divide both the right- and left-hand sides of equation (6.6) by the asset's current price, P_i, to obtain

$$\frac{P_i}{P_i} = E\left[m \times \frac{\text{payoff}_i}{P_i}\right]$$

$$1 = E\left[m \times (1 + r_i)\right]. \qquad (6.7)$$

A special case of equation (6.7) occurs when the payoffs are constant. That would give us a risk-free asset, so the price of a risk-free bond is simply $1/(1 + r_f) = E\left[m \times 1\right]$.

It turns out that we can write the risk premium of an asset in a relation very similar to the SML of the CAPM in equation (6.2):[8]

$$E(r_i) - r_f = \frac{\text{cov}(r_i, m)}{\text{var}(m)}\left(-\frac{\text{var}(m)}{E(m)}\right)$$

$$= \beta_{i,m} \times \lambda_m, \qquad (6.8)$$

---

[7] And, beyond the scope of this book, there are many useful statistical techniques for estimating m based on statistical "projections" similar to the estimation methods for ordinary least squares regressions based on the notation in equation (6.4).

[8] See, for example, Cochrane (2001) for a straightforward derivation.

where $\beta_{i,m} = \text{cov}(r_i, m)/\text{var}(m)$ is the beta of the asset with respect to the SDF. Equation (6.8) captures the "bad times" intuition that we had earlier from the CAPM. Remember that m is an index of bad times. The *higher* the payoff of the asset is in bad times (so the higher $\text{cov}(r_i, m)$ and the higher $\beta_{i,m}$), the *lower* the expected return of that asset. The higher beta in equation (6.8) is multiplied by the price of "bad times" risk, $\lambda_m = -\text{var}(m)/E(m)$, which is the inverse of factor risk, which is why there is a negative sign. Equation (6.8) states directly the intuition of Lesson 6 from the CAPM: higher covariances with bad times lead to *lower* risk premiums. Assets that pay off in bad times are valuable to hold, so prices for these assets are high and expected returns are low.

Just as the CAPM gives rise to assets having betas with respect to the market, multiple factors in the SDF in equation (6.4) gives rise to a multi-beta relation for an asset's risk premium:

$$E(r_i) = r_f + \beta_{i,1}E(f_1) + \beta_{i,2}E(f_2) + \ldots + \beta_{i,K}E(f_K), \qquad (6.9)$$

where $\beta_{i,k}$ is the beta of asset i with respect to factor k and $E(f_k)$ is the risk premium of factor k. For macro factors, f_1 could be inflation and f_2 could be economic growth, for example. Bad times are characterized by times of high inflation, low economic growth, or both. For an example for multiple investment factors, f_1 could be the market portfolio and f_2 could be an investing strategy based on going long value stocks and short growth stocks. Value stocks outperform growth stocks in the long run (see chapter 7). Bad times are characterized by low market returns, value stocks underperforming growth stocks, or both.

4.3. MULTIFACTOR MODEL LESSONS

The key lessons in the multifactor world are in fact the same from the CAPM:

	CAPM (Market Factor)	**Multifactor Models**
Lesson 1	Diversification works. The market diversifies away idiosyncratic risk.	Diversification works. The tradeable version of a factor diversifies away idiosyncratic risk.
Lesson 2	Each investor has her own optimal exposure of the market portfolio.	Each investor has her own optimal exposure of each factor risk.
Lesson 3	The average investor holds the market.	The average investor holds the market.

continued

	CAPM (Market Factor)	Multifactor Models
Lesson 4	The market factor is priced in equilibrium under the CAPM assumptions.	Risk premiums exist for each factor assuming no arbitrage or equilibrium.
Lesson 5	Risk of an asset is measured by the CAPM beta.	Risk of an asset is measured in terms of the factor exposures (factor betas) of that asset.
Lesson 6	Assets paying off in bad times when the market return is low are attractive, and these assets have low risk premiums.	Assets paying off in bad times are attractive, and these assets have low risk premiums.

The $64,000 question with multifactor pricing kernel models is: how do you define bad times? For the average investor who holds the market portfolio, the answer is when an extra $1 becomes very valuable. This interprets the SDF as the marginal utility of a *representative agent*. We will come back to this formulation in chapter 8 when we characterize the equity risk premium. Times of high marginal utility are, for example, periods when you've just lost your job so your income is low and any extra dollars are precious to you. Your consumption is also low during these times. In terms of the average, representative consumer, this also corresponds to a macro factor definition of a bad time: bad times are when GDP growth is low, consumption is low, or economic growth in general is low. Times of high marginal utility could also be defined in relative terms: it could be when your consumption is low relative to your neighbor or when your consumption is low relative to your past consumption. In chapter 2, we captured the former using a catching up with the Joneses utility function and the latter with a habit utility function.

During 2008–2009, the financial crisis was a bad time with high volatility and large financial shocks. So volatility is an important factor, and the next chapter shows that many risky assets perform badly when volatility is high. Factors can also be tradeable, investment styles. Some of these include liquid, public market asset classes like bonds and listed equities. Others include investment styles that are easily replicable and that can be implemented cheaply (but often are not when they are delivered to customers) and in scale, like value/growth strategies.[9]

---

[9] There is a third type of factor based solely on statistical principal components, or similar (dynamic) statistical factor estimations of the APT. A pioneering example of these is Connor and Korajczyk (1986). These generally lack economic content, and so I do not discuss them here.

5. Failures of the CAPM

The CAPM is derived using some very strong assumptions. It's worth taking a moment to examine these assumptions and discuss what happens when they are relaxed.

1. Investors have only financial wealth.

   As Part I of this book has emphasized, investors have unique income streams and liabilities, and their optimal portfolio choice has to take these into consideration. Liabilities are often denominated in real terms—we want to maintain a standard of living even if prices rise, for example. Income streams are usually risky, and income declines during periods of low economic growth. This makes variables like inflation and growth important factors because many investors' income and liabilities change as the macro variables change.

   One particular important factor that drives asset returns is human capital, or labor income risk.[10] In an influential paper, Jagannathan and Wang (1996) found large improvements in the performance of the CAPM when labor income risk is taken into account.

2. Investors have mean-variance utility.

   As chapter 2 emphasizes, more realistic utility functions often have an asymmetric treatment of risk because investors are generally more distressed by losses than pleased by gains. We should expect, then, to find deviations from the CAPM among stocks that have different measures of downside risk. Ang, Chen, and Xing (2006) show that stocks with greater downside risk have higher returns. A large number of papers show that other higher moment risk, like skewness and kurtosis, also carry risk premiums.[11]

3. Single-period investment horizon.

   By itself an investment horizon of one period is a minor assumption. Merton (1971, 1973) provides a famous extension of the CAPM to the dynamic case. In this setting, the CAPM holds in each single period.

   While the long investment horizon is an inconsequential assumption for the CAPM theory, there is a huge implication when we extend portfolio choice to a dynamic, long-horizon setting. As Part I of this book has shown, the optimal strategy for long-term investors is to rebalance (see chapter 3).

---

[10] Mayers (1973) is the seminal first reference. See also Constantinides and Duffie (1996), Jagannathan, Kubota, and Takehara (1998), Storesletten, Telmer, and Yaron (2007), and Eiling (2013).

[11] These effects come in two forms. First, there is the risk premium associated with individual stock higher moments. These are properties of each individual stock. See Mitton and Vorkink (2007), Boyer, Mitton, and Vorkink (2010), and Amaya et al. (2012) for skewness risk premiums of this form. Second, there is the risk premium coming from how stock returns covary with higher moments of the aggregate market. Harvey and Siddique (2000), Dittmar (2002), and Chang, Christoffersen, and Jacobs (2013) show that there are risk premiums for co-skewness and co-kurtosis, which result from the co-movement of stock returns with skewness and kurtosis moments of the market portfolio.

The average investor, who holds the market portfolio by definition, does not rebalance.

4. Investors have *homogeneous* expectations.

This assumption ensures that all investors hold the same MVE portfolio in the CAPM world and that, in equilibrium, the MVE portfolio becomes the market portfolio. In the real world, though, people obviously do not all share the same beliefs; they have *heterogeneous* expectations. By itself, the homogeneous expectations assumption is not important: a version of the CAPM holds where the expected returns are simply averages across the beliefs of all investors.[12] But, in combination with the next assumption, heterogeneous expectations can produce significant deviations from the CAPM.

5. No taxes or transactions costs.

Taxes matter. Chapter 12 shows that taxes affect expected returns and can be regarded as a systematic factor. Transactions costs, meanwhile, also vary across securities. We should expect that for very illiquid markets with high transactions costs, there may be more deviations from the CAPM. This is indeed the case, and chapter 13 discusses various liquidity premiums in more detail.

There is another effect of transaction costs when trading frictions are combined with heterogeneous investors. If investors cannot short, then investor beliefs matter. Optimists may prevail in pricing because the pessimists' beliefs are not impounded into stock prices. Pessimists would like to short but cannot, and so stock prices reflect only the belief of optimists. Thus, investor beliefs become a systematic factor. While there are behavioral versions of this story, the original setting of Miller (1977), where this concept was developed, was a rational setting. Related to this assumption is the next one, since when individuals move prices, markets are likely to be illiquid and there are many trading frictions:

6. Individual investors are price takers.

The informed investor is trading and moving prices because he has some knowledge that others do not have. But when these trades are large, they move prices, which leads us to. . . .

7. Information is costless and available to all investors.

Processing and collecting information is not costless, and certain information is not available to all investors. Information itself can be considered a factor in some economic settings, as in Veldkamp (2011). The CAPM applies in a stylized, efficient market; we should think that additional risk premiums can be collected in more inefficient securities markets, especially where information is very costly and not available to many investors. As we explore in the next few chapters, this is indeed the case; several deviations from the

---

[12] See Williams (1977).

CAPM are strongest in stocks that have small market capitalizations and trade in illiquid markets where information is not promulgated efficiently.

In summary, we expect that when the assumptions behind the CAPM are violated, additional risk premiums should manifest themselves. These include macro factors, which should affect investors' nonfinancial considerations, effects associated with the asymmetric treatment of risk, illiquidity and transactions costs, and taxes. We should expect failures of the CAPM to be most apparent in illiquid, inefficient markets. The assumption, in particular, of perfect information is one of the reasons why modern economists no longer believe that markets are efficient in the form the original CAPM specified.

6. The Fall of Efficient Market Theory

Today, economists do not believe in perfectly efficient markets.[13] In fact, markets cannot be efficient in their pure form. The modern notion of market near-efficiency is developed by Sanford Grossman and Joseph Stiglitz (1980), which forms part of the collection of papers for which Stiglitz was awarded his Nobel Prize in 2001. Grossman and Stiglitz describe a world in which markets are nearly efficient, and in doing so they address a conundrum that arises from the costless information assumption of the CAPM. Suppose that it is costly to collect information and to trade on that information, as it is in the real world. Then, if all information is in the price already, why would anyone ever invest in gathering the information? But if no one invests in gathering the information, how can information be reflected in security prices so that markets are efficient? It is then impossible that markets be efficient in their pure form.

Grossman and Stiglitz develop a model in which markets are near-efficient. Active managers search for pockets of inefficiency, and in doing so cause the market to be almost efficient. In these pockets of inefficiency, active managers earn excess returns as a reward for gathering and acting on costly information. In the assumptions of the CAPM discussed above, we should expect these pockets of inefficiency to lie in market segments that are illiquid, with poor information dissemination and where outsized profits may be hard to collect because trading on these anomalies will likely move prices. Whether active managers actually do earn excess returns for their investors (rather than for themselves) is a topic that we cover extensively in the third part of this book.

---

[13] The "classical" notions of weak, semi-strong, and strong efficiency were laid out by Fama (1970) and are obsolete. Fama was awarded the Nobel Prize in 2013. In that year, the Nobel Prize committee also gave Robert Shiller the prize, representing the opposite viewpoint of behavioral, or non-rational, influences on financial markets.

The near-efficient market of Grossman and Stiglitz fits closely with the multiple factor risk framework of the APT developed by Ross (1976). In Ross's multifactor model, active managers and arbitrageurs drive the expected return of assets toward a value consistent with an equilibrium trade-off between risk and return. The factors in the APT model are systematic ones, or those that affect the whole economy, that agents wish to hedge against. In their purest form the factors represent risk that cannot be arbitraged away, and investors need to be compensated for bearing this risk.

Despite the modern notion that markets are not perfectly efficient, a large literature continues to test the *Efficient Market Hypothesis* (EMH). The implication of the EMH is that, to the extent that speculative trading is costly, active management is a loser's game and investors cannot beat the market.[14] The EMH does give us a very high benchmark: if we are average, we hold the market portfolio and indeed we come out ahead simply because we save on transactions costs. Even if we know the market cannot be perfectly efficient, tests of the EMH are still important because they allow investors to gauge where they may make excess returns. In the Grossman–Stiglitz context, talented investors can identify the pockets of inefficiency where active management efforts are best directed.

The EMH has been refined over the past several decades to rectify many of the original shortcomings of the CAPM including imperfect information and the costs associated with transactions, financing, and agency. Many behavioral biases have the same effect and some frictions are actually modeled as behavioral biases. A summary of EMH tests is given in Ang, Goetzmann, and Schaefer (2011). What is relevant for our discussion is that the deviations from efficiency have two forms: rational and behavioral. For an asset owner, deciding which prevails is important for deciding whether to invest in a particular pocket of inefficiency.

In a rational explanation, high returns compensate for losses during bad times. This is the pricing kernel approach to asset pricing. The key is defining those bad times and deciding whether these are actually bad times for an individual investor. Certain investors, for example, benefit from low economic growth even while the majority of investors find these to be bad periods. In a rational explanation, these risks premiums will not go away—unless there is a total regime change of the entire economy. (These are very rare, and the financial crisis in 2008 and 2009 was certainly not a regime change.) In addition, these risk premiums are scalable and suitable for very large asset owners.

In a behavioral explanation, high expected returns result from agents' under- or overreaction to news or events. Behavioral biases can also result from the inefficient updating of beliefs or ignoring some information. Perfectly rational investors, who are immune from these biases, should be able to come in with sufficient capital and remove this mispricing over time. Then it becomes a question of

[14] See Ellis (1975) for a practitioner perspective.

how fast an asset owner can invest before all others do the same. A better justification for investment, at least for slow-moving asset owners, is the persistence of a behavioral bias because there are barriers to the entry of capital. Some of these barriers may be structural, like the inability of certain investors to take advantage of this investment opportunity. Regulatory requirements, for example, force some investors to hold certain types of assets, like bonds above a certain credit rating or stocks with market capitalizations above a certain threshold. If there is a structural barrier to entry, then the behavioral bias can be exploited for a long time.

For some risk premiums, the most compelling explanations are rational (as with the volatility risk premium), for some behavioral (e.g., momentum), and for some others a combination of rational and behavioral stories prevails (like value/growth investing). Overall, the investor should not care if the source is rational or behavioral; the more appropriate question is whether she is different from the average investor who is subject to the rational or behavioral constraints and whether the source of returns is expected to persist in the future (at least in the short term). We take up this topic in detail in chapter 14, where I discuss factor investing.

7. The 2008–2009 Financial Crisis Redux

The simultaneously dismal performance of many risky assets during the financial crisis is consistent with an underlying multifactor model in which many asset classes were exposed to the same factors. The financial crisis was the quintessential bad time: volatility was very high, economic growth toward the end of the crisis was low, and there was large uncertainty about government and monetary policy. Liquidity dried up in several markets. The commonality of returns in the face of these factor risks is strong evidence in favor of multifactor models of risk, rather than a rejection of financial risk theory as some critics have claimed. Assets earn risk premiums to compensate for exposure to these underlying risk factors. During bad times, asset returns are low when these factor risks manifest. Over the long run, asset risk premiums are high to compensate for the low returns during bad times.

Some commentators have argued that the events of 2008 demonstrate the failure of diversification. Diversification itself is not dead, but the financial crisis demonstrated that asset class labels can be highly misleading, lulling investors into the belief that they are safely diversified when in fact they aren't. What matters are the embedded factor risks; assets are bundles of factor risks. We need to understand the factor risks behind assets, just as we look past the names and flavors of the things that we eat to the underlying nutrients to ensure we have enough to sustain us. We take on risk to earn risk premiums in the long run, so we need to understand when and how that factor risk can be realized in the short run. Some have criticized the implementation of diversification through mean-variance utility, which assumes correlations between asset classes are constant when in fact correlations tend to increase during bad times.[15] Factor exposures can and do vary through time, giving rise to time-varying correlations—all the more reason to understand the true factor drivers of risk premiums.

---

[15] Models of portfolio choice with time-varying correlations are developed by Ang and Bekaert (2002, 2004), for example. Chua, Kritzman, and Page (2009) provide an analysis of increasing correlations during the financial crisis.

CHAPTER 7

Factors

Chapter Summary

Factors drive risk premiums. One set of factors describes fundamental, economy-wide variables like growth, inflation, volatility, productivity, and demographic risk. Another set consists of tradeable investment styles like the market portfolio, value-growth investing, and momentum investing. The economic theory behind factors can be either rational, where the factors have high returns over the long run to compensate for their low returns during bad times, or behavioral, where factor risk premiums result from the behavior of agents that is not arbitraged away.

1. Value Investing

Historically speaking, value stocks beat the pants off growth stocks. Value stocks have low prices in relation to their net worth, which can be measured by accounting book value. Growth stocks are relatively costly in comparison to book value. Figure 7.1 plots the returns of value stocks (stocks with high book-to-market ratios) versus growth stocks (stocks with low book-to-market ratios). I plot the returns to the *value-growth strategy*, which goes long value stocks and short growth stocks.[1] Although value investing has on average done well, it sometimes loses money. For example, note the pronounced drawdown during the tech boom of the late 1990s. There was another drawdown during the financial crisis in 2008. Value stocks also did poorly in 2011.

Why does value investing work? Was the value strategy—the returns of value stocks in excess of growth stocks—a systematic factor? If so, what determined the value risk premium?

In the context of the previous chapter on factor theory, assets are buffeted by risk factors. The risk factors offer premiums to compensate investors for bearing

---

[1] The data for this strategy, as for all the other Fama–French strategies in this chapter are from http://mba.tuck.dartmouth.edu/pages/faculty/ken.french/data_library.html.

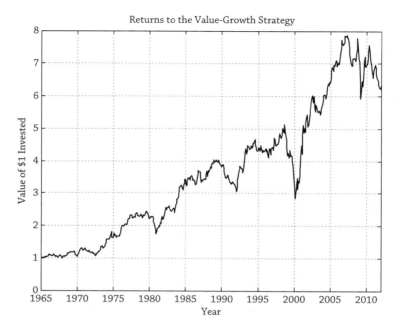

Figure 7.1

losses during bad times. I discuss the economic stories behind the factors from a rational and behavioral perspective and the implications of these stories for asset owners.[2]

There are two types of factors. There are macro, fundamental-based factors, which include economic growth, inflation, volatility, productivity, and demographic risk. The second type is investment-style factors like the market factor of the capital asset pricing model (CAPM) and the value strategy of this motivating example. Investment factors include both *static factors*, like the market, which we simply go long to collect a risk premium, and *dynamic factors*, which can only be exploited through constantly trading different types of securities. (In chapters 17 and 18, I show that many hedge funds and private equity investments are essentially bundles of dynamic factors.) The two types of factors are linked, and macro factors are often embedded in the performance of investment factors. I turn to economy-wide macro factors first.

2. Macro Factors

It is intuitive that macro factors pervasively affect all investors and the prices of assets.[3] When economic growth slows or inflation is high, all firms and investors

---

[2] A very comprehensive study of factor risks is Ilmanen (2011).

[3] The first study to consider macro factors as systematic sources of risk in the cross section of equities was Chen, Roll, and Ross (1986).

in the economy are affected—it is just a question of degree. Most consumers dislike low growth and high inflation because it is more likely they will be laid off or they are less able to afford the same basket of goods and services in real terms. A few investors, such as debt collectors, benefit from slow growth, and a few other investors, including owners of oil wells, benefit from high inflation induced by surging commodity prices. In general, though, bad outcomes of macro factors define bad times for the average investor.

The *level* of the factor often does not matter as much as a *shock* to a factor. Many macro factors are persistent: when inflation is low today, we know that it will be very likely low next month. The fact that it is then low at the end of the month is no surprise. What is surprising are any movements in inflation not anticipated at the beginning of the period. Thus, we often need to look at *unexpected changes* to macro factors.

Asset prices respond to these factors *contemporaneously*. As inflation is increasing or unexpected adverse inflation shocks hit the economy, we enter a bad time and asset prices fall. The risk premium over the long run compensates investors for the losses endured when bad times of high inflation occur in the short run.

The three most important macro factors are growth, inflation, and volatility.

2.1. ECONOMIC GROWTH

Risky assets generally perform poorly and are much more volatile during periods of low economic growth. However, government bonds tend to do well during these times. If an investor is in a position to weather recessions relatively comfortably, then that person should tilt more heavily toward risky assets such as equities. In doing so she'll enjoy higher returns, on average, and over the long run these will make up for losses during periods of low growth.[4] If an investor cannot bear large losses during recessions, she should hold more bonds, especially government bonds. Her portfolio will likely perform much better during recessions but worse over the long run. This is the price the investor pays for low exposure to growth risk.

Table 7.2 reports means and volatilities of large stocks, small stocks, government bonds, and corporate bonds (investment grade and high yield) conditional on economic recessions and expansions defined by the National Bureau of Economic Research (NBER). I also report means and volatilities conditional on low and high real GDP growth and low and high consumption. These are computed simply by dividing the sample into two sets, above and below the median, respectively. Table 7.2 shows that, during recessions, stock returns fall: the mean return for large stocks is 5.6% during recessions and 12.4% during expansions. The difference in returns across recessions and expansions is more pronounced for the

---

[4] A related variable to GDP growth is real consumption growth. It turns out that real consumption is very smooth and actually does not vary much across recessions and expansions, unlike GDP growth. We will look at the effects of consumption risk in chapter 8 when we discuss the equity risk premium.

Table 7.2 **Means and Volatilities Conditional on Factor Realizations**

	Large Stocks	Small Stocks	Govt Bonds	Corporate Bonds	
				Investment Grade	High Yield
Means					
Full Sample	11.3%	15.3%	7.0%	7.0%	7.6%
Business Cycles (1)					
Recessions	5.6%	7.8%	12.3%	12.6%	7.4%
Expansions	12.4%	16.8%	5.9%	6.0%	7.7%
Real GDP (2)					
Low	8.8%	12.2%	10.0%	9.7%	7.0%
High	13.8%	18.4%	3.9%	4.4%	8.2%
Consumption (3)					
Low	5.6%	5.6%	9.6%	9.1%	7.1%
High	17.1%	25.0%	4.4%	5.0%	8.2%
Inflation (4)					
Low	14.7%	17.6%	8.6%	8.8%	9.2%
High	8.0%	13.0%	5.4%	5.3%	6.0%
Volatilities					
Full Sample	16.0%	23.7%	10.6%	9.8%	9.5%
Business Cycles					
Recessions	23.7%	33.8%	15.5%	16.6%	18.1%
Expansions	14.0%	21.2%	9.3%	7.8%	6.8%
Real GDP					
Low	16.9%	23.7%	12.2%	11.8%	12.1%
High	14.9%	23.7%	8.5%	7.0%	6.0%
Consumption					
Low	17.5%	23.8%	11.9%	11.6%	11.8%
High	13.8%	22.7%	8.9%	7.4%	6.6%
Inflation					
Low	15.5%	21.9%	9.6%	8.2%	7.7%
High	16.4%	25.4%	11.5%	11.1%	11.0%

Returns are from Ibbotson Morningstar and are at the quarterly frequency
The sample is 1952:Q1 to 2011:Q4.
(1) Business cycles are defined by NBER recession and expansion indicators.
(2) Real GDP is quarter-on-quarter
(3) Consumption is quarter-on-quarter real personal consumption expenditures
(4) Inflation is quarter-on-quarter CPI-All Items

riskier small cap stocks at 7.8% and 16.8%, respectively. Government bonds act in the opposite way, generating higher returns at 12.3% during recessions compared to 5.9% during expansions. Investment-grade corporate bonds, which have relatively little credit risk, exhibit similar behavior. In contrast, high-yield bonds are much closer to equity, and their performance is between equity and government bonds; in fact, high-yield bonds do not have any discernable difference in mean returns over recessions and expansions.

We can see a similar pattern if we look at periods of low or high growth, as measured by real GDP or consumption growth. For example, large stocks return 8.8% during periods of low real GDP growth and 5.6% during periods of low consumption growth. During periods of high real GDP growth and high consumption growth, large stock returns average 13.8% and 17.1%, respectively. Consistent with the behavior across NBER recessions and expansions, government bonds tend to do relatively well during periods of low growth, averaging 10.0% during periods of low real GDP growth compared to 3.9% during periods of high real GDP growth.

All asset returns are much more volatile during recessions or periods of low growth. For example, large stock return volatility is 23.7% during recessions compared to 14.0% during expansions. While government bonds have higher returns during recessions, their returns are also more volatile then, with a volatility of 15.5% during recessions compared to 9.3% during expansions. It is interesting to compare the volatilities of assets over the full sample to the volatilities conditional on recessions and expansions: volatility tends to be very high during bad times.

2.2. INFLATION

High inflation tends to be bad for both stocks and bonds, as Table 7.2 shows. During periods of high inflation, all assets tend to do poorly.[5] Large stocks average 14.7% during low inflation periods and only 8.0% during periods of high inflation. The numbers for government bonds, investment grade bonds, and high yield bonds are 8.6%, 8.8%, and 9.2%, respectively, during low inflation periods and 5.4%, 5.3%, and 6.0%, respectively, during high inflation periods. It is no surprise that high inflation hurts the value of bonds: these are instruments with fixed payments, and high inflation lowers their value in real terms. It is more surprising that stocks—which are real in the sense that they represent ownership of real, productive firms—do poorly when inflation is high. We'll take a closer look at the inflation-hedging properties of equities in chapter 8, but for now, suffice to say that high inflation is bad for both equities and bonds. Part of the long-run risk premiums for both equities and bonds represents compensation for doing badly when inflation is high. (In chapter 11, we'll further explore the inflation hedging properties of different asset classes.)

---

[5] Deflation, which is not examined here, is also a bad time when assets tend to have low returns.

2.3. VOLATILITY

Volatility is an extremely important risk factor. I measure volatility risk using the VIX index, which represents equity market volatility.[6] Here's a table correlating changes in VIX with stock and bonds returns on a monthly frequency basis from March 1986 to December 2011:

	VIX Changes	Stock Returns	Bond Returns
VIX Changes	1.00	−0.39	0.12
Stock Returns	−0.39	1.00	−0.01
Bond Returns	0.12	−0.01	1.00

The correlation between VIX changes and stock returns is −39%, so stocks do badly when volatility is rising. The negative relation between volatility and returns is called the *leverage effect*.[7] When stock returns drop, the financial leverage of firms increases since debt is approximately constant while the market value of equity has fallen. This makes equities riskier and increases their volatilities. There is another channel where high volatilities lead to low stock returns: an increase in volatility raises the required return on equity demanded by investors, also leading to a decline in stock prices. This second channel is a time-varying risk premium story and is the one that the basic CAPM advocates: as market volatility increases, discount rates increase and stock prices must decline today so that future stock returns can be high.[8]

Bonds offer some but not much respite during periods of high volatility, as the correlation between bond returns and VIX changes is only 0.12. Thus, bonds are not always a safe haven when volatility shocks hit. In 2008 and 2009, volatility was one of the main factors causing many risky assets to fall simultaneously. During this period, risk-free bonds did very well. But during the economic turbulence of the late 1970s and early 1980s, bonds did terribly, as did equities (see chapter 9). Volatility as measured by VIX can also capture uncertainty—in the sense that investors did not know the policy responses that government would take during the financial crisis, whether markets would continue functioning, or whether their own models were the correct ones. Recent research posits uncertainty risk itself as a separate factor from volatility risk, but uncertainty risk and volatility risk are highly correlated.[9]

---

[6] The VIX index is a measure of option volatilities on the S&P 500 constructed by the Chicago Board Options Exchange. The VIX index captures a variety of risks related to higher movements, including volatility itself, but also jump risk and skewness risk. But the main components captured in the VIX index are volatility and the volatility risk premium.

[7] A term coined by Fischer Black (1976).

[8] See equation (6.2) in chapter 6. For evidence of this time-varying risk premium channel, see Bekaert and Wu (2000).

[9] See, for example, Anderson, Ghysels, and Juergens (2009) for stocks and Ulrich (2011) for bonds.

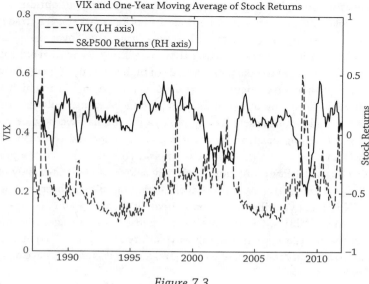

Figure 7.3

Figure 7.3 plots the VIX index (left-hand side axis) in the dashed line and a one-year moving average of stock returns (on the right-hand side axis) in the solid line. Volatility tends to exhibit periods of calm, punctuated by periods of turbulence. Figure 7.3 shows spikes in volatility corresponding to the 1987 stock market crash, the early 1990s recession, the Russian default crisis in 1998, the terrorist attacks and ensuing recession in 2001, and a large spike in 2008 corresponding to the failure of Lehman Brothers. In all of these episodes, stock returns move in the opposite direction from volatility, as shown during the financial crisis.

The losses when volatility spikes to high levels can be quite severe. Partitioning the sample into high and low periods of volatility changes gives us an average return for large stocks of –4.6% during volatile times and 24.9% during stable times. This compares to an overall mean of 11.3% (see Table 7.2). Investors allergic to volatility could increase their holdings of bonds, but bonds do not always pay off during highly volatile periods—as the low correlation of 0.12 between VIX changes and bond returns in the table above shows.

Stocks are not the only assets to do badly when volatility increases. Volatility is negatively linked to the returns of many assets and strategies. Currency strategies fare especially poorly in times of high volatility.[10] We shall see later that many assets or strategies implicitly have large exposure to volatility risk. In particular, hedge funds, in aggregate, sell volatility (see chapter 17).

Investors who dislike volatility risk can buy volatility protection (e.g., by buying put options). However, some investors can afford to take on volatility risk by

[10] See Bhansali (2007) and Menkhoff et al. (2012a).

selling volatility protection (again, e.g., in the form of selling put options). Buying or selling volatility protection can be done in option markets, but traders can also use other derivatives contracts, such as volatility swaps. Investors are so concerned about volatility, on average, that they are willing to pay to avoid volatility risk, rather than be paid to take it on. Periods of high volatility coincide with large downward movements (see Figure 7.3) and assets that pay off during high volatility periods, like out-of-the-money puts, provide hedges against volatility risk.

We often think about assets having *positive* premiums—we buy, or go long, equities, and the long position produces a positive expected return over time. Volatility is a factor with a *negative* price of risk. To collect a volatility premium requires *selling* volatility protection, especially selling out-of-the-money put options. The VIX index trades, on average, above volatilities observed in actual stocks: VIX implied volatilities are approximately 2% to 3%, on average, higher than realized volatilities. Options are thus expensive, on average, and investors can collect the volatility premium by short volatility strategies. Fixed income, currency, and commodity markets, like the aggregate equity market, have a negative price of volatility risk.[11]

Selling volatility is not a free lunch, however. It produces high and steady payoffs during stable times. Then, once every decade or so, there is a huge crash where sellers of volatility experience large, negative payoffs. Figure 7.4 plots the cumulated returns of a volatility premium (swap) index constructed by Merrill Lynch. There are steady returns until 2007, with the few blips corresponding to some small losses during 1998 (Russian default crisis) and 2001 and 2002 (9/11 tragedy and economic recession, respectively), and also during the summer of 2007 (subprime mortgage-backed losses just prior to the financial crisis). But between September and November 2008 there are massive losses close to 70%. These were the darkest months in the financial crisis, and most of the losses across all types of risky assets during 2008 were concentrated during these months (see Table 6.1). The huge crash causes volatility selling to have a large negative skewness of −8.26 over the whole sample. Taking data prior to the financial crisis ending December 2007, the skewness is only −0.37, so prior to 2007 selling volatility looked like easy money.

---

[11] For a negative volatility risk premium in fixed income markets, see Simon (2010) and Mueller, Vedolin, and Yen (2012); currency markets, see Low and Zhang (2005); commodity markets, see Prokopczuk and Wese (2012); and the aggregate stock market, see Bakshi and Kapadia (2003) and Ang et al. (2006). For individual stocks, the volatility risk premium can be positive (some agents really like individual stock risk), see Driessen, Maenhout, and Vilkov (2009). One explanation why individual stocks can carry positive risk premiums but the volatility risk premium is significantly negative at the aggregate level is that much of a stock's variation is idiosyncratic (see also chapter 10). In portfolios, the stock-specific, idiosyncratic movements are diversified away leaving only market volatility risk, which has a negative risk premium. In the discussion in the main text, volatility risk refers to both "smooth" movements in time-varying volatility (*diffusive* risk) and abrupt changes (*jump* risk). More sophisticated models differentiate between the two; see Pan (2002).

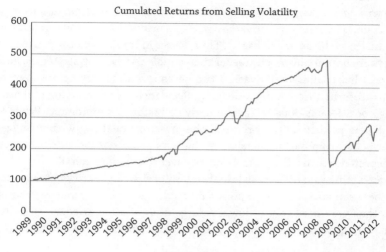

Figure 7.4

Unfortunately, some investors who sold volatility prior to the financial crisis failed to anticipate that a crash like the one of 2008 would materialize. But it did, and the abysmal returns of many assets resulted to a great extent from them being exposed to volatility risk. While forecasting when a crash will take place is always hard, if not impossible, investors might have known from past data that a crash of this type will happen from time to time. For example, volatility had spiked to these levels during the Great Depression. In fact, during the 1930s, volatility was not only extremely high, but it remained high for a much longer period than the 2008–2009 experience.

Only investors who can tolerate periods of very high volatility—which tend to coincide with negative returns on most risky assets—should be selling volatility protection through derivatives markets. Selling volatility is like selling insurance. During normal times, you collect a premium for withstanding the inevitable large losses that occur every decade or so. The losses endured when volatility spikes represent insurance payouts to investors who purchased volatility protection.

In chapter 4, I showed that rebalancing as a portfolio strategy is actually a short volatility strategy. Thus, the simple act of rebalancing will reap a long-run volatility risk premium, and the person who does not rebalance—the average investor who owns 100% of the market—is long volatility risk and loses the long-run volatility risk premium.[12] A long-run, rebalancing investor is exposed to the possibilities of fat, left-hand tail losses like those in Figure 7.4. There are two differences, however. Rebalancing over assets (or strategies or factors as in chapter 14) does not directly trade volatility risk. That is, rebalancing over stocks

_____

[12] Sharpe (2010) calls a non-rebalancing strategy an adaptive allocation policy.

trades *physical* stocks, but Figure 7.4 involves trading *risk-neutral*, or option, volatility. Trading volatility in derivatives markets brings an additional volatility risk premium that rebalancing does not. Thus, losses in trading volatility in derivative markets are potentially much steeper than simple rebalancing strategies. Second, pure volatility trading in derivatives can be done without taking any stances on expected returns through delta-hedging. Rebalancing over fundamental asset or strategy positions is done to earn underlying factor risk premiums. While there is only weak predictability of returns, the investor practicing rebalancing gets a further boost from mean reversion as she buys assets with low prices that have high expected returns. Chapters 4 and 14 cover this in more detail.

Constructing valuation models with volatility risk can be tricky because the relation between volatility and expected returns is time varying and switches signs and is thus very hard to pin down. A large literature has tried to estimate the return–volatility trade-off as represented in equation (6.1) repeated here:

$$E(r_m) - r_f = \bar{\gamma}\sigma_m^2, \tag{7.1}$$

where $E(r_m) - r_f$ is the market risk premium and σ_m^2 is the variance of the market return. According to CAPM theory, $\bar{\gamma}$ represents the risk aversion of the average investor.

Is the coefficient, $\bar{\gamma}$, relating the market volatility or variance to expected returns, which is supposedly positive in theory, actually positive in data? In the literature, there are estimates that are positive, negative, or zero. In fact, one of the seminal studies, Glosten, Jagannathan, and Runkle (1993), contains all three estimates in the same paper! Theoretical work shows that the risk–return relation can indeed be negative and change over time.[13] What is undisputed, though, is that when volatility increases dramatically, assets tend to produce losses. Only an investor who can tolerate large losses during high-volatility periods should consider selling volatility protection.

2.4. OTHER MACRO FACTORS

Several other macro factors have been investigated extensively in the literature and deserve attention from asset owners.

Productivity Risk

A class of *real business cycle models* developed in macroeconomics seeks to explain the movements of macro variables (like growth, investment, and savings) and asset prices across the business cycle. In these models, macro variables and asset prices vary across the business cycle as a rational response of firms and agents adjusting to *real shocks*. The label "real" in "real business cycle" emphasizes

---

[13] See, for example, Backus and Gregory (1993), Whitelaw (2000), and Ang and Liu (2007).

that the business cycle is caused by real shocks and is not due to market failures or insufficient demand as in the models of John Maynard Keynes (1936).
Real business cycle models have inflation, but inflation is *neutral* or has no real
effects. These models are *production economies* because they involve optimizing
firms producing physical goods, in addition to agents optimizing consumption
and savings decisions, but the firms are subject to shocks that affect their output.
One particularly important shock that affects firm output is a *productivity shock*.
The early literature, like Kydland and Prescott (1982), did not have asset prices.
(Kydland and Prescott won the Nobel Prize in 2004.) The next generation of models, like Jermann (1988), put them in. The newest papers, like Kaltenbrunner
and Lochstoer (2010), capture realistic, and complicated, dynamics of shocks and
agents' behavior.

Because these models are designed to work at business cycle frequencies, they
are less relevant for investors who have short horizons. But for long-horizon
investors—like certain pension funds, sovereign wealth funds, and family
offices—the productivity factor should be considered. Asset returns reflect
long-run productivity risk. At the time of writing, Europe is still in the throes of
its sovereign debt convulsions, and an important issue is the future productive
capacity of European economies. In Figure 7.5, I plot a five-year average of productivity shocks and stock returns. I use a five-year average because the productivity
variable is used in economic models that are designed to explain business cycle
variation, which has a frequency of three to six years. The productivity shocks
are alternatively called *Solow residuals* after Robert Solow (1957) or *total factor
productivity* (TFP) shocks. I take the TFP shocks constructed by Fernald (2009),

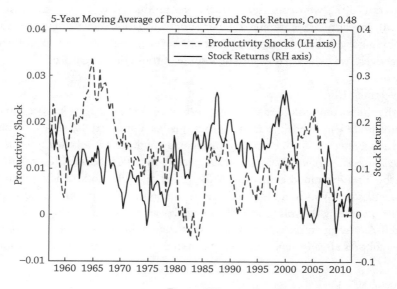

Figure 7.5

who follows the method of Basu, Fernald, and Kimball (2006).[14] Figure 7.5 shows that when there are periods of falling productivity, like the 1960s and 1970s, stock prices tend to fall. In the 1980s and 1990s (the computer revolution), productivity shocks are positive and stocks tend to appreciate. The correlation of the five-year moving averages of TFP shocks and stock returns is high, at 48%. So stocks are exposed to productivity risk; when productivity slows down, stock returns tend to be low.

Productivity risk is just one source of shocks that enter the new generation of *dynamic stochastic general equilibrium* (DSGE) macro models. This mouthful conveys the complexity of this class of models. In DSGE models, the economy is dynamic (as the name indicates) and the actions of agents (consumers, firms, central banks, and governments), technologies (how firms produce), and institutions or markets (the way that agents interact) cause economic variables to change. Asset prices are set from the complex interaction of all of these players and technologies. The DSGE models allow us to think about how shocks from these factor risks are transmitted across the economy. An important part of DSGE models are the actions of policy makers—government policy matters, as the financial crisis showed. Monetary policy and government shocks are important factors that influence asset prices and constitute their own sources of risk. We come back to some of these factors in the next few chapters. Current DSGE models nest both the real business cycle models pioneered by Kydland and Prescott, and they also include *new-Keynesian models*, where prices do not immediately adjust and inflation is *non-neutral*.

DSGE models describe business cycle fluctuations well, and we know asset returns vary over the business cycle. A benchmark model today is Smets and Wouters (2007), who specify seven shocks: productivity (as we have just discussed), investment, preferences, labor supply, inflation, government spending, and monetary policy. In chapters 8 and 9 covering equities and fixed income, respectively, we delve further into how some of these risks are priced.[15]

Demographic Risk
Another important risk for a very long-term investor is *demographic risk*. This can be interpreted as a shock to labor output, just as a productivity shock is a shock to firm production. A slow-moving variable, demography is a factor in economic *overlapping generations* (OLG) models. A given individual follows a life-cycle model, like the kind examined in chapter 5. Take, for example, an individual who progresses through youth, middle-age, and retirement. Labor income is earned and saved only during the young and middle-aged periods, and dis-saving occurs when retired. As any given age cohort progresses through the three stages, they join two other cohorts already alive who were born in previous generations. Thus, several

[14] Available at http://www.frbsf.org/csip/tfp.php.
[15] While most DSGE models do not study how these risks affect asset prices, the newest incarnations of these models, like Rudebusch and Swanson (2012), do.

generations overlap at any given time. A demographic shock changes the composition of a given cohort relative to other cohorts through such events as war (like World Wars I and II), a baby boom (like the generation born in the two decades following World War II), or infectious disease (Spanish Flu in 1918).

Several OLG models predict that demographic composition affects expected returns. Theory suggests two main avenues for this to occur. First, the life-cycle smoothing in the OLG framework requires that when the middle-aged to young population is small, there is excess demand for consumption by a relatively large cohort of retirees. Retirees do not want to hold financial assets: in fact, they are selling them to fund their consumption. For markets to clear, asset prices have to fall.[16] Abel (2001) uses this intuition to predict that as baby boomers retire, stock prices will decline. The predictions are not, however, clear cut: Brooks (2002), for example, argues that the baby boom effect on asset prices is weak. The second mechanism where demography can predict stock returns is that, since different cohorts have different risk characteristics, asset prices change as the aggregate risk characteristics of the economy change. In an influential study, Bakshi and Chen (1994) show that risk aversion increases as people age and, as the average age rises in the population, the equity premium should increase.

In testing a link between demographic risk and asset returns, it is important to use international data; using only one country's demographic experience is highly suspect because demographic changes are so gradual. The literature employing cross-country analysis includes Erb, Harvey, and Viskanta (1997), Ang and Maddaloni (2005), and Arnott and Chaves (2011). There is compelling international empirical evidence that demography does affect risk premiums.

Political Risk

The last macro risk that an asset owner should consider is *political* or *sovereign risk*. Political risk has been always important in emerging markets: the greater the political risk, the higher the risk premiums required to compensate investors for bearing it. Political risk was thought to be of concern only in emerging markets.[17] The financial crisis changed this, and going forward political risk will also be important in developed countries.[18]

3. Dynamic Factors

The CAPM factor is the market portfolio, and, with low-cost index funds, exchange-traded funds, and stock futures, the market factor is tradeable. Other

---

[16] This is the main economic mechanism in, for example, Geanakoplos, Magill, and Quinzii (2004).

[17] Harvey (2004) finds little evidence, for example, that political risk is reflected in developed countries.

[18] For a recent paper showing how political risk affects equity risk premiums, see Pástor and Veronesi (2012).

factors are tradeable too. These factors reflect macro risk and at some level should reflect the underlying fundamental risks of the economy. Macro factors like inflation and economic growth, however, are not usually directly traded (at least not in scale, with the exception of volatility), and so dynamic factors have a big advantage that they can be easily implemented in investors' portfolios.

I present examples of dynamic factors using the best-known example of a tradeable multifactor model introduced by Fama and French (1993). I interchangeably use the words "style factors," "investment factors," and "dynamic factors." Sometimes these are also called "smart beta" or "alternative beta," mostly by practitioners.

3.1. FAMA AND FRENCH (1993) MODEL

The Fama–French (1993) model explains asset returns with three factors. There is the traditional CAPM market factor and there are two additional factors to capture a size effect and a value/growth effect:

$$E(r_i) = r_f + \beta_{i,MKT}E(r_m - r_f) + \beta_{i,SMB}E(SMB) + \beta_{i,HML}E(HML), \qquad (7.2)$$

where two new factors, SMB and HML, appear alongside the regular CAPM market factor.

Let us briefly recap the effect of the CAPM market factor (see chapter 6). When the market does poorly, stocks that have high exposures to the market factor (stocks with high betas, $\beta_{i,MKT}$) also tend to do badly. That is, high beta stocks tend to tank in parallel when the market tanks. But over the long run, the CAPM predicts that stocks with high betas will have higher average returns than the market portfolio to compensate investors for losses when bad times hit—defined by the CAPM theory as low returns of the market.

Robert Merton (1973), Stephen Ross (1976), and others developed the theoretical multifactor model framework in the 1970s, but it took another two decades for an explosion of studies to demonstrate that factors other than the market mattered empirically. Two of these effects—size and value—are in the Fama–French model. Fama and French did not discover these effects; they just provided a parsimonious model to capture their effects. Unfortunately for the original authors, most of the credit for these risk factors now gets assigned to Fama and French.

In equation (7.2), the first factor in addition to the market factor in the Fama–French model is SMB, which refers to the differential returns of small stocks minus big stocks (hence SMB), where small and big refer simply to the market capitalization of the stocks. (Fama and French were clearly not marketers, so the labels on the factors are a tad banal.) The SMB factor was designed to capture the outperformance of small firms relative to large firms.

The other factor in the Fama–French model is the HML factor, which stands for the returns of a portfolio of high book-to-market stocks minus a portfolio of low book to market stocks. The book-to-market ratio is book value divided by market capitalization, or the inverse of equity value normalized by book value.

In essence, a value strategy consists of buying stocks that have low prices (normalized by book value, sales, earnings, or dividends, etc.) and selling stocks that have high prices (again appropriately normalized). Academics often normalize by book value. Thus, value stocks are stocks with low prices relative to book value. Growth stocks have high prices relative to book value. The value effect refers to the phenomenon that value stocks outperform growth stocks, on average. One can normalize prices by measures other than book value—which practitioners do when they build their (often proprietary) value factors.

Fama and French's *SMB* and *HML* factors are constructed to be *factor mimicking portfolios*. They are constructed to capture size and value premiums, respectively and use the (CAPM and multifactor) concept of diversification to ensure that the factors capture size and value effects by averaging across many stocks. These factors are long–short portfolios and take positions away from the market portfolio.[19] The average stock, however, only has market exposure since every stock can't be small and every stock can't be large. Let's examine this point more closely because it is intimately related with the profound CAPM insight that the average investor holds the market.

Suppose ~~Buffet~~, I mean Huffet, is a value stock, headed by a manager who likes to buy companies trading for less than their fundamental value, measured, say, by book value. In the Fama–French model in equation (7.2), Huffet has a positive *HML* beta, $\beta_{i,HML}$. Value stocks, on average, do better than growth stocks. Relative to the CAPM, the expected return on Huffet is adjusted upward by $\beta_{i,HML} \times E(HML)$. Since *HML* is constructed to have a positive risk premium (remember, it goes long high book-to-market stocks, which are value stocks with high returns, and goes short low book-to-market stocks, which are growth stocks with low returns), the Fama–French nudges Huffet's risk premium upward to account for its "valueness."

Now consider a growth firm, ~~Enron~~, sorry Inron, which has grown rapidly through a series of acquisitions. Inron has a negative *HML* beta. Relative to the CAPM, the expected return on Inron is adjusted downward, since now $\beta_{i,HML} \times E(HML)$ is negative; because Inron is anti-value, or a growth stock, it carries a lower return.

In the Fama–French model, the *SML* and *HML* betas are centered around zero. The market is actually size neutral and value neutral. Just as the average investor holds the market, the average stock does not have any size or value tilt. It just has market exposure. Furthermore, in the CAPM, the average beta of a stock is one, which is also the beta of the market. The market itself could be affected by macro factors, like GDP growth, inflation, and the factors discussed in the

---

[19] The *SMB* and *HML* factors are sometimes given as examples of alternative (or smart) beta. I prefer to use the term dynamic factors because technically beta has the strict meaning of measuring exposure to a factor, rather than the factor itself. We invest in factor portfolios, not betas.

previous sections. The Fama–French model (7.2) prices value stocks like Huffet and growth stocks like Inron relative to the market.

One important assumption in the CAPM and Fama–French models is that the betas are constant. Empirical evidence shows that exposures of some assets to systematic factors vary over time and, in particular, increase during bad times.[20] The variation of betas themselves can be a source of risk. That betas tend to increase during bad times undoubtedly caused the negative returns of risky assets to be larger during the financial crisis than they otherwise would have been had their betas remained constant.

3.2. SIZE FACTOR

The size effect was discovered by Banz (1981), with similar results in Reinganum (1981), and refers to the fact that small stocks tended to do better than large stocks, after adjusting for their betas. The past tense is appropriate here, because since the mid-1980s there has not been any significant size effect.

Figure 7.6 plots the value of $1 invested in the *SMB* strategy after taking out the market effect beginning in January 1965 to December 2011 in the solid line.[21]

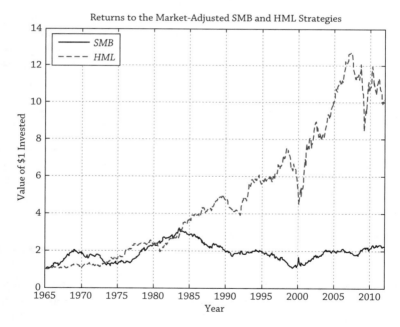

Figure 7.6

[20] See Ang and Chen (2002).

[21] *SMB*, *HML*, and *WML* data for Figures 7.6 and 7.7 are from http://mba.tuck.dartmouth.edu/pages/faculty/ken.french/data_library.html.

The compound returns of *SMB* reach a maximum right around the early 1980s—just after the early Banz and Reinganum studies were published. Since the mid-1980s there has been no premium for small stocks, adjusted for market exposure. International evidence since the mid-1980s has also been fairly weak. Examining international data, Dimson, Marsh, and Staunton (2011) state that if researchers today were uncovering the size effect, "the magnitude of the premium would not command particular attention, and would certainly not suggest there was a major 'free lunch' from investing in small caps." Fama and French (2012) also find no size premiums in a comprehensive international data set over recent periods.

There are two responses to the disappearance of the size effect. First, the original discovery of the size premium could have just been data mining. Fischer Black (1993) made this comment immediately after Fama and French's paper was released. The "discovery" of the size effect was then an example of Rosenthal's (1979) "file drawer problem," which is now a "hard drive problem" (and turning into a "cloud problem"). Researchers store on their hard drives 95% of the results that are statistically insignificant (using a standard p-value of 0.05 to judge significance) and only publish the 5% that are statistically significant. The discoverers of the size premium accidentally fell into the 5% category and were just lucky. One telling outcome of data mining is that an effect appears significant *in sample*, where the models are originally estimated, but it fails *out of sample*, where the models are tested after their discovery. Banz's size effect, therefore, might never have truly existed in the first place, and its finding by Banz and Reinganum was pure luck.[22]

The second response is that actually the size effect was there and actions of rational, active investors, acting on news of the finding, bid up the price of small cap stocks until the effect was removed.[23] In this context, the disappearance of the size effect represents the best of the Grossman–Stiglitz (1980) near-efficient market in which practitioners quickly exploit any anomaly. Viewed this way, size does not deserve to be a systematic factor and should be removed from the Fama–French model.

It should be noted that small stocks do have higher returns, on average, than large stocks. The effects of other factors, like value and momentum, which we discuss below, are also stronger in small stocks.[24] Small stocks also tend to be more illiquid than large stocks. The pure size effect refers to the possible excess returns of small stocks after adjusting for CAPM betas. The weak size effect today means that an asset owner should not tilt toward small stocks solely for higher risk-adjusted returns. There may only be a case for preferring small caps based on

---

[22] Harvey, Liu, and Zhu (2013) examine hundreds of factors explaining stock returns and investigate the effects of data mining on identifying factors.

[23] Schwert (2003), among others, present this argument.

[24] See Loughran (1997) for size–value interactions and Chen, Hong, and Stein (2007) for size–momentum interactions.

wanting to pursue higher returns without being able to short the market (to re-move small caps' market exposures) or an investor could tilt to small caps because she wishes high returns but cannot lever. The unconstrained, investment-only reason for small caps, however, is not compelling.

3.3. VALUE FACTOR

Unlike size, the value premium is robust. Figure 7.6 graphs cumulated returns on the value strategy, *HML*. Value has produced gains for the last fifty years.[25] There are several notable periods where value has lost money in Figure 7.6, some extend-ing over several years: the recession during the early 1990s, the roaring Internet bull market of the late 1990s, and there were large losses from value strategies in the financial crisis over 2007–2008. The risk of the value strategy is that although value outperforms over the long run, value stocks can underperform growth stocks during certain periods. It is in this sense that value is risky.

The benefits of value have been known since the 1930s. Graham and Dodd published a famous book, *Security Analysis*, in 1934, that serves as a guide to identifying firms with low prices relative to their fundamental value. Academics and practitioners proxy fundamental value today by various balance sheet vari-ables or transformations thereof. Graham and Dodd were at Columbia Business School, where I teach, and a strong value-investing tradition continues at my in-stitution today with the Heillbrunn Center for Graham & Dodd Investing. Modern academic research into the value effect began with Basu (1977), and the last few decades have seen an explosion of papers offering various explanations for the value premium. These explanations, like most of the finance literature, fall largely into two camps: the rational and the behavioral.

3.4. RATIONAL THEORIES OF THE VALUE PREMIUM

In the rational story of value, value stocks move together with other value stocks after controlling for market exposure (and in fact covary negatively with growth stocks). All value stocks, therefore, tend to do well together or they do badly to-gether. Finding a value stock that doesn't move together with the pack is like finding the sourpuss not thrashing at a heavy metal concert. Just as the eupho-ria can't last, and some fans experience throbbing migraines the next day, value doesn't always earn high returns. Value is risky, and the riskiness is shared to a greater or lesser degree by all value stocks. Some value risk can be diversified by creating portfolios of stocks, but a large amount of value movements cannot be diversified away. (In fact, Fama and French exploit this *common covariation* in constructing the *HML* factor.) In the context of the APT, since not all risk can be

---

[25] Interestingly, a few authors including Ang and Chen (2007) show that value did not exist in the first half of the twentieth century.

diversified away, the remaining risk must be priced in equilibrium, leading to a value premium.

The Fama–French model itself is silent on why value carries a premium. In contrast, the CAPM provides a theory of how the market factor is priced and even determines the risk premium of the market (see equation (7.1) and also chapter 7). To go further, we need to delve into an economic reason for why the value premium exists.

In the pricing kernel formulation, any risk premium exists because it is compensation for losing money during bad times. The key is defining what those bad times are. Let's look at Figure 7.6 again. The bad times for value do not always line up with bad times for the economy. Certainly value did badly during the late 1970s and early 1980s when the economy was in and out of recession. We had a recession in the early 1990s when value also did badly, and the financial crisis in 2008 was unambiguously a bad time when value strategies posted losses. But the bull market of the late 1990s? The economy was booming, yet value stocks got killed. Rational stories of value have to specify their own definitions of bad times when value underperforms, so that value earns a premium on average.

Some factors to explain the value premium include investment growth, labor income risk, nondurable or "luxury" consumption, and housing risk. A special type of "long-run" consumption risk also has had some success in explaining the value premium.[26] During some of the bad times defined by these factors, the betas of value stocks increase. This causes value firms to be particularly risky.[27]

Firm Investment Risk

A key insight into the behavior of value and growth firms was made by Berk, Green, and Naik (1999). They build on a *real option* literature where a manager's role is to optimally exercise real investment options to increase firm value.[28] A firm in this context consists of assets in place plus a set of investment options that managers can choose (or not) to exercise. The CAPM is a linear model, and it turns out that CAPM does not fully work when there are option features (see also chapter 10). Berk, Green, and Naik show that managers optimally exercise investment options when market returns are low. These investment options are dynamically linked to book-to-market (and size) characteristics, giving rise to a value premium. Value firms are risky; their risk turns out to be the same conventional bad times risk as the CAPM or other macro-based factors. Be a value investor only if you can stomach losses on these firms during these bad times.

---

[26] For a labor income risk explanation, see Santos and Veronesi (2006). Parker and Julliard (2005) and Lustig and van Nieuwerburgh (2005) consider luxury consumption and housing risk, respectively. For "long-run" consumption risk, see, for example, Bansal, Dittmar, and Lundblad (2005).

[27] For time-varying betas of value stocks, see Lettau and Ludvigson (2001b), Petkova and Zhang (2005), Lewellen and Nagel (2006), Ang and Chen (2007), and Ang and Kristensen (2012).

[28] This literature was started by McDonald and Siegel (1985).

Lu Zhang has written a series of papers explaining the value premium in terms of how value firms are risky as a result of their underlying production technologies. An important paper is Zhang (2005), which builds on the *production-based asset pricing* framework introduced by Cochrane (1991, 1996). Cochrane teaches us to look at firm investment to study firm returns. The gist of the Cochrane–Zhang story is as follows. Value firms and growth firms differ in how flexible they are and how quickly they can respond to shocks. During bad times, value firms are risky because they are burdened with more unproductive capital. Think of value firms as making stodgy widgets, and when a bad time comes, they cannot shift their firm activities to more profitable activities—they are stuck making widgets. They wish to cut back on capital, but they cannot sell their specialized widget-manufacturing equipment. In economists' jargon, they have *high and asymmetric adjustment costs*. Growth firms, however, can easily divest because they employ hotshot young employees and the great bulk of their capital is human capital, not stodgy widget-making factories. Thus, value firms are fundamentally riskier than growth firms and command a long-run premium.

Rational Implications for Asset Owners

The literature is still debating whether the bad times defined by these theories are truly bad times. But this academic debate is not that relevant to an asset owner; bickering over a Cochrane–Zhang story versus a story about another risk factor is not what the asset owner contemplating a value tilt should be doing.

Remember that the average investor holds the market portfolio. The asset owner should take these rational theories and ask, given that each factor defines a different set of bad times, are these actually bad times for me? If I do not need to eat less during periods when investment growth is low, then this is not as bad a time for me as it is for the average investor. Thus, I have a comparative advantage in holding value stocks and can harvest the value premium. Other investors are not comfortable holding value stocks (and should hold growth stocks instead) because they cannot afford to shoulder the losses generated by value stocks during bad times. Overall, the average investor holds the market even though some investors prefer value stocks and some investors prefer growth stocks. Which type you are—value or growth—depends on your own behavior during each of these bad times.

3.5. BEHAVIORAL THEORIES OF THE VALUE PREMIUM

Most behavioral theories of the value premium center around investor *overreaction* or *overextrapolation* of recent news. The standard story was first developed by Lakonishok, Shleifer, and Vishny (1994). Investors tend to overextrapolate past growth rates into the future. The posterchild growth stock example at the time of writing is Apple Inc. (AAPL), which has achieved tremendous growth over the last few years by introducing a series of must-have products. Investors mistake Apple's past high growth for future high growth. Growth firms, in general, have had high growth rates. The prices of these firms are bid up too high, reflecting excessive optimism. When this growth does not materialize, prices fall, leading to returns on growth stocks being low relative to value firms. The story here is that value stocks are not fundamentally riskier than growth firms, as in the rational stories. Value stocks are cheap because investors underestimate their growth prospects. Conversely growth firms are expensive because investors overestimate their growth prospects.

The value effect can also be produced by investors with other psychological biases. Barberis and Huang (2001) generate a value effect by employing two psychological biases: *loss aversion* and *mental accounting*. Loss aversion we have seen before, in chapter 2. Since investors suffer from losses more than they rejoice from equivalent gains, a loss following a loss is more painful than just a single loss. As for mental accounting, here agents look at each stock individually rather than considering overall gains and losses on their portfolios. The Barberis–Huang story of value is that a high book-to-market ratio stock is one that has achieved its relatively low price as the result of some dismal prior performance. This burned the investor who now views it as riskier and thus requires higher average returns to hold the stock.

The crucial question that behavioral models raise is: why don't more investors buy value stocks and, in doing so, push up their prices and remove the value premium, just as investors appear to have done with the size premium (at least according to the Grossman–Stiglitz interpretation)? Put another way, why aren't there more value investors? It can't be ignorance; the message of Graham and Dodd has spread far and wide since the 1930s, as demonstrated by the cult-like fervor of Berkshire Hathaway annual meetings, where value guru Warren Buffet holds court, or at the Graham & Dodd Breakfast conferences at Columbia Business School.

Perhaps investors think value investing is too difficult. Yet simple strategies of academics sorting stocks on a book-to-market basis are available even to the smallest retail investor using stock screens freely available on the Internet. Perhaps it is the legacy of the efficient market theory developed in the 1970s (see chapter 6)— but active managers have never believed in truly efficient markets, and now academics no longer believe in them either.

Maybe not enough institutions have sufficiently long horizons to effectively practice value investing. The value effect documented here, though, is different from the "deep value" practiced by some investors, including Buffet. That requires five- to ten-year horizons. The book-to-market value effect described here is a three- to six-month effect. But perhaps even this horizon is too long for most "long-horizon" investors.

Behavioral Implications for Asset Owners

The relevant question that an asset owner should ask from a behavioral standpoint is simple: do you act like the market, or do you have the ability not to overextrapolate or overreact? If you know you overextrapolate, do you overextrapolate less than the average investor? If you act like everyone else, then simply hold the market portfolio. If you overreact more, perhaps unconsciously, then you tilt toward growth stocks. If you can go against the crowd, then value investing is for you.

3.6. VALUE IN OTHER ASSET CLASSES

Value in essence buys assets with high yields (or low prices) and sells assets with low yields (or high prices). While in equities the strategy is called value-growth investing, the same strategy of buying high-yielding assets and selling low-yielding assets works in all asset classes but goes by different names. Many commentators view these different asset-class strategies as distinct, but they share many features. In fixed income, the value strategy is called *riding the yield curve* and is a form of the duration premium (see chapter 9). In commodities it is called the *roll return*, and the sign of the return is related to whether the futures curve is upward- or downward-sloping (see chapter 11).

In foreign exchange, the value strategy is called *carry*. This is a popular strategy that goes long currencies with high interest rates and shorts currencies with low interest rates. Traditionally, the former have been countries like Australia and New Zealand, and the latter have been countries like Japan and more recently the United States. In these cases, we can use versions of equation (7.2) within each asset class. For example, adapting Lustig, Roussanov, and Verdelhan (2011), we could capture the carry (or "value") returns of a foreign currency by using

$$E(FX_i) = \beta_{i,FX}E(HML_{FX}), \tag{7.3}$$

where FX_i is the foreign carry return of country i, $\beta_{i,FX}$ is the loading of currency i on the carry factor HML_{FX}, which is formed by going long currencies with high interest rates minus currencies with low interest rates. There is no conceptual difference between the value strategy in currencies in equation (7.3) and the value strategy in equities in equation (7.2) in terms of viewing low prices as equivalent to high yields.

Value strategies turn out to have some common components across asset classes, as shown by Koijen et al. (2012) and Asness, Moskowitz, and Pedersen (2013). While we have compelling stories, both rational and behavioral, of value strategies within equities, bond, and currency markets, we have few theories to link the risk premiums of value strategies across markets.[29] Nevertheless, value is a pervasive factor and theoretically can be implemented cheaply and in size by

---

[29] See chapter 9 for bonds and chapter 11 for commodities. Burnside et al. (2010) develop a disaster-based explanation of the carry trade, similar to the disaster explanations of the equity premium (see chapter 8).

a large investor. For small investors, there are low-cost index products for value strategies in equity, fixed income, and currency markets as well. The pervasiveness of value across many different asset classes turns out to be something an asset owner should exploit in factor investing, which we come back to in chapter 14.

3.7. MOMENTUM

Another standard investment factor is momentum. This burst onto the academic scene with Jegadeesh and Titman (1993) in the same year that Fama and French were capturing size and value factors.[30] Industry professionals like Richard Driehaus, a star mutual fund manager, had already been practicing momentum for decades.[31] Jegadeesh and Titman (1993) noted that Value Line, a vendor of financial data, has been providing price momentum signals in its publications since the 1980s.

Momentum Investing

Momentum is the strategy of buying stocks that have gone up over the past six (or so) months (winners) and shorting stocks with the lowest returns over the same period (losers). The momentum effect refers to the phenomenon that winner stocks continue to win and losers continue to lose. We call the momentum factor *WML*, for past winners minus past losers. (It is also called *UMD*, for stocks that have gone up minus stocks that have gone down.) The momentum strategy, like size and value, is a cross-sectional strategy, meaning that it compares one group of stocks (winners) against another group of stocks (losers) in the cross section, rather than looking at a single stock over time. Winners and losers are always relative—stocks win or lose relative to each other, and the market as a whole can go up or down.

Momentum returns blow size and value out of the water. Figure 7.7, which plots cumulated returns from January 1965 to December 2011, for *SMB*, *HML*, and *WML* speaks for itself. The cumulated profits on momentum strategies have been an order of magnitude larger than cumulated profits on size and value. Momentum is also observed in every asset class: we observe it in international equities, commodities, government bonds, corporate bonds, industries and sectors, and real estate.[32] In commodities, momentum is synonymous with commodities

---

[30] Momentum had appeared in the literature with Levy (1967) but was ignored until Jegadeesh and Titman's (1993) work.

[31] As recounted by Schwager (1992).

[32] See Asness, Moskowitz, and Pedersen (2012) for momentum in equities, government bonds, currencies, and commodities. The standard momentum effect based on past returns is weak in Japanese equities, but versions of momentum do work in Japan; see Chaves (2012). For momentum in corporate bonds and real estate, see Jostova et al. (2013) and Marcato and Key (2005), respectively. Menkhoff et al. (2012b) is a detailed look at momentum in currencies.

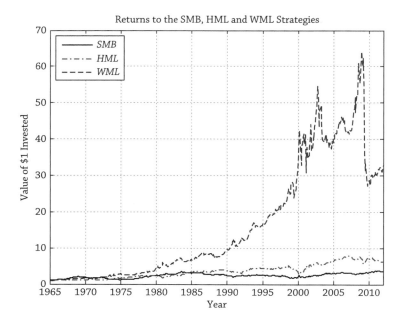

Figure 7.7

trading advisory funds. Momentum is also called "trend" investing, as in "the trend is your friend."

Momentum returns are not the opposite of value returns: in Figure 7.7, the correlation of *HML* with *WML* is only −16%. But many investors who claim that they are growth investors are actually momentum investors, especially mutual funds (see chapter 16), as pure growth underperforms value in the long run. There is one sense in which momentum is the opposite of value. Value is a *negative feedback strategy*, where stocks with declining prices eventually fall far enough that they become value stocks. Then value investors buy them when they have fallen enough to have attractive high expected returns. Value investing is inherently stabilizing. Momentum is a *positive feedback strategy*. Stocks with high past returns are attractive, momentum investors continue buying them, and they continue to go up! Positive feedback strategies are ultimately destabilizing and are thus subject to periodic crashes, as Figure 7.7 shows and as I discuss below.

The presence of momentum does not contradict the advice that I gave on rebalancing in chapter 4 for long-horizon investors. Momentum is primarily a *cross-sectional strategy* within an asset class: it looks at a particular group of stocks (those with past high returns) relative to another group of stocks (those with past low returns). Rebalancing, in contrast, should be done primarily at the asset class or strategy level because rebalancing requires the assets or strategies to exist over the long run while individual equities can disappear. Momentum manifests across asset classes, as does value.[33] It can be part of a long-run investor's opportunistic strategy (the Merton (1969) long-run hedging demand portfolio).

Momentum is often used as an investment factor, added onto the Fama–French model:[34]

$$E(r_i) = r_f + \beta_{i,MKT}E(r_m - r_f) + \beta_{i,SMB}E(SMB) + \beta_{i,HML}E(HML) + \beta_{i,WML}E(WML)$$
$$(7.4)$$

The same intuition applies as with the Fama–French model. The momentum beta, $\beta_{i,WML}$, is centered around zero. Winner stocks have positive momentum betas; their risk premiums are adjusted upward using equation (7.4). Loser stocks have negative momentum betas; their risk premiums are adjusted downward. The market, neither a relative winner nor a relative loser, is simply the market.

Characterizing Momentum Risk

Figure 7.7 shows that despite the large return, on average, of momentum strategies, momentum is prone to periodic crashes. Some of these have lasted for extended periods. Daniel and Moskowitz (2012) examine these in detail. Of the eleven largest momentum crashes, seven occurred during the Great Depression in the 1930s, one occurred in 2001, and the other three occurred during the financial crisis in 2008. The loser stocks then were tanking financials: Citi, Bank of America, Goldman, and Morgan Stanley, and some others hard hit by circumstances, like General Motors. Loser stocks have a tendency to keep losing, and lose they would have, were it not for Uncle Sam riding to their rescue. Government bailouts put a floor underneath the prices of these stocks, and they consequently skyrocketed. Since momentum strategies were short these stocks, momentum investors experienced large losses when these stocks rebounded. It is notable that the other big momentum drawdowns were concentrated during the Great Depression when policymakers also had great influence on asset prices. Momentum seems to reflect monetary policy and government risk during extraordinary times. These have also been times of high volatility.

What else explains momentum? Tantalizing suggestions in the literature suggest that at least some portion of momentum profits correlates with macro factors. Momentum profits, for example, vary over the business cycle and depend on the state of the stock market, and there is a link with liquidity.[35] In the rational story of momentum (which is still far from being fully fleshed out in the literature), asset owners should examine how they behave facing the various sources of macro risk discussed earlier.

---

[33] See Blitz and Van Vliet (2008).

[34] Carhart (1997) was the first to do this.

[35] See Chordia and Shivakumar (2002), Cooper, Gutierrez, and Hameed (2004), and Pástor and Stambaugh (2003), respectively.

The most widely cited theories are behavioral. In the main behavioral theories, momentum arises because of the biased way that investors interpret or act on information. Suppose good news on a stock comes out. Momentum can be generated in two ways. First, investors could have delayed overreaction to this news, causing the price to persistently drift upward. Second, investors could underreact to the news. The price initially goes up, but it does not go up as much as it should have to fully reflect how good the news actually was. Investors then learn and cause the stock to go up again the next period. Behavioral explanations, then, fall into two camps: momentum is an overreaction phenomenon, or it is an underreaction phenomenon. Distinguishing between these camps is difficult and still bedevils the literature.[36]

The seminal overreaction models are Barberis, Shleifer, and Vishny (1998) and Daniel, Hirshleifer, and Subrahmanyam (1998). Barberis, Shleifer, and Vishny's investors suffer from *conservatism bias*, which causes them to overreact to information because they stick doggedly to their prior beliefs. This causes momentum. In the Daniel, Hirshleifer, and Subrahmanyam model, investors also have psychological biases giving rise to momentum. In this model, investors are *overconfident* and overestimate their abilities to forecast firms' future cash flows. They also have biased *self-attribution*: when they are successful, it must be due to their skill, and when they are unsuccessful, it must be due to bad luck. Informed, overconfident investors (think of retail investors and overconfident hedge fund managers) observe positive signals about some stocks that perform well. These overconfident investors attribute the good performance to their own skill, leading to overconfidence. Based on increased confidence, they overreact and push up the prices of stocks above their fundamental values, generating momentum.

The standard reference for the underreaction theory is Hong and Stein (2000). Hong and Stein rely on "bounded rational" investors who have limited information. Momentum in Hong and Stein's model is caused by "news watchers" who receive signals of firm value but ignore information in the history of prices. Other investors trade only on past price signals and ignore fundamental information. The information received by the news watchers is received with delay and is only partially incorporated into prices when first revealed to the market. This causes underreaction.

In both the underreaction and overreaction models, prices eventually reverse when they revert to fundamentals in the long run.

Implications for Asset Owners

In the context of these behavioral stories, the asset owner should think about what types of psychological biases that she has and how these biases differ from those of the average investor. Do you overreact (or underreact) in a way similar

---

[36] See, for example, Jegadeesh and Titman (2001).

to the market? You should also think about how the market's psychological biases can change. Momentum strategies are negatively skewed; the skewness of the momentum strategy in Figure 7.7 is –1.43. At a minimum, the investor should be able to tolerate large drawdowns induced by momentum strategies. Historically, these declines are concentrated in periods when policymakers have interrupted natural progressions of momentum, as in the Great Depression and the financial crisis.

4. Value Investing Redux

Factor risks represent bad times for an investor. There are two main types of factors—macro factors and investment factors. Assets are exposed to factor risks. The higher the exposure for a factor with a positive risk premium (the higher the asset's beta), the higher the asset's expected return.

The value strategy is an example of an investment style factor. In a rational story, value produces losses during bad times, and value stocks are risky. These bad times could coincide with bad times of the economy, as proxied by poor economic growth or poor returns of the market, or they could correspond with bad outcomes of other factors like firm investment. The average investor dislikes these bad times and requires a risk premium to hold value stocks. Thus, value stocks earn high returns to compensate investors for lousy returns during bad times. In behavioral stories, value stocks have high returns because investors underestimate the growth rates of value stocks. They overextrapolate the past growth rates of growth, or glamour, stocks, leading to growth stocks being overpriced and value stocks underpriced. If these behavioral biases are not arbitraged away, value stocks have high excess returns.

In the next two chapters, we turn to characterizing the factor risk–return trade-offs of the bread-and-butter asset classes, equities and fixed income, which can be considered factors in their own right.

CHAPTER 8

Equities

Chapter Summary

Equities have historically exhibited high returns relative to bonds and cash (bills). The equity risk premium is a reward for bearing losses during bad times, which are defined by low consumption growth, disasters, or long-run risks. Equities are a surprisingly poor hedge against inflation. While theory suggests that equity risk premiums are predictable, predictability is hard to detect statistically. Equity volatility, however, is much more forecastable.

1. The Lost Decade

The 2000s were the Lost Decade for stock returns. Figure 8.1 plots the cumulated returns of $1 invested at January 1, 2000 through December 31, 2010 in the S&P 500, Treasury bonds, or Treasury bills (which I call cash). The performance of stocks was dismal. Stock returns started to decline in late 2000 and then the terrorist attacks of September 11, 2001, and the subsequent recession sent stock returns into a tailspin. By September 2002, stocks ended up cumulatively losing more than 40 cents of that initial $1 investment. Stocks recovered over the mid-2000s but lost money again in 2007 as subprime mortgages started to deteriorate. Then came the global financial crisis. In 2008, stocks lost 37% of their value. As policymakers stabilized financial markets and the economy began to improve, stocks bounced back in 2009. But the initial $1 invested in stocks at the beginning of the decade had grown to only $1.05 by December 31, 2010. Investors would have done better simply holding Treasury bills, which cumulated to $1.31 at December 31, 2010. Bonds, however, trounced stocks and bills, finishing the decade at $2.31.

While stocks did poorly in the Lost Decade, they have exhibited a high risk premium relative to bonds and cash over long periods. Figure 8.2 plots average returns (on the y-axis) and volatilities (on the x-axis) for nineteen countries and the world from 1900 to 2010 for stocks and bonds as reported by Dimson, Marsh, and Staunton (2011). The countries are Australia, Belgium, Canada, Denmark,

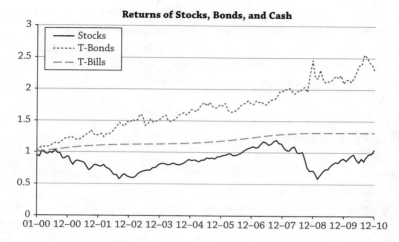

Figure 8.1

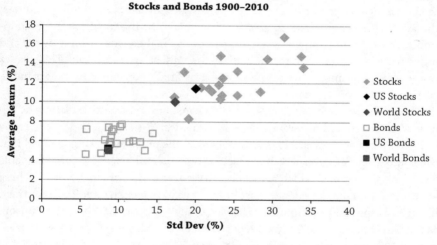

Figure 8.2

Finland, France, Germany, Ireland, Italy, Japan, the Netherlands, New Zealand, Norway, South Africa, Spain, Sweden, Switzerland, the United Kingdom, and the United States. The United States and the world are highlighted separately. Notice in Figure 8.2 how equities around the world congregate toward the upper right-hand corner of the graph, while bonds around the world are grouped together at the lower left-hand corner. Stocks, therefore, have yielded much higher returns than bonds over long periods of time, but with more volatility. In the United States, the equity return has been 11.4% compared to 5.2% for bonds. Equity return volatility was 20.0% compared to 8.6% for bonds. Thus, over the long run, there has been a considerable equity premium in excess of bonds, but it comes with significantly higher volatility.

Going forward, will the equity premium continue to be high? Or will the next ten years be another Lost Decade for stocks? To answer these questions, we must understand what factors explain equity return performance and volatility and ascertain whether these risk factors will persist in the future. These are issues of how the *aggregate market* is priced and moves over time.

2. The Equity Risk Premium

In previous chapters we've described how risk premiums arising from factor risks compensate investors for bearing losses during bad times. One of those factors, described in chapter 7, was *consumption*—which was part of a broader set of variables capturing economic growth in general. In a *consumption-based asset pricing model*, all risk is summarized by consumption—bad times occur when society, or all agents in the economy, are consuming less. We summarize all agents in society by assuming a *representative agent*, which we can think about as the average person or investor. To compensate investors for holding equities, the average investor earns an *equity risk premium*. In the most basic consumption models, there is only one factor, per capita real consumption growth, and other factors matter only to the extent they affect consumption. This makes sense because ultimately we care about what is finally consumed by agents in the economy.

The *equity premium puzzle* is that, using consumption as a risk factor, the equity premium should be very modest. How modest? In 1985, a paper written by Rajnish Mehra and Edward Prescott challenged the profession. They claimed that the equity premium over risk-free assets should be well below 1% for reasonable levels of risk aversion, which are levels of risk aversion between 1 and 10. These are the risk aversion levels that most individuals have (see chapter 2). In contrast, historically the equity premium has been very high. Over 1900–2010, the Dimson, Marsh, and Staunton (2011) data reported in Figure 8.2 show that the average return of U.S. equities in excess of bonds was 6.2% and in excess of bills was 7.4%. The world equity premium in excess of bonds was 5.0% and in excess of bills was 6.0%. Thus, equities have historically had much higher returns than predicted by simple economic models.

Mehra and Prescott titled their paper, "The Equity Premium: A Puzzle," and it quickly spawned a new literature.[1] They based their model on Lucas (1978), which is one of the most influential papers in financial economics and was a factor in Robert Lucas's Nobel Prize in 1995. Prescott himself would go on to win the Nobel in 2004 for advancements in macroeconomic modeling.

---

[1] A recent summary is Mehra (2006).

Lucas showed how asset prices responded to an economy's factors and that these prices were set by agents' optimal consumption and market clearing. In Mehra and Prescott's adaptation of Lucas, the factor was consumption, and there was a representative agent with constant relative risk aversion (CRRA) preferences (see chapter 2).[2] Just as the capital asset pricing model prices all assets through exposure through the market factor, consumption-based asset pricing explains the returns of all assets through exposure to the consumption factor. The relation between the consumption factor, though, and how it enters the risk premiums of individual assets is a transformation that depends on the representative agent's degree of risk aversion.

To gain intuition why the returns of equity are anomalously high relative to this simple setting, Table 8.3 reports log returns of the S&P 500 with real consumption growth over June 1947 to December 2010. The Sharpe ratios are approximately 0.3 using either a nominal short rate of 5% or a real short rate of 2%. Table 8.3 shows that the volatilities of equity returns and consumption growth do not line up: equity volatility is high, around 17%, while consumption volatility is low, around 2%. Equity returns are also poorly correlated with real consumption growth, with a correlation of below 15%. Thus, when bad times of low consumption growth occur, equity returns do not tend to fall. Since equities do not exhibit losses when agents experience bad times, as measured by times of slowing consumption, the equilibrium risk premium should be low.

A skeptical reader might now be asking, "So what?" Consumption does not move around very much, and there are better proxies for economic growth (see chapter 7). I have also told you that most agents do not have mean-variance type utility functions, of which CRRA is an example (see chapter 2). Is this equity

Table 8.3

	Log S&P 500 Returns, Consumption Growth		
	Nominal Stock Returns	Real Stock Returns	Real Consumption Growth
Mean	10.4%	7.1%	3.3%
Stdev	16.5%	16.6%	1.7%
Sharpe Ratio	0.328	0.308	
	with 5% nom	with 2% real	

[2] In the context of factor theory (see chapter 6), Mehra–Prescott's world has a nonlinear pricing kernel, which is given by how the representative agent responds (at the margin) to changes in real consumption growth.

premium puzzle—that equity returns are high relative to this highly stylized, artificial, Mehra–Prescott economy—purely academic, or does it have relevance for how we invest assets in the real world?

The equity premium puzzle is important because many investors hold large amounts of equities based on the historical record of high returns. Will such returns persist going forward, as in our motivating example, or will equity returns permanently enter a new phase that looks more like an enduring version of the 2000s' Lost Decade? Understanding the reasons for the equity premium provides a rational basis for deciding whether we should continue to hold lots of equities in the future, rather than simply continuing to do so because that's what we have done in the past. While economists have developed many explanations, I cover four that are most relevant for investors.

3. Explanations for the Equity Premium Puzzle

3.1. MARKET RISK AVERSION IS (SOMETIMES) VERY HIGH

The first resolution to the equity premium puzzle is that the market's risk aversion is extremely high. It can be shown that a lower bound for the risk aversion of the market, γ, or the representative agent's risk aversion, is given by

$$\gamma > \frac{Sharpe\ Ratio}{\sigma_c}, \tag{8.1}$$

where *Sharpe Ratio* denotes the Sharpe Ratio of the equity market portfolio and σ_c is the volatility of real consumption growth.[3]

The lower bounds for risk aversion given by the data in Table 8.3 are approximately 20. These are much larger than the upper bounds of "reasonable" risk aversion levels of 10 claimed by Mehra and Prescott and discussed in chapter 2. If we compute the implied risk aversion levels exactly assuming lognormal consumption growth, then risk aversion of the average investor to match the equity premium is above 120. Estimates like these are pervasive throughout the literature beginning with the seminal work of Hansen and Singleton (1983).

Maybe the representative agent's risk aversion is high, perhaps even above 120. This is problematic for the obvious reason that individuals do not have risk aversion that high. There is a second reason labeled the *risk-free rate puzzle* due to Philippe Weil (1989). While very high risk aversion can match the equity premiums in data, high risk aversions also raise the risk-free rate in the Mehra–Prescott model. A very risk-averse representative agent would demand a high premium to

---

[3] See Cochrane (2001) for a derivation. This is a special case of a more general bound on the pricing kernel (see chapter 6) developed by Hansen and Jagannathan (1991). Lars Hansen received his Nobel Prize in 2013.

hold equities, but this agent wishes to have extremely smooth consumption paths over time. Risk-free rates need to be very high to induce them not to smooth consumption. It turns out that the question, "why are equity returns so high?" is the flipside of the question, "why are risk-free rates so low?" If we're *over* compensated for investing in equities, we're *under*compensated for investing in bonds.

A class of models with *time-varying risk aversion* can explain the equity premium puzzle. Let us illustrate how they work by looking at the model of *habit utility*. We have come across these utility functions before, in chapter 2, where they were used to construct utility of wealth relative to some level, rather than using the utility of wealth itself. In habit utility, the utility of the representative agent depends on consumption relative to past consumption or a *habit level*. A canonical model is by Campbell and Cochrane (1999).

Consider a young college graduate who is accustomed to sleeping on sofas, sharing apartments, and driving second-hand cars. She gets a job as a barista. Then she suddenly gets laid off. This is, of course, a bad time, but it does not hurt that much because she is already used to her frugal lifestyle. Her consumption has not declined by much relative to her habit. Now suppose that upon graduation she lands a high-flying job (on Wall Street, I guess). Her consumption increases because her income is now very high. She moves into her own place with a wonderful view, buys a brand new car, and starts a wardrobe of designer clothing. Her consumption habit has increased. Now when she is suddenly laid off, this is a *very* bad time. She actually might have more money from some savings than as a barista, but her habitual consumption level is very high, and so the drop in her consumption relative to her habit hurts a lot. Her *marginal utility* is very high because she is used to having high consumption and has to go back to low consumption. In habit models, it is not the consumption decrease per se that matters; what matters instead is the consumption decrease relative to habit.

Habit models allow *local* risk aversion to be very high. When recessions hit, risk aversion can shoot up to very high levels—the risk aversions of 20 or even 100 required by equation (8.1)—but the increase is temporary. In economists' jargon, marginal utility is very high during recessions as consumption approaches habit; the agent really values that extra $1, and the curvature of the utility function is very steep. Although consumption itself barely falls during recessions, the small reductions in consumption bring agents perilously close to their habits. Thus, agents become very risk averse during bad times, generating high equity risk premiums. Equity prices fall in recessions to generate high future returns.

In good times, consumption is far above habit. Risk aversion is low, and equity premiums are small. In these good times, marginal utility is low, and the representative agent's utility function is very flat. During booms, equities are expensive, and there is not much room for future appreciation; hence, future expected returns are low. Since expected returns are high during bad times and low during good times, another benefit of time-varying risk aversion models is that they match how equity returns can be predicted over time, a subject that we cover in section 5 below. Overall, the very high risk aversion during bad times dominates the low risk aversion during good times, resulting in a high long-run equity risk premium.

If time-varying risk aversion, which increases dramatically during bad times, is responsible for the equity risk premium, then investors should ask the following question before holding large equity stakes: In bad times, say, of low consumption growth in the basic Mehra–Prescott model or bad times more generally in a multifactor context, do you behave in a less risk-averse fashion than the market?

Most investors and the representative investor, by construction, become much more risk averse during recessions: bad times are spooky, so everyone gets scared—but to greater or lesser degrees. The question is whether you can tolerate these bad times better than the average investor. The Norwegian sovereign wealth fund certainly can since it has stable cash flows, no immediate liabilities, and a well-functioning governance structure. Supreme Court Justices are well situated to tolerate bad times since their income stream is risk free (unless they have borrowed money to the hilt). And many private wealth management clients also find bad times for the economy hurt less for them than for the average investor. These special types of investor have lower risk aversions during downside events and can tolerate larger losses during bad times. They can hold more equities. In doing so, they will earn higher average returns.

3.2. DISASTER RISK

Disaster models take bad times to the extreme. The bad times are really, really bad: they represent catastrophic declines in consumption. In this explanation, the equity premium is the reward to compensate for rare catastrophes.[4] This story was introduced by Rietz (1988) and immediately dismissed by Mehra and Prescott (1988) as lacking empirical evidence. But the disaster explanation has made a recent roaring comeback beginning with Barro (2008), who examined the data much more thoroughly. Catastrophes are labeled "black swans" by Nassim Taleb (2004) in the popular literature, although he would object to having them treated in a rational paradigm.[5] They cannot be predicted or at least are very hard to predict, and for disasters to account for high equity risk premiums, the disasters must be very bad indeed.

---

[4] More generally, they do not need to be large, sudden negative jumps per se. They can be a series of persistent, large losses in the left-hand tails. Martin (2012) shows that asset prices reflect the possibility of extraordinary bad news that nests but does not necessarily need the assumption of aggregate disaster risk.

[5] The recent financial crisis cannot be considered as an example of an averted disaster to explain the equity premium. While there was a downturn in economic growth and consumption, the downturn happened as a result of the crash in financial prices, rather than the other way round. In disaster models, sharp contractions of consumption happen contemporaneously with falls in asset prices.

Mehra and Prescott's original skepticism was not without merit. Looking only at U.S. data, there has not been a large drop in consumption, except for the Great Depression in the 1930s, and even then it was not catastrophic.[6] Looking more broadly at data from other countries and using a long time series, however, Barro and Ursua (2011) document some sizeable drops in consumption and GDP—even for countries that are large and developed today. For example, Barro and Ursua report that Germany's consumption declined by 41% in 1945 and Japan's fell by 50% during World War II. The United States and the United Kingdom have been more tranquil, with the largest decline being 16% for the United States in 1921 and 17% for the United Kingdom in 1945. But these are exceptions. For many countries, macroeconomic disasters have been truly calamitous. Russia's consumption fell 71% in World War I and the Russian Revolution and again by 58% during World War II (poor Russia!). China's GDP (not consumption) fell 50% from 1936 to 1946, and Turkey's consumption fell 49% during World War II.

The disaster explanation is also labeled a *peso problem*, which refers to a very low probability event that is not observed in the sample. The U.S. equity premium is high because it reflects the probability of a disaster, but so far we have not observed that disaster. The first published use of the term "peso problem" appears in Krasker (1980) in the context of the phenomenon that the Mexican peso traded at a steep discount on the forward market during the early 1970s. It appeared to be mispriced, but market participants were expecting in a devaluation that eventually occurred in August 1976. Researchers only looking at the early 1970s sample would have concluded that an asset price—the forward peso—appeared anomalous because a crash had not occurred in the sample available to them. Likewise, the U.S. equity premium may appear too high because we have not observed a disaster in the U.S. sample.

If equities command a risk premium because of infrequent crash risk, then the pertinent question to ask an investor is how he can weather such disasters. Of course, there are some disasters so ruinous that an entire society disappears, and a new one takes its place, such as the Russian Revolution in 1918 and the rise of modern Communist China, where all domestic investors are wiped out. (This by itself should be a good reason for diversifying across countries as mean-variance investing advocates; see chapter 3.) The fact that we have not seen a truly terrible consumption disaster in the United States should give us pause. The extreme advice implied by this theory is that equity investors should stockpile AK-47s and MREs in their basements in case society collapses. Before the cataclysm comes, equity returns will be high; that equity returns are in fact high, on average, foretells the cataclysm to come. We just haven't seen it yet.

---

[6] For the entire economy. Certainly it was catastrophic for certain individuals like the Joad family, in John Steinbeck's *Grapes of Wrath*.

My interpretation of the disaster theory for asset owners is that it reemphasizes the importance of downside outcomes, as I stressed in chapter 2. There, I stressed that mean-variance utility does not cut it in capturing how investors respond to bad events. The disaster story says that those bad events can indeed be very bad, and they are systematically very bad for the entire economy. We need to think about how investors behave in these bad outcomes—a joint statement about the utility function and the data-generating process, which must capture disaster events. Investors who are relatively the best off in severe economic crashes (all investors will be affected adversely during disasters; it is a question of how much) are in the best position to hold large amounts of equities. The overall message is that investors need to think about how bad these events can be, how they can respond to meeting their liabilities, and how they react to these risks when these bad events arrive.

Disasters suggest that another explanation for the high equity premium is that it is a result of markets that have survived ex post. In the early 1900s, you could have invested in China or Russia, and you would have lost everything. You could also have invested in Hungary, Czechoslovakia (which were together part of the Austro-Hungarian Empire), Poland, and Greece, but you would not have been able to trade equities again in those countries until the late twentieth century. Jorion and Goetzmann (1999) argue that the realized equity premium is high because we compute the equity return on countries that have survived. Had we computed the returns including all the countries whose markets disappeared, then the premiums would be much lower. Thus, survivorship bias makes the equity premium too high. The true equity premium, which is the one that is relevant for the future, is lower.

I believe this argument only increases the mystery of the equity premium. The equity premium is measured relative to bonds or bills, and sovereign bonds in many countries fared worse than equities. If you invested in German equities in 1900, there were long periods during which markets were closed (like the credit crisis of the early 1930s, World War II, and the occupation by the Allies after World War II), but equity markets survived and eventually German equity holders did well. Holders of German bonds got nothing. First they were ravaged by hyperinflation in the 1920s, and then there was a default on Reichsmark claims when the Deutschmark was introduced in 1948. Of course, in some countries, including Russia and China, both equity holders and debt holders were wiped out. But, in many countries with structural breaks, equity holders eked out a (sometimes modest) long-term return while bond holders were decimated. If the equity premium is measured relative to bonds, this survivorship bias of markets exacerbates the equity premium puzzle. The historical superiority of equities relative to bonds in disasters does carry some implications for factor investing, which I discuss in chapter 14.

3.3. LONG-RUN RISK

Real consumption growth, which we observe in data, has an autocorrelation close to zero. The data in Table 8.3, for example, exhibit a quarterly autocorrelation of 0.08. The basic Mehra–Prescott model assumes that the consumption shocks are independent and identically distributed (i.i.d.), or that they cannot be forecasted. In an influential article, Bansal and Yaron (2004) change this assumption to specifying that the mean of consumption growth is not constant but wanders around so slowly that it is extremely hard to distinguish between an i.i.d. process and this slow, persistent process where there is a small amount of forecastability.[7] This changing consumption process is what Bansal and Yaron call long-run risk.[8] Bansal and Yaron also alter the basic CRRA preference in the Mehra–Prescott framework so that the representative agent cares much more about long-run risks.[9] The Bansal–Yaron long-run risk model has been adapted to many different contexts and explains a wide variety of stylized facts including the equity premium puzzle and the risk-free rate puzzle of this section.[10]

Europe at the time of writing is a wonderful example of the long-run risk story at play. Current shocks, say, from a particular raucous parliamentary vote in some euro zone country, have an effect on today's expectation about future economic growth. But they also have an effect on economic growth ten to twenty years in the future. The vote could diminish current productivity, but lowering current productivity might keep Europe on a low-growth path for a long time. Long-run risks exist. The special preferences Bansal and Yaron employ differentiate between the short-run and the long-run effect of these shocks. Equities are particularly sensitive to long-run risk, not surprisingly, because equity is a long-lived (in fact, perpetual) security.

The second channel that Bansal and Yaron employ is that the fundamental consumption factor exhibits time-varying volatility. Agents dislike volatility components and asset prices reflect the volatility risk. As volatility increases, asset valuation declines. The Bansal–Yaron model has separate risk compensations for consumption growth and for consumption volatility.

---

[7] Bansal and Yaron (2004) also specify that the volatility of the conditional mean of consumption varies over time.

[8] Predictability in consumption growth had been considered before, but allowing for simple autocorrelated consumption growth actually makes the equity premium puzzle worse with CRRA utility because it smooths out consumption, requiring even higher degrees of risk aversion to match the data. See Dunn and Singleton (1986) for an early attempt.

[9] Specifically, the representative agent wishes to have smooth consumption paths, but the way that these consumption paths are smoothed is different from risk aversion, which measures how an agent treats different risky betas at a given moment in time. These are called Epstein and Zin (1989) preferences, and they are also used in the disaster framework.

[10] See Bansal (2007) for a summary of this literature that was already large by then.

There are three lessons for an asset owner:

1. Many assets can lose money in the short run.
   This is the standard channel of how we should evaluate risk.
2. What appears safe in the short run can, in fact, be quite risky over the long run.
   The market cares about long-run risk, and small adjustments made today can result in large effects in twenty to thirty years time. In the context of factor model theory, assets with large exposures to long-run risk (high long-run risk betas) need to have high returns. It turns out that assets with high long-run risk betas include value stocks and other popular investment strategies such as currency carry trades.[11] How much long-run risk can you tolerate as an investor?
3. Volatility as a risk factor matters.
   In Bansal–Yaron, it is consumption volatility, but in a more general setting, it is macro volatility. Volatility risk is different from consumption (macro) risk. It carries its own risk premium. We discussed volatility as a risk factor in chapter 7.

3.4. HETEROGENEOUS INVESTORS

One criticism of Mehra–Prescott involved the assumption of the representative agent. The world has *heterogeneous* investors, not a single representative agent.[12] Perhaps the representative agent isn't really representative. This was first shown by Jerison (1984), in a paper that never got published but was expanded and extended by Kirman (1992). Jerison and Kirman show that in some circumstances the preferences of the representative agent are not the (weighted) average of preferences of individual agents in the economy. To be blunt, if all agents in the economy prefer bananas over apples, it is possible to construct a representative agent who prefers apples over bananas. Furthermore, how that representative agent feels about apples versus bananas in different states of the world leads to the same prices as the economy where individual agents optimize and prefer bananas over apples. Thus, rejecting a representative agent model with implausibly high risk aversion may not say anything about how a true heterogeneous agent economy works.

The profession remains wedded to representative agent models, though. Some of the reasons are historical and due to tractability; representative agent models are much easier to solve than heterogeneous agent models. But one good reason is that, in a world full of heterogeneous agents, there is still economic meaning for a representative agent even though he may not be the "average" agent, where the average is a simple average or even an average taken over wealth. In fact, some

---

[11] See Bansal, Dittmar, and Lundblad (2005) and Bansal and Shaliastovich (2010), respectively.
[12] Heterogeneous agent models were first examined by Bewley (1977).

solution methods of heterogeneous agent models are solved this way by constructing a representative agent with special weights, where the weights do not necessarily correspond to wealth or income.[13] The weights on some agents may be zero. Agents with small proportions of total wealth in heterogeneous agent models can have very large effects in determining prices.

In this context, the representative agent should not be interpreted as the average agent, but as the *marginal* agent. Prices are set through how the marginal agent responds to small changes in factor shocks, which is different from how the average agent responds. For the asset owner weighing optimal equity allocations, the context of the previous sections—whether bad times for me correspond to bad times for the average agent or whether my risk aversion increases when the risk aversion of the average agent increases—are identical except that we ask the questions in the context of the agents determining prices at the margin. For example, can I absorb losses during bad times more than the asset managers forced to liquidate at fire-sale prices? Am I exposed to the same margin calls as hedge funds?

In heterogeneous agent models, a new factor arises that determines risk premiums. Asset prices now depend on the cross-sectional distribution of agent characteristics. This can be the cross-sectional distribution (across agents) of wealth, beliefs, labor income shocks, or other variables in which investors differ.[14] In Constantinides and Duffie (1996), agents exhibit heterogeneity by how much they earn. They also cannot completely hedge the risk of job loss (as in the real world). Constantinides and Duffie show that if income inequality increases during recessions (more formally, the cross-sectional variance of idiosyncratic labor income shocks increases), as it does in data, the equity premium will be high. Intuitively, in recessions, the probability of job losses increases and equities drop in value. That is, equities are poor hedges for insuring against the risk of losing your job and won't pay off when your boss has fired you and you need to eat. These considerations make equities quite unattractive and mean that equities must exhibit a high return in equilibrium to induce investors to hold them.

The income shocks that workers face in the Constantinides and Duffie world are an example of *market incompleteness*. This refers to risks that cannot be hedged or removed in aggregate and thus, in effect, serve to increase the total amount of risk that all agents (or the implied representative agent) face. A similar effect can be engineered by constraints, such as those on borrowing.[15] During bad times, some investors may face binding funding constraints that force them to behave

---

[13] These are called Negishi (1960) weights.

[14] Models with heterogeneity in risk aversion, which give rise to the factor of a cross-sectional wealth distribution, were developed by Dumas (1989) and Wang (1996). For models with heterogeneity in beliefs, see David (2008).

[15] See, among many others, Constantinides and Duffie (1996) and Constantinides, Donaldson, and Mehra (2002).

in an extremely risk averse way, which manifests in their selling equities. An investment bank, for example, cannot roll over its debt or there are outflows from an asset manager. Both of these situations can similarly raise the aggregate risk aversion of the economy during bad times.

For an asset owner contemplating a large position in equities, heterogeneity implies that she should think not only about how she is different from the market (or the marginal or representative agent) but also what kind of investor she is relative to the full distribution of investors. The behavior of these other investors and how they interact affects asset prices. The main intuition of bad times survives in these heterogeneous agent models—the equity premium is high because some agents (they do not have to be numerous, but when they matter, they matter a lot) find that equity is unattractive for their set of bad times. These may not be bad times for her, and if so, she should hold an above-average allotment of equities.

The problem in applying the insights of heterogeneous agent models to investment policy is that the world is so heterogeneous. It is unclear what dimensions—risk aversion, wealth, loss capacity, leverage capacity, (lack of) liabilities, income, or aversion to downside events—we should emphasize. It is often difficult, if not impossible, to measure cross-sectional characteristics of investor types, which the heterogeneous agent economies predict should be useful candidate factors. Since a representative agent often arises in these models anyway, my advice is to concentrate on the first three explanations of the equity risk premium in terms of considering how you differ from the market. The implication from heterogeneous agent models is that you may interpret the "market" as the "marginal investor" as well as the "average investor."

4. Equities and Inflation

4.1. STOCKS ARE A BAD INFLATION HEDGE

Equity is a real security, in the sense that it represents a claim on real, productive assets of firms. But it turns out that equities actually are not a real security in the sense that "real" means "inflation adjusted" or the opposite of "nominal." In fact quite the opposite: equities are bad at hedging inflation risk.[16]

That may surprise you but take a look at Figure 8.4, which graphs correlations between inflation and stock returns, excess stock returns relative to T-bills (cash), and T-bill returns from 1926 to 2010. Inflation hedging is about the co-movement of assets with inflation, not about long-run average returns. The correlations are computed over various horizons measured in years on the x-axis. I use log returns and log inflation changes so that the long-horizon returns are sums of the short frequency, one-month returns (see the appendix).

---

[16] An early reference on the negative relationship between equity returns and inflation is Lintner (1975).

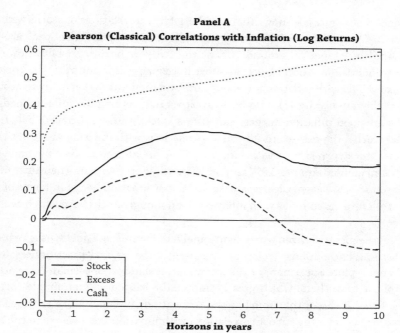

Panel A
Pearson (Classical) Correlations with Inflation (Log Returns)

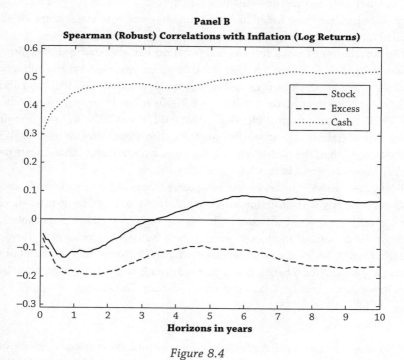

Panel B
Spearman (Robust) Correlations with Inflation (Log Returns)

Figure 8.4

Panel A of Figure 8.4 shows that the short-term correlations of stocks with inflation are low—below 10%. Moving out to four to five years, they peak around 30% and then taper off around 20% at the ten-year horizon. T-bills, however, are a wonderful inflation hedge. At short horizons, below one year, the correlations of T-bills with inflation are above 20% and then increase steadily to around 60% at the ten-year horizon. Because raw stock returns are poor inflation hedges, T-bills are good inflation hedges, and excess stock returns subtract T-bills from stock returns, the excess stock return correlations with inflation are lower than the raw stock correlations with inflation. They are around zero below one year, reach a maximum around 10% around years three to four, and then turn negative around year seven. Clearly, stocks are a poor inflation hedge in terms of the way stock returns co-move with inflation, even though stocks have a high average return.[17]

The true picture is even worse than Panel A of Figure 8.4. Panel A uses Pearson, or classical, correlations, which most of the literature and practitioners focus on. Panel B plots Spearman, or robust, rank correlations. Spearman correlations are robust to outliers, which greatly impact the calculations of simple correlations. Panel B shows that some of the correlations in Panel A are spurious and caused by outliers; the robust correlations with inflation are lower than the simple correlation measures in Panel A. Notably the correlations of excess stock returns are now negative for all horizons and after one year, range between −20% and −10%.

The correlation of stock returns and inflation has also changed over time, as shown in Figure 8.5. Figure 8.5 plots the rolling ten-year classical and robust correlations of excess stock returns and inflation. For some of the 1940s and 1950s, the correlation was positive, but from the 1950s it has been negative. Recently, post-2000, the correlation is barely positive (still below 10%), at least measured by simple correlations, but it remains negative after accounting for outliers. While it has changed sign, the correlation of excess stock returns and inflation has never reached above 20% and in fact has gone below −40%.

T-bills are a good inflation hedge, producing three- to five-year (simple and robust) correlations with inflation close to 0.5 because short-term interest rates directly reflect expected inflation. This is through the Fisher hypothesis and through the actions of monetary policy, which we cover in chapter 9. However, a good inflation hedge does not necessarily mean an overall high nominal or real return; a good inflation hedge is an asset that tends to move together with inflation. In terms of returns, T-bills just beat inflation. The average return of T-bills

---

[17] Ang, Brière, and Signori (2012) also find that within the cross section of equities, it is difficult to find individual stocks that can hedge inflation risk by computing stock inflation betas. Konchitchki (2011) finds more success in finding individual stocks that correlate highly with inflation using accounting data.

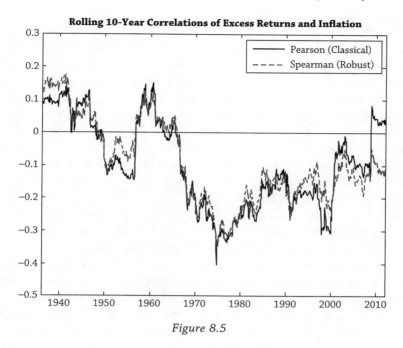

Figure 8.5

in the sample is 3.5%, and the long-run average inflation rate is 2.9%. In comparison, equities have an average return of 9.3% and handily beat inflation in the long run. Equity does well—the equity premium is high (see sections 2 and 3). But equity does not co-move with inflation, and this makes equity a bad inflation hedge.

The negative relation of equities and inflation is not particular to the United States. Bekaert and Wang (2010) regress asset returns around the world onto inflation. A good inflation hedge should have an inflation beta of one. Bekaert and Wang find that inflation betas of equities are generally negative for all developed markets, with an average of −0.25. Even when they are positive in certain developed countries, the inflation betas are low and far from one. For example, the North American inflation beta is −0.42 and the EU inflation beta is 0.27. Interestingly, emerging markets do have positive inflation betas close to one, with an average of 1.01.

High inflation is good for those who owe and bad for their creditors. Corporate debt is denominated almost exclusively in nominal terms and high inflation reduces the debt outstanding in real terms. This is beneficial for borrowers at the expense of lenders. Most companies issue debt, which means that the equity market is itself leveraged. So we would expect that high inflation benefits shareholders at the expense of bondholders. This only exacerbates the puzzle.

4.2. WHY ARE STOCKS A BAD INFLATION HEDGE?

There are a number of reasons why stocks do badly in periods of high inflation. I will examine two rational stories in the context of Ang and Ulrich (2012), where I develop a model where equities are influenced by the same factors driving bond prices and an equity-specific cash flow factor.

First, high inflation reduces future firm profitability. Inflation is negatively associated with real production; see, for example, Fama (1981). Rising inflation reduces profit margins because, while firms can pass through cost increases to consumers continuously, they can only do so in stages. These are called "*menu costs*" and, empirically, price rigidity is pervasive, as Nakamura and Steinsson (2008) show. This is a *cash flow* effect.

Second, there is also a *discount rate* effect. Times of high inflation are bad times when risk is high. This causes expected returns to be high in a factor story. Even in the consumption-only world of Mehra and Prescott, the historical record has seen high inflation episodes occurring with recessions when growth is slow (stagflation). Thus, when inflation is high, expected returns on equity increase, and this cuts equity prices. Thus, equity prices tend to fall with large inflation increases, resulting in a low correlation between *realized* inflation and *realized* equity returns. If this were always true, the correlation between inflation and equity should be -1. It is not because there are other factors driving equity prices that are not perfectly correlated with inflation.

The behavioral explanation of equities' shortcoming as an inflation hedge was proposed by Modigliani and Cohn (1979). According to this account, investors suffer from *money illusion*, and they discount real dividends using nominal discount rates instead of using real discount rates. Thus when inflation is high, the market's irrational expectation causes the market to be undervalued relative to the fundamental value. Thus, in times of high inflation, there are realized low returns on the market leading to low correlations of inflation with stock returns.

Under both the rational and behavioral explanations, equity has low returns during high inflation periods and is a bad inflation hedge. Inflation is a risk factor, but inflation causes equities to perform badly, not well. Consequently, any investor forecasting high inflation in the future relative to what the average investor believes is advised to lower holdings of equities.

5. Predicting Equity Risk Premiums

Active investors spend a lot of effort trying to forecast equity returns. But the consensus view in financial theory is that, while equity risk premiums vary over time, movements are hard to predict. Thus, I advise most investors not to time the market, and this is behind my advice in chapter 4 to rebalance back to constant weights or exposures.

5.1. THEORY SAYS EQUITY RISK PREMIUMS ARE PREDICTABLE

Consider the Gordon (1963) *Dividend Discount Model*, which states that the equity price, P, is the present value of future discounted dividends:

$$P = \frac{D}{E(r) - g}, \tag{8.2}$$

where D is the expected dividend next period, $E(r)$ is the discount rate, and g is the growth rate of dividends. Equation (8.2) is a valuation formula. Holding D fixed, prices today are high because $1/(E(r) - g)$ is low: either future expected returns are low, future growth is high, or both. The common wisdom is that high prices occur because growth will be high. For example, at the time of writing, the high share prices of Apple Inc. (AAPL) and Facebook Inc. (FB) suggest that the future growth of these companies will continue. But generally, high prices forecast low growth. (This is the *value effect*; see chapter 7).

The Gordon model in equation (8.2) can be equivalently expressed as

$$\frac{D}{P} = E(r) - g, \tag{8.3}$$

which states that high dividend yields are caused by high future expected returns, low future growth, or both. We could also write

$$E(r) = \frac{D}{P} + g, \tag{8.4}$$

which states that the expected return is the dividend yield plus the cash flow growth. Equation (8.4) says that dividend yields should help forecast expected returns, and this has been examined in finance since Dow (1920).

Academics have examined *variance decompositions* of dividend yields, which are computed by taking variances of both sides of equation (8.3). By doing so we can decompose movements of dividend yields into movements due to expected returns or discount rates, $E(r)$, or movements due to g, and movements due to the co-movement of both:

$$\mathrm{var}\left(\frac{D}{P}\right) = \mathrm{var}\left(E(r)\right) + \mathrm{var}(g) - 2\mathrm{cov}\left(E(r), g\right).$$

For the discussion below, let's assume that you can ignore the covariance term so we write:[18]

$$\mathrm{var}\left(\frac{D}{P}\right) \approx \mathrm{var}\left(E(r)\right) + \mathrm{var}(g). \tag{8.5}$$

---

[18] Serious studies do not ignore the covariance term. They assign the covariance term to the other variance terms through orthogonalization (usually Cholesky) procedures.

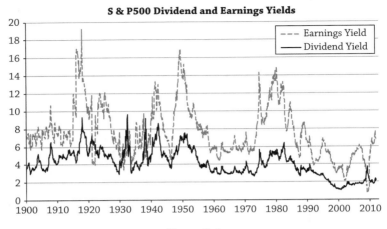

S & P500 Dividend and Earnings Yields

Figure 8.6

It seems obvious that dividend yields move over time. Figure 8.6 plots dividend yields and earnings yields of the S&P 500 from January 1900 to December 2011. Both series move in tandem, with the correlation being 73%. Since price appears in the denominator of dividend yields and earnings yields, the yield measures tend to be high when the equity market is in the doldrums, like during the Great Depression, the early 1950s, the late 1970s and early 1980s, and 2001. In 2008 when equities fell during the financial crisis, dividend yields were very low. But, during this period earnings yields moved in the opposite direction because earnings contracted a lot, but dividend payouts were sticky.

"What drives dividend yield variation?" turns out to be the same question as "what predicts returns?" Suppose cash flows are unpredictable, or i.i.d.. Then in equation (8.4), expected returns are predictable by the dividend yield: when dividend yields are high or prices are low, future expected returns are high. Equation (8.5) says that all dividend yield movements are driven by discount rate variation. Now suppose everything comes from cash flows and discount rates are constant. Equation (8.4) says that expected returns would change over time if we can forecast the future cash flows of companies, and equation (8.5) says that all variation in dividend yields comes from changing cash flows.

Do dividend yields move around because discount rates move, cash flows move, or both? Academic opinion is divided. John Cochrane, in his presidential address to the American Finance Association in 2011, gave a one-sided view and stated that all variation of dividend yields comes from expected returns, not cash flows. This used to be the prevailing opinion in finance due to Campbell (1991) and Cochrane (1992), even though contemporaneous dissenters argued that returns were not predictable (e.g., Goetzmann and Jorion in 1993). The Campbell–Cochrane view is that dividends are i.i.d. and dividend yields predict expected returns, not future cash flows. In the Bansal and Yaron (2004) framework to explain the equity premium, however, it is exactly the opposite. In Bansal and Yaron's world, almost all dividend yield variation comes from cash flows, and there is essentially no discount rate channel.[19] The risk premiums are still predictable according to equation (8.4), but they are driven only by predictable cash flows.

I have a stake in this literature and, unlike such "true believers" in discount rate predictability as Cochrane, my research documents the existence of cash flow predictability.[20] In Ang and Liu (2007), I show that since both dividend yields and equity return volatility vary over time (see also section 6 below), it *must* be the case that risk premiums also exhibit predictable components. Overall, my opinion is that the truth lies somewhere in between the Cochrane and the Bansal–Yaron extremes: there is both cash flow and discount rate predictability, but it is hard to detect both (see below).

What an investor should take away is that dividend yields vary over time, and, as a result, expected returns and cash flows are predictable. In the discount rate story, low prices mean high returns in the future and times of low prices are good times to buy equities. If we can forecast high future cash flows according to the cash flow story, we want to hold equities. A smart investor might be able to use these facts to her advantage.

5.2. THEORY SAYS TIME-VARYING EQUITY RISK PREMIUMS ARE HARD TO ESTIMATE

Theory says equity risk premiums are predictable, but theory also says that the amount of predictability is small. Thus, it is hard to statistically detect predictability in data and even harder to trade on it.

Predictability Regressions
A common statistical model to capture predictability is a *predictability regression*:

$$r_{t+1} = c + b \cdot X_t + \varepsilon_{t+1}, \tag{8.6}$$

where r_{t+1} is the market excess return and X_t is a set of predictive variables. The predictors range from the economically intuitive factors, like macro factors, to more esoteric variables, like sentiment-based factors based on Twitter or Facebook.[21] In regression (8.6), the strength of predictability is measured by the statistical significance of the predictive coefficient, b. Econometricians like to see high t-statistics, or low p-values, with a standard cut-off of a p-value of 5% called "statistically significant." If the returns and the predictive instruments have been standardized, that is, set to zero mean and a variance of one, then b represents

---

[19] There is a discount rate channel in Bansal and Yaron because there is stochastic volatility and the risk-free rate is time varying. But the variation in these components is small.

[20] See Ang and Bekaert (2007), Ang (2012b), and Ang and Zhang (2012).

[21] See Bollen, Mao, and Zeng (2011) and Karabulut (2011), respectively.

a correlation between a predictive variable today and next-period returns. In this case, the regression R^2 is simply given by squaring the correlation coefficient, b^2.

We are also interested in *long-horizon predictability*, which we can measure statistically by extending the regression (8.6) to multiple periods of returns on the left-hand side. We use log returns so we can add them. For example, for a three-period excess return we have

$$r_{t+3} + r_{t+2} + r_{t+1} = c + b \cdot X_t + \varepsilon_{t+3,3}. \tag{8.7}$$

Because we have limited data, we generally run long-horizon regressions using *overlapping* data. That is, when we consider the timing of the variables at time $t+1$ predicting returns over the next three periods, we predict the one-period excess returns from $t+1$ to $t+4$, r_{t+4}, r_{t+3}, and r_{t+2}. Thus, considering the two regressions with right-hand side variables at t and $t+1$, we overlap the one-period returns r_{t+3} and r_{t+2} on the left-hand side. This overlap is behind the complicated notation, $\varepsilon_{t+3,3}$, in the residuals of (8.7), which denotes that the residuals are realized at $t+3$, but they involve returns over the last three periods (the second term in the subscript). The overlapping data turn out to induce some very nasty statistical properties that cause regular ordinary least squares statistical inference to highly overstate how much true predictability there is in data. This is not just a problem for geeky econometricians; it has large implications for investors, as we shall see.

How much predictability should we expect? Not much. Ross (2005, 2012) and Zhou (2010) show that the R^2 in the predictive regression (8.6) should be very low. Technically, Ross and Zhou show that the regression R^2 is bounded by the variance of the pricing kernel (see chapter 6), and the factors entering the pricing kernel, like consumption, are generally not volatile.[22] Ross computes a bound of 8% and Zhou's bound is even lower. We should expect R^2s to be low and typically below 5%. That is, 95% of the movements of the market should be unpredictable, and any strategy that claims to predict future returns with high R^2s should be viewed with great suspicion. The low degree of predictability is consistent with the near-efficient markets of Grossman and Stiglitz (1980) in chapter 6: profitable market-timing strategies are rare and statistically hard to detect.

The data bear this out. Empirically, it is hard to find robust statistical evidence of predictability. Table 8.7 reports correlation coefficients of next-period returns on various predictors at the beginning of the period. The base unit of measurement is one-quarter, so the one-period ahead return in regression in (8.6) is over the next quarter. I also run long-horizon regressions of the form (8.7) over one year, two years, and five years. These are also reported as correlation coefficients. Table 8.7 reports robust t-statistics that account for the overlapping observation

---

[22] Denoting the pricing kernel as m, Ross (2005) shows that the regression R^2 is bounded by $R^2 \le (1 + r_f)^2 \text{var}(m)$. Zhou (2010) derives a more restrictive bound of $R^2 \le \rho_{z,m}^2 (1 + r_f)^2 \text{var}(m)$, where $\rho_{z,m}^2$ is the multiple correlation between the predictive variables z and the pricing kernel m.

Table 8.7

		1 Qtr	1 Year	2 Years	5 Years	Sample	Source
Dividend Yield	Correlation	0.12	0.23	0.33	0.49	Jan 1926 - Dec 2011	CRSP
	t-stat	(1.12)	(1.25)	(1.48)	(1.95)		
(10-Yr) Earnings Yield	Correlation	**0.18**	**0.33**	**0.41**	**0.48**	Jan 1926 - Dec 2011	Shiller (2000) updated
	t-stat	**(2.23)**	**(2.55)**	**(2.79)**	**(2.31)**		
Volatility VIX	Correlation	0.12	0.10	0.13	-0.16	Jan 1986 - Dec 2011	CBOE
	t-stat	(0.96)	(0.63)	(0.75)	(-0.47)		
Past Volatility [Over Last Quarter]	Correlation	0.05	0.09	0.13	0.06	Sep 1963 - Dec 2011	CRSP
	t-stat	(0.55)	(0.65)	(0.78)	(0.17)		
Lagged 1-Year Return [Past 12 Mths to Past 1 Mth]	Correlation	-0.01	-0.05	-0.13	-0.26	Dec 1926 - Dec 2011	CRSP
	t-stat	(-0.12)	(-0.26)	(-0.55)	(-1.39)		
T-Bill Rate	Correlation	-0.07	-0.12	-0.15	-0.22	Sep 1926 - Dec 2011	Ibbotson
	t-stat	(-1.23)	(-1.17)	(-1.05)	(-0.97)		
Consumption-Wealth Ratio	Correlation	**0.16**	**0.30**	**0.42**	0.53	Mar 1953 - Dec 2011	Lettau and Ludvigson (2001a) updated
	t-stat	**(2.92)**	**(2.62)**	**(2.23)**	(1.34)		

continued

Table 8.7 (continued)

		1 Qtr	1 Year	2 Years	5 Years	Sample	Source
Term Spread [10 Yr Tsy minus 3 Mth T-bill]	Correlation	0.11	0.23	0.27	0.35	Mar 1953 - Dec 2011	Federal Reserve Bank of St Louis
	t-stat	(1.60)	(1.84)	(1.66)	(1.61)		
Credit Spread [AAA minus BAA]	Correlation	0.02	0.08	0.12	0.20	Dec 1918 - Dec 2011	Federal Reserve Bank of St Louis
	t-stat	(0.15)	(0.34)	(0.44)	(0.67)		
GDP Growth [Past 1 Year]	Correlation	0.01	-0.13	-0.11	-0.08	Jun 1947 - Dec 2011	BEA
	t-stat	(0.17)	(-1.37)	(-1.25)	(-0.84)		
Inflation [Past 1 Year]	Correlation	-0.07	-0.12	-0.10	-0.03	Mar 1914 - Dec 2011	Federal Reserve Bank of St Louis
	t-stat	(-1.07)	(-0.94)	(-0.58)	(-0.09)		
Industrial Production [Past 1 Year]	Correlation	-0.01	-0.04	0.02	-0.04	Dec 1919 - Dec 2011	Federal Reserve Bank of St Louis
	t-stat	(-0.06)	(-0.25)	(0.08)	(-0.20)		
Oil Price [Past 1-Year Change]	Correlation	-0.10	-0.18	-0.16	-0.11	Dec 1945 - Dec 2011	Federal Reserve Bank of St Louis
	t-stat	(-1.20)	(-1.20)	(-1.08)	(-0.78)		
Unemployment Rate	Correlation	0.12	0.22	0.19	0.22	Dec 1947 - Dec 2011	Bureau of Labor Statistics
	t-stat	(1.86)	(1.85)	(1.08)	(0.75)		

problem and the problem of time-varying volatility, which also causes regular ordinary least squares to overreject the null of predictability too often.[23] Table 8.7 considers a variety of variables used in the literature ranging from macro variables, interest rates and spreads, and past excess returns.

Table 8.7 shows that it is very hard to predict returns. I highlight in bold in Table 8.7 all correlation coefficients that are significant at the 95% level—that is, they have p-values smaller than 0.05 (or equivalently they have t-statistics greater than 1.96 in absolute value). There are only two variables that have statistically significant correlations at the 95% level: Shiller's (2000) cyclically adjusted ten-year earnings yield and the deviations from long-run consumption-wealth trends constructed by Lettau and Ludvigson (2001a) known as "cay." The latter has look-ahead bias (it is constructed using information not available to investors at the time), so should be interpreted with caution because it cannot be used in an investable strategy.[24] The dividend yield has borderline predictive ability at the five-year horizon, with a t-statistic of 1.95. Thus, it is very hard to predict returns, just as Ross and Zhou say it should be.

The Shiller inverse price–earnings ratio that does so well in Table 8.7 and the borderline dividend yield at the five-year horizon is consistent with the Gordon model intuition in equation (8.4). High yields mean low prices. Low prices result from future cash flows being discounted at high expected returns. Consequently, the low price today forecasts that future returns tend to be high. Note that the only significant variables in Table 8.7 are these *valuation* ratios. Other predictors are documented in an extensive academic literature over different time horizons and samples.[25] Overall, it is hard to predict returns.

Be Wary of Long-Horizon R^2s

Many commentators argue that there is substantial evidence of long-horizon predictability in data. Table 8.7 does not show this. It is there, but, again, it is hard to detect. You cannot conduct statistical inference at long horizons by using standard R^2 measures. The overlapping observations in equation (8.7) cause long-horizon R^2s to be grossly inflated; the simple R^2s appear to indicate substantial predictability, but it isn't actually there. For example, take the dividend yield correlation of 49% with excess returns over the next five years. This implies an $R^2 = (0.49)^2 = 24\%$. This looks enormous, especially given that financial theory predicts that the regression R^2s should be close to zero.

---

[23] The t-statistics in Table 8.7 are computed using Hodrick (1992) standard errors, which Ang and Bekaert (2007) show have the correct statistical properties and do not overreject the null of predictability. There are many versions of robust standard errors that still are not "robust" enough, including the commonly used Hansen and Hodrick (1980) and Newey and West (1987) standard errors, in the sense that they do not have correct size properties.

[24] See Brennan and Xia (2005).

[25] See a summary article by Rapach and Zhou (2011), who show that combinations of variables can do a better job than individual variables at forecasting equity returns.

Investors cannot rely on long-horizon R^2s because they are *spurious*. This means that while the true predictability is very weak (we say that there is a small degree of predictability in *population*), the regression R^2s are much larger in *small samples*. Small samples here can mean hundreds or thousands of years. The intuition for this spurious effect is that the overlapping observations in equation (8.7) artificially induce dependence—the three-period long-horizon return from t to $t+3$ overlaps two periods with the three-period long-horizon return from $t+1$ to $t+4$—and the problem gets worse as the horizons get longer.[26] Valkanov (2003) and Boudoukh, Richardson, and Whitelaw (2008), among others, derive the correct small sample R^2 distributions and show they are hugely biased upward; using the simple R^2 always overstates, often grossly so, long-horizon predictability. The robust t-statistic corrections get the calculations right; R^2s do not. The moral of the story is that there is not that much predictability in the data—which is as it should be according to theory—and it is also hard to detect at long horizons.

Predictability Comes and Goes

A final twist makes it even harder for investors to predict returns in practice: the predictive coefficients themselves (the b parameter in equation (8.7)) vary over time. Statistical models that can accommodate this *parameter instability* do so by allowing the coefficients to undergo structural breaks or to change slowly over time.[27] Henkel, Martin, and Nardari (2011) capture regime-dependent predictability. They find that predictability is weak during business cycle expansions but very strong during recessions. Thus, predictability is counter-cyclical and is observed most during regimes of economic slowdowns. [28]

Implications for Investors

There are time-varying risk premiums, but they are difficult to estimate. If you attempt to take advantage of them, do the following:

1. Use good statistical techniques.

    Overstating statistical significance, for example, by using the wrong t-statistics and thereby making predictability look "too good," will hurt you when you implement investment strategies. One manifestation of spuriously high R^2 in fitted in samples is that the performance deteriorates markedly

---

[26] The literature on spurious regressions calls these *partially aggregated variables*.

[27] See, for example, Paye and Timmermann (2006) and Lettau and Van Nieuwerburgh (2008) for structural breaks in predictability relations. Dangl and Halling (2012) allow the predictive coefficient to change slowly following a random walk specification. The coefficients of predictability change in Johannes, Korteweg, and Polson (2011) as investors learn over time.

[28] For a summary of regime changes and financial markets, see Ang and Timmermann (2012).

going out of sample. Consistent with the spurious high R^2s, Welch and Goyal (2008) find that the historical average of excess stock returns forecasts better than almost all predictive variables. Use smart econometric techniques that combine a lot of information, but be careful about data mining and take into account the possibility of shifts in regime.[29]

2. Use economic models.

Notice that the best predictors in Table 8.7 were valuation ratios. Prediction of equity risk premiums is the same as prediction of economic value. If you can impose economic structure, do it. Campbell and Thompson (2008), among others, find that imposing economic intuition and constraints from economic models helps.[30]

3. Be humble.

If you're trying to time the market, then have humility. Predicting returns is hard. Since it is difficult to statistically detect predictability, it will also be easy to delude yourself into thinking you are the greatest manager in the world because of a lucky streak (this is *self-attribution bias*), and this overconfidence will really hurt when the luck runs out. You will also need the right governance structure to withstand painful periods that may extend for years (see chapter 15). Asset owners are warned that there are very few managers who have skill, especially among those who think they have skill (see also chapters 17 and 18 on hedge funds and private equity, respectively).

Since the predictability in data is weak, investors are well served by taking the i.i.d. environment as a base case. This means dynamic asset allocation with rebalancing to constant weights (or exposures) along the lines of chapter 4. If there is some mean reversion of returns in the data, as suggested by the low returns that follow high prices, and vice versa, then rebalancing back to constant weights will be advantageous. Recall that rebalancing is a counter-cyclical strategy; it buys when equities have fallen in price, so the equity position is increased when expected returns are high and sells when equities have risen in price, so the equity position is reduced when expected returns are low. You can do better than this if you can predict the future, but you probably can't. At least rebalancing will get you going in the right direction—the truly optimal (ideal) strategy will only be *more* aggressive than rebalancing. If you can't do constant rebalancing, then you are highly unlikely to be able to undertake the optimal investment strategy when the true data-generating process of the equity risky premium exhibits predictability.

---

[29] See Timmermann (2006) for a summary on optimal forecast combination.

[30] Ang and Piazzesi (2003) impose no-arbitrage constraints and find these improve forecasts of interest rates. Campbell and Thompson (2008) impose that forecasts of equity risk premiums are positive by truncating at zero. A more general approach is Pettenuzzo, Timmermann, and Valkanov (2013), who impose bounds on Sharpe ratios.

6. Time-Varying Volatility

In contrast to the weak predictability of equity risk premiums, there is a great deal of predictability in aggregate market volatilities.[31]

First, the volatility of equities is relatively high and much higher than *fundamental* volatilities of dividends (and also of consumption as a factor, as mentioned in section 2). This is labeled *"excess volatility"* by Robert Shiller (1981). From January 1935 to December 2010, the standard deviation of log returns is 16.0%. In contrast, the standard deviation of dividend growth is 9.6%, and thus return volatility is higher than fundamental volatility. However, taking earnings as fundamentals gives a different story. The volatility of earnings growth is 36.0%, and there is no excess volatility puzzle. But earnings cannot be directly used to value equity because they are generated by a firm owned by both debt and equity holders (it is also an accounting construct and not an actual cash flow payment).[32] Dividends accrue only to stockholders. The fact that equity return volatility is higher than dividend volatility is a reflection that some predictability of risk premiums is coming from discount rates and not from cash flows in the Cochrane versus Bansal–Yaron debate.

Models to predict volatility were created by Robert Engle (1982) and are called ARCH models (for "<u>a</u>uto<u>r</u>egressive <u>c</u>onditional <u>h</u>eteroskedasticity"). This is a mouthful and means that conditional volatility changes over time ("heteroskedasticity" is Greek for "different dispersions") in such a way that it is mean-reverting ("autoregressive"). The model was extended by Bollerslev (1986) to *GARCH*, for "<u>g</u>eneralized <u>a</u>utoregressive <u>c</u>onditional <u>h</u>eteroskedasticity," and that is the name used by industry and the literature. The GARCH model revolutionized volatility modeling, especially for risk management. Engle was awarded the Nobel Prize in 2003.

In the basic GARCH model, conditional variance, σ_t^2, follows:[33]

$$\sigma_t^2 = a + b\sigma_{t-1}^2 + c\varepsilon_{t-1}^2. \tag{8.8}$$

The main effect in equation (8.8) is that volatility depends on itself and is thus persistent (through b, which is close to one), or autoregressive, and it is also affected by past shocks (through c). Thus, large shocks—like those in 1987 (stock market crash), 1998 (Russian default and emerging markets crisis), and 2008

---

[31] Most of this predictability in equity volatility comes from equity volatility predicting itself. There is little predictive ability of macro variables to forecast market volatility, as Paye (2012) shows.

[32] There are many earnings models, but one seminal paper that links the dividend discount model with what are now called *residual income models* is Miller and Modigliani (1961). These are the same Miller and Modigliani who received the Nobel prize in 1985 for (the irrelevance of) capital structure. My paper on this is Ang and Liu (2001).

[33] There have been many extensions in the literature for different past volatility dependence, asymmetry, including jumps, and so on.

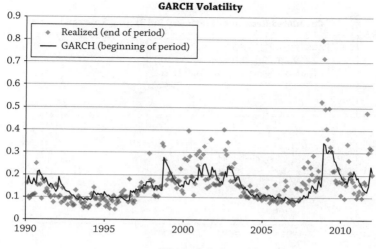

Figure 8.8

(Lehman default)—lead to higher future volatility. Once these hit, volatility remains high for a certain period of time before mean-reverting. This allows the GARCH model to capture periods of turbulence and quiet. We see this in Figure 8.8, which plots GARCH forecasted volatility with realized volatility (computed using realized daily returns over the month), both at the monthly frequency, from January 1990 to December 2012. The correlation of GARCH volatility at the beginning of the month with realized volatility over the next month is 63%. Compare this correlation with the barely 5% correlations that we were expecting to predict future equity risk premiums! Volatility is quite predictable in equity markets.

If volatility is so predictable, then volatility trading should lead to terrific investment gains. It does. Despite my pessimism on predicting expected returns of the previous section, I am far more enthusiastic on strategies predicting volatilities.

Panel A of Figure 8.9 contrasts cumulated returns from January 1986 to December 2011 of a static 60% equities–40% T-bill strategy with a volatility timing strategy based on VIX, which is also overlaid on the graph. The static strategy is the mean-variance portfolio weight given in equation (2.10) in chapter 2, which for convenience is repeated here:

$$w = \frac{1}{\gamma} \frac{\mu - r_f}{\sigma^2}, \tag{8.9}$$

where the risk aversion, γ, is calibrated to produce a 60%/40% portfolio over the whole sample. The volatility timing strategy replaces market volatility, σ, in the denominator of equation (8.9) with the VIX, so that it becomes time varying.

Panel A

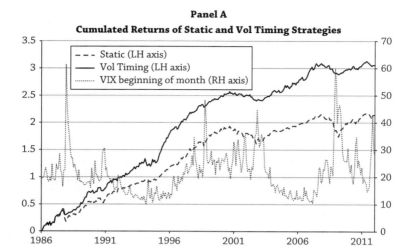

Panel B

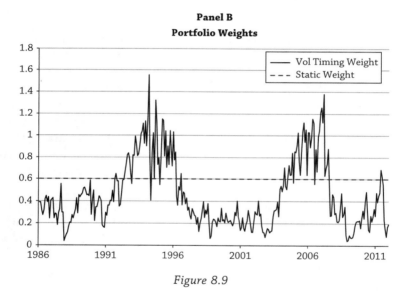

Figure 8.9

I hold the numerator equal to the mean excess return over T-bills, $\mu - r_f$, over the whole sample just as in the 60%–40% strategy. That is, the volatility timing strategy only changes volatility and holds the mean fixed. In Figure 8.9, I use the known VIX at the beginning of the current month. There are plenty of examples of volatility strategies, and important references include Fleming, Kirby, and Ostdiek (2001) and Kirby and Ostdiek (2012). The most sophisticated versions of volatility forecasts combine information from past returns using GARCH-type models, models estimated on realized volatilities, and stochastic volatility models estimated from option prices (see, e.g., Andersen et al. (2006)).

Panel A of Figure 8.9 shows that the cumulated returns (left-hand axis) of the volatility timing and the static 60%/40% strategy. I have scaled the returns of both so that they have a target volatility of 10%. The figure shows that the volatility strategy decisively beat the static strategy and was less prone to drawdowns during the early 2000s and the 2008 financial crisis. During these periods VIX (right-hand axis) was high and the volatility timing strategy shifted into T-bills. It thus partly avoided the low returns occurring when volatility spiked. The cumulated return at the end of the sample is 3.06 for the volatility timing strategy compare to 2.14 for the static 60%/40% strategy. Volatility strategies perform strongly.

An obvious question: if volatility timing does so well, why doesn't everyone do it? Volatility timing requires nimbleness. Panel B of Figure 8.9 shows that the portfolio weights move all over the place. Portfolio weights in equities range from more than 1.5 to nearly zero (as during 2008). Most large investors would have trouble moving in and out of stocks so rapidly or even managing large equities futures positions if done synthetically. So this is not a strategy for all investors.

A deeper question is: what beliefs are implied by the average investor, the representative agent, who holds 100% in the market portfolio and cannot flit in and out of equities by definition? If we rearrange equation (8.9) for the representative agent who holds $w = 1$ in the market portfolio, then we obtain the capital market line of chapter 6 (see equation (6.1)), repeated here:

$$\mu - r_f = \gamma \sigma^2, \tag{8.10}$$

and high volatilities should correspond to very high future returns (but be accompanied by low contemporaneous returns). We see little predictive power of volatilities in Table 8.7 and overall little evidence of predictability. What the portfolio choice of equation (8.9) is missing, which was used to derive equation (8.10) under the assumption that the representative agent holds 100% of the market, is terms representing liabilities and the long-horizon investment opportunities of chapter 4. Grouping both of these into "hedging terms," we have

$$w = \frac{1}{\gamma} \frac{\mu - r_f}{\sigma^2} + \text{hedging terms}, \tag{8.11}$$

and the hedging terms must be playing very important roles for the representative agent. Guo and Whitelaw (2006) argue that the hedging terms completely dominate the simple linear risk–return relation and offset the effects of volatility.

A closing comment is that the modern practice of risk management almost exclusively measures risk in (souped-up versions of) GARCH models. I believe risk management is the flipside of expected returns. That is, volatility must be linked with risk premiums, and together they determine valuations. This arises naturally

in economic models and is the point made by Ang and Liu (2007). The next generation of risk management models should embed valuation metrics. When volatility
spikes, prices fall. But when prices are low, discount rates tend to be high, and this
predicts that returns going forward will be high (see equation (8.4)). We see little
direct relation between volatility and future returns (see Table 8.7) because of the
hedging terms in equation (8.11) and the fact that the relation between volatility
and the risk premium is nonlinear (see also chapter 6). When volatility is high and
prices are low, risk is high as measured by high volatility, but these are times of
high risk premiums. In terms of valuations, these are times of low risk and opportunities to buy. Of course, one of the main messages from this chapter is that
forecasting the risk premium is an inherently difficult exercise.

7. The Lost Decade Redux

The Lost Decade of the 2000s was certainly brutal for stock returns relative to
bonds and even T-bills (cash). But over much longer time periods, there has been a
considerable equity risk premium relative to bonds and bills. While the equity risk
premium is high, equity returns are volatile—and even excessively volatile relative
to fundamentals like consumption, dividend, and other macro volatility measures.
So low returns over a decade are not unexpected. In fact, it is precisely because
equities can perform poorly over extended periods and over bad times in general
that equities earn a risk premium. These bad times include periods of low growth,
disasters, long-run risks, and high inflation, among other factor risks. I expect the
equity premium to be high going forward but over the long run. Over the short
run, investors holding equities should steel themselves for the possibility of poor
returns. You earn high returns over the long run to compensate for the possibility
of poor performance during bad times in the short run.

The equity risk premium is predictable. But theory and empirical evidence
suggest that the predictability is hard to detect. Investors should ignore the
weak predictability in data and rebalance to constant weights. If they do wish
to exploit time-varying risk premiums, then they should be careful to use robust statistical inference, economic models, and restrictions where possible and
do it in a framework of good governance structures. The constant rebalancing
strategy is naturally countercyclical, and any strategy that takes advantage of
mean-reverting risk premiums will use a more aggressive strategy than simply
maintaining constant weights.

CHAPTER 9

Bonds

Chapter Summary

The level factor, which shifts the yields of all bonds, is the crucial factor in fixed income investments. The level factor is affected by risks associated with economic growth, inflation, and monetary policy. Corporate bonds do not just reflect credit risk; as predicted by theory, volatility risk is an important factor and corporate bond returns correlate highly with equity returns. Illiquidity risk is also an important factor in bond returns.

1. U.S. Downgrade

On Friday August 5, 2011, Standard & Poor's downgraded the credit rating of the United States from AAA to AA+, keeping its rating outlook at "negative."[1] The ratings agency was concerned about political risk, especially the ability of U.S. lawmakers to cut spending or raise revenue to even stabilize, let alone reduce, the nation's growing debt. "The downgrade," Standard & Poor's said, "reflects our view that the effectiveness, stability, and predictability of American policy-making and political institutions have weakened at a time of ongoing fiscal and economic challenges." Standard & Poor's AAA rating for the United States dated back to 1941 and was unshaken even by World War II. The agency had never before downgraded the country.

Global stock markets declined on Monday, August 8, when trading resumed after the announcement. But U.S. Treasury bonds rose in price. Figure 9.1 shows that the yield on ten-year Treasuries closed on Monday at 2.40% after closing the previous Friday at 2.58%. By the close of trading on Friday August 12, the yield was even lower, at 2.24%.

Why did U.S. bond yields drop? If the United States was supposed to be riskier (at least according to Standard & Poor's), Treasury yields should have risen as

---

[1] See http://www.standardandpoors.com/ratings/articles/en/U.S./?assetID=1245316529563.

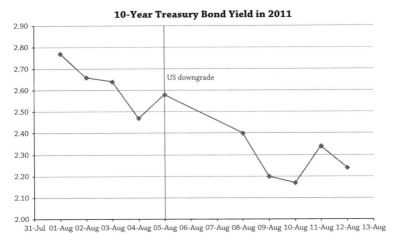

Figure 9.1

a result of investor demands for a greater risk premium to compensate for the higher likelihood of default. If higher credit risk could not explain the movements of U.S. Treasuries at the time of the downgrade, what could?

In this chapter we examine the risk and return trade-offs of fixed income securities. We first assume that Treasuries are risk free and discuss the factors driving risk-free bond returns. We then consider corporate bonds, which add the dimension of credit risk, and other types of risks.

2. Monetary Policy and the Level Factor

Understanding the factors affecting bonds requires understanding the most important player in bond markets—the Federal Reserve, America's central bank, known as the Fed.

2.1. THE FEDERAL RESERVE

Monetary policy is one of the primary drivers behind interest rates because of the way monetary policy responds to macro factors. Monetary policy is officially set by the Federal Open Market Committee (FOMC), a Fed panel with membership comprising the Fed Chair, the seven members of the Federal Reserve Board, and five of the twelve regional Federal Reserve Bank presidents (the president of the Federal Reserve Bank of New York always sits on the committee, a "first among equals").[2] The current Fed Chair, Janet Yellen, was appointed on February 1,

---

[2] The convoluted setup of the Fed was the result of a series of compromises between politicians in the rural and west versus the east and between politicians and businesses, as described at length

2014. The previous Fed Chair was Ben Bernanke who served from February 1, 2006 to January 31, 2014. Before Bernanke, Alan Greenspan was the Fed Chair from August 11, 1987 to January 31, 2006.

The Fed traditionally implements monetary policy by intervening in the Federal funds market. This is where banks (*depository institutions*) lend or borrow money (*Fed funds*) overnight through the Fed to maintain reserve requirements. Banks with *excess reserves* lend them to other banks that need money. This market is bilateral, meaning banks needing funds seek out banks willing to lend funds on a one-to-one basis, and banks pay different rates for funds depending on who is lending and who is borrowing. Each pair of banks, therefore, borrows or lends at a different *Fed funds rate*. The *effective Fed funds rate* is the volume-weighted average of these rates across the banks. The Fed intervenes in this market through *open market operations* (a fancy term for buying and selling bonds) so that the market rates bear some resemblance to the *target federal funds rate*, which is set by the FOMC. Since December 16, 2008, the Fed has specified a *range* for the target federal funds rate of 0% to 0.25%.

Monetary policy is conducted at the very shortest end of the yield curve—the overnight market—and only among banks. But the Fed ultimately wants to influence the long end of the yield curve, with maturities of ten to thirty years and also the prices of corporate and agency debt in addition to those of long-term Treasuries. The way short-end monetary policy ultimately affects the economy is through the *transmission mechanism*.[3] Since the financial crisis, the Fed has conducted *nonconventional* monetary policy by directly buying or selling long-dated Treasuries and a large variety of (sometimes very) risky credit instruments. *Quantitative easing* falls in this series of nonconventional programs. Before the financial crisis, experts would have called you crazy if you had suggested that monetary policy would now be conducted by the direct purchase of commercial paper (CP), agency debt, and debt of government-sponsored enterprises (Fannie Mae, Freddie Mac, and the Federal Home Loan Banks), residential mortgage-backed securities, commercial mortgage-backed securities, collateralized debt obligations, and so on, plus direct loans to JP Morgan Chase ("Maiden Lane"), AIG ("Maiden

---

in Meltzer (2003). The locations of the Federal Reserve Banks largely correspond to the main areas of economic activity at the time of the creation of the Federal Reserve System in 1913: Atlanta, Boston, Chicago, Cleveland, Dallas, Kansas City, Minneapolis, New York City, Philadelphia, St. Louis, and San Francisco. The one exception is the former capital of the Confederacy, Richmond, which was selected largely because it was in the home constituency of Carter Glass, the Democratic congressman who helped write the Fed's enabling legislation. The regional Federal Reserve Banks are owned by commercial banks, but the stock is not tradeable. The Federal Reserve Board of Governors is an independent federal agency. For more information on Fed governance, see Gerdesmeier, Mongelli, and Roffia (2007), who also compare the Fed with the European Central Bank and the Bank of Japan. Full disclosure: I have received consulting fees from the Federal Reserve Board of Governors and the Federal Reserve Bank of New York.

[3] The standard reference is actually by the former Fed Chair, Bernanke and Blinder (1988).

Lane II" and "Maiden Lane III"), Citigroup, and Bank of America. In my opinion, unconventional monetary policy is likely to become conventional, and interventions in the Fed funds market will be just one of many weapons in the Fed's arsenal.

For now, let's concentrate on conventional monetary policy. It may seem incredible that the Fed can affect the yields of thirty-year corporate bonds by influencing interest rates in a bank-to-bank market where funds are lent overnight, but these monetary policy actions turn out to be one of the most important drivers of all bond prices.

2.2. THE LEVEL FACTOR

Figure 9.2 plots the Fed funds rate in the solid line and the three-month T-bill rate in the dashed line from July 1954 to December 2011. The correlation between the two series is 0.99: whatever happens in the Fed funds market is mirrored in the T-bill market almost one for one. Since the 1950s, interest rates have a remarkable triangle-shaped pattern: they reached a maximum during the late 1970s and early 1980s when three-month T-bills topped 15%.[4] During the 1970s, inflation soared

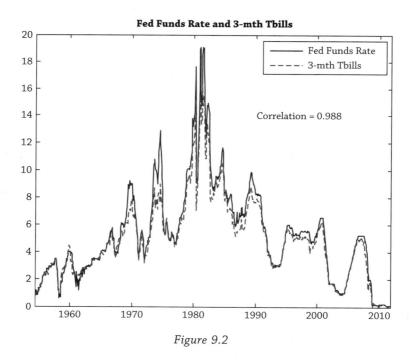

Figure 9.2

---

[4] On average, the T-bill yield has been *lower* than the Fed funds rate, as can be seen in Figure 9.2. This is partly because the Fed funds market, consisting of banks, has credit risk whereas the Treasury

(*the Great Inflation*) until Fed Chair Paul Volcker brought it under control in the 1980s. (I describe the inflation experience in more detail in chapter 11 where I discuss "real" assets.) There have been notable cycles around this broader up and down interest-rate trend. The Fed cut interest rates sharply after the 9/11 attacks, and the economy was in recession for most of 2001. The Fed held interest rates low for two years after these events, around 1%, and started to raise them again in 2003. Most recently, the Fed cut interest rates during the global financial crisis of 2008 and 2009, although interest rates already had begun to fall in 2007. They have remained almost zero (below 25 basis points) since, giving the Fed a *zero lower bound* problem: how do you conduct monetary policy when the policy rate cannot go any lower? This is one reason that quantitative easing and other nonconventional monetary policy programs have been introduced.[5]

Very often, long-term Treasuries move in tandem with short-term Treasuries. Figure 9.3 plots the Fed funds rate and the ten-year Treasury yield from July

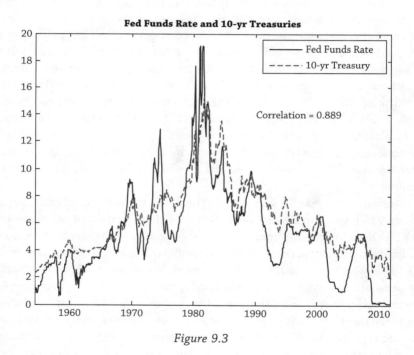

Figure 9.3

market is risk free, Standard & Poor's opinion notwithstanding. Also, T-bills can be used as collateral, which increases T-bill prices and reduces T-bill yields, while Fed funds cannot. Finally, the T-bill market is much larger and more liquid than the Fed funds market.

[5] Conducting monetary policy when policy rates are at zero had been well studied before the financial crisis because the problem has afflicted Japan for the past twenty plus years. It is called *zero interest-rate policy*. One of the ways to conduct monetary policy in this environment is quantitative easing, which the Fed practiced during and after the financial crisis (see, e.g., Goodfriend (2000)).

1954 to December 2011. The correlation is 0.89, lower than the almost perfect correlation for the Fed funds rate and T-bills but still very high. Treasury yields have the same triangle pattern as the short end of the yield curve, but there are some periods of pronounced differences between the short and long ends of the curve. Below we discuss what drives this *term spread*, but notice that the whole yield curve displays a strong degree of commonality with the Fed funds rate.

The strong co-movement of the Fed funds rate and the entire Treasury yield curve is captured by a *level factor*. The level factor simply describes the tendency of all bond yields to move up and down together, largely in line with the Fed funds rate. Level factor movements constitute the vast majority—above 90%—of movements across all maturities in the yield curve (or the *term structure of interest rates*).[6] The exposure to level is known as *duration*. This is analogous to beta in equity markets, which measures exposure to the market equity factor (see chapter 6). Duration is the beta of bonds with respect to level shifts of interest rates. Other factors influencing bond returns are *slope* or the *term spread*, which describes the movements of the long end of the yield curve relative to the short end, and *curvature*, which allows the middle of the yield curve to move independently of the level and term spread. But the most important factor is level.

Factors are extremely important in fixed income. It is instructive to compare fixed income with equities in this regard. In equities, idiosyncratic risk is large, constituting 80% to 90% of return variance, and systematic factor risk is small (10% to 20%). Intuitively, each company is different—firms have different managers, plants, employees, and production technologies even when they operate in the same sector. In fixed income, the idiosyncratic risk component is quite small—often less than 1% for risk-free Treasuries. Systematic factor risk, especially level, dominates.

Consider a five-year Treasury bond. This bond is highly correlated (approximately 98%) with the six-year bond, which is highly correlated (approximately 98%) with the seven-year bond. The risk-free cash flow streams of these bonds are fixed, as we assume that the Treasury will pay. Thus, the only uncertainty is the rate at which the cash flows are discounted. The seven-year bond is subject to the same discount rate as a one-year bond, plus a rate prevailing between years one and seven (this is called the *forward rate*). Similarly, the six-year bond is subject to the short-term one-year discount rate, plus a rate prevailing between years one and six. Thus, whatever affects the short-term rate gets propagated through the yield curve—each long-term bond moves in response to the one-year rate as well as shocks that affect longer maturities. The short, one-period rate affects *all* bond prices. This is why the level factor, or the level shift, is so important in fixed income.

Idiosyncratic risk does increase as you move through the risk spectrum of fixed income from sovereigns, to agencies, to investment grade corporate bonds, and

---

[6] See, among others, Litterman and Scheinkman (1991).

then to high-yield bonds, but for all of these bonds, the main effect is the level factor. To understand fixed income investments, therefore, investors have to understand the level factor. The level factor acts like the Fed funds rate, so we need to understand how the Fed sets monetary policy.

2.3. THE TAYLOR (1993) RULE

The current goals of the Fed are outlined in the 1977 Federal Reserve Reform Act. The Fed

> shall maintain long run growth of the monetary and credit aggregates commensurate with the economy's long run potential to increase production, so as to promote effectively the goals of *maximum employment, stable prices*, and *moderate long-term interest rates*.

The italics are mine. The last of these three goals gets relatively little attention but, in my opinion, empowers the Fed to take actions that will reduce uncertainty. During the financial crisis, the Fed undertook *extraordinary measures* to stabilize the monetary system and the economy, which certainly reduced volatility. This was done under Section 13(3) of the 1913 Federal Reserve Act, which authorizes the Fed to lend money to anyone "in unusual and exigent circumstances." Prior to the financial crisis, it was last invoked during the Great Depression. The first two considerations of "maximum employment" and "stable prices" are called the *dual mandate*, which some scholars consider a contradiction (a "dueling mandate").[7] Although "low inflation" is not necessarily "stable prices," the stable price mandate has been traditionally interpreted as a low inflation mandate.[8] Many central banks, including the European Central Bank, do not have a mandate for economic growth and only have a mandate for price stability. Since the financial crisis, many central banks, including the Fed, have added a *financial stability* mandate.

We know a great deal but far from everything about the Fed's decision-making process. Minutes of FOMC meetings are made public three weeks later. But detailed transcripts along with other materials, which include detailed internal forecasts, are only available after a five-year lag. Even then, anyone who has served on committees knows that often the actual (often dirty) work happens before the committee meeting between select groups of people, so minutes or transcripts do not necessarily capture what is really going on. While some researchers have used

[7] See, for example, the study of Labonte (2012) done for Congress, which criticizes the dual mandate. De Long and Summers (1988) make a case for the dual mandate.

[8] See Goodfriend (1999). Since January 2012, the Fed considers that "inflation at the rate of 2 percent, as measured by the annual change in the price index for personal consumption expenditures, is most consistent over the longer run with the Federal Reserve's statutory mandate." See http://www.federalreserve.gov/newsevents/press/monetary/20120125c.htm.

these minutes, transcripts, and other materials to describe Fed behavior,[9] an important alternative is a reduced-form model developed by the Stanford University economist John Taylor in 1993.

The famous *Taylor rule* states that the Fed funds rate should be set to move together with inflation and economic activity. Its original formulation was

$$FF_t = r^* + \pi_t + 0.5(\pi_t - \pi^*) + 0.5Gap_t, \qquad (9.1)$$

where FF denotes the Fed funds rate, r^* is the long-run real interest rate, π is the current inflation rate, and π^* is the target inflation rate. The output gap, which is the difference between real and potential GDP, is denoted as *Gap*. The Taylor rule is used both as a descriptive tool (what has the Fed done?) and a prescriptive tool (what should the Fed do?).

The Taylor rule captures the dual mandate of the Fed by describing how it moves the Fed funds rate in response to changes in the output gap and inflation. There is a positive coefficient of 0.5 (the coefficient differs in data and subsequent theories) on the output gap. As the output gap shrinks and economic activity slows, the Fed lowers the Fed funds rate to spur economic growth. The coefficient on inflation, π, in equation (9.1) is 1.5, but it is split up between the first term, $r^* + \pi$, and the second, $0.5(\pi - \pi^*)$. The first term is the sum of the real rate and inflation and should be the simple nominal short rate according to the *Fisher Hypothesis* (see below). The second term is the deviation of current inflation from its long-term target. As inflation increases, the Fed raises the Fed funds rate to rein in rising prices. As the total coefficient on inflation is greater than 1.0, when inflation increases, the Fed moves interest rates more than one for one. This means that the Fed raises *real rates* when inflation increases. This is called the *Taylor principle*.

Many versions of the Taylor rule describe the Fed's reaction to inflation and economic growth. These models can use different definitions of inflation (GDP deflator, CPI-All, core CPI, PPI, etc.) or of economic growth (GDP growth, output gap, industrial production growth, employment, etc.); the important concept in equation (9.1) is that the Fed responds to general movements in inflation and growth. Variants developed since Taylor (1993) can use forward-looking measures like surveys or agents' expectations (*forward-looking rules*) and past data beyond just current inflation and output (*backward-looking rules*). Versions of the rule can also account for occasions when the Fed partially adjusts to information (*partial adjustment rules*).[10] The difference between the actual Fed funds rate and what the

---

[9] See, for example, the recent study of Weise (2012), who examines the transcripts to characterize Fed behavior during the 1970s. Romer and Romer (2000) show that the Fed's internal forecasts are far superior to commercial forecasts.

[10] There is an equivalence among some forms of these different basic Taylor rules, and the forward-looking, backward-looking, and partial adjustment versions, as Ang, Dong, and Piazzesi (2007) explore.

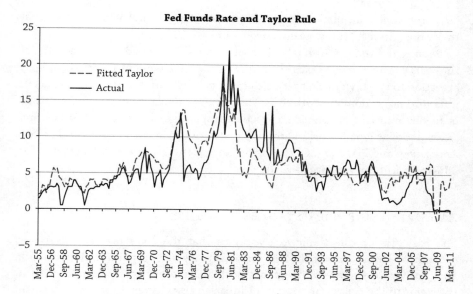

Fed Funds Rate and Taylor Rule

Period: 1955Q1 - 2011Q1

	Coeff	Std Error	t-stat
Const	0.97	0.06	15.51
GDP	0.26	0.07	3.58
CPI	1.09	0.41	2.66
R^2	0.52		

Figure 9.4

Fed is predicted to do according to the Taylor rule in equation (9.1) is referred to as a *monetary policy shock*. Thus, the monetary policy shock captures the discretion of the Fed in acting beyond what the Taylor rule prescribes in responding to movements in inflation and output.

Figure 9.4 graphs a version of the Taylor rule compared to the actual Fed funds rate from March 1951 to March 2011. Estimates of Taylor rule coefficients are also reported proxying economic growth with real GDP growth and inflation with CPI inflation, both defined as year-on-year changes. The coefficients on economic growth and inflation are both positive, consistent with the Taylor (1993) predictions, and the R^2 is over 50%, indicating a good fit. Figure 9.4 shows that monetary policy shocks can be large and persistent. The Taylor rule indicates that the Fed should have set interest rates to be much higher during the 1970s and reduced interest rates by more during the 1980s. Fed funds rates largely conformed to Taylor rule predictions during the 1990s. In the early 2000s, the Fed funds rate was much lower than predicted. During the financial crisis in 2009, the Taylor rule predicted that Fed funds rates should have been negative—precisely when the Fed embarked on its unconventional monetary policy programs. More recently, in

2011, the Taylor rule model advocated interest rates to be much higher than what they were (interest rates were effectively zero).

Because the Fed has such a big impact on bond prices and because the Taylor rule tells us (for the most part) what the Fed will do, bond investors should pay attention to the Taylor rule as it helps them get their arms around the impact of inflation and economic growth risks. The Fed also sets short-term interest rates to be higher or lower than predicted by a pure response to only macro variables, and this is monetary policy risk. Monetary policy risk is important for bond prices: Ang, Dong, and Piazzesi (2007) estimate that monetary policy risk accounts for 25% to 35% of the variance of yield levels.

2.4. CHANGING POLICY STANCES

The basic Taylor rule framework assumes that the Fed's *reaction function* is constant—that is, the way the Fed responds to a given output or inflation shock does not vary over time, although obviously the shocks vary in size. But what if the *stance* of the Fed toward output or inflation risk changes over time? In equation (9.1), this is captured by time-varying coefficients on growth and inflation, rather than constant coefficients of 0.5 and 1.5, respectively, in the benchmark Taylor (1993) model. In addition to potentially changing Fed stances with respect to macro risk, which of the Fed's dueling mandates—full employment or stable prices—has been given precedence by the Fed?

These are the questions that Ang et al. (2011) investigate. They find that the Fed policy stances—the policy coefficients on output and inflation in the Taylor rule—have evolved a great deal over time, mostly with respect to inflation rather than output. These changing policy stances also have a big impact on long-term bond prices.

Figure 9.5 estimated by Ang et al. (2011) shows that the monetary policy loading on output has not moved very much from around 0.4, whereas the inflation loading has changed substantially from close to zero in 2003 to approximately 2.4 in 1983. Figure 9.5 shows that during the 1960s and 1970s, the response to inflation was less than 1.0. According to the Taylor principle, the coefficient on inflation should be greater than 1.0, otherwise *multiple equilibria* occur. This is economist talk for very volatile and unfortunate macro outcomes—like the high inflation and low economic growth (*stagflation*) of the 1970s.[11] The Fed became much more aggressive in battling inflation during the 1980s, when Volcker brought the inflation beast under control. In the early 2000s, the inflation loading was again very low but rose quickly in the mid-2000s.

---

[11] This view is argued by Taylor (1999) and Clarida, Gali, and Gertler (2000), among others. For a theory view of how multiple equilibria can arise and why this is bad, see Benhabib, Schmitt-Grohe, and Uribe (2001).

Time-Varying Taylor Rule Coefficients

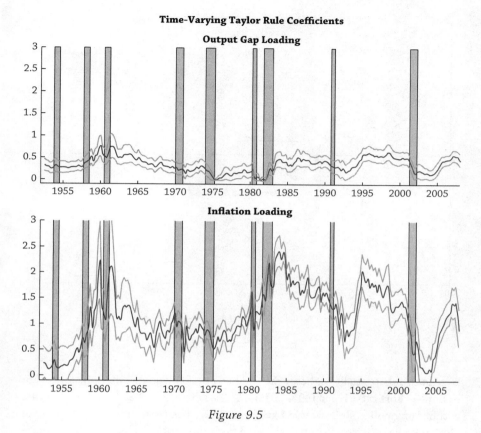

Figure 9.5

One question that Ang et al. can address is the existence of a *Greenspan put* (and after him a *Bernanke put*), which refers to the propensity of the Fed to open the spigots and provide liquidity whenever the economy experiences bad shocks—thereby, in the view of some critics, rescuing investors from their own risky decisions and encouraging ever-greater recklessness. Some commentators, including John Taylor, raised the possibility that short-term interest rates were held too low for too long after the Fed lowered interest rates in response to the 9/11 terrorist attacks and the 2001 recession.[12] Figure 9.6 from Ang et al. (2011) plots the path of the short rate after 2001 compared with what it would have been had the Fed maintained its output and inflation stances in 2000. The difference between the solid line (data) and the dashed line (which is the counterfactual) is a quantitative measure of the Greenspan put. Interest rates from 2002 to 2005 would

[12] See Taylor, J., "How Government Created the Financial Crisis," *Wall Street Journal* op-ed, Feb. 9, 2009.

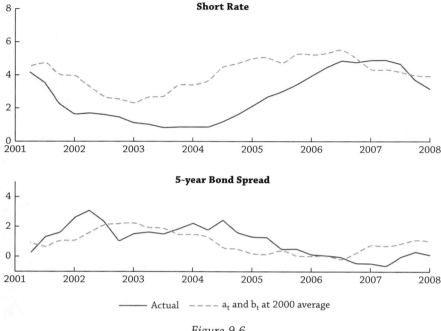

Figure 9.6

have been substantially higher if the Fed had not changed its inflation stance. For example, short rates reach 0.9% in June 2003, whereas at this time the short rate without any policy shifts would have been 2.7%. The bottom panel in Figure 9.6 plots the five-year bond spread, showing both the actual spread and the one pre-dicted had the Fed not been so accommodating. They are very similar. Thus, the Greenspan put does not explain any part in the flattening of the yield curve in the early 2000s (the *Greenspan conundrum*).

The message for investors is that not only are macro risks, growth and in-flation, important for bonds, but investors should take into consideration the actions of the Fed. Fed risk includes monetary policy shocks, which are deviations of Fed behavior from what would normally be expected of Fed policy with respect to output and inflation, and also changing policy stances, especially with regard to how the Fed responds to inflation risk.

2.5. NEW MONETARY POLICY

We live in the post-financial crisis world, and discussion of monetary policy risk for bond prices cannot be complete without discussing how an investor should react to the Fed's new unconventional monetary tools, which will in all likelihood become conventional. These programs have taken many forms in addition to quantitative easing and fall under an alphabet soup of acronyms, including the

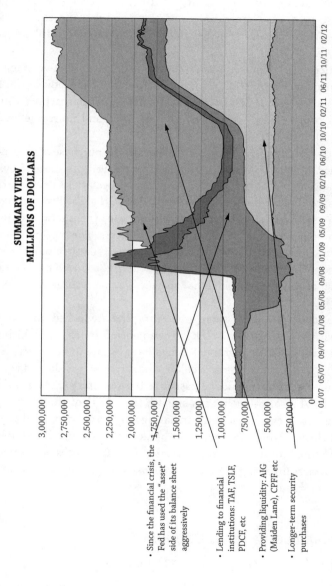

Figure 9.7

Money Market Investor Funding Facility (MMIFF), the Asset-Backed Commercial Paper Money Market Mutual Fund Liquidity Facility (AMLF), the Commercial Paper Funding Facility (CPFF), the Primary Dealer Credit Facility (PDCF), the Term Securities Lending Facility (TSLF), and the Term Auction Facility (TAF). The Money Market Investor Funding Facility (MMIFF) was never used. Strangely, the MBS Purchase Program seemed not to get an acronym. And the Fed also loaned money to primary dealer affiliates and banks: JP Morgan, Citibank, and Bank of America.

Since the financial crisis, the Fed has expanded its balance sheet very aggressively and bought many risky assets. Figure 9.7 shows the explosion in the Fed balance sheet since September 2008, which at April 2012 is approaching $3 trillion. Traditional "plain vanilla" Treasuries have declined and mortgage-backed securities now total almost $1 trillion.

For unconventional monetary policy, defined here as the purchase of risky non-Treasury securities, to have a permanent effect after the Fed has ceased buying, the buying programs must have either altered investor expectations or risk premiums or there must be some segmentation in the market so that the Fed can change prices in one part of the market or yield curve without the other markets or parts of the yield curve fully adjusting to offset the Fed's effects. The original version of segmented markets was the *preferred habitat theory* or clientele model developed by Culbertson (1957) and Modigliani and Sutch (1966a, 1996b). The most recent incarnation of this theory, which has spawned a new, resurgent literature, is Vayanos and Vila (2009).

In the Vayanos and Vila model, there are agents who are locked into, or prefer, bonds of a particular maturity. Think here of pension funds, say, which like long-dated Treasuries because they must hedge long-term liabilities. There are also arbitrageurs, who are able to take speculative positions across the yield curve. Think here of hedge funds or the (now-emasculated) proprietary trading desks of investment banks. While arbitrageurs can smooth the effects of shocks at a particular maturity induced, say, by the Fed purchasing long-term bonds, Fed actions have permanent effects across the yield curve because they change the supply of bonds available to those investors locked into long-term Treasuries of that maturity. Thus, asset owners investing in fixed income instruments might consider the effects of relative supply as a factor.

3. Term Spread (Long-Term Bonds)

3.1. RISK AND RETURNS OF LONG-TERM BONDS

Bond yields and prices are inversely related, so bond returns are high in times of falling yields, and vice versa. Since Figures 9.2 and 9.3 document the general pattern that interest rates rose until the early 1980s and then fell, it is not surprising that bonds generally did relatively poorly up until the early 1980s and then had high returns since the early 1980s. Table 9.8 lists means, volatilities, and Sharpe ratios across maturities from January 1952 to December 2011 of excess bond returns, computing excess returns using the T-bill rate as the short rate. Like many researchers, I use the post-1951 sample because bond yields were pegged at artificially low yields by the Fed until the 1951 Treasury Accord between the U.S. Treasury and the Federal Reserve. This was a legacy of World War II when interest rates were held low so the government could borrow cheaply. The Treasury Accord freed the Fed from being forced to purchase bonds issued by the Treasury and gave the Fed independence.[13] I split the sample at the end of 1982 because the Fed temporarily targeted monetary reserves in its conduct of monetary policy from October 6, 1979 to October 9, 1982.[14]

Table 9.8 shows that from 1952 to 1982, excess returns of bonds of five- to ten-year maturities were zero, on average, and excess returns of bonds with maturities greater than ten years were actually negative, at −0.62%. But since 1983, bonds have done very well as an asset class. Bonds with maturities of five to ten years and greater than ten years have returned 5.85% and 8.48% in excess of the T-bill rate from 1983 to 2011. Thus, the overall positive returns of these bonds of 1.91% and 2.97%, respectively, over the full sample are mostly due to the general decline in all interest rates post-1980. Over the full sample, bond returns increase, on average, with maturity: excess returns are 0.59% for bonds of less than one-year maturity and increase to 2.97% for bonds with maturities greater than ten years. Table 9.8 also separately breaks out 2000–2011, the Lost Decade for stock returns. (Stock returns are reported in the last column of Table 9.8.) Since 2000, bonds have been a terrific investment relative to stocks: bonds with maturities greater than ten years have returned 7.18% in excess of T-bills compared to −0.39% for U.S. equities.

The Sharpe ratios reported in Table 9.8 generally decrease across maturities starting from above 0.7 for bonds of maturities less than one year to around 0.3 for long-term bonds. Because average returns increase with maturities, the falling Sharpe ratios as maturities lengthen are due to the much greater volatility of long-term bond returns relative to short-term bond returns. This is in itself surprising—a ten-year bond should reflect the macro and financial environment over ten years, and given mean reversion of interest rates and the tendency of economic shocks to die out, this implies that long-term bonds should have significantly lower volatilities than short-term bonds. They don't. Volatilities of long-term bonds are only a little lower than short-term bonds. The large volatility of long-term bonds is indeed excessive compared to simple economic models

---

[13] For an account of joint monetary and fiscal policy in the years after World War II, see Eichengreen and Garber (1991).

[14] The Taylor rule is still appropriate over this sample, as Cook (1989) shows the short-term interest rate is a good instrument to proxy the Fed's actual monetary targeting operating procedure during this period.

Table 9.8

		Treasury Returns						Stocks
	1-12 mths	1-2 years	2-3 Years	3-4 Years	4-5 Years	5-10 Years	> 10 Years*	Stocks
Excess Returns								
1952-1982	0.47%	0.56%	0.54%	0.36%	0.04%	-0.01%	-0.62%	5.93%
1983-2011	0.72%	1.58%	2.29%	2.93%	3.28%	3.96%	5.66%	7.00%
2000-2011	0.53%	1.45%	2.43%	3.30%	4.03%	4.59%	7.18%	-0.39%
1952-2011	0.59%	1.05%	1.39%	1.60%	1.61%	1.91%	2.97%	6.45%
Volatilities								
1952-1982	1.03%	2.50%	3.66%	4.36%	4.96%	5.85%	8.48%	14.09%
1983-2011	0.48%	1.50%	2.55%	3.54%	4.43%	5.71%	9.76%	15.45%
2000-2011	0.41%	1.31%	2.35%	3.37%	4.34%	5.27%	10.41%	16.36%
1952-2011	0.81%	2.08%	3.18%	4.00%	4.73%	5.81%	9.27%	14.76%
Sharpe Ratios								
1952-1982	0.46	0.22	0.15	0.08	0.01	0.00	-0.07	0.42
1983-2011	1.51	1.05	0.90	0.83	0.74	0.69	0.58	0.45
2000-2011	1.31	1.11	1.04	0.98	0.93	0.87	0.69	-0.02
1952-2011	0.73	0.51	0.44	0.40	0.34	0.33	0.32	0.44

Data: CRSP Fama bond total returns, S&P 500 total returns

*Data missing Sep 1962 to Nov 1971

with just mean-reverting short rates. This phenomenon is the *bond excess vola-tility puzzle* and was documented by the same economist, Robert Shiller (1979), who documented excess volatility in stock markets (See chapter 8).[15] Long-term bond yields also exhibit large excess sensitivity to macroeconomic announcement shocks.[16] Long-term bonds exhibit relatively large volatility and are sensitive to movements in macro and other factors because they exhibit large risk premi-ums. That is, long-term bonds are very sensitive to factor risk, and to adequately describe factor risk premiums for bonds, we need to explain how factor risk premiums are related across the yield curve.

3.2. MACRO-FACTOR TERM STRUCTURE MODELS

While conventional monetary policy operates on the short end of the yield curve, it influences the long end as well. Bond prices at the long end of the yield curve, however, are (largely but not completely now due to quantitative easing) set by markets, and thus the Fed has much less control of these long-term bonds than over the price of Fed funds. Figure 9.2 shows the three-month T-bill has almost identical movements with the Fed funds rate, which the Taylor rule tells us re-sponds to macro factors. The same macro factors, or the level factor, will affect the entire yield curve through *no arbitrage*.

While prices of two different stocks can diverge wildly because they have dif-ferent managers and operations, risk-free bonds with different maturities cannot have prices too far out of whack with each other. This is because bonds only dif-fer in terms of their maturity since their cash flows are risk free. Bond markets are chock full of arbitrageurs who pounce on the slightest profitable opportuni-ties when prices of bonds with a particular maturity move out of line with prices of bonds with similar maturities. While there are some limited arbitrage opportu-nities in bond markets (no one believes—not even ivory-tower academics—that markets are perfectly efficient; see chapter 6), bonds must move in a tight fashion with other bonds. Otherwise, the profit opportunities grow too big, and like in a game of whack-a-mole, smart investors quickly bash their mallets down to remove them. We capture this phenomenon with models where investors receive returns for holding bonds commensurate with their risk, and as a close approximation, we assume bond prices are determined by the *absence* of arbitrage. These are called *term structure models*. The key insight of this class of models is that bond yields are linked to each other—across maturities and across time.

Take, for example, a two-year Treasury note. Investing for a two-year period, we can just go and buy the two-year T-note. We can also invest our money over a

[15] Early economic models with *constant* risk premiums were not only unable to explain excess volatilities of long-term bonds, they could not even explain why the yield curve sloped upward, on average (see Backus, Gregory, and Zin (1989) and den Haan (1995)).

[16] See Gürkaynak, Sack and Swanson (2005).

two-year horizon by buying a three-month T-bill. In three months, the T-bill expires, but then we invest the proceeds in another three-month T-bill. If we *roll over* three-month T-bills over seven successive quarters, we will have reached the same horizon as directly investing in a two-year T-note. The two strategies are not identical—we are subject to roll-over risk when we invest in a series of T-bills, whereas we know the yield today on the two-year Treasury note. Nevertheless, the price of a three-month T-bill cannot move too far from the price of a two-year Treasury note. If the roll-over strategy is very cheap compared to the two-year Treasury note, arbitrageurs will buy T-bills and sell notes. Conversely, if T-bills are too expensive compared to notes, investors will sell T-bills and buy notes. Following this logic, the price of any long-term bond must be related to the price of any short-term bond.

Risk Premiums

We can decompose the movements of long-term yields into pure "expectations" components and components that embed risk premiums. According to the *Expectations Hypothesis* originally developed by one of the great economists of the early twentieth century, Irving Fisher (1896),

$$\text{Nominal long yield} = \underbrace{\text{average of expected short rates}}_{\text{Expectations Hypothesis}} + \text{risk premiums.} \quad (9.2)$$

If we interpret the three-month T-bill as the short rate, then the two-year Treasury note yield should be the average of eight three-month T-bill yields: the current three-month T-bill, the future three-month T-bill yield that will prevail in three months time, the future three-month T-bill yield that will start in six months time, and so on, up to the end of two years. This is the Expectations Hypothesis component. In the real world, this does not hold. One three-month T-bill today and seven future, roll-over three-month T-bill positions do not, on average, equal the two-year Treasury yield.[17] There is risk in the rolled-over T-bill positions: the macro-economy may change and inflation may spike, volatility may change, or investors may become suddenly more risk averse. Not surprisingly, the risk premium components, especially in long-term Treasuries, can be quite large.

Another decomposition is based on the *Fisher Hypothesis*, also by Fisher (1930):

$$\text{Nominal long yield} = \underbrace{\text{real yield} + \text{expected inflation}}_{\text{Fisher Hypothesis}} + \text{risk premiums} \quad (9.3)$$

The pure Fisher Hypothesis states that the long yield is equal to the real yield and expected inflation and ignores the risk premium components. Like

---

[17] There is a very large literature testing the Expectations Hypothesis beginning with Fama and Bliss (1987) and rejecting it overwhelmingly for the United States.

the Expectations Hypothesis, the Fisher Hypothesis is rejected in the data. Nevertheless, the risk premiums, both relative to the Expectations Hypothesis and the Fisher Hypothesis, must be closely related across bonds of similar maturities; a ten-year bond must move, by our smart whack-a-mole investors, in a manner similar to a bond of maturity of nine years.

Term structure models specify the types of risk premiums and how they change. Thus, they capture how the two-year Treasury yield can deviate from an average of current and future T-bill rates (deviations from the Expectations Hypothesis), and how the long yield differs from the real rate and expected inflation (deviations from the Fisher Hypothesis). These models have three ingredients:

1. The underlying risk factors,
2. How the short rate moves, and
3. How the short rate and factor risk premiums affect long-term bonds.

The dynamics of the short rate in (2) can be interpreted as modeling how the Fed sets (or is implied to set) the interest rates at the shortest end of the yield curve in terms of risk factors (inflation and output according to the Taylor rule). The risk premiums specified in (3) compensate investors for maturity or duration risk, monetary policy risk, uncertainty, macro risk coming from inflation and growth shocks, and other risks. The key result is that the risk premiums differ across maturities and across time.[18] The workhorse models of today are the class of *affine term structure models*, which embody time-varying volatility, macro and latent factors, and what turns out to be very important to match the dynamics of yields in data—time-varying risk premiums.[19]

Term structure models derive both the dynamics of the entire cross section of bonds across maturities relative to each other, that is, the term structure of interest rates at a given point in time and specify how the term structure of interest rates evolves across time. In the context of equations (9.2) and (9.3), term structure models specify how risk premiums change across maturities. In a term structure model, the ten-year risk premium and, hence, yield is a function of the underlying factors and must move in such a way that it does not move "too much" (in a fashion consistent with no arbitrage) relative to the nine-year yield. The same must be true for the nine-year yield relative to the eight-year yield, and so on. Thus, the term structure model naturally picks up the notion of strong systematic

---

[18] The no arbitrage assumption in term structure models implies that investors receive the same *risk-adjusted* compensation across all bonds.

[19] The affine class of term structure models was formalized by Duffie and Kan (1996), but the first model was a pure Gaussian model developed by Vasicek (1977). Oldrich Vasicek played an important role in the development of the index fund industry (see chapter 17). A famous heteroskedastic model, also a special case of the affine framework, is Cox, Ingersoll, and Ross (1985). Time-varying risk premiums are essential in matching deviations from the Expectations Hypothesis, as Dai and Singleton (2002) show. For a summary of term structure models, see Piazzesi (2010).

factor dependence of yields so that yield dynamics at a particular maturity are tightly bound to other maturities. The affine term structure models do this in a very tractable way so that bond yields are affine (constant plus linear) functions of risk factors. This makes the models straightforward to use in many applications from asset allocation to derivative pricing. The risk premiums in these models change over time—so the shape of the yield curve can take different shapes in recessions and expansions or in times of low or high volatility.

The first generation of term structure models employed only latent variables. That is, they described the yield curve by using only variables that were not observable macro factors and were "filtered" out from the bond yields themselves. These models did provide interpretations for what these latent factors represented by their action on the yield curve: the level, slope, and curvature factors, with the most important of these being the level factor (see Figure 9.2 and 9.3).[20] A sizeable macro-finance literature now characterizes the movements of yields and risk premiums using macro factors, including economic growth and inflation, partly inspired by Ang and Piazzesi (2003).

Monika Piazzesi and I wrote the first draft of this paper in 1998 while we were PhD students at Stanford University. At the time, we could not foresee the big bump in our citation counts that it would generate (we got lucky). We brought together the Taylor policy rule and factor dynamics for inflation and output that were widely used in macro models, with time-varying risk premium models in finance that were able to closely match bond prices. An advantage of the model is that it explicitly showed how monetary policy risk was priced in the yield curve. We have since worked on other macro-finance term structure models together, with our students, and other co-authors.

3.3. MACRO RISK PREMIUMS IN LONG-TERM BONDS

The macro-finance literature shows that macro factors play a very important part in the dynamics of the yield curve and the excess returns of bonds. Ang and Piazzesi find that the variance of bond yields at various points on the yield curve has the following attributions to output, inflation, and other (including monetary policy) factors:

	Inflation	Output	Other Factors (Including Monetary Policy)
Short End	70%	13%	17%
Middle	62%	11%	27%
Long End	32%	6%	62%

[20] Other labels are, of course, used. The canonical study of Dai and Singleton (2000), for example, labels the three factors "level," "central tendency," and "volatility." The third factor has slightly different dynamics depending on the particular affine specification employed.

At the short end of the yield curve, macro factors explain approximately 85% of the variation of yield levels decreasing to 40% of long-term bond yields. Of the macro factors, yield movements are most sensitive to inflation and inflation risk, which is not surprising because bonds are nominal securities. Monetary policy plays a large role in the "other factors," and monetary policy risk is priced in long-term bonds, but Ang and Piazzesi use other latent factors that may represent other risk factors.

Ang, Bekaert, and Wei (2008) decompose yields into real yields, expected inflation, and risk premiums based on the Fisher decomposition in equation (9.3). In their sample, they find that the short rate is 5.4% and the long yield is 6.3%, which can be decomposed as:

	Real Rate	Expected Inflation	Risk Premium	Total
Short End	1.2%	3.9%	0.3%	5.4%
Long End	1.3%	3.9%	1.1%	6.3%

Thus, most of the upward-sloping nominal yield curve (going from 5.4% to 6.3% in the Ang–Piazzesi sample) is explained by risk premiums rather than by real rates. The variance of the long yield is 20% attributable to variations of real rates, 70% due to movements in expected inflation, and 10% due to changes in risk premiums. Thus, expected inflation and inflation risk are extremely important determinants of long-term bond prices.

The risk premiums on long-term bonds also vary through time. Risk premiums are *counter-cyclical*: long-term bond yields are high relative to short rates during recessions because agents demand large compensation for taking on risk. The short rate is *pro-cyclical* because of the Taylor rule; the Fed lowers short rates in recessions to stimulate economic activity. During expansions, the opposite relations hold. Bonds do badly during recessions, where they have low prices and high yields. Investors feel most risk averse during these times of high marginal utility (see chapter 6). They demand higher risk premiums, which are reflected in a steeper yield curve. We tend to see steeper yield curves during other hard times like periods of high inflation, which tend to coincide with times of low economic activity. Bad times are also times of low productivity, and they could be times when other supply shocks hit the economy, like oil price shocks.[21]

The counter-cyclical risk premiums of long-term bonds manifest themselves in the ability of the term spread to predict recessions. Recessions have upward-sloping yield curves when the risk premiums on bonds are the highest. Correspondingly, the peaks of expansions are when risk premiums are the lowest,

---

[21] See Piazzesi and Schneider (2006), Wachter (2006), and Rudebusch and Swanson (2012).

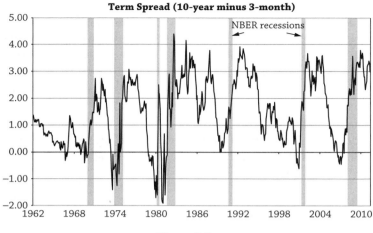

Figure 9.9

and the yield curve is downward sloping. Thus, the term spread is a counter-cyclical indicator of future economic activity, and low, especially negative, term spreads forecast economic slowdowns.[22] Figure 9.9 plots the ten-year Treasury minus the three-month T-bill term spread and shades the National Bureau of Economic Research recessions. The term spread has been negative prior to every recession since the 1960s.[23]

3.4. OTHER FACTORS

While macro factors and monetary policy account for a substantial part of yield curve movements, they do not explain everything. During the financial crisis of 2008–2009, there was a pronounced *flight to safety* as many investors moved into risk-free Treasuries and sold off risky assets including corporate bonds and equities. One measure of liquidity is the *on-the-run/off-the-run* spread. When Treasuries are newly issued, they are most liquid and called "on the run." But as time passes and new Treasuries are issued, the old ones become "off the run." On-the-run bonds are in higher demand by investors, so their yields are lower, on average, than off-the-run bonds. The on-the-run/off-the-run effect is a liquidity measure because it involves instruments with the same credit risk (zero, assuming

[22] Some papers in this literature include Harvey (1988), Estrella and Mishkin (1998), and Ang, Piazzesi, and Wei (2006).

[23] At the time of writing, these are December 1969 to November 1970, November 1973 to March 1975, July 1981 to November 1982, July 1990 to March 1991, March 2001 to November 2001, and December 2007 to June 2009.

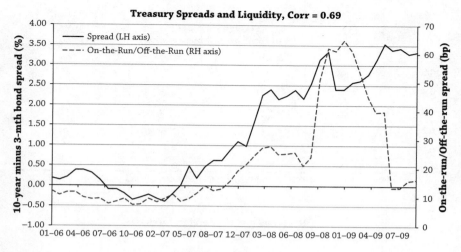

Figure 9.10

Treasuries are risk free) but different volumes and prices.[24] The effect is, however, influenced by how and when the Treasury brings to market new issues.

Figure 9.10 plots the ten-year Treasury minus three-month T-bill term spread (left-hand axis) with the on-the-run/off-the-run spread (on the right-hand axis) from January 2006 to October 2009. Higher on-the-run/off-the-run spreads indicate periods of greater illiquidity. During this sample, the correlation between the term spread and the illiquidity spread was a lofty 69%. Figure 9.10 shows that the term spread tracks the rise in illiquidity from 2007 to 2009. However, the term spread remains elevated after the economy stabilizes and the financial crisis passes post-2009, whereas the illiquidity spreads fall and the market recovers its liquidity. Nevertheless, the demand for Treasuries during times of illiquidity and high volatility, or the flight-to-safety effect, was an important factor driving Treasuries during the financial crisis.

Recently several researchers have focused on the effect of different investors, particularly foreign investors, on the dynamics of the yield curve. The top panel of Figure 9.11 graphs the proportion of Treasuries held by foreign investors (excluding official holdings in central banks), showing this has increased from below 10% during the 1960s to over 50% today. (The largest of these foreign positions is China's; see chapter 1.) The bottom panel of Figure 9.11 plots net new issues by the Treasury and foreign demand for Treasuries, both normalized by GDP. The panel shows that both are cyclical and the effects have been increasing over time. Foreign demand had a local peak in the mid-2000s and also during the financial crisis in 2008. Fed Chair Ben Bernanke himself suggested that these

---

[24] See Amihud and Mendelson (1991) and Krishnamurthy (2002).

Panel A
Foreign Holdings
(% of total amount outstanding)

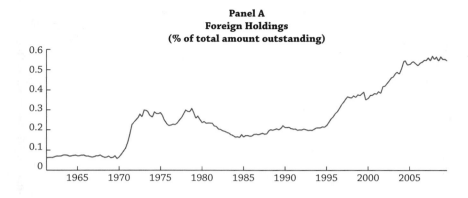

Panel B
Net Issues and Net Foreign Purchases
(% of US GDP)

Figure 9.11

developments could be affecting bond prices, saying in 2007 that "strong foreign demand for U.S. long-term debt has been one factor tending to reduce the term premium."[25]

The modern clientele models based on Vayanos and Vila (2009) predict that the smaller the supply or the greater the demand, all else equal, the higher the prices of Treasuries and the lower their yields. The Vayanos–Vila framework would interpret certain classes of investors such as foreigners as demanding certain maturities for exogenous reasons—in China's case, this could be to manage its exchange rate—and this foreign demand affects bond prices. Greenwood and Vayanos (2010), Hamilton and Wu (2012), and Krishnamurthy and Vissing-Jørgensen (2012) find supply effects in Treasuries consistent with the clientele model. Thus, actions by the Fed such as quantitative easing must be weighed along with demand from investors. This is related to how outstanding supply should affect optimal holdings of fixed income. We return to these topics in chapter 14 on factor investing.

[25] Speech by Fed Chair Ben Bernanke in 2007 at the Fourth Economic Summit, Stanford Institute for Economic Policy Research, Stanford University, http://www.federalreserve.gov/newsevents/speech/bernanke20070302a.htm.

4. Credit Spread (Corporate Bonds)

So far our analysis has assumed that bonds are risk free. Corporate bonds are affected by all the factors that affect risk-free bonds, but in addition we must consider credit, or default, risk. It turns out that the corporate bond spread, which is the difference in yields between corporate bonds and Treasuries, contains more than just credit risk.

4.1. RISK AND RETURNS OF CORPORATE BONDS

Figure 9.12 graphs corporate bond yield spreads over Treasuries from January 1973 to December 2011. Risk increases as we move from AAA (very safe) to Caa (high yield, or junk). There is a pronounced commonality among the corporate bond spreads, especially for the investment grade bonds, which are those with ratings Baa and upward. Figure 9.12 also shows that these corporate spreads vary with the economic cycle, with increases during the mid-1970s recession, the early-1980s recession, and the early-2000s recession and a noticeable spike during the most recent recession caused by the financial crisis. The figure also shows that for junk bonds, the level of the yield spread and its volatility are much higher than for investment-grade bonds.

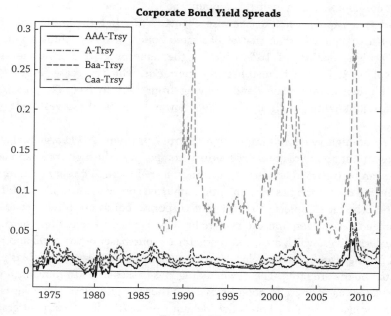

Figure 9.12

Table 9.13

	AAA	Aa	A	Baa	Caa	Trsys
Corporate Bond Returns Jan 1987 to Dec 2011						
Yields						
Mean	6.20%	6.35%	6.72%	7.35%	15.45%	5.26%
Corp Spread	0.93%	1.09%	1.45%	2.09%	10.19%	
Excess Returns over Treasuries						
Mean	0.32%	0.42%	0.43%	1.04%	0.86%	
Stdev	2.61%	2.92%	4.00%	4.70%	16.00%	
Sharpe	0.124	0.143	0.109	0.221	0.054	

High yields, however, do not translate into high returns. Table 9.13 lists corporate bond yield spreads and realized returns from January 1987 to December 2011. The realized credit premium has been fairly modest and much lower than the credit spreads. Yield spreads for AAA bonds above Treasuries are 0.93%, but realized average excess returns over Treasuries are about one third, at 0.32%. For Baa-rated bonds, yield spreads are 2.09%, and mean excess returns are approximately half this amount, at 1.04%. For junk bonds, the credit spread is a gaping 10.19% (see also Figure 9.12), but the mean excess return is actually lower than that of Baa-rated bonds, at 0.86%. Junk bonds also have a high volatility of 16%, which is the same order of magnitude as equity volatility. Table 9.13 also lists Sharpe ratios, which increase from 0.08 to 0.22 for investment-grade bonds moving from AAA to Baa. The Sharpe ratios for junk-rated bonds is only 0.07, lower than all the investment-grade classes.

Why do high yields not imply high returns? Ilmanen (2011) argues that the modest credit premium in realized returns compared to the high credit spreads in yields can be traced to, among other things, a credit and illiquidity premium (of around 30–60 base points) and an option-adjusted spread (of around 70–100 base points). The latter reflects the fact that corporate bonds are often issued with embedded derivatives, and the raw credit spreads need to adjust for the cost of these derivatives, which are often costly for the purchaser of the bond and beneficial for the issuer. Ilmanen also points out that there is a systematic bias in the way the bonds are rated. The downgrading bias causes firms to move into more risky classes as their credit deteriorates, and thus the junk class "overcounts" defaults because many junk bonds that default were originally investment grade at issue. Nevertheless, a large amount of the credit risk premium reflects, naturally, credit risk.

4.2. DEFAULT MODELS

Structural models of default risk are originally due to Robert Merton (1974). These models are based on the same type of intuition as the Black–Scholes (1973) option pricing formula. In fact, one of the first applications of the Black–Scholes option pricing model covered in the original paper of Fisher Black and Myron Scholes was the valuation of corporate bonds.

Structural default models work by simulating out the value of the firm. If the value of the firm drops below a pre-determined barrier, the firm defaults. At default, bondholders recover a fraction of the face value of debt. The simulations of firm value can be solved analytically in simple cases but need to be solved numerically in more complex versions. In the original default models, the barrier was *exogenously* given at the face value of debt. In recent structural default models, the default boundaries are *endogenous*, as the firm can optimally choose when to default to maximize shareholder value. Bond holders themselves can also decide when to pull the trigger and initiate firm bankruptcy when a firm is in financial distress.[26]

The key insight from default models is that debt is a put option on the firm's assets. Denote the value of the firm as V, which is the value of the underlying assets of the firm (*enterprise value*). Assume that a firm issues debt with a face value of $100. At the maturity of the debt, the payoffs to the bondholders are:

	Firm Value $V < \$100$	Firm Value $V > \$100$
Payoff to Bondholder	V	$100

If the firm is worth less than $100, the bondholders get the whole firm, which is worth V. If the firm is worth more than $100, the bondholders are paid $100, and then shareholders get the residual value of $(V-\$100)$. Pictorially, we can illustrate this as:

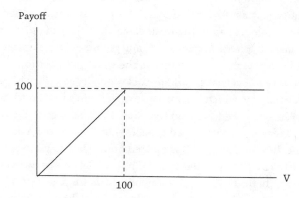

---

[26] The first paper with an endogenous default boundary was Leland (1994). Broadie, Chernov, and Sundaresan (2007) consider the case where either equity holders or bondholders can initiate default.

These payoffs can be equivalently summarized as:

	Firm Value $V < \$100$	Firm Value $V > \$100$
Hold a Risk-Free Bond	$100	$100
Write a Put with Strike $= \$100$	V – $100	0
Total	V	$100

Thus, the payoff to a corporate bondholder is equivalent to the bondholder holding a risk-free bond and selling a put with strike price equal to the face value of the debt. Thus, bondholders have written a put option on the firm's assets. Corporate bondholders are *short volatility*. Equity holders, conversely, hold a call option on the firm's assets and are long volatility.

From this decomposition, we can see that

$$\text{Risk-Free Bond} + \text{Put} = \text{Corporate Bond.}$$

Or, rearranging we have

$$\text{Corporate Bond} - \text{Risk-Free Bond} = \text{Short Put Option.} \qquad (9.4)$$

The corporate bond spread is hence the value of a short put option on the assets of the borrower with a strike price equal to the face value of the debt. The credit spread increases with volatility, leverage, and maturity.

The intuition behind the fact that the credit spread is a put option is that equity holders have limited liability and are paid second after bond holders. Equity holders have borrowed the par value of debt ($100 in the above example) from creditors. Equity holders can walk away from their obligations and put the firm to creditors when the firm value is low. It is in this sense that they own a put option. By put–call parity, equity holders have a call option on the firm—equity owners are long volatility just as debt holders are short volatility. Another way to view this is that equity holders get all the upside, which is the call option on the firm's assets. *Bond holders only have downside risk*, and get none of the upside. Thus, bond holders price in the downside risk, which is the short put position.

Equation (9.4) predicts that credit spreads widen as volatility increases. Figure 9.14 plots VIX volatility, which is a measure of volatility from option prices, with the Baa minus Treasury credit spread (Baa-Tsy) in Panel A and VIX volatility with the Caa minus Treasury credit spread (Caa-Tsy) in Panel B from January 1986 to December 2011. In each panel, VIX is plotted on the left-hand axis and the credit spreads are plotted on the right-hand axis. The correlations between volatility and credit spreads are high: 64% for Baa-Tsy and 56% for Caa-Tsy. Thus, volatility is a crucial factor for corporate bonds, and high volatility occurs contemporaneously with high credit spreads and lower realized returns. Note that in both panels in Figure 9.14, the temporary jump in volatility due to the 1987 crash was not

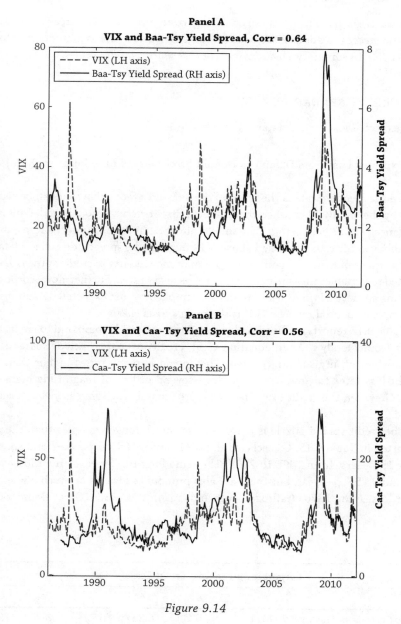

Panel A

VIX and Baa-Tsy Yield Spread, Corr = 0.64

Panel B

VIX and Caa-Tsy Yield Spread, Corr = 0.56

Figure 9.14

reflected in higher corporate bond spreads; this affair was concentrated in equity markets. In both the early 1990s recession and the early 2000s recession, junk Caa-Tsy spreads started to increase before investment grade Baa-Tsy spreads, and volatility started to increase before both credit spreads started to increase. In the financial crisis, in contrast, there was a large contemporaneous increase in volatilities and credit spreads in 2007 and 2008 and then a decrease as markets stabilized post-2009. In summary, *credit investments are short volatility trades.*

4.3. CREDIT SPREAD PUZZLE

The expected loss from default is given by

$$\text{Expected Loss from Default} = \text{Default Probability} \times (1 - \text{Recovery Rate}),$$
(9.5)

where the recovery rate is the fraction of the bond's face value that can be recovered by the bondholders when the firm defaults. Structural models of default give guidance for various factors that should affect default and recovery rates, most notably volatility, as discussed above. Although credit spreads do reflect default risk, it turns out that a significant fraction of movements in credit spreads is unrelated to variables measuring default and recovery rates. Furthermore, corporate spreads are several times wider than those implied by just expected default losses in simple structural models. This is the *credit spread puzzle.*[27]

Table 9.15 reports credit spreads above Treasury yields compared to credit loss rates from Moody's. As in equation (9.5), credit loss rates include losses from default net of any sums recovered. The spread is many times higher than the credit loss rates for investment grades—several orders of magnitude higher in fact. However, the credit loss rates are approximately the same as yields for junk bonds.

The credit spread puzzle is observed over much longer samples than the one reported in Table 9.15. Giesecke et al. (2011) study U.S. corporate bond spreads over 150 years, from 1866 to 2008. They find long-run average credit losses are around 0.75% per year, but there are also pronounced waves of much higher default losses: the 1870s (railroad boom and crash), the 1930s (Great Depression),

Table 9.15

Corporate Spreads and Credit Losses (%)					
	Aaa	Aa	A	Baa	Caa
Corp Spreads vs Trsys 1987–2011	6.20	6.35	6.72	88.20	15.40
Credit Loss Rates 1982–2008 (Moody's)	0.00	0.03	0.02	0.12	13.34
Credit Loss = Default and Recovery					

[27] See Huang and Huang (2012) for a summary of the credit spread puzzle.

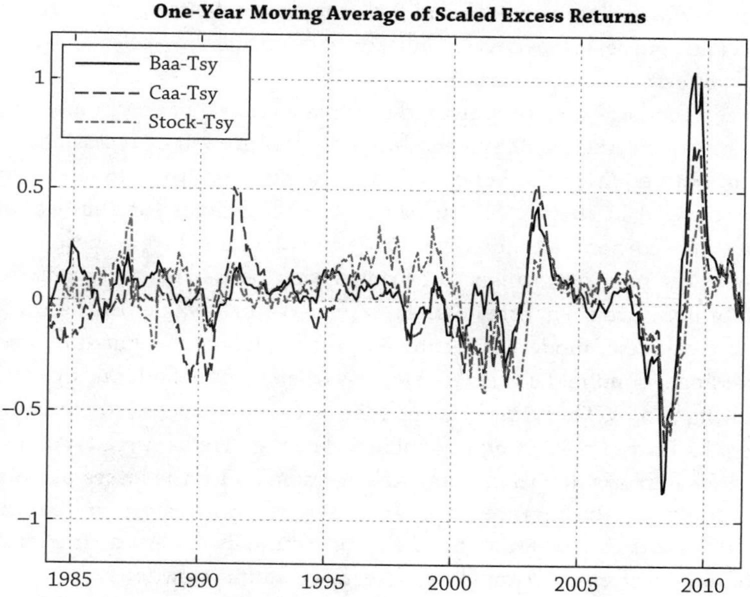

One-Year Moving Average of Scaled Excess Returns

Figure 9.16

and 2001–2001 (dot-com bust). The average credit spread is 1.5%, resulting in a roughly 80 basis point premium for default risk.

The credit spread puzzle is analogous to the equity premium puzzle in chapter 8. New models explain the pronounced difference between credit loss rates and credit spreads by high-and time-varying risk premiums and can jointly match the high equity risk premium and the high credit spread. Corporate bonds and equity must be related as both securities divide up the total value of firms. Corporate bondholders are paid first, while equity holders are residual claimants. Thus, if firm values vary over time, we should expect the changing value of corporate bonds and equity to be linked. Bad times, where firm values shrink enough to jeopardize bondholder claims, result in poor returns for both equity and bonds. (This is the area of $V < 100$ in the example of section 4.2.)

Figure 9.16 plots rolling one-year excess returns over Treasuries for Baa investment grade, Caa high yield, and equities from July 1983 to December 2011. The excess returns have all been scaled so that they have the same volatility as excess equity returns, which is 16.2% in the sample. Figure 9.16 shows a pronounced commonality of corporate bond returns and equity returns; the correlation over the sample between Baa and equities is 48% and the correlation between Caa and equities is 65%. Figure 9.16 shows that after 2005, the co-movement is even higher, particularly during the financial crisis. Both equities and corporate bonds suffered terrific losses during 2008 and 2009 and then bounced back in 2009 and

2010. Post-2005, there is a 65% and 84% correlation between Baa and equities and Caa and equities, respectively. Thus, *corporate bonds are (scaled-down) versions of equity returns.*

Some of the same intuition, then, that explains the equity premium can be extended to explain the credit spread puzzle.[28] Slow growth or recessions are bad times for both equities and bonds. (This is the same macro channel for equities that we covered in chapter 8.) But these same bad times for equities are also bad times for corporate bonds. There are more defaults during these bad times because of the poor performance of firms during recessions, and equity holders choose to liquidate their firms earlier to preserve firm value. In the context of the structural credit models of section 4.2, the boundary of liquidation *rises* during recessions. Bondholders also recover less when firms default during recessions than during booms. Thus, corporate bond investors are exposed to the same types of macro bad times risks as equity holders. The high credit spreads compared to realized defaults are due to investor risk aversion, since the losses on corporate bonds come right during recessions—precisely when investors can afford them least. To harvest the corporate bond risk premium, as modest as it is, investors must be able to stomach strong losses during economic slowdowns.

4.4. LIQUIDITY RISK IN CORPORATE BONDS

Liquidity risk—the ability to easily trade at low cost—is an important factor for corporate bond returns. Collin-Dufresne, Goldstein, and Martin (2001) argue that

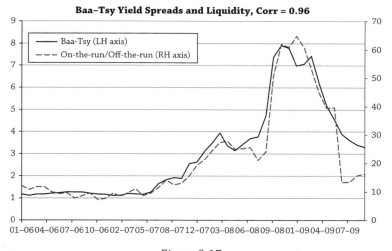

Figure 9.17

[28] See Chen, Collin-Dufresne, and Goldstein (2007) and Chen (2010) for models along these lines.

liquidity, macroeconomic, and aggregate financial condition risks account for up to 40% of all credit spread changes. Longstaff, Mithal, and Neis (2005) show that almost all of the nondefault components of credit spreads are attributable to liquidity. Liquidity certainly played a very important role in the returns of corporate bonds during the financial crisis. Figure 9.17 plots the Baa-Treasury yield spread (left-hand axis) together with the on-the-run/off-the-run liquidity factor (right-hand axis) from January 2006 to October 2009. (Figure 9.17 for corporate spreads is similar to Figure 9.12 for Treasury term spreads.) Movements in the credit spread uncannily mirror the changes in illiquidity; the correlation between the two series is 96%![29] *Corporate bonds have large exposures to illiquidity risk.*

5. U.S. Downgrade Redux

In August 2011 when the United States was downgraded for the first time in history by Standard & Poor's, Treasury yields actually fell. If U.S. credit risk had increased with everything else equal, investors should have demanded a higher risk premium for holding Treasuries, resulting in higher yields rather than lower ones. An important factor for bond prices, especially Treasuries, is illiquidity and volatility risk. U.S. Treasuries have a flight-to-quality characteristic that investors embrace during bad times. In the turmoil of the ongoing European debt crisis, investors poured money into Treasuries as a safe haven, pushing down Treasury yields despite the U.S. downgrade.

Liquidity, however, turns out to be a secondary characteristic of Treasury bond prices. The most important factor for all fixed income instruments is the level factor—which simply acts to shift all yields up or down. The level factor is well described by the actions of the Fed reacting to economic growth and inflation changes. As economic growth accelerates or inflation rises, the Fed raises interest rates to cool the economy. Thus, bond prices reflect economic factor risk, especially inflation risk, along with the risk of unanticipated monetary policy shocks.

In this chapter, we treated Treasuries as risk free. As the U.S. downgrade in August 2011 implied, U.S. Treasuries may not be totally risk free. We deal with risky sovereign debt in chapter 14, including the implications for optimal portfolio choice.

Corporate bonds are exposed to the same risks as risk-free debt but also reflect default risk. The credit risk premium, however, has been fairly modest and much smaller than the equity risk premium. Investing in corporate bonds turns out to be equivalent to a short volatility strategy; as volatility increases, credit spreads also increase. Thus, credit strategies are highly exposed to volatility risk.

---

[29] Friewald, Jankowitsch, and Subrahmanyam (2012) show that the impact of liquidity on corporate bond spreads increases during periods of crises, especially for junk bonds.

Corporate bond returns, especially junk bond returns, have historically closely re-sembled equity returns. This is intuitive because firm values fall during bad times of slow economic growth, slashing the value of equity and corporate debt alike. In addition, liquidity risk in corporate bonds is a major risk factor.

But overall, fixed income is mainly about level. Level reflects Fed risk: how the Fed responds to inflation and output changes, and the Fed's unanticipated monetary policy actions. Watch the Fed.

CHAPTER 10

Alpha (and the Low-Risk Anomaly)

Chapter Summary

Alpha—the average return in excess of a benchmark—tells us more about the set of factors used to construct that benchmark than about the skill involved in beating it. A positive alpha under one set of factors can turn negative using a different set. Whatever the benchmark, alpha is often hard to detect statistically, especially when adjustments for risk vary over time. The risky anomaly—that stocks with low betas and low volatilities have high returns—appears to be a strong source of alpha relative to standard market-weighted benchmarks and value-growth, momentum, and other dynamic factors.

1. GM Asset Management and Martingale

Jim Scott and Brian Herscovici of General Motors (GM) Asset Management, which manages GM Pension Fund, were entranced as Bill Jacques, the CIO of Martingale Asset Management, gave a pitch on his firm's low volatility strategy.[1]

Low volatility seemed too good to be true.

Jacques claimed that stocks with low risk, as measured by past volatility or past beta, had higher returns than stocks with high risk. This was contrary to generally accepted financial theory: the capital asset pricing model (CAPM), for example, stated that there should be a positive relation between risk and return. Martingale's low volatility strategy was constructed to exploit this risk anomaly.

---

[1] This is based on the case "GM Asset Management and Martingale's Low Volatility Strategy," 2012, Columbia CaseWorks ID #110315. I have known Scott and Jacques for some time. I have taught a class with Scott on quantitative investments, which is basically what quant hedge funds do. Jacques contacted me out of the blue after I wrote a report on the Norwegian sovereign wealth fund in 2009 with William Goetzmann and Stephen Schaefer. In the report, I cited a Harvard Business School case study about Martingale written by Luis Viceira (another adviser to Martingale). Jacques phoned me one morning, swung by my office later the same day, and then immediately invited me to be part of Martingale's academic advisory board.

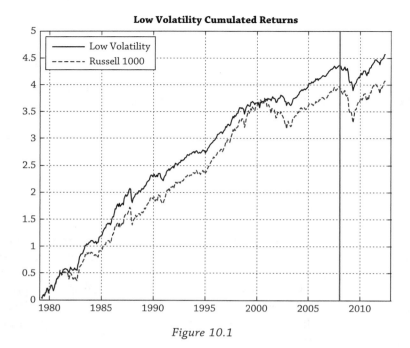

Figure 10.1

Figure 10.1 graphs cumulated returns on Martingale's Low Volatility LargeCap+ strategy based on the Russell 1000 from January 1979 to April 2012. Up until December 2007, the returns are simulated by Martingale's analysts. From January 2008, indicated in Figure 10.1 by the vertical line, performance is live.

Over the full sample, Martingale's volatility strategy beat the Russell 1000 by 1.50%. It had done even better after going live, generating an average outperformance of 1.83% since 2008. Using one-month T-bill rates as the risk-free benchmark, the low volatility strategy had a mean excess return of 8.59% and a standard deviation of 12.22%, which gave the volatility strategy a Sharpe ratio of 8.59/12.22 = 0.70 over the full sample. In comparison, the Sharpe ratio of the Russell 1000 was 0.45. Adjusted for market risk, Martingale's performance was even more impressive; running a CAPM regression using the Russell 1000 as the market portfolio produced an alpha of 3.44% with a beta of 0.73

Scott and Herscovici, however, were not immediately swayed by these numbers and Jacques's enthusiastic presentation. Was low volatility a good fit for GM? Tracking error was closely monitored at GM Asset Management, and the Martingale product had a historic tracking error of 6.16% versus the Russell 1000. This was relatively high; other U.S. equity strategies that the group typically considered had tracking errors below 6%. Scott, as managing director of GM Asset Management's global public markets business, insisted that the equities group would need to offset that risk or convince the investment committee that a change of benchmark was warranted. However, what ultimately mattered for GM was meeting its pension fund liability. Herscovici, a global equities portfolio manager, believed that "the low volatility strategy has two main factors consistent with GM's direction to reduce surplus volatility: lower risk and a higher correlation to pension liabilities."

Most of all, Scott and Herscovici wondered what explained this anomaly. If it offered such a great opportunity, why weren't a lot of other investors doing it? And would it persist going forward?

2. Active Management

Alpha is often interpreted as a measure of skill. That is debatable. It is first and foremost a statement about a benchmark.

2.1. DEFINITION OF ALPHA

Alpha is the average return in excess of a benchmark. Thus, the concept of alpha requires first defining a benchmark against which alpha can be measured.

We define the excess return, r_t^{ex}, as the return of an asset or strategy in excess of a benchmark as

$$r_t^{ex} = r_t - r_t^{bmk}, \tag{10.1}$$

for r_t the return of an asset or strategy and r_t^{bmk} the benchmark return. Sometimes we refer to the excess returns, r_t^{ex}, as *active returns*. This terminology assumes that the benchmark is *passive* and can be produced without any particular investment knowledge or even human intervention. Common passive benchmarks are market-weighted portfolios, like the S&P 500 or the Russell 1000, which investors can track by buying low-cost index funds.

We compute the alpha by taking the average excess return in equation (10.1):

$$\alpha = \frac{1}{T} \sum_{t=1}^{T} r_t^{ex}, \tag{10.2}$$

where there are T observations in the sample.

The other two terms that we need to define are *tracking error* and the *information ratio*. Tracking error is the standard deviation of the excess return; it measures how disperse the manager's returns are relative to the benchmark:

$$\text{Tracking Error} = \bar{\sigma} = \text{stdev}(r_t^{ex}). \tag{10.3}$$

Tracking error constraints are imposed to ensure a manager does not stray too far from the benchmark (see chapter 15 on agency issues in delegated portfolio management). The larger the tracking error, the more freedom the manager has. If the benchmark is risk adjusted, then academics like to call tracking error *"idiosyncratic volatility"* (see sections 3 and 4, below).

Finally, the information ratio is the ratio of alpha to tracking error:

$$\text{Information Ratio} = IR = \frac{\alpha}{\sigma}. \tag{10.4}$$

Alpha by itself could be produced by a manager taking large amounts of risk. The information ratio divides the alpha by the risk taken, so it is *the average excess return per unit of risk.* Information ratios above one are not common—although many hedge funds trying to raise money claim to have them. (Since the financial crisis, information ratios on many funds and strategies have come down substantially.)

A special case of equation (10.4) is when the benchmark is the risk-free rate, r_t^f. (Note that the risk-free rate is known at the beginning of the period and applies from t–1 to t.) Then, the alpha is the average return in excess of the risk-free rate, $\alpha = \overline{r_t - r_{ft}}$ (where the upper bar denotes the sample average of the excess return), and the information ratio coincides with the Sharpe ratio (see chapter 2),

$$\text{Sharpe Ratio} = SR = \frac{\overline{r_t - r_{ft}}}{\sigma},$$

where σ is the volatility of the asset.[2]

2.2 BENCHMARKS MATTER

Martingale's low volatility strategy is based on the Russell 1000 universe of large stocks, so naturally Jacques takes the Russell 1000 as his benchmark. This is also a convenient benchmark for the asset owner because large investors can buy Russell 1000 index funds for less than 10 basis points per year. Jacques is running an active strategy with relatively high fees and his volatility strategy must offer compelling returns (higher returns, lower risk, or both) relative to the Russell 1000 to attract investors.

A combination of assets or asset classes can also serve as a benchmark. One of Scott and Herscovici's concerns is that Jacques's low volatility strategy has a high tracking error, of 6.16%, relative to the Russell 1000. The tracking error is high because Martingale's product has a low beta of 0.73 relative to the same index. Beta is measured by regressing excess returns of the fund (using T-bills as the risk-free asset) on excess returns of the Russell 1000 (which is the regression implied by the CAPM; see chapter 6):

$$r_t - r_t^f = 0.0344 + 0.7272(r_t^{R1000} - r_t^f) + \varepsilon_t,$$

---

[2] In practice, volatilities of excess returns or raw returns are generally almost the same—unless risk-free rates are very volatile, which happens in some emerging markets.

where r_t^{R1000} represents the return of the Russell 1000 and ε_t is the residual of the regression.

The $\alpha = 3.44\%$ per year in this CAPM regression is the average excess return of the low volatility strategy relative to a *market-adjusted portfolio*. Put another way, we can rewrite the CAPM regression using a benchmark portfolio of a risk-free asset and 0.73 of the Russell 1000:

$$r_t = 0.0344 + \underbrace{0.2728r_t^f + 0.7272r_t^{R1000}}_{r_t^{bmk}} + \varepsilon_t,$$

That is, suppose the benchmark $r_t^{bmk} = 0.27r_t^f + 0.73r_t^{R1000}$ consists of a portfolio holding 27% in the risk-free asset and 73% in the Russell 1000. The low volatility strategy outperforms this benchmark by 3.44% per year. The information ratio of the low volatility strategy with this *risk-adjusted benchmark* is a very high 0.78.

If we assume a naive benchmark of just the Russell 1000, we falsely assume that the beta of the low volatility strategy is one (when in fact it is 0.73). With the Russell 1000 benchmark we have

$$r_t = 0.0150 + \underbrace{r_t^{R1000}}_{r_t^{bmk}} + \varepsilon_t,$$

so the alpha is 1.50% per year. The information ratio of the low volatility strategy relative to the naive Russell 1000 benchmark is just 0.24. This is not the correct risk-adjusted benchmark because the beta of the low volatility strategy is not one.

Thus, even with a simple Russell 1000 portfolio, failing to adjust the benchmark for risk can make a huge difference in the alpha!

Ideal Benchmarks

What are the characteristics of a sound benchmark? It should be:

1. Well defined

    Produced by an independent index provider, the Russell 1000 is verifiable and free of ambiguity about its contents. Thus it ably defines the "market portfolio" for GM and Martingale.

2. Tradeable

    Alpha must be measured relative to tradeable benchmarks, otherwise the computed alphas do not represent implementable returns on investment strategies.

    So the benchmark should be a realistic, low-cost alternative for the asset owner. The Russell 1000 is a natural passive benchmark for Martingale's low volatility strategy because low-cost mutual fund and ETF versions are available (see chapter 16).

3. Replicable

Both the asset owner and the funds manager should be able to replicate the benchmark. Martingale is certainly able to replicate the returns of the Russell 1000 benchmark because it bases its strategy on the Russell 1000 universe. GM Asset Management, the client, is also able to replicate the Russell 1000, either by internally trading it or by employing a Russell 1000 index fund provider. Thus, both Martingale and GM face a common, low-cost option.

Certain benchmarks can't be replicated by the asset owner because they are beyond the asset owner's expertise. Such nonreplicable benchmarks are not viable choices and make it difficult or impossible to measure how much value a portfolio manager has added because the benchmark itself cannot be achieved by the asset owner. There are some benchmarks, like absolute return benchmarks, that can't even be replicated by the fund manager. In these cases, the fund manager is disadvantaged because she may not even be able to generate the benchmark in the first place.

4. Adjusted for risk

Sadly, most benchmarks used in the money management business are not risk adjusted.

Taking the Russell 1000 as the benchmark assumes the beta of Jacques's strategy is one, but the actual beta of the volatility strategy is 0.73. This risk adjustment makes a big difference in the alpha; with the true beta of 0.73, the alpha of the low volatility strategy is 3.44% per year compared to 1.50% when the beta is one.

When we compute Martingale's beta, we assume that the investor can construct the benchmark portfolio ($r_t^{bmk} = 0.27r_t^f + 0.73r_t^{R1000}$) of T-bills and the Russell 1000 and rebalance it every month. GM Asset Management can easily do this, but some risk-adjusted benchmarks are beyond the reach of less sophisticated clients. We also estimate the beta using data from the whole sample. That is, the beta of 0.73 is the beta generated by Martingale after the fact—at the beginning of the sample, it was not obvious that Martingale would actually trade to generate a beta of 0.73.

And even though Martingale endorses the Russell 1000 as its benchmark, beta-adjusted or not, what if this is the wrong adjustment for risk? We know that there are more risk factors than just the equity market (see chapter 7): dynamic factors like value-growth, momentum, credit, and volatility risk also exist. Perhaps we should adjust for some of these as well? In section 3 we extend risk adjustments to multiple sources of risk.

2.3 CREATING ALPHA

A portfolio manager creates alpha relative to a benchmark by making bets that deviate from that benchmark. The more successful these bets are, the higher the alpha.

Grinold's (1989) "fundamental law" of active management makes this intuition formal. It states that the maximum information ratio attainable—since it ignores transactions costs, restrictions on trading, and other real-world considerations—is given by:

$$IR \approx IC \times \sqrt{BR}, \qquad (10.5)$$

where IR is the information ratio; IC is the *information coefficient*, which is the cor-relation of the manager's forecast with the actual returns (how good the forecasts are); and BR is the breadth of the strategy (how many bets are taken). Breadth is the number of securities that can be traded and how frequently they can be traded. High information ratios are generated by a manager finding opportunities—and many of them—where she can forecast well. Grinold and Kahn (1999) state that "it is important to play often (high breadth, BR) and to play well (high IC)."

The fundamental law has been quite influential in active quantitative portfolio management because it offers a guideline as to how good asset managers have to be at forecasting, how many bets they have to make, or both to generate alpha. Suppose we require an information ratio of 0.5 and we make bets every quarter. A stock market timer trading just the aggregate market has narrow breadth be-cause there are few assets—sometimes just stocks and bonds—to trade. Making only four bets a year, the stock market timer's bets have to be very accurate. She needs an IC of 0.25 to obtain an information ratio of $0.50 = 0.25 \times \sqrt{4}$. The cross-sectional strategies of value, size, and momentum (see chapter 7) have great breadth because hundreds of stocks can be traded. These strategies can have very low ICs, often just 2% to 5%, to be highly profitable. Stock selectors doing value, size, or momentum strategies making four hundred independent bets per year need only ICs of 0.025 to generate information ratios of $0.50 = 0.025 \times \sqrt{400}$. In short, you can be very talented at forecasting and make those bets really count, or you can have a very small edge but make a lot of bets. Both lead to high information ratios.

Grinold's fundamental law is derived under mean-variance utility, and so all the shortcomings of mean-variance utility apply (see chapter 3).[3] In particular, by using mean-variance utility, the Grinold–Kahn framework ignores downside risk and other higher moment risk while assuming that all information is used optimally. A crucial assumption is that the forecasts are independent of each other. Nevertheless, the fundamental law is useful to frame the active manage-ment process. Alpha begins with raw information; we process that information into forecasts and then optimally and efficiently construct portfolios that balance

---

[3] The fundamental law is itself an approximation in the mean-variance framework. A better ap-proximation to equation (10.5) is made by Hallerbach (2011). Extensions to the fundamental law allow time-varying signals for the forecasts (Ye (2008)), correlated forecasts (Buckle (2004)), and incorporate estimation risk (Zhou (2008)).

return forecasts against risk. The key to generating alpha is forecasting. That requires superior information or superior ability to process public information.

While the fundamental law was intended originally as a portfolio construction tool, Knut Kjær, the founding CEO of Norges Bank Investment Management, which manages the Norwegian sovereign wealth fund, also used the intuition of the fundamental law as a management style. Since alpha is created by finding many different forecasts that are independent, Kjaer's philosophy was to delegate widely to specialized managers. He tried to ensure that they act as independently as possible. He explained:[4]

> To achieve the greatest possible level of independence for decisions on active investments, these must be delegated to many different groups and individuals. This delegation must be real, without intervention from superiors, provided that the individual employee stays within the agreed structure and risk limits. . . . The sense of ownership which derives from responsibility and an absence of intervention from superiors is an important motivation and driving force for the development of this expertise.

There are two very important limitations of the fundamental law. The first is that ICs are assumed to be constant across BR. The first manager whom you find may truly have a high IC, but the one hundredth manager whom you hire probably does not. As assets under management increase, the ability to generate ICs diminishes. Indeed, the empirical evidence on active management, which I cover in Part III of this book, shows *decreasing returns to scale*: as funds get bigger, performance deteriorates. This effect is seen in mutual funds, hedge funds, and private equity.[5] Thus, ICs tend to fall as assets under management rise.

Second, it is difficult to have truly independent forecasts in BR. Manager decisions tend to be correlated and correlated bets reduce BR. An equity manager with overweight positions on 1,000 value stocks offset by underweight positions in 1,000 growth stocks has not placed 1,000 different bets; he's placed just one bet on a value-growth factor. Hiring one hundred different fixed income managers who are all "reaching for yield" by buying illiquid bonds gets you not one hundred different bets but rather a single bet on an illiquidity factor. Correlated factor bets tend to dominate at the overall portfolio level—a reason why top–down factor investing is so important (see chapter 14).

Despite its influence in industry, Grinold's fundamental law makes only scant appearance in the academic literature. This is because Grinold's framework is a statistical model devoid of economic content. It says nothing about where positive

---

[4] NBIM Annual Report, 2007, "Ten Years of NBIM."
[5] See Chen et al. (2004), Fung et al. (2008), and Kaplan and Schoar (2005), respectively.

risk-adjusted opportunities are; it only provides a method of systematically evaluating them. I cover a promising area of alpha in section 4.

3. Factor Benchmarks

Consider the CAPM applied to asset (or strategy or fund) i:

$$E(r_i) - r_f = \beta_i(E(r_m) - r_f), \tag{10.6}$$

where $E(r_i)$ is the expected return of asset i, r_f is the risk-free rate (U.S. T-bills), β_i is the beta of asset i, and $E(r_m)$ is the expected return of the market portfolio. Let's assume the beta is 1.3, $\beta_i = 1.3$, so we can write equation (10.6) as

$$E(r_i) = r_f + 1.3E(r_m) - 1.3r_f,$$

and, rearranging, we have

$$\underbrace{E(r_i)}_{\$1} = \underbrace{-0.3r_f + 1.3E(r_m)}_{\$1}. \tag{10.7}$$

Applying the CAPM assumes that we can produce the same return as \$1 in asset i by holding a short position in T-bills of –\$0.30 and a levered position in the market of \$1.30. Note that we have \$1 on both the left-hand side and right-hand side of equation (10.7). Thus, the CAPM implies a *replicating portfolio*: a combination of risk-free assets and the market has the same expected return as the asset under the CAPM. Thus, the beta of the asset is actually a *mimicking portfolio weight*.[6]

Factor benchmarks are a combination of investment portfolios, or factors, on the right-hand side that give the same return as the asset on the left-hand side. The factor benchmark describes the systematic components of asset i's return.

The alpha of asset i is any expected return generated in excess of the short \$0.30 in T-bills and the long \$1.30 position in the market portfolio:

$$E(r_i) = \alpha_i + \underbrace{[-0.3r_f + 1.3E(r_m)]}_{E(r^{bmk})}, \tag{10.8}$$

where the benchmark consists of the risk-adjusted amount held in equities and the risk-free rate, $r^{bmk} = -0.3r_f + 1.3r_m$. Since the benchmark in this case comes from the CAPM, alpha is the average return in excess of the return predicted by the CAPM.

---

[6] Equation (10.7), which can be estimated in a regression (see below), takes the perspective of matching \$1 invested in the asset on the left-hand side with the factor benchmark on the right-hand side. An alternative approach is to scale both the left- and right-hand sides so that they have the same volatility. This would match risk exposures rather than dollars invested.

3.1 FACTOR REGRESSIONS

We can estimate the risk-adjusted benchmark, or equivalently the mimicking portfolio, using factor regressions.

CAPM Benchmark

To illustrate, consider the grand master of value investing, Warren Buffett. Taking monthly returns on Berkshire Hathaway from 1990 to May 2012, I run the following CAPM regression:

$$r_{it} - r_{ft} = \alpha + \beta(r_{mt} - r_{ft}) + \varepsilon_{it}, \tag{10.9}$$

where ordinary least squares assumes that the residuals ε_{it} are independent of the market factor. Estimating the CAPM regression in equation (10.9) implicitly yields the CAPM-implied mimicking portfolio weights. The estimates for Berkshire Hathaway are

	Coefficient	T-stat
Alpha	0.72%	2.02
Beta	0.51	6.51
Adj R^2	0.14	

This implies that the CAPM benchmark consists of 0.49 in T-bills and 0.51 in the market portfolio, $r^{bmk} = 0.49r_f + 0.51r_m$, and that $1 invested in Berkshire Hathaway is equivalent to

$$(1 - 0.51) = \$0.49 \text{ in T-bills}$$
$$+ \$0.51 \text{ in the market portfolio.}$$

Relative to this benchmark portfolio, Buffett is adding

$$+ 0.72\% \text{ (alpha) per month.}$$

This is impressive performance! Buffett is generating an alpha of $0.0072 \times 12 = 8.6\%$ per year with a risk of approximately half that of the market ($\beta = 0.51$). The alpha estimated using a market portfolio benchmark in equation (10.9) is often called Jensen's alpha, after Michael Jensen's pioneering 1968 study of mutual fund performance. (No, mutual funds generally don't beat the market; see chapter 16.)

The alpha is also statistically significant, with a high t-statistic above two. The cutoff level of two corresponds to the 95% confidence level, a magic threshold for statisticians. Buffett is special. Most factor regressions do *not* produce significant alpha estimates. The adjusted R^2 of the CAPM regression is 14%, which is also relatively high. For most stocks, CAPM regressions produce R^2s of less than 10%.[7]

---

[7] CAPM regressions tend to produce low R^2s because idiosyncratic risk is large in stock returns. Economically, there are tremendous diversification benefits in creating portfolios. See chapter 3.

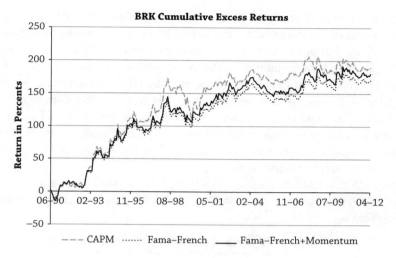

Figure 10.2

The high R^2 indicates the fit of the CAPM benchmark is very good compared to the typical fit for a CAPM regression for an individual stock.

The excess return generated by Berkshire Hathaway relative to the CAPM risk-adjusted benchmark is

$$r^{ex} = r_i - r^{bmk}$$

$$= r_i - (0.49r_f + 0.51r_m).$$

The average of the excess returns is the alpha, $\alpha = E(r^{ex}) = 0.72\%$ per month. Figure 10.2 plots the cumulative excess returns of Berkshire Hathaway. The solid line corresponds to the CAPM benchmark. Note that the slope of the cumulative excess returns flattens in the more recent period, especially since the mid-2000s. In 2012, Berkshire Hathaway has a capitalization over \$220 billion. In the early 1990s, Berkshire's market capitalization was less than \$10 billion. As Berkshire Hathaway has grown bigger, its average excess returns have shrunk. Buffett himself said in 2011,

> The bountiful years, we want to emphasize, will never return. The huge sums of capital we currently manage eliminate any chance of exceptional performance. We will strive, however, for better-than-average results and feel it fair for you to hold us to that standard.[8]

Even Berkshire Hathaway is subject to the law of decreasing returns to scale.

Size and Value-Growth Benchmarks

Eugene Fama and Kenneth French, two of the most influential scholars in finance, introduced a benchmark in 1993 that extended the CAPM to include factors that

---

[8] Berkshire Hathaway's 2010 shareholder letter.

captured a size effect (small companies outperform large companies) and a value-growth effect (value stocks do better than growth stocks). They labeled their size factor "*SMB*," for s̲mall stocks m̲inus big s̲tocks, and their value-growth factor "*HML*," for h̲igh book-to-market stocks m̲inus l̲ow book-to-market stocks. Value stocks are stocks with depressed prices, and the *HML* factor normalizes these prices (market value) relative to book value. Hence value stocks are stocks with high book-to-market ratios. Chapter 7 covers the Fama–French model and the economics behind the size and value premiums. (Although the size effect is much weaker today, it is still instructive to include *SMB* to explain some of Berkshire Hathaway's performance, as I show below.)

The *SMB* and *HML* factors are long–short factors. They are mimicking portfolios that consist of simultaneous $1 long and $1 short positions in different stocks. That is,

$$SMB = \underbrace{\$1 \text{ in small caps}}_{\text{Long}} - \underbrace{\$1 \text{ in large caps}}_{\text{Short}}$$

and so *SMB* is designed to capture the outperformance of small companies versus large companies. The *HML* factor picks up the outperformance of value stocks versus growth stocks:

$$HML = \underbrace{\$1 \text{ in value stocks}}_{\text{Long}} - \underbrace{\$1 \text{ in growth stocks}}_{\text{Short}}.$$

The Fama–French benchmark holds positions in the *SMB* and *HML* factor portfolios, along with a position in the market portfolio as in the traditional CAPM.

Fama and French extended the CAPM regression in equation (10.9) to include a size factor and a value factor. The Fama–French benchmark can be estimated by running the following regression:

$$r_{it} - r_{ft} = \alpha + \beta(r_{mt} - r_{ft}) + sSMB_t + hHML_t + \varepsilon_{it}, \tag{10.10}$$

which adds the *SMB* and *HML* factors to the standard market factor.

The *SMB* and *HML* factor loadings are given by s and h, respectively. If a stock co-moves neither with small nor large stocks, it's a medium-size stock, and s would be zero. As it starts moving with small stocks s becomes positive, and if it moves together with large stocks, s is negative. Likewise, h measures how much a stock is acting like other value stocks: positive hs indicate the stock has a value orientation, and negative hs indicate the stock is acting like a growth stock. The market itself is neither small nor big and neither value nor growth, so the market has zero s and h loadings.

Estimating the Fama–French regression for Berkshire Hathaway yields the following coefficients:

	Coefficient	T-stat
Alpha	0.65%	1.96
MKT Loading	0.67	8.94
SMB Loading	−0.50	−4.92
HML Loading	0.38	3.52
Adj R^2	0.27	

Buffett's alpha has fallen from 0.72% per month (8.6% per year) with the CAPM benchmark to 0.65% per month (7.8% per year). Controlling for size and value has knocked nearly 1% off Buffett's alpha.

First, note that the market beta has moved from 0.51 in the pure CAPM regression to 0.67 in the Fama–French specification. This is an indication that adding the *SMB* and *HML* factors is doing something—the market beta would stay the same only if the *SMB* and *HML* factors would have *no* ability to explain Buffett's returns.

The *SMB* factor loading in the Fama–French regression is $s = -0.50$. The negative sign indicates that Berkshire Hathaway is acting the opposite way from a small stock (remember, *SMB* is long small stocks and short large stocks). That is, Berkshire Hathaway has large stock exposure. Note that being large counts against Buffett's outstanding performance because large stocks, according to the Fama–French model, tend to underperform small stocks.

The *HML* loading of $h = 0.38$ says that Berkshire Hathaway has a strong value orientation; it tends to move together with other value stocks.

Thus, the negative *SMB* and positive *HML* factor loadings suggest that Berkshire Hathaway is a large, value investor. Duh, of course it is! It doesn't take the finance cognoscenti to know that this is the investing technique that Buffett has touted since founding Berkshire Hathaway in the 1960s. It is comforting that an econometric technique yields the same result as common sense. But the statistical technique gives us the appropriate benchmark to compute Buffett's risk-adjusted alpha.

The surprising result in the Fama–French regression is that Buffett is still generating considerable profits relative to the size- and value-factor controls: Buffett's monthly alpha of 0.65% is still outsized; the Fama–French model reduces the CAPM alpha by less than 1% per year. This is not because the size and value factors are inappropriate risk factors. Quite the contrary. The Fama–French regression has an adjusted R^2 of 27%, which is large by empirical finance standards, and much higher than the adjusted R^2 of 14% in the CAPM benchmark. The size and value factors, therefore, substantially improve the fit relative to the CAPM benchmark. Buffett's performance is clearly not merely from being a value investor, at least the way value is being measured relative to the CAPM.

The benchmark implied by the Fama–French regression estimates is:

$$(1 - 0.67) = \$0.33 \text{ in T-bills}$$
$$+ \$0.67 \text{ in the market portfolio}$$
$$- \$0.50 \text{ in small caps} + \$0.50 \text{ in large caps}$$
$$+ \$0.38 \text{ in value stocks} - \$0.38 \text{ in growth stocks}$$

In addition to this benchmark, Buffet is generating

$$+ 0.65\% \text{ (alpha) per month.}$$

Again, the factor loadings can be translated directly to a benchmark portfolio, only now the portfolio contains (complicated) long–short positions in small/large and value/growth stocks. But it still represents $1 of capital allocated between factor portfolios. Every time we run a factor regression, we are assuming that we can create a factor benchmark portfolio.

Adding Momentum

The momentum effect—that stocks with high returns in the past continue their upward trend and stocks with lousy past returns continue to deliver lousy returns—can be added to the factor benchmark. Momentum is observed in many asset classes and is a systematic factor (see chapter 7). Buffett famously eschews momentum investing, basing his investment decisions on a company's fundamentals instead of past growth and price movements. Three of his famous quotes are:

The investor of today does not profit from yesterday's growth.
Focus on the underlying conditions that cause price, rather than price itself.
It's far better to buy a wonderful company at a fair price than a fair company at a wonderful price.

We add a momentum factor, *UMD*, constructed by taking positions in stocks that have gone up minus stocks that have gone down, to the Fama–French benchmark:[9]

$$r_{it} - r_{ft} = \alpha + \beta(r_{mt} - r_{ft}) + sSMB_t + hHML_t + uUMD_t + \varepsilon_{it}, \qquad (10.11)$$

where the new *UMD* factor has a loading (or beta) of u. Estimating this regression, we have

	Coefficient	T-stat
Alpha	0.68%	2.05
MKT Loading	0.66	8.26
SMB Loading	−0.50	−4.86
HML Loading	0.36	3.33
UMD Loading	−0.04	−0.66
Adj R^2	0.27	

[9] First done by Carhart (1997).

These estimates are very close to the Fama–French regression estimates. Consistent with Buffett's avowed eschewal of momentum investing, the UMD loading is close to zero ($u = -0.04$) and statistically insignificant. Note that the adjusted R^2 of this regression is 27%, exactly the same as the Fama–French regression, implying that adding the momentum factor has not improved the fit of the factor regression. Buffett's alpha has even improved slightly by adding the momentum factor ($\alpha = 0.68\%$ per month) compared to the Fama–French regression ($\alpha = 0.65\%$ per month).

For completeness, the mimicking portfolio implied by this Fama–French plus momentum benchmark is:

$$(1 - 0.66) = \$0.37 \text{ in T-bills}$$
$$+ \$0.66 \text{ in the market portfolio}$$
$$- \$0.50 \text{ in small caps} + \$0.50 \text{ in large caps}$$
$$+ \$0.36 \text{ in value stocks} - \$0.36 \text{ in growth stocks}$$
$$- \$0.04 \text{ in past winning stocks} + \$0.04 \text{ in past losing stocks}$$

Buffet is also adding:

$$+ 0.68\% \text{ (alpha) per month.}$$

Figure 10.2 shows cumulative excess returns relative to the Fama–French benchmark in the dashed line and the Fama–French plus momentum benchmark in the solid line. Both lie below the CAPM benchmark, which is mainly a consequence of lowering Buffett's alpha by including the *HML* value-growth factor.

3.2 DOING WITHOUT RISK-FREE ASSETS

Benchmark portfolios need not include risk-free assets.

CalPERS

CalPERS is the largest public pension fund in the United States and had $246 billion of assets at June 30, 2011.[10] A benchmark for this pension fund might be a passive portfolio of index funds in stocks and bonds—the benchmark that the Canada Pension Plan has adopted through its Reference Portfolio. A stock-bond benchmark can be run extremely cheaply—for close to zero—and is a viable yardstick for judging whether active management is adding value.

A benchmark regression for CalPERS' returns would be

$$\underbrace{r_{it}}_{\$1} = \alpha + \underbrace{\beta_s r_{st} + \beta_b r_{bt}}_{\$1} + \varepsilon_{it}, \tag{10.12}$$

[10] Data and additional information for this section is from "California Dreamin': The Mess at CalPERS," Columbia CaseWorks, #120306 and "Factor Investing: The Reference Portfolio and Canada Pension Plan Investment Board," Columbia CaseWorks #120302.

where r_{it} is the return of CalPERS, r_{st} is the S&P 500 equity market return, and r_{bt} is a bond portfolio return—in this case, the Ibbotson Associates long-term corporate bond total return index. To obtain a benchmark portfolio, we require the restriction that

$$\beta_s + \beta_b = 1.$$

That is, the portfolio weights must sum to one. Then, $1 placed into CalPERS on the left-hand side of equation (10.12) can be replicated by a portfolio of stocks and bonds (with portfolio weights, which also must sum to one) on the right-hand side, plus any alpha generated by the CalPERS' funds manager.

Estimating equation (10.12) on CalPERS' annual returns from 1990 to 2011, we get the following:

	Coefficient	T-stat
Alpha	−1.11%	−1.16
Bond Loading	0.32	13.97
Stock Loading	0.68	13.97
Adj R^2	0.90	

The high adjusted R^2 of 90% is amazing: CalPERS' returns are extremely well explained by this mimicking portfolio of 32% bonds and 68% stocks!

The point estimate of CalPERS alpha is negative, at −1.11% per year. Should we immediately fire the CalPERS funds manager and put everything into low-cost index funds? Formally, we can only make the statement that "we fail to reject the hypothesis that CalPERS adds value relative to the 32% bonds/68% stocks benchmark portfolio at the 95% level" because the t-statistic is less than two in absolute value.

CalPERS, however, is an expensive fund. In 2011 its internal estimate of its expense ratio was upward of 0.50%, while expense ratios inferred from its annual reports exceed 0.80%. (What a travesty that it does not explicitly report its expense ratio in its annual report!) These expense ratios are much higher than those of industry peers. The median expense ratio of the largest pension plans studied by Bauer, Cremers, and Frehen (2009) was 0.29%; at the largest 30% of defined benefit plans, the expense ratios are just 0.15%. Thus, CalPERS is three to four times more expensive than median fund in Bauer, Cremers, and Frehen's sample, and nearly nine times more expensive than the largest 30% of pension plans! Expense ratios for managing typical index stock or bond funds at CalPERS' scale are way below 0.10%. (The Norwegian sovereign wealth fund had an expense ratio of 0.06% in 2012.) So yes, given that CalPERS could run a benchmark stock-bond portfolio for close to zero, perhaps it should consider firing its funds manager and going completely index.

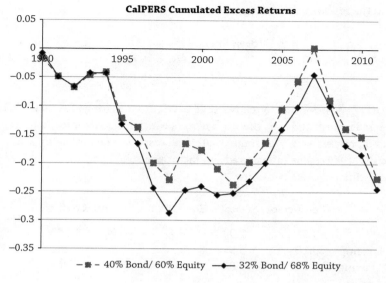

Figure 10.3

Figure 10.3 plots cumulative excess returns for CalPERS. The estimated 32% stocks/68% bonds benchmark portfolio is shown in the solid line and a standard 40% stocks/60% bonds portfolio is overlaid for comparison. Note the similarity. CalPERS performance improves during 2000–2007. But during the financial crisis in 2008, things completely fall apart, and the fund's performance continued to deteriorate in 2010 and 2011. A large part of this dismal showing was due to CalPERS' failure to rebalance in 2008 and 2009: it sold equities rather than buying them when prices were low (see chapter 4 on the optimality of rebalancing as a long-term strategy).

Real Estate
Canada Pension Plan considers real estate to have many characteristics in common with fixed income and equities—so much in common that the plan doesn't consider real estate a separate asset class. But can real estate exposure be replicated by a factor portfolio of stocks, bonds, and, potentially, listed REITs (see chapter 11), which offer indirect real estate exposure?

Real estate returns are complicated because they are not tradeable. Leaving aside this problem—which I deal with in chapter 11 along with other illiquid investments—I take quarterly real estate returns from the National Council of Real Estate Investment Fiduciaries from June 1978 to December 2011 (my left-hand side variable). I consider factor benchmark regressions using S&P 500 stock returns, Ibbotson long-term corporate bond returns, and the FTSE NAREIT index returns (my right-hand side variables).

I run the following factor regressions:

$$r_{it} = \alpha + \beta_{REIT}REIT_t + \beta_b r_{bt} \qquad\qquad + \varepsilon_{it},$$
$$r_{it} = \alpha \qquad\qquad\quad + \beta_b r_{bt} + \beta_s r_{st} + \varepsilon_{it}, \qquad (10.13)$$
$$r_{it} = \alpha + \beta_{REIT}REIT_t + \beta_b r_{bt} + \beta_s r_{st} + \varepsilon_{it}.$$

where $REIT_t$ is the return to the NAREIT portfolio consisting of traded REITs, r_{bt} is the bond return, and r_{st} is the stock return, which have factor loadings of β_{REIT}, β_b, and β_s, respectively. We require that, in all cases, the factor loadings add up to one so that they can be interpreted as a factor portfolio benchmark.

The estimated coefficients are:

	Coefficient	T-stat	Coefficient	T-stat	Coefficient	T-stat
Alpha	−0.51%	−1.02	−0.43%	−0.90	−1.50%	−1.05
REIT Loading	0.30	5.92			0.12	1.81
Bond Loading	0.70	14.0	0.65	12.7	0.26	3.75
Stock Loading			0.35	6.95	0.61	11.6

For all of these factor benchmarks, direct real estate does not offer significant returns in excess of a factor benchmark. In fact, the point estimates are negative

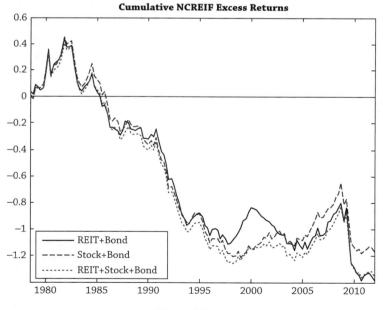

Figure 10.4

and around 0.50% per quarter. Interestingly, the factor benchmark consisting of just bonds and stocks indicates that the optimal combination of stocks and bonds to mimic real estate is 35% stocks and 65% bonds.

Figure 10.4 graphs cumulative excess returns of direct real estate relative to these factor benchmarks. While there was some value added in the early 1980s relative to these REIT, bond, and stock factors, the factor benchmarks did much better than direct real estate from the mid-1980s to the early 2000s. Direct real estate picked up relative to the factor benchmarks in the mid-2000s, coinciding with the period's property boom. Figure 10.4 clearly shows the crash in real estate markets in 2008 and 2009 toward the end of the sample.

3.3 TIME-VARYING FACTOR EXPOSURES

William Sharpe, one of the inventors of the CAPM, introduced a powerful framework to handle time-varying benchmarks in 1992. He called it *"style analysis."* In our context, style analysis is a factor benchmark where the factor exposures evolve through time.[11]

To illustrate time-varying factor exposures in the spirit of Sharpe's style analysis, consider four funds:

LSVEX: LSV Value Equity. LSV is a "quantitative value equity manager providing active management for institutional investors" and was named after its founding academics: Josef Lakonishok, Andrei Shleifer, and Robert Vishny.[12]

FMAGX: Fidelity Magellan. One of the most famous retail mutual funds, it grew to prominence under superstar manager Peter Lynch in the 1980s and 1990s.

GSCGX: Goldman Sachs Capital Growth. How can we not include a Goldman Sachs name?

BRK: Berkshire Hathaway. Since we've been using Buffett's example, let's stay with it.

I use monthly data from January 2001 to December 2011.

Here are the Fama–French and momentum factor regressions using *constant* factor weights:

---

[11] Computing standard errors for alphas when factor loadings vary over time, and even when the alphas themselves vary over time, is tricky, as Ang and Kristensen (2012) show. For a summary of style analysis, see ter Horst, Nijman, and de Roon (2004).

[12] See http://www.lsvasset.com/about/about.html.

	LSVEX	FMAGX	GSCGX	BRK
Alpha	0.00%	−0.27%	−0.14%	0.22%
t-stat	0.01	−2.23	−1.33	0.57
MKT Loading	0.94	1.12	1.04	0.36
t-stat	36.9	38.6	42.2	3.77
SMB Loading	0.01	−0.07	−0.12	−0.15
t-stat	0.21	−1.44	−3.05	−0.97
HML Loading	0.51	−0.05	−0.17	0.34
t-stat	14.6	−1.36	−4.95	2.57
UMD loading	0.2	0.02	0.00	−0.06
t-stat	1.07	1.00	−0.17	−0.77

The only alpha that is statistically significant is Fidelity Magellan, which is −0.27% per month or −3.24% per year. Poor investors in Fidelity lose money, and their losses are statistically significant. Berkshire Hathaway's alpha estimate is positive but insignificant. Our analysis in section 3.1 had a significantly positive alpha but we started in 1990. Now, starting ten years later in 2001, we don't even obtain statistical significance for Buffett. Detecting statistical significance of outperformance is hard, even in samples of more than ten years.

Looking at the factor loadings, LSV seems to be a big value shop—with a large HML loading of 0.51 (with a massive t-statistic of 14.6). Berkshire Hathaway is still value, too, with an HML loading of 0.34. Fidelity is a levered play on the market, with a beta of 1.12. Since none of the UMD loadings are large or significant, none of these funds are momentum players.

Style analysis seeks to rectify two potential shortcomings of our analysis so far:

1. The Fama–French portfolios are not tradeable.[13]
2. The factor loadings may vary over time.

Style Analysis with No Shorting

Style analysis tries to replicate the fund by investing passively in low-cost index funds. The collection of index funds that replicate the fund is called the "style weight."

To illustrate, let's take the following index ETFs (see chapter 16 for 40-Act funds):

---

[13] GM Asset Management has implemented tradeable versions of the Fama–French portfolios. See Scott (2012) for further details and chapter 14 on factor investing. Cremers, Petajisto, and Zitzewitz (2012) argue that the nontradeability of the Fama–French indices leads to distortions in inferring alpha.

SPY: SPDR S&P 500 ETF, which is designed to mimic the S&P 500;

SPYV: SPDR S&P 500 Value ETF, which tracks the S&P 500 value index; and

SPYG: SPDR SP& 500 Growth ETF, which replicates the S&P 500 growth index.

These low-cost index ETFs are tradeable, unlike the Fama–French portfolios. They belong to the SPDR (pronounced "spider") family of ETFs sponsored by State Street Global Advisors.

Our benchmark factor regression for fund i (but I avoid the i subscripts to make the notation clearer) is

$$r_{t+1} = \alpha_t + \beta_{SPY,t}SPY_{t+1} + \beta_{SPYV,t}SPYV_{t+1} + \beta_{SPYG,t}SPYG_{t+1} + \varepsilon_{t+1}, \quad (10.14)$$

where we impose the restriction

$$\beta_{SPY,t} + \beta_{SPYV,t} + \beta_{SPYG,t} = 1,$$

so that the factor loadings, or factor weights, sum to one. The factor weights on the right-hand side of equation (10.14) constitute a replicating portfolio for fund i.

The main idea with style analysis is that we use actual tradeable funds in the factor benchmark. I used SPDR ETFs in equation (10.14), but I could have used other ETFs or index mutual funds for the benchmark portfolio.

Note the timing in equation (10.14). The weights are estimated using information up to time t. The return of the fund over the next period, $t+1$, is equal to the replicating portfolio formed at the beginning of the period at time t plus a fund-specific residual, ε_{t+1}, and the fund alpha, α_t for that period. The weights can change over time. Equation (10.14) asks, "Can we find a robot that makes time-varying investments in SPY, SPYV, and SPYG that, together, match the returns of Buffett?"

Figure 10.5 graphs the factor weights (or style weights) of the four funds. I estimate the factors using data over the previous sixty months, $t - 60$ to t, to form the benchmark weights at time t. In addition to imposing that the factor weights sum to one, I also constrain the factor weights to be all positive (so there is no shorting). The first factor weight is estimated at January 2006.

Panel A of Figure 10.5 shows that LSV is merely a combination of the market (SPY) and value (SPYV). Fidelity Magellan starts off in 2006 as a combination of all three ETFs but, at the end of 2012, ends up being all growth (SPYG). Goldman's growth fund is mostly market exposure (SPY) and growth (SPYG) at the beginning of the sample and at the end of the sample is just growth (SPYG). Buffett's factor exposure is the most interesting. He starts off in 2006 being strongly value (SPYV). During the financial crisis, he switches styles to become growth. Then as the crisis subsides, he goes back to being a strong value manager.

Panel A

Factor Weights

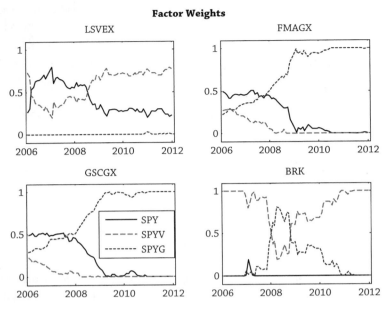

Panel B

Cumulated Excess Returns

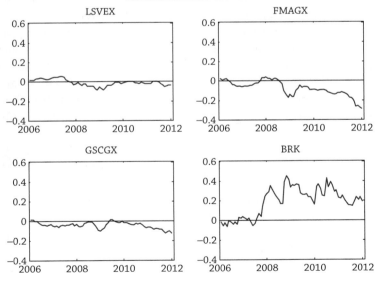

Figure 10.5

The excess return for $t+1$ is the return of the fund at the end of the period, t to $t+1$, minus the benchmark portfolio formed using the weights at time t:

$$r_{t+1}^{ex} = r_{t+1} - \underbrace{[\beta_{SPY,t}SPY_{t+1} + \beta_{SPYV,t}SPYV_{t+1} + \beta_{SPYG,t}SPYG_{t+1}]}_{r_{t+1}^{bmk}}.$$

I graph the excess returns in Panel B of Figure 10.5. The cumulated excess returns are zero for LSV. Fidelity Magellan's returns trend downward (recall that Magellan significantly subtracts value in the full-sample regressions). Goldman's growth fund also has zero cumulative excess returns. The only fund with an upward trend is Berkshire Hathaway.

Style Analysis with Shorting

What if we allow shorting? In Figure 10.6, I allow the investor to take short positions in the ETFs. I use the following factor regression:

$$r_{t+1} - r_{f,t+1} = \alpha_{i,t} + \beta_{SPY,t} (SPY_{t+1} - r_{f,t+1}) + h_t (SPYV_{t+1} - SPYG_{t+1}) + \varepsilon_{t+1}.$$
$$(10.15)$$

This is the "ETF version" of the Fama–French (1993) regression that we estimated in equation (10.10), without the *SMB* factor, except that we allow the factor loadings to change over time. The *SPYV-SPYG* is an investment that goes long the value SPYV ETF and simultaneously shorts the growth SPYG ETF. Thus, it is analogous to the *HML* factor.

The factor loadings plotted in Panel A of Figure 10.6 show the strong value bias of LSV, with a positive h loading on the *SPYV-SPYG* factor. Magellan becomes more of a growth fund over time, with increasingly negative h loadings, as does Goldman's growth fund. Berkshire Hathaway's changing factor loadings from value to growth to value can be seen in its negative h loadings during 2008 and 2009.

Allowing shorting does not much change the cumulated excess returns in Panel B of Figure 10.6. But allowing shorting, not surprisingly, reduces the alphas. Magellan's trend line for cumulated excess returns becomes more negative when shorting is allowed. Although Buffett's excess returns are positive, they are shifted downward in Figure 10.6, Panel B, compared to the corresponding long-only picture in Figure 10.5, Panel B.

My final comment is that the problems of statistical inference with time-varying portfolio benchmarks are serious. It is hard enough to detect statistical significance with constant portfolio benchmarks, and estimated time-varying styles will have even larger standard errors.[14]

---

[14] See comments by DiBartolomeo and Witkowski (1997).

Panel A

Factor Weights, with Shorting

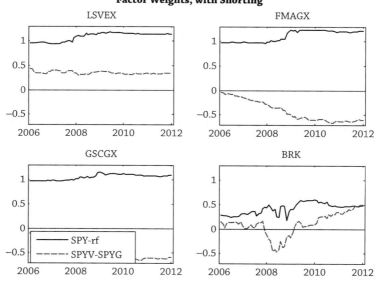

Panel B

Cumulated Excess Returns, with Shorting

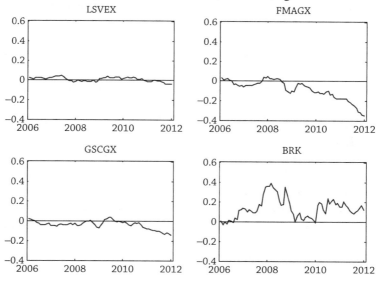

Figure 10.6

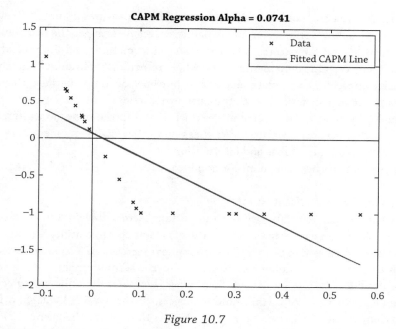

Figure 10.7

3.4 NON-LINEAR PAYOFFS

With alphas and information ratios, any manager can appear to have talent when he actually doesn't.

Alphas are computed in a *linear* framework. There are many *nonlinear* strategies, especially those involving dynamic option strategies, that can masquerade as alpha.[15] To give an extreme (and admittedly stylized) example, consider Figure 10.7. It is produced by selling put options on the market portfolio in a small sample, just using Black–Scholes (1973) prices. The returns on these put options are recorded with crosses. I then run a CAPM regression with these simulated returns. The "alpha" appears to be positive—ta da!—but we know that in the Black–Scholes world there is no extra value created in puts or calls. The alpha is purely illusory. This is not a result of a small sample, even though small samples exacerbate the problem. *No nonlinear strategy can be adequately captured in a linear framework.*[16] This is a serious problem because many common hedge fund strategies, including merger arbitrage, pairs trading, and convertible bond arbitrage, have payoffs that resemble nonlinear option volatility strategies.[17]

---

[15] This was first shown in a seminal paper by Dybvig and Ingersoll (1982). Technically, this is because any factor model used (Dybvig and Ingersoll used the CAPM) implicitly allows the pricing kernel to be negative and permits arbitrage (see chapter 6). The linear pricing kernel correctly prices all benchmark assets (stocks) but incorrectly prices nonlinear payoffs like derivatives.

[16] For a more formal treatment see Lhabitant (2000), Lo (2001), and Guasoni, Huberman, and Wang (2011). You can *always* beat a market Sharpe ratio (or information ratio) by selling volatility.

[17] See Mitchell and Pulvino (2001), Gatev, Goetzmann, and Rouwenhorst (2006), and Agarwal et al. (2011), respectively.

Why do dynamic, nonlinear strategies yield false measures of alpha? Because buying and selling options—or any dynamic strategy—changes the distribution of returns.[18] Static measures, like the alpha, information, and Sharpe ratios, capture only certain components of the whole return distribution. Often, short volatility strategies can inflate alphas and information ratios because they increase negative skewness. These strategies increase losses in the left-hand tails and make the middle of the distribution "thicker" and appear to be more attractive to linear performance measures. Skewness and other higher moments are not taken into account by alphas and information ratios.

There are two ways to account for nonlinear payoffs.

Include Tradeable Nonlinear Factors

Aggregate market volatility risk is an important factor, discussed in chapters 7 through 9, and an easy way to include the effects of short volatility strategies is to include volatility risk factors. Other nonlinear factors can also be included in factor benchmarks. By doing so, the asset owner is assuming that she can trade these nonlinear factors by herself. Sometimes, however, the only way to access these factors is through certain fund managers. In chapter 17, I will show how controlling for nonlinear factors crucially changes the alphas of hedge funds. Fung and Hsieh (2001), among many others, show that hedge fund returns often load significantly on option strategies.

Examine Nontradeable Nonlinearities

It is easy to test whether fund returns exhibit nonlinear patterns by including nonlinear terms on the right-hand side of factor regressions. Common specifications include quadratic terms, like r_t^2, or option-like terms like $\max(r_t, 0)$.[19] The disadvantage is that, after including these terms, you do not have alpha—we always need tradeable factors on the right-hand side to compute alphas.

But we must move beyond alpha if we want evaluation measures that are robust to dynamic manipulation. These will not be alphas, but they can still be used to rank managers and evaluate skill. One state-of-the-art measure has been introduced by Goetzmann et al. (2007).[20] With long enough samples, this measure cannot be manipulated in the sense that selling options will not yield a false measure of performance.

The Goetzmann et al. evaluation measure is

$$\frac{1}{1-\gamma} \ln \left(\frac{1}{T} \sum_{t=1}^{T} (1 + r_t - r_{ft})^{1-\gamma} \right), \tag{10.16}$$

---

[18] This is true even of simple rebalancing; see chapter 4.

[19] These can be traced to Treynor and Mazuy (1966) and Henriksson and Merton (1981), respectively.

[20] For some other notable manipulation-free performance measures, see Glosten and Jagannathan (1994) and Wang and Zhang (2011).

where γ is set to three. Funds can be ranked on this measure from high to low, with the best funds having the highest values. Equation (10.16) harks back to chapter 2 on utility functions, and indeed it is a CRRA or power utility function. (More precisely, it's the certainty equivalent of a CRRA utility function.) Goetzmann et al. report that Morningstar uses a variant of this measure:

$$\left(\frac{1}{T} \sum_{t=1}^{T} \frac{1}{(1 + r_t - r_{ft})^2} \right)^{-\frac{1}{2}} - 1,$$

which is also a CRRA utility function with risk aversion $\gamma = 2$.

3.5 DOES ALPHA EVEN EXIST?

Since alpha is based on a benchmark and estimates of alpha are very sensitive to that benchmark, is there even such a thing as true alpha? It could just be a wrong benchmark. The academic literature calls this a *joint hypothesis problem*, and the search for alpha is the same as the testing for market efficiency.[21] In a major contribution, Hansen and Jagannathan (1997) show that it is always possible to find an ex-post benchmark portfolio that produces no alpha. This is less useful ex ante, but it shows that a benchmark portfolio can always be constructed where no alpha exists after the fact. Since Grossman and Stiglitz (1980), the profession recognizes that perfectly efficient markets cannot exist (see chapter 6)—so there is alpha— but as the analysis of this section has shown, even for a recognized master of investing like Buffett, alpha can be very hard to detect statistically.

The joint hypothesis problem—that alpha and the benchmark are simultaneously determined—is the key problem for asset owners. It is of little use for an academic to say that Fidelity has no alpha, when the asset owner cannot access the complicated size, value-growth, and momentum factors used to compute that alpha. For that asset owner, Fidelity may be providing alpha. For another asset owner, Fidelity may well be adding negative alpha because she can do all the appropriate factor exposure (and implement the underlying replicating factor benchmark portfolios) on her own.

Choosing the right set of factors, then, is the most relevant issue for asset owners, and I return to this topic in chapter 14. Alpha is primarily a statement about the factor benchmark (or lack of a factor benchmark). We now have enough knowledge of risk adjustments to judge different alpha opportunities, and so we turn to one source of alpha that has recently stirred up debate.

---

[21] For a summary of this large literature, see Ang, Goetzmann, and Schaefer (2011).

4. Low Risk Anomaly

The low-risk anomaly is a combination of three effects, with the third a consequence of the first two:[22]

1. Volatility is negatively related to future returns;
2. Realized beta is negatively related to future returns; and
3. Minimum variance portfolios do better than the market.

The risk anomaly is that risk—measured by market beta or volatility—is negatively related to returns. Robin Greenwood, a professor at Harvard Business School and my fellow adviser to Martingale Asset Management, said in 2010, "We keep regurgitating the data to find yet one more variation of the size, value, or momentum anomaly, when the Mother of all inefficiencies may be standing right in front of us—the risk anomaly."

4.1 HISTORY

The negative relation between risk (at least measured by market beta and volatility) and returns has a long history. The first studies showing a negative relation appeared in the late 1960s and early 1970s.[23] Friend and Blume (1970) examined stock portfolio returns in the period 1960–1968 with CAPM beta and volatility risk measures. They concluded (my italics):

> The results are striking. In all cases risk-adjusted performance is dependent on risk. *The relationship is inverse and highly significant.*

Haugen and Heins (1975) use data from 1926 to 1971 and also investigate the relation between beta and volatility risk measures and returns. They report (my italics):

> The results of our empirical effort do not support the conventional hypothesis that risk—systematic or otherwise—generates a special reward. Indeed, our results indicate that, over the long run, *stock portfolios with lesser variance in monthly returns have experienced greater average returns than "riskier" counterparts.*

---

[22] Some references for the third are Haugen and Baker (1991), Jagannathan and Ma (2003), and Clarke, de Silva, and Thorley (2006). I cover references for the others below.

[23] In addition to the papers in the main text, also see Pratt (1971), Sodolfsky and Miller (1969), and Black (1972).

Most of these results were forgotten. But these old results recently have come roaring back.

4.2 VOLATILITY ANOMALY

I was fortunate to write one paper that helped launch the new "risk anomaly" literature in 2006 with Robert Hodrick, one of my colleagues at Columbia Business School, and two of our former students, Yuhang Xing and Xiaoyan Zhang, who are now professors at Rice University and Purdue University, respectively. We found that the returns of high-volatility stocks were "abysmally low." So low that they had zero average returns. This paper now generates the most cites per year of all my papers and has spawned a follow-up literature attempting to replicate, explain, and refute the results.[24]

First, should there even be a relation between volatility and returns? The whole point of the CAPM and the many multifactor extensions (see chapter 7) was that stock return volatility itself should not matter. Expected returns, according to these models, are determined by how assets covary with factor risks. Idiosyncratic volatility, or tracking error (see equation (10.3)), should definitely *not* have any relation to expected returns under the CAPM. But in markets that are segmented due to clientele effects—where some agents cannot diversify or where some agents prefer to hold some assets over others for exogenous reasons— idiosyncratic volatility should be positively related to returns. Intuitively, agents have to be paid for bearing idiosyncratic risk, resulting in a positive relation between idiosyncratic risk and volatility in equilibrium. In later models with "noise traders," who trade for random reasons unrelated to fundamental valuation, higher volatilities are associated with higher risk premiums.[25]

The Ang et al. (2006) results show exactly the opposite.

Particularly notable is the robustness of the negative relation between both idiosyncratic and total volatility with returns. We employed a large number of controls for size, value, leverage, liquidity risk, volume, turnover, bid–ask spreads, co-skewness risk, dispersion in analysts' forecasts, and momentum. We also did not find that aggregate volatility risk explained our result—even though volatility risk is a pervasive risk factor (see chapter 7). In subsequent work, Ang et al. (2009), we showed that the volatility effect existed in each G7 country and across all developed stock markets. We also controlled for private information, transactions costs, analyst coverage, institutional ownership, and delay measures, which

---

[24] Volatility makes many appearances, of course, in tests of cross-sectional asset pricing models before Ang et al. (2006), but most of them are negative results or show a slight positive relation. For example, in Fama and MacBeth's (1973) seminal test of the CAPM, volatility is included and carries an insignificant coefficient. Eric Falkenstein (2012) recounts that he uncovered a negative relation between volatility and stock returns in his PhD dissertation in 1994, which was never published.

[25] For clientele models, see Merton (1987). For noise trader models, see DeLong et al. (1990).

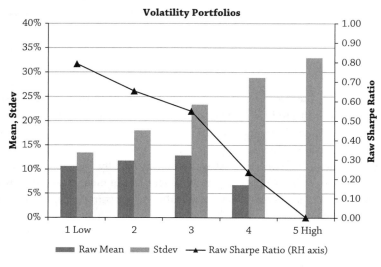

Figure 10.8

recorded how fast information is impounded into stock prices. Skewness did not explain the puzzle.

Lagged Volatility and Future Returns

To see the volatility anomaly, I take U.S. stocks, rebalance quarterly from September 1963 to December 2011, and form quintile portfolios. I construct monthly frequency returns. I sort on idiosyncratic volatility using the Fama–French (1993) factors with daily data over the past quarter. (Ranking on total volatility produces very similar results.) I market weight within each quintile similar to Ang et al. (2006, 2009).

In Figure 10.8, I report the mean and standard deviations of the quintile portfolios on the left-hand axis in the two bars. The volatilities increase going from the low- to high-volatility quintiles, by construction. The average returns are above 10% for the first three quintiles, fall to 6.8% for quintile 4, and then plummet to 0.1% for the highest volatility stocks. High volatility stocks certainly do have "abysmally low" returns. The right-hand axis reports raw Sharpe ratios, which are the ratios of the means to the standard deviations. These monotonically decline from 0.8 to 0.0 going from the low- to high-volatility quintiles.

Contemporaneous Volatility and Returns

Do stocks with high volatilities also have high returns over the same period used to measure those volatilities?

I examine this question in Figure 10.9 by forming portfolios at the end of the period based on realized idiosyncratic volatilities. I then measure realized returns over the same period. Note that these are not tradeable portfolios. Figure 10.9

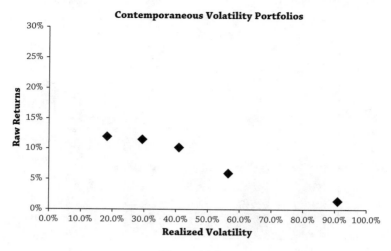

Figure 10.9

plots the average realized volatility and average realized returns of these quintile portfolios; there is still a negative relation between contemporaneous volatility and returns. Thus, the most volatile stocks *currently* lose money (which we cannot forecast), and they also tend to lose money in *the future* as well (which is predictable).

4.3 BETA ANOMALY

The first tests of the CAPM done in the 1970s did find positive relations between beta and expected returns, but they did not find that pure forms of the CAPM worked. Black, Jensen, and Scholes (1972), for example, found the relation between beta and returns to be "too flat" compared with what the CAPM predicted, but at least the relation was positive.

Fama and French wrote a major paper in 1992 that struck at the heart of the CAPM. While their main results showed that size and value effects dominated beta in individual stocks, they noted that "beta shows no power to explain average returns." In fact, their estimated relation between beta and returns was statistically insignificant. Worse, the point estimates indicated that the relation between beta and returns was negative.

Lagged Beta and Future Returns
In Figure 10.10, I form quintile portfolios rebalancing every quarter based on betas estimated over the previous quarter using daily returns. The portfolios are equal weighted so as to form the largest differences in returns and Sharpe ratios, and returns are at the monthly frequency.

The beta anomaly is that stocks with high betas tend to have lower risk-adjusted returns. Panel A of Figure 10.10 shows that the average returns across

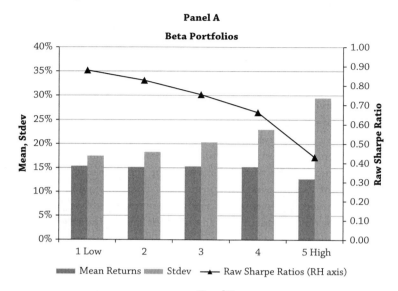

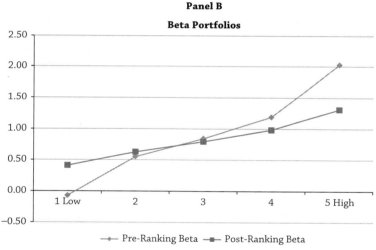

Figure 10.10

the beta quintiles are approximately flat, around 15% for the first four quintiles and slightly lower at 12.7% for quintile 5. The beta anomaly is not that stocks with high betas have low returns—they don't. Stocks with high betas have high volatilities. This causes the Sharpe ratios of high beta stocks to be lower than the Sharpe ratios of low-beta stocks. The right-hand axis of Panel A shows that the raw Sharpe ratios drop from 0.9 to 0.4 moving from the low- to the high-beta quintile portfolios.

In Panel B of Figure 10.10, I plot the pre-ranking and post-ranking betas. The pre-ranking beta is the beta over the previous three months, which is used to rank the stocks into portfolios. The post-ranking beta is the realized beta over the next three months after the portfolios have been formed. Panel B graphs the average pre-ranking betas of each portfolio with the average post-ranking betas. There is considerable noise in estimating betas at both ends, which is why the post-ranking beta line is much flatter than the pre-ranking betas. Betas are noisy! There is, however, still a large spread in post-ranking betas of over 1.0 between the highest and lowest beta portfolios.

Contemporaneous Beta and Returns

The CAPM does *not* predict that lagged betas should lead to higher returns. The CAPM actually states that there should be a *contemporaneous* relation between beta and expected returns. That is, stocks with higher betas should have higher average returns over the same periods used to measure the betas and the returns (see chapter 7 for more on factor theory).

Figure 10.11 examines the contemporaneous relation between betas and average returns by graphing average realized returns and average realized betas of portfolios formed at the end of each three-month period. It shows, perhaps surprisingly, that there is a positive contemporaneous relation between beta and returns.[26] This is exactly what the CAPM predicts!

Can we reconcile the negative relation between past betas and future returns and the positive contemporaneous relation between betas and realized returns? If we could find the future beta, future betas line up with future returns in keeping

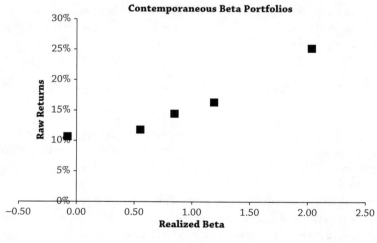

Figure 10.11

[26] See also Ang, Chen, and Xing (2006). Consistent with the early studies like Black, Jensen, and Scholes (1972), Figure 10.11 also shows that the estimated security market line is "too flat," especially near the *y*-axis.

with what the CAPM tells us. But Figure 10.10, Panel B, shows that it is hard to predict future betas. Past betas do a lousy job at predicting future betas. There is large variation in betas, and there is substantial sampling error.[27]

Studies that estimate betas from other information tend to find positive risk relations. Buss and Vilkov (2012) estimate betas from options and find them to be better predictors of future betas than betas estimated from past returns. Their betas estimated from option-implied information yield a positive risk–return relation. Cosemans et al. (2012) use valuation information from accounting balance sheets to compute betas along with past returns. They also estimate a positive relation between betas and returns. Thus, the real mystery in the low-beta anomaly is actually not so much that beta does not work; it is that we have such difficulty in predicting future betas, especially with past betas.

4.4 RISK ANOMALY FACTORS

It is a straightforward extension to use these portfolio results to create a benchmark factor for the risk anomaly.

Betting against Beta

Frazzini and Pedersen (2010) construct a betting-against-beta (BAB) factor that goes long low-beta stocks and short high-beta stocks. Constructing a factor to trade the beta anomaly cannot be done just by taking differences of the portfolios in Figure 10.10. Remember, the differences in average returns across the beta quintiles are tiny—what's large are the differences in Sharpe ratios across betas. Frazzini and Pedersen form their BAB factor by scaling the low- and high-beta portfolios by their betas:

$$BAB_{t+1} = \frac{r_{L,t+1} - r_f}{\beta_{L,t}} - \frac{r_{H,t+1} - r_f}{\beta_{H,t}}, \qquad (10.17)$$

where $r_{L,t+1}$ is the return of the low-beta portfolio and $r_{H,t+1}$ is the return of the high-beta portfolio. The betas of the low-beta and high-beta portfolio at the beginning of the period (the pre-ranking betas) are given by $\beta_{L,t}$ and $\beta_{H,t}$, respectively.

Figure 10.12 shows what is going on. The horizontal line labeled "Data" is the empirical pattern of flat average returns with lagged betas in contrast to the upward-sloping line that is predicted by the "Standard CAPM." The long position in the low-beta portfolio is levered. It takes the position where it hits the

---

[27] Blume (1975) was one of the first to document this. For formal statistics for calculating the paths of time-varying alphas and betas and their standard errors, see Ang and Kristensen (2012).

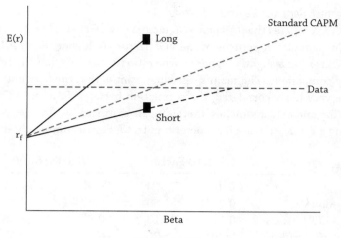

Figure 10.12

"Data" line and levers it up to the square marked "Long." The short position in the high-beta portfolio is marked "Short." The *BAB* portfolio does not take the entire position in the high-beta portfolio; it combines it with the risk-free asset to obtain the position marked Short. In effect, the Long and Short portfolios are unit beta positions in the low- and high-beta portfolios.

Frazzini and Pedersen use just two beta portfolios in creating their *BAB* factor. They have little choice. In Figure 10.10, the first quintile portfolio has a pre-ranking beta close to zero. Levering up this portfolio results in a position close to infinity. Thus, one is forced to create very small numbers of portfolios—two or three at most—in the *BAB* factor. One advantage of the volatility portfolios is that they can be directly traded without using the risk-free asset because there are pronounced differences in expected returns, not only volatilities, across the volatility quintiles.

Volatility Factor
I construct a volatility factor, *VOL*, similar to Frazzini and Pedersen's *BAB*:

$$VOL_{t+1} = \sigma_{\text{target}} \times \left(\frac{r_{L,t+1} - r_f}{\sigma_{L,t}} - \frac{r_{H,t+1} - r_f}{\sigma_{H,t}} \right), \qquad (10.18)$$

where $\sigma_{L,t}$ and $\sigma_{H,t}$ are the pre-ranking volatilities of the low- and high-volatility portfolios. While the *BAB* factor scales to unit betas, the *VOL* factor scales to a target volatility. I use the first and fifth quintile portfolios with returns $r_{L,t}$ and $r_{H,t}$, respectively. I set the target volatility $\sigma_{\text{target}} = 15\%$.

Betting-against-Beta and Volatility Factors

Figure 10.13 compares the *BAB* and *VOL* factors from October 1963 to December 2011.[28] The cumulative returns of the *VOL* factor are higher than *BAB*, and the volatility factor has a slightly higher Sharpe ratio (0.6 vs. 0.5), but the two factors are largely comparable. The main surprising result is that the beta and volatility effects are very lowly correlated; the correlation between *BAB* and *VOL* is −9%. The volatility and beta anomalies, therefore, are distinct.

Running a Fama–French plus momentum factor regression, we obtain

	BAB Factor		**VOL Factor**	
	Coeff	T-stat	Coeff	T-stat
Alpha	0.33%	1.89	0.42%	4.37
MKT Loading	−0.17	−4.13	0.87	38.8
SMB Loading	0.29	5.20	−0.63	−20.3
HML Loading	0.48	7.85	0.20	5.73
UMD Loading	0.09	2.35	0.13	6.00

The alpha for the *BAB* factor is 0.33% per month (4% per year) and the *t*-statistic of 1.89 corresponds to a *p*-value of 0.06. So this is borderline statistically significant at the standard 95% level. The *VOL* factor's alpha is slightly

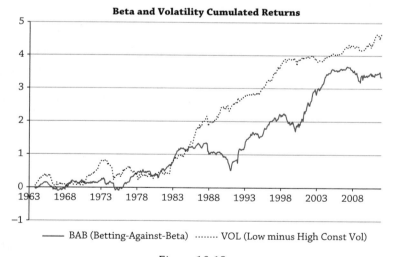

Figure 10.13

[28] I construct a *BAB* factor similar to Frazzini and Pedersen (2012) except I do not follow their step in shrinking the betas. Specifically, betas are computed in one-year rolling regressions using daily frequency returns. There are two beta portfolios created at the end of each month, and the *BAB* factor is constructed using equation (10.14) using the pre-ranking portfolio betas.

higher, at 0.42% per month (5% per year) but is much more statistically significant with a *t*-statistic of 4.37. Note that both *BAB* and *VOL* have significant value tilts (positive *HML* loadings) and momentum tilts (positive *UMD* loadings). The big difference is that the *BAB* factor carries a negative *SMB* loading, whereas it is positive for the *VOL* factor. That is, the beta anomaly manifests more in small stocks. In contrast, the volatility anomaly is more pervasive in large stocks, which are usually easier to trade because they are more liquid.

So should you do low volatility, or should you do low beta? This is not an either–or choice. You should do both.

4.5 EXPLANATIONS

We are still searching for a comprehensive explanation for the risk anomaly. In my opinion, the true explanation is a combination of all of the explanations listed below, plus potentially others being developed.

Data Mining
Some papers in the literature rightfully point out some data mining concerns with the original results in Ang et al. (2006). There is some sensitivity in the results to different portfolio weighting schemes and illiquidity effects.[29] For the most part, however, the low-risk anomaly is fairly robust. A recent survey article by Chen et al. (2012) argues that "idiosyncratic volatility is a common stock phenomenon" and is not due to microstructure or liquidity biases.

The best argument against data mining is that the low-risk effect is seen in many other contexts. Ang et al. (2006) show that the effect appears during recessions and expansions and during stable and volatile periods. Ang et al. (2009) show that it takes place in international stock markets. Frazzini and Pedersen (2011) show that low-beta portfolios have high Sharpe ratios in U.S. stocks, international stocks, Treasury bonds, corporate bonds cut by different maturities and credit ratings, credit derivative markets, commodities, and foreign exchange. Cao and Han (2013) and Blitz and de Groot (2013) show that the low-risk phenomenon even shows up in option and commodity markets, respectively. Low risk is pervasive.

Leverage Constraints
Many investors are leverage constrained—they wish to take on more risk but are unable to take on more leverage.[30] Since they cannot borrow, they do the next best thing—they hold stocks with "built-in" leverage, like high-beta stocks. Investors bid up the price of high-beta stocks until the shares are overpriced and deliver low

---

[29] See Bali and Cakici (2008) and Han and Lesmond (2011), respectively.

[30] Black (1972) was the first to develop a theory of the CAPM for when investors cannot lever. Frazzini and Pedersen (2011) apply a leverage-constraint story to explain the low-beta anomaly.

returns—exactly what we see in data. In CAPM parlance, the voracious demand of leverage-constrained investors for high-beta stocks flattens the security market line (see chapter 6). The leverage constraint story, however, does not explain the underpricing of low- beta stocks relative to the market, only the overpricing of high-beta stocks. Thus, it cannot explain why low-beta or low-volatility assets have higher returns than the market portfolio, but it can explain why some low-beta assets have positive alphas. This story also predicts that leverage-constrained institutions should be attracted to high-risk stocks. In reality, though, institutional investors tend to underweight high-risk stocks; stocks with high idiosyncratic volatility are predominantly held and traded by retail investors.[31]

Agency Problems

Many institutional managers can't or won't play the risk anomaly. In particular, the use of market-weighted benchmarks itself may lead to the low volatility anomaly.[32]

Figure 10.14 draws a theoretical relation between beta and expected returns in the diagonal solid line marked "CAPM" (the security market line). The data relation between returns and beta is the horizontal line marked "Data." Consider stock A, which has positive alpha, and B, which has negative alpha. Unconstrained investors simply buy low and sell high. They buy A, which offers a high return relative to the CAPM, and they sell B, whose return is too low relative to the CAPM.

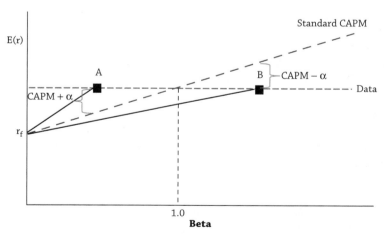

Figure 10.14

[31] For an academic reference, see Han and Kumar (2011). Taking 13-F filings as of June 30, 2012 on Russell 1000 holdings, Martingale calculates that institutions hold 46.5% low-risk stocks and 53.5% high-risk stocks compared to a balanced 50%/50% split.

[32] See Greenwood et al. (2010) and Baker, Bradley, and Wurgler (2011).

In a perfect world, these unconstrained investors would bid up the price of A until it no longer has any excess returns. And they would sell B until its returns reach a fair level relative to the CAPM. In this perfect world, the risk anomaly disappears.

Now consider a long-only investor subject to tracking error constraints that place limits on how much she can deviate from benchmark (see equation (10.3)). This investor cannot short. This investor does *not* invest in A, even though A is offering high returns relative to the CAPM. The returns of A are higher than the CAPM predicts. Stock A would even perform in line with the market. But, by investing in A, she takes on significant tracking error.

What about stock B? Stock B has negative alpha. To make money, she needs to short stock B, and she cannot do so. The best that she can do is to avoid buying stock B, thus making at most a small active bet relative to the market portfolio. The tracking error constraint also limits the underweight position in stock B that she can hold. If the "Data" line is in fact just slightly upward sloping rather than perfectly flat, then she actually has an incentive to buy B rather than sell it short because B could outperform the market.

Thus, the use of tracking error with these benchmarks makes it hard to bet against low volatility or low beta. Tracking error is a binding constraint for GM Asset Management. It is also a binding constraint for most institutional asset owners. One obvious solution is to change the benchmarks, and there are certainly more appropriate factor benchmarks available (see section 3 and chapter 14). But changing benchmarks at GM is a lengthy process requiring approval of the investment committee. It opens up a broader issue of how all benchmarks "depend on funded status and on the health of the parent," as Scott explains.

Frazzini, Kabiller, and Pedersen (2012) even argue that low-risk factors play a part in explaining the superior performance of Berkshire Hathaway—a company well known for its ability to go against the crowd and avoid common agency issues. They find that Buffett's alpha declines from 12.5% from 1976 to 2011 using the Fama–French and momentum benchmark we've been using in this chapter to 11.1% when including the *BAB* factor. If they add another factor measuring the underlying quality of companies, Buffett's alpha falls to 7.0%. So some of Buffett's investing prowess is due to Buffett selecting stocks with low risk, but most of Buffett's investment prowess comes from ferreting out gems with high underlying quality—true skill that is unrelated to just holding low-volatility stocks.

Preferences

If asset owners simply have a preference for high-volatility and high-beta stocks, then they bid up these stocks until they have low returns. Conversely, these investors shun safe stocks—stocks with low volatility and low betas—leading to low prices and high returns for these shares. Thus, "hopes and dreams" preferences, where the hopes and dreams are represented by high-volatility and high-beta stocks, could explain the risk anomaly.[33]

Hou and Loh (2012) comprehensively examine many explanations of the low volatility anomaly. They arrange their explanations into three broad groups: (i) lottery preferences, (ii) market frictions including illiquidity, and (iii) "other," which is a broad category that includes uncertainty, short-sales constraints, financial distress, investor inattention, growth options, earnings shocks, and other variables. Hou and Loh find that when individual explanations are taken alone, each explains less than one-tenth of the volatility anomaly. But taken as groups, the most promising explanation is lottery preferences. When individual lottery preference stories are taken together, they explain close to half of the low volatility puzzle. But close to half of the puzzle remains unexplained.

Agents disagreeing with each other (heterogeneous preferences) combined with the inability to short could also account for some of the risk anomaly. Hong and Sraer (2012) show that when disagreement is low and everyone takes long-only positions, the CAPM holds. But when disagreement is high, some agents want to sell short and they cannot. High beta stocks become overpriced. Large enough disagreement causes the relation between beta and returns to be downward sloping.[34]

5. GM Asset Management and Martingale Redux

Martingale's low volatility strategy is attractive compared to the market portfolio. It delivers alpha relative to the Russell 1000 benchmark of 1.50% per year. Adjusting the Russell 1000 for risk increases that alpha to 3.44% per year. Alpha is all about the benchmark. What if we changed the benchmark of the Martingale's strategy to be the low volatility strategy itself? Then, there wouldn't be any alpha of course, as alpha morphs into the benchmark (or beta, as some in industry like to call it). This is not just philosophical—GM Asset Management might be in a position to internally do low volatility strategies. But low-risk strategies appear to have significant alpha relative to standard market capitalization benchmarks and sophisticated factor benchmarks that control for risk using dynamic value-growth and momentum factors along with the market portfolio.

Yet alpha is not the only consideration for GM Asset Management. Martingale's alpha comes with high tracking error relative to the Russell 1000 benchmark. In fact, the ubiquitous tracking error constraints employed in

---

[33] For stories along these lines, see Boyer, Mitton, and Vorkink (2010), Bali, Cakici, and Whitelaw (2011), and Ilmanen (2012).

[34] See also Jiang, Xu, and Yao (2009) for the relation between earnings uncertainty and low volatility.

the asset management industry may partly give rise to the risk anomaly in the first place.

Will the risk anomaly persist? I am hoping that it goes away as soon as possible, and I have a large academic stake in this debate. As much as I enjoy seeing new explanations being proposed (including some of my own), the risk anomaly is an enigma. If it does disappear, then the low-risk trades already put on by the smart money will pay off handsomely—low-volatility or low-beta stocks have returns that are too high and prices that are too low. Capital should be drawn to these stocks, driving up their prices and removing the anomalous returns. If that happened, current low-risk anomaly investors would enjoy large capital gains.

But I doubt this will happen. Low-volatility strategies are far from predominant, as most institutional investors appear to be underweight low-risk stocks. More fundamentally, the fact that we see the risk anomaly in many markets—U.S. and international, stocks, bonds, commodities, foreign exchange, and derivatives—suggests that the effect is pervasive and requires a deep explanation. As Greenwood says, the low-risk anomaly is the mother of all inefficiencies.

CHAPTER 11

"Real" Assets

Chapter Summary

Many "real" assets, including inflation-indexed bonds (linkers), commodities, and real estate, turn out not to be that "real." While a single linker provides a constant real return, linkers as an asset class have almost no correlation with inflation. Among commodities, only energy has been a decent inflation hedge. Gold, surprisingly, has been a poor inflation hedge. Real estate has some, but certainly far from complete, inflation-hedging ability. Boring Treasury bills (T-bills), in contrast, are the best at hedging inflation.

1. How Real Is Real Estate?

Carole was a consultant to a mid-sized pension fund holding a traditional portfolio of 60% equities and 40% bonds.[1] For a long time the fund was too small to consider direct real estate investments, but recently, thanks to large employer contributions, the fund had swelled. The trustees, worried about the threat of inflation, believed that investing in real estate could offer some protection against its ravages.

Were the trustees right? Is direct real estate a good inflation-hedging asset? Carole knew this was not only about number crunching. Real estate seemed to differ from the other asset classes—equities and bonds—in the fund's portfolio. Although direct real estate could have a static allocation, it requires active management, typically by a professional. What's more, bricks and mortar require ongoing capital spending if the asset is to remain competitive. The fund already had a passive allocation to traded real estate investment trusts (REITs), which had underlying real estate exposure. Are REITs different from direct real estate? Carole had to consider these additional challenges as well.

---

[1] This example is based on the case "Is Real Estate Real?" CaseWorks ID#111704.

The fund's liabilities increased when inflation was high and, to minimize the variation in the difference between assets and liabilities (which is *surplus*, see chapter 1), the trustees wanted some assets that have high returns when inflation is high. In fact, the trustees' top concern was finding assets whose returns correlated highly with inflation. If real estate turned out not to provide adequate inflation protection, then what other real assets should Carole consider?

In this chapter, we cover the properties of assets traditionally thought to hold their value during times of high inflation, especially the "real" assets of real bonds, commodities, and real estate. I distinguish between inflation hedging—the correlation of returns and inflation—and the long-run returns of assets. An asset having a long-run return much higher than inflation can be a very poor inflation hedge; inflation hedging is a statement about a co-movement, while the latter is a statement about a long-term mean. As we shall see, most real assets turn out not to be so "real."

2. Inflation

2.1. RISING AND FALLING INFLATION

Figure 11.1 plots inflation measured by year-on-year changes in the Consumer Price Index (CPI; for all urban consumers, all items) from January 1952 to December 2012. The U.S. inflation experience since the second half of the twentieth century is marked by an increase in inflation through the 1960s and 1970s, which the economic historian Allan Meltzer (2005) calls the *Great Inflation*, and then a low inflation experience after the mid-1980s. Inflation reached a peak of over 14% in 1980. Meltzer calls the Great Inflation "the climactic monetary

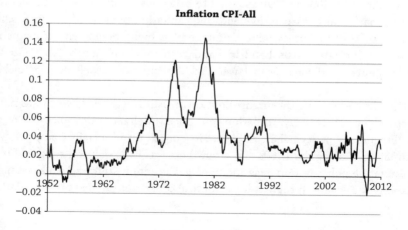

Figure 11.1

event of the last part of the 20th century" and its effect was devastating: it contributed to the destruction of the world's system of fixed exchange rates (known as *Bretton Woods* for the town in New Hampshire where the system was agreed), it bankrupted much of the savings and loan industry, and it was an experience shared by all developed countries to greater or lesser degrees.

The United States had high inflation after World War II, and a bout of inflation during the Korean War in the early 1950s, but in both cases policymakers quickly brought it under control. In fact, in 1954 and 1955, inflation was actually negative. Thus the Great Inflation erupted in the mid-1960s from a time of stable and low inflation. Why did rising prices get so out of hand in the 1960s and 1970s, and how did policymakers bring inflation under control again in the 1980s?[2]

Three things caused inflation to get out of control.

First, policymakers used the wrong models. In the 1960s, economists believed in the Phillips (1958) curve, which plotted a tradeoff between unemployment and inflation. Economists believed unemployment could be reduced by raising inflation, but over time it became clear that there was no such tradeoff. During the 1960s and 1970s, *both* unemployment and inflation rose. The *Rational Expectations* revolution in economics in the 1970s spearheaded by Friedman and Lucas (who won Nobel Prizes in 1976 and 1995, respectively) explained that the Phillips curve was unstable and could not be effectively exploited by policymakers.

Second, economists were divided on how to respond to higher inflation. They recognized it was a problem, but some thought the Fed was not responsible. *Cost push inflation*, which arose in the price of natural resources such as oil, was thought to be outside the Fed's control, whereas *demand pull inflation*, caused by an overheating economy, was thought to be under the Fed's control. Most economists believed the era's underlying inflation was of the cost push variety. Even some economists who thought the Fed could control inflation did not recommend that the Fed embark on disinflation because of the large *sacrifice ratios*—the reductions in GDP required to bring down inflation—and advocated instead that society learn to live with high inflation because of the unacceptably high costs of unemployment. Unfortunately, high unemployment happened anyway in the late 1970s hand in hand with inflation (*stagflation*), and unemployment would have been lower had the inflation problem been tackled earlier.

The third reason was the intense political pressure on the Fed, which was not as independent as it is today. "Inflation continued," Meltzer writes, "because of the unwillingness of policymakers to persist in a political and socially costly policy of disinflation. During the 1960s and after, there was little political support for an anti-inflation policy in Congress and none in the administration." This last point is especially relevant: if there is little political consensus on how to end inflation,

---

[2] In particular see DeLong (1997), Sargent (1999), Meltzer (2005), and Nelson (2005).

it will persist. Inflation can be as much a political risk as it is an economic one (see also chapter 7 for inflation risk and political risk as factors).

Inflation was finally brought under control by Fed Chairman Paul Volcker, who was appointed by President Jimmy Carter and served from August 6, 1979, to August 11, 1987. When Volcker took office, the public was ready to endure the pain required to cure the inflation disease. Volcker brought inflation under control by jacking up the Fed funds rate above 19% in the early 1980s. The economy careened into recession, but inflation was brought under control. This period is the *Volcker disinflation*. There are several lessons for asset owners in this experience: committed monetary policy can control inflation, doing so can be painful, and inflation risk is intertwined with monetary policy risk (see chapter 9 on fixed income).

Figure 11.1 shows that not only has the level of inflation varied considerably, but the volatility of inflation has also changed over time, exhibiting high and low volatility periods. This sort of volatility clustering is described well by Engel's (1982) popular model of GARCH volatility. In fact, although GARCH models are now overwhelmingly applied on financial returns (see chapter 8), his first application was inflation! From the mid-1980s to the early 2000s, the volatility of inflation declined dramatically, especially compared to the very high inflation volatility of the 1960s and 1970s. Economists dubbed the later, quiet period *the Great Moderation*. The fall in volatility was not only observed in inflation; volatility declined in all macro series: GDP growth, investment, consumption, sales, unemployment, and so on. (Volatility of asset returns, however, did not fall.)

The decline in inflation and other macroeconomic volatility was accepted by many as a permanent regime change. In 2003, at the Fed's rarefied Jackson Hole symposium—an annual retreat of central bankers, policymakers, and academics—conference delegates debated whether the Great Moderation was due to structural changes in the economy, good monetary policy, or plain good luck. All three played some role.[3] Central bankers gave themselves a hearty round of congratulations for a new era of successful monetary policy, but the uptick in volatility since the financial crisis has shown how wrong most economists were. Inflation volatility, like other macroeconomic volatilities, changes over time, and asset owners must be prepared to live with it. The worst thing is to become complacent.

2.2. THERE IS NO SINGLE INFLATION RATE

While prices of all goods and services generally rise and fall together, inflation means different things to different investors because investors do not consume the same basket of goods and services. Two especially important inflation rates

[3] See Stock and Watson (2002).

for individuals are for medical care and higher education. The former is part of the CPI bundle and is separately tabulated by the Bureau of Labor Statistics; clearly the elderly and sick consume more medical care than the average consumer. The latter is measured by the Higher Education Price Index and is distributed annually by Commonfund, a nonprofit institution specializing in asset management for endowments and foundations. (Higher education expenses do enter the CPI bundle, but I use the Higher Education Price Index for this analysis as it is more relevant for university endowments.) Figure 11.2 plots both series, together with CPI, from 1984 to 2008.

Figure 11.2 shows that both medical care costs and higher education expenses have been increasing faster than the overall rate of inflation as measured by the vanilla CPI. From 1984 to 2008, the average annual CPI increase has been 3.1% while the average inflation rate for medical care and higher education has been 5.3% and 4.0%, respectively. Due to the effect of compound interest, a 1% difference over twenty to thirty years can really kill you (literally, in the case of inadequate medical care). A basket of $10,000 worth of general goods and services at the beginning of 1984 would cost $21,600 at the end of 2008, but $10,000 worth of medical care in 1984 would cost $36,100 in 2008.

The difference between the CPI and an investor's own consumption basket is called *basis risk*, and Figure 11.2 shows that it can be substantial. There are ways to hedge against basis risk, but the most important is to first hedge against a general rise in all prices. Then an investor can tilt her portfolio to assets that may have higher exposures to medical care risk, for example, if her liabilities or

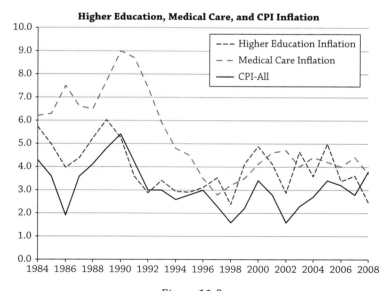

Figure 11.2

considerations reflect that risk. To accomplish this, she might invest in health care companies. Like factor investing in general (see chapter 14), finding assets that hedge inflation risk is specific to the inflation index that is relevant to the investor.

Let's examine some assets usually considered to have some value as a hedge against inflation. We start with one that is not normally considered an inflation hedge and is ignored by many textbooks and investors.

3. Treasury Bills

Figure 11.3 is the same CPI inflation series as Figure 11.1, except it overlays the year-on-year returns of cash, or T-bills, in the dotted line. From 1952 to 2012, T-bills have returned 4.8% per year, about 1% above average inflation for the period, which was 3.7%. Crucially, the correlation of T-bill returns and inflation has been high, at 70.1%. We have seen high correlations of T-bill returns and inflation before—chapter 8 portrayed equity as a poor inflation hedge and in passing presented evidence that T-bills hedge inflation marvelously. Of all the "real" assets considered in this chapter—real bonds, commodities, and real estate—T-bills have had the highest correlation with inflation.

Of course, the long-term return of T-bills has been much lower than other asset classes. But inflation hedging is all about the co-movement of asset returns with inflation, not the average return. T-bills are highly correlated with inflation because monetary authorities respond to inflation in setting the short-term interest rate—technically the Fed funds rate, but the T-bill rate moves almost one for one with the Fed funds rate (see chapter 9). Furthermore, according to the Fisher

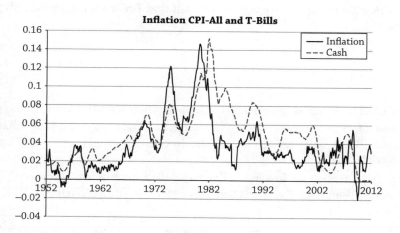

Figure 11.3

Hypothesis, the T-bill rate reflects *expected* inflation. Movements in expected inflation account for a large part of overall movements in total inflation because of inflation's persistence—if inflation is high today, it is likely to be high next month.

Investors need to be concerned about two things in holding cash as an inflation-hedging tool. First, Figure 11.3 shows that cash returns *lag* inflation. This is most clearly seen in the huge spike in inflation in the late 1970s; the increase in T-bill yields did not come until the early 1980s. It is impossible for a policy authority to respond with perfect foresight to contemporaneous inflation shocks given that all our macro data is collected with a lag.[4] But once inflation shocks occur, inflation is persistent. Inflation shocks are thus reflected in T-bill yields with a lag. Unless inflation is extraordinarily high (hyper-inflation has never occurred in the United States and is extremely unlikely despite the doomsayers), this lag is inconvenient and modestly costly, but it is not a reason to avoid cash as a real asset.

The second reason is. At the time of writing and at end of the sample in Figure 11.3, T-bill returns were effectively zero. This is exactly where the Fed wanted short-term interest rates to be at this time: the economy was still tender after the global financial crisis of 2008 and 2009 and the Great Recession that followed. Inflation was 3.0% at December 2011 and thus lay square in the middle of the Fed's preferred 2% to 4% policy range. The real interest rate, which is the difference between the T-bill yield and inflation, was negative, and significantly so. Reinhart and Rogoff (2011) and Reinhart and Sbrancia (2011) label this *financial repression*. It is effectively a tax imposed on bond (and cash) investors by policymakers who channel the benefits to other purposes and people (like shoring up the financial system and subsidizing managers and owners of large financial institutions). Given the ocean of government debt sloshing around worldwide, financial repression is likely to stay a while. This second reason is a statement about the relatively low long-run return of T-bills and that an investor may desire other assets with higher long-run average returns, not that T-bills are not a good inflation hedge.

4. Real Bonds

A real bond is a bond whose principal or coupon is indexed to inflation. In this way the investor is protected against inflation because the payouts grow as inflation increases. Bond payments, therefore, remain constant in real terms. Real bonds are called *linkers*.

The U.S. version of linkers is *Treasury Inflation-Protected Securities* (TIPS), which have been issued by Uncle Sam since 1997. As of December 31, 2011, the

---

[4] "Forecasting" current economic conditions is called *nowcasting*, and econometricians have developed sophisticated models to do this. See Giannone, Reichlin, and Small (2008).

Treasury has issued $739 billion of TIPS, which represents 7.5% of all outstanding marketable Treasury securities.[5] Officially, these bonds are now referred to as *Treasury Inflation Indexed Securities*, but market participants and all the literature, except for official government publications, continue to use the name TIPS.

Many sovereigns have issued real bonds. The first linker was issued by Massachusetts in 1780 to raise money for the Revolutionary War.[6] Inflation was extremely high while patriots were fighting the British, and the bonds were invented partly to allay the anger of soldiers in the revolutionary army who were dismayed by the declining purchasing power of their (already meager) pay. An important linkers market is in Great Britain, where the Bank of England first issued *Inflation-Linked Gilts* in 1981. This market was immediately successful because of high inflation in the United Kingdom during that time (significantly higher than U.S. inflation, and the Great Inflation lasted longer in the United Kingdom than in the United States). The U.S. market, in contrast, was highly illiquid for the first few years (see below). Linkers now account for approximately a quarter of all outstanding debt issued by the U.K. government.

TIPS pay a fixed coupon payment that is indexed to CPI with a lag of three months.[7] The interest rate on TIPS is fixed, but the bond's principal is regularly adjusted for inflation, with the result that investors receive increasing interest payments when inflation rises. The principal can also fall with inflation, but it can never go below the original face value of the bond. This *deflation put* usually has little value for a long-maturity TIPS bond that has a high principal balance. Such a bond has already experienced a period of high inflation. For this bond, deflation would have to be extremely severe for its principal to fall back to par. In contrast, during times of low inflation and deflation, the deflation put is valuable for short-maturity TIPS.[8] These bonds have low principal balances, and, when deflation occurs, their principals cannot go below par. Such a period occurred during 2008 and 2009. Inflation during parts of 2009 was actually negative (see Figure 11.1 and 11.3), and newly issued TIPS during that time were extra valuable because of the high value in their deflation puts.

4.1. REAL BONDS FOR RETIREMENT?

An investor buying and holding a TIPS bond when it is first issued receives a constant real yield due to the inflation indexation.[9] If the TIPS bond is held to pay

---

[5] Monthly Statement of the Public Debt of the United States, Dec. 31, 2011.

[6] See Humphrey (1974) and Shiller (1993).

[7] Since CPI is released with a two-week delay, there is actually a two and a half month lag between the actual release of CPI and the indexation adjustment.

[8] Jacoby and Shiller (2008) show that the value of the deflation put can be large.

[9] Well, not quite. There is still the reinvestment risk associated with the coupons of the bond. One would technically need to buy and hold a TIPS zero-coupon bond to receive a constant real yield. The text ignores this consideration.

off a liability coming due at the maturity of the bond, the investor purchasing the TIPS has eradicated inflation risk. (This is an example of immunization; see chapter 4.) If a retired person can purchase a series of TIPS maturing in different years, then she has locked in a stream of payments that are constant in real terms. This allows her to meet her living expenses in the future, impervious to the effects of inflation. Thus it seems that TIPS are an ideal retirement savings mechanism for retail investors. Zvi Bodie, a professor at Boston University specializing in investment management and pensions, advocates that retail investors should hold close to 100% TIPS in their retirement portfolios.[10]

There are several problems with Bodie's advice.

First, purchasing a single TIPS bond provides an inflation hedge for future cash flows immunized at a moment in time—subject to the small indexation lag and the important caveat that the CPI is the right inflation measure for that investor. But perfect cash flow matching assumes that the investor can predict all her future liabilities to immunize them today. Often, she can't really know for certain what liabilities she will face down the road, and some of those retirement expenses are the result of choices about where she works, how long she works, her health, and other considerations along the way.

Second, most investors do not save a lump sum at a moment in time for retirement. Instead, an investor saves a portion of his income at a time over many years. The real yield curve changes across time. As real yields change, the value of the TIPS portfolio also changes, and it changes in such a way such that the TIPS portfolio returns have low correlations with inflation, as I show below. This wouldn't matter if the investor could perfect forecast his retirement liabilities and he cares only about hedging them using TIPS, but in many situations we care about wealth today as well as wealth at retirement: taking out a mortgage, having a financial cushion to start a business, or even splurging on vacation are all decisions that are impacted by investors' total wealth today.

The third problem with retail investors holding only real bonds for retirement is that at the time of writing in 2013, TIPS are paying negative real yields. If real yields are negative, to secure a payment of $100 that is immune from inflation risk in five years requires an investor to put away more than $100 today. Negative real rates mean that TIPS subtract wealth, instead of adding wealth, from investors. In a world of negative real rates, investors investing in risk-free real assets must be prepared to see safe investments decline, not increase, in purchasing power. This critique applies not only to individuals saving for retirement but for all endowments, foundations, and sovereign wealth funds wishing to preserve spending in real terms. While real rates on risk-free bonds may be negative, there are positive expected real risk premiums in other asset classes and strategies (see chapter 7).

A final consideration is that TIPS have sovereign risk. Sovereign risk includes both the risk of a government explicitly defaulting on a real bond—which may

---

[10] Bodie makes his case in a series of papers and books, most recently in Bodie and Taqqu (2012).

be minimal for the United States but is not negligible for other markets—but also the risk that the government implicitly defaults by changing the definition of inflation. The Argentinian government, for example, took direct control of its statistics institute in 2007 and since then the discrepancy between its official inflation figures and those reported by independent economists has been up to 15%. Up to 2013, this doctoring has saved the Argentinian government $2.5 billion in linkers payments.[11] The United States periodically changes its inflation basket. While these changes are geared towards keeping the basket relevant for the typical consumer, the basket can change in a way that makes it less relevant for you. This is *time-varying basis risk*. In some countries, however, governments have redefined inflation to the detriment of all consumers. I consider sovereign credit risk in chapter 14 as part of factor investing.

This is not to say that real bonds are not good investments. I recommend that they be used as part of an overall portfolio, rather than constituting the majority of individuals' retirement savings. And whether and how much an investor should hold must be a factor decision, not a decision based on the false notion that real bonds are "real," which I now show.

4.2. REAL BONDS ARE LOUSY INFLATION HEDGES

Almost all investors investing in TIPS hold a portfolio of TIPS, and the composition of that portfolio changes over time (unlike a perfectly immunized bond portfolio). Investors often hold a fixed proportion of their portfolio in TIPS, treating TIPS as an asset class, or as part of an overall bond portfolio. Investing in TIPS this way, as opposed to using individual TIPS bonds to immunize (usually partially unknown) future cash flows, results in TIPS being a poor inflation hedge. Real bonds, unfortunately, are not so real.

Table 11.4 reports means and standard deviations of TIPS and nominal Treasuries from March 1997 to December 2011. The bond portfolios are the BarCap U.S. Treasury and U.S. TIPS benchmarks. The full sample statistics are listed in the top panel of Table 11.4. TIPS show a mean return of 7.0%, exceeding the average Treasury return of 6.2%. TIPS volatility of 5.9% is also higher than the Treasury volatility of 4.7%. TIPS and Treasuries tend to move together, with a correlation of 64%, and the correlations of both TIPS and Treasuries with inflation is low. Far from offering good inflation protection, TIPS' correlation with inflation is just 10%.

The first few years of the TIPS market during the late 1990s and early 2000s were characterized by pronounced illiquidity (as I detail below), so the second panel of Table 11.4 takes data from when the TIPS market was mature and starts at July 2007. In this sample the same stylized facts hold: TIPS have higher average returns than Treasuries (8.4% vs. 7.2%, respectively), TIPS and Treasuries have a relatively high correlation of 45%, and TIPS are poor at hedging inflation with

---

[11] See *Economist*, "The IMF and Argentina: Motion of Censure," Feb. 9, 2013.

Table 11.4

TIPS and Treasury Returns Mar 1997 to Dec 2011						
	TIPS	*Tsys*	*Tsys-TIPS*	*Monthly Inflation*	*TIPS-Infl*	*Tsys-Infl*
Mean	7.02	6.24	−0.78	2.35	4.67	3.89
Stdev	5.89	4.70	4.65	1.33	5.90	5.16
Mean/Stdev	1.19	1.33	−0.17			
Correlations with						
Tsys	64%					
Inflation	10%	−22%	−35%			

TIPS and Treasury Returns Jul 2007 to Dec 2011						
	TIPS	*Tsys*	*Tsys–TIPS*	*Monthly Inflation*	*TIPS–Infl*	*Tsys–Infl*
Mean	8.44	7.25	−1.65	1.79	6.65	5.46
Stdev	7.71	5.17	7.10	1.71	7.63	6.02
Mean/Stdev	1.09	1.40	−0.23			
Correlations with						
Tsys	45%					
Inflation	16%	−37%	−44%			

a correlation between TIPS and inflation of only 16%. To understand why TIPS covary so little with inflation even though they are indexed to inflation, let us examine the different factors driving real bond returns.

4.3. REAL YIELDS

Real yields are surprisingly volatile. I say "surprisingly" because before real bonds were issued, many economists believed that real yields set in traded markets would be like the real interest rates theories in textbooks at that time. In simple economic models, real rates should reflect demographic trends, the growth of economic output, savers' time preferences and attitudes toward risk, and the opportunity costs of firms investing in real production.[12] All of these change

---

[12] Ramsey (1928) was the first to characterize the real rate as a function of consumers' preferences and output growth. Another early contribution was Fisher (1930), who derived that the real interest rate should reflect the marginal benefits of real firm investments.

smoothly, if at all, over time. Thus, before linkers were issued, many economists believed linkers would be the most boring of markets! The father of modern empirical asset pricing, Eugene Fama, argued in 1975 that the real rate was constant. He wrote the paper at a time when linkers were not available. Now that we have linkers, he was obviously wrong; Table 11.4 shows that real rates are volatile, and in fact approximately as volatile as nominal rates.

In Panel A of Figure 11.5, I plot real yields of five- and ten-year TIPS from the St. Louis Federal Reserve Bank from January 2003 to December 2011. On average, the real term structure is slightly upward sloping, but the real term spread between ten- and five-year maturities TIPS was approximately zero from 2006 to 2008 and was negative in 2008. The figure shows that real rates move around quite a bit: the five-year real rate moved from close to zero at the beginning of 2008 to over 4% that same year during some of the worst months of the financial crisis.

Panels B to D of Figure 11.5 graph the nominal Treasury yield and the TIPS yield for the five-, ten-, and twenty-year maturities, respectively. TIPS yields soared during the financial crisis as Treasury yields fell at the end of 2008. At this time there was a flight to quality as many investors flocked to safe Treasuries and sold other risky assets, including TIPS. Since both TIPS and Treasuries are backed by the full faith and credit of the U.S. government, both have the same near-zero default risk. Why would TIPS have sold off? Treasuries are the traditional tried-and-true, and Treasuries have roles in many places where TIPS do not (or where TIPS are rarely used) such as for collateral, meeting margin calls and, most of all, guaranteeing good liquidity. I discuss liquidity risk as a factor in TIPS below.

Panels A and B of Figure 11.5 show that the five-year real rate was negative and around −1% at December 2011. The ten-year TIPS yield (Panel C) was slightly below zero at this time. A negative real rate may seem surprising. Why would anyone want to buy a security and see it lose value in real terms over time? It is not a surprise from an economic point of view, however. While the older generation of models, which predate modern linkers markets, had trouble explaining the volatile real rates we see in the real world (newer models generate volatile real rates as investors' assessments of risks change and firms' financing and production opportunities change), they did accommodate the possibility of negative real rates.

In production models, the real rate represents how much future output is worth today: a real rate of 2% means that one widget today is worth 1.02 widgets next year. Usually this is positive because consumers are willing to forego output today for greater output in the future. The economy expands, on average, and there are positive production opportunities. With negative real rates, consumers want to consume today because output in the future is expected to be lower. Thus negative real rates can reflect shrinking future output opportunities—and a negative real rate is the ultimate bearish signal. This is the *production* interpretation of the real rate.

Panel A

TIPS Yields

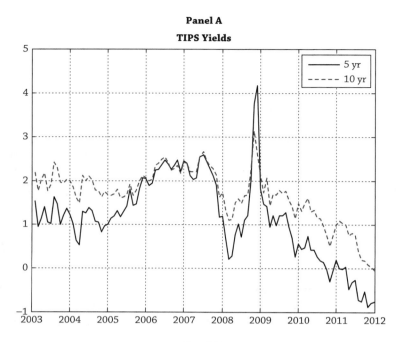

Panel B

5-Yr Yields

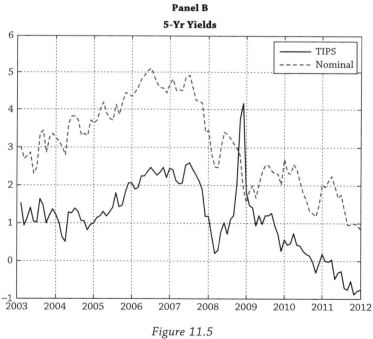

Figure 11.5

Panel C

10-Yr Yields

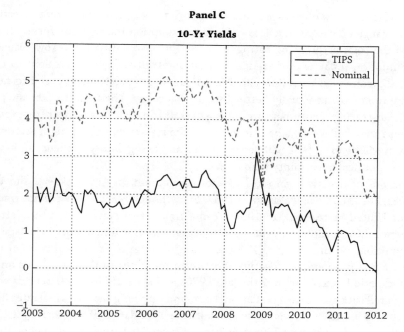

Panel D

20-Yr Yields

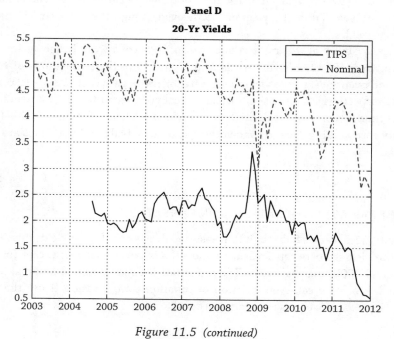

Figure 11.5 (continued)

A related *consumption* explanation is that the real rate is a price that investors use to gauge how expensive it is to shift consumption today to the future. It reflects the cost of foregoing eating today and instead eating tomorrow. Usually, consumption today is preferred, so eating one fruit today is equivalent to eating 1.02 fruits next year. But with a negative real rate, consumers prefer to save: eating tomorrow is actually better than eating today. This reflects extreme *precautionary saving*. Consumers are willing to shift consumption to later from today because they believe very bad times are a-coming—taxes will be high, economic growth will be low, there will be even more undue regulatory burdens, and even greater political uncertainty than today.

Periods of negative real rates are not uncommon. In Ang, Bekaert, and Wei (2008), I estimate real yields since 1952. Even though real yields were not traded in the United States prior to 1997, I can estimate real rates using a term structure model (see chapter 9), which ties together inflation and nominal yields, with assumptions on time-varying risk premiums, to infer the term structure of real rates. I find pronounced negative short-term real rates in the late 1950s and a second period extending over the late 1970s and early 1980s. Both periods were associated with accelerating inflation. I also find very long-maturity real rates have not turned negative. This is consistent with the TIPS data in the more recent sample where the twenty-year TIPS yield has not turned negative: on December 2011, the twenty-year TIP had a yield of 0.53% even though the five-year TIP had a negative yield.

The variability of real rates is one reason TIPS are a weak hedge against inflation. Over the sample for the data in Figure 11.5, the correlations of five-, ten-, and twenty-year TIPS yields with inflation are negative, at −23%, −12%, and −13%, respectively. As inflation increases, real yields tend to fall: unfortunately at the time investors most desire high real yields—when inflation is high—they are not forthcoming. Due to time-varying real rates, real bond portfolios are not so real.

4.4. BREAK-EVEN INFLATION COMPENSATION

In Figure 11.5, Panels B through D, Treasuries always have higher yields than TIPS and the distance between Treasuries and TIPS is fairly constant, except for the 2008 and 2009 financial crisis. The difference between nominal and real bond yields is labeled break-even inflation or inflation compensation (I use the two terms interchangeably, as the literature does):

$$\text{Nominal yield} = \text{Real yield} + \text{Break-Even Inflation}$$
$$\text{or Nominal yield} = \text{Real yield} + \text{Inflation Compensation}$$

$$(11.1)$$

Break-even inflation in Panels B to D of Figure 11.5 is represented by the distance between the TIPS yield (sold line) and the Treasury yield (dashed line). Taking out the financial crisis in 2008 and 2009, break-even inflation is fairly stable. For example, for the ten-year maturity TIPS and Treasury bonds in Panel C, break-even inflation was 2.44% from July 2004 to December 2007, and from January 2010 to December 2012, it was 1.79%. For the twenty-year maturity bonds in Panel D, the corresponding numbers for the two periods are 2.66% and 2.35%.

TIPS yields are set by the market relative to Treasuries yields, for reasons that are not entirely clear, such that break-even inflation is fairly stable. During and after the financial crisis, the nominal yield on long-term bonds was pushed down partly by quantitative easing and other nonconventional monetary policies (see chapter 9) and partly as a flight-to-quality response by investors seeking the safety of Treasuries versus risky European and other sovereign debt. Except for the 2008 to 2009 period, the market prices TIPS yields at an approximately constant discount to Treasuries. Since Treasury yields are very low, this leads to negative real yields.

Break-even inflation, or inflation compensation, can be decomposed into two terms:

$$\text{Break-Even Inflation} = \text{Expected Inflation} + \text{Risk Premium}. \qquad (11.2)$$

If the risk premium is constant, then break-even inflation moves one-for-one with expected inflation. But since risk premiums vary over time, break-even inflation cannot be used directly as a measure of future expected inflation. When the variation in the inflation risk premium is small, changes in TIPS yields relative to the benchmark Treasury curves are statements of the market's expectations about future inflation.[13] Inflation risk premiums, however, change. Ang, Bekaert, and Wei (2008) show they were especially large during the Great Inflation of the 1960s and 1970s, during the late 1980s when the economy was booming, and during the mid-1990s (see also chapter 9 on fixed income).

Using the decomposition of break-even inflation in equation (11.2), we can interpret the negative break-even inflation rates during the financial crisis as the market pricing in negative future inflation, or negative risk premiums, or both. Can we say which it is?

Inflation surveys turn out to be one of the best methods of forecasting inflation and beat many economic and term structure models, as Ang, Bekaert, and Wei (2007) show. Inflation expectations have been fairly stable for the sample considered in Figure 11.5, except in the financial crisis. At December 2008, the median

[13] Fleckenstein, Longstaff, and Lustig (2010) argue that TIPS and Treasuries are mispriced relative to each other with TIPS being cheap and Treasuries being expensive. They claim this is the "largest arbitrage ever documented in the financial economics literature."

forecast from the Survey of Professional Forecasters predicted current CPI head-line inflation during that quarter to be −2.6%, coming back to 2.0% during 2009. Thus the negative break-even inflation rates over 2008 and 2009 were consistent with market participants forecasting dire, Japan-like deflation scenarios during that time. At the same time, the flight to safety in Treasuries, which forced up Treasury prices and drove down Treasury yields, was consistent with Treasuries having a negative risk premium. Investors so desperately wanted Treasuries that they were willing, on a risk-adjusted basis, to pay to hold them (there was a negative risk premium) rather than demanding to be paid to hold them (the nor-mal positive risk premium). So both the deflation scenario and the negative risk premiums were important.

4.5. ILLIQUIDITY

An important factor in TIPS markets is illiquidity risk. The TIPS market was illiq-uid during the first few years after TIPS were introduced, up to around the early mid-2000s, and is still much less liquid than Treasuries.[14] Since many of the in-vestors preferring TIPS are pension funds and retail investors, Sack and Elasser (2004) predict the TIPS market will remain more illiquid than the Treasuries market, where there is a larger concentration of active fund managers.

Researchers estimate the TIPS illiquidity risk premium was around 1.0% for the five-year TIPS and between 0.5% and 1.0% for ten-year TIPS up until around 2003 and 2004. In 2004, illiquidity risk premiums fell substantially to well below 0.5% for both the five- and ten-year TIPS. They dramatically spiked to above 2.5% during the financial crisis, and after 2009 have gone back to below 0.5%.

The illiquidity risk premium makes TIPS yields higher than what they would be if they had the same liquidity as Treasuries. That is, liquidity-adjusted real yields would be *lower*, and thus even more negative at December 2011, than what we ob-serve in TIPS markets. Liquidity-adjusted inflation compensations would be also *higher* than the raw inflation compensations. Thus if negative real rates reflect in-vestors' expectations of very bad times in the future, the bad times are predicted to be even worse after adjusting for liquidity risk.

4.6. TIPS AND TAXES

Interest payments on TIPS, like the interest paid on conventional Treasury bonds, are subject to Federal income tax. Any inflation-adjusting increases in the princi-pal of TIPS are also taxable. The tax code does not differentiate between real and nominal income—it is just income—so the investor's after-tax yield is exposed to inflation risk. During periods of high inflation, the tax levied on the increased

[14] See D'Amico, Kim, and Wei (2009), Gürkaynak, Sack, and Wright (2010), and Pflueger and Viceira (2011).

inflation-adjusted principal constitutes a loss of purchasing power; investors lose out on an after-tax basis when inflation is high. But during periods of deflation, the TIPS principal shrinks (at least until it reaches par value). This deflation adjustment is tax-deductible and is an offset to the TIPS interest income. Thus there is an after-tax benefit of deflation but an after-tax inflation penalty. Inflationary periods are much more common than deflationary ones, so the net tax effect, on average, is negative.

Because of this, TIPS are best held in tax-deferred accounts. (Taxes are discussed in chapter 12.) The retail version of TIPS is the I Savings Bond (I-Bond, for short). I-Bonds are real zero-coupon bonds. The interest and principal adjustments are paid at maturity or upon redemption by the investor. While interest on I-Bonds is subject to federal income tax, that tax is paid only at redemption.[15] The interest paid is added back to the bond value, so there is a benefit from tax-deferred growth. The indexed principal is not taxed. Accordingly, individual investors should hold I-Bonds—rather than TIPS—in after-tax accounts. Individuals, however, can purchase only $10,000 of I-Bonds per year. I-Bonds also are not tradeable in secondary markets—if you want to cash out, you must redeem them.

4.7. SUMMARY

1. The TIPS asset class is a poor inflation hedge.

    The correlation of TIPS returns with inflation is close to zero. One reason "real" bonds are not so real is that real yields are volatile. The result is that TIPS are poorly correlated with inflation. While a single TIPS can be an inflation hedge, an investment strategy based on a rebalanced portfolio of TIPS is not.
2. Real yields can be negative for extended periods of time.

    Negative real yields mean a loss of purchasing power. You need to put aside a larger sum of money today than the cash flows you need to meet in the future.
3. An individual's portfolio for retirement should not hold only TIPS.

    The exception is when the individual knows her future cash flow needs exactly and can immunize them immediately. Otherwise, the need to save over time opens up the investor to time-varying real rates, and then TIPS have little ability to hedge inflation risk. Even when you know your future cash flows exactly, you bear basis risk if your price basket of goods and services is not the CPI basket.
4. Liquidity is an important factor in TIPS markets.

---

[15] If you use I-Bonds to pay for education expenses and you meet certain income limits and other restrictions, you will not pay any tax.

During bad times, you will have much less liquidity than traditional Treasury securities. Liquidity-adjusted real rates are lower than observed real rates.
5. Hold TIPS in tax-deferred accounts.

If you want to hold linkers in an after-tax account as an individual, buy I-Bonds.

5. Commodities

Commodities are touted as natural hedges for inflation risk, especially because commodity prices enter many inflation indices.[16] Commodity prices affect many items in the CPI basket. For example, oil prices directly affect gasoline, which has its own category in the CPI basket. Agricultural commodities, including wheat and corn, enter the price of food, which is another category in the CPI basket.

Commodities have become quite popular among institutional investors since the mid-2000s. Many institutions were attracted to them by the research of Erb and Harvey (2006) and Gorton and Rouwenhorst (2006), who showed that commodities had attractive returns and low correlations to stocks, bonds, and other traditional asset classes. These authors noted the good inflation-hedging ability of commodities.[17] Yet, as we'll see, only certain commodities—those linked with energy—have positive correlations with inflation, and those correlations are far from perfect.

5.1. COMMODITY FUTURES

Despite the popular belief that commodities are good for hedging inflation, the baseline case in economics is that in perfect markets with no extraction costs, prices of exhaustible commodities like gold and oil should have no correlation with inflation.[18] Actual prices of exhaustible commodities should follow random walks, and forward prices should rise at the risk-free rate. The intuition is that in this perfect world, producers can costlessly adjust their production to shocks and all demand shocks—whether permanent or transitory—have permanent effects on the remaining supply of these commodities. For nonexhaustible commodities, new supplies are always being created, so the normal demand and supply mechanisms, which may not involve the general price level, are at play. There is no underlying economic foundation that says commodities must be (automatically)

---

[16] See Bodie (1983) and many others.

[17] The Commodity Futures Modernization Act of 2000 also made it easier for institutional investors to take commodity positions.

[18] Hotelling (1931) was the first to show this. Weinstein and Zeckhauser (1975) and Pindyck (1980) show this under uncertainty.

linked with inflation. Perhaps it is no surprise, then, that most commodities turn out not to have any relationship with inflation.

In the real world, of course, gold and oil prices do not follow random walks. The perfect-world case is still useful because it allows us to see the effect of production frictions and how the behavior of investors and producers causes commodity prices to change in a predictable fashion. Today's economic models show that commodity prices reflect production costs. These vary over time, and, once you start production, you can't get your money back (they are *irreversible investments*), which impart an option value to delay production in the presence of uncertainty. Commodity prices also are driven by supply shocks to current and future substitutes, technological change—for example, a clean energy breakthrough that makes oil obsolete—and time-varying storage costs.[19] Some papers emphasize the role of speculators and other types of investors.[20] Speculators, for example, can cause commodity prices to temporarily swing away from fundamentals. Many of these factors do not have a direct bearing on inflation.

That many factors influence commodity prices means plenty of scope for active management in commodity investments. Commodity markets exhibit the same value and momentum effects, and other cross-sectional predictability phenomena, as equities and bonds.[21] Commodity Trading Advisors (CTAs), in fact, are often a byword for momentum-style trading. These value and momentum effects are manifestations of standard investment factors (see Chapter 7). In addition, commodity prices respond to hedging pressure, relative scarcity, and demand and supply imbalances, as predicted by economic models.[22] Open interest and other asset prices, including exchange rates, also forecast commodity prices.[23]

5.2. COMMODITY FACTORS

Commodities are usually not held physically by financial investors because of storage costs. Instead, investors gain commodity exposure through futures markets. An exception is the small group of investors who directly hold precious metals, but even in this case most investors seeking precious metal exposure (directly or indirectly through intermediated funds) invest through futures. Even for producers, the storage costs of some commodities, like electricity, are close to infinity.

Table 11.6 lists the performance of various commodity futures investments from the Goldman Sachs Commodity Index (GSCI) along with their correlations

[19] Carlson, Khokher, and Titman (2007) show that these effects give rise to stochastic volatility and determine the shape of the forward curves.

[20] Keynes (1923) and Hicks (1939) developed the first model of this type. Another seminal paper is Deaton and Laroque (1992).

[21] See Asness, Moskowitz, and Pedersen (2013).

[22] An important paper in this literature is Bessembinder (1992). Relative scarcity or demand in one commodity also spills over into other commodities, as Casassus, Liu, and Tang (2013) show.

[23] See Chen, Rogoff and Rossi (2010) and Hong and Yogo (2012).

Table 11.6

	GSCI	Precious Metals	Gold	Crude	Energy	Light Energy	Non-Energy	Agriculture	Inflation
					GSCI Commodity Indices 1986:01–2011:12				
Mean	8.92	7.77	7.25	9.53	12.65	6.68	5.41	2.37	2.80
Stdev	20.71	15.99	15.39	32.95	32.90	14.30	12.55	18.35	1.12
Sharpe [raw]	0.43	0.49	0.47	0.29	0.38	0.47	0.43	0.13	
Correlations									
with Inflation	29%	2%	1%	23%	26%	25%	8%	–4%	
with Ind Prod	11%	–7%	–9%	3%	9%	12%	9%	9%	
with Bonds	–9%	0%	4%	–13%	–10%	–9%	–5%	1%	
with Stocks	14%	–3%	–10%	4%	7%	24%	30%	20%	
with VIX	–18%	–4%	–1%	–11%	–13%	–23%	–21%	–12%	

to stocks, bonds, and various macro factors. The overall GSCI is a weighted combination of various commodities. With an approximate exposure of 80% to various types of oil and gas, this index heavily weights energy.

From January 1986 to December 2011, the GSCI has returned 8.9% with a standard deviation of 20.7%. The raw Sharpe ratio, without subtracting a risk-free rate, is 8.9%/20.7% = 0.43. For comparison, the raw Sharpe ratios on stocks and bonds were 0.66 and 0.94, respectively, during this period. The low correlations of commodity future returns with stocks and bonds (at 14% and −9%, respectively) make commodities compelling investments. There is tremendous diversification potential in adding commodities to traditional stock and bond portfolios (see chapter 3).

Commodities offer some inflation protection, but they certainly are not a perfect hedge. The overall GSCI correlation with inflation is 29%. This reflects the relatively good inflation-hedging performance of energy futures. The correlations of crude oil and energy overall (which lumps crude oil, Brent crude oil, unleaded gas, heating oil, gas oil, and natural gas together) with inflation are 23% and 26%, respectively. Nonenergy futures are poor inflation hedgers. Agriculture, for example, has only a −4% correlation with inflation. Precious metals, which include gold, and gold on its own have low correlations of only 2% and 1%, respectively, with inflation.

Table 11.6 also lists correlations of commodities with industrial production growth (measured year on year) and the VIX volatility index. Commodity returns, especially energy and agriculture, are higher when economic growth is high. The correlations with economic growth are around 10% and so are lower than the correlations with inflation. It is notable that precious metals have slight negative correlations with growth—indicating that precious metals have some value as insurance when the economy performs poorly, but the correlations are below 10% in absolute value. Volatility is also a factor: the correlation of GSCI with VIX is −18%, which comes through energy and agricultural commodities performing poorly when volatility is high. Precious metals, in contrast, have almost no correlation with inflation.

In summary, only energy commodities have hedged inflation and even then the correlations are far from one. Energy and agricultural futures tend to perform badly when growth is low and volatility is high. Precious metals, in contrast, move fairly independently of macro factors.

5.3. SPOT, CASH, AND ROLL RETURNS

Commodity futures returns have three parts and all of them are important:

1. *Spot* return

    This is the return earned by changing physical commodity prices in spot markets.

2. *Cash* or *collateral* return

    The cash return is the interest earned on the collateral (or the margin) investors are required to post to trade futures contracts.

3. *Roll* return

    Investors desiring constant exposures to commodities must roll over their exposures to new futures contracts as the old ones expire. As they sell futures contracts that are about to expire and buy new ones, they incur capital gains or losses.

Table 11.7 breaks the average total returns of the GSCI into spot, cash, and roll return components. Figure 11.8 plots the rolling two-year average of these return components over time. From January 1970 to December 2011, the average 11.3% GSCI total return included a spot return of 6.4%, a cash return of 5.6% and a –0.7% roll return. During the 1980s, however, the spot return was negative, at –0.4%, but overall commodity futures returns were still positive because the losses in commodity spot markets were offset by high interest earnings on collateral, with a cash return of 9.1%, and a positive roll return of 2.4%. In the 2000s, the roll return was –7.5%, but spot commodity markets did well, at 13%, so the total GSCI return was positive.

Figure 11.8 shows that the variation in the spot return is much larger than the variation in the roll and cash returns. We can decompose the variation of total GSCI returns into:

$$\text{var(total return)} = \text{var(spot)} + \text{var(cash)} + \text{var(roll)}$$

100%   100.0%   0.2%   6.0%

$$+ \ 2\text{cov(spot, roll)} + 2\text{cov(spot, cash)} + 2\text{cov(roll, cash)}$$

       2 × –3.4%   2 × 0.2%   2 × 0.1%

                                                   (11.3)

Table 11.7

	Average Returns of GSCI Commodities Index			
	Spot	*Cash*	*Roll*	*Total*
1970s	11.1%	6.6%	4.0%	21.6%
1980s	–0.4%	9.1%	2.4%	11.1%
1990s	0.8%	5.0%	–0.5%	5.3%
2000–2011	13.0%	2.3%	–7.5%	7.8%
1970–2011	6.4%	5.6%	–0.7%	11.3%

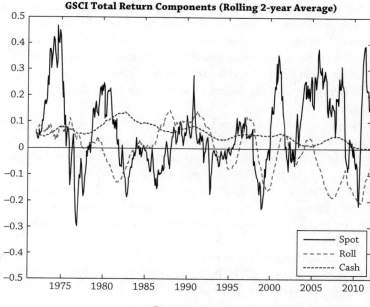

Figure 11.8

The cash and the roll components play important roles in the overall return of commodities, but the variance in the commodity future return is almost entirely due to movements in underlying spot markets. Thus all the risk is coming from spot markets. But to understand the expected returns, you need to understand all the factor drivers of all three spot, cash, and roll components.

Spot commodity markets are affected by production factors and investor behavior discussed in Section 5.1.

Interest rate factors determine the cash return (see chapter 9). Because you do not earn negative interest rates on collateral (at least not yet), the cash return is always positive.

The roll return depends on the slope of the futures curve. When the futures curve is upward sloping, called *contango*, there is a negative roll return.[24] When markets are in contango, an investor must replace the currently expiring futures contract with the next-maturity contract that is more expensive. This involves selling low and buying high, and so the roll loses money. A downward-sloping futures curve is called *backwardation*. When markets are *backwardated*, the investor sells the expiring futures at a high price and is able to buy the next-maturity contract at a low price. Selling high and buying low in backwardated futures markets makes money. But not always, because commodity markets can quickly change between backwardation and contango.

---

[24] See Mouakhar and Roberge (2010) for optimized roll strategies.

Whether the futures market is in contango or backwardated depends, among other things, on the usual elements of supply and demand plus the cost of storage, inventory imbalances, and *convenience yield*. The latter refers to the reward producers receive for storing a commodity, which investors do not receive: being able to keep production on schedule, the ability to profit from increasing production at short notice, and the ability to profit from temporary shortages in the commodity.

Returns on commodities depend crucially on the behavior of long-dated futures, so commodity investors need to keep an eye on the shape of the futures curve. In Table 11.7, the negative roll return in the 2000s was due to highly backwardated oil markets in 2008. The movement of the oil futures from contango in 2007 to backwardated in 2008, causing negative roll returns, was a double whammy for many investors who were already hurt by falling oil prices (negative spot returns) during that period. Most other commodity markets at that time were in contango.

Investors expecting positive commodity returns when commodity prices are increasing in spot markets will be in for a nasty surprise when their investments in futures turn out to be quite different from the spot returns. The United States Oil Fund is one of the largest exchange-traded funds (ETFs) with approximately $1.3 billion net assets as of July 2012 (see chapter 16 for details on 40-Act funds) and is designed to track the price of oil.

The USO doesn't hold physical oil: it holds oil futures and is forced to roll every thirty days. Figure 11.9 plots the one-year moving average of USO returns versus crude oil spot returns from April 2007 to December 2012. There are pronounced discrepancies between the crude oil spot return and the USO return; on

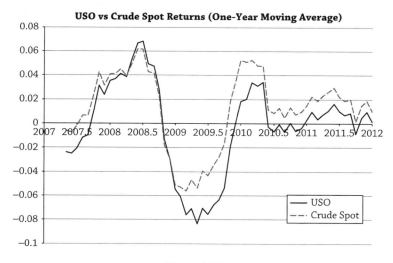

Figure 11.9

average, the USO return is 1.4% lower. This is due to the roll, as the cash return during this span was close to zero. The shape of the futures curve—contango or backwardation—determines the sign of the roll return. In addition, large investors forced to roll on pre-determined schedules have to pay large transactions costs. Bessembinder et al. (2012) estimate that ETFs pay about 30 basis points on average per roll, or approximately 4.4% per year in oil futures markets. ETFs need liquidity for the roll, and this is the premium they must pay for it in the futures markets.

5.4. GOLD

Gold is not a good inflation hedge. A case can be made for gold in an investor's diversified portfolio, but it cannot be made on the basis that gold is a real asset.

There are two popular misconceptions about gold: first, that gold is an inflation hedge in terms of how gold moves with inflation (the correlation of gold with inflation); and second, that the long-run performance of gold handily beats inflation (the return of gold, on average, is greater than inflation). Let's examine both. Using data from Global Financial Data, I plot the real price appreciation of gold in Panel A of Figure 11.10 from September 1875 to December 2011. The real price appreciation is defined to be the price of gold divided by CPI. I normalize the index to be 1.0 at the beginning of the sample. The correlation of annual returns of gold and inflation is 23% in Figure 11.10. To repeat: gold is far from a perfect inflation hedge.

If the long-run returns of gold were exactly the same as inflation, then the graph of gold's average real return over time should be exactly a horizontal line. From 1875 to the early 1930s, the price of gold declined in real terms. In 1933 real gold prices suddenly jumped upward when President Franklin Roosevelt signed Executive Order 6102 forbidding the private holdings of gold—one of many attempts to stabilize the financial system during the Great Depression. In 1934 the United States defaulted. The 1934 Gold Reserve Act changed the value of a U.S. dollar from $20.67 per troy ounce to $35. This was an economic default but not legal default. Reinhart and Rogoff (2008) label it an explicit default: the United States reduced the value of its debt payments relative to an external measure of value (at that time, all major currencies were backed by gold).

Real gold prices started rising dramatically in the early 1970s, when the Bretton Woods system of fixed exchange rates broke down. In 1979 and 1980, the real price of gold skyrocketed from below 0.5 to above 3.0 as Fed Chairman Volcker jacked up interest rates to end the Great Inflation. Once inflation stabilized, gold lost much of its value in real terms. Since 2000, however, real gold prices have relentlessly marched upward. At the end of the sample at December 2011, the real price was above 2.0.

The time variation in real gold prices in Panel A of Figure 11.10 unequivocally rejects the hypothesis that gold returns are driven only by inflation. Gold has not

Panel A

Panel B

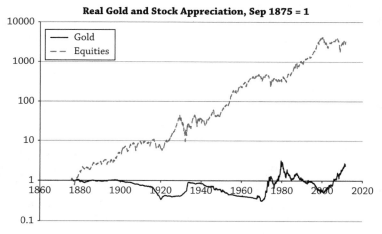

Figure 11.10

been an inflation hedge over the past 130 years. Erb and Harvey (2013), however, document that over the extremely long run, gold may have a higher return than the inflation rate (the mean effect), even though gold does not correlate highly with inflation (the inflation hedging ability). Erb and Harvey compare the pay of a U.S. Army private today with that of a legionary during the reign of Augustus (27 BC to 14 AD), the first emperor of the Roman Empire. Erb and Harvey find the pay of U.S. army privates and Roman legionnaires very similar when stated in ounces of gold. They also find the pay of a U.S. army captain approximately the same as that of a Roman centurion, when expressed in gold. So, over centuries, gold tracks inflation, at least in preserving the long-run level of military pay. If only we could live so long.

Sadly, these extremely long horizons are not relevant for most investors. Only a few institutions—the Catholic Church, the Padmanabhaswamy Temple in Kerala, India (founded in the sixteenth century and possessor of $22 billion in gold),[25] and certain universities such as the University of Bologna (the world's first, founded in the eleventh century)—have survived for many centuries. But having survived for centuries does not mean these institutions' planning horizons are centuries-long. The long-term investors of today—pension funds, endowments, family offices, sovereign wealth funds—do not plan 1,000 years ahead.[26]

Gold may serve valid roles in an investor's portfolio, but being an inflation hedge is not one of them (at least for horizons less than a century). So why invest in gold?

Gold is often regarded as a safe haven, and Erb and Harvey (2012) show that gold can serve as catastrophe insurance. Tiny increases in the likelihood of disaster raise the gold price substantially. Thus gold could serve as a hedge for disaster risk—which is also one of the main explanations for the high equity-risk premium (see chapter 8).

Ray Dalio, a superstar hedge fund manager who popularized risk parity (which is a special case of mean-variance investing; see chapter 3), makes an argument that gold "is a very under-owned asset" and that if many investors move to increase their holdings of gold to the level reflective of gold's market capitalization in a world wealth portfolio, the gold price should increase.[27] At first glance, this is a silly argument. All the gold in the world—whether in the ground, stored in a vault, or even resting in a shipwreck on the seabed—is already owned by someone. Dalio's argument can work only if there are market participants who buy to increase their holdings of gold to market capitalization weights and are completely insensitive to the price they pay. That is, some investors must have *perfectly inelastic* demand curves. There may be some institutions like this—some central banks, the growing rich and middle-class populations in emerging markets, and perhaps some pension funds that (mistakenly) believe gold is an inflation hedge. Erb and Harvey (2012) estimate that the market weight of gold as a fraction of total wealth ranges between 2% and 10%, depending on whether you count only the gold held by investors or the entire gold supply, which includes gold yet to be mined and gold held by central banks.

When I look at Panel A of Figure 11.10, I am struck by the very long-term mean reversion exhibited by the real price of gold. The correlation of twenty-year real

[25] Jake Halpern, "The Secret of the Temple," *New Yorker*, April 30, 2012.

[26] Perhaps Norway is an exception. The Norwegian sovereign wealth fund pays out approximately 4% of the fund to the Norwegian government each year (the Handlingsregel). The Norwegian government fully funded the construction and is meeting a large part of the operational costs, of the Svalbard Global Seed Vault, which seeks to preserve seeds of plants around the world in a remote, secure underground cavern near the North Pole. It is insurance for the world in case of a global catastrophe.

[27] Ward, S., "Observing a Bipolar World," *Barron's*, March 12, 2011.

returns of gold with lagged twenty-year real returns of gold is –63%—a stagger-ing number in absolute value terms. When the real price of gold has been high, the subsequent long-term performance of gold has been low. This should be a warning to all asset owners adding to their gold holdings now. The classic error of an in-vestor chasing returns is to invest after past returns have been high, while current prices are high. Subsequent returns often end up disappointingly low.

I close with a look at the real performance of gold relative to equities in Panel B of Figure 11.10. The line for gold is exactly the same as in Panel A, except the scale on the y-axis has been drawn to be logarithmic. Panel B overlays the real price of equities also starting at 1.0 at September 1875. The equity market simply clobbers gold in real terms.

6. Real Estate

Real estate is all about space. To be more specific, real estate investing is about creating and maintaining structures to remove physical space between people and institutions. There are two core models in urban economics that articulate the fundamental sources of demand and supply for real estate. Central to both is the concept of *spatial equilibrium*, which states that people and firms invest in real estate in such a way that they are indifferent about where they locate.[28] Agents' utility and, ultimately, real estate values, are affected by the amenities provided by real estate—which include proximity to customers and suppliers, human cap-ital spillovers, and the innate advantages of geography, including gorgeous views and nice weather. Real estate values are also affected by workers' income, housing costs, and transportation costs.

The Alonso (1964), Mills (1967), and Muth (1969) model explains real estate prices *within* a given city in terms of distance to centers of production: as transpor-tation costs increase, real estate prices fall. The second workhorse model, Rosen (1979) and Roback (1982), explains how real estate prices differ *across* different cities and metropolitan areas because of different incomes, amenities, and produc-tivity levels. Higher land values are the price of entry to metropolitan areas with more productive firms or better amenities (which includes more cultural activities, less crime, better schools, and more comfortable weather).

The realtors' mantra of "location, location, location" gets it only half right. Location certainly is the primary driver in the Alonso-Mills-Muth model, but it matters because of transportation costs. The Rosen-Roback model emphasizes that it is not location per se but the interaction of location's advantages (enabling trade or production, for example) with the productive capabilities of firms and workers and other macro factors.

---

[28] See Glaeser (2008) for a summary.

Asset owners with real estate investments should start with urban economics as their foundation (no pun intended). Urban economics allows us to:

1. Understand macro factors

    Economic models are especially good at explaining how endogenous variables—which in this context are real estate prices, where people live, and how much housing they consume—are determined from exogenous variables, like geography, or slow-moving conditions like productivity levels. Economic models give insight into the fundamentals behind prices, including aggregate demand factors and supply restrictions. The emphasis on the macro drivers is especially important because real estate holdings are long-horizon investments, with a median holding period for individual institutional properties of over a decade.[29]

2. Place real estate in its context

    Real estate prices, like all prices, are determined in equilibrium. I live in New York City where real estate prices are high, average wages are high, and the cost of living is high. From the point of view of a worker, the high wage is good. From the point of view of an employer, the high wage is bad. Why don't firms shift away from New York and lower their wage bill? In equilibrium real estate prices can be high and wages can be high only if the city enables all workers and firms to be jointly more productive. What creates this productivity? What sustains it? What will cause the productivity to disappear? Real estate can only be understood as part of an economic whole.

3. Evaluate policy

    Government policy matters in equity and fixed income markets (see chapters 8 and 9, respectively), but in real estate, policy is crucial. The value of real estate cannot be divorced from the regulations governing its use. Economic models are especially good at measuring the effects of exogenous policy changes (through *comparative statics* exercises). An extremely important determinant of real estate prices is the supply of real estate. In the "superstar cities," which include San Francisco, Boston, and the like clustered on the coasts, the supply of new housing and office space is more tightly restricted by regulation.[30] This creates scarcity, which drives up prices. Atlanta, on the other hand, has few supply restrictions, and real estate prices are low compared to cities on the coasts. Government policy matters from city to city, but it is as important in determining real estate prices within cities. If policy regarding supply is changed, all else equal, economic models allow us to predict which areas benefit and which areas suffer and by how much.

---

[29] Fisher and Young (2000) report a median sale period of eleven years for the properties in the National Council of Real Estate Investment Fiduciaries (NCREIF) database.

[30] See Glaeser and Ward (2009). The "superstar cities" of Gyourko, Mayer, and Sinai (2012), alas, do not include New York because of the limited data availability of their sample, which starts in 1950.

6.1. DIRECT OR INDIRECT?

I concentrate my analysis on institutional direct real estate investment and indirect real estate investment through REITs. REITs are mutual fund-like vehicles allowing broad ownership of real estate assets. Many REITs are publicly traded. REITs have to satisfy many restrictions: most notably, they are required to distribute at least 90% of their taxable income each year to shareholders as dividends. REITs are one of the few ways retail investors can access commercial real estate markets and were created by Congress in 1960 through the Real Estate Investment Trust Act. Congress did not have the high-minded intention of allowing the masses access to the diversification benefits of commercial real estate; the REIT Act was originally a rider attached to An Act to Amend the Internal Revenue Code with Respect to the Excise Tax on Cigars and was passed after adept lobbying by the real estate industry so that developers could tap the equity market for additional funds.[31]

Since direct real estate and REITs both involve buildings and land that generate cash flows, one would think the returns of these two approaches would be highly correlated.[32] Surely direct and indirect physical holdings of real estate must be driven by common fundamentals in the long run. But they are not, and this is called the *REIT puzzle*.

Table 11.11 reports means, standard deviations, autocorrelations, and cross-correlations of direct and indirect real estate returns along with equity returns from the beginning of 1978 to the end of 2011 at the quarterly frequency. The direct property returns are from the National Council of Real Estate Investment

Table 11.11

	Mean	*Stdev*	*Autocorrelation*
NCREIF	0.0221	0.0225	0.7806
REIT	0.0347	0.0918	0.1070
S&P 500	0.0301	0.0823	0.0711

	Correlation Matrix		
	NCREIF	REIT	S&P 500
NCREIF	1.0000	0.1520	0.0900
REIT		1.0000	0.6265
S&P 500			1.0000

[31] See Brandon (1998) and Graff (2001).

[32] For a theoretical basis of this proposition, see Carlson, Titman, and Tiu (2010).

Fiduciaries (NCREIF), which collects property data from its members. NCREIF computes a value-weighted index based on appraisals on a quarterly basis. The indirect property returns are the FTSE NAREIT All Equity returns, also at the quarterly frequency. I compare these property returns with S&P 500 equity returns.

Table 11.11 shows that NCREIF returns are very smooth (the quarterly autocorrelation is 78% and volatility is just 2.2%) compared to REIT and equity returns, which have autocorrelations close to zero and volatilities around 8% to 9%. Notably, the correlation between REIT and equity returns is high, at 63%, while the correlation between NCREIF and REIT returns is low, at 15%. Thus REITs resemble equities more than they resemble direct real estate. Hartzell and Mengden, who were industry practitioners at Salomon Brothers, were the first to document this phenomenon in 1986, and they generated substantial discussion about the underlying nature of real estate returns. Was real estate indeed a separate asset class, or was it just a different version of equity (and debt)?

This debate continues in real estate economics today. My takeaways for asset owners from this long literature are:

Direct Real Estate Returns Are Not Returns

The NCREIF series (and the corresponding widely used Investment Property Databank series in Europe) have many data biases because the values are not based on market transactions. REIT returns, in contrast, are investable returns. There are two important and large biases:[33]

1. Smoothing bias

   Using appraisals (done at most once or twice a year) artificially induces smoothness,[34] which is why the autocorrelation of the NCREIF series is so much higher than REITs or equities in Table 11.11.
2. Selection bias

   The properties that you see sold are not representative of the entire stock. For example, perhaps only the best properties are sold because those are the ones a developer is sprucing up, while the foreclosed crummy ones are not being sold.[35]

---

[33] There are two minor biases in addition to these two main ones. The first is an index construction bias, which is that repeat-sales indexes, which are developed to deal with appraisal bias, are equal-weighted cross-sectional estimators. But returns of equal-weighted portfolios are arithmetic averages of cross-sectional individual asset returns. I warned you that this was technical! The second is that the time a property is on the market differs in "hot" versus "cold" real estate markets. A paper that deals with all four biases is Fisher et al. (2003).

[34] See Geltner (1991) and Ross and Zisler (1991).

[35] See Munneke and Slade (2000).

In addition, REITs are levered while NCREIF returns are reported on an unlevered basis. Researchers have developed many methods to move from appraisals to transaction-level (and repeat-sales) indices, to desmooth real estate returns, to take into account selection bias, and to remove other illiquidity biases. The effects of these biases are enormous. Lin and Vandell (2012), for example, report that for a one-year holding period, the variance of direct real estate returns should be three times higher than the raw variance reported in Table 11.11. Pagliari, Scherer, and Monopoli (2005) argue that there is no difference in direct and indirect real estate returns after adjusting for leverage and sector composition and also adjusting direct real estate returns for appraisal smoothing.

Smoothing and selection biases are shared by all illiquid assets—including private equity—and I discuss methods of dealing with them in chapter 13. I use NCREIF returns for now, but you've been warned: these are not actual returns.

In the Long Run, Direct and Indirect Real Estate Returns Move Together

Direct and indirect real estate returns are linked in the long run. Figure 11.12 graphs the correlation of long-horizon log NCREIF returns with long-horizon log REIT returns. At the one-quarter horizon, the correlation is around 0.22, which reflects the low correlation between NCREIF and REIT returns in Table 11.11. (Quarterly returns in Table 11.11 are arithmetic returns but I use log returns in Figure 11.12; see the appendix.) After twelve quarters, the correlation tapers to

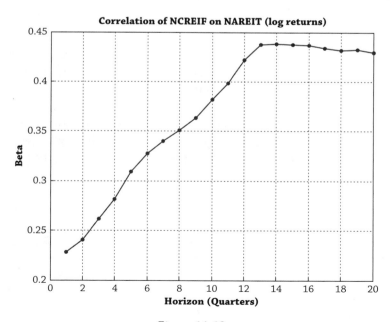

Figure 11.12

around 0.43. Thus there are some long-horizon common components in NCREIF and REIT returns. Econometric studies also document strong evidence that public real estate markets lead private real estate markets, which is to be expected since price discovery should happen in markets that are liquid.[36]

The astute reader will be wondering at this point, if direct and indirect real estate do move together in the long run, is real estate a separate asset class given that the correlation between REITs and equities is so high (63% in Table 11.11)? CPPIB, the manager of the CAN$162 billion Canada Pension Plan, does not consider real estate a separate asset class; CPPIB practices factor investing when it invests in real estate and thinks of real estate as comprising equity and debt characteristics.[37] In chapter 10, we also found that real estate did not seem to yield additional returns in excess of stocks, bonds, and REITs in factor benchmarks. But CPPIB is an exception: most investors regard real estate to be a separate asset class (or even factor). REITs cannot be the basis for this statement, given the high correlation of REIT returns with equities in Table 11.11. The statement is usually made using direct real estate returns—but as we know, direct real estate returns are not returns.[38] Although REIT and NCREIF returns do exhibit some commonality in the long run, the long-horizon correlations are far from one as Figure 11.12 shows. Thus:

Direct and Indirect Real Estate Are Different

Listed REITs seem to have one major advantage over direct real estate: they are liquid. But as of June 30, 2012, there were only 150 REITs traded on the New York Stock Exchange with a collective market capitalization of $545 billion. This is an average market capitalization of $3.6 billion for each REIT—smaller than many big real estate developments in the world's leading cities. The FTSE NAREIT All Equity REITs Index had a total market capitalization of $562 billion. In contrast, Florance et al. (2010) estimate that the (direct investment) commercial real estate market in the United States totaled over $9 trillion at the end of 2009, even though the market lost over $4 trillion from 2006 to 2010.

If REITs have such a big liquidity advantage, why is the amount of money invested through REITs well below one-tenth of the total commercial real estate market? Why aren't REITs more popular?

Structurally, REITs are different from direct real estate. Prior to the early 1990s, the REIT industry was very small because REITs were forced to retain external advisors to select and execute investment strategies. In 1986, REITs were allowed to select and manage their own assets and during the early 1990s many

[36] See Gyourko and Keim (1992), Barkham and Geltner (1995), and Oikarinen, Hoesli, and Serrano (2011).

[37] See the case "Factor Investing: The Reference Portfolio and Canada Pension Plan Investment Board," Columbia CaseWorks #120302. Assets under management as of March 31, 2012.

[38] See Mei and Lei (1994) and Ling and Naranjo (1997, 1999).

reorganized to bring these roles in-house.[39] The post-1990s is called the *new REIT era* for this reason.

Even today, however, the legal structure of REITs makes them different from direct real estate investment. Graff (2001) persuasively argues that there are still large agency costs associated with REITs imposed by their legal requirements.[40] (See Part III of this book for agency problems in delegated asset management.) The 75% income test (relaxed somewhat in 1986) requiring that proportion of REIT income to be derived from real estate investments gives REIT managers greater incentives to commit capital to overpriced acquisitions than managers of private real estate partnerships. In addition, REIT managers collect a perpetuity in the form of management fees, while closed-end funds are usually scheduled to liquidate after a prespecified term and open-ended funds are supposed to liquidate after requests from investors. The 5–50 test to preserve the exemption of REITs from double taxation where each group of five or few investors cannot own more than 50% of the voting stock means that REITs cannot be taken over to remove poorly performing incumbent management. That REITs have higher average returns than NCREIF returns in Table 11.11 is consistent with the notion that REITs are riskier than direct real estate, and their higher returns compensate for the extra risk.

The legal structure of REITs can also lead to differences with direct real estate even when there are no agency considerations. The requirement that REITs pay out 90% of their income each year means REIT managers gravitate to properties already generating quality cash flows rather than investing in developments that require cash today to create cash flows in the future. On the other hand, there has been tremendous innovation in REITs recently with an abundance of issues in many new sectors, like health care, data centers, and storage. NCREIF is traditionally wedded to the "core" sectors of apartment, retail, office, and industrial partly because these new sectors are small—the markets for self-storage centers and server farms are tiny compared to the office market.

Overall, however, I believe these agency and legal differences are secondary. There are more similarities, especially over the long run, between REITs and direct real estate. This is as expected from economic theory, where underlying both are buildings and land, and this is borne out in empirical tests. The large divergences in short-run returns between direct real estate and REITs are mostly due to direct real estate returns not being returns.

6.2. REAL ESTATE AND INFLATION

The literature is sharply divided on whether real estate is a good hedge for inflation. Fama and Schwert (1977) were the first to state that real estate was a perfect

---

[39] See Decker (1998) and Ambrose and Linneman (2001).
[40] See also Sagalyn (1996) who documents agency problems in REITs.

hedge for both expected and unexpected inflation. Fama and Schwert, however, used the housing component in the CPI, as they lacked direct real estate return data. For direct real estate, the results seem to be inconclusive. On the one hand, Goetzmann and Valaitis (2006) argue that direct real estate is a good inflation hedge. On the other hand, Huang and Hudson-Wilson (2007) find "that the conventional wisdom that real estate, as an asset class, is an effective inflation hedge is overly generous." It is clear from the literature that REITs do not hedge inflation in the short run.[41] Gyourko and Linneman (1998), for example, note that REITs are perverse inflation hedges.

I believe real estate offers some inflation protection but is far from an effective inflation hedge. That is, real estate is only partially real.

In Figure 11.13, I plot correlations of direct and indirect real estate returns with inflation over various horizons. I also overlay correlations of equity returns with inflation for comparison. We saw in chapter 8 that equity was a poor inflation hedge. Panel A plots classical (Pearson) correlations. REIT return correlations with inflation are slightly higher than equity correlations, but only just, and these increase from just above 0.1 at the one-quarter horizon to around 0.4 at the five-year horizon. NCREIF correlations are around 0.4 at the one-quarter horizon and decrease slightly to 0.3 at the five-year horizon. NCREIF returns, as I emphasized before, should not be trusted at short horizons due to illiquidity biases. It is comforting, though, that at long horizons, where the illiquidity biases are mitigated, the correlations for both REIT and NCREIF returns are both around 0.3 to 0.4. Real estate provides a partial inflation hedge at long horizons but not at short horizons.

Panel A of Figure 11.13 is an overly generous representation. In Panel B, I graph robust (Spearman) correlations. These are lower than the Pearson correlations in Panel A. Both the REIT and stock correlations with inflation are negative at short horizons, with correlations around −0.1. (This is consistent with the findings for equities in chapter 8.) After one year, REIT correlations with inflation are a little higher than stock correlations. At the five-year horizon, the correlation of REIT returns with inflation is approximately 0.4, very similar to the number in Panel A. The robust calculations in Panel B for the NCREIF series have brought down the correlations with inflation significantly. Now the NCREIF correlations with inflation are around 0.2 at the one-quarter horizon, have a hump-shaped pattern increasing to around 0.3, and end at the five-year horizon back around 0.2.

In Panel C of Figure 11.13, I graph correlations of inflation with a common real estate factor from June 1980 to December 2011. I construct this real estate factor

---

[41] Glascock, Lu, and So (2002) argue that this is because the observed negative relation between REIT returns and inflation is statistically spurious and explained by other macro factors, especially monetary policy shocks. This is similar to Fama's (1981) argument on why equities are a poor hedge to inflation (see chapter 8). Case and Wachter (2011) take a contrary view and argue that REITs are good inflation hedges, but they do not define inflation-hedging ability as a correlation (or beta) with inflation.

Panel A

Correlations with Inflation (Log Returns)

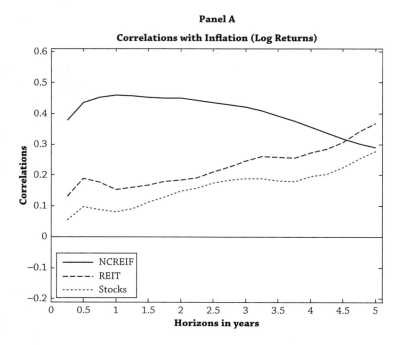

Panel B

Spearman (Robust) Correlations with Inflation (Log Returns)

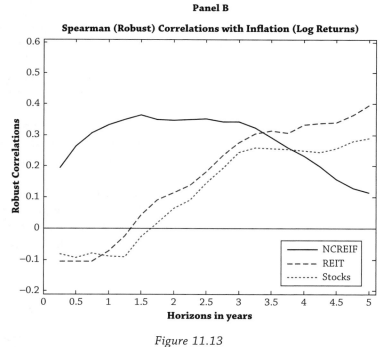

Figure 11.13

Panel C

Common Real Estate Factor Correlations with Inflation (Log Returns)

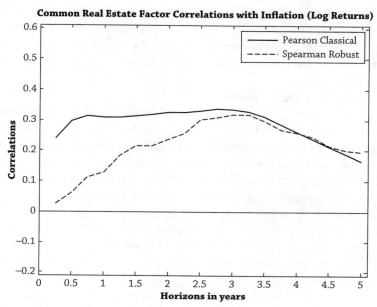

Figure 11.13 (continued)

in Ang, Nabar, and Wald (2013), where I extract common movements in real estate returns from REITs and two direct real estate indices based on the NCREIF database (one is an appraisal-based property index and one is a transaction-based index). All the indices are adjusted to have the same sector composition and leverage (delivered REIT returns). The goal is to capture joint movements in an overall real estate cycle while allowing specific real estate sectors freedom to move up and down relative to that overall cycle. Panel C, not surprisingly, shows that the correlation of the real estate cycle with inflation is between the NCREIF and REIT correlations in Panels A and B. The robust correlations are close to zero at short horizons. They peak around 0.3 at the three-year horizon and end at 0.2 at the five-year horizon.

In summary, real estate is not that real. It provides some inflation protection at long horizons but not at short horizons.

7. How Real Is Real Estate? Redux

I've shown that real estate is partly, but far from completely, real.

Carole has several considerations in writing her report in addition to just the inflation-hedging ability of direct real estate. In particular,

1. Idiosyncratic risk is large.

    Since there are no return series for direct real estate, benchmarking a single real estate investment or a portfolio of real estate properties is an important problem. Moreover, the "return" from the fund's real estate portfolio can differ significantly from a benchmark index—and neither represents true returns. This is also related to . . .

2. Heterogeneity across properties.

    Carole's fund is likely buying only a few properties, and in an extreme case only one. While we have talked about property at an "index" level, there can be large differences across property sectors and even across properties within a given sector. Different property sectors offer different inflation-hedging abilities. Huang and Hudson-Wilson (2007) find that office is the best property sector at hedging inflation risk and retail one of the worst.

3. Investment vehicles typically involve high leverage.

    Real estate investment is more than just a real estate play. Most real estate investment vehicles bundle fixed income factors as well. This is all the more reason for thinking about factors and looking through the "real estate" label.

4. Active management.

    Bond and stock investments can be passive. But direct real estate investment can be done actively only to maintain and enhance returns. Active management requires selecting a manager, which in turn means agency issues. I take up these considerations in Part III of the book.

If real estate is not that real, what drives real estate returns? We circle back here to the baseline models in urban economics—property market fundamentals matter, and movements in consumer or producer prices are just one of many factors affecting spatial equilibriums. Other macro factors, including interest rates and economic growth, also play a role.[42]

The micro level matters, too. Direct real estate returns comprise both income components and capital gains, but cash components matter more in the short run due to the illiquid nature of direct real estate. A long-term lease that has inflation-indexed rents and is triple net (where all operating expenses such as taxes, insurance, utilities, and maintenance are paid by the tenant) is a perfect income inflation hedge. The worst income inflation hedge is a long-term contract with a fixed rent where the landlord is responsible for all expenses.

So what is a real asset? The best one in this chapter turns out to be cash (T-bills), in terms of moving together with inflation. *Cash is too often underestimated as an inflation hedge.* But T-bill returns are lower than the expected returns of other asset classes. Carole should note that real bonds are definitely not that real, and gold is badly overrated as an inflation hedge. It is challenging to find

---

[42] See Chan, Hendershott, and Sanders (1990).

assets that deliver steady real returns—but that is exactly why these assets have risk premiums in the long run. Factor theory says that these assets carry risk premiums because they do not pay off during bad times, when investors most desire cash flows. Times of high inflation are bad times. That most risky assets, including "real" assets, are not perfect inflation hedges is why these assets have long-run risk premiums.

CHAPTER 12

Tax-Efficient Investing

Chapter Summary

Tax-efficient asset management confronts investors with a traditional asset allocation problem—how much of each asset to hold—and also an asset location problem. The traditional asset allocation problem concerns how much you should put into bonds. But taking account of taxes means having to figure out how much of your bonds you put in tax-deferred accounts versus taxable ones. Taxes also affect asset prices, a fact that can be exploited by a savvy tax-exempt investor.

1. Pre-Tax and After-Tax Returns

Duncan was as confused as ever after talking to his financial planner, who doubled as his accountant. His thriving business was generating cash, but success brought a new set of problems: taxes, which Duncan acknowledged was a good problem to have.

Duncan pondered a list of investments provided by his financial planner in the form of the following table:

	Pre-Tax Expected Return
Private Equity Fund	10.00%
Tactical Trading Hedge Fund	12.00%
Corporate Bond	7.00%
Municipal Bond	5.00%

His accountant emphasized that these were not the relevant numbers Duncan should be considering (not least because they did not consider the underlying factor risks; see chapter 7). "There's an old saying in this business," he told Duncan. "It's not what you make. It's what you keep that counts." In 2013, Duncan was subject to a marginal 39.6% Federal income tax. He paid a 23.8% tax rate on long-term capital gains (20% capital gains rate plus a Medicare surtax of 3.8%). So the take-home returns on these investments at the margin were forecast to be:[1]

	Tax Treatment	Post-Tax Expected Return
Private Equity Fund	Long-Term Capital Gains Tax 23.8%	7.62%
Tactical Trading Hedge Fund	Short-Term Capital Gains Tax 39.6%	7.25%
Corporate Bond	Income Tax 39.6%	4.23%
Municipal Bond	Tax-Exempt 0%	5.00%

Taxes had a major effect! The tactical trading hedge fund looked marvelous at first, with a pre-tax expected return of 12%. But it generated a lot of short-term capital gains, which are taxed as regular income; on an after-tax basis, the private equity fund and tactical trading fund had similar returns. The municipal bond looked terrible from a pre-tax perspective, offering only a 5% yield. But it beat the corporate bond after tax because municipal bonds are tax exempt.

Now suppose Duncan has a choice of holding these assets in his retirement accounts, which defer taxes, as well as in his personal accounts, which are subject to the usual income and capital gains levies. If the assets were in a retirement account, Duncan could rightly focus only on pre-tax returns. The tactical trading hedge fund would dominate, and he would prefer corporate bonds over municipal bonds. But if Duncan could only put his money in a taxable account, the private equity fund looks more attractive and municipal bonds dominate corporate bonds. (Again, all of this discussion ignores risk.) Duncan, however, can allocate to either his retirement account or his taxable account, or both. He thus faced both an *asset allocation decision* (how much of each type of asset to hold) as well as an *asset location decision* (in which account—taxable or tax deferred—to hold these assets).

Taxes are a first-order issue in asset management. There are a lucky few for whom taxes do not matter or are a second-order consideration. Pension funds, for example, are tax-exempt. Tax considerations are usually secondary for sovereign wealth funds, which typically pay some taxes, but not much, depending on the nature of bilateral taxation agreements. But for other investors, taxes are front and center.

---

[1] This example ignores state income taxes. I live in New York City and have the privilege of paying New York State tax and New York City tax. Both jurisdictions tax long-term capital gains as ordinary income. On the other hand, Duncan could live in Texas and not worry about state income tax.

2. After-Tax Returns

I start by showing the effect of taxes on savings vehicles with different tax treatments. I adapt the treatment in chapter 3 of Scholes et al. (2005), a marvelous book on *Taxes and Business Strategy* for the MBA classroom. Myron Scholes, the Nobel Prize winner and primary author of the book, asserted not very convincingly, "I said I was not an expert with regard to taxes," under cross-examination by the Justice Department in 2003 over an abusive tax shelter associated with his hedge fund, Long-Term Capital Management (LTCM). Scholes and other LTCM partners paid $40 million in fines and penalties associated with the transaction.[2] LTCM blew up in 1998 and was bailed out by a consortium of banks coordinated by the Federal Reserve Bank of New York. Scholes's second hedge fund after LTCM, Platinum Grove Asset Management, was forced to halt investor withdrawals (it invoked *gates*, see chapter 17) after losing close to 40% of its value in 2008 during the financial crisis.[3]

In our examples below, we assume an income tax rate of 39.6%, a capital gains rate of 23.8%, and that each asset earns a constant annual return of 12%. We start with $1,000 invested in each asset in year zero. Consider the following investments:

Bond Fund: where all distributions are taxed as ordinary income and there are no capital gains or losses. After n years, $1,000 initially invested in the bond fund cumulates to

$$1,000 \times (1 + 0.12(1 - 0.396))^n, \tag{12.1}$$

where every year the investor can only keep 60.4c of each dollar earned by the fund. This is the lowest after-tax accumulation of all the strategies we consider.

Non-Deductible IRA: where contributions are not tax deductible (that is, contributions are made with after-tax dollars) but earnings are not taxed until retirement, at which point they are taxed as income. In this case, the non-deductible IRA cumulates to

$$\underbrace{1,000 \times (1 + 0.12)^n}_{\text{Pre-tax accumulation}} - \underbrace{0.396[1,000 \times (1 + 0.12)^n - 1,000]}_{\text{Taxed at withdrawal as income}}. \tag{12.2}$$

Compared to the bond fund, the non-deductible IRA accumulates at the pre-tax return of 12% rather than the after-tax return of $(1 - 0.396) \times 0.12 = 7.2\%$.

---

[2] Johnston, D. C., "Economist Questioned on Tax Shelter Role," *New York Times,*" July 10, 2003. Browning, L., and D. C. Johnston, "Hedge Fund Is Censured and Ordered to Pay Taxes," *New York Times*, Aug. 28, 2004.

[3] Kishan, S., "Scholes's Platinum Grove Fund Halts Withdrawals after Losses," Bloomberg, Nov. 6, 2008.

At withdrawal, the earnings are taxed as ordinary income. The current limit for non-deductible IRA contributions is $5,000 for those age forty-nine or younger and $6,000 for those fifty and older.

Equity Fund: pays capital gains annually. In this case, the earnings are taxed each year at the 15% capital gains rate:

$$1,000 \times (1 + 0.12(1 - 0.238))^n. \tag{12.3}$$

This category of funds includes assets whose prices are marked up to market value at year end, even when no sale has occurred.

Non-Dividend Paying Stock: There is a reason why Warren Buffet has never allowed Berkshire Hathaway to pay a dividend. This investment is similar to the non-deductible IRA, except the earnings are taxed as a capital gain rather than as income:

$$\underbrace{1,000 \times (1 + 0.12)^n}_{\text{Pre-tax accumulation}} - \underbrace{0.238[1,000 \times (1 + 0.12)^n - 1,000]}_{\text{Taxed at withdrawal as captial gain}}. \tag{12.4}$$

Tax Exempt or Tax Deferred: After n years, a tax-exempt investment simply cumulates to

$$1,000 \times (1 + 0.12)^n. \tag{12.5}$$

The formula is exactly the same for a municipal bond (although in practice a municipal bond's average return would be much lower, see Section 3) as for a tax-deductible retirement account. Every dollar contributed to the latter is equivalent to $(1 - 0.396) = \$0.60$ after tax. But, at withdrawal, the pension is taxed as regular income at the full 39.6% rate. Thus we have

$$1,000 \times \frac{1}{(1 - 0.396)}(1 + 0.12)^n(1 - 0.396) = 1,000 \times (1 + 0.12)^n \tag{12.6}$$

as the return on a pension investment, which is exactly the same as equation (12.4). This category also includes 529 college savings plans.

We know immediately that the bond fund is always the worst and that the tax-exempt or tax-deferred fund is always the best (remember, everything in this simple example earns 12% with certainty). This implies that people should not be holding bonds in taxable accounts, unless they are very risk averse and their entire portfolio, both taxable and tax-deferred, is dominated by bonds. What about the other investments?

The after-tax accumulations of the various investments are:

Year	Bond Fund	Non-Deductible IRA	Equity Fund	Non-Dividend Paying Stock	Tax Exempt
0	1000.00	1000.00	1000.00	1000.00	1000.00
10	2013.22	2271.93	2398.83	2604.66	3105.85
20	4053.07	6222.36	5754.36	7588.48	9646.29
30	8159.74	18491.79	13803.71	23067.46	29959.92

The non-dividend paying stock dominates the bond fund, the non-deductible IRA, and the equity fund. It is second only to the tax exempt strategy. It works so well because of the lower capital gains rate. From this perspective Warren Buffet is right not to pay dividends. But so many companies do![4] Why? The standard explanations are dividend clientele and signaling hypotheses, since paying dividends by itself loses money for shareholders. There may also be benefits to paying out cash rather than managers wasting it on white elephant projects in the firm.[5]

It is interesting that the non-deductible IRA and the equity fund switch positions between years 20 and 30. For short horizons, the equity fund dominates. For example, at the 10-year horizon, the equity fund cumulates to $2,399 versus $2,272 in the non-deductible IRA. So if you're saving for a short time period, forget the Roth IRA; just put your money directly into a mutual fund. But at longer horizons, the non-deductible IRA comes out ahead. At 30 years, the non-deductible IRA cumulated amount is $18,492, which trounces the $13,804 in the equity fund. (If you're twenty-five years old and reading this book, sock the maximum permissible into your non-deductible IRA every year.) The intuition for this is that the non-deductible IRA has earnings that compound at the higher pre-tax rate of 12% (see equation (12.2)), whereas the mutual fund compounds at the after-tax rate of 9.1% (see equation (12.3)). This is offset in the short run by the higher income tax rate for non-deductible IRAs and the lower capital gains rate for mutual fund investments. But over time, the "interest on the interest" dominates in the non-deductible IRA. Such is the beauty of compounding.

Clearly, taxes matter. This simple example shows that:

1. The most important lesson is to save in a way that is sheltered from taxes. Everything else is secondary.

---

[4] Fewer companies now are paying dividends but those that do pay out big ones. In fact, while the number of firms paying dividends has dropped over the past few decades, the sum of dividends paid by all companies has increased in both nominal and real terms. See Fama and French (2001) and DeAngelo, DeAngelo, and Skinner (2004).

[5] See Allen and Michaely (1995) for a literature summary, which is a little dated but still relevant.

2. After maxing out your tax-exempt account, optimal allocation decisions can be quite complicated. They can depend on time horizon and tax rates. Different investment vehicles will have different tax implications. The tax treatment interacts with the returns the assets generate to make the joint optimal allocation and location decision complex.

3. Individuals need to focus on after-tax returns, not pre-tax returns. Unfortunately, most of the financial industry only reports pre-tax returns.

The first lesson is crucial. You can save directly in a tax-deferred pension. Or you can find an asset that pays you a tax-exempt return. One extremely important asset class that does this is municipal bonds, which allow money to accumulate tax-free in a taxable account.

3. Municipal Bonds

3.1. CHARACTERISTICS OF THE MUNI MARKET

Municipal bonds, or munis, are bonds issued by states, municipalities, 501(c)(3) nonprofit corporations (named for the section of the Internal Revenue Code granting them a tax exemption), and other tax-exempt entities. This market is large: at the end of 2011 there were $3.7 trillion in muni securities outstanding, about a third the size of the U.S. Treasury market. The coupons and original issue discount (OID) on regular munis are exempt from Federal income tax. In addition, individuals are exempt from state income tax on muni coupons and OID on bonds issued by tax-exempt authorities in the investor's home state. But some munis are subject to federal income tax and the alternative minimum tax, so individuals have to be careful.[6]

The tax-exempt muni market is unique to the United States. In other countries, investors holding state bonds pay national income taxes. Munis are exempt from federal taxes here due to the separation of the federal and state governments in the constitution (federalism). In *Pollack v. Farmers' Loan and Trust* (1895), the Supreme Court interpreted the constitution as not allowing the Federal government to tax the states. Put simply, one government could not tax another. But in 1988 the Supreme Court overturned the constitutional basis for the tax exemption in *South Carolina v. Baker*, so the muni exemption is now the purview of Congress. Periodically there are calls to rescind it, but it will take an extremely brave Congress to do so.[7]

---

[6] There are taxable munis, of which one important class is Build America Bonds. See Ang, Bhansali, and Xing (2010a).

[7] The calls to rescind the tax exemption of municipal debt are not a recent phenomenon: Ott and Meltzer (1963) report that there were 114 resolutions to repeal the municipal tax exemption from 1920 to 1943.

At issue, OID and interest coupons are equivalent. The issuer can trade off paying a higher coupon with a steeper discount. Thus if the interest is tax exempt, the OID must also be tax-exempt. Issuers take advantage of this equivalence of OID and interest: in muni-land, only about 10% of straight bonds are par bonds, whereas the great majority of corporate bonds are issued at par.[8]

Individuals are the main holders of municipal bonds. Figure 12.1 plots the holdings of municipal bonds using data from the flow of funds from 1952 to 2012. Household holdings include both direct holdings and indirect holdings through mutual funds, exchange-traded funds (ETFs), and closed-end funds (see chapter 16). Households hold close to 80% of munis and have done so since the early 1990s. Of this 80%, about half is directly held and 30% is held indirectly. Banks used to own up to 50% of munis in the 1970s, but since most of their tax breaks for holding munis were eliminated, bank holdings of munis have been below 10%.[9]

Individuals benefit from holding munis because they pay no income tax on muni interest or OID. Consequently, an individual holding a muni bond is willing

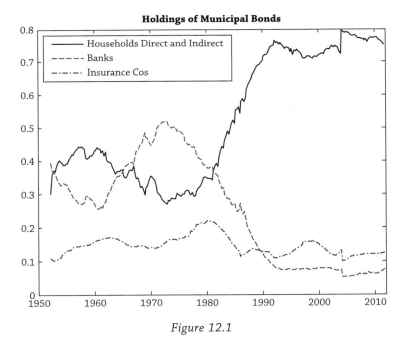

Figure 12.1

[8] See Ang, Bhansali, and Xing (2010b, Table 1).

[9] There are still bank-qualified muni issues, which are restricted to issues less than $10 million in size. Banks can tax deduct 80% of the carrying costs of these munis. The 2009 Recovery Act temporarily allowed banks to deduct 80% of the carry costs up to 2% of the bank's total assets (this is called the 2% de minimus rule) for a much wider set of bonds and raised the $10 million bank qualified size limit to $30 million.

to tolerate a lower yield, and muni yields are, on average, lower than the yields of federally taxable bonds such as Treasuries and corporate bonds. Tax benefits are the distinguishing characteristic of munis, and naturally these benefits are built into their high prices (or low yields).

Ang, Bhansali, and Xing (2012) decompose municipal yield spreads into credit, liquidity, and tax components:

$$\underbrace{\text{Muni} - \text{Tsy}}_{-0.92\%} = \underbrace{\text{Credit Risk}}_{0.01\%} + \underbrace{\text{Illiquidity Risk}}_{1.12\%} + \underbrace{\text{Tax Benefit}}_{-2.05\%} \qquad (12.7)$$

As you can see, muni yields take a big hit (−2.05%) as a result of their tax benefit; in effect, muni bond issuers are able to transfer some of their borrowing costs to Uncle Sam, who makes up the difference in the form of a tax giveback. Credit risk is negligible (0.01%). Illiquidity risk is high (1.12%).

Equation (12.7) emphasizes what munis bring to the table versus Treasuries. Overall muni interest rates are influenced by the same factors driving interest rates in general—which we discussed in chapter 9. The fundamental, market-wide forces of economic growth, inflation, monetary policy, and associated risk premiums matter here as well.

But there are other factors affecting munis, so let's examine each in turn.

3.2. ILLIQUIDITY

The muni market is disgustingly inefficient.

Information in the municipal market is dreadful. Contrast an investor obtaining financial reports on a listed company. She can do it for free with a mouse click, in a standardized format going back years, and compare this data with that of other companies. It is hard, and for the most part impossible, to do the same for the town where she lives, or for the school district which educates her children. Or for her county or state. Various organizations, including government and industry groups, have expended great efforts to make information more accessible to muni investors, but information quality, accessibility, and dissemination generally remain poor.[10]

From a political standpoint, this is appalling. Taxpayers, after all, have a right to know. Is my school district borrowing money at a rate competitive with the school district across the river? If I can see a leverage ratio for the companies I invest in, why can't I quickly see the leverage ratio for my town?

---

[10] There is no penalty for noncompliance with Governmental Accounting Standards Board (GASB) standards. Only thirty-eight states require state and local government entities to use GASB. Certain states, like Kansas, New Jersey, and Washington, set their own accounting standards and some government entities within those states keep three sets of books: the GASB standard so that they are able to receive a clean GAAP opinion by auditors, the state standard, and their own accounts.

Poor information also impairs liquidity, and liquidity in muni markets is abysmal. Transaction costs are high, price adjustment is slow, and different buyers pay different prices for the same bond. The bonds themselves are overly complex, and this further reduces liquidity. The way muni bonds are issued in series is ironically designed to minimize liquidity: it takes a large issue and then chops it up into several small issues (thirteen, on average, but with 5% of series issues containing more than twenty-five separate securities). Each small issue has a different maturity, different coupon, and perhaps even different embedded derivatives. There are literally a million or so different bonds in the muni market. Over 60% of them contain hard-to-value embedded derivatives. Contrast this with the large, deep U.S. Treasury market. U.S. Treasuries, unlike munis, are simple and easy to value, and there are relatively few issues with large sizes.

As a result of all this, individual investors often get fleeced when buying munis. Investors need to pay attention to recent comparable bond prices, released through the Municipal Securities Rule Marking Board, but the vast array of bond types and features makes these securities hard to compare; in addition to different maturities, coupons, and discounts/premiums, munis can be sinkable, callable, putable, refunded, conduit, bundled with other contingent claims, subject to alternative minimum tax, taxable, bank-qualified, and so on.

Round-trip transaction costs for individuals average 2% to 3% but can easily reach 5%. This is more than double what institutions pay, roughly twice as much as what it costs to trade a corporate bond, and many times what it costs to trade a stock. Green, Hollifield, and Schürhoff (2007) show that dealer markups over the reoffering price can be high as 5%—roughly a year's return on a typical muni bond. (The reoffering price is often represented to issuers as the price at which the bonds are sold to the public.) Biais and Green (2005) show that, remarkably, it is twice is as expensive to trade munis today as it was in the 1920s, when muni bonds were actively traded on the New York Stock Exchange. Given the huge advances in technology, what other securities cost more to trade today than they did 100 years ago?

Figure 12.2 shows just how illiquid muni markets are. Dividing up all municipal bond transactions into ten buckets by the number of trades per year, excluding the bonds that never trade and taking bonds transactions which occur ninety days after issue, the 10% most illiquid bonds trade once every five to six years. The typical municipal bond trades once or twice per year. Even the most liquid bonds trade once every two days, on average. Muni bonds are extremely illiquid.

It's tragic that these bonds, which appeal mainly to individual investors, are so hideously inefficient and unfriendly. Reforming this market would immensely benefit the common man as well as save billions in taxpayer dollars by lowering issuer costs. But muni reform is hard: the Securities and Exchange Commission (SEC) does not regulate this market and cannot impose mandatory disclosure requirements or minimal accounting standards, as it can with regular securities. In fact, the main framework for the regulation of capital markets in the U.S. (the

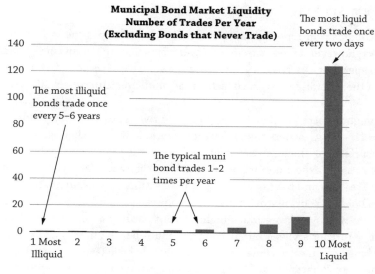

Figure 12.2

1933 Securities Act and the 1934 Exchange Act) specifically exempts all municipal securities from their provisions except for the antifraud statutes. The SEC
does what it can, but it is greatly hamstrung.[11] In the words of SEC Commissioner
Elisse Walter, muni investors have often been treated as "second class citizens."[12]
The muni market has poor information and terrible liquidity partly because the
muni market is segmented by states. Congress cannot simply mandate better disclosure, set up a muni market regulator, or dictate what types of bonds states can
issue—these are state matters, and the U.S. constitution, along with a vast body
of court rulings, limit what the federal government can do.

Richard Green and I, through The Hamilton Project, Brookings Institution,
have proposed that municipalities could eliminate a great many inefficiencies by
acting collectively.[13] Municipalities could band together and thereby obtain better access to better financial advice, have more resources, and help each other in a
way that they cannot do on their own. The potential benefits are enormous. From
equation (12.7), if munis had the same liquidity as Treasuries, then municipalities
would be borrowing at rates 1% lower than currently. This is a saving to taxpayers
of more than $30 billion per year.

---

[11] The SEC itself calls for legislative change to better police these markets. See the SEC "Report on
the Municipal Securities Market," July 31, 2012. The report makes for some very sad reading of cases
where the SEC has been able to take action.

[12] "Regulation of the Municipal Securities Market: Investors are Not Second Class Citizens," Speech
by SEC Commissioner Elisse B. Walter, Oct. 28, 2009.

[13] See Ang and Green (2011). This also contains a good summary of muni market inefficiencies and
is a reference for the numbers reported in this section.

3.3. TERM SPREAD

The decomposition reported in equation (12.7) was across the yield curve. The tax effect, however, varies with maturity. In particular, the muni curve has always been steeper than the Treasury curve, but the steepness has varied over time. This is one of the outstanding stylized facts in the muni literature and is called the *muni puzzle*.

We might expect muni yields, y_{muni},, to be related to Treasury yields, y_{tsy}, by $y_{\text{muni}} = (1 - \tau)y_{\text{tsy}}$, where τ is a relevant tax rate.[14] An individual can earn 4%, say in Treasuries, but the after-tax yield she receives is $(1 - 0.396) \times 0.04 = 2.4\%$. Thus, we might expect a muni bond to deliver the same 2.4% yield to make the taxable Treasury and the tax-exempt muni investments equivalent after-tax. This relation holds at short maturities less than one year, but it fails at long maturities. Long-term muni yields are much higher than this simple tax relation predicts.[15] There is a further stylized fact beyond the muni puzzle: muni yield curves have never sloped downward, while Treasuries regularly have (see chapter 9).

Various explanations have been proposed for the muni puzzle, with my sometime co-author Richard Green's (1993) among the most compelling. Green is able to construct a risk-free portfolio of taxable Treasuries so that income is transformed and treated as capital gains. Essentially, Green shows how to construct taxable bond portfolios to lessen the effect of taxes, making the muni puzzle less pronounced than it should be relative to a naïve analysis. Green modestly refers to his model as "a simple analysis" (which he puts in the title), but it requires some sophistication to follow.

Investors trade on the muni puzzle and it is called the MOB trade, for municipals-over-Treasury bonds. There are many ways to implement this strategy; a basic one is simply to buy long-term munis and sell short-term munis, hence you are exposed to the muni term spread. You fund this by taking offsetting positions in the Treasury term structure: selling long-term Treasury bonds and buying short-term Treasury notes. Then you leverage this, a lot.

Panel A of Figure 12.3 plots the twenty-year minus one-year term spread in munis (AAA) and the after-tax Treasury term spread from January 1990 to June 2011 and shows the spread for munis has been higher than the spread for Treasuries. But it has varied over time and dramatically narrowed during 2008. Panel B plots the difference between the two series. There have been pronounced increases in the muni slope relative to the after-tax Treasury slope before, as in 1992 and 1994, but nothing in the post-1990 sample is as dramatic as 2008. If the

---

[14] This is formulated by Miller (1977).

[15] Another way of stating the muni puzzle is that marginal tax rates implied by the ratio of the muni curve to the Treasury curve are much smaller than they should be given federal income tax rates. Estimates of implied tax rates from other muni prices, however, are high. Longstaff (2011) estimates implied tax rates around 38% using muni swaps. Ang, Bhansali, and Xing (2010) estimate marginal tax rates that exceed over 100% using muni market discount bonds.

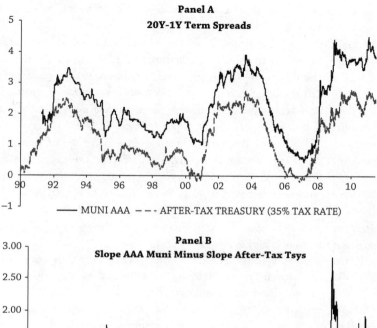

Figure 12.3

picture reminds you of volatility risk, you are spot on. As volatility spiked, the MOB trade suffered, along with other carry trade and risky asset strategies (see chapter 7). Many muni bond funds, some of which were very highly levered, took severe losses in 2007 and 2008 on the MOB trade.

3.4. CREDIT RISK

On December 19, 2010, Meredith Whitney, a noted banking analyst and CEO of Meredith Whitney Advisory Group LLC, appeared on *60 Minutes* and predicted "hundreds of billions" in losses from municipal bond defaults starting in 2011. Her comments drew a lot of attention. But we have yet to see the tidal wave of defaults in munis. Whitney may be early, but she raises a provocative point. Given that this asset class is perceived as being so low in risk, how much credit risk do munis really have?

Municipalities enter bankruptcy all the time. Orange County, California, caused a huge stir when it entered bankruptcy in 1994. In 2013, the City of Detroit filed for bankruptcy—the largest municipal bankruptcy in history with debts close to $20 billion. Since the financial crisis, scattered defaults among municipalities have arisen partly from the fall in house prices and the legacy of the subprime crisis. A partial list is as follows: in 2008, City of Vallejo, California; in 2009, City of Prichard, Alabama; in 2011, City of Central Falls, Rhode Island, City of Harrisburg, Pennsylvania, Jefferson County, Alabama; and in 2012, City of Stockton, California. But, overall, credit risk in munis is extremely low. The decomposition estimated by Ang, Bhansali, and Xing (2012) in equation (12.7) shows that credit risk plays a negligible part in municipal bond spreads, but this is for the sample used by Ang, Bhansali, and Xing since the mid-1990s. Perhaps muni risk now is higher?

Moody's reports only four defaults among towns, cities, or counties from 1970 to 2009, and only fifty-four defaults of municipal entities over the same period.[16] The average five-year cumulative default for investment grade muni debt is 0.03% compared to 1% for investment-grade corporate. Thus, credit risk in munis has been very low—an order of magnitude lower than credit risk for investment grade corporate debt. Moody's also reports that the recovery rates when a default occurred were 60 cents on the dollar, compared to 38 cents for investment grade corporate debt. Hempel's (1971) study gave special attention to the many municipal defaults that occurred during the 1920s and 1930s and also found that default rates were much lower, and recovery rates much higher, than for corporate debt.

Whitney's prediction may yet come true. States have gone bankrupt before.[17] In the early 1830s and 1840s, eight states and one territory defaulted: Arkansas, Florida Territory, Indiana, Louisiana, Maryland, Michigan, Mississippi, and Pennsylvania. U.S. states during that era were the emerging markets of the time, and there was heavy borrowing for infrastructure that could not be paid back ("canals to nowhere," in the words of John Cochrane).[18] Some states, like Florida and Mississippi, repudiated completely. In Charles Dickens's 1843 novel, *A Christmas Carol*, the protagonist Ebenezer Scrooge has a nightmare in which his wealth has withered into a "mere United States security." Scrooge was not

---

[16] U.S. Municipal Bond Defaults and Recoveries, 1970–2009, Moody's Investors Service, Feb. 2010.

[17] For more details see Ang and Longstaff (2013), who also compare the credit risk of U.S. states with the credit risk of Eurozone nations. U.S. states are sovereign borrowers in a currency union, just as Eurozone nations are. Germany, however, is not going to send troops to prevent a country from leaving the Eurozone, while the United States had Gettysburg.

[18] http://johnhcochrane.blogspot.com/2012/02/sargent-on-debt-and-defaults.html

dreaming about Treasuries but these state issues that were widely held in the United Kingdom at the time.

In the 1870s and 1880s, ten states defaulted, including some two-time losers: Alabama, Arkansas, Florida, Georgia, Louisiana, Minnesota, North Carolina, South Carolina, Tennessee, and Virginia. All were adversely affected by the Civil War except Minnesota, which went bankrupt because it failed to meet payments on railroad bonds ("railroads to nowhere").

And then finally, in 1933, Arkansas defaulted, again. Arkansas has the dubious distinction of being the only state to default three times.

In all these defaults, there was no bankruptcy mechanism. States are sovereign entities under the constitution (in particular, under the Eleventh Amendment). Furthermore, the federal government did not step in to offer aid. Will the Feds intervene in a state default in the future? I doubt it. New York City almost defaulted in 1975. New York City is notable because its metropolitan area has a gross domestic product larger than most states (and most countries). The mayor at the time, Abraham Beame, appealed to the federal government and President Ford for assistance, which was denied. The *Daily News* had the pithy headline, "FORD TO CITY: DROP DEAD." There is no federal obligation to provide a muni bailout, there never has been a bailout, and in my opinion a federal bailout will not happen when the next state defaults (hopefully not Arkansas for the fourth time).

I think Whitney is right in one respect: there will be defaults amounting to "hundreds of billions of dollars." I do not believe, however, that the defaults will be substantial in muni bond markets. State and muni governments will default implicitly (these are not legal defaults but defaults on social contracts) by reducing or eliminating services and benefits to residents. States and municipalities will cut public pension payments—which may be explicit defaults depending on how pension obligations rank in the liability pecking order. These defaults have already started. The full force of muni downsizing, however, will not be borne by muni bond holders.

3.5. ADVICE FOR INVESTORS

I summarize with the following recommendations:

1. Overall for muni interest rates, the same factors operate as in other fixed income markets: economic growth, inflation, monetary policy, volatility, and so on.
2. The tax-exempt status is the distinguishing characteristic of munis. Investors benefit from the tax exemption but need to be choosy because . . .
3. There are huge illiquidity and information shortcomings in muni markets. Try to avoid buying individual munis unless you know what you are doing. And even if you know what you are doing, pay attention to comparable prices and

shop around. The opacity of muni markets means investors have to be especially vigilant—you will likely be ripped off and, given the poor transparency in the muni market, you won't even know it.

4. If you're a small investor, hold munis through low-cost mutual funds or ETFs (see chapter 16).

5. The MOB trade is not an "arbitrage." The same factors driving term spreads, such as volatility, are at play as in regular fixed-income markets. But there is a large added dose of illiquidity risk. See point 3 above.

6. Credit risk is likely to remain small. Of course, be smart about what kind of munis you buy. See point 3 again.

I close with a muni investment strategy. Many investors buying munis, including pass-through institutional investors like mutual funds, do so to avoid paying taxes. Munis are tax-exempt only at issue. Investors trading munis in secondary markets have to pay taxes. For example, if an investor purchases a par bond for a price less than par on the secondary market, he has to pay income tax on the difference between purchase price and the par value at maturity. This is taxation on *market discount* (as opposed to the no taxation on OID, which at issue is equivalent to tax-exempt coupon interest). Ang, Bhansali, and Xing (2010b) show that there are some very cheap munis with market discounts. Buying cheap market discount munis is like buying second-hand time shares. Everyone wants the new condo, but you get the exact same one for 50% less on the secondary market. Investors are reluctant to buy market discount munis because they are averse to tax—and many major muni mutual funds don't wish to pass on taxes to retail investors and thus avoid purchasing these bonds. The pricing anomaly is likely to persist because the muni market is fragmented: even if you were to know about this effect, you may not be offered the deals at cheap enough prices.

4. Tax-Efficient Allocation

The optimal asset allocation decision (ideally an optimal factor allocation decision, see chapter 14) concerns how much of each asset to hold. The optimal location decision is about where to hold these assets. The simplest choice is between a taxable or tax-deferred account. There are other asset locations: joint accounts with spouses and/or children, charitable vehicles, and many different kinds of trusts.

The optimal location problem is complicated because of the existence of *dynamic tax strategies*, and in some cases there are pure *tax arbitrages*. Some of these tax arbitrages are legal but permitted only to a certain extent, others are prohibited outright, and some are allowed but prohibited in "pure" forms and so fall into a murky area. For example, universities are prevented from issuing tax-exempt debt—they borrow at a rate lower than the federal government (see Section 3)—and then using that money to buy stocks. But, money is fungible. So the money in the university's endowment that would have gone to building the dormitory can be allocated to equities, so the dormitory gets built anyway and is used as collateral for the university's muni bond issue. A second example is an individual who receives a tax deduction for the interest on a mortgage. She could borrow using a home equity loan and invest that money in dividend-paying stocks. Money is again fungible. This allows her to allocate the money she is saving for her son's college tuition to equities. Then she borrows money with a home equity loan and uses those proceeds for the money she would have put into her son's college savings fund. One of the largest tax arbitrages (in terms of the cost to the federal government) is the mortgage deduction, which the IRS limits to a mortgage of no more than $1 million.

4.1. TAX TIMING OPTIONS

In 1983, George Constantinides published a major paper showing how the one-year cut-off between short-term capital gains (which are taxed as income) and long-term capital gains gave rise to tax-timing options. Constantinides showed that it is optimal to realize losses immediately as they arise and to defer (to infinity ... and beyond!) the realization of capital gains.[19] The loss is deductible at income tax rates, and the deferment delays paying capital gains taxes. Furthermore, the tax strategy is separable from the portfolio choice problem.

There are some strong conditions in Constantinides' original paper, but they have been relaxed in follow-on work.[20] For example, in Constantinides' basic model there are no constraints on buying or selling. If there are short sale constraints, then the asset allocation decisions depend on the tax basis (in a complicated fashion). In the original model, there was no limit on tax rebates for capital losses. In the current tax code, only $3,000 of losses can be offset against ordinary income (but amounts in excess of $3,000 can be carried over to future tax years). With such a constraint, it may be optimal to realize gains and pay taxes to regain the option of using new losses against other income. But overall the basic idea holds: realize the loss as soon as you can (but with transactions costs it may pay to wait) and try to defer capital gains. So come the end of the tax year, sell your losers.

This advice sounds like the opposite of rebalancing, which I advocated in chapter 4. Rebalancing buys losers. Tax timing sells losers. How are these consistent with each other? The Constantinides tax timing option is different from the underlying asset allocation decision. Suppose there is a 40% allocation to equities, which an investor has implemented using the AA Index Fund. Then at the end

---

[19] Deferring to infinity is not academic. In many circumstances, when you leave appreciated securities to your heirs, the basis is reset at your death.

[20] See, for example, DeMiguel and Uppal (2005), Gallmeyer and Srivastava (2011), and Marekwica (2012).

of the tax year suppose there is a loss. Rebalancing would say buy more equities. The tax timing option says sell AA index Fund. The investor proceeds to sell AA Index Fund, thus realizing the loss which is deductible, and then buys the same amount and more of BB Market ETF. Economically, AA Index Fund is equivalent to BB Market ETF. For tax purposes, they are different. Doing this, the investor has both rebalanced and harvested the tax losses.

4.2. TAX-EFFICIENT ASSET ALLOCATION

The asset allocation and asset location problems are potentially complex given the potential interactions and dynamic tax strategies. There are two common approaches:

1. To specify the joint asset allocation and asset location problem and to solve the two problems simultaneously. An example is Dammon, Spatt, and Zhang (2004).
2. To ignore the interaction between the two decisions and implement ad hoc rules. Usually the asset allocation problem is solved first and then, taking the asset allocation as a given, the asset location problem is solved.

The second method is by far the more popular in the financial services industry. For example, Vanguard says:[21]

> Consider placing the most tax-efficient holdings (such as tax-managed, index, and tax-exempt funds) in your taxable accounts while holding tax-inefficient investments in your tax-advantaged accounts—such as IRAs or employer plans.

It turns out that industry is right (partly). The optimal location problem is separable from the asset allocation problem, and the overall allocation problem can be done by considering only taxable accounts, rather than a considerably more complex joint problem over taxable and tax-deferred accounts. Jennifer Huang (2008), in a paper that was her PhD dissertation, was the first to show this.

Huang's model aligns with popular industry advice, with an extremely important caveat which I detail below. Investors place assets with the highest tax rates in the tax-deferred account to maximize the tax benefit. Bonds are highly taxed because coupons are taxed as income (at 36.9%). So these are placed in the tax-deferred account. Stocks with no dividends are subject only to the long-term capital gains tax (at 23.8%). So stocks are placed in taxable accounts.

---

[21] https://personal.vanguard.com/us/insights/taxcenter/how-to-be-tax-savvy-investor

The major result in Huang (2008) is that she is able to compute the optimal allocation with tax effects, which industry models rarely do (or if they do, rarely do
correctly). Moreover, Huang does it only using a taxable account. Huang's insight
is that you can convert any tax-deferred return into a taxable return. A holding of
an asset in a tax-deferred account is equivalent to a levered holding of the same
asset in a taxable account. We've already seen this in equation (12.6): \$1 con-
tributed pre-tax to a pension fund is worth $1/(1 - 0.396) = \$1.66$ in a taxable
account. The taxable portfolio levers up the tax-deferred portfolio to generate the
same return. Anything that the investor can do in a tax-deferred account, the same
investor can undo (or re-do) in his taxable account.

Huang's procedure is to compute the equivalent taxable wealth, which is the
sum of wealth already in the taxable account, W^T, and then convert all the tax-
deferred wealth, W^D, to an equivalent amount in taxable wealth. She redefines
total wealth, W, as the sum of

$$w = w^T + Z \times W^D, \tag{12.8}$$

where Z is the appropriate factor that converts the tax-deferred wealth to the
taxable equivalent. Most popular industry advice, unfortunately, does not perform optimal allocation calculations on equivalent taxable wealth amounts as per
equation (12.8).

Now the standard Merton (1971, 1973) solution applies to total wealth, W,
as in chapter 4. The asset allocation and asset location decisions are separable.
What makes them so is that there is an appropriate adjustment, Z, which transforms the value of the tax-deferred wealth to taxable wealth and vice versa.
The asset allocation problem hence requires an adjustment for the impact of tax
deferment.

The key driver in Huang's analysis is the ability to sell short in the taxable
account. Small investors will not be able to do this, but large and sophisticated
investors certainly can. If investors cannot borrow in the taxable account, then
investors may prefer to hold lower taxed assets in the tax-deferred account as this
lowers the volatility of the tax benefit. The basic analysis in Huang also misses
Constantinides-style tax timing. This can be incorporated. The factor Z in equation (12.8) that converts taxable to tax-deferred wealth can be modified to take
into account tax option benefits, where Z now captures *effective* tax rates rather
than *statutory* tax rates. In theory, all these effects can be captured in Huang's
framework. The downside, however, is that in practice, Huang's Z factor may be
difficult to compute.

With the answer to optimal location and optimal asset allocation in hand, we
circle back to a question involving muni bonds. If the main benefit of munis
is the tax exemption, what about holding munis in a taxable account instead
of Treasury or corporate bonds in a tax-deferred account? Dammon, Spatt, and
Zhang (2004) examine this question and come to the conclusion that it if you

want to hold bonds, it is better to hold taxable bonds in a tax-deferred account rather than holding tax-exempt bonds in a taxable account. The exception is if you are so risk averse and subject to constraints (like the ones above), that you need to hold bonds in both the taxable and tax-deferred accounts. So the case for munis for a moderately risk tolerant investor should be made on the basis of factor exposure, as I have advocated for any other asset class (see chapters 7 to 10), not the tax exemption per se.

4.3. TAXES AND DYNAMIC FACTORS

Taxes have a significant effect on dynamic trading strategies, especially strategies that have high turnover and generate plentiful short-term capital gains (which are taxed as income). Bergstresser and Pontiff (2009) and Israel and Moskowitz (2011) examine the effect of taxes on the value-growth and momentum factors described in chapter 7. Not surprisingly, since the dynamic factors involve continual trading, taxes reduce the value-growth and momentum premiums. Bergstresser and Pontiff document that the tax-exempt value-growth premium of 3.5% is reduced to 1.8% for a high income resident of New York State using the tax rates investors were subject to between 1927 and 2009. The same investor would reap an after-tax momentum premium of 8.1% while a tax-exempt investor undertaking the momentum strategy would have enjoyed a return of 10.5%. Value-growth and momentum investing are tax inefficient because of the large dividends that value stocks generate and the high turnover of the momentum strategies.

Taxable asset owners implementing dynamic factor strategies should be encouraged that while the value-growth and momentum premiums are diminished, they are still present on an after-tax basis. There is ample scope for tax optimization of these strategies. Israel and Moskowitz (2011) find that tax optimization induces large improvements to value and momentum styles. I also advise taxable asset owners to locate these dynamic factor strategies, as far as possible, in tax-exempt accounts and consider tax-optimized versions of these factors in taxable accounts.

4.4. TRUSTS

Trusts do not exist solely to avoid or defer taxes; some trusts are designed primarily to protect assets from profligate family members rather than to minimize paying Uncle Sam. Some trusts are designed to actually disinherit family members and to preserve estates. But most trusts are set up with some intention of minimizing taxes, especially the estate tax (called the "death tax" by those who advocate removing all estate taxes).

At the time of writing in 2013, the estate tax exemption is $5.25 million per spouse, or $10.5 million per married couple.[22] The top tax rate assessed for estates in excess of these amounts is 40%. Ultra high net worth asset owners have many trusts they can play with: grantor retained annuity trusts (GRATs), charitable remainder unitrusts, and their close cousins charitable lead trusts, intentionally defective grantor trusts (IDGTs, which are called "I Dig It" trusts), and dynasty trusts—just to name a few. GRATs are very popular among the wealthy and it would be rare to find an ultra-high net worth asset owner without at least one GRAT in her estate. Along with these instruments are family partnerships or corporate structures with valuation and control discounts, which set a different value of the shares for tax purposes than more realistic market values.

While the rules for these are very complicated (that is why you hire your tax attorney), they have three key economic components:

1. Alternative location

    They offer taxpayers another asset location with a tax break. GRATs are initially set up by a donation to a tax-advantaged trust.

2. The trust generates income

    The trust takes advantage of income compounding at tax-advantaged rates (see Section 1). In a GRAT, the trust pays money to the person setting up the trust, which is taxable, but any appreciation in excess of a hurdle rate (which is computed by the IRS, is adjusted every month, and is based on a market interest rate) flows back into the trust. Thus assets with high expected returns are ideally held in GRATs. They compound tax free.

3. The trust transfers to beneficiaries

    At death, assets in the trust are transferred to beneficiaries and are not subject to the gift tax. (In 2012, the IRS permitted a parent to transfer up to $5.12 million to a child tax free.) The GRAT is set up with a specific maturity (at least two years), and one risk is that if the grantor dies before the trust matures, then the value of the trust is included in her estate—but this would have been exactly the same situation if the GRAT had not been set up, so the grantor's estate has not lost anything (except the lawyer's fees in setting up the GRAT).

Absent the probability of dying before the expiration of the trust, computing optimal allocations to a GRAT can be handled in Huang's model. With appropriate assumptions on the expected returns and dividend streams of the assets, we can

---

[22] An exemption of $5 million was introduced in 2010 under the Tax Relief, Unemployment Insurance Reauthorization, and Job Creation Act (TRA), but at the time of passage the exemption was temporary. In 2013, the American Taxpayer Relief Act made the TRA exemption permanent and indexed it to inflation.

compute a taxable value of money in the GRAT (equation (12.8)). This calculation is more difficult than the simple case because it involves valuing payments in excess of a (pre-determined but stochastic) hurdle rate. Different trusts will have different taxable income conversion factors. Conceptually, Huang's basic model is unchanged.

One disadvantage of trusts is that they can be hard to dismantle. (Many are *irrevocable*.) Of course, not being able to touch your money could be an advantage, but it is a form of liquidity constraint. The standard Merton models, and Huang's tax-adjusted extension of Merton's models, do not take into account illiquidity risk or constraints. In chapter 13, we discuss asset allocation models that do.

4.5. TAXES, CONSUMPTION, INVESTMENT, AND OTHER DECISIONS

Investors also use taxes to their advantage in timing consumption and investment decisions. Some of these can be pure tax arbitrages. A famous example is the pension tax arbitrage of Black (1980) and Tepper (1981). They show that a corporate defined pension fund allows a corporation to engage in a form of tax arbitrage by allowing the corporation (the plan sponsor) to borrow money, take a tax deduction for the interest, and then invest the proceeds in the pension plan. Pension funds are tax exempt and are a natural clientele for highly taxed assets like corporate bonds and U.S. Treasuries. The corporation gets a tax break for the pension fund contribution, and the pension fund gets to house highly taxed assets in a tax-efficient vehicle. Moreover, since the corporation is actually a stock, the Black-Tepper tax arbitrage allows the corporation to harvest an equity risk premium by investing in bonds!

Frank (2002) presents evidence that corporations do undertake the Black-Tepper strategy and shows that there is a positive relation between the amount held by the company's pension plan in bonds and the tax benefit. But the Black-Tepper strategy is vastly inefficiently taken up. Company pension plans seem to hold way too much equity, at least solely according to tax arguments. Perhaps this is optimal according to other arguments, as chapter 1 discusses.

Pension fund contributions are deductible by corporations. Firms strategically time the contributions when tax rates are high. This practice now has limits because contributions when the plan is more than 150% overfunded cannot be deducted under the 1987 Tax Act. The 1990 Tax Act also raised the excise tax to 50% on a corporation taking out assets from an overfunded pension plan. The same concept applies to individuals—deductions for contributions to charities, pensions, and so on are more valuable when tax rates are high.

On a final morbid note, the ultimate economic decision is timing one's death to minimize, or in some cases entirely avoid, income taxes. In the U.S. in 2010, there was no estate tax. Anecdotal evidence suggested that people tried to postpone their deaths until 2010 so their heirs could reap the windfall.[23] Serious academic studies show that people do time deaths to avoid taxes, either postponing or hastening death.[24] (Deaths are *elastic* with respect to taxes.) While death and taxes are both inevitable, people evidently do exercise some control over the one to minimize the other.

4.6. ARE INVESTORS TAX EFFICIENT?

No.

Tax-efficient allocation implies that we should see investors hold heavily taxed assets (corporate bonds and Treasuries) in tax-deferred accounts and lightly taxed assets (stocks) in taxable accounts. But investors generally don't do this. Poterba and Samwick (2002), Bergstresser and Poterba (2004), and others find that asset allocations in taxable and tax-deferred accounts are very similar. More than one-third of U.S. investors could cut their taxes by shifting heavily taxed assets to tax-deferred accounts and vice versa. The data show that wealthier households (and these are more heavily taxed) are more tax-efficient but not as tax efficient as they should be.

The Constantinides tax timing options imply that investors should be ready to realize losses and defer gains. Investors tend to do the opposite. Barber and Odean (2003) find that investors realize gains far more than they realize losses. They also locate large amounts of bonds in taxable accounts. Barber and Odean also find investors are far from being fully tax efficient.

An important question for many individual investors is whether they should allocate savings to paying off a mortgage early or to contribute to a tax-deferred account. Both are tax advantaged: the mortgage interest payment is tax deductible, and the pension saving is tax-exempt. Where should a household put that extra $1: paying off the mortgage or saving in a pension? According to Amromin, Huang, and Sialm (2007), the answer is that, assuming you have a low (optimally refinanced) mortgage interest rate, you should not pay off the mortgage early; instead, contribute to the pension. You maintain the benefit of the mortgage tax deduction and allow the pension to earn the pre-tax return (see equation (12.6)). Most households do the opposite, possibly because they are reluctant to participate in markets as lenders or borrowers; Shakespeare's adage "neither a borrower nor a lender be" costs them money.

Hopefully after reading this chapter, your investment portfolio will become more tax efficient.

---

[23] Saunders, L., "Rich Cling to Life to Beat Tax Man," *Wall Street Journal*, December 30, 2009.
[24] See Kopczuk and Slemrod (2003) and Gans and Leigh (2006).

5. Taxes as a Factor

Taxes clearly affect individuals' behavior, but do taxes affect asset prices? Originally there were two schools of thought. Miller and Scholes (1978—yes, the same Nobel Prize winning Scholes who asserted his own lack of tax expertise) said that although a given individual is affected by taxes, the average investor is not and taxes are not a factor. Intuitively, investors sort themselves into two groups: those with low tax rates, who tend to hold assets with high tax burdens such as high-dividend stocks, and highly taxed investors who hold assets with low tax burdens, such as stocks that pay no dividends.[25] In this way, taxes should become irrelevant for equilibrium pricing.

The other school of thought is that the representative investor is subject to taxes, and equity evaluations are affected (inversely) by tax burdens. Increases in tax burdens should be compensated by higher expected returns. The first model along these lines was by Brennan (1970). The empirical evidence has strongly settled the debate in favor of this camp. Taxes are a factor.

There are two ways taxes induce pricing effects.[26] There is a *dividend tax penalty*, where high dividend yield stocks are disadvantaged because of the higher rate of tax levied on dividends than on capital gains. In addition, stocks that have done well provide shareholders with accrued capital gains. Investors with too many shares of a stock that has appreciated in the past sell fewer shares than would otherwise be the case in order to avoid paying capital gains tax. There is no effect for investors buying because buying does not trigger capital gains. Thus prices of stocks with large accrued capital gains must be higher, and thus expected returns lower, to induce more selling by investors who are locked in. This is an example of *tax capitalization*, and it can lead to long-term reversals.

Sialm (2009) shows that tax effects exist in both the time series and cross-section of equity returns. Sialm computes an expected tax yield, which is the sum of taxes on dividends, short-term capital gains yields, and long-term capital gains yields. The capital gains yields component is small, as expected from the Constantinides (1983) tax-timing option. Sialm shows that when tax yields are high, aggregate market valuations are low. This is a time-series effect. In the cross section, Sialm shows that stocks with high tax yields (high dividend paying stocks) have higher returns. These returns are in excess of the Fama–French size, value, and momentum factors. This control is very important because stocks with high tax burdens are likely to have dividend payments, and these are more likely to be value stocks—which we know already have high returns (see chapter 7). Sialm

---

[25] Miller and Modigliani (1961) also predicted that investors in high tax brackets would be attracted to stocks with low dividend yields and vice versa. The paper does not focus on equilibrium with taxes; its major result is that the value of the firm is independent of the firm's dividend policy and was cited in the Nobel Prizes awarded to Modigliani in 1985 and Miller in 1990.

[26] This discussion follows Klein (2000).

finds that the stocks with the high tax burdens have average returns 2.5% higher, after controlling for the Fama–French effects, than stocks with low tax burdens.

The fact that taxes affect expected returns does not mean that the clientele sorting predicted by Miller and Scholes (1978)—where different types of investors are drawn to stocks with high or low dividend yields—does not occur. Institutions prefer to own stocks that pay dividends and individual investors are drawn to non-dividend paying stocks. Graham and Kumar (2006) show, however, that while taxes do induce clientele effects in individual investors, the effects are much smaller than non-tax-based investor characteristics such as age and wealth.

The average, representative investor is affected by taxes, so tax as a factor is ideally exploited by a tax-exempt investor. By definition, individuals buying stocks with high tax yields will be paying more tax. But tax-exempt investors will not, and they should use their comparative advantage.

6. Pre-Tax and After-Tax Returns Redux

Duncan's accountant is right in emphasizing after-tax returns over pre-tax returns. The latter are relevant for holding assets in a taxable account. But Duncan may be able to hold the assets in a tax-deferred account. Thus Duncan faces both an asset allocation problem and an asset location problem.

The overriding rule is to maximize savings in tax-deferred vehicles first and to hold assets with the most onerous tax treatments (corporate bonds and high dividend paying stocks) in tax-deferred vehicles. This aligns with popular industry advice, but to do it properly requires computing an adjustment to convert tax-deferred wealth to taxable wealth so that a standard asset allocation problem can be solved over taxable wealth. The optimal asset location decision implies we should not observe the same mix of stocks and bonds in tax-deferred and taxable accounts. Sadly, most investors are very far from being tax efficient.

Taxes are a factor for asset prices. The fact that muni bonds have lower yields, on average, is evidence that asset prices reflect tax effects. Munis have historically had little credit risk. Muni yield curves have never sloped downward and are more steeply sloped than Treasuries. But munis are extremely illiquid and the market is hugely inefficient.

Taxes also affect equity prices. Stocks with high tax burdens have higher returns than stocks with low tax burdens, in excess of those predicted by the standard value/growth, momentum, and other factor premiums.

CHAPTER 13

Illiquid Assets

Chapter Summary

After taking into account biases induced by infrequent trading and selection, it is unlikely that illiquid asset classes have higher risk-adjusted returns, on average, than traditional liquid stock and bond markets. However, there are significant illiquidity premiums within asset classes. Portfolio choice models incorporating illiquidity risk recommend only modest holdings of illiquid assets and that investors should demand high-risk premiums for investing in them.

1. Liquidating Harvard

No one thought it could happen to Harvard.[1]

In 2008, Harvard University's endowment—the world's largest—fell victim to the worldwide plunge in asset prices triggered by the financial crisis. In contrast to its 15% average annual returns since 1980, Harvard's endowment suffered its worst decline in history, falling 22% between July 1 and October 31, 2008. More than $8 billion in value had been wiped out in three months.

Concerned with the impending budget shortfall due to the collapse in the endowment, Harvard University President Drew Faust and Executive Vice President Edward Forst sounded the alarm by sending a memo to the Council of Deans on December 2, 2008. They asked each school to cut expenses and compensation and to scale back ambitions in the face of reduced revenue. As bad as the reported losses were, they cautioned that the true losses were even worse: "Yet even the sobering figure is unlikely to capture the full extent of actual losses for this period, because it does not reflect fully updated valuations in certain managed asset classes, most notably private equity and real estate."[2]

---

[1] This is based on "Liquidating Harvard," Columbia CaseWorks ID #100312.

[2] Financial Update to the Council of Deans, December 2, 2008, from Faust and Forst.

Harvard relied on endowment earnings to meet a large share of university expenses. In its fiscal year ending June 30, 2008, more than one-third of operating revenue came from endowment income. For some of the university's individual departments, the proportion was even higher: the Radcliffe Institute for Advanced Study derived 83% of its revenue from the endowment, the Divinity School 71%, and the Faculty of Arts and Sciences 52%.

Harvard Management Company (HMC), the funds manager of Harvard's endowment, was one of the early adopters of the *endowment model*, which recommends that long-term investors hold lots of illiquid, alternative assets, especially private equity and hedge funds. Advocated by David Swensen in his influential book, *Pioneering Portfolio Management*, the endowment model was based on the economic concept of diversification originally attributable to Harry Markowitz (1952; see chapter 3). Through diversification, a portfolio of many low-correlated assets has a risk-return trade-off superior to that of conventional portfolios consisting of only stocks and bonds. Swensen went further and advocated holding large proportions of illiquid private equity and hedge funds. Not only were these assets supposed to have low correlations to stocks and bonds, but they potentially carried an illiquidity risk premium.

Swensen argued that in liquid markets, the potential for making excess returns (or "alpha"; see chapter 10) was limited. In these markets, crowded with thousands of active managers vying for an edge, information is freely available and almost everyone has access to it. Illiquid asset markets, like venture capital and private equity, had large potential payoffs for investors who had superior research and management skills. Swensen argued that alpha was not competed away in illiquid assets because most managers have short horizons. University endowments, with their longer horizons, would seem to have an advantage in illiquid assets. Swensen recommended that long-term institutions with sufficient resources who can carefully select expert managers in alternative, illiquid assets could achieve superior risk-adjusted returns.

Dutifully following Swensen's advice, many endowments, including Harvard, loaded up with illiquid assets during the 1990s. In 2008, HMC held 55% of its portfolio in hedge funds, private equity, and real assets. Only 30% was in developed-world equities and fixed income, with the remainder of its portfolio in emerging-market equities and high-yield bonds.

In its desperate need for cash, HMC tried to sell some of its $1.5 billion private equity portfolio, which included marquee names such as Apollo Investment and Bain Capital. But buyers in secondary markets demanded huge discounts. Nina Munk, a journalist writing in *Vanity Fair*, recounts a surreal conversation between the CIO of HMC, Jane Mendillo, and a money manager specializing in alternative investments:[3]

[3] Nina Munk, "Rich Harvard, Poor Harvard," *Vanity Fair*, August 2009.

FUNDS MANAGER: Hey look, I'll buy it back from you. I'll buy my interest back.

MENDILLO: Great.

FUNDS MANAGER: Here, I think it's worth you know, today the [book] value is a dollar, so I'll pay you 50 cents.

MENDILLO: Then why would I sell it?

FUNDS MANAGER: Well, why are you? I don't know. You're the one who wants to sell, not me. If you guys want to sell, I'm happy to rip your lungs out. If you are desperate, I'm a buyer.

MENDILLO: Well, we're not desperate.

But in truth Harvard was desperate.

The reaction to Faust and Forst's cost-cutting memo was swift and sharp. Faculty, students, and alumni were incredulous. Alan Dershowitz, a famous professor at Harvard Law School, said:[4] "Apparently nobody in our financial office has read the story in Genesis about Joseph interpreting Pharaoh's dream. . . . You know, during the seven good years you save for the seven lean years."

All the short-term decisions for Harvard leaders and Mendillo at HMC were painful: slashing budgets, hiring freezes, and the postponement of the university's planned Allston science complex. Asset-liability management for Harvard University had failed. In the longer term, was the endowment model with illiquid, alternative assets still appropriate?

2. Illiquid Asset Markets

2.1. SOURCES OF ILLIQUIDITY

Vayanos and Wang (2012) provide a taxonomy of how illiquidity arises due to market imperfections:

1. Clientele effects and participation costs

    Entering markets can be costly; investors often must spend money, time, or energy to learn their way around and gain the necessary skills. In many large, illiquid asset markets, only certain types of investors with sufficient capital, expertise, and experience can transact.

2. Transaction costs

    These include commissions, taxes, and, for certain illiquid assets, the costs of due diligence, title transfers, and the like, as well as the bread-and-butter costs incurred for trading. It also includes fees paid to lawyers, accountants, and investment bankers. Academics sometimes assume that investors can

---

[4] Quoted by Munk, N., "Rich Harvard, Poor Harvard," *Vanity Fair*, August 2009.

trade whenever they want as long as they pay (sometimes a substantial) a transaction cost, but this is not always true because of . . .

3. Search frictions

For many assets, you need to search to find an appropriate buyer or seller. Only certain investors have the skills to value a complicated structured credit product, for example. Few investors have sufficient capital to invest in skyscrapers in major metropolitan areas. You might have to wait a long time to transact.

4. Asymmetric information

Markets can be illiquid because one investor has superior knowledge compared with other investors. Fearing they'll be fleeced, investors become reluctant to trade. When asymmetric information is extreme—all the products are lemons, and no one wants to buy a lemon—markets break down.[5] Many liquidity freezes are caused by these situations. The presence of asymmetric information also causes investors to look for nonpredatory counterparties, so information is a form of search friction.

5. Price impact

Large trades will move markets.

6. Funding constraints

Many of the investment vehicles used to invest in illiquid assets are highly leveraged. Even investing in a house requires substantial leverage for most consumers. If access to credit is impaired, investors cannot transact in illiquid asset markets.

2.2. CHARACTERISTICS OF ILLIQUID MARKETS

Illiquid asset markets are characterized by many, and sometimes all, of the market imperfections on this list. I refer to these effects as "illiquidity." On the basis of this reasoning, all assets are at least somewhat illiquid—even the large-cap equities that trade many times every second—but of course some assets are much more illiquid than others. Illiquidity manifests as infrequent trading, small amounts being traded, and low turnover. Intervals between trades in illiquid markets can extend to decades. Table 13.1, adapted from Ang, Papanikolaou, and Westerfield (2013), lists average intervals between trading and turnover for several asset classes.[6] First, note that . . .

---

[5] The lemons market was first described by George Akerlof (1970), who was awarded the Nobel Prize in 2001.

[6] See Ang, Papanikolaou, and Westerfield (2013) for additional references behind the numbers in Table 13.1 and other references in this section.

Table 13.1

Asset Class	Typical Time between Transactions	Annualized Turnover
Public Equities	Within seconds	Well over 100%
OTC (Pinksheet) Equities	Within a day, but many stocks over a week	Approx 35%
Corporate Bonds	Within a day	25–35%
Municipal Bonds	Approx 6 months, with 5% of muni bonds trading more infrequently than once per decade	Less than 10%
Private Equity	Funds last for 10 years; the median investment duration is 4 years; secondary trade before exit is relatively unusual	Less than 10%
Residential Housing	4–5 years, but ranges from months to decades	Approx 5%
Institutional Real Estate	8–11 years	Approx 7%
Institutional Infrastructure	50–60 years for initial commitment, some as long as 99 years	Negligible
Art	40–70 years	Less than 15%

Most Asset Classes Are Illiquid

Except for "plain-vanilla" public equities and fixed income, most asset markets are characterized by long periods, sometimes decades, between trades, and they have very low turnover. Even among stocks and bonds, some subasset classes are highly illiquid. Equities trading in pink-sheet over-the-counter markets may go for a week or more without trading. The average municipal bond trades only twice per year, and the entire muni-bond market has an annual turnover of less than 10% (see also chapter 11). In real estate markets, the typical holding period is four to five years for single-family homes and eight to eleven years for institutional properties. Holding periods for institutional infrastructure can be fifty years or longer, and works of art sell every forty to seventy years, on average. Thus most asset markets are illiquid in the sense that they trade infrequently and turnover is low.

Illiquid Asset Markets Are Large

The illiquid asset classes are large and rival the public equity market in size. In 2012, the market capitalization of the NYSE and NASDAQ was approximately

$17 trillion. The estimated size of the U.S. residential real estate market is $16 trillion, and the direct institutional real estate market is $9 trillion. In fact, the traditional public, liquid markets of stocks and bonds are smaller than the total wealth held in illiquid assets.

Investors Hold Lots of Illiquid Assets

Illiquid assets dominate most investors' portfolios. For individuals, illiquid assets represent 90% of their total wealth, which is mostly tied up in their house— and this is before counting the largest and least liquid component of individuals' wealth, human capital (see chapter 5). There are high proportions of illiquid assets in rich investors' portfolios, too. High net worth individuals in the United States allocate 10% of their portfolios to "treasure" assets like fine art and jewelry. This rises to 20% for high net worth individuals in other countries.[7]

The share of illiquid assets in institutional portfolios has increased dramatically over the past twenty years. The National Association of College and University Business Officers reported that, in 2011, the average endowment held a portfolio weight of more than 25% in alternative assets versus roughly 5% in the early 1990s. A similar trend is evident among pension funds. In 1995, they held less than 5% of their portfolios in illiquid alternatives, but today the figure is close to 20%.[8]

Liquidity Dries Up

Many normally liquid asset markets periodically become illiquid. During the 2008 to 2009 financial crisis, the market for commercial paper (or the *money market*)—usually very liquid –experienced "buyers' strikes" by investors unwilling to trade at any price. This was not the first time that the money market had frozen: trading in commercial paper also ceased when the Penn Central railroad collapsed in 1970. In both cases, the money market needed to be resuscitated by the Federal Reserve, which stepped in to restore liquidity.

During the financial crisis, illiquidity also dried up in the repo market (which allows investors to short bonds), residential and commercial mortgage-backed securities, structured credit, and the auction rate security market (a market for floating rate municipal bonds; see chapter 11). The last example was one of the first markets to become illiquid at the onset of the financial crisis in 2008 and at the time of writing in 2013 is still frozen. This market is dead in its present form.

Illiquidity crises occur regularly because liquidity tends to dry up during periods of severe market distress. The Latin American debt crisis in the 1980s, the Asian emerging market crisis in the 1990s, the Russian default crisis in 1998, and of course the financial crisis of 2008 to 2009 were all characterized

---

[7] See "Profit or Pleasure? Exploring the Motivations Behind Treasure Trends," Wealth Insights, Barclays Wealth and Investment Management, 2012.

[8] See Global Pension Asset Study, Towers Watson, 2011.

by sharply reduced liquidity, and in some cases liquidity completed evaporated in some markets. Major illiquidity crises have occurred at least once every ten years, most in tandem with large downturns in asset markets.

2.3. SUMMARY

Illiquid asset classes as a whole are larger than the traditional liquid, public markets of stocks and bonds. Even normally liquid markets periodically become illiquid. Most investors' wealth is tied up in illiquid assets. Thus asset owners must consider illiquidity risk in the construction of their portfolios. Doing this requires estimating risk-return trade-offs of illiquid assets, but measuring illiquid asset returns is not straightforward.

3. Illiquid Asset Reported Returns Are Not Returns

As Faust and Forst note in their memo to Harvard's Council of Deans, the true illiquid asset losses were greater than the reported ones, which leads us to an important corollary. *Reported illiquid asset returns are not returns.* Three key biases cause people to overstate expected returns and understate the risk of illiquid assets:

1. Survivorship bias,
2. Infrequent sampling, and
3. Selection bias.

In illiquid asset markets, investors must be highly skeptical of reported returns.

3.1. SURVIVORSHIP BIAS

Survivorship bias results from the tendency of poorly performing funds to stop reporting. Many of these funds ultimately fail—but we only rarely count their failures. This makes true illiquid asset returns worse than the reported data.

Here's an analogy: Suppose we wanted to test the hypothesis that smoking is bad for you. We're going to run our tests only on a sample of smokers that have puffed cigarettes for at least twenty years and are in good health today. Lo and behold, we conclude that this *select* group of smokers has a slightly better mortality rate than the general population. Is this a valid conclusion? Of course not! We have taken a *biased sample* of smokers blessed with longevity who are, so far, invulnerable to the detrimental effects of tobacco. If you were to take up smoking today, what are the odds that you would end up in this lucky group twenty years later? Or would you die from emphysema (or heart disease, or lung cancer, etc.) before the experiment could be repeated in twenty years' time?

Surviving funds in illiquid asset management are like those lucky, long-lived smokers. We observe the returns of surviving funds precisely because they are still around, and they are generally above average. All of the unlucky illiquid managers disappear and thus stop reporting returns. Of course, these nonsurvivors have below-average returns.[9] Industry analysis of buy-out funds, venture capital funds, or [insert your favorite illiquid asset class] tends to encompass only firms that have survived over the period of the analysis. But do we know that the small venture capital firm we're investing in today will be around ten years later? Existing firms and funds, by dint of being alive today, tend to have better-than-average track records. This produces reported returns of these illiquid assets that are too good to be true.

The only way to completely remove the effect of survivorship bias is to observe the entire population of funds. Unfortunately, *in illiquid asset markets we never observe the full universe.*

We can gauge the impact of survivorship bias with mutual funds, which are required to report their returns to the Securities and Exchange Commission because they fall under the 1940 Investment Act. This allows us to see the whole mutual fund universe, at least when the funds become registered, and to compute the effect of survivorship bias. (I provide more details in chapter 16.) Survivorship bias knocks at least 1% to 2% off the estimates of expected returns of mutual funds if we fail to include dead funds in our sample. However, industry often bases its conclusion only on funds in existence at a given point in time. When we separately compare defunct and live funds, the survivorship effect can go above 4%. Take these as lower bounds for illiquid asset managers. Chapters 17 and 18, covering hedge funds and private equity, respectively, show that managers of these investment vehicles often further massage (or manipulate) returns because standardized disclosure is not required and the underlying asset values are not readily observable. In chapter 17, I show that the effect of survivorship and reporting biases for hedge funds is even larger than for mutual funds.

There are data biases other than survivorship bias: for funds specializing in very illiquid assets, reporting returns to database vendors is almost always voluntary. This introduces *reporting biases*.[10] Survivorship bias results when your fund is in the database now and you stop reporting returns because you know your returns are going to be low. Reporting bias also occurs when you don't start reporting your returns in the first place because your fund never achieves a sufficiently attractive track record.

[9] Jorion and Goetzmann (1999) argue that survivorship bias partly explains the high equity premium (see chapter 8): Countries where we have long histories of equity returns are, by definition, those countries where equity investments have prospered.

[10] See Ang, Rhodes-Kropf and Zhao (2008).

3.2. INFREQUENT TRADING

With infrequent trading, estimates of risk—volatilities, correlations, and betas—
are too low when computed using reported returns.

To illustrate the effect of infrequent trading, consider Figure 13.2. Panel A plots
prices of an asset that starts at $1. Each circle denotes an observation at the end

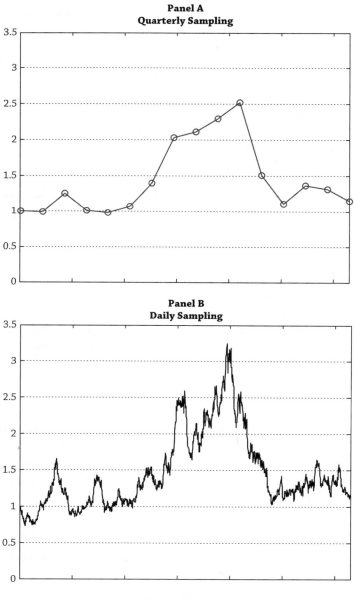

Figure 13.2

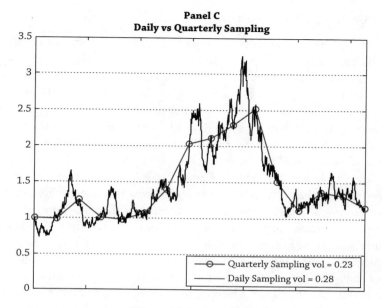

Panel C
Daily vs Quarterly Sampling

Figure 13.2 (continued)

of each quarter. I produced the graphs in Figure 13.2 by simulation and deliberately chose one sample path where the prices have gone up and then down to mirror what happened to equities during the 2000s' Lost Decade. The prices in Panel A appear to be drawn from a series that does not seem excessively volatile; the standard deviation of quarterly returns computed using the prices in Panel A is 0.23.

The true daily returns are plotted in Panel B of Figure 13.2 These are much more volatile than the ones in Panel B. Prices go below 0.7 and above 3.0 in Panel B with daily sampling, whereas the range of returns in Panel A is between 1.0 and 2.5 with quarterly sampling. The volatility of quarterly returns, computed from (overlapping) daily data in Panel B is 0.28, which is higher than the volatility of quarterly-sampled returns of 0.23 in Panel A.

For a full comparison, Panel C plots both the quarterly and daily sampled returns and just overlays Panels A and B in one picture. Infrequent sampling has caused the volatility estimate using the quarterly sampled returns to be too low. The same effect also happens with betas and correlations—risk estimates are biased downward by infrequent sampling.[11]

---

[11] See Geltner (1993) and Graff and Young (1996) for infrequent observation bias on the effect of betas and correlations, respectively. Geltner estimates that betas are understated by a factor of 0.5 for real estate returns. This is not a "small sample" problem, which goes away when our sample becomes very large; it is a "population" problem as the next section explains.

3.3. UNSMOOTHING RETURNS

To account for the infrequent trading bias, we need to go from Panel A of Figure 13.2, which samples quarterly, to Figure B, which samples daily. That is, the quarterly observed returns are too smooth, and we need to tease out the true, noisier returns. This process is called *unsmoothing* or *de-smoothing*, and the first algorithms to do this were developed by David Geltner (1991), a noted professor of real estate at MIT, and Stephen Ross and Randall Zisler (1991). Ross is the same professor who developed multifactor models (see chapter 6) and Zisler is a real estate professional who started his career as an academic. Ross and Zisler's work originally grew out of a series of reports written for Goldman Sachs in the late 1980s. This methodology has been extended in what is now an extensive literature.

Unsmoothing is a *filtering problem*. Filtering algorithms are normally used to separate signals from noise. When we're driving on a freeway and talking on a cell phone, our phone call encounters interference—from highway overpasses and tall buildings—or the reception becomes patchy when we pass through an area without enough cell phone towers. Telecommunication engineers use clever algorithms to enhance the signal, which carries our voice, against all the static. The full transmission contains both the signal and noise, and so the true signal is less volatile than the full transmission. Thus standard filtering problems are designed to remove noise. The key difference is that unsmoothing *adds* noise back to the reported returns to uncover the true returns.

To illustrate the Geltner-Ross-Zisler unsmoothing process, denote the true return at the end of period t as r_t, which is unobservable, and the reported return as r_t^*, which is observable. Suppose the observable returns follow

$$r_t^* = c + \phi r_{t-1}^* + \varepsilon_t, \tag{13.1}$$

where ϕ is the autocorrelation parameter and is less than one in absolute value. Equation (13.1) is an AR(1) process, where "AR" stands for autoregressive and the "1" denotes that it captures autocorrelation effects for one lag. Assuming the observed returns are functions of current and lagged true returns (this is called a "*transfer function*" or an "*observation equation*" in the parlance of engineers), we can use equation (13.1) to invert out the true returns. If the smoothing process only involves averaging returns for this period and the past period, then we can filter the observed returns to estimate the true returns, r_t, from observed returns, r_t^*, using:

$$r_t = \frac{1}{1-\phi} r_t^* - \frac{\phi}{1-\phi} r_{t-1}^*. \tag{13.2}$$

Equation (13.2) unsmooths the observed returns. If our assumption on the transfer function is right, the observed returns implied by equation (13.2) should have zero autocorrelation. Thus, the filter takes an autocorrelated series of observed returns and produces true returns that are close to IID (or not fore-castable). Note that the variance of the true returns is higher than the observed returns:

$$\text{var}(r_t) = \frac{1 + \phi^2}{1 - \phi^2}\text{var}(r_t^*) \geq \text{var}(r_t^*), \qquad (13.3)$$

since $|\phi| < 1$, so we are adding variance to the observed returns to produce estimates of the true returns.

Another way to interpret the unsmoothing process in equations (13.1) and (13.2) is that it is equivalent to assuming that the smoothed, or reported, return follows:

$$r_t^* = (1 - \phi)r_t + \phi r_{t-1}^*, \qquad (13.4)$$

and thus the unsmoothed return at time t, r_t^*, is a weighted average of the un-smoothed, or true, return at time t, r_t, and the lagged unsmoothed return in the previous period, r_{t-1}^*. Thus the smoothed returns only slowly update—they partly reflect what is happening in the true returns, but there are lags induced from the appraisal process.

The unsmoothing process has several important properties:

1. Unsmoothing affects only risk estimates and not expected returns.

   Intuitively, estimates of the mean require only the first and last price observation (with dividends take "total prices," which count reinvested dividends).[12] Smoothing spreads the shocks over several periods, but it still counts all the shocks. In Figure 13.2, we can see that the first and last observations are unchanged by infrequent sampling; thus unsmoothing changes only the volatility estimates.

2. Unsmoothing has no effect if the observed returns are uncorrelated.

   In many cases, reported illiquid asset returns are autocorrelated because illiquid asset values are appraised. The appraisal process induces smoothing because appraisers use, as they should, both the most recent and comparable sales (which are transactions) together with past appraised values (which are estimated, or perceived, values). The artificial smoothness from the appraisal process has pushed many in real estate to develop pure transactions-based, rather than appraisal-based indexes.[13] Autocorrelation also results from more

---

[12] Technically taking means of both the right and left sides in equation (13.2) results in the same means in large samples.

[13] This literature includes both repeat-sales methodologies (see Goetzmann (1992)) and con-structing indexes using only transactions (see Gatzlaff and Geltner (1998) and Fisher, Geltner, and Pollakowski (2007)). Some of these methods adjust for the different characteristics of individual homes in creating these indices, like whether an apartment or a house is for sale, whether it is

shady aspects of subjective valuation procedures—the reluctance of managers to mark to market in down markets.

In many cases, we expect the true illiquid asset returns to be autocorrelated as well.[14] Illiquid asset markets—like real estate, private equity, timber plantations, and infrastructure—are markets where information is not available to all participants, information does not spread rapidly, and capital cannot be immediately deployed into new investments. Informationally inefficient markets with slow-moving capital are characterized by persistent returns.[15]

3. Unsmoothing is an art.

The unsmoothing example in equations (13.1) and (13.2) uses the simplest possible autocorrelated process, an AR(1), to describe reported returns. Many illiquid assets have more than first-order lag effects. Real estate, for example, has a well-known fourth-order lag working with quarterly data arising from many properties being reappraised only annually.[16] A good unsmoothing procedure takes a time-series model that fits the reported return data well and then with a general transfer function assumption, the filter for true returns in equation (13.2) becomes a very complicated function of present and past lagged observed returns.[17] Doing this properly requires good statistical skills. It also requires underlying economic knowledge of the structure of the illiquid market to interpret what is a reasonable lag structure and to judge how much unsmoothing is required.

close to the water or far, or whether the house has two stories or one. These are called *hedonic* adjustments. These methods have been applied to create indexes in other illiquid markets, like art (Goetzmann (1993) and Moses and Mei (2002)), stamps (Dimson and Spænjers (2011)), and wine (Krasker (1979) and Masset and Weisskopf (2010)). The aggregation process in constructing indexes of illiquid asset returns induces further smoothing. Indexes combine many individual indications of value, either market transactions or appraised values, and typically the values are appraised at different points throughout the year. Note that if $\phi = 0$, then equations (2) and (3) coincide and unsmoothed returns are exactly the same as reported returns. Figure 13.2, which shows the effects of infrequent observations, is produced with a year-on-year autocorrelation of 0.4.

[14] When the true returns are autocorrelated, the horizon matters in stating volatilities, correlations, and Sharpe ratios. From point 1, the means are unaffected. See Lo (2002) for formulas to convert the risk measures for different horizons.

[15] See Duffie (2010) and Duffie and Strulovici (2012).

[16] This is noted in the seminal Geltner (1991) and Ross and Zisler (1991) papers.

[17] We want an ARMA(p, q) model, which captures the effect of p lagged autocorrelated terms (the "AR" effect for p lags) and where innovations to those returns in past periods continue to have an effect on present returns. The latter are referred to as moving average terms (the "MA" effects for q lags). Both Geltner (1991) and Ross and Zisler (1991) consider richer time-series processes than just an AR(1). Okunev and White (2003) and Getmansky, Lo, and Makarov (2004) develop unsmoothing algorithms to hedge fund returns with higher-order autocorrelation corrections.

Unsmoothed Real Estate Returns

To illustrate the effects of unsmoothing, Figure 13.3 plots direct real estate returns from the National Council of Real Estate Investment Fiduciaries (NCREIF),
which constructs an institutional property index from data reported by its
members.[18] Because this is an appraisal index, NCREIF real estate returns are
highly autocorrelated. From March, 1978 to December, 2011, the first-order autocorrelation of NCREIF returns is 0.78. The raw reported data is shown in the solid
line. I graph unsmoothed returns in the squares applying the filter of equations
(13.1) and (13.2). All returns are at the quarterly frequency.

Unsmoothing produces a dramatic effect. The minimum reported return during the real estate downturn in the early 1990s is –5.3% during the quarter
ending December 1991. The corresponding unsmoothed return is –22.6%. During
the financial crisis, NCREIF returns reached a low of –8.3% in December 2008.
The unsmoothed return during this quarter is –36.3%. The volatility of the raw
NCREIF returns is 2.25% per quarter, whereas the volatility of the unsmoothed
returns is 6.26% per quarter. This approximates the volatility of stock returns,
which is around 7.5% per quarter. Correlation (and hence beta) estimates are
also affected by unsmoothing: the correlation of raw NCREIF returns with the
S&P 500 is 9.2% and this rises to 15.8% once the unsmoothing correction is
applied.

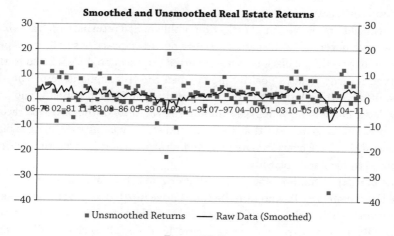

Figure 13.3

[18] Unsmoothing corrections produce similar effects in other illiquid markets. Campbell (2008),
for example, estimates that unsmoothing increases the volatility of art market returns from 6.5%
to 11.5%.

3.4. SELECTION BIAS

Sample selection bias results from the tendency of returns only to be observed when underlying asset values are high.

Buildings tend to be sold when their values are high—otherwise, many sellers postpone sales until property values recover. This causes more transactions to be observed when the underlying real estate values are high.

In private equity, selection bias is acute. In buyout funds, companies are taken public only when stock values are high. Many venture capital investments are structured over multiple rounds. Better-performing companies tend to raise more money in more rounds. The venture capitalist tends to sell a small company, and the transaction is recorded, when the company's value is high. Distressed companies are usually not formally liquidated, and these "zombie" companies are often left as shell companies. When observing old companies without recent transactions, it is not clear whether these companies are alive and well or whether they are zombies.

To illustrate the selection bias problem, consider Figure 13.4, which is adapted from Korteweg and Sorensen (2010). Panel A shows the full universe of returns of an illiquid asset marked by dots. These returns (on the *y*-axis) are plotted contemporaneous with market returns (on the *x*-axis). In the full universe, there is no alpha, and the intercept of the line summarizing the relationship between the illiquid asset and the market goes through the origin (this line is called the security market line (SML; see chapter 6). The slope of the SML is the beta of the illiquid asset and is a measure of risk.

Panel B illustrates the sample selection problem. Bad returns, which are shaded gray, are not observed in the databases—we record transactions only when prices are high. Now only the black dots are reported. An estimated SML fitted to these observed returns yields a positive alpha when the true alpha is zero. The slope of the fitted SML is flatter than the slope of the true SML in panel A, and hence we underestimate beta. When we compute the volatility of the observed returns, we only count those returns that are high, and so the volatility estimate is biased downward. Thus we overestimate expected return, and we underestimate risk as measured by beta and volatility.

The statistical methodology for addressing selection bias was developed by James Heckman (1979), who won the Nobel Prize in 2000 for inventing these and other econometric techniques. Studies that use models to correct for these biases do not take such an extreme view as Figure 13.4 they allow the threshold above which returns are observed to vary over time and depend on company or property-level characteristics.[19] The model of risk is sometimes extended to multifactor

---

[19] See also Cochrane (2005) for selection bias models applied to venture capital and Fisher et al. (2003) for real estate. Korteweg, Kräussl, and Verwijmeren (2012) find that correcting for selection bias decreases the Sharpe ratio of art from 0.4 to 0.1.

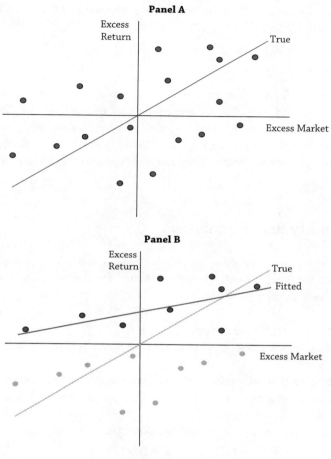

Figure 13.4

models (see chapters 6 and 7), rather than just using the market portfolio as the sole risk factor.

The effect of selection bias can be enormous. Cochrane (2005) estimates an alpha for venture capital log returns of over 90% not taking into account selection bias, which reduces to −7% correcting for the bias. Korteweg and Sorensen (2005) estimate that expected returns for the same asset class are reduced downwards by 2% to 5% per month (arithmetic returns) taking into account selection bias. The effect of selection bias in real estate is smaller, perhaps because the underlying volatility of real estate returns is lower than private equity. Fisher et al. (2003) implement selection bias corrections for real estate. They estimate that average real estate returns reduce from 1.7% to 0.3% and standard deviation estimates increase by a factor of 1.5. The small means of real estate returns are due to their sample period of 1984 to 2001, which includes the real estate downturn in the early 1990s and in the early 2000s. They miss the bull market in real estate during the mid-2000s.

3.5. SUMMARY

Treat reported illiquid asset returns very carefully. Survivors having above-average returns and infrequent observations, and the tendency of illiquid asset returns to be reported only when underlying valuations are high, will produce return estimates that are overly optimistic and risk estimates that are biased downward. Put simply, reported returns of illiquid assets are too good to be true.

4. Illiquidity Risk Premiums

Illiquidity risk premiums compensate investors for the inability to access capital immediately. They also compensate investors for the withdrawal of liquidity during illiquidity crises.

Harvesting Illiquidity Risk Premiums
There are four ways an asset owner can capture illiquidity premiums:

1. By setting a *passive allocation* to *illiquid asset classes*, like real estate;
2. By choosing securities within an asset class that are more illiquid, that is by engaging in *liquidity security selection*;
3. By acting as a *market maker* at the individual security level; and
4. By engaging in *dynamic strategies* at the aggregate portfolio level.

Economic theory states that there should be a premium for bearing illiquidity risk, although it can be small.[20] In models where illiquidity risk has small or no effect on prices, illiquidity washes out across individuals. A particular individual may be affected by illiquidity—illiquidity can crimp his consumption or affect his asset holdings (as in the asset allocation model with illiquidity risk that I present below)—but other agents will not be constrained, or they trade at different times. Different agents share risk among themselves, which mutes the impact of illiquidity. Thus in equilibrium the effects of illiquidity can be negligible.[21]

Whether the illiquidity risk premium is large or small is an empirical question.

[20] This large literature begins with a seminal contribution by Demsetz (1968). See summary articles by Hasbrouck (2007) and Vayanos and Wang (2012).

[21] For models of this kind, see Constantinides (1986), Vayanos (1998), Gârleanu (2009), and Buss, Uppal, and Vilkov (2012). In contrast, Lo, Mamaysky, and Wang (2004) and Longstaff (2009), among others, argue that the illiquidity premium should be large.

4.1. ILLIQUIDITY RISK PREMIUMS ACROSS ASSET CLASSES

Figure 13.5 is from Antti Ilmanen's (2011) wonderful book, *Expected Returns*, and plots average returns on illiquidity estimates. The average returns are computed from (reported) data over 1990 to 2009. The illiquidity estimates represent Ilmanen's opinions. Some private equity investments are more liquid than certain hedge funds, and some infrastructure investments are much less liquid than private equity, so it is hard to pigeon-hole these asset classes in terms of illiquidity. Nevertheless, Figure 13.5 seems to suggest a positive relation between how illiquid an asset class is and its expected return. Figure 13.5 represents "conventional" views among most market participants that there is a reward to bearing illiquidity across asset classes.

This conventional view is flawed for the following reasons:

1. Illiquidity biases.

    As Section 3 shows, reported data on illiquid assets cannot be trusted. The various illiquidity biases—survivorship, sampling at infrequent intervals, and selection bias—result in the expected returns of illiquid asset classes being overstated using raw data.

2. Ignores risk.

    Illiquid asset classes contain far more than just illiquidity risk. Adjusting for these risks makes illiquid asset classes far less compelling. Chapter 10 showed that the NCREIF real estate index (despite the artificial rosiness of its raw returns) is beaten by a standard 60% equity and 40% bond portfolio. Chapters 17 and 18 will show that the average hedge fund and private equity fund, respectively, provide zero expected excess returns. In particular, after adjusting for risk, most investors are better off investing in the S&P 500 than in a portfolio of private equity funds.

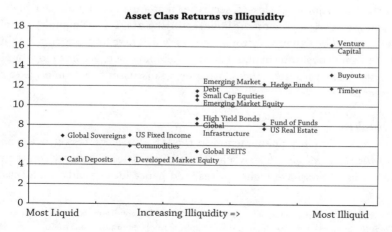

Figure 13.5

3. There is no "market index" for illiquid asset classes.

No investor receives the returns on illiquid indexes. An asset owner *never* receives the NCREIF return on a real estate portfolio, for example. The same is true for most hedge fund indexes and private equity indexes. In liquid public markets, large investors can receive index market returns and pay close to zero in fees. In contrast, NCREIF is not investable as it is impossible to buy all the underlying properties in that index. Since all asset owners own considerably fewer properties than the thousands included in NCREIF, they face far more idiosyncratic risk. While this large amount of idiosyncratic risk can boost returns in some cases, it can also lead to the opposite result. Returns to illiquid asset investing can be far below a reported index.

4. You cannot separate factor risk from manager skill.

Tradeable and cheap index funds in bond and stock markets allow investors to separate systematic returns (or factor returns; see chapter 7) from management prowess. In illiquid markets, no such separation is possible: *investing in illiquid markets is always a bet on management talent*. The agency issues in illiquid asset markets are first-order problems, and I discuss them in Part III of this book. Agency problems can, and often do, overwhelm any advantages that an illiquidity risk premium may bring.

Taking into account data biases, the evidence for higher average returns as asset classes become more illiquid is decidedly mixed, as Ang, Goetzmann, and Schaefer (2011) detail.[22] But while there do not seem to be significant illiquidity risk premiums *across* classes, there are large illiquidity risk premiums *within* asset classes.

4.2. ILLIQUIDITY RISK PREMIUMS WITHIN ASSET CLASSES

Within all the major asset classes, securities that are more illiquid have higher returns, on average, than their more liquid counterparts. These illiquidity premiums can be accessed by dynamic factor strategies which take long positions in illiquid assets and short positions in liquid ones. As illiquid assets become more liquid, or vice versa, the investor rebalances. (Chapter 14 discusses how to allocate to these and other factors.)

U.S. Treasuries

A well-known liquidity phenomenon in the U.S. Treasury market is the *on-the-run/off-the-run bond spread*. Newly auctioned Treasuries (which are "on the run") are more liquid and have higher prices, and hence lower yields, than seasoned

---

[22] Nevertheless, there are common components in illiquidity conditions across asset classes: when U.S. Treasury bond markets are illiquid, for example, many hedge funds tend to do poorly. See, for example, Hu, Pan, and Wang (2012).

Treasuries (which are "off the run").[23] The spread between these two types of bonds varies over time reflecting liquidity conditions in Treasury markets.[24] (For more details, see chapter 9.)

There were pronounced illiquidity effects in Treasuries during the 2008 to 2009 financial crisis. Treasury bonds and notes are identical, except that the U.S. Treasury issues bonds with original maturities of twenty to thirty years and notes originally carry maturities of one to ten years. But after ten years, a Treasury bond originally carrying a twenty-year maturity is the same as a Treasury note. If the maturities are the same, whether this particular security is bond or a note should make no difference. During the financial crisis Treasury bond prices with the same maturity as Treasury notes had prices that were more than 5% lower—these are large illiquidity effects in one of the world's most important and liquid markets.[25]

Corporate Bonds

Corporate bonds that trade less frequently or have larger bid–ask spreads have higher returns. Chen, Lesmond, and Wei (2007) find that illiquidity risk explains 7% of the variation across yields of investment-grade bonds. Illiquidity accounts for 22% of the variation in junk bond yields; for these bonds, a one basis point rise in bid–ask spreads increases yield spreads by more than two basis points.[26]

Equities

A large literature finds that many illiquidity variables predict returns in equity markets, with less liquid stocks having higher returns.[27] These variables include bid–ask spreads, volume, volume signed by whether trades are buyer or seller initiated, turnover, the ratio of absolute returns to dollar volume (commonly called the "Amihud measure" based on his paper of 2002), the price impact of large trades, informed trading measures (which gauge adverse, informed trading; see below), quote size and depth, the frequency of trades, how often there are "zero" returns (in more liquid markets returns will bounce up and down), and return autocorrelations (which are a measure of stale prices).[28] These are all illiquidity characteristics, which are properties unique to an individual stock. There are

---

[23] The on-the-run bonds are more expensive because they can be used as collateral for borrowing funds in the repo market. This is called *"specialness."* See Duffie (1996).

[24] See Goyenko, Subrahmanyam, and Ukhov (2011).

[25] See Musto, Nini, and Schwarz (2011).

[26] See also chapter 9, Bao, Pan, and Wang (2011), Lin, Wang, and Wu (2011), and Dick-Nielsen, Feldhutter, and Lando (2012).

[27] See the summary article by Amihud, Mendelson, and Pedersen (2005).

[28] Sorting stocks on all these variables results in spreads in average returns. But some of these illiquidity measures produce spreads in expected returns opposite to an illiquidity risk premium. Stocks with higher than average (normalized) volume, for example, tend to have lower future returns as shown by Gervais, Kaniel, and Mingelgrin (2001).

also illiquidity risk betas. These are covariances of stock returns with illiquidity measures, like market illiquidity or signed volume.

Estimates of illiquidity risk premiums in the literature range between 1% and 8% depending on which measure of illiquidity is used. However, Ben-Rephael, Kadan, and Wohl (2008) report that these equity illiquidity premiums have diminished considerably—for some illiquidity measures the risk premiums are now zero! In pink sheet stock markets, which are over-the-counter equity markets, Ang, Shtauber, and Tetlock (2013) find an illiquidity risk premium of almost 20% compared to about 1% for comparable listed equities.

Illiquid Assets

There are higher returns to hedge funds that are more illiquid, in the sense that they place more restrictions on the withdrawal of capital (called lockups, see chapter 17) or for hedge funds whose returns fall when liquidity dries up.[29] Franzoni, Nowak, and Phalippou (2012) report that there are significant illiquidity premiums in private equity funds—typically 3% (for further details, see chapter 18). In real estate, Liu and Qian (2012) construct illiquidity measures of price impact and search costs for U.S. office buildings. They find a 10% increase in these illiquidity measures leads to a 4% increase in expected returns.

Why Illiquidity Risk Premiums Manifest within but Not across Asset Classes

To my knowledge, we have yet to develop formal equilibrium models explaining the large illiquidity risk premiums within asset classes but not across asset classes.

Perhaps the reason is limited integration across asset classes. There are significant impediments to switching capital and investment strategies seamlessly even across liquid stock and bond markets.[30] Investors put asset classes into different silos and rarely treat them consistently as a whole. This happens on both the sell-side, where fixed income, equity desks, and other divisions rarely talk with each other, and on the buy-side, where each asset class is managed by separate divisions. (Canada Pension Plan's factor investing strategy is a notable exception to this, as I discuss in chapter 14.) The potential mispricing of illiquidity across asset classes could reflect institutional constraints, slow-moving capital, and limits to arbitrage.[31]

On the other hand, perhaps asset class illiquidity risk premiums might be small because investors overpay for illiquid asset classes; they chase the illusion of higher returns and bid up the prices of these illiquid assets until the illiquidity premiums to go away. Lack of integrated asset class markets cause investors to make ill-informed decisions for illiquid asset classes. In contrast, within asset classes— especially the more liquid stock and bond markets—illiquidity-shy investors are

[29] See Aragon (2007) and Sadka (2010), respectively.

[30] See Kapadia and Pu (2012) for evidence of lack of integration across stock and bond markets.

[31] See Merton (1987), Duffie (2010), and Shleifer and Vishny (1997), respectively.

willing to pay for the privilege to trade as soon as they desire. As investors compete within an asset class, they covet and pay up for liquidity.

4.3. MARKET MAKING

A market maker supplies liquidity by acting as an intermediary between buyers and sellers.[32] Liquidity provision is costly. Market makers need capital to withstand a potential onslaught of buy or sell orders, and at any time they can be transacting with investors who have superior information. In compensation for these costs, market makers buy at low prices and sell at prices around "fair value." Investors transacting with the market maker pay the *bid–ask spread*.

In liquid stock and bond markets, market making is now synonymous with high frequency trading by investors who build massive computer infrastructure to submit buy and sell orders within fractions of a second. More than 70% of dollar trading volume on U.S. equity exchanges is believed due to high frequency traders.[33] Many successful hedge funds specialize in high frequency trading (see chapter 17).

Many asset owners cannot collect illiquidity risk premiums by building high-frequency trading systems, nor would they wish to enter this business (directly or indirectly). But there is a way large asset owners can do a low-frequency version of market making.

Dimensional Funds Advisors (DFA) is a funds management company that started in 1981 by specializing in small-cap equities. DFA's strategies have deep roots in academic factor models, and its founders, David Booth and Rex Sinquefield, roped in the big guns of the finance literature, Fama, French, and others, in building the company. From the start, DFA positioned itself as a liquidity provider of small stocks, and market making was an integral part of its investment strategy.[34] When other investors seek to urgently offload large amounts of small stocks, DFA takes the other side and buys at a discount. Similarly, DFA offers small-cap equities at a premium to investors who demand immediate liquidity.

Large asset owners, like sovereign wealth funds and large pension funds, are in a position to act as liquidity providers, especially in more illiquid markets. They can accept large blocks of bonds, shares, or even portfolios of property at discount and sell these large blocks at premiums. They can do this by calculating limits within their (benchmark tracking error) constraints on how much they are willing to transact. That is, they can provide liquidity in different securities up to a certain amount so that they do not stray too far from their benchmarks. Buyers and sellers will come to them as they develop reputations for providing liquidity.

---

[32] O'Hara (1995) provides a summary of theoretical models of market making.

[33] See Zhang (2010).

[34] See Keim (1999) and the Harvard Business School case study, Dimensional Fund Advisors, 2002, written by Randolph Cohen.

Secondary Markets for Private Equity and Hedge Funds

Exchanges for secondary transactions in hedge funds and private equity have sprung up, but these markets are still very thin.[35] Many transactions do not take place on organized secondary market platforms.

There are two forms of secondary markets in private equity. First, in secondary (and tertiary) market buyout markets, private equity firms trade private companies with each other. These markets have blossomed: in 2005, secondary buyouts represented around 15% of all private equity buy-out deals.[36] From the perspective of asset owners (limited partners [LPs]), this market provides no exit opportunities from the underlying private equity funds and is at worst a merry-go-round of private equity firms swapping companies in circular fashion. At best, more transactions at market prices (assuming there is no finagling between the transacting funds) allow asset owners to better value their illiquid investments. The LPs are still stuck in the fund, but they might receive some cash when a company in their fund's portfolio is sold to another private equity firm.

Secondary markets for LPs, which allow them to exit from private equity funds, are much smaller and more opaque. Even industry participants acknowledge this market "still remains relatively immature ... and still represents a very small percentage of the primary market."[37] Bid-ask spreads in these transactions are enormous. As Cannon (2007) notes, the secondary market for LPs was dominated in the 1990s by distressed sellers. Specialized firms on the other side of these deals got discounts of 30% to 50%; there was a reason these firms were called "vultures." In the 2000s, discounts fell to below 20% but shot up during the financial crisis. Harvard University found this out when it tried to disinvest in private equity funds during 2008 and faced discounts of 50%.

Discounts for hedge funds are much smaller than private equity. This reflects the fact that hedge funds investors can, in most cases, access capital at predetermined dates after lockups have expired and notice requirements have been satisfied (unless the hedge fund imposes gates). Reflecting this greater underlying liquidity, hedge fund discounts in secondary markets in 2007 and 2008 were around 6% to 8%.[38] (A few hedge funds that are closed to new investors actually trade at premiums.)

The nascent secondary markets for private equity and hedge funds are tremendous opportunities for large asset owners to supply liquidity. Secondary private equity is like second-hand cars that are still brand new. When you drive a new car off the lot, it immediately depreciates by a quarter, even though it is exactly the same as a car sitting in the dealer's inventory. Secondary private equity is still private equity, and you can get it a lot cheaper than direct from the dealer.

---

[35] An academic study of this market is Kleymenova, Talmor, and Vasvari (2012).

[36] Report of the Committee on Capital Markets Regulation, 2006,

[37] From the introduction to Luytens (2008) written by Andrew Sealey and Campbell Lutyens.

[38] See Ramadorai (2012).

Adverse Selection

A market maker faces a risk that a buyer has nonpublic information, and the stock is selling at a price that is too high or too low relative to true, fundamental value. A buyer knowing that the stock will increase in value will continue to buy and increase the price. In this case, the market maker has sold too early and too low. This is *adverse selection*. Glosten and Milgrom (1985) and Kyle (1985)—the papers that started the market-making microstructure literature—developed theories of how the bid–ask spread should be set to incorporate the effects of adverse selection. DFA provides some examples of how to counter adverse selection. To avoid being exploited, DFA trades with counterparties that fully disclose their information on stocks. At the same time, DFA itself operates in a trustworthy way by not front running or manipulating prices.[39]

4.4. REBALANCING

The last way an asset owner can supply liquidity is through dynamic portfolio strategies. This has a far larger impact on the asset owner's total portfolio than liquidity security selection or market making because it is a top-down asset allocation decision (see chapter 14 for factor attribution).

   Rebalancing is the simplest way to provide liquidity, as well as the foundation of all long-horizon strategies (see chapter 4). Rebalancing forces asset owners to buy at low prices when others want to sell. Conversely, rebalancing automatically sheds assets at high prices, transferring them to investors who want to buy at elevated levels. Since rebalancing is counter-cyclical, it supplies liquidity. Dynamic portfolio rules, especially those anchored by simple valuation rules (see chapters 4 and 14), extend this further—as long as they buy when others want to sell and vice versa. It is especially important to rebalance illiquid asset holdings too, when given the chance (see also below).

   Purists will argue that rebalancing is not strictly liquidity provision; rebalancing is an asset management strategy. Rebalancing, in fact, can only occur in the context of liquid markets. But prices exhibit large declines often because of blowouts in asymmetric information, or because funding costs rapidly increase so that many investors are forced to offload securities—some of the key elements giving rise to illiquidity listed at the start of Section 2. Brunnermeier (2009) argues that these effects played key roles in the meltdown during the financial crisis. In the opposite case, rebalancing makes available risky assets to new investors, potentially with lower risk aversions than existing clientele or those who chase past high returns, or to investors who load up on risky assets when prices are high because they have abundant access to leverage and they perceive asymmetric information is low. In this general framework, *rebalancing provides liquidity*.

---

[39] See MacKenzie (2006).

Large asset owners give up illiquidity premiums by sheepishly tracking standard indexes. When indexes change their constituents, asset owners demand liquidity as they are forced to follow these changes. Index inclusion and exclusion induce price effects of 3% to 5%, and these effects have become stronger in more recent data.[40] Large asset owners should be collecting index reconstitution premiums instead of paying them. They can do this by using their own proprietary benchmarks. Candidate indexes could emphasize illiquidity security characteristics but more generally would be built around harvesting factor risk premiums (see chapter 14). Even an index without illiquidity tilts allows asset owners to harvest a liquidity premium collected from all the other investors forced to track standard indexes.

4.5. SUMMARY

Of all the four ways to collect an illiquidity premium: (i) holding passive allocations to illiquid asset classes, (ii) holding less liquid securities within asset classes, (iii) market making at the individual security level, and (iv) dynamic rebalancing at the aggregate level; the last of these is simplest to implement and has the greatest impact on portfolio returns.

5. Portfolio Choice with Illiquid Assets

In deciding on how much of their portfolios to devote to illiquid assets, investors face many considerations specific to their own circumstances. Investors have different horizons. Illiquid markets don't have tradeable indices, so investors have to find talented active portfolio managers. Then they face agency issues and evaluating and monitoring portfolio managers requires skill. Thus the premium for bearing illiquidity risk might be individual-specific. Computing these illiquidity premiums requires asset allocation models with liquid and illiquid assets. These models also prescribe an optimal amount of illiquid assets to hold.

Practitioners generally use one-period investment models—usually the restrictive Markowitz (1952) mean-variance model with ad hoc adjustments (yes, most of the industry is still using models from the 1950s; see chapter 3)—which are inappropriate for illiquid asset investing. The fact that you cannot trade an illiquid asset now but will do so in the future makes illiquid asset investing a dynamic, long-horizon problem. There are two important aspects of illiquidity—large transaction costs and long times between trading—that have been captured in portfolio choice models with illiquid assets.[41]

---

[40] See chapter 15 and the literature on index reconstitution effects summarized by Ang, Goetzmann, and Schaeffer (2011).

[41] Parts of this are based on Ang (2011) and Ang and Sorensen (2012).

5.1. ASSET ALLOCATION WITH TRANSACTIONS COSTS

George Constantinides (1986) was the first to develop an asset allocation model where the investor had to pay transaction costs. Selling $100 of equities, for example, results in a final position of $90 with 10% transactions costs. Not surprisingly, the investor trades infrequently—to save on transactions costs. Constantinides proved that the optimal strategy is to trade whenever risky asset positions hit upper or lower bounds. Within these bounds is an interval of no trading. The no-trading band straddles the optimal asset allocation from a model that assumes you can continuously trade without frictions (the Merton 1971 model; see chapter 4).[42]

The no-trade interval is a function of the size of the transactions costs and the volatility of the risky asset. Constantinides estimates that for transactions costs of 10%, there are no-trade intervals greater than 25% around an optimal holding of 25% for a risky asset with a 35% volatility. (I bet Harvard wished it could have received just a 10% discount when it tried to sell its private equity investments in 2008.) That is, the asset owner would not trade between (0%, 50%)—indeed, very large fluctuations in the illiquid asset position. Illiquid asset investors should expect to rebalance very infrequently.

Constantinides' model can be used to compute an illiquidity risk premium, defined as the expected return of an illiquid asset required to bring the investor to the same level of utility as in a frictionless setting. This is the risk premium the investor demands to bear the transactions costs and is a certainty equivalent calculation (see chapter 2). For transaction costs of 15% or more, the required risk premium exceeds 5%. Compare this value with (the close to) zero additional excess returns, on average, of the illiquid asset classes in data.

A major shortcoming of the transaction costs models is that they assume trade is always possible by paying a cost. This is not true for private equity, real estate, timber, or infrastructure. Over a short horizon, there may be no opportunity to find a buyer. Even if a counterparty can be found, you need to wait for due diligence and legal transfer to be completed and then the counterparty can get cold feet.[43] Many liquid assets also experienced liquidity freezes during the financial crisis where no trading—at any price—was possible because no buyers could be found.

---

[42] Chapter 4 discusses extensions of Constantinides (1986) to double bands, contingent bands, and rebalancing to the edge or center of the bands.

[43] For some illiquid assets, investors may not be even willing to transact immediately for one cent; some investments do not have liability limited at zero. For example, on June 30, 2008, a real estate investment by CalPERS was valued at negative $300 million! See Corkery, M., C. Karmin, R. L. Rundle, and J. S. Lublin, "Risky, Ill-Timed Land Deals Hit CalPERS," *Wall Street Journal*, Dec. 17, 2008.

5.2. ASSET ALLOCATION WITH INFREQUENT TRADING

In Ang, Papanikolaou, and Westerfield (2013), I develop an asset allocation model in which the investor can transact illiquid assets only at randomly occurring liquidity events. This notion of illiquidity is that usually illiquid assets are just that—illiquid and cannot be traded. But when the liquidity event arrives, investors can trade.

I model the arrival of liquidity events by a Poisson arrival process with intensity λ. The interval between liquidity events is $1/\lambda$. For real estate or private equity, intervals between trading would occur every ten years or so, so $\lambda = 1/10$. As λ increases to infinity, the opportunities to rebalance become more and more frequent and in the limit approach the standard Merton (1981) model where trading occurs continuously. Thus λ indexes a range of illiquidity outcomes.

Poisson arrival events have been used to model search-based frictions since Peter Diamond (1982), who won his Nobel Prize in 2010. The following year, he was nominated to serve on the Federal Reserve Board of Governors, but Republican opposition blocked his confirmation.

Illiquidity risk causes the investor to behave in a more risk-averse fashion toward both liquid and illiquid assets. Illiquidity risk induces time-varying, endogenous risk aversion. Harvard discovered in 2008 that although it is wealthy, it cannot "eat" illiquid assets. Illiquid wealth and liquid wealth are not the same; agents can only consume liquid wealth. Thus the solvency ratio of illiquid to liquid wealth affects investors' portfolio decisions and payout rules—it becomes a state variable that drives investors' effective risk aversion.

The takeaways from the Ang, Papanikolaou and Westerfield model are:

Illiquidity Markedly Reduces Optimal Holdings
Start with the bottom line in Panel A of Table 13.6, which reports a baseline calibration where the investor holds 59% in a risky asset that can always be traded. This weight is close to the standard 60% equity allocation held by many institutions. As we go up the rows, the asset becomes more illiquid. If the risky asset can be traded on average every six months, which is the second to last line, the optimal holding of the illiquid asset contingent on the arrival of the liquidity event is 44%. When the average interval between trades is five years, the optimal allocation is 11%. For ten years, this reduces to 5%. Illiquidity risk has a huge effect on portfolio choice.

Rebalance Illiquid Assets to Positions Below the Long-Run Average Holding
In the presence of infrequent trading, illiquid asset wealth can vary substantially and is right-skewed. Suppose the optimal holding of illiquid assets is 0.2 when the liquidity event arrives. The investor could easily expect illiquid holdings to vary from 0.1 to 0.35, say, during nonrebalancing periods. Because of the right-skew, the average holding of the illiquid asset is 0.25, say, and is greater than the optimal

Table 13.6

Panel A	
Average Time Between Liquidity Events (or Average Turnover)	*Optimal Rebalance Value*
10 Years	0.05
5 Years	0.11
2 Years	0.24
1 Year	0.37
$\frac{1}{2}$ Year	0.44
Continuous Trading	0.59

Panel B	
Average Time Between Liquidity Events (or Average Turnover)	*Illiquidity Risk Premium*
10 Years	6.0%
5 Years	4.3%
2 Years	2.0%
1 Year	0.9%
$\frac{1}{2}$ Year	0.7%
Continuous Trading	0.0%

rebalanced holding. The optimal trading point of illiquid assets is lower than the long-run average holding.

Consume Less with Illiquid Assets

Payouts, or consumption rates, are lower in the presence of illiquid assets than when only comparable liquid assets are held by the investor. The investor cannot offset the risk of illiquid assets declining when these assets cannot be traded. This is an *unhedgeable* source of risk. The investor offsets that risk by eating less.

There Are No Illiquidity "Arbitrages"

In a mean-variance model, two assets with different Sharpe ratios and perfect correlations produce positions of plus or minus infinity. This is a well-known bane of mean-variance models, and professionals employ lots of ad hoc fixes, and arbitrary constraints, to prevent this from happening. This does not happen when one asset is illiquid—there is no arbitrage. Investors do not load up on illiquid assets because these assets have illiquidity risk and cannot be continuously traded to construct an "arbitrage."

Investors Must Demand High Illiquidity Hurdle Rates

How much does an investor need to be compensated for illiquidity? In Panel B of Table 13.6, I compute premiums on an illiquid asset required by an investor to bear illiquidity risk. Let's define the illiquidity premium, or hurdle rate, as a certainty equivalent (see chapter 2). Suppose an investor holds two liquid assets and replaces one asset with another that is identical except for being illiquid. The illiquidity premium is the increase in the expected return of the illiquid asset so that the investor has the same utility as the case when all assets are liquid.

When liquidity events arrive every six months, on average, an investor should demand an extra 70 basis points. (Some hedge funds have lockups around this horizon.) When the illiquid asset can be traded once a year, on average, the illiquidity premium is approximately 1%. When you need to wait ten years, on average, to exit an investment, you should demand a 6% illiquidity premium. That is, investors should insist that private equity funds generate returns 6% greater than public markets to compensate for illiquidity. As Section 3 discusses, most illiquid assets are not generating excess returns above these hurdle rates (see also chapter 11).

The Ang, Papanikolaou, and Westerfield (2013) model is highly stylized. Given the other issues the model misses, like agency conflicts of interest (see chapter 15), cash flow management issues of capital calls and distributions, and asset–liability mismatches, the true illiquidity hurdle rates are even higher than those reported in Table 13.6.

5.3. SUMMARY

Portfolio choice models with illiquid assets recommend holding only modest amounts of illiquid assets. Investors should demand high illiquidity risk premiums.

6. Liquidating Harvard Redux

6.1. THE CASE FOR ILLIQUID ASSET INVESTING

Large, long-term investors often cite their large amounts of capital and their long horizons as rationales for investing in illiquid assets. Size and patience are necessary but not sufficient conditions for illiquid asset investing; these conditions simply aren't adequate justifications in themselves. Since illiquid asset classes do not offer high risk-adjusted returns, the case for passively them is not compelling. Illiquid investing also poses huge agency problems; asset owners, for example, find it tough to monitor external managers. Many institutions face "fiefdom risk" as illiquid assets are run as separate empires within an organization, detrimentally affecting how the aggregate portfolio is allocated.

In addition, investors in illiquid markets face high idiosyncratic risk because there is no "market" portfolio. It is exactly this large idiosyncratic risk, however, that is the most compelling reason for investing in illiquid assets.

Suppose you are a skilled investor (assume you have true alpha; see chapter 10) and have a choice between investing in (i) a market where prices quickly reflect new information, almost everyone sees the same information, and news gets spread around very quickly, or (ii) a market where information is hard to analyze and even harder to procure, only a select few have good information, and news takes a long time to reach everyone. Obviously you pick (ii). This, in a nutshell, is the Swensen (2009) justification for choosing illiquid assets. The argument is not that illiquid asset classes have higher risk-adjusted returns. Empirical evidence suggests they don't.

Investing in illiquid assets allows an investor to transfer idiosyncratic risk from liquid equity and bond markets, which are largely efficient, to markets where there are large information asymmetries, transactions costs are punishing, and the cross-sections of alpha opportunities are extremely disperse. These are the markets, in other words, where you can make a killing!

The Swensen case crucially relies on one word: "skilled." Whereas skilled investors can find, evaluate, and monitor these illiquid investment opportunities, assuming they have the resources to take advantage of them, unskilled investors get taken to the cleaners. If you are unskilled, you lose. Harvard, Yale, Stanford, MIT, and a few other select endowments have the ability to select superior managers in illiquid markets because of their size, their relationships, and their commitment to support these managers through long investment cycles. What about the others? An endowment specialist says, "It's a horror show. [Performance has] been flat to even negative. The strong get stronger and the weak get stuck with non-top quartile managers and mediocre returns and high fees."[44]

6.2. INVESTMENT ADVICE FOR ENDOWMENTS

Thomas Gilbert and Christopher Hrdlicka at the University of Washington are probably the world's only endowment management theorists. In a 2012 paper, they provocatively argue that the optimal allocation policy for successful universities is to hold large amounts of fixed income, not risky assets, and by extension not illiquid risky assets.

Gilbert and Hrdlicka model universities as creators of "social dividends," which are research and teaching. Universities can invest internally, in research and

---

[44] Quoted by Stewart, J. B., "A Hard Landing for University Endowments," *New York Times*, Oct. 12, 2012.

teaching projects, or they can invest externally through the endowment. If the endowment is taking on external risk—via equities, for example—this signals that the university does not have enough good internal risky projects generating social dividends. If the endowment is invested in safe assets, through bonds, the university takes on risk through internal research and teaching projects. Gilbert and Hrdlicka argue that a university endowment's large investment in risky assets is a sign that it does not have enough fruitful research and teaching assignments!

Harvard, with its large endowment heavily invested in risky illiquid assets, would take issue with Gilbert and Hrdlicka. An endowment allows a university to be more independent, rather than depend entirely on grants from government or private foundations. As Dershowitz argues, the endowment could be used as a rainy day account to be tapped precisely during times like 2008. Harvard's endowment has historically yielded a predictable stream of cash for operating budgets, but 2008 blew this predictability away. Harvard claims its endowment allows for future generations to share in its riches, saying, "Although their specific uses vary, endowment funds have a common purpose: to support activities not just for one year, or even one generation, but in perpetuity."[45] The price of education, however, has been rising in real terms (see chapter 11), and if education is costlier in the future than in the present, being stingy on research and teaching now makes no sense because it substitutes a more expensive good in the future for a cheaper one today.[46]

Henry Hansmann, a professor at Yale Law School, describes large private universities as "institutions whose business is to run large pools of investment assets. . . . They run educational institutions on the side, that can expand and contract to act as buffers for investment pools."[47] He contends that a large part of why universities like large endowments is prestige, pursued as its own objective. Journalist Kevin Carey puts it another way, echoing the cadences of the Book of Common Prayer when he says that large endowments per se are "aspiration without limit, accumulation without end."[48]

6.3. LIQUIDATE HARVARD?

Did Harvard generate excess returns, or an illiquidity risk premium, from its large investments in illiqui , alternative assets? Yes. Harvard could extract value from illiquid asset investir g not because illiquid asset classes have a large risk premium but because it is a skillful investor. And it is one of the few investors able to do so.

---

[45] "About HSPH: Endowment Funds: What Are Endowment Funds?" Harvard School of Public Health, http://www.hsph.harvard.edu/about/what-are-endowment-funds

[46] See Hansmann (1990).

[47] "Q&A. Modest Proposal. An Economist Asks, Does Harvard Really Need $15 Billion?" New York Times, Aug. 2, 1998.

[48] Kevin Carey, "The 'Veritas' About Harvard," Chronicle of Higher Education, Sept. 28, 2009.

But this didn't help Harvard solve its cash crunch. The worst failing of Harvard was in basic asset–liability management. Even without using the asset allocation models with illiquidity risk or the advice given by Gilbert and Hrdlicka, Harvard should have recognized that its assets did not match its liabilities. In technical terms the duration of its liabilities was shorter than the duration of its assets.

Harvard faced five choices:

1. Liquidate a portion of the endowment.

    But a lot of the endowment is illiquid and cannot be sold.
2. Cut expenses.

    Universities are like government bureaucracies: big, bloated, and ineffi-cient. You can hardly fire anyone. So there is a limit to how much can be cut.
3. Increase donations.

    It's embarrassing to ask for funds to replace those lost as a result of mismanagement.
4. Increase other revenue.

    Harvard could rescind its need-blind financial-aid policy. But it turns out this doesn't save much money.
5. Borrow.

Harvard did (5). It issued $2.5 billion in bonds and more than doubled its lev-erage ratio between 2008 and 2009. It did try to cut expenses and deferred its Allston campus expansion. Was the endowment a rainy day fund Joseph could use to save his family and all of Egypt, as suggested by Dershowitz? No. Harvard actu-ally *reduced* its payout ratio in 2009, preferring to keep as much of the endowment intact as it could.[49] Maybe Hansmann is right in suggesting that prestige maximi-zation is the driving motivation in endowment management. After all, everyone likes to be well-endowed.

---

[49] Brown et al. (2013) show that most universities do the same thing: they hoard endowments when bad times come.

CHAPTER 14

Factor Investing

Chapter Summary

There are many factor strategies—value investing, momentum, and short volatility strategies, to name but a few—that beat the market. To determine which factors we should choose, factor investing asks: how well can a particular investor weather hard times relative to the average investor? Answering this question helps an investor reap long-run factor premiums by embracing risks that lose money during bad times but make up for it the rest of the time with attractive rewards. When factor investing can be done cheaply, it raises the bar for active management.

1. Passive-Aggressive Norway

Norwegians were shocked by their sovereign wealth fund's performance during the 2008 and 2009 financial crisis. Officially the Norwegian Government Pension Fund—Global, the fund was formed in 1990 to invest state revenues from oil and gas reserves in the North Sea. At the end of 2012, Norway's fund stood at $650 billion, or more than $130,000 per Norwegian. The fund is larger than Norway's annual economic output.

The fund's returns were humming along nicely at the start of 2007. Figure 14.1 plots cumulated returns from January 2007 to September 2009, encompassing the worst of the financial meltdown. While there were some rumblings and negative returns starting in the summer of 2007 as subprime mortgage prices declined,[1] the market started to plummet in 2008. Figure 14.1 shows that cumulated returns starting in 2007 reached –17% in October 2008, a month after Lehman Brothers went bankrupt. Thanks to frantic efforts by Washington to prop up the banking system and other major players, the Norwegian fund posted

---

[1] In August 2007, a crisis occurred for hedge funds specializing in quantitative investing techniques; see chapter 17.

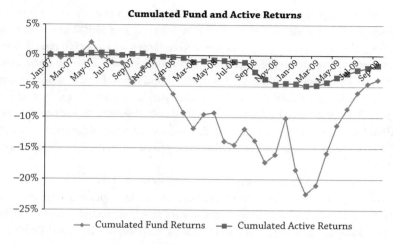

Cumulated Fund and Active Returns

Figure 14.1

positive returns in December 2008. Then the first quarter of 2009 was a roller coaster downward as these measures proved inadequate and policymakers put on further programs to stabilize the financial system. February 2009 was the lowest cumulated return marked in Figure 14.1, at –22%. From there, fund returns gradually climbed back.

Surprisingly, Norwegians weren't that upset by the large losses of the overall fund. It had been a long journey bringing the fund's asset allocation from 100% bonds when the fund was first formed, to 40% equities in 1998, and then to 60% equities in the 2007 to 2009 period. (Since 2011, the fund has had a maximum allocation to real estate of 5% coming from the bond allocation.) The public was well informed of the risks, and parliamentarians had made investment decisions understanding that large holdings of equities brought the risk of large losses. The reward was that, over the long run, equities would earn a return higher than bonds.[2] After all, financial markets have always tended to bounce back.

What Norwegians were angry about were the negative returns generated by *active management*. The fund's manager, Norges Bank Investment Management (NBIM), was supposed to produce returns in excess of a benchmark provided by the Ministry of Finance. The active return is the fund return minus the benchmark return. Figure 14.1 showed that post-2007, cumulated active returns reached –5% during the worst months of the financial crisis. Many members of the public had been expecting active management to steadily add value—after all, wasn't that why those portfolio managers at NBIM were paid so much more than regular bureaucrats? Perhaps the extra fees paid to NBIM for active management were a waste of money, and the fund should be *passively managed* using low-cost index funds.

[2] This is the equity premium, which is discussed in chapter 8.

The Norwegian fund is always in the public eye, and the actions and words of the responsible officials at the Ministry of Finance and NBIM are closely scrutinized by the press. The outcry at the active losses was special, partly because the losses occurred alongside contracting economic growth and the uncovering of other financial excesses—Norway, despite its stolid reputation, was not spared the effects of the financial crisis. Also, Norwegian parliamentarians are financially sophisticated; they have to be, as they are ultimately responsible for the nest egg of a nation. (Ask the average member of Congress what's the difference between active and passive management and he'll think you're referring to different exercise routines.)

The Ministry of Finance wisely did not immediately yank NBIM's active mandate despite the public outcry. Instead, it commissioned a four-month, in-depth study of the fund. William Goetzmann (Yale University), Stephen Schaefer (London Business School), and I were tasked with evaluating NBIM's historical performance, assessing its strategic plans for active management and its risk budgeting process and describing and evaluating investing strategies that played to Norway's comparative advantages as a large, patient, and transparent investor. Released at the end of 2009 and presented in January 2010 at a public meeting introduced by the King of Norway, the report was quickly dubbed the "Professors' Report," or more conventionally, Ang, Goetzmann, and Schaefer (2009).

We found that a major part of the fund's active returns before, during, and after the financial crisis could be explained by systematic factors. It was right for Norway to collect these risk premiums in the long run, which compensated Norway for losses during bad times like the financial crisis. Many of these factors could be collected more cheaply by *passive management*. The report recommended that NBIM's active mandate should not be rescinded but that the Norwegian fund should go beyond equities and bonds in its asset allocation: Norway should adopt a top–down approach of factor investing, especially for *dynamic factors*.

2. Factors Really Matter

2.1. WHAT IS A FACTOR?

Factors are investment styles that deliver high returns over the long run. The risk premiums don't come for free, however, as factors can underperform in the short run ("*bad times*"). Factor losses are associated with bad economic outcomes, like times of high inflation and slow economic growth. Equities and bonds are examples of factors whose risk premiums are obtained by simply buying assets (*long-only* positions), hence they are *static* factors.[3] Other

---

[3] Of course, you would want to rebalance equity and positions over time, as chapter 4 advocates, to maintain constant risk exposures to equity and bond market risk. You can rebalance over both static factors and dynamic factors.

factors require *dynamic* trading involving *long-short* positions, where we constantly have to adjust portfolio weights. Just like their static factor cousins, dynamic factor strategies—like value-growth investing, momentum, and short volatility strategies—don't always make money, and investors have to brace for stomach-turning stumbles. It is precisely for suffering these losses that factors accrue risk premiums. Assets embed different combinations of factor risks, just as foods mix different types of nutrients.

The simplest factors are the equity and bond indexes that Norway selects as its benchmark returns. It's easy to invest in these factors by buying cheap index funds.[4] The traditional approach to asset management has been to build on an equity-bond mix by adding other asset classes, notably subclasses of equities and bonds such as emerging markets and high-yield bonds, or *alternative assets* like real estate, private equity, and hedge funds. (This is referred to, incorrectly in the context of its original incarnation by Swensen (2009), as the *endowment approach*; see chapter 13.[5]) Even without adding alternative asset classes, the equity-bond factor decision is the most important one taken by funds. And it explains the majority of the variation in performance.

2.2. RETURN DECOMPOSITION

To be concrete, I denote r as a fund's return. We subtract and add the benchmark return, r_{bmk}, to obtain a return in excess of the benchmark, which is the active return, and the benchmark return:

$$r = \underbrace{(r - r_{bmk})}_{\text{Active Return}} + \underbrace{r_{bmk}}_{\text{Benchmark Return}} . \qquad (14.1)$$

The poor active returns, $r_{active} = r - r_{bmk}$, were what the Norwegians were up in arms about in 2008 and the beginning of 2009. The benchmark returns, r_{bmk}, are the result of the asset allocation decision (later it will be a factor decision) taken by the Ministry of Finance. Benchmark returns are often called passive returns, especially if they can be implemented by passive index funds as in Norway's case. The active returns, r_{active}, result from the decisions of NBIM to deviate from the benchmark.

Gary Brinson, Randolph Hood, and Gilbert Beebower, all practitioners, wrote a major study in 1986 showing that approximately 90% of a typical fund's return

---

[4] See chapters 6 to 9 for economic theory underlying these risk premiums.

[5] Chapters 17 and 18 argue that hedge funds and private equity are not asset classes, respectively. Chapter 10 covers a factor decomposition of real estate.

variance is explained by the asset allocation decision. Their result is stated in terms of variances:[6]

$$\underbrace{\text{var}(r)}_{100\%} = \underbrace{\text{var}(r_{active})}_{\sim 10\%} + \underbrace{\text{var}(r_{bmk})}_{\sim 90\%}, \tag{14.2}$$

where approximately 90% of the variance of total returns, var(r), is accounted for by the variance of passive or benchmark returns.

For Norway, the effect of factors is even more dramatic than the set of funds studied by Brinson, Hood, and Beebower. Figure 14.2 reports the variance attribution of Norway's fund returns into its active returns and benchmark returns for the whole fund, and the equities and fixed income portfolio components of the fund as computed in the Professors' Report. From January 1998 to September 2009, 99.1% of variation in the fund's returns was explained by the equity-bond decision taken by Parliament. For the equities and bond portfolios, the passive benchmark accounted for 99.7% and 97.1% of return variation, respectively. Norway's factor attributions are so high because NBIM worked under very strict risk constraints that allowed it only extremely small deviations from the benchmark. In effect, Norway is a huge index fund.

The asset allocation decision—the asset classes where you collect your risk premiums—is by far the most important decision in understanding the fluctuations of your fund over time. If you want to explain why your fund's performance is different relative to your competitor's, however, your fund's benchmark allocation becomes less important.[7] Many endowments, for example, have similar asset allocation policies (see chapter 1), and thus the active bets taken by Harvard are a major determinant in whether Harvard beats Yale in one particular year. But for just your fund compared to itself over time, the most important investment decision you make is the top–down choice on asset allocation.

2.3. MORE SOPHISTICATED RETURN DECOMPOSITIONS

Risk managers often use more sophisticated return decompositions by drilling down into asset-class or position-level data.[8] (These are derived by subtracting and adding one just as in equation (14.1).) In all of these decompositions, the asset class decision is the most important taken by the fund.

---

[6] There is a covariance term in equation (14.2) that is folded into either the active or the benchmark component. The covariance term is zero if the benchmark is risk-adjusted (see chapter 10), in which case the benchmark return represents exposure to *systematic risk* and the active return corresponds to *idiosyncratic risk*.

[7] See Hensel, Ezra, and Ilkiw (1991) and Ibbotson and Kaplan (2000). Brown, Garlappi, and Tiu (2010) report that 70% of the (time-series) variance of endowment returns is due to passive policy decisions.

[8] See also Karnosky and Singer (1994) and Lo (2008).

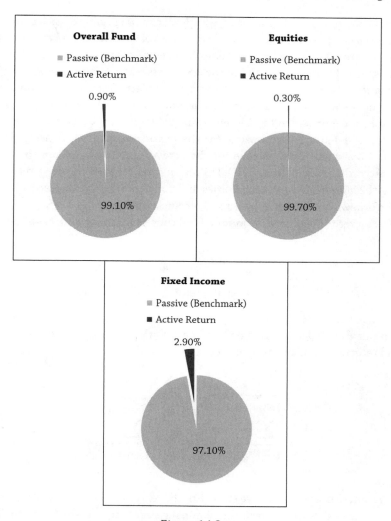

Figure 14.2

A decomposition of a total fund return into a benchmark return, a component where the asset classes in the benchmark are timed (called *tactical asset allocation*) and a component where securities are picked within each asset class (called *security selection*) is given by:

$$r_i = r_{bmk} + r_{timing} + r_{selection}. \tag{14.3}$$

In its full glory, this can be written as

$$r = \sum w_i r_i = \underbrace{\sum w_i^b r_i^b}_{r_{bmk}} + \underbrace{\sum (w_i - w_i^b) r_i^b}_{r_{timing}} + \underbrace{\sum w_i (r_i - r_i^b)}_{r_{selection}},$$

where the weights in each asset class, w_i, apply at the beginning of each period and the returns generated by each asset class, r_i, are realized at the end of the period. The sums are taken across asset classes indexed by i. The superscript bs denote the weights (w_i^b) and returns (r_i^b) of the asset classes in the benchmark.

Equation (14.3) has partitioned the active returns into a timing and selection component. One advantage of this decomposition is that we can assign each separate source of return to different responsible parties. In Norway's case, the Ministry of Finance is responsible for the passive benchmark decision. NBIM, the fund manager, is responsible for the active decision away from the benchmark. According to equation (14.3), NBIM can generate positive active returns by timing the allocations between equities and bonds or by choosing securities that outperform within the equities or fixed income asset classes.

Here's a return decomposition for a fund concerned about returns in excess of inflation:

$$\underbrace{r - \pi}_{\text{Real Return}} = \underbrace{(r - r_f)}_{\text{Risk Premium}} + \underbrace{(r_f - \pi)}_{\text{Real Cash Return}}, \qquad (14.4)$$

where π is the inflation rate and r_f is the risk-free return on U.S. T-bills. A real return can also be decomposed using a benchmark, r_{bmk}, with asset class weights w_i and returns r_i, similar to equation (14.3):

$$r - \pi = \underbrace{(r_f - \pi)}_{\text{Real Cash Return}} + \underbrace{\sum w_i^b (r_i^b - r_f)}_{\text{Strategic Asset Allocation}}$$
$$+ \underbrace{\sum (w_i - w_i^b) r_i^b}_{\text{Tactical Asset Allocation}} + \underbrace{\sum w_i (r_i - r_i^b)}_{\text{Security Selection}}. \qquad (14.5)$$

If we aim to beat inflation, we start with the real cash return in equation (14.5), which is the difference between the nominal risk-free return and inflation. Then strategic asset allocation aims to pick asset classes that produce returns in excess of the nominal risk-free return, and it is now an active decision.[9] In Norway's case, the strategic asset allocation is the constant equity-bond mix. For other funds, the strategic asset allocation slowly varies over time. The tactical asset allocation and security selection components are the same as the last two terms in equation (14.3). Even though both the strategic asset allocation and tactical asset allocation involve changing asset class weights, practitioners use the term "tactical" to distinguish the shorter-term changes in the asset class holdings from the more slowly moving strategic allocations.

[9] Chapter 4 interprets strategic and tactical allocation in the context of long-run portfolio choice. Equation (14.5) is stated as a return in excess of inflation. When we replace inflation with a liability, the decomposition reflects a *surplus* return, or a return in excess of liabilities.

Norway seeks to maximize its international purchasing power. The fund's spending rule set by Parliament is approximately 4%. This can be interpreted as a long-run real return (this is probably too optimistic; see chapter 11).[10] The expanded return decomposition in equation (14.5) indicates that the Ministry of Finance, and hence Parliament, is making active decisions in real terms. First, by choosing a currency basket, it decides on a cash return. In 2013, at the time of writing, investors seeking positive real returns are disadvantaged by negative cash returns (T-bill yields are lower than inflation). Second, members of Norway's Parliament decide on fixed benchmark weights in different asset classes (w_i^b) which have (hopefully positive) returns in excess of cash ($r_i^b - r_f$). The other two components in equation (14.5) are the benchmark-timing and security selection components, for which NBIM takes responsibility.

2.4. DYNAMIC FACTORS

A large body of academic literature, and long investing experience, has uncovered certain classes of equity, debt, and derivative securities that have higher payoffs than the broad market index. Stocks with low prices relative to fundamentals (value stocks) beat stocks with high prices relative to fundamentals (growth stocks) over long periods, giving rise to a *value-growth* premium. Over the long run, stocks with past high returns (winners) outperform stocks with low or negative past returns (losers), leading to *momentum* strategies. Securities that are more illiquid trade at low prices and have high average excess returns, relative to their more liquid counterparts. Thus there is an *illiquidity* premium.[11] Bonds that have higher default risk tend to have higher average returns reflecting a *credit risk* premium. And because investors are willing to pay for protection against high volatility periods, when returns tend to crash, sellers of *volatility protection* in option markets earn high returns, on average.

We combine long positions in these classes of securities with underweight or short positions in the securities that underperform. Thus we can collect dynamic risk premiums. A partial list is:

Value-Growth Premium = Value stocks minus growth stocks
Momentum Premium = Winning stocks minus losing stocks
Illiquidity Premium = Illiquid securities minus liquid securities
Credit Risk Premium = Risky bonds minus safe bonds
Volatility Risk Premium = Selling out-of-the-money puts offset by stocks or calls to produce market-neutral positions

---

[10] For further details on payout policies from sovereign wealth funds and endowments, see chapter 1.

[11] At least within asset classes. There is scant evidence of illiquidity premiums across asset classes, as discussed in chapter 13.

These are *dynamic factors*, because they involve time-varying positions in securities that change over time. *Dynamic* factors involve taking simultaneous *long* and *short* positions, whereas we can earn the *static* equity and bond risk premiums by taking just long positions.

Dynamic factor premiums, just like their long-only counterparts, are not a free lunch. As chapter 7 explains, while dynamic factors often beat the market over long periods of time, they can grossly underperform the market during certain periods—like the 2008–2009 financial crisis. All factor risk premiums exist in the long run because they compensate the investor for bearing losses during bad times. The factors are not appropriate for everyone because factor strategies are risky.

An important concept of dynamic factors is that they remove market exposure. Optimally constructed value-growth nets out the market portfolio and is exposed to the returns of value stocks less the returns of growth stocks. Similarly, by going long winners and short losers, momentum removes the market portfolio. In practice, factor portfolios need not be constructed with an equal number of stocks or equal dollars in opposite long-short positions. (These are called *unbalanced portfolios*.) There is no need to take short positions, but the fewer the short positions, the greater the market exposure. Put another way, the fewer short positions, the greater the correlation of the factors with the market portfolio. For example, many vehicles invest in value stocks, but they usually only take long positions. Without netting out growth stocks, the main driver of returns of these funds is the market portfolio. As the number of short positions in growth stocks increases, more market movements are removed and the more the factor reflects the *difference* between value stocks and growth stocks.

Industry often uses the terms *smart beta*, *alternative beta*, or *exotic beta* for dynamic factors. I'll stick with the term "factors" because, in asset pricing theory, beta has the strict meaning of measuring exposure to a risk factor. (These risk factors actually have a beta of one with respect to themselves.) Beta measures the magnitude of the exposure to a risk factor: we invest in factors, not betas.

Factors Define Bad Times

Each factor defines a different set of bad times. Value strategies got crushed during the financial crisis. They also got slammed during the roaring 1990s Internet bull market. In the late 1990s and early 2000s, venerable value managers, like Warren Buffet of Berkshire Hathaway, Jeremy Grantham who heads GMO Asset Management, and Julian Robertson who ran the hedge fund Tiger Management, became old-fashioned laggards. Grantham almost had to sell or close his firm. Robertson did close his fund in 2000 but went on to seed the funds of many of his associates (these hedge funds are affectionately known as "tiger cubs").

The financial crisis was a bad time for many factors. Liquidity evaporated in commercial paper markets, mortgage-backed securities markets (especially for subprime mortgages), markets involving securitized fixed income products, and the repo market (which allows investors to borrow short-term funds). As investors clamored for liquid assets, illiquid securities tanked and there were heavy losses for illiquidity risk strategies. Investors sought safety, so risky bonds nose-dived and credit spreads shot upward. Volatility "reached for the sky!" benefiting the purchasers of volatility protection but inflicting heavy losses on providers of it. Momentum strategy portfolios plummeted in spring 2009 when battered financial firms, shorted by momentum strategists, were buoyed by waves of bailouts and easy money.

It is precisely because factors episodically lose money in bad times that there is a long-run reward for being exposed to factor risk. *Factor premiums are rewards for investors enduring losses during bad times.*

Factors Dominate in Large Portfolios

In very large portfolios, it is very hard to find excess returns that are not related to factors. Many mispricing opportunities (or *alpha;* see chapter 10) are not scalable—we expect small pockets of inefficiency to lie in areas of the market that are illiquid or where information is not freely available. Manager decisions, both internal and external, tend to be correlated as it is hard to find truly independent portfolio strategies. Large investors hold tens of thousands of securities, and security-specific bets are swamped at the portfolio level by macro-economic and factor risks. This is not to say that large-scale security selection is impossible, but in general the bigger the portfolio, the harder it gets. A farmer, for example, may certainly be able to select a farm with the best soil and conditions for planting (farm equals security selection). But if there's a severe drought, having chosen the best farm is not going to help (rain is the factor).

Thousands of correlated individual bets by managers effectively become large bets on factors. An equity manager going long 1,000 value-oriented stocks and underweighting 1,000 growth stocks does not have 1,000 separate bets; he has one big bet on the value-growth factor. A fixed-income manager who squeezes out the last bits of yield by finding 1,000 relatively illiquid bonds funded by short positions in 1,000 liquid bonds (through the repo market) has made one bet on an illiquidity factor.

2.5. FACTOR ATTRIBUTION

In the Professors' Report, we showed that about 70% of all active returns on the overall fund can be explained by exposures to systematic factors. Panel A of Figure 14.3 graphs cumulated active returns for the Norwegian fund from January 1998 to September 2009. The figure shows the regime shift in 2008 that erased all of Norway's cumulated active returns since the beginning of the sample.

Panels B and C of Figure 14.3 plot illiquidity and volatility factors, which explain a large part of the active returns of the fund. Panel B plots an *illiquidity factor,*

Panel A
Overall Fund Cumulated Active Returns

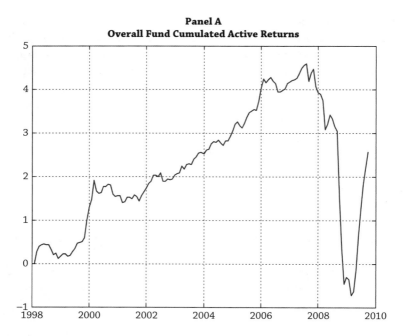

Panel B
Liquidity On-the-Run/Off-the-Run

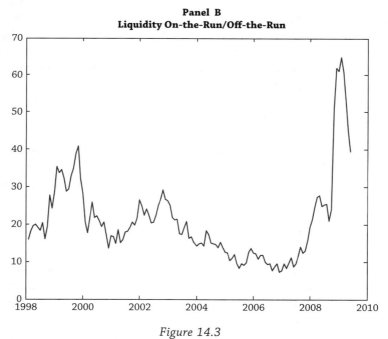

Figure 14.3

Panel C
Cumulated Returns on VOL

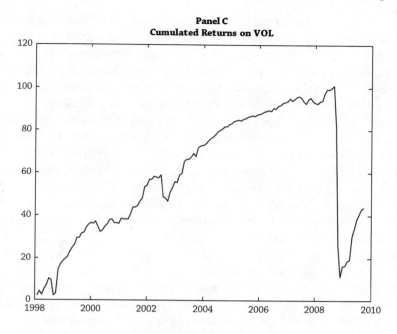

Panel D
GPFG Active Returns

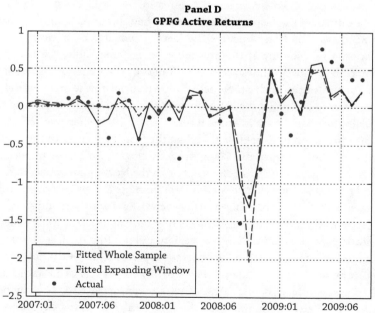

Figure 14.3 (continued)

which is formed by taking the differences in yields between liquid newly issued government bonds (on-the-run) and relatively illiquid seasoned government bonds (off-the-run). Higher values indicate more illiquid markets. Illiquidity spreads widened in 1998 as a result of the Russian default crisis and the failure of Long-Term Capital Management, a large hedge fund (see chapter 17). The second dramatic widening at the end of the sample is due to the financial crisis. The illiquidity spread grew dramatically in the latter part of 2008 after the failure of Lehman Brothers and reached its greatest extent in January 2009. As the financial system stabilized over the last few months in 2009, illiquidity risk fell. The volatility risk factor in Panel C represents returns from selling volatility (see chapters 1 and 7). Returns from the volatility strategy fell off a cliff in 2008, wiping out ten years of cumulated gains. The negative active returns during the 2008–2009 financial crisis coincided with both more illiquid markets (Panel B) and pronounced losses on short volatility strategies (Panel C).

In Panel D of Figure 14.3, I ask whether the negative active returns over 2008–2009 could have been anticipated. This is a different question than whether the negative active returns could have been perfectly forecast. ("Prediction is very difficult, especially if it's about the future," said Nobel laureate physicist Nils Bohr.) The figure graphs the actual active returns each month in dots and the active returns explained by factor exposures in the solid lines. There are two lines: one estimates the factor exposures over the full sample and the other uses rolling windows. The latter updates the factor exposures each month and uses information available only at the prevailing time. Remarkably, the two lines almost coincide.[12] The two lines account for much of the variation in actual active returns: they track the fairly stable active returns prior to the onset of the financial crisis, they follow down the large losses during the financial crisis, and factors also explain the bounce back in active returns in late 2009 when markets stabilize.

My interpretation of Panel D is that, had the factor exposure of the fund been properly communicated prior to 2008, the active losses during the financial crisis would not have caused such a strong reaction in the Norwegian public. Had the responsible parties warned that sooner or later markets always become illiquid and volatility shoots upward (but that bearing such risks is worth it, and things eventually turn out fine), then the negative active returns in 2008 might have been within anticipated loss limits. The Norwegians did not find the losses from equity positions, however large, surprising because they were aware of the downside risk.

The Professors' Report showed that Norway's active returns have large exposure to systematic, dynamic factors that are appropriate for Norway because the factors earn risk premiums over the long run. The factor exposures, however, did not come about through a process that deliberately chose which factor premiums should be harvested and optimally determined the sizes of the factor

---

[12] Interestingly, the estimation using the expanding window predicts much more severe losses in September 2008 than what actually occurred. This is consistent with NBIM's skill in managing time-varying factor exposures by changing either internal or external investment strategies.

exposures. We recommended that the Norwegian fund take a top–down, intentional approach to factor exposures. That is, Norway should practice dynamic factor investing; the fund's benchmarks should also include dynamic factors just as they do static, long-only bond and equity factors.

3. The Factor Recipe

Just as eating right requires looking through foods to their underlying nutrients, investing right requires looking through asset class labels to underlying risk exposures. Assets are bundles of factors, and assets earn returns because of their underlying exposures to factor risks. (Chapter 6 covers factor theory in more detail.)

3.1. SELECTING FACTORS

The Professors' Report to the Norwegian Ministry of Finance lists four criteria for determining which factors investors should choose. A factor should:

1. Be justified by academic research

    The factors should have an intellectual foundation, and only factors with the strongest support in academic research should be included in an investor's benchmark. Research should demonstrate compelling rational logic or behavioral stories or both in explaining why the risk premiums arise. We do not need unanimity concerning the mechanism that generates the risk premium—which, if you've met financial economists, you know is impossible. (Economists are even divided over the source of the equity risk premium, for example [see chapter 8], but I am highly confident that equities have higher returns than bonds over the long run and that equities are a risk factor.) On this criterion, value-growth, momentum, and short volatility strategies are appropriate risk factors. New research can identify new factors, or qualify earlier consensus on known factors, or even disqualify factors and can inform investment policy accordingly.

2. Have exhibited significant premiums that are expected to persist in the future

    Not only should we have some understanding as to why the risk premium has existed in the past, but we should have some basis for believing that it will prevail in the future (at least in the short term). Factors are systematic by definition—they arise from risk or behavioral tendencies that will likely persist (again in the short term) even if everyone knows about the factors, and many investors are pursuing the same factor strategies.[13]

---

[13] This chapter does not discuss the factors that are used by many (mean-variance) risk models. Most of these factors are constructed based on decompositions of a covariance matrix of (residual) returns and are not based on economic theory generating risk premiums.

3. Have return history available for bad times

Factor risk premiums exist because they reward the willingness to suffer losses during bad times. Having some data points to measure worst-case scenarios is necessary for assessing risk–return trade-offs and risk management (see below). We also want a reasonable length of data to perform these exercises.

4. Be implementable in liquid, traded instruments

As in Canada Pension Plan Investment Board's (CPPIB) Reference Portfolio, factor strategies should be dirt cheap, something best accomplished by constructing them from liquid securities. Scalability is an important requirement for large investors.

Factor strategies often involve leverage. You need to overweight value stocks and simultaneously underweight or short growth stocks. Going long value and short growth is a *dynamic leverage* strategy. Even if shorting is not possible, factor strategies still work: Israel and Moskowitz (2013) show that there are still significant value and momentum factor premiums available even if an investor cannot short, but the profitability of these factor strategies is dented by 50% to 60%.

Limiting ourselves to liquid securities might make it seem impossible to construct a factor illiquidity premium, but this is not so. You can collect an illiquidity premium by taking long positions in (relatively) illiquid assets and short positions in (relatively) liquid assets, all in liquid markets. It turns out that illiquidity premiums within (liquid) asset classes are much larger than illiquidity premiums across asset classes involving private equity, hedge funds, and other illiquid assets (see chapter 13). These types of illiquid assets also present tricky principal-agent problems and can be accessed only in murky markets where scant information is available.

The four criteria deliberately exclude the trendy factor du jour. A factor should be considered for a benchmark only if it is widely recognized. A factor that predicts returns by some statistical analysis of social networking data (yes, there are some, see chapter 8) is best left to active management. Many of the factors that we recognize today—like value-growth and momentum—were originally labeled as anomalies, or alpha, as they could not be explained by existing risk factors. As the literature matured and there was growing acceptance of these strategies by institutional investors, they became beta, or were treated as factor premiums in their own right.

Factors Can Appear and Disappear

The set of factors is not static. Options trading on centralized markets was introduced in the late 1960s, and these markets blossomed after the seminal option pricing formula of Black and Scholes (1973). Before then, it was not possible to obtain large-scale exposure to volatility risk. The high yield bond market rose to prominence in the late 1970s and 1980s, due largely to the financier Michael

Milken, the "Junk Bond King" (who went to prison for securities fraud). Prior to this we could not access a high yield, or junk, credit risk premium. Finally, we could only collect the carry factor in foreign exchange markets when the world's currencies became untethered from gold and freely floated in 1970s.[14]

There is no consensus on the complete set of factors. Academic studies using statistical analysis suggest that a limited number, usually less than ten, can capture most variation in expected returns.[15] These are, however, statistical and not economic descriptions of data. Some factors, like CPPIB's bond and equities, and some dynamic factors like value-growth and momentum, are tried and true. I recommend that even if you can confidently identify and invest in ten or more factors, don't. Keep things simple. Start with a select few. The point is that putting a factor into a fund's benchmark removes a component from the active return that doesn't really belong there and can be obtained more cheaply.

Some factors disappear. The *size effect*—that small stocks outperform large stocks—was brought to investors' attention by Banz in 1981 and reached its peak just after that. There are good academic justifications why small stocks might do better than large stocks: smaller stocks are more illiquid, they are less likely to be followed by analysts, so information is scarcer, small stocks don't have the same operating cushions that large firms do, and they operate in riskier segments of the economy. Since the mid-1980s, however, there has been no size premium after adjusting for market risk (see chapter 7). That is, small stocks do have higher returns than large stocks but not after taking out their exposure to the market factor. The creation of small stock mutual funds allowed the ordinary investor to participate and bear size-related risk. Thus the risk-bearing capacity of the economy changed after industry created new products to capitalize on the size premium. Those industry developments caused size to disappear. Those early investors in small caps experienced a bonanza. Prices of small stocks rose back to long-run equilibrium and early investors enjoyed a tidy risk-adjusted capital gain.

As I write, there is a flurry of new products created by industry to exploit many factor risk premiums. I take a special interest in funds taking advantage of the high average returns to low risk stocks, or *the risk anomaly*, which I describe in chapter 10. Stocks with low volatilities, or low (past) betas, seem to be too cheap as they have anomalously high returns. Low volatility could be a factor, according to the criteria I lay out, but admittedly the academic literature on the risk anomaly is still much smaller than the literature on value-growth, momentum, and selling volatility protection. As the asset management industry creates products to trade low volatility risk—as it has been doing with gusto (although perhaps not as cheaply as asset owners would wish)—new investors may increase their holdings of low risk stocks. Perhaps then prices of low risk stocks will rise to where they

---

[14] Accominotti and Chambers (2013) report that carry worked even worked during the 1920s and 1930s, and many countries were on the gold standard for some of this time.

[15] See Connor and Korajczyk (1993) and Jones (2001).

should be, giving early low volatility investors a handsome capital gain, and the risk anomaly will go the same way as size.[16] I'd really like this to happen because the low risk mystery will then be resolved, but I'm not expecting it.

3.2. FACTORS => ASSETS

An asset owner should take a stand on which risk factors are appropriate and then implement those factor exposures with appropriate assets. Figure 14.4 illustrates this process. Some risk factors are themselves asset classes, like plain-vanilla stocks and bonds, which can be implemented cheaply. These are passive factors earned by simply going long the equity or bond market.

Many dynamic factors cut across asset class boundaries. Value-growth strategies buy cheap securities with high yields and sell expensive securities with low yields. Foreign exchange's version of value-growth is *carry*: carry strategies go long currencies with high interest rates and short currencies with low interest rates.[17] In fixed income, buying high-yielding bonds with long maturities funded by low-yielding bonds with short maturities is called *riding the yield curve* and is related to the *duration* risk premium (see chapter 9). In commodities, positive *roll returns* are accomplished by buying cheap long-dated futures contracts that increase in price as their maturities decrease (see chapter 11). And finally, in equities, value-growth is, well, value-growth.

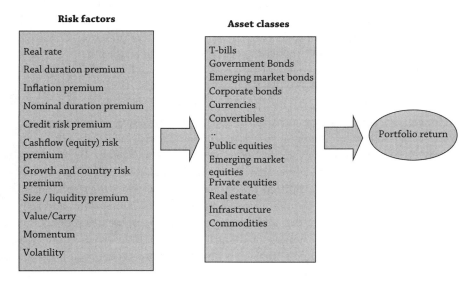

Figure 14.4

---

[16] See also Cochrane (2013b).

[17] Or perhaps value-growth might be better described as carry in equity markets.

Momentum strategies overweight assets that have recently risen in price and underweight assets that have fallen in price.[18] Momentum is pervasive and observed in equities, fixed income, foreign exchange, real estate, commodities (where it is often called CTA, for the type of fund which often pursues it), within and across asset classes, and in asset classes all over the world.[19] Similarly, selling volatility protection can be done in options markets where the underlying securities are equities, fixed income, commodities, or foreign exchange. An investor should decide on whether momentum or volatility strategies are appropriate and then implement them with appropriate asset classes in the cheapest way possible.

3.3. CANADA PENSION PLAN INVESTMENT BOARD

CPPIB, the fund manager of the Canada Pension Plan, uses two simple factors—stocks and bonds.[20] CPPIB holds many other asset classes—it is chock full of private equity, infrastructure and other sexy, illiquid assets, but it does not consider them to be asset classes. CPPIB looks through "private equity" and other labels and treats these investments as a combination of its two factors, stocks and bonds.

Figure 14.5, Panels A and B show factor investing à la CPPIB (which it calls the "total portfolio approach") and are drawn from CPPIB's 2013 annual report. Consider a private equity (buyout) investment in Panel A. CPPIB does not have a separate allocation to private equity and theoretically could hold almost all its portfolio in private equity subject to staying within the overall risk limits for the fund. In this particular example, $1 invested in the private equity fund is economically equivalent to $1.30 invested in public equities and a short position in bonds. This private equity investment is levered, and CPPIB accounts for this by the − $0.30 position in fixed income. In reality, CPPIB performs a more complicated matching procedure that involves pairing the private equity fund by sector and geographic region, with adjustments for the artificially low volatility of reported private equity returns (see chapter 11).

Panel B illustrates a factor investing decision for real estate. In this example, $1 invested in the real estate deal is economically equivalent to $0.40 in public equities and $0.60 of debt. Again, CPPIB's process is a bit more complicated: it assigns real estate to one of three risk classes (low, core, or high), and does some

---

[18] This is a *cross-sectional* strategy that takes positions in different assets at a point in time. This is different from *time-series* momentum, which refers to the tendency of a particular asset to keep rising if it has had past high returns.

[19] An exception is that momentum is very weak in over-the-counter equities markets, as Ang, Shtauber, and Tetlock show (2013).

[20] This is drawn from the case "Factor Investing: The Reference Portfolio and Canada Pension Plan Investment Board," CaseWorks ID #120302.

matching by geography and industry, but the general idea is that real estate is a bundle of risk factors.

The matching procedure in Figure 14.5 is not just academic. CPPIB funds the investment in private equity by transfers from its factor portfolios of equities and bonds. This benchmark portfolio is called the Reference Portfolio, and it can be managed by twelve to fifteen people using cheap, passive index funds. The factor Reference Portfolio at writing is 65% equities and 35% bonds, with further breakdowns for domestic and foreign equities, and domestic and (hedged) foreign sovereign bonds.[21] The factors in the Reference Portfolio are chosen so that the

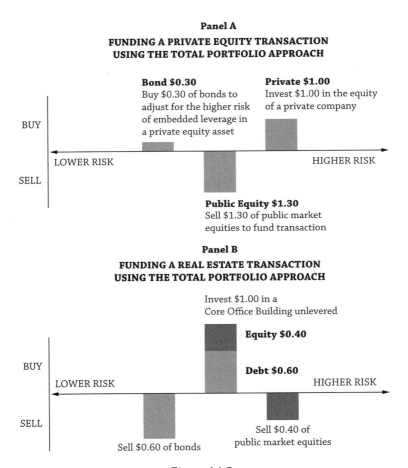

Panel A

FUNDING A PRIVATE EQUITY TRANSACTION USING THE TOTAL PORTFOLIO APPROACH

Bond $0.30
Buy $0.30 of bonds to adjust for the higher risk of embedded leverage in a private equity asset

Private $1.00
Invest $1.00 in the equity of a private company

BUY

LOWER RISK   HIGHER RISK

SELL

Public Equity $1.30
Sell $1.30 of public market equities to fund transaction

Panel B

FUNDING A REAL ESTATE TRANSACTION USING THE TOTAL PORTFOLIO APPROACH

Invest $1.00 in a Core Office Building unlevered

Equity $0.40

BUY

LOWER RISK   **Debt $0.60**   HIGHER RISK

SELL

Sell $0.60 of bonds

Sell $0.40 of public market equities

Figure 14.5

[21] The Reference Portfolio was revised on April 1, 2012. Prior to that date it was still 65% equities and 35% fixed income, but the equity portfolio was divided into domestic, foreign developed, and emerging market equities, and the bond portfolio comprised domestic fixed income, domestic real bonds, and (hedged) foreign sovereign bonds.

Panel C

AS AT MARCH 31, 2013			Asset Mix		Exposure Mix
ASSET CLASS	($ billions)	(%)	($ billions)	(%)
CANADIAN EQUITIES	15.3	8.4%	17.6%	9.6%
Public	13.1	7.2%		
Private	2.2	1.2%		
FOREIGN DEVELOPED MARKET EQUITIES	64.0	34.9%	89.4	48.7%
Public	35.4	19.3%		
Private	28.6	15.6%		
EMERGING MARKET EQUITIES	12.4	6.7%	12.1	6.6%
Public	10.6	5.7%		
Private	1.8	1.0%		
FIXED INCOME	60.7	33.1%	53.2	29.0%
Non-marketable bonds	24.4	13.3%		
Marketable bonds	28.1	15.3%		
Inflation-linked bonds	0.4	0.2%		
Other debt	8.6	4.7%		
Money markets and debt financing	(0.8)	− 0.4%		
FOREIGN SOVEREIGN BONDS	−	0.0%	11.2	6.1%
REAL ASSETS	31.1	16.9%		
Real estate	19.9	10.8%		
Infrastructure	11.2	6.1%		
TOTAL[1]	183.5%	100.0%	183.5	100.0%

[1] Excludes non-investment assets such as premises and equipment and non-investment liabilities.

Figure 14.5 (continued)

fund has a reasonable chance of meeting the liabilities of the Canada Pension Plan. The factor decision in the Reference Portfolio is taken at the very top by the board of CPPIB.

The management team of CPPIB is responsible for any deviations from the Reference Portfolio, which they are required to justify. As David Denison, the former CEO of CPPIB, explained:

> Our decision to vary from the Reference Portfolio is our responsibility. If we want to build up a real estate team—we have to recover that cost. Do we really want to spend those extra dollars? We have to have the conviction that it will yield, net of costs, incremental returns for the Canada Pension Plan fund.

The example investments in Figure 14.5 in private equity (Panel A) and real estate (Panel B) are made by CPPIB because the portfolio managers think they can create value, net of costs, above the Reference Portfolio. Put simply, CPPIB is hunting for alpha. Viewed in this fashion, the factor decompositions in Figure 14.5 are *factor-mimicking portfolios* (see chapter 7), and the alpha is the return CPPIB can generate over and above the factor exposures. These factor-mimicking portfolios are how the investments in private equity, real estate, infrastructure, and other nonfactor assets are funded. The alpha (net of costs) that CPPIB generates justifies having more than 900 employees in active management around the world in Toronto, London, and Hong Kong, rather than a bare-bones staff of fifteen managing a few index funds.

Panel C of Figure 14.5 is CPPIB's asset mix and exposure mix at March 31, 2013. At this date, CPPIB managed CAN\$183 billion. The fund holds 0.0% in foreign sovereign bonds, one of the Reference Portfolio's factors, but its economic exposure to foreign government bonds is 6.1%, which it achieves through its real estate, private equity, and infrastructure deals. Similarly, CPPIB holds 16.9% of its portfolio in real estate and infrastructure and yet it reports 0.0% economic exposure in these asset classes. For CPPIB, real estate and infrastructure are merely vehicles for obtaining Reference Portfolio factor exposure and are themselves not asset classes. Finally, CPPIB holds 34.9% of its portfolio in foreign developed market equities, but its economic exposure is 48.7%. The economic factor exposure in equities is far higher as it includes the implied equity exposure from real estate and infrastructure investments.

CPPIB's governance structure is crucial in allowing the organization to pursue factor investing and hire talented people (see Part III of the book for delegated investing). The Reference Portfolio means that management is "fully accountable for every dollar that we spend. ... This keeps management focused and accountable," says Denison. CPPIB can do this partly because it is independent of political meddling. There are no ex-officio government officials on its board. CPPIB does not submit its investment strategy or business plans for government approval, nor does it need approval for its compensation policies. The independence structure of CPPIB is enshrined in the fund's enacting legislation and changing its independence charter is, in the words of Donald Raymond, its senior vice-president and chief investment strategist, "more difficult than changing the Canadian constitution."

When I've taught my case study on CPPIB, some quip that CPPIB's factor investing procedure is "complicated." Isn't it just easier to find and invest in a private equity deal? If you do that, you are implicitly giving yourself long equity exposure combined with short credit exposure. That is, you're getting the factor exposures anyway. The difference is that CPPIB handles and tries to explicitly control the factor risk. A major advantage of factor investing is that you know what the fundamental drivers are behind your assets and understand the circumstances under which your portfolio may do badly. It more accurately identifies alpha. During the financial crisis, many "alternative assets" tanked right along with equities; we should recognize these factor exposures ex ante rather than being surprised ex post. As the Professors' Report recommends, it is better to get a top–down handle on factor exposure than having it result haphazardly from ad hoc, bottom–up decisions.

One valid criticism of CPPIB's factor investing procedure is that it doesn't go far enough! The factors in the Reference Portfolio are simple: static equities and bonds. There are no dynamic factors in CPPIB's benchmark, at least not yet.

3.4. HOW ARE YOU DIFFERENT FROM AVERAGE?

How do we allocate to factors, especially dynamic factors?

The skeptics will facetiously reply that we can allocate to dynamic factors just as badly as we do regular asset allocation. They have a point. Industry is besotted with mean-variance analysis (see chapter 3), which is great for those rare investors with mean-variance preferences. (I don't know any, do you?) In mean-variance land, you still have to assign means and variances, along with correlations, to all the assets, and there is not much difference between using factors and regular asset classes.[22] This is really a statement about the shortcomings of mean-variance optimization.

As Part I of this book stresses, modeling the investor is about identifying her bad times, and how well she can handle losses when losses materialize in bad times. We capture these notions with *utility functions*: a rich array defines bad times as low wealth, when your consumption falls below what you're used to, and even when your neighbor bests the performance of your own portfolio (see chapter 1). Factors perform badly during bad times, as they did for Norway in 2008 and 2009. The key in factor investing is comparing how the bad times encapsulated in factors compare to the bad times of an investor. Each investor will have a different set of bad times defined by her liabilities, income stream, how she tolerates losses (or not), and other salient investor characteristics.[23]

We can, and should, use all the impressive machinery of utility functions and fancy optimization in allocating to factors. I am, however, not a big fan of blindly applied brute-force mathematical procedures. I now lay out a procedure for thinking about factor investing that focuses on an individual's bad times. We start with a very special investor who actually takes on no dynamic factor risk whatsoever . . .

Mr. Market

The market is the quintessential typical investor—the market, by definition, embodies the average effect. *The average investor holds the market portfolio,* a passive, long-only collection of all available securities held with market capitalization

---

[22] As Kaya, Lee, and Wan (2011) and Idzorek and Kowara (2013) claim. Even in a mean-variance factor context, using factors does shrink, considerably, the number of means, variances, and correlations that need to be estimated, so there are some important differences between unconstrained approaches and factor models. See chapter 3.

[23] See Cochrane (1999, 2013a).

weights. Thus the average investor collects no dynamic factor risk premiums because Mr. Market holds all securities and does not continuously trade.

If you are average, then you're done! And if you use cheap index funds, you'll outperform two-thirds of active managers (see chapter 16). What the mean-variance framework and the equilibrium Capital Asset Pricing Model (CAPM) get spot-on right is that the market portfolio is well diversified; in fact, the market is the most diversified portfolio you can passively construct.

If you are different from average, then you will optimally *NOT* hold market weights. How you tilt away from the market will depend on your investor-specific characteristics. The important question is: "How are you different from average?" Do you have a longer horizon than the typical investor, as Norway does? Are you terrified of highly volatile periods because you need to meet a fixed liability stream? Do you tremble when the market crashes because your income is directly linked to market performance, so you get double-whacked as your financial wealth comes crashing down just as you lose your job?

Each factor defines a different set of bad times. The investor should ask, for example, whether the bad times defined by the value-growth factor are bad times for me? And if they are bad for me, do they hurt less than for a typical market participant?

There are three steps, then, in the factor allocation process:

1. How am I different from average?

    Identify your comparative advantages. The Professors' Report enumerated these for the Norwegian fund: (1) transparency and a long-term mandate, (2) large size, (3) long-term horizon and the lack of immediate cash liabilities, and (4) the fund manager NBIM is capable, has a strong public service ethos, and mitigates the problem of agency which is the central challenge of delegated investment management.

    Identify your comparative disadvantages. Size is a two-edged sword for Norway, and being large means small-scale alpha opportunities do almost nothing for the overall portfolio. If you're an endowment, perhaps you can't afford big losses because your university will have trouble meeting payroll (this happened to Harvard, see Chapter 13).[24] Or do you tend to go-with-the-flow and lavish attention on the latest hot stock?

2. What losses during bad times can I bear?

    In each factor's definition of bad times, assess your risk-bearing capacity. This is essentially your risk aversion with respect to each factor. If you are so risk-averse you can't afford any losses during a factor's set of bad times, then you should take the opposite positions in those factors. That is, perhaps you should be doing growth instead of value, or buying volatility protection instead of selling it.

---

[24] See "Liquidating Harvard," Columbia CaseWorks ID #100312.

3. Rebalance!

Mr. Market is special in another way: *the average investor never rebalances.* As Chapter 4 explains, for everyone who rebalances by buying low and selling high, there must be someone on the other side who loses money by buying high and selling low. During the financial crisis, CalPERS did a terrible job at rebalancing and sold equities when equity prices were at their lowest, and expected returns were at their highest.[25] Who was on the other side? Norway was the world's biggest buyer of equities in the last quarter of 2008.

Rebalancing is tricky because, for dynamic factors, you don't necessarily want to rebalance to dollar positions. In fact, for strict long-short dynamic factor positions, your dollar position is zero! But you want to rebalance as it forces you to cut your exposure when things have gone well, and add exposure in the opposite case, bringing you back to your optimal exposure to dynamic factors. You need to decide on rebalancing to risk exposures, volatility weights, exposures determined by contributions to risk or value-at-risk, etc. (I cover some of these cases in Chapter 4.) Pick a set of (risk) weights, then rebalance.

If you're good at rebalancing, you're ready for *factor timing*. Many factors are predictable (although the degree of predictability is very small, see Chapter 8), and you can exploit mean reversion in factor returns by incorporating valuation information in your investment process. You want to add more factor exposure beyond what rebalancing implies when those factors are cheap. Rebalancing already forces you to buy low and sell high; with factor timing you can buy even more when factor strategies become dirt cheap.

In my view of factor investing, *it is optimal for investors to hold non-market weighted portfolios*. Traditional asset management, as exemplified by Norway, (often unwittingly) takes on large amounts of factor risk. An influential article by Charles Ellis (1975) calls active management a "loser's game" because for every winner there is a loser and after transactions costs, there are only losers, on average. Active management can be a (relatively expensive) way to access factors, and it is optimal for investors to have different factor exposures. Active management, expressed through factor risks, may not be a loser's game. While for every person on one side of a factor trade, there is a person on the other side, both investors are happy because they improve their risk–return profiles by offsetting factor positions. For example, certain investors are happy to forego the premium for selling volatility to avoid periodic crashes. Instead, they purchase protection that pays off when volatility spikes. This makes everyone better off.

Investors find rebalancing standard stock-bond positions hard, and rebalancing dynamic factor positions is even harder. As Chapter 4 discusses, behavioral tendencies make investors most likely to give up on factor strategies after a string of

---

[25] See "California Dreamin': The Mess at CalPERS," Columbia CaseWorks ID#120306 and Chapter 15. Also see Ang and Kjær (2011).

recent stinging losses, which is the worst time to dis-invest because the low prices mean expected returns are high. Retail investors are especially prone to invest *pro-cyclically*, instead of *counter-cyclically*. One reason Vanguard has yet to introduce pure momentum factor funds is that small investors are likely to lose their shirts in poor factor timing.[26] George "Gus" Sauter, the former CIO of Vanguard says, "We have data that show that with narrowly defined investments, investors are not invested in them on the way up. They pile in at the top and then ride them on the way down." An initial allocation to factor strategies is not enough; you must have the conviction to rebalance.

CAPM

The *CAPM* is a good place to show how the process works.[27] According to the CAPM, investors should hold the market portfolio with risk-free T-bills, as shown in Figure 14.6. Tracing out the combination of T-bills, which is the intercept on the y-axis, with the market portfolio, shown in the circle, yields the capital allocation line (CAL). Investors hold portfolios on this line. There is a special investor who holds a 100% market portfolio (Mr. Market). If you are more risk-averse than the market, you will hold less than 100% of the market and lie to the left of the market

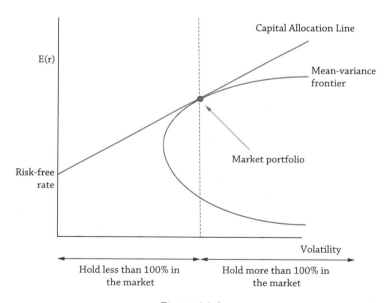

Figure 14.6

---

[26] Personal conversation with Sauter at the 2012 World Investment Forum. The quote is from Clark, K., "Listen Up, Bond Investors: Vanguard Investment Chief Gus Sauter Sees Low Returns Ahead for Some of His Most Popular Products," CNNmoney.com, December 2012.

[27] See Chapter 6 for an exposition of the CAPM.

portfolio on the CAL. If you are less risk-averse than the market, then you will lever up the market portfolio and short T-bills. In this case, your portfolio will lie to the right of the market on the CAL.

Investors who are more risk-averse than Mr. Market will earn lower average returns than the market. They're perfectly fine with this because they're more risk averse, so they sacrifice the higher returns for the safety of lower-yielding T-bills. (These investors have optimal betas of less than one.) If you are more risk-seeking than Mr. Market, you will earn higher average returns than the market portfolio. You don't feel the pain of bad times as much as the average investor, enabling you to earn higher returns. (Investors more risk tolerant than Mr. Market hold portfolios with betas greater than one.) Thus, whether you have large or small holdings of market factor risk depends on whether you are more risk-averse or more risk-seeking than the market investor. In equilibrium, any person who is more risk-averse than Mr. Market is balanced by a person less risk-averse than Mr. Market.

The CAPM gives us directions on how to construct the optimal factor portfolio, which turns out to be the market-capitalization weighted portfolio of all risky assets (the market factor, of course!). It seems easy now, but when the CAPM was initially derived in the early 1960s there was no way to gain market factor exposure. It took twenty to thirty years until retail investors could gain cheap access to the market factor portfolio thanks mainly to the Vanguard Group (see chapter 17).

Value-Growth
Let's do an example of a dynamic factor allocation by taking value-growth.

There are two main theories of the value-growth premium. Rational stories define different bad times when value stocks underperform growth stocks. Some of these stories, as chapter 7 details, describe situations in which the market portfolio does badly (this is a *conditional CAPM*), so if you're already wary of bad market draws you should definitely stay away from value. We saw this happen during 2008 and 2009. But other rational stories define bad times in terms of low investment growth, or when "long run" consumption growth is low. When these episodes happen, you ask whether you can shoulder the losses in value-growth strategies more easily than the market. If so, value-growth is for you.

In the behavioral stories, value firms are neglected because investors inordinately focus on high-flying growth stocks. They overextrapolate past high growth into the future, causing them to overestimate future growth opportunities. Stocks with past high growth are bid up too high, and thus value stocks are relatively cheap. According to this line of reasoning, are you drawn to hot stocks that are in the news because they have been recently successful? If you are, you are not a good candidate for value-investing. On the other hand, if you can stomach investing in stocks out of favor or close to distress, then value investing might be your thing.

This approach is very different from slamming a value-growth factor into a mean-variance optimizer. We start with the needs and characteristics of the asset owner (his *utility function*, in the language of an economist). We compare his bad outcomes with the bad times as defined by the value-growth factor. This requires an economic understanding, not just a statistical optimization procedure, of why these risk premiums exist. The appropriateness of a factor strategy depends on whether the investor can tolerate the factor's bad times more readily than the average investor, or how he differs in behavior from the average investor.

3.5. SUMMARY

Factor investing compares how you feel about bad times to how the average investor feels. If you are average—and there is nothing wrong with being average—hold the market portfolio. If you differ from average, you tilt to dynamic factor risk exposures. You hold factors whose losses during bad times can be endured more easily by you relative to the typical investor. Or you might hold negative positions in factors—which is equivalent to buying insurance against factor losses.

4. Dynamic Factor Benchmarks

Dynamic factors imply nonmarket capitalization weighted holdings, which change through time. Unlike the CAPM, there is no unique way to construct an optimal dynamic factor portfolio.

4.1. MECHANICS

Consider three stocks, which we label "Growth," "Neutral," and "Value" with market weights 20%, 50%, and 30%, respectively.[28] We assume that these are the only three stocks traded, and we have given these labels on the basis of the stock prices relative to fundamental value. We construct a value-growth factor that is long the value stock and short the growth stock. Suppose the desired portfolio is 100% equities with a loading of 5% on the value-growth portfolio. The optimal benchmark is the market portfolio plus the value-growth:

	Market Portfolio	Value-Growth Factor	Benchmark Portfolio
Value	0.20	0.05	0.25
Neutral	0.50		0.50
Growth	0.30	−0.05	0.25
Sum Weights	1.00	0.00	1.00

[28] This is drawn from Section IIIB of Ang, Goetzmann, and Schaefer (2009).

The value-growth factor picks up the differences in returns between the value stock and the growth stock and is a long-short portfolio (in jargon it is *a zero-cost mimicking portfolio*). The weight of exposure to value-growth, which is 0.05, is chosen by the investor.

The desired portfolio is a combination of the market weights now adjusted for the value-growth exposure. Note that the optimal portfolio is not a market-weighted portfolio; it overweights value and is tilted away from growth to achieve the desired exposure. In practice, the desired portfolio may have negative weights if the loading on value-growth is high enough, which would require dynamic leverage of the overall portfolio.

Now suppose that the value stock has done well and its new, higher price makes it Neutral. "New Neutral" (formerly Value) moves from a market capitalization weight of 0.20 to 0.40. The old Neutral stock has declined in price from a 50% weight to 30%, making it "New Value." The Growth stock retains its original characterization—it's still a growth stock and therefore keeps its original weighting of 30%. The value-growth factor changes: it drops the old value stock (which is now neutral) and brings on board the new value stock (which was previously neutral). Now we have:

	Market Portfolio	Value-Growth Factor	Benchmark Portfolio
New Neutral (Formerly Value)	0.40		0.40
New Value (Formerly Neutral)	0.30	0.05	0.35
Growth	0.30	−0.05	0.25
Sum Weights	1.00	0.00	1.00

The optimal portfolio reflects the change. In a pure market portfolio benchmark, there is no rebalancing to take account of the dynamic value-growth effect. The factor benchmark does this.

Although highly stylized, our simple example illustrates three key points about factor benchmarks:

1. The desired exposure to the value-growth factor is set by the investor (here, a weighting of 5%).
2. The benchmark portfolio is no longer market-weighted and instead reflects the value-growth exposure desired by the investor.
3. The benchmark portfolio is "passive" in the sense that it is based on a set of systematic rules but is "dynamic" in the sense that its composition changes over time.

All the major index companies put out nonmarket weighted indexes, as do some asset management companies. Arnott, Hsu, and Moore (2005), for example, construct portfolios with securities weighted by various metrics of fundamental value and offer a way to collect a value premium.[29] These exposures are not determined directly by the investor but are a first step in collecting dynamic risk premiums. True factor investing calls for an individual-specific benchmark, and there has been an increasing trend to customization in the index business.

4.2. GM ASSET MANAGEMENT

The dynamic factors involve trading, and thus minimizing costs and turnover, are essential components in constructing factor benchmarks. The largest investors have constructed and trade their own factor portfolios.

GM Asset Management, the fund manager of the parent company's pension plan, has built in-house dynamic factor portfolios for value and momentum.[30] James Scott (2012), the managing director of GM Asset Management's global public markets business, says that their approach is "consistent with the management of alpha and risk at the plan level and surplus plan management as suggested by Ang, Goetzmann and Schaefer (2009)."

GM Asset Management starts with an institutionally-investible universe. They do not short any growth stocks or loser stocks—they either underweight them relative to market weight or hold them at a zero weight. Their measure of fundamental value takes an average of Book/Price, Forward Earnings/Price, Price/Sales, Trailing Earnings/ Price, and Trailing Cash Flow/Price. They define momentum as the past twelve month return (but drop the most recent month, following standard academic practice, to avoid a reversal effect). Portfolios are rebalanced monthly and designed for low turnover. The factor portfolios have only small exposures to value and momentum, reflecting GM Asset Management's desire for only small factor exposures (they have tight *tracking error*). They have built U.S. value and momentum portfolios, as well as international versions.

GM Asset Management benchmarks all its equity managers to these in-house factor portfolios. Managers have to prove they are generating excess returns beyond those available passively from the factor benchmarks. They assess managers by a regression:

$$r_{active} = r - r_{mkt} = b_0 + b_1 r_{mkt} + b_2 r_{size} + b_3 r_{value-growth} + b_4 r_{momentum} + \varepsilon,$$
(14.6)

where r_{mkt} is a standard market-weighted aggregate benchmark, r_{size} proxies for the size effect (they take the Russell 2000 minus the Russell 1000), and

---

[29] See comments by Perold (2007), Jun and Malkiel (2008), and West (2010).

[30] For further details see "GM Asset Management and Martingale's Low Volatility Strategy," Columbia CaseWorks ID #110315. This section reflects conversations with Scott.

$r_{value-growth}$ and $r_{momentum}$ are the returns of their in-house value-growth and momentum factor portfolios. The factor exposures are the coefficients b_1 to b_4, and the manager's active return comprises a true alpha, b_0, plus movements due to market, size, value-growth, and momentum exposures.

Academics will recognize equation (14.6) as an industry version of Fama and French (1993).[31] GM Asset Management believes that market, value, and momentum are sources of risk premiums, and they can obtain all this exposure very cheaply through their own index factor portfolios. GM Asset Management likes tilts to value and momentum but wants to select managers who can deliver stock selecting prowess in excess of these factor exposures (they want to see $b_0 > 0$, $b_3 > 0$, and $b_4 > 0$). They believe that size does not contribute to a risk premium, consistent with the lack of a size effect we now observe in data. They also would like to see a fund manager not take excessive market risk. Thus, all else equal, they prefer to see managers with benchmark-like exposures to the market and size ($b_1 \approx 0$ and $b_2 \approx 0$).

GM Asset Management uses the factor benchmarks as just one tool to select and evaluate managers. GM Asset Management also finds their approach useful in controlling factor exposures at the total equity portfolio level. They use this tool only internally; they do not give factor benchmarks to their managers. In fact, most portfolio managers would feel extremely uncomfortable being given a factor benchmark that combines the value and momentum effects. Perhaps the widespread adoption of factor benchmarks will change this.

4.3. RAISING THE BAR FOR ACTIVE MANAGEMENT

We could go beyond GM Asset Management and evaluate all managers, not just equity managers, using factor benchmarks. In an ideal implementation of factor investing, we would give customized factor benchmarks directly to managers instead of passive market-based indexes.

For example, we could evaluate:

A private equity manager using a benchmark incorporating EQUITY MARKET + BOND MARKET + LIQUIDITY + CREDIT factors. CPPIB does this, but uses only the first two factors.

A corporate bond manager using BOND MARKET + CREDIT + VOLATILITY factors. If we can obtain credit exposure cheaply elsewhere, the manager should be giving us something extra to justify her fees.

A value equity manager using EQUITY MARKET + VALUE-GROWTH. GM Asset Management does this now, except it does not give the factor benchmark to the manager.

---

[31] Fama and French (1993) have market, size, and value-growth factors. Carhart (1997) augments this with a momentum factor.

By taking into account factor exposures, we raise the bar for active management. We want to pay active managers well when they create value (see chapter 15), but we need to ensure the returns they generate are higher, net of fees, than what we can get more cheaply in low-cost dynamic factor benchmarks.

4.4. RISK–RETURN FACTOR ANALYSIS

An important part of factor allocation is to look at the distribution of portfolio returns with different exposures to the factors. This is where fancy statistical analysis is useful. Many investors do this with the long-only factors like equity and bonds, where simulations are employed to compute risk–return trade-offs for a select few combinations of equity-bond mixes. We can extend this process to dynamic factor allocation. Most investors dislike downside outcomes more than they like upside gains (they have *loss aversion* utility functions, see chapter 2), so I recommend concentrating on downside risk measures.

The Professors' Report illustrated this for the factor weights implied by NBIM, along with less and more aggressive allocations than what they implicitly did during the financial crisis. Factor allocation usually produces returns that are highly left-skewed. That is, they can occasionally produce some very large losses. Viewing the potential of these losses as a function of the size of the factor exposures allows investors to calibrate their desired holdings to the factor risks.

4.5. FACTORS AND GOVERNANCE

Few in Norway dispute that factors are important and deserve close attention. A major challenge, however, is deciding who sets the factor exposures. The factor decision, like all investment strategy considerations, cannot be divorced from the governance structure.

The Professors' Report recommended that asset owners categorize factors by horizon and within each horizon bucket set appropriate performance reviews and investment strategy. Figure 14.7 contains three (simplified) horizons: short-term,

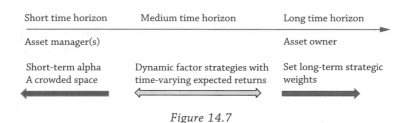

Figure 14.7

medium-term, and long-term.[32] Most fund managers, especially active managers seeking alpha, have short time horizons and work in a crowded space. At the other end, asset owners represented by boards, a Ministry of Finance, trustees, or investment committees usually set long-term asset allocation weights. For Norway and CPPIB, this is the long-term equity-bond allocation set at the highest levels, which are Parliament and the board, respectively.

Dynamic factor strategies occupy the middle ground as their verification horizons are in the order of two to five years. Value strategies, for instance, under-performed for up to five years during the late 1990s in the midst of the Internet mania. Many short-term asset managers harvest factor risk premiums (which sometimes masquerade as alpha). If the asset owner does not know the factor exposures, then she can be surprised and angry—as the Norwegian public was with NBIM—when the factors perform badly. *Factor benchmarks do not penalize a manager for losses that are due to poor factor performance.*

Asset owners also benefit from explicit factor benchmarks if they choose to set portions of their portfolio to factor exposures. The ATP Group, Denmark's largest pension fund, is responsible for financing the retirement of most working Danes. ATP divides its financial assets into a hedging portfolio, which is managed to match the funds' liabilities, and an investment portfolio, whose aim "is to gen-erate an absolute return that is sufficient to preserve the long-term purchasing power of pensions."[33] The investment portfolio is itself divided into risk groups: interest rates, credit, equities, inflation-linked assets, and commodities. ATP re-balances these factors to maintain approximate risk allocations (it practices a form of *risk parity*; see chapter 3). It also practices factor timing. The factor benchmarks allow ATP to invest counter-cyclically, so that factor exposures are increased as a factor strategy looks attractive.

Problems arise if neither the asset owner nor the fund manager takes respon-sibility for dynamic factors in the medium-term gray area. Many asset owners, for example, just gave up on volatility strategies after large losses in 2008, which was right at the time a counter-cyclical investor would have been increasing exposure (see chapters 2 and 4). Bringing a volatility risk factor, like all dynamic factors, into the fund's overall benchmark would enhance asset owners' ability to commit to the factor strategy over the long haul.

4.6. SUMMARY

Factor investing leads to optimal nonmarket capitalization indexes. Investors ought to be able to invest in cheap factor portfolios and customize their factor ex-posures to investor-specific circumstances and characteristics. Innovation in the asset management industry is taking us closer to this optimal case.

---

[32] Figure 14.7 is adapted from Knut Kjær.

[33] From the 2011 annual report of the ATP Group.

5. Macro-Factor Investing

So far we have taken an investment, or style, approach to factor investing as our factors have all been tradeable investing strategies. An alternative approach to factor investing can be based on (nontraded) macro factors. This is academically purer but much harder to implement.

This is because asset classes do not move one-for-one with macro factors, and in fact, many of their movements are perverse or at least unintuitive. Equities, for example, are a claim on real assets yet a terribly inadequate choice for tracking inflation (see chapter 8). Real estate is a better inflation hedge but it is only partially "real" (see chapter 11). Bond prices reflect inflation risk, but other factors, including monetary policy risk and illiquidity risk are important drivers of long-term bonds (see chapter 9).

Academic Model

Taking a macro view requires a framework for how macro factors simultaneously affect many asset classes. Ang and Ulrich (2012) is one model that could be used for macro-factor investing. We develop a model where real bonds, nominal bonds, and equities are jointly determined by two macro factors—inflation and economic growth—along with a factor capturing how the Fed sets monetary policy. If there is an inflation shock, for example, the model shows how the prices of all asset prices move. Macro factors are responsible for a lot of the variation in expected returns; for example, economic growth accounts for approximately 60% of variation in the equity risk premium, while expected inflation accounts for 40% of variation in real rates and 90% of variation in nominal bonds.

Bridgewater Associates

A practitioner framework where macro factors affect asset prices has been developed by Bridgewater Associates, a large hedge fund. Bridgewater's All Weather Strategy considers inflation and economic growth as macro factors, as shown in Figure 14.8. Although Bridgewater deviated from its originally intended strategy during the financial crisis, it is worth examining their overall framework. Bridgewater estimates how different assets perform during periods when growth is high or low, or when inflation is rising or falling. They fill in a 2 × 2 matrix corresponding to these scenarios. In Figure 14.8, they expect that nominal bonds do well when growth and inflation are falling. Equities, on the other hand, outperform when growth is high and inflation is subdued. This is clearly a much more simplified version compared to a formal model like Ang and Ulrich (2012), but the idea is the same: we want to see how assets react when macro factors change.

Bridgewater's All Weather Strategy

	GROWTH	INFLATION
RISING	**25% of Risk** • Equities • Corporate Spreads • Commodities • EM Debt Spreads	**25% of Risk** • Inflation-Linked Bonds • Commodities • EM Debt Spreads
FALLING	**25% of Risk** • Nominal Bonds • Inflation-Linked Bonds	**25% of Risk** • Nominal Bonds • Equities

Figure 14.8

Alaska Permanent Fund Corporation

Table 14.9 reports the asset allocation of Alaska's sovereign wealth fund, officially the Alaska Permanent Fund Corporation, which is funded by mineral lease rentals and royalties.[34] Alaska places its asset classes into different groups based on how they respond to different macro-factor risks. The company exposure category contains equities, naturally, and "benefits from times of growth and prosperity." But corporate bonds go into the same category—not in a separate fixed income allocation. Chapter 9 shows that corporate bonds are affected by many of the factors that affect equity—if a company is doing poorly, both bondholders and shareholders suffer. The correlations between corporate bond returns and stock returns, both in excess of Treasury bonds, turn out to be high: at 48% for Baa grade bonds and 65% for high-yield bonds (see Figure 9.17 and Section 4.3 of chapter 9). Alaska does not consider them separate asset classes as they respond in the same way to macro risk.

Alaska is also interesting because it follows the Merton (1971) model outlined in chapter 4 for long-horizon investing. It has a special opportunities class, with a target allocation of 18%. Long-horizon investors take positions in a portfolio that is optimal for short-run investors, called the *myopic* portfolio, as well as an opportunistic portfolio (Merton actually labels it a *long-run hedging demand* portfolio) in which the long-horizon investor takes advantage of time-varying expected returns. When there are special deals for distressed assets, or it believes there are good deals in more illiquid investment opportunities that Alaska can exploit because of its long horizon, it invests through its Special Opportunities allocation. If there are no such attractive opportunities, the allocation not invested resides in the Company Exposure asset class.

---

[34] Adapted from http://www.apfc.org/home/Content/investments/assetAllocation2009.cfm

Table 14.9

Alaska Permanent Fund Asset Allocation at April 2012		
Asset Class	Weights	Comment
Cash	2%	Aim: To meet expected liabilities and manage liquidity needs from rebalancing
Interest Rates	6%	Examples: Safe sovereign bonds Aim: To provide insurance against severe equity market correlations and to provide high liquidity
Company Exposure	55%	Examples: Global equities, corporate bonds, bank loans, private equity Aim: Benefit from times of growth and prosperity
Real Assets	19%	Examples: Real bonds, real estate, infrastructure Aim: Hedge inflation risk
Special Opportunities	18%	Examples: Absolute and real return mandates, emerging markets, distressed debt Aim: Take advantage of special investment opportunities The allocation is not fixed, and the allocation not invested resides in the company exposure risk class

In summary, Alaska's macro-factor investing looks through asset class labels by categorizing the way different asset classes react to economic growth, inflation, and other macro risks.

6. Sovereign ("Risk-Free") Bonds

My factor investing advice—to start with the market portfolio and see how your preferences differ from the average investor—must allow for an important exception: sovereign bonds that are "safe" assets. I recommend not holding, or starting from, market weights for risk-free bonds. Factor investing, however, still applies to these assets. Indeed, the special nature of these investments means that taking factors into account is especially valuable.

6.1. DO NOT HOLD MARKET WEIGHTS IN SOVEREIGN BONDS

In simple economic models, safe assets issued by governments are in *zero net supply*. There are no aggregate weights for risk-free assets because, for every person with a long position in risk-free assets, someone is shorting to provide that long position. Risk-free assets have meaningful prices, but these are prices in which parties contract with each other to borrow or lend.[35] All other risky securities—stocks, corporate bonds, and so on—are in *positive net supply* and represent real wealth. Thus, for corporate bonds, I recommend starting with the standard factor investing procedure.[36]

This same concept applies to all government debt, not only short-term T-bills. *Ricardian equivalence* is the name given to the principle that any liability of a government has to be repaid at some point ("tax now or tax later"), and in simple economic models without frictions, government debt is not net wealth: if we wrote down an aggregate balance sheet for the economy across generations, we would also see zero net supply.

The profession has moved beyond these simple cases and shown that government debt can be net wealth and fulfills many purposes other than borrowing or lending.[37] The simple economic models are useful to show that *the baseline case for investing in sovereign safe assets should not be market weights*. Market weights for sovereign debt are not very meaningful. To determine optimal holdings of safe assets, we should understand the roles that safe assets play and why governments issue debt, how much, and how often they default.

6.2. FACTORS IN SAFE ASSETS

Government debt, like any other asset, is simply a bundle of risk factors. The problem is that so many risk factors, some acting at cross purposes, are at work in safe assets. Look at what the International Monetary Fund (IMF) says:[38]

> Safe assets are used as a reliable store of value and aid capital preservation in portfolio construction. They are a key source of liquid, stable collateral in private and central bank repurchase (repo) agreements and in derivatives markets, acting as the lubricant or substitute of trust in financial transactions. As key components of prudential regulation, safe assets provide banks with a mechanism for enhancing their capital

---

[35] A major paper by Cox, Ingersoll, and Ross (1985) shows there are few restrictions on the risk-free interest rate process in equilibrium. They assume all safe bonds are in zero net supply.

[36] Aren't corporate bonds similar in that for every company that issues (sells) bonds there is a buyer? Why are corporate bonds net wealth? Miller and Modigliani (1958, 1961) tell us that in frictionless markets, there is no difference been corporate bonds and equities. We know this world is far from reality, but the main point that corporate bonds and equity are both claims on a risky corporation that generates profitable investment opportunities, on average, remains the same. This is not true for risk-free government debt.

[37] David Ricardo, after whom Ricardian equivalence is named, was one of the giants who established economics as a field in the early 1800s. The seminal reference is Barro (1974), who overcomes Ricardian equivalence by assuming distortionary taxes. Lucas and Stokey (1983) is another standard reference. A summary article is Ricciuti (2003).

[38] IMF, Global Financial Stability Report, 2012.

and liquidity buffers. As benchmarks, safe assets support the pricing of other riskier assets. Finally, safe assets have been a critical component of monetary policy operations.

Whew! Let's just discuss a few factors:

Credit Risk

An ideal store of value has zero default risk. The private sector, then, has great difficulty creating enough safe assets (the literature calls these *information-insensitive assets*) to meet demand.[39] But sovereign debt also has credit risk. Sovereigns default all the time.[40] Tomz and Wright (2013) compute that there is a 1 in 50 chance that a given country is in default at any time, but for the post-1980 sample the annual probability of default more than doubles, to 4%. Investors lose around 40% (the *haircut*) when sovereigns default, but there is wide variation with a range of 30% to 75%.[41]

Even the United States has defaulted. Twice. In 1934, it slashed the value of a dollar from $20.67 per troy ounce of gold to $35. Reinhart and Rogoff (2008) classify the U.S. abrogation of the gold clause as a default, which it was because at the time all major currencies were backed by gold. Then, in a little-known episode in April and May 1979, T-bill investors did not receive their interest payments on time.[42] The Treasury blamed processing problems and the failure of Congress to act on the debt ceiling (the latter is a perennial problem). At first, the Treasury did not want to pay any additional interest, which triggered a class-action lawsuit. The government paid only after much lobbying.

If we were to rank countries on credit risk, then we might rank three (I've randomly selected these) countries in order of most safe to least safe as: Norway, United States, and Brazil.

Collateral

Safe assets are used as collateral to borrow money or short other assets.[43] Ranking the debts of countries on the ability to use them as collateral we have: the United States (Treasuries are by far the largest source of such collateral), followed by Norway and Brazil depending on specific circumstances (like whether you're a Norwegian or Brazilian investor).

---

[39] See Gorton (2010).

[40] Reinhart and Rogoff (2011) is a comprehensive treatise. They show that from the 1930s to the 1950s, nearly half of countries were in default.

[41] See Sturzenegger and Zettelmeyer (2008) and Cruces and Trebesch (2013).

[42] Zivney and Marcus (1989) examine this interesting episode.

[43] A model of the collateral role for safe assets is Gorton and Ordonez (2013).

Transactions

Safe assets function like money for carrying out transactions.[44] The word central bankers use for this is *liquidity* (which is different from the notion of an illiquidity premium, discussed in chapter 13).[45] A major aim of monetary policy during the financial crisis, at least in the United States, was to alleviate liquidity shortages (see chapter 9). If we were to rank countries whose debt is the most useful in facilitating transactions to the least, it would be United States, and then Norway and Brazil again, with the order of the latter two depending on circumstances.

Another related role of risk-free assets, particularly currency (the sovereign bond with an instantaneous maturity), is a numeraire. We like to think of values as being independent of the units we use to measure them (your height is the same whether you measure it in inches or centimeters, for example), and numeraires transfer values from one unit to another. However, the choice of numeraire matters. Norway can report its return in local currency, U.S. dollars, or a currency basket. Each choice has consequences for the fund's volatility and perceived risk by the public.

Macro Factors

Chapter 9 discusses in detail how economic growth and inflation influence interest rates and hence safe asset prices. High economic growth makes countries more likely to honor their commitments, all else equal. Ranking countries from high growth to low, we have Brazil and then United States and Norway. If we order our countries from low to high inflation, with low inflation better for safe asset investors but high inflation better for investors with an eye to investment returns (see below), we have United States, Norway, and then Brazil.

Reserve Status

"Exorbitant privilege" was the phrase used by Valery Giscard D'Estaing, the French finance minister in 1960, for the role of the U.S. dollar as a reserve currency and the ability of the U.S. to print all the dollars it wanted. The U.S. dollar is still the world's leading reserve asset, and our other two countries would then rank Norway and, as a distant third, Brazil.

Caballero and Farhi (2013) argue that demand for reserve assets, especially U.S. sovereign bonds, has been steadily increasing. The supply of safe U.S. assets is limited by the health of the federal budget and the fact that the United States is shrinking as a proportion of the world economy. Our exorbitant privilege is that we can borrow cheaply through large reserve demand among foreigners, especially in emerging markets. As crises erupt, the U.S. government is likely to encounter

---

[44] This literature dates back to Sidrauski (1967) and Tobin (1969). A recent example is Krishnamurthy and Vissing-Jørgensen (2012).

[45] Important early references are Woodford (1990) and Holmstrom and Tirole (1998). There is a huge resurgence of papers on this topic after the financial crisis.

fiscal challenges and just when foreigners really want reserve protection, it might not be forthcoming.[46]

Summary

The flipping order of our three countries in each of these considerations show-cases the problem of how safe assets embody so many factor risks. Market weights capture none of these effects; some investors prefer safety, others most value liquidity, and still others want investment opportunities from rosy macro fundamentals.

Figure 14.10 compares the market weights of the United States, the Euro area, and Japan, in Panels A to C, respectively, using the Citi Yieldbook database. I over-lay Currency Composition of Official Foreign Exchange Reserves weights, which are the weights of central banks and reserve managers reporting to the IMF, along with gross domestic product (GDP) weights of each country adjusted for

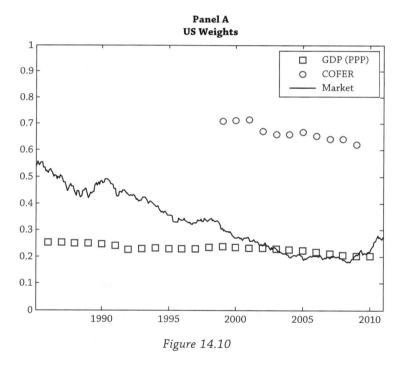

Panel A
US Weights

Figure 14.10

---

[46] This is a new incarnation of the Triffin dilemma, named after the economist Robert Triffin. Under Bretton Woods, major currencies were backed by gold, and the U.S. dollar had the same role as gold. Triffin argued this was unstable because the supply of safe assets would become in-sufficient, or foreign dollar holdings would be too large for the United States to support at the statutory peg. Triffin was prescient and Bretton Woods collapsed in the early 1970s. See Obstfeld (2011).

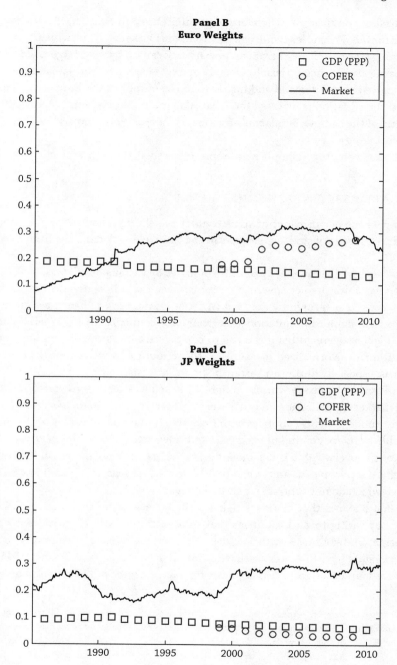

Figure 14.10 (continued)

purchasing power parity. There are huge differences. In Panel A, the reserve demand for U.S. Treasuries is much higher than the market weights, which have been declining since 1985 apart from an upward tick caused by new, large issuances of debt after the financial crisis. In Panel B, market weights of Euro-area safe debt is well above reserve demand and higher than the output of the Euro area. Panel C shows the situation is reversed for Japan. Japan's market weight is about 30% at the end of the sample, but Japan's fraction of the world economy is less than 10% and shrinking.

Market weights are simply inappropriate for sovereign safe assets.

6.3. SAFE ASSET WEIGHTING SCHEMES

I compare the performance of some country-weighting schemes for government bonds for the set of sovereign issuers in the Citi Yieldbook database from 1990 to 2010.[47]

In Table 14.11, Panel A, I examine countries by various macro variables. Many macro variables predict sovereign returns: over the full sample, countries that are poorer, as measured by nominal GDP per capita, tend to have lower returns. There is a significant inflation risk premium; countries with higher inflation have higher sovereign bond returns to compensate investors for bearing higher inflation risk. Normalized measures of the amount of government debt predict returns, especially during and after the financial crisis.

In Panel B, I consider various weighting schemes from macro variables, along with market capitalization and GDP weights. Starting with market weights, I overweight (underweight) countries with favorable (unfavorable) values of the macro variable at the beginning of each year and track returns over the next year. The sign of the overweights is dependent on the sign of the predictive coefficients in Panel A. I report means and standard deviation of returns, along with raw Sharpe ratios (which do not subtract a risk-free rate, see chapter 2).

Panel B shows that market weights actually have done fairly well. We can do better by tilting toward countries that have faster growth, countries with high inflation, and countries with low debt/GDP ratios.[48] Since the financial crisis, GDP weights have done very well, with raw Sharpe ratios of 1.73 compared with 1.58 for market weights. This accounts for a large degree of the recent popularity

---

[47] I construct year-on-year returns in U.S. dollars with a constant duration of 5.0 taking only developed countries. The macro data are from the IMF. Regressions in Panel A use country fixed effects. In Panel B, I set the maximum deviation from the market weight at 5% and do not allow short positions. Thus a country with a market weight of 7% has weights between 2% and 12%, and a country with a market weight of 2% is allowed to take weights between 0% and 7%. Rebalancing is done annually.

[48] The Debt/GDP measure is a nonlinear characteristic because very low measures are bad, but also very high measures are bad. Nonlinearity is much less pronounced in the developed country sample, which is used in Table 14.12.

of GDP weights for safe assets—the Norwegian fund is included in the herd.[49] This is a nice fact, but it lacks a coherent story.

GDP weights are a solution in search of a problem. What factor are you trying to capture with GDP weights? If it is capacity to pay, or credit risk, then we are better off using solvency ratios or political risk measures. If it is investment potential, then we should design a proper return-enhancing index based on the macro predictors in Panel A of Table 14.11. It can't be liquidity, as the largest GDP countries tend to have more liquid sovereign bond markets (China is an important exception). Finally, if we want to overweight countries with higher economic growth potential, then we should do GDP growth rather than GDP levels.

6.4. OPTIMAL WEIGHTS OF SAFE ASSETS

The factor investing method starts by listing the factors that matter for an asset owner. Is liquidity the most important? Perhaps we want to emphasize credit-worthiness. Or we prefer our fund to hold only reserve countries. Or maybe the

Table 14.11

Predictive Regressions of Sovereign Bond Returns				
	Panel A			
	1990-2010		2007-2010	
	Beta	t-stat	Beta	t-stat
Real GDP growth	0.573	1.24	1.530	1.64
Nominal GDP per capita USD	−0.945	−2.16	0.927	0.98
GDP (PPP) `	−0.603	−1.48	0.098	0.10
GDP (PPP) per capital	−0.451	−1.01	1.181	1.26
GDP (PPP) share of world	−0.604	−1.48	0.098	0.10
Inflation rate	1.864	3.79	0.832	0.88
Unemployment rate	0.041	0.09	−1.960	−2.12
Govt expenditure/GDP	−0.157	−0.34	−2.347	−2.57
Govt net lending/borrowing/GDP	1.364	2.74	2.316	2.54
Govt net debt/GDP	−0.899	−1.92	−1.726	−1.79
Govt gross debt/GDP	−0.692	−1.60	−0.616	−0.65
Current a/c/GDP	0.294	0.64	1.780	1.92

continued

[49] The Norwegian SWF uses GDP weights but requires NBIM "to take account of differences in fiscal strength between countries in the composition of government bond investments."

Table 14.11 (**continued**)

		Panel B					
		1990-2010			2007-2010		
	Sign	Mean	Std	Raw SR	Mean	Std	Raw SR
Real GDP growth	+	7.58	7.31	1.04	6.87	3.83	1.79
Nominal GDP per capita USD	-	7.80	7.92	0.98	6.42	4.45	1.44
GDP (PPP)	-	7.99	8.61	0.93	6.67	3.58	1.86
GDP (PPP) per capita	-	7.64	8.27	0.92	6.33	4.26	1.49
GDP (PPP) share of world	-	7.99	8.60	0.93	6.70	3.54	1.89
Inflation rate	+	7.97	7.89	1.01	6.59	3.58	1.84
Unemployment rate	+	7.43	7.87	0.94	6.14	4.47	1.37
Govt expenditure/GDP	-	5.41	5.88	0.92	7.31	3.77	1.94
Govt net lending/borrowing/GDP	+	5.72	6.66	0.86	7.01	3.67	1.91
Govt net debt/GDP	-	7.16	7.05	1.02	6.81	3.25	2.09
Govt gross debt/GDP	-	7.27	7.14	1.02	6.96	3.01	2.31
Current a/c/GDP	+	7.58	7.64	0.99	6.77	4.31	1.57
Market		7.35	7.49	0.98	6.47	4.10	1.58
GDP weighted		7.63	6.84	1.11	6.31	3.64	1.73
Mktcap/GDP weighted		7.23	6.04	1.20	6.55	6.59	0.99

number one priority is the return potential. The country weights should reflect the importance of these factors. Market capitalization or GDP weights will probably not accomplish that. Investors should decide on the factors, then reflect the importance of these factors by sovereign weights.

What about the optimal holdings of safe assets within a given country? Figure 14.12 plots the market values of all U.S. Treasury issues at December 31, 2011, using data from Bloomberg. Panel B removes U.S. T-bills and uses only longer-dated U.S. T-notes and T-bonds.[50] If you used a market weighted index, your holdings are skewed toward short-dated maturities because the U.S. Treasury

---

[50] At issue, Treasury notes have maturities between two and ten years, while Treasury bonds have maturities between twenty and thirty years. When issued, T-bills carry maturities less than one year.

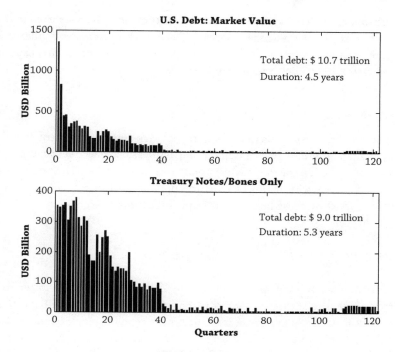

Figure 14.12

issues most of its debt with short maturities.[51] Do you really want a maturity structure like Figure 14.12 if you are bound to market weights?

The level factor, or the average interest rate across maturities, is by far the most important factor for fixed income (see chapter 9). The level factor accounts for 90% or more of the variation of safe asset returns and yields.[52] We could create a level factor portfolio quite easily by taking select bonds across the maturity structure. Exposure to the level factor is labeled *duration*, and once the level factor is constructed, an investor selects an appropriate duration target.[53]

An objection might be: but if you select a few bonds (somewhat arbitrarily), aren't you missing out on a lot of issues? Yes. But a dirty secret is that most investors never hold all the bonds in fixed income indexes. In many cases, it is impossible to hold all the securities because some issues just don't trade or are

---

[51] There are few theories on how a government should select a maturity structure for its debt. The leading paper is Angeletos (2002), who shows how to derive an optimal maturity structure that ensures against fiscal shocks and allows the government to smooth taxes.

[52] See Litterman and Scheinkman (1991).

[53] Term structure movements across countries are highly correlated, as Kose, Otrok, and Whiteman (2003) and Jotikasthira, Le, and Lundblad (2010) show. Setting one duration target across all countries is a reasonable thing to do.

held disproportionately by a few investors. Investors have often resorted to *factor replication* to track fixed income indexes.[54] They track fixed income indexes well despite owning only a fraction of the bonds because factors dominate, especially the level factor, in fixed income portfolios.

6.5. SUMMARY

Rarely should an investor base his holdings of risk-free, government bonds on market capitalization weights or outstanding issue sizes. Safe assets collect many different sources of factor risk, many at odds with one another. The factor investing approach starts with listing the factors that are most important for an asset owner and reflecting these factors in the optimal country weights.

7. Passive-Aggressive Norway Redux

As part of the active management review in 2009, NBIM wrote a letter to the Ministry of Finance stating:[55] "Active management will expose the Fund to systematic risk factors to a greater or lesser extent. The management and control of systematic risk must therefore be part of our management task." NBIM acknowledged the importance of factors but wanted them to be under its control. This is an important debate about where the factor decision should be made. In another letter dated February 2, 2012, to the Ministry of Finance, NBIM wrote:

> The investment strategy should be designed in such a way that the Fund can harvest risk premia dynamically. . . . Norges Bank believes that the strategic benchmark index should not be adjusted to take account of systematic risk premia for equity investments.

As I write this, the Ministry of Finance has not made a final recommendation on whether the dynamic factor decision should be at the asset owner level (Parliament) or at the fund manager level (NBIM). (The issue was discussed in the Ministry's 2013 report to Parliament.) Nevertheless, NBIM has gone ahead and introduced factors into its internal benchmarks. In 2012, NBIM introduced an *operational benchmark* for equities that explicitly takes into account systematic risk factors. There are just two factors so far: value-growth and size. (Note that I believe size by itself does not yield a risk premium in excess of market exposure.) I anticipate there will be reporting of exposures to the systematic risk factors so that the ultimate owners of the fund, the Norwegian people, are informed of the

[54] The quality of many fixed income indexes is far below equity indexes. See Goltz and Campani (2011).

[55] Letter to the Ministry of Finance dated December 23, 2009.

factor risks taken by NBIM and a repeat of the 2008–2009 controversy can be averted. At the very least, the public will be better informed about the risks of such an event.

David Blitz at Robeco, an asset management firm, and other practitioners have already dubbed the passive harvesting of dynamic factors "the Norway model."[56] In the public presentation of the Professors' Report, I said factor investing is "passive but dynamic" and "index but active." Factor investing aggressively pursues passive investments. It is a way of accessing returns based on a strong historical and academic foundation in a cost-effective manner. It is scalable. It can be done simply and without the agency issues and information problems of illiquid asset markets. It allows investors to pay only for active management that produces results unavailable passively. Many investors might consider following Norway and aggressively harvest dynamic factor risk premiums in a cheap, passive way.

---

[56] Blitz, D., "Strategic Allocations to Factor Premiums: The Next Big Thing?" Robeco Insight, October 7, 2012. See also Chambers, Dimson, and Ilmanen (2011).

DELEGATED PORTFOLIO
MANAGEMENT

CHAPTER 15

Delegated Investing

Chapter Summary

What is best for the asset owner (principal) is usually not best for the delegated fund manager (agent). Principal-agent conflicts can be mitigated by appropriate governance structures and contracts. Effective boards can advocate for principals' interests. Boards should build processes for investment decisions rather than making those decisions.

1. New York State Common Retirement Fund

The New York State Common Retirement Fund (NYSCRF) had $140.6 billion in assets and more than a million participants in 2011, making it one of the largest pension plans in the world.[1] This large pile of assets is controlled by just one man—the state comptroller, an elected official who serves as the sole trustee.

Over the years, many had tried to reform the governance of New York's pension system, but despite repeated scandals, all such attempts failed. All that power vested in one person is an invitation for trouble, and that's just what it has produced over the decades. Edward Regan, for example, was comptroller from 1979 to 1993 and was investigated in 1989 by the New York Commission on Government Integrity for directing state business to investment banks and lawyers who had donated to his political campaign. H. Carl McCall served as comptroller from 1993 to 2002 and came under fire for writing to companies in which the pension fund had invested, asking them to consider the resumes of his friends and family members. He even used state letterhead. McCall also was accused of directing pension fund legal business toward campaign contributors. McCall's successor, Alan Hevesi, was forced to resign in 2006, eventually pleading guilty to accepting

---

[1] This example is based on the case "Who Watches the Watchman? New York State Common Retirement Fund," Columbia CaseWorks ID#110307.

$1 million in placement fees in exchange for directing NYSCRF pension money to certain investment firms. Hevesi went to prison.

Thomas DiNapoli, appointed in 2007 to fill out Hevesi's remaining term as comptroller, introduced a number of reforms to improve transparency and prevent fraud. DiNapoli used outside advisors, consultants, and legal experts and established committees of professionals to advise him on the retirement system, investments, real estate, and actuarial valuations. Yet ultimately these structures and individuals were all merely advisory; the comptroller retained absolute control.[2]

The NYSCRF was subject to the same principal-agent issues as corporate pension plans, including the self-interest of managers and the misalignment of manager and beneficiary incentives. But as a public pension plan, the NYSCRF had additional principal-agent problems related to the conflicting interests of taxpayers and politicians, since taxpayers bore residual responsibility for the plan's liabilities.[3] Public agencies often face limits on the salaries that can be paid to employees, and thus the most talented investment managers, in general, are not available to public pension plans. The legislative and political process can also hamper the management of a public pension fund.

Eric Schneiderman, New York's attorney general, has criticized the sole trustee model. "Being a sole trustee gives more power than a good comptroller should want and more power than a corrupt comptroller should have," he said.[4]

But a board of trustees, instead of just one all-powerful trustee, has its own disadvantages. Trustees appointed by politicians, government officials, or unions may not have investment expertise and could be dominated by special interest groups. Or they could simply be crooks.

What is the right governance model for NYSCRF?

2. Principal-Agent Problem

Asset owners do not usually manage their own wealth. Instead, they employ an asset manager. This gives rise to an *agency problem*. The asset owner is the *principal*, who delegates portfolio management responsibility to the fund manager, who is the *agent*. The terms "principal" and "agent" come from common law.

[2] Strictly speaking, the state comptroller has direct, full control over all assets except real estate. Under Section 423(b) of the New York State Retirement and Security Law, all real estate transactions need approval from the Real Estate Advisory Committee. But the members of the committee are appointed by the comptroller! For further information on the sole trustee function and other responsibilities of the comptroller, see Sanzillo (2012).

[3] Under Article V, Section 7 of the New York State constitution, the public pension liabilities rank among the most senior of all unsecured state debt. Put another way, state pensions have the same seniority as general obligation New York state bonds.

[4] Editorial, "From Pay-to-Play to Jail," *New York Times*, April 16, 2011.

The problem of agency was introduced to economics by Ross (1973)—the same Stephen Ross who developed the theory of the multifactor model (see chapter 6). Agency problems are everywhere: they arise between employers and employees, landlords and tenants, clients and attorneys, patients and physicians, the public and politicians, and so on. In the context of asset management, the principal is the owner of the funds while the agent is the fund manager or advisor.

2.1. AGENCY PROBLEMS

Agency problems in delegated asset management arise because the asset owner (principal) and the fund manager (agent) have different utilities or risk aversions, incentives, horizons, skills, information sets, or interests. In addition, the principal's ability to monitor the agent is limited. In the cases where monitoring is possible, it could be expensive, it can be done only infrequently, and the asset owner may not understand the information being uncovered in the monitoring process. Principals lack the ability to judge whether the agent has talent or whether the agent is doing a good job. Even when a talented fund manager is employed, the principal does not know if the agent is working or shirking.

There are two key agency problems, with the terminology for both originating from insurance:

Adverse selection arises when the principal cannot verify the agent's skills. The manager is always better informed than the asset owner. The manager claims to have alpha, but the asset owner is naturally skeptical. The asset owner cannot verify whether the manager is the next Warren Buffett or the next Bernie Madoff.

In the insurance context, adverse selection arises when individuals have more information than the insurer, so only individuals who know they are terminally ill are more likely to purchase life insurance. Not taking into account the adverse selection results in the insurer charging too low a premium.

Moral hazard arises when the principal cannot observe the effort put in by the agent and the agent has or can acquire superior information than the principal has. The asset owner hires the budding Warren Buffett. But the asset owner can't monitor him. Instead of adding value to the asset owner's portfolio, Warren is in fact adding value to his own portfolio and ignoring the asset owner's. Worse, budding Warren is churning and front-running, thereby actually losing money for the asset owner.

In the insurance context, moral hazard arises (for example) when the insurer has sold an insurance policy covering theft. But the insurer can't monitor the individual buying the policy, who now leaves his front door wide open, since he's not bearing the loss. The insurer will end up underpricing the coverage if it does not take into account moral hazard.

Economists have studied ways to mitigate agency problems. Principals and agents can write contracts or construct governance mechanisms (economists call these *games*). The contract must make it worthwhile for talented, good agents to work (the jargon for this is the *participation constraint*). The contract must also provide the right incentives for these agents to work hard, lest the talented fund managers spend their time playing golf (this is called the *incentive compatibility constraint*). The contract maximizes the principal's value, and the contract takes into account the participation and incentive compatibility constraints.

Often the talented fund manager will be able to generate value that the asset owner cannot. This surplus will be split between the fund manager and the asset owner in a *bargaining game*. In some cases, the fund manager may extract all the value, leaving the asset owner with nothing. A cynic would say the technical term for this is *Wall Street*. Fred Schwed's famous book, *Where Are the Customer's Yachts?*, is as relevant today as it was when it was published in 1940:

> Once in the dear dead days beyond recall, an out-of-town visitor was being shown the wonders of the New York financial district. When the party arrived at the Battery, one of his guides indicated some handsome ships riding at anchor. He said, "Look, those are the bankers' and brokers' yachts."
>
> "Where are the customers' yachts?" asked the naïve visitor.

I will show over the next few chapters that in several investment vehicles—mutual funds, hedge funds, and private equity—the average fund manager adds zero to, or subtracts value from, an asset owner using an appropriate benchmark. That is, the fund manager collects, on average, all the surplus. In some cases, however, the fund manager may still add value because the asset owner may not be able to implement the benchmark herself. In other cases, the client wants someone to hold his hand and the fund manager helps him stay the course (see chapter 4).

2.2. OPTIMAL CONTRACTS IN GENERAL AGENCY PROBLEMS

Solving principal-agent problems and finding optimal contracts is difficult. Two Nobel Prizes have been awarded in this area: James Mirrlees received one in 1996 for solving models involving both adverse selection and moral hazard. (He is best known for his result, cited by the Nobel committee, that the optimal marginal tax rate for the rich should be 0%.) Leonid Hurwicz, Eric Maskin, and Roger Myerson were awarded the 2007 Nobel for developing the field of mechanism design, an area closely linked with agency theory. Many principal-agent problems can be interpreted as games and solved using the insights developed by these authors.[5]

---

[5] Textbook treatments of this material are Salanie (1997) and Bolton and Dewatripont (2005).

Several principles from agency theory can help us design systems to get fund managers to act in the best interests of asset owners. One general principle is that the fund manager has to "look more like the asset owner" and by doing so will "act more like the asset owner:"

Outcome-based contracts enable the fund manager to share the principal's reward. These types of contracts include *bonuses* paid if a certain outcome is obtained—for example, when outperforming a benchmark. Another type of outcome-based contract is a *relative performance* contract, where the agent is paid for outperforming a peer group.

Behavior-based contracts allow the asset owner to more closely monitor what the fund manager is doing, constraining his behavior and curbing his opportunities to exploit and deceive his employer. Examples of such restrictions include not allowing a manager to trade derivatives contracts or specifying the amount of risk or leverage a manager can take on. At the same time, effort can be rewarded.

Inference-based contracts are based on the principle that the fund manager should receive disproportionately high rewards for outcomes that are more likely if she is diligent and disproportionately low rewards for outcomes that are likely only if she shirked or was negligent. This principle means that, in general, nonlinear contracts are optimal.

Reputation is important. Agents know that their reputation is essential for winning new clients and maintaining professional standing. So the desire to preserve a spotless reputation helps keep agents in line. Even a single serious allegation can do real damage.

In the asset management industry, certain types of contracts are prohibited by law for certain types of investment managers. For example, under the 1970 amendment to the Investment Advisers Act of 1940, mutual fund performance fees can only be symmetric (see chapter 16). This rules out nonlinear inference-based contracts for mutual funds. On the other hand, some contracts that permeate industry generally are not optimal, as I explain later. One of these turns out to be benchmarking using basic asset class indexes.

In asset management, *implicit contracts* turn out to be as important as *explicit* ones. Asset managers receive compensation on assets under management, so the ability to attract flows from future clients is a powerful long-term incentive and in many cases is even more powerful than the explicit incentives in the manager's contract with existing clients.[6] Explicit contracts are under the control of the principal, whereas implicit contracts are subject to market forces. Incentive schemes arising from implicit contracts are often of a winner-takes-all variety, which leads to excessive risk taking.

---

[6] Fund flows in mutual funds, hedge funds, and private equity are examined by Chevalier and Ellison (1998), Fung et al. (2008), and Kaplan and Strömberg (2009), respectively. For all of these cases, assets under management increase when past returns have been high.

The key insight of agency theory boils down to this: the agent is out to screw you, not because the agent dislikes you but because the agent is human and therefore cares first and foremost about himself. As asset owner, you recognize this and can design a system (a management structure, a contract, or a governance system) that can mitigate these effects, and in the best case the tendencies of the agent to enrich himself work to your advantage. For example, you know the agent wants to maximize his own profit, so you allow him to earn some in a way that increases your earnings (the outcome-based contract). Another example: you pay enough so that the best agents come work for you, but you make sure they are adding value for your portfolio and not for their own (the behavior-based contract). Agency theory is about recognizing the conflicts between the principal and agent and working with the agent in the presence of these conflicts to enhance the principal's interests.

What if you don't get the contract right? Well, as Martin Wolf said, "With the 'right' fee structure mediocre investment managers may become rich as they ensure that their investors cease to remain so."[7]

3. Delegated Portfolio Management

We now turn to the special set of agency issues in delegated portfolio management.

Asset management generally has multiple principal-agency issues, many of them in conflict with each other. Consider the principal-agent relationships involved in NYSCRF summarized in Figure 15.1. In relationship (1), the comptroller is the sole trustee of the fund, and so is the agent of beneficiaries, who are the asset owners. The comptroller is responsible for overseeing internal fund managers and selecting external fund managers in relationship (2), and these agents are better informed than the comptroller (adverse selection), and the comptroller cannot observe their efforts in running the fund 100% of the time (moral hazard). The comptroller is aided by consultants, but this adds another agency dimension—relationship (3) between the comptroller as principal and the consultant as agent. The consultants themselves, in relationship (4), may be principals in their dealings with fund managers, like those employed to search and screen for best-in-class fund managers.

The taxpayer lurks in the background and is actually the ultimate principal. Government, through the taxpayer, hires the public sector employees— relationship (5). NYSCRF, like many public funds, targets certain economic priorities deemed to be important by the state. The fund, for example, takes a special investment interest in New York businesses. Thus, in some cases, the

---

[7] Wolf, M., "Why Today's Hedge Fund Industry May Not Survive," *Financial Times*, March 18, 2008.

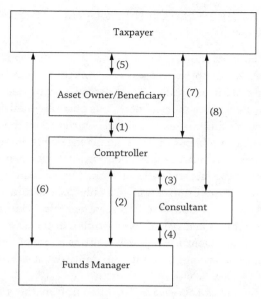

Figure 15.1

fund managers may be agents—relationship (6)—of the taxpayer. The comptroller himself is elected by New York residents, so he is an agent of the taxpayer in relationship (7). And finally, in relationship (8), some consultants working on NYSCRF matters are engaged by government rather than the comptroller, and so they serve as agents ultimately of the taxpayer and not the comptroller.

There are usually several layers of intermediation between the asset owner and the ultimate portfolio manager, and each layer brings additional principal-agent conflicts (and additional fees). For the current setup of NYSCRF, the beneficiaries as principal go through the comptroller, who then is principal to the fund manager. A given fund manager may himself outsource to fund managers beneath him. Not surprisingly, the ultimate goals of the asset owner carry less and less weight going down the chain of agents. Performance also suffers. Chen, Hong, and Kubik (2010) study intermediation in mutual funds (see chapter 16). Intermediation is actually very common in the mutual fund industry, where more than a quarter of funds outsource management to unaffiliated advisory firms (Vanguard's outsourcing to Wellington is a good example). Chen, Hong, and Kubik find that mutual funds managed externally underperform those managed internally.

Although all of these principal-agent relationships concern portfolio management issues, let's focus on the ones closest to the fund manager, where actual investments are being managed. In this case, there are two key differences between the standard principal-agent relationship and the delegated portfolio management one.

3.1. UNIQUENESS OF DELEGATED PORTFOLIO MANAGEMENT AGENCY ISSUES

A large part of what portfolio managers do is acquire information. The manager who takes a fundamental approach pores over company reports and visits firms to gain insights into a company, while a quant manager writes code to analyze data to forecast future stock price movements. Thus portfolio management typically involves the search for an information signal, which can be the basis for action. This makes the agency problems in portfolio management different from stand-ard agency problems, which are usually about direct performance—for example, how many widgets is the factory worker making? In standard agency problems, the agent does not acquire information and only decides how many widgets to make. The second difference from standard agency problems is that the fund man-ager controls both returns and risk of the portfolio. In the classical formulations of agency problems, the agent usually only controls a rate of output (how many widgets do you make on average?), not its variability (what's the range of widgets we're likely to make today?).[8]

What the asset owner can observe is also different from the standard principal-agent setup. In the standard moral hazard problem, *effort* or *action* is unob-servable. The principal is unsure of how much the factory worker is slacking or working. But the factory owner does know that the worker is either slacking or working, or more generally somewhere in the spectrum between totally slacking off or all-out working. The *choice set* or the *action set* of the worker is limited. In the portfolio management problem, the asset owner does not know the full set of portfolios that could have been selected but (sometimes) observes the final portfolio selected. That is, the reverse of the standard principal-agent set-up oc-curs: *the asset owner observes the action chosen but not the action set*. The very first paper in the delegated portfolio management field, Bhattacharya and Pfleiderer (1985) solved these issues and found that the principal needed a *nonlinear* con-tract to hire the best agents and ensure the best agents made the right portfolio selection.

The marked differences between standard principal-agent problems and dele-gated portfolio management problems have caused the field of delegated portfolio management to develop relatively slowly compared to other areas of contract the-ory. In Stracca's (2006) excellent survey, he says that because of these differences, "the literature has reached more negative rather than constructive results and the search for an optimal contract has proved to be inconclusive even in the most sim-ple settings."[9] Stracca is correct—economists have not yet developed a sure-fire

---

[8] In some problems the agent controls the variance (what's the maximum and minimum number of widgets you make each shift?), but the agent does not control both the mean and variance, which the fund manager does.

[9] See also the literature survey by Bhattacharya et al. (2008). A somewhat dated, but lucid, review is by Lakonishok et al. (1992).

way to guarantee that you won't get screwed by your portfolio manager. But the situation is not all dismal. I believe many useful principles are available to asset owners, but some of these unfortunately are neglected in industry practice.

3.2. IRRELEVANCE RESULT

A common way to reward a fund manager is to pay her for beating a benchmark, which is typically set to be an asset class index like the S&P 500. The agent's compensation is typically structured in a *linear* way, so she gets a base salary and then some fraction or multiple of the outperformance. We often choose linear contracts not because they are optimal (they generally aren't), but because they are convenient. In standard agency problems, linear contracts satisfy the participation constraint (a high enough base salary entices the talented agents to come to work) and the incentive-compatibility constraint (as the talented agent has an incentive to work hard).

Amazingly, the linear contract does not get the manager to behave in an optimal way for the asset owner. This *Irrelevance Result*, discovered by Stoughton (1993) and Admati and Pfleiderer (1997), states that *linear contracts have no useful role in delegated portfolio management*. The agent, who controls both the mean and risk of the portfolio, can always undo what the principal wants to achieve. Put another way, the "Irrelevance Result" is that the manager's effort does not depend on how much he gets paid. This is remarkable because linear payments for outperformance of asset class indices are so common, yet they are not beneficial to asset owners.

The setup of Stoughton-Admati-Pfleiderer is very realistic: the principal selects from multiple agents, just like the asset owner has a multiplicity of (supposedly talented) fund managers to choose from, all hawking their own brand of alpha, and there is hidden effort which arises because asset owners cannot look over the shoulders of all the fund managers they hire to determine whether or not they are shirking. The linear benchmarks based on the S&P 500, or similar asset class benchmarks, do not optimally share risk, do not allow the principal to achieve optimality, weaken a manager's incentives to expend effort, are not useful in screening out bad managers, and play no role in aligning manager preferences with the investor's.

The Irrelevance Result highlights the importance of the optimal portfolio of the asset owner. We cannot talk about the agency relation between the fund manager and the asset owner without first determining the optimal portfolio for the asset owner. In chapter 14, we saw that this must be based on a foundation of factor risk. Thus there are two decisions that cannot be delegated to agents: the level of risk to be taken and the key sources of risk premiums to be exploited, which both depend on the characteristics of the investor and her liabilities, income, and wealth (see Parts I and II of this book). Getting this benchmark right is step one so that all agency distortions can be measured relative to it.

The Irrelevance Result says that even if we have the right benchmark for the asset owner, the benchmark is irrelevant for the fund manager's actions when she is paid using a linear contract. But we can give the agent a different benchmark.

3.3. OPTIMAL DESIGN OF BENCHMARKS

One way to break the Irrelevance Result is to use a *smarter* benchmark. The benchmarks in the simple Stoughton-Admati-Pfleiderer setups are simple, *static* asset class benchmarks, like a traditional S&P 500 index. If we insist on using a linear contract, then it is possible to hire the best agent, and get the best agent to optimally put in effort, by changing the static benchmark to a smarter *dynamic* benchmark. This is what Ou-Yang (2003) shows.[10] Ou-Yang creates an *active* benchmark where the number of shares in each asset varies over time, rather than using a passive index where the number of shares invested in each asset is fixed.

The factor benchmarks, which chapter 14 considers, do precisely this. In dynamic benchmarks, the number of shares varies over time and in a factor benchmark the time variation is engineered to optimally maximize exposure to factor risk. Although this is not exactly the same optimal benchmark that Ou-Yang's setup would predict (and Ou-Yang's optimal benchmark can be difficult to compute), the overall concept is that we should move toward giving delegated portfolio managers smarter dynamic benchmarks if we retain linear payment structures. At the very least, we know from the Irrelevance Result that the static benchmark does not create any value for the asset owner.

Factor benchmarks also pick up common or aggregate shocks over which agents have no control and then relative performance evaluations offer better risk-sharing because they filter out the common shocks and reward or penalize the actions over which the agent does have control. Factor benchmarks, if chosen correctly, also make it harder for agents to "fake skills" that masquerade as excess returns (or alpha; see chapter 10) relative to passive indexes.[11] In particular, investment strategies with highly skewed payoffs, like those exposed to volatility risk, are best measured with dynamic factors that explicitly account for nonlinear risk.

The basic setting in the Irrelevance Result is a one-shot delegation model, where the asset owner finds portfolio managers over a single period. In that sense, it is similar to the Capital Asset Pricing Model. The single period is often not a constraint, as chapter 4 shows, because dynamic problems are simply a series of

---

[10] This paper is also remarkable because it is the first principal-agent model where the agent's action affects both the return (drift) and the risk (diffusion) simultaneously, which is the key issue in the delegated portfolio management problem, and Ou-Yang succeeds in deriving an optimal linear contract breaking the Irrelevance Result.

[11] Makarov and Plantin (2012) argue that is optimal for agents to fake alpha by taking on tail risk that cannot be correctly measured by static indexes.

one-period problems if we can rebalance. For large investors, however, there is a two-, or sometimes three- or four-, stage process where an asset allocation decision (which should be a factor allocation decision) is made at the highest level and then asset managers are chosen who specialize in single asset classes. This two-stage process generates misalignments of interest that are costly to the asset owner.

Static asset class benchmarks introduce further costs in addition to the Irrelevance Result in a multistage delegated setting.[12] Van Binsbergen, Brandt, and Koijen (2008) show that smarter, nonstatic benchmarks can overcome the disadvantages of decentralized investment management. These benchmarks often involve leverage and unusual positions of sector, or subasset class, holdings and would be hard to use in practical settings. However, the general idea remains valid: the static, asset class benchmarks so common in the industry today are bad for asset owners. The industry should move to smarter benchmarks. Factor benchmarks, therefore, have a significant role to play both as a tool for investment performance and as a tool for ameliorating agency issues.

3.4. OPTIMAL CONTRACTS

The Irrelevance Result says that linear contracts do not get the fund manager to act in the interests of the asset owner. So we could move to *nonlinear* performance contracts.

Nonlinear Contracts

The pioneering work of Bhattacharya and Pfleiderer's (1985) paper, which opened up the field of delegated asset management, derived an optimal nonlinear contract. It was quadratic and penalized both negative and positive deviations of the return away from the benchmark. It is natural to expect that compensation should be lower when managers underperform. Quadratic contracts seem unnatural because they also result in lower compensation when the manager has outperformed. And the greater the outperformance, the larger the penalty![13] We don't see quadratic contracts in the real world (at least not yet). But we do see plenty of nonlinear contracts in hedge funds and other alternative asset vehicles. Even if a wrong benchmark is chosen, leading the manager to shirk, having an option-type performance fee will help in motivating the manager to increase her effort.[14] Thus nonlinear contracts should be more widely embraced.

---

[12] This was first analyzed by Sharpe (1981).

[13] Quadratic contracts penalize excess volatility. In the real world, volatility constraints are imposed using tracking-error constraints. Constraints do play an important role in optimal contracts as I further elaborate in Section 3.4.

[14] This is shown by Li and Tiwari (2009).

General agency theory predicts that constraints form important parts of behavioral-based contracts and will mitigate agency problems for principals. In the Stoughton-Admati-Pfleiderer world, portfolio managers were unrestricted in the portfolio positions they could take. This allowed them to perfectly control both the return and risk of the portfolio and completely eliminate the effects of the incentive fee. Restrictions could be placed as schemes to induce manager effort. Placing restrictions allows us to move beyond the Irrelevance Result in some cases, and we see many restrictions on what managers can do in the real world. There are restrictions on portfolio risks (duration, tracking error, betas, concentration, and so on) and on what can and cannot be held (universe, derivatives, and so on). Theory shows that constraints form an important part of an optimal contract.[15]

Transparency and Disclosure

In choosing an investment manager, there is one other important consideration for an asset owner and this should go, wherever possible, into the optimal contract. Suppose there are two types of investors: skilled investors (Warren Buffets) and unskilled investors, (Bernie Madoffs). Bernie Madoffs cannot produce true alpha, but they are clever. They can mimic high returns that look similar to the Warren Buffetts for a time, say by selling options (see chapter 10), but they will go bust eventually. Foster and Young (2010) show that *no compensation contract can separate skilled from unskilled managers solely on the basis of their track records.* This is in contrast to the manipulation-proof portfolio evaluation measures that we discussed in chapter 10 that did allow us to (eventually) detect true skill statistically. But any compensation contract that filters out the mimicking Bernie Madoffs also deters all the truly skilled Warren Buffetts from participating. This seems to place the asset owner in a bind: if you can detect the Bernie Madoff, you won't be able to hire the Warren Buffett. But if you can hire the Warren Buffett, you may be hiring the Bernie Madoff.

The key to moving past the depressing Foster and Young (2010) conclusion is noting that in their analysis, the compensation contract is a function based solely on past returns generated by the manager. This looks very general: it nests bonuses, clawbacks, and all linear and nonlinear contracts. But it restricts the asset owner to looking at past returns. An immediate implication is that we need to look beyond past returns. We need *transparency* of managers' positions and strategies, and we should take into account reputation and all other information pertinent to their investment management business. Institutional investors should be familiar with the *separately managed account* as a way of making the manager's trades completely transparent.

---

[15] See Dybvig, Farnsworth, and Carpenter (2010) and He and Xiong (2011).

Disclosure is fundamental in addressing agency conflict in delegated invest-ment management. Many studies show that greater transparency in fee pay-ments lowers agency costs and results in better performance for investors.[16] Unfortunately, fund managers use obfuscation of fees to their advantage. Bund-ling, or making fees more opaque, results in lower returns to investors and higher payments to fund managers. Financial advisors often receive kickbacks from mutual fund companies and so have incentives to steer investors into poorly per-forming products, or ones ill-suited for asset owners. The more transparent these kickbacks are, the better the asset owner can see the distortions that other agency relations place on her welfare.

The Agent Has a Career, Too

Agents serve current principals, but they also wish to nurture relationships with future principals. That is, agents also have *career concerns*. Chevalier and Ellison (1999) study the labor market of mutual fund managers. They find that younger managers are more likely to be fired when performance is bad. Younger man-agers do not want to differ from the status quo—they hug benchmarks and want to hold more conventional portfolios. This is all the more reason to use smart, factor benchmarks: a young manager who acts in the principal's best interest by taking on nonlinear factor risk when this factor risk is not reflected in a run-of-the-mill S&P 500 benchmark is likely to be rewarded with termination when her performance dips below the S&P 500. Factor benchmarks benefit both agents and principals.

3.5. PAYING FINANCIAL ADVISORS AND ASSET MANAGERS

There are several methods of payment:

Commissions: Many financial advisors act as brokers and receive compen-sation—which can be substantial—for products they sell to their clients. This gives advisors an incentive to steer clients to the wrong funds. It also encourages financial advisors to recommend excessive trading to their clients to maximize fees. Bergstresser, Chalmers, and Tufano (2009) show that broker-sold funds un-derperform direct-sold funds, even before subtracting any distribution charges! Brokers exhibit no evidence of market timing ability, or superior asset allocation skills, for their clients. I interpret Bergstresser, Chalmers, and Tufano's sad re-sults as a prime example of the principal-agent problem: brokers put their own interests first. Investors should try never to compensate their financial advisors this way.

---

[16] See, for example, Gabaix and Laibson (2006), Stoughton, Wu, and Zechner (2011) and Edelen, Evans, and Kadlec (2012). Some economists, like Carlin and Manso (2010), have built models for the optimal amount of fee obfuscation that a fund manager should practice to deceive asset owners!

Fee Based on AUM: The fee based on assets under management (AUM) is the most common form of advisory fee, representing 85% of advisory-firm revenue.[17] Fees based on AUM predominate in institutional settings. The problem with fees set as a percentage of assets is that if the market does well, the AUM grows even if the agent does nothing. Why should the asset owner pay for time and effort *not* spent with the advisor or fund manager?

The history of AUM-based fees is interesting. The first independent investment adviser, Arthur Clifford, began his practice in Pasadena, California, in 1915 and charged *fixed* fees for his services.[18] This was in contrast to the commission-based fees, which brought large conflicts of interests. Across the country, in Boston, Theodore Scudder started Scudder, Stevens & Clark in 1919 to provide independent advice to clients. It charged fees of 1% of all transaction amounts—a commission-based scheme. Scudder found this did not generate enough revenue and was contrary to the firm's philosophy as it encouraged churning. So he switched to the much more profitable model of charging a *proportional* 1% fee on assets. In both cases, Clifford and Scudder were revolutionary because everyone else was charging commission-based fees. For a long time investment advice by commission-free advisors was limited to wealthy clients. Unfortunately, it was Scudder's proportional fees rather than Clifford's fixed fees that became the model for the industry.

Institutions paid fees largely based on (mainly brokerage) commissions up until the 1960s. At that time, a few institutions did charge 1% but offset those fees with brokerage commissions.[19] The Morgan Bank took the lead in charging fees of 0.25% of assets in the late 1960s, and it was predicted that Morgan would lose business. Only one account actually left, and Morgan became a leader for the whole industry. Gradually the proportional fees started ratcheting upward (rather than downward, as might have been expected from competition) to current levels.

Today fees based on AUM are high at 1% for individuals and a little less than 50 basis points for institutions. As Charles Ellis (2012) says, "investors already own those assets, so investment management fees should really be based on what investors are getting in the returns that managers produce." In the context of agency theory, Ellis is saying the fixed fee to induce agent participation is way out of line. But the incentive fee reflecting the value truly added by the agent is much too low. An investor would be fine paying large fees, if those fees resulted in added performance that increases the AUM, rather than fees that immediately reduce AUM. For institutions especially, this means that more fees should be incentive based and fees based on AUM should be much, much smaller. Individuals

---

[17] Survey by FA Insight of Tacoma in 2010. Reported in "How to Pay Your Financial Adviser," *Wall Street Journal*, December 12, 2011.

[18] This is drawn from Charles Schwab's 2007 book, *The Age of Independent Advice: A Remarkable History*.

[19] See Ellis (2012).

should also move away from fees based on AUM, but I do not recommend a large proportion of incentive fees, as I explain below.

From the standpoint of the financial advisor, a disadvantage of fees based on AUM is that it subjects a lot of the advisor's income to the vagaries of the market. In the parlance of factor theory, the factor choice should be the decision of the client, not the financial advisor. Yet the financial advisor is being paid as a function of factor risk not under her control.

Percentage of Net Worth and Income: This is like the fee based on AUM, except it allows the financial advisor to levy a proportional fee on (usually) a much bigger number. The advantage for the financial advisor is that it enables him to charge fees to clients that would not normally satisfy minimum AUM levels. Thus it opens up new clients to serve but with the same disadvantage for the clients as the fee based on AUM. Why would the investor want to pay for time not spent with you?

Flat Fee: Agency theory says that the flat fee should be set high enough to attract the best financial advisors. This is an attractive option for the client. The disadvantage is that there is no incentive fee to induce effort. That is, the client might be able to attract the best financial advisor. But with no incentive fee, the world's best financial advisor may be playing golf instead of working for you. As long as the flat fee is high enough to satisfy the participation constraint, however, this may be optimal, as I explain below.

Hourly Fee: This is rare, but it does remunerate on actual effort put in by the agent. This makes financial advisor compensation more like a lawyer's. A typical "low-cost" hourly fee is $300.[20]

Pay on Outperformance Relative to a Benchmark: This is also rare but gaining traction. This is exactly the incentive fee advocated by agency theory. It is subject to the Irrelevance Result. You need the right benchmark, and the benchmark itself is not sufficient with a linear contract. Thus all the same conclusions of Sections 3.3 and 3.4 apply. I recommend, though, that this remain a small part of advisor compensation for the following reasons.

Financial advisors perform a large variety of tasks, including often acting as principals themselves in a further delegated principal-agent asset management problem. In addition, they serve as therapists, legal and tax advisors, family counselors, and mediators. Many financial planners will argue that these are in fact more important than actually managing the client's portfolio. (My arguments in chapter 4 back this up. Even the act of rebalancing is as much a psychological one as an economic decision.)

The multidimensional role of financial advisors, which is not shared by most delegated fund managers in institutional contexts (including hedge fund and private equity managers, which I discuss in chapters 17 and 18, respectively),

---

[20] Pollock, M. A., "How to Find Low-Cost Investing Help," *Wall Street Journal*, June 4, 2012.

makes financial advisor compensation special. I follow Holmstrom and Milgrom (1991) in recommending that incentive payments that are common in institutions *not* be a major part of the compensation structure of financial advisors. Holmstrom and Milgrom show that when an agent has several different tasks to perform—as financial advisors do—then incentivizing the agent to perform well on one task diverts attention from other tasks. The agent then focuses disproportionate time or effort on the tasks that are compensated well. When the agent is asked to multitask, or the tasks are not easily measured, the optimal incentive contract is closer to a fixed wage without any incentive contracts. Holmstrom and Milgrom argue this is in fact why we do not observe incentive payments, or only very small ones, in many situations. For individual investors, a financial advisor provides services on many dimensions that are hard to measure, and so financial advisor compensation fits squarely in the Holmstrom and Milgrom category. Only a minor part of compensation for a financial advisor should be incentive based.

At the same time, there are too many disadvantages of fees based on AUM or as a percentage of net worth and income. For a small retail investor, my advice is to find one of the growing number of financial advisors who charge flat or hourly fees. Make sure you're paying enough to get the best financial advisors to work for you. Pay extra for services that the flat fee does not cover.

Benchmarks, however, are still important. The benchmark allows the investor to see what value is being added by the financial advisor, even though the advisor is receiving little incentive compensation relative to the benchmark. The benchmark should be something an investor can do on her own at low cost, without the advisor: a simple combination of index funds, a "default" target-date fund (although these have many disadvantages; see chapter 5), or a simple factor portfolio for the more sophisticated investor (see chapter 14). Most financial advice results in clients underperforming simple benchmarks: in a study of the Oregon University System, Chalmers and Reuter (2012b) report that investors using brokers underperform those not using brokers by in excess of 1.5%.[21] Broker fees paid by clients account for 0.9% of this, and the rest comes from brokers recommending riskier portfolios stuffed with expensive products that do not perform as well as simple benchmarks. Pay well when advice is good, but to recognize good advice you need a transparent and demanding benchmark.

3.6. SUMMARY

There is often a multiplicity of agency relations in asset management. The role of consultants, for example, often lends another set of agency issues rather than

---

[21] Karabulut (2010) and Mullainathan, Noth, and Schoar (2012) also find little value-added from the average financial advisor. Like Chalmers and Reuter (2012b), they also show that financial advice is associated with lower risk-adjusted returns.

resolving existing ones between asset owners and fund managers. Solving one agency relation can exacerbate another.

I offer several recommendations:

1. By themselves, linear contracts with traditional static (S&P 500-like) benchmarks are useless and in the worst case cause managers to destroy value. (This is the Irrelevance Result.)
2. Smarter benchmarks, particularly factor benchmarks, will ameliorate agency issues when used in linear contracts.
3. Nonlinear, option-like compensation contracts can optimally motivate fund managers.
4. Constraints play an important role in contracts, with fewer constraints for more talented fund managers.
5. Disclosure is paramount: optimal contracts should be as transparent as possible.
6. The 1% fee for individuals (or 50 basis point institutional fee) based on AUM is exorbitant. Minimize payments based on AUM.
7. Incentive fees for financial advisors should only represent a fraction of total compensation. Retail investors should pay flat fees or by the hour.
8. Benchmark your financial advisor by using a simple, fixed combination of index funds.

4. Boards

A large number of principals are often represented by a board, just as in a corporate setting. Boards have long been known to be a good monitoring system to temper the opportunism of agents and a large literature in corporate finance, both theoretical and empirical, emphasizes the importance of independent directors on boards.[22] Effective boards advocate for the principals' interests. By monitoring and interpreting information, boards mitigate principal-agent problems.[23]

While boards themselves are agents of those they represent, like beneficiaries, family members of a family office, and an entire nation for a sovereign wealth fund, in this section I concentrate on the board as principal and discuss its role in relation to a fund manager as its agent.

I pay special attention to the concerns of NYSCRF in this section. Edward Regan, who served as comptroller from 1979 to 1993, attempted to change the NYSCRF's governance structure to a board and tried to reform himself out of a job as sole trustee. He recalled,

---

[22] See Fama and Jensen (1983) and Hermalin and Weisbach (2003) for summaries.

[23] Monitoring and constraints are substitutes. Almazan et al. (2004) find that investment restrictions on mutual funds are more likely when their boards are less independent.

In the 1980s, when I was the comptroller, I proposed legislation calling for a small board of investment experts for the pension fund, representing local governments and active and retired state government workers. Within weeks of its introduction, however, the bill was the subject of amendments intended to grant additional seats to favored interest groups. So I withdrew my support.[24]

Having a pension board dominated by special interests groups, especially with a majority of representatives lacking professional investment knowledge, would be a recipe for disaster. How should NYSCRF select a board, assuming we select a board model as the optimal governance structure?

4.1. BOARD MEMBERSHIP

Corporate finance theory and empirical data suggest that independent boards add the most value.[25] I discuss two models NYSCRF could emulate: the Canada Pension Plan Investment Board (CPPIB) and the New Zealand Superannuation Fund (NZSF), the sovereign wealth fund of New Zealand.[26] Both have boards independent of their governments.

CPPIB is a dedicated fund manager whose job is to invest the assets of the Canada Pension Plan to "maximize investment returns without undue risk of loss." It is set up at "arm's length from governments." Under the terms of the 1997 Canada Pension Plan Investment Board Act, CPPIB is governed by a twelve-person board of directors. They are appointed by the Federal Finance Minister in consultation with the provinces (except Quebec, which does not participate), and with the assistance of a nominating committee, for a term of three years. Terms are staggered such that no more than half the directors' terms expire in any one year. Directors are eligible for reappointment, with a maximum service of three terms. Directors must have investment expertise, "with a proven financial ability or relevant work experience such that the board will be able to effectively achieve its objects." Additionally, directors must be "representative of the various regions of Canada." There are no government officials on the board. CPPIB does not submit investment strategy or business plans to the government for approval; nor does it require government approval for compensation policies or

---

[24] Regan, E. V., "Too Much Money for One Man," *New York Times*, March 5, 2011.

[25] Gordon (2007) shows that independent directors are much more valuable than insiders at adding value to firms. The earlier literature, like Hermalin and Weisbach (1991) found little relation between board independence and higher firm value, but now there are many papers showing this link. Independent directors also are associated with better outcomes regarding CEO turnover, executive compensation, fraud, opportunistic timing of stock option grants, and investment efficiency. See Bebchuk and Weisbach (2010) for references.

[26] More details are available in the case, "Factor Investing: The Reference Portfolio and Canada Pension Plan Investment Board," Columbia CaseWorks ID#120302.

pay levels. To change the governance structure of CPPIB and its mandate requires approval by the federal government and two-thirds of the provinces representing two-thirds of the population. Senior vice president and chief investment strategist Donald Raymond comments, this is "more difficult than changing the Canadian constitution."

In many ways, NZSF is similar to CPPIB.[27] NZSF invests government contributions to New Zealand Superannuation. In 2029, the New Zealand government began making withdrawals from the NZSF to help meet the cost of pension benefits. NZSF is an independent crown entity. It is overseen by an independent board, called the Guardians Board, who operate at arm's length from the government but make quarterly reports to the Minister of Finance. The NZSF has a "double arm's length structure" from the government. First, the New Zealand government appoints an independent Nominating Committee. The government does not control the pool of candidates, making this the first arm of independence. The Nominating Committee identifies candidates for the Guardians Board. The Minister of Finance must select members from the list made by the Nominating Committee. The Guardians and management of NZSF decide investment policy and make investment decisions independent of government, which is the second arm of independence.

In both CPPIB and NZSF, board members are selected for skills and experience. This certainly helps, but I believe it is not a prerequisite. In some cases, recruiting investment professionals can shift the board away from the fund's base constituency and weaken legitimacy and the ability to communicate effectively with the fund's asset owners. Investment professionals who are especially close with financial intermediaries may in fact generate more agency problems, and potentially higher costs, in steering business toward those intermediaries.[28]

This has happened, for example, at Dartmouth College, where members of the board and endowment investment committee have been accused of enriching their own investment management firms.[29] Tellus Institute, a not-for-profit research and policy organization, puts Dartmouth in the spotlight for its large number of trustees and committee members involved in running money for the university.[30] It singled out the conflict of interests involved when CIO Davis Russ left in 2009. The investment committee chair and trustee Stephen Mandel played the CIO role on a voluntary part-time basis, but at the same time Mandel's firm, Lone Pine Capital LLC, managed money for Dartmouth's endowment. "It

---

[27] See information at http://www.nzsuperfund.co.nz/

[28] See Ang and Kjær (2011). Levit (2012) shows that in some situations, the expertise of some board members can actually subtract value.

[29] Diamond, R., "Dartmouth Board Members are Accused of Enriching Own Firms," *Pensions & Investments*, May 28, 2012.

[30] Tellus Institute, 2010, "Educational Endowments and the Financial Crisis: Social Costs and Systemic Risks in the Shadow Banking System, A Study of Six New England Schools."

dawned on me that we seemed to be spending hundreds of millions on conflicted transactions," said a former trustee of Dartmouth.[31] In September 2009, 4% of Dartmouth's endowment was in Mandel's fund.

Another governance model that I recommend NYSCRF not follow is that of CalPERS, the large state pension fund in California. CalPERS is beset by political interference.[32] Its board is not independent of government. On the contrary, it has four government ex-officio members. Six of the thirteen board members are from unions. Thus there are not many board members directly and independently representing beneficiaries.

The main requirement for board members should be independence; director competence should be continually upgraded by education, and this process itself enables principals to better monitor and evaluate agents.

4.2. WHAT BOARDS SHOULD DO

Own Factor Risk Sources and Exposures

Two things cannot be outsourced by boards, and these are the two most important decisions in asset management: the level of risk to be taken and the key sources of factor risk premiums to be exploited.[33] These decisions must be made based on the characteristics of the asset owner (see Part I) with an emphasis on how these characteristics allow the investor to collect long-run factor risk premiums or insure against short-run factor risk calamities (see Part II). The board of CPPIB, for example, owns the Reference Portfolio. The Reference Portfolio is the capstone of CPPIB's strategic risk-taking framework and is, in effect, a factor exposure decision. It is a passive factor mix that is reasonably expected to match its liabilities and can be implemented in low-cost, passive vehicles. (CPPIB practices factor investing; see chapter 14.) Through the choice of the Reference Portfolio, the board of CPPIB has pinned down its desired level of risk and the factor risk premiums to be exploited in the long run.

Build Processes to Make Investment Decisions, But Do Not Make Investment Decisions

Boards should build processes for a fund manager to make investment decisions, rather than make direct investment decisions themselves. Elroy Dimson, a prominent U.K. finance professor, asks how often a board or committee should meet

---

[31] Quoted in Wee, G., "Leon Black Investing Dartmouth Money Stirs Ethics Debate," Bloomberg, Jan. 7, 2013.

[32] Several instances are outlined in "California Dreamin': The Mess at CalPERS," Columbia CaseWorks ID#120306, 2012.

[33] Chapter 14 discusses these points in the context of factor investing.

if the primary role of an investment committee is to set investment objectives, make asset allocation decisions, and select money managers—in other words to produce alpha? The answer is simple: NEVER.[34]

The board has hired the asset manager (agent) to make these decisions. And the fund manager is closer to markets and has better information than the board. The board must anchor and own the long-run investment strategy, but it does not implement that strategy. For the asset manager to do that well, there has to be communication and reporting set up so that the asset owner can trust the manager. The asset owner should put in place processes so that the asset manager can make investment decisions, but the board should not make investment decisions itself.

This advice aligns with theory. Aghion and Tirole (1997) show that if the principal intervenes and overrules the agent's choices, he reduces the agent's incentives to make good choices, and thus the agent is less incentivized to create value. Constant intervention destroys the opportunities and incentives for lower levels to learn. Always second-guessing the manager undercuts autonomy and any performance incentives arising from it. And of course, intervention is destructive to firm culture and leads to a lot of wasted effort and politicking.

Set Consistent Goals

The board has the responsibility to create an environment where a professional investment culture can flourish, consistent with the comparative advantages of the investor, investment beliefs and strategy, and the institution's ability to implement. The last is crucial. CPPIB has empowered its investment manager (agent) and given it an active investment mandate. The Reference Portfolio serves as the benchmark to measure the active performance. The Reference Portfolio represents a low-cost, investable alternative to active management and it is transparent, demanding, and simple.

To implement the active mandate, CPPIB pays its managers well (although nowhere near the highest levels of Wall Street); the board supports its manager and gives it appropriate resources to pursue active management. Most of the funds are managed internally, at great savings to beneficiaries. Although sufficient pay is part of creating a strong investment culture, it is certainly not the only consideration. Equally important is the board's ability to assess and support the manager's ability to build and retain skills. At the opposite extreme, the large state pension fund of CalPERS is hamstrung by many state constraints, especially on pay. Joseph Dear, CIO of CalPERS, has said the CPPIB model is not "politically feasible"

[34] Elroy Dimson, quoted by Arnold Wood, presentation slides "Behavioral Insights: Origins of Imperfect Choices," 2011.

in California and so CalPERS is forced to outsource more active management, with fewer savings for California state workers.[35] A similar problem is that a board may give an investment manager a mandate for active management, but without giving sufficient resources to pursue that goal, the board sets up the agent to fail. There must be consistency in the goals for both the principal and the agent.

Set Clear Boundaries
There should be bright lines between what the board (principal) does and what the manager (agent) does.

At CPPIB, the division of responsibility between the board and management is clear. The board sets the Reference Portfolio—the factor risk decision—and management takes responsibility for any deviation from it in trying to beat the Reference Portfolio benchmark. The board sets constraints on how much deviation is possible from the Reference Portfolio, consistent with constraints being part of the optimal contract in Section 3.4, with other constraints on the portfolio holdings. CPPIB's structure allowed management to put in place human resource policies that supported the execution of this strategy, including a compensation system that is performance based and allows CPPIB to attract talented people. These human resource policies could be justified in the context of the Reference Portfolio—if CPPIB's active management outperformed the passive Reference Portfolio, net of costs, these policies add value.

NZSF also has a clear division of responsibilities between the Board of Guardians (principal) and management (agent). Like CPPIB, the board does not make investment decisions. The Guardians set investment policy, decide on an appropriate level of risk, approve and monitor investment strategies, appoint the custodians, and deal with other oversight matters but leave investment decisions to management. Management advises the Guardian Board on investment policy and implements the agreed investment strategies.

Avoid Ad-Hoc Modifications to Long-Term Strategy
Many ad hoc responses induce pro-cyclical behavior.

During the financial crisis from 2007 to 2009, many boards resorted to panic selling and abandoned rebalancing. CalPERS' equity portfolio shrank from more than $100 billion in 2007 to just $38 billion in 2009.[36] Stock lending blew up and CalPERS sold equities to raise cash. CalPERS also sold stocks to meet its commitments to private equity and real estate partners. The CalPERS board became skittish. The forced selling occurred at precisely the wrong time, when prices were

[35] "Maple Revolutionaries: Canada's Public Pension Funds Are Changing the Deal-Making Landscape," *The Economist*, March 3, 2012, p. 86.
[36] This material is drawn from "California Dreamin': The Mess at CalPERS," Columbia CaseWorks ID#120306, 2012.

lowest and expected returns were highest. The CalPERS board did not establish a formal rebalancing policy until 2009.

The opposite problem is that boards are often attracted to asset classes or strategies that have done well and enter after a period of strong gains when future expected returns are low. This also tends to generate pro-cyclical investing. As real estate returns were heating up during the mid-1990s, CalPERS followed aggressively and ramped up its real estate allocations from a 5% low in 2005 to a peak of more than 9% in 2008—just as real estate was crashing. In 2001, CalPERS' loan-to-value ratio in its real estate portfolio was only 19%. By 2004, the leverage CalPERS was using in its real estate transactions had reached 41% and was projected to reach 50%. In addition to juicing its real estate investments with more leverage, the board jumped on the real estate band wagon and delegated decisions to outside partners so that deals would not get caught up in "red tape." But CalPERS retained the risk. CalPERS only began an external due-diligence process for its real estate investments in January 2008, which was after the market had peaked and many real estate investments had already soured.

Joseph Dear, CIO of CalPERS, described CalPERS' real estate investments as "a disaster."[37] CalPERS' real estate holdings lost over 70% of their value between 2008 and 2010. Some of the individual deals are sorry stories indeed. In New York, CalPERS lost $500 million after lenders took control of the Stuyvesant Town-Cooper Village property in which it had foolishly invested. In 2005, CalPERS bought 9,000 lots of residential housing in Mountain House, California, from Trimark Communities. By 2008, CalPERS was forced to value the deal at negative $305 million (an "asset" with a negative value!) due to the losses suffered plus the interest it paid on the leverage. That same year, Mountain House was declared the most "underwater" community in America.[38] All of this pro-cyclicality was due to poor judgment, lack of risk controls, and a failure to set risk boundaries: these shortcomings created the worst possible alignments between CalPERS and its real estate investment advisors. In addition, complexity and high costs obscured CalPERS' true underlying factor risk exposure.

Norway's sovereign wealth fund has so far had the opposite experience. It was the largest buyer of equities in the fourth quarter of 2008 and it was able to cling to its rebalancing rule while others abandoned theirs. Norway had decided on a process for rebalancing, rather than having a board make rebalancing decisions.[39] But Norway also experienced poor active returns during 2008 and 2009. At the time, many in Norway called for the active mandate to be rescinded from its fund manager, NBIM. But the Ministry of Finance did not act in haste. I was one of three researchers asked to analyze the fund's investments as part of building

[37] Creswell, J., "Pensions Find Riskier Funds Fail to Pay Off," *New York Times*, April 1, 2012,

[38] As determined by American CoreLogic, a real estate data company. See Streitfield, D., "A Town Drowns in Debt as Home Values Plunge," *New York Times*, Nov. 10, 2008.

[39] See more details in Ang and Kjaer (2011).

consensus for change.[40] In keeping with our report, the active mandate was not removed and the fund came through the experience more robust. In contrast to CalPERS, Norway was not caught up in the real estate bubble. The Ministry of Finance had studied the feasibility of real estate investment during the span of rising property prices in the mid-2000s. It approved the fund's investments in real estate only in 2010, after real estate had crashed.[41] And when it did so, it moved cautiously—placing a 5% limit of real estate on the total portfolio, aiming to do as much as possible in-house for cost savings, and adding properties slowly.

As an investor, Norway moves slower than a supertanker. Usually long lags are a disadvantage, but the delays induced by Norway's need for broad-based consensus are an advantage: they allow the effects of business cycle variation to be mitigated and they partly counteract the tendency for pro-cyclical investment behavior. The Norwegian Ministry of Finance builds the framework for NBIM, its agent, to make investment decisions, but the Ministry of Finance does not itself make investment decisions. These decision processes are owned by Parliament, which represents the ultimate principals—the Norwegian people. The lengthy decision-making process avoids the tendency to make ad hoc modifications to long-term strategy. It helps Norway stay the course.

Face Up to Noncommercial Considerations
Many public pension funds and sovereign wealth funds have important noncommercial considerations. The board may want to take account of these in setting its investment objectives and strategies. Noncommercial considerations can hinder investment performance, but can be important to give the board legitimacy in the eyes of the underlying owner. The board itself, after all, is an agent. Any loss from this constraint should be measured.

In reforming NYSCRF, these noncommercial goals could be considered. (It would be even better if the noncommercial goals were eliminated as constraints can only reduce investment returns; see chapter 3.) The role of the NYSCRF as a public asset should be reflected in the board's investment policies. In the case of NZSF, a wider mandate comes from its enabling legislation, which states that the Guardians must invest the fund in a manner consistent with best-practice portfolio management, maximizing return without undue risk, and avoiding prejudice to New Zealand's reputation as a responsible member of the world community. The Guardian Board has determined that excluding companies manufacturing cluster munitions and nuclear weapons is consistent with the latter.[42] CPPIB, in contrast, has no noncommercial considerations and has an investment-only objective.

---

[40] Ang, Goetzmann and Schaefer (2009). It recommended the fund take up factor investing; see chapter 14.

[41] http://www.regjeringen.no/en/dep/fin/press-center/press-releases/2010/Government-Pension-Fund-Global-to-invest-in-real-estate.html?id=594019

[42] http://www.nzsuperfund.co.nz/news.asp?pageID=2145831983&RefId=2141737352

The Board Should Benchmark Itself

Finally, decisions at the board level should be measured and benchmarked, just as the performance of the manager is measured and benchmarked. This is not often done, but boards need to measure themselves.

5. Agency Issues as a Factor

Since agency issues are pervasive, it is not surprising that agency issues affect prices.[43] Agency contracting issues, especially those affecting large institutions, give rise to short-term persistence, long-term reversals, momentum effects, and other patterns in risk premiums.[44]

An obvious effect is that *herding* arises when managers all follow the same benchmark. Herding can also arise from career or reputational concerns, even when managers have different contracts.[45] When many managers want to buy or sell the same stocks at the same time, prices are affected. A large literature, beginning with Harris and Gurel (1986) and Shleifer (1986), documents index reconstitution effects.[46] When a stock moves into an index such as the S&P 500, the price of that stock jumps as many investors, both index and active managers benchmarked to the S&P 500, buy on the same day. After inclusion, the newly added stock has higher correlations with the S&P 500 than before inclusions. The opposite effects occur when stocks are removed from the S&P 500. The literature estimates price effects of 3% to 5%, and these have become stronger since the 1990s.[47] Stocks widely held by institutions have lower returns, and institutional flow has predictive power for stock returns.[48]

Vayanos and Woolley (2013) show that delegated portfolio management can give rise to momentum and long-term reversals. Suppose a negative news shock hammers the fundamental value of stocks. Investment funds holding these stocks experience losses. This triggers outflows by investors who now regard these managers as less talented than they originally thought. They withdraw

---

[43] The first papers to show that delegated portfolio management can affect risk premiums were Roll (1992) and Brennan (1993).

[44] In addition to the other references in this section, see Dasgupta, Prat, and Verado (2010) and Cuoco and Kaniel (2010).

[45] See Scharfstein and Stein (1990).

[46] Shleifer (1986) originally hypothesizes these effects are due to downward-sloping demand curves, but they are also consistent with herding as a subsequent literature has emphasized.

[47] This literature is summarized in Ang, Goetzmann, and Schaeffer (2011). Boyer (2012) finds inclusion (and exclusion) effects in the BARRA value and growth indices, along with greater movement with these indices after they have been included in the index. Boyer finds the effect exists only after 1992, which is when the BARRA indices were introduced.

[48] See Gompers and Metrick (2001), Leippold and Rohner (2009), and Lou (2012), among many others.

funds, but the withdrawal is sticky, so it occurs over several periods. As a consequence of the flows, funds sell assets, and this further depresses prices. Eventually prices dip below fundamental values, expected returns eventually rise, and flows come back into the funds originally dumping the stocks. Consistent with delegated portfolio management being behind momentum effects, we see momentum in every large, liquid asset class: stocks, bonds, commodities, and currencies.[49] These asset classes are where institutions dominate. But we do not observe momentum in over-the-counter stock markets, where individuals dominate and where there are few institutional investors, as Ang, Shtauber, and Tetlock (2013) show.

Principal-agent issues are pervasive, and having good governance or good structures to mitigate agency issues are comparative advantages that an asset owner should capitalize on. An asset owner with the ability to stay the course, with a board that can support a manager over the long haul, or a board that is in a position to collect risk premiums cheaply, does not look like the average investor. These investors can harvest the various factor risk premiums outlined in chapter 7 and are good candidates for factor investing. In fact, trying to harvest certain factor risk premiums such as volatility, which involve disastrous drawdowns once every decade or so, without good governance structures can destroy institutions when losses occur. Many institutions should envy CPPIB, which has independence enshrined by law, a board that trusts the manager, a factor approach, the ability to hire and pay the best people, and can partner with the best managers in the world.

Large investors might be in a position to choose not to be part of the herd. Some part of herding is caused by many investors having the same explicit or implicit contracts. These investors can choose factor benchmarks other than the common S&P 500 or similar long-only market-weighted benchmarks. In doing so, these special asset owners provide liquidity to, and reap liquidity premiums from, those investors forced to rebalance to standard indices. Naturally this requires a degree of internal maturity and trust between principal and agent and, by definition, a type of high-quality principal-agent relation that the average investor does not possess.

6. New York State Common Retirement Fund Redux

Clearly having just one person in charge of the vast assets of NYSCRF is not optimal. As a *New York Times* editorial said, "What the comptroller's office needs is an independent, financially savvy board of directors to approve the awarding

---

[49] See Asness, Moskowitz, and Pedersen (2013).

of investment contracts—with the single goal of protecting and increasing state pension assets, invested for more than a million workers and retirees."[50]

But one cannot simply adopt a board without thinking through the complete governance structure of how the board is appointed, the membership of the board, the role of the board in relation to the government, the broader role of the pension fund assets in relation to the finances of state government as a whole, and the powers of the board and its relation with its agent (fund managers or CEO). A board by itself is no panacea.

Principal-agent theory helps us to recognize the conflicts between the principal and agent and to design a system so that the principal can work with the agent in the presence of these conflicts to enhance the principal's interests. When applied to the problem of delegated portfolio management, principal-agent theory suggests that the board of NYSCRF should own the two most important decisions: the *level* of risk to be taken and *where* the risks should be taken. There should be consistency of goals and a clear demarcation of responsibilities between the board and its fund manager. If the board of NYSCRF gives its fund manager an active mandate, then adequate support and resources should be made available so that the fund manager can achieve that goal. It is important for the board to avoid ad hoc modifications of long-term strategy, which often lead to pro-cyclical investment behavior.

Delegated portfolio agency theory says that the benchmark choice is extremely important. In fact, according to the Irrelevance Result, traditional static benchmarks are useless at motivating fund managers (with linear contracts) and in the worst cases cause managers to destroy value. Smarter benchmarks, like factor benchmarks, can ameliorate agency issues. Constraints, disclosure, transparency, and reputation play an important role in asset management contracts. Contracts need to be designed to engage the best portfolio managers (to enable the best portfolio managers to participate) but also give the best portfolio managers incentives to expend effort in creating value for the principal. This involves nonlinear incentive fees.

The overall message from agency theory is that the asset owner should not be surprised that the agent's primary concern is not for the principal. Greg Smith, a former executive director of Goldman Sachs, caused a ruckus by resigning and then publishing a scathing op-ed in the *New York Times* on March 14, 2012, criticizing Goldman's "toxic and destructive" culture which, he said, placed the client a distant second (well, maybe third or fourth):

> I don't know of any illegal behavior, but will people push the envelope and pitch lucrative and complicated products to clients even if they are not the simplest investments or the ones most directly aligned with the client's goals? Absolutely. Every day, in fact.

[50] Editorial, "From Pay-to-Play to Jail," *New York Times*, April 16, 2011.

The asset owner should not be surprised that, according to Smith, the agent (Goldman) took advantage of principals (clients). That's simply what the agent does. The principal's first job is to wake up to this fact; common sense tells us self-interest is paramount, and therefore agents often do not look out for the principal. Then the principal should use agency theory to minimize the ways in which the agent can take advantage of her and in fact use the agent's motives to the principal's advantage.

CHAPTER 16

Mutual Funds and Other 40-Act Funds

Chapter Summary

Mutual fund managers are talented, but on average none of that skill enriches asset owners. The average mutual fund underperforms the market after fees, investors chase funds with high past returns only to end up with low future returns, and larger mutual funds do worse than smaller funds. While the Investment Company Act of 1940 gives significant protection to ordinary investors, most mutual funds are run for the benefit of mutual fund firms rather than investors.

1. Janus

Those heady, growth-crazed days of the late 1990s! The Internet boom was in full force and, driven by investor mania, stocks with even the flimsiest fundamentals were soaring. Pets.com, with its endearing sock puppet and a balloon in the 1999 Macy's Thanksgiving Day Parade, went public in February 2000. The stock hit a high of $14 on the first day of trading. From then on, it was a downward spiral; shares fell below $1 in August and the company declared bankruptcy in November. Webvan Group went public in November 1999 and was valued at over $1.2 billion at its peak. But the company expanded its grocery delivery service too fast and filed for Chapter 11 protection in July 2001. During the late 1990s, investors were enamored with anything Internet related: just adding ".com" to a company's name resulted in a 75% return in excess of the market in the ten days after the name change—even if the company had no involvement with the Internet prior to the name change.[1]

The Janus mutual fund company epitomized the Internet bubble. Janus was hot. Year after year, enticed by outsized returns on high-flying growth stocks, money poured into Janus funds. In 1996, Janus was one of first fund companies to open a website so investors could peruse its funds. In 1997, the manager of the Janus Worldwide Fund, Helen Young Hayes, was named Fund Manager of the Year

---

[1] See Cooper, Dimitrov, and Rau (2001).

by Morningstar. Scott Schoelzel, another Janus portfolio manager, was named Manager of the Year by *Mutual Fund Magazine* in 1998. That same year the magazine rated Janus "Family of the Year." Janus was the envy of every active mutual fund company. Even President Bill Clinton had part of his IRA in a Janus fund.[2]

One of the most famous funds was Janus Twenty, designed to invest in only twenty to thirty stocks selected for their growth potential. Panel A of Figure 16.1 graphs Janus Twenty's assets under management (AUM) and returns. From January 1995 to December 1999, the fund's AUM mushroomed from $2.5 billion to $36.9 billion. Thanks to the Internet boom, returns averaged 40% per year. Then in 2000, Internet growth stocks crashed. Janus Twenty was hit harder than most funds with its concentrated growth positions, and it returned −32.4% in 2000. Despite this terrible performance, Janus Twenty's AUM was approximately flat at around $35 billion—money continued to flow into the fund based on the high returns generated over the *previous* year. Only in 2001 did the fund record significant negative outflows, and the fund's AUM leveled out after 2003 at approximately $10 billion, a third of its peak size.

Nearly all of Janus's funds were like the Janus Twenty and owned large positions in the same booming growth companies, including Cisco, Nokia, Sun Microsystems, and America Online. Panel B of Figure 16.1 shows that the firm's AUM rose from $50.3 billion at December 1996 to a peak of $257.8 billion at December 1999.[3] Despite the crash of Internet stocks in 2000, the firm's AUM at December 2000 increased slightly, to $257.8 billion, as investors continued to pile in. Investors chased *past* returns even though current returns were lousy. Only in the following year did Janus experience outflows.

In 2001, Enron Corp., an energy company that claimed it was generating high earnings but really was engaged in an elaborate accounting fraud, blew up. Janus's funds owned more than 5% of Enron. In 2002, Janus was also the largest shareholder in Tyco International in 2002, whose share price plunged when it was hit by a corporate scandal. Tyco executives Chairman and CEO Dennis Kozlowski and CFO Mark Swartz were eventually sent to prison for stealing money.

In 2003, Janus was caught up in a Securities and Exchange Commission (SEC) investigation into market timing. Janus had allowed favored clients to trade more frequently and ahead of other investors, generating profits for themselves while raising the cost burden on other investors in the funds.[4] Janus paid $262 million in fines to settle the charges.

Despite these travails, Janus never posted a loss. In fact, its operating profit margins (the ratio of operating income to revenue) never fell below 10%, as shown in Panel B of Figure 16.1 (During the peak years of the late 1990s, Janus

---

[2] Elkind, P., "The Hidden Face of Janus," *Fortune*, Jan 22, 2001.

[3] Data in Figure 16.1 are from 10-K filings of Stilwell Financial and Janus Capital Group.

[4] Janus was one of several mutual fund companies that engaged in this odious practice. It was uncovered by Eric Zitzewitz (2006), a professor at Dartmouth College.

Panel A
Janus Twenty AUM and Returns

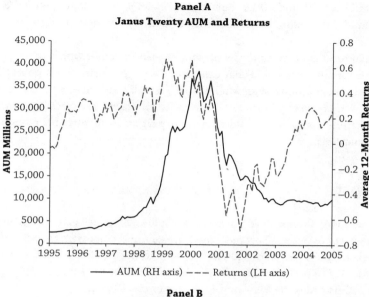

AUM (RH axis) --- Returns (LH axis)

Panel B
Janus AUM and Operating Margin

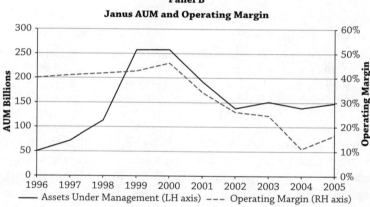

Assets Under Management (LH axis) --- Operating Margin (RH axis)

Figure 16.1

was enjoying operating margins above 40%.) For comparison, the juggernaut of retailing efficiency, Wal-Mart Stores Inc., generates operating margins slightly above 5%.[5] Janus was partly saved by its INTECH division, which managed money using quantitative trading techniques (including a version of the rebalancing premium; see chapter 4). INTECH constituted less than 3% of Janus's AUM in the late 1990s and grew to over 35% of its AUM in 2006. But the main savior of Janus was its surprisingly loyal investors. Despite poor performance and SEC investigations, enough money remained so that Janus still ranked in the top ten mutual

---

[5] Wal-Mart's operating margin in 2011 was 5.9%.

fund families in the mid-2000s. Figure 16.1, Panel B shows that Janus's AUM settled around $150 billion in 2003. Since fees are levied directly on AUM, Janus
remained profitable.

Mutual fund companies throw off lots of cash, much of which they spend on
employee remuneration, and that can be cut when performance is poor. Clients,
meanwhile, stick around even when things go badly. "It's pretty hard to mess up
a mutual fund company," said an executive at a mutual fund research firm.[6] "You
can't kill these companies," said another expert at an investment advisory and
management firm.[7]

2. 40-Act

The Investment Company Act of 1940 has allowed the delegated asset management industry to flourish, protects the little guy, and empowers the SEC to police
the market.[8] I use the term "40-Act" to refer to the 1940 Act itself, subsequent
amendments (1970) and rules issued by the SEC under the act.

The SEC provides the following summary of the 40-Act:[9]

> This Act regulates the organization of companies, including mutual
> funds, that engage primarily in investing, reinvesting, and trading in se-
> curities, and whose own securities are offered to the investing public. The
> regulation is designed to *minimize conflicts of interest* that arise in these
> complex operations.

The italics are mine. The 40-Act is designed to mitigate principal-agent
problems that arise in delegated investing, which we discussed in chapter 15.
Companies covered under the 40-Act are called *registered investment companies*,
and they can solicit money directly from the general public (through *public offerings*). For this privilege, registered investment companies must adhere to
minimum standards to "minimize conflicts of interest." The SEC explains the
40-Act's role in accomplishing this:

---

[6] Quoted by Nocera, J., "Janus Funds: Everybody Loves a Loser," *New York Times*, May 28, 2005.

[7] Quoted by Effinger, A., and S. V. Bhaktavatsalam, "Healey Rules $400 Billion Empire with Stakes
in 28 Funds," Bloomberg Markets, Jul 9, 2012.

[8] The backbone of U.S. financial market regulation consists of the 40-Act, the Securities Act of
1933, and the Securities Exchange Act of 1934. The latter created the SEC. All this regulation was
created as a response to the stock market crash of 1929 and the Great Depression. The entire apparatus
was conceived as part of President Franklin Roosevelt's New Deal and designed to make markets safe
for the ordinary investor.

[9] From http://www.sec.gov/about/laws.shtml#invcoact1940

The Act requires these companies to disclose their financial condition and investment policies to investors when stock is initially sold and, subsequently, on a regular basis. The focus of this Act is on disclosure to the investing public of information about the fund and its investment objectives, as well as on investment company structure and operations.

The 40-Act emphasizes disclosure so that asset owners have information to make informed choices; disclosure minimizes information asymmetry and reduces *adverse selection* and *moral hazard*. The 40-Act further stipulates how the fund manager can be paid and specifies the governance structure of registered investment companies. Thus, it sets *behavior-based contracts* that place restrictions on what managers can do.

The SEC ends with a warning:

> It is important to remember that the Act does not permit the SEC to directly supervise the investment decisions or activities of these companies or judge the merits of their investments.

The 40-Act only establishes a barebones framework that helps investors make informed decisions; it does not guarantee that those decisions will be smart.

2.1. REGISTERED INVESTMENT COMPANIES

The 40-Act covers four types of registered investment companies: (i) *mutual funds*—the vehicle that built Janus into a powerhouse, (ii) *closed-end funds*, (iii) *unit investment trusts* (UITs), and (iv) *exchange-traded funds* (ETFs), which are the newest of the four and rapidly growing in popularity. All of these are tax pass-through vehicles so that investors, not the funds, are taxed. There are two main investing styles practiced by registered investment companies: *passive* managers closely track benchmarks, usually at low cost (warning: some index funds are expensive!), while *active* managers, like Janus, try to add value by picking and choosing stocks, thereby deviating significantly from their benchmarks.

Figure 16.2 graphs net assets invested in each of these types of investment companies from the Investment Company Institute (ICI), the industry association of U.S. investment companies. At the end of 2011, investment companies held a total of $11.6 trillion, the bulk of which (90%) was held in mutual funds.

A great many people own shares in registered investment companies—especially mutual funds. At end of 2011, 44% of all U.S. households held investments in mutual funds, and registered investment companies managed 23% of U.S. households' financial assets.

Mutual funds issue shares directly from the fund itself or indirectly through a broker. The *net asset value* (NAV) is the value of the fund's assets minus liabilities. Dividing the NAV by the number of shares is the price at which investors can

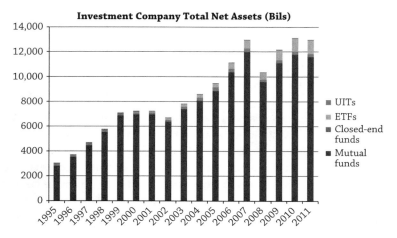

Figure 16.2

buy or sell shares in the mutual fund, not including fees. Mutual fund shares are redeemable daily at the NAV.[10] Mutual funds are said to be *open-ended* because investors can purchase or redeem shares from the issuer, so the number of outstanding shares can rise (or fall) over time.

Although mutual funds hold the most assets of all registered investment company types, their share has been slowly shrinking. In 2000, mutual funds accounted for 96% of all investment company assets, but by the end of 2011 this proportion had declined to 90%.

In contrast to mutual funds, shares of **closed-end funds** are not redeemable and are fixed in number. (There can be secondary issues after the fund's inception, and the fund may offer to repurchase shares, but these are usually infrequent occurrences.) These shares trade on a secondary market after initial public offering (IPO). Closed-end funds are allowed to invest in more illiquid securities than mutual funds (which have to provide daily liquidity).

Mutual funds and closed-end funds are managed by *registered investment advisors*, which are separate entities from the funds. Investment advisors are compensated through fees paid by the fund shareholders. Often, the registered investment advisor works for the *fund sponsor*. The fund sponsor is usually an asset management company, like Janus, that creates and markets many registered investment companies. Funds that have the same brand name or manager are called *mutual fund families* (or *complexes*). The Janus fund family includes all funds marketed under the Janus name, like the Janus Twenty Fund, but Janus also sponsors funds in different fund families as with its INTECH funds.

Sometimes a fund sponsor can outsource management of a fund to a third-party (a *subadvisory firm*). These externally managed funds are usually marketed

[10] The provision of this *daily liquidity* by mutual funds is costly to the fund shareholders, as shown by Edelen (1999), Coval and Stafford (2007), and Chen, Goldstein, and Jiang (2010).

under the umbrella of a fund family. For a while, American Skandia Insurance Co. used Janus as subadvisor to manage its funds. American Skandia terminated the relationship in 2002, after Janus's disastrous losses in the bursting of the tech bubble.[11] Mutual fund companies use unaffiliated subadvisors to gain access to specialized managers, and these subadvisors in turn gain access to a different distribution channel.[12] Chen, Hong, and Kubik (2010) show that funds managed externally underperform funds that are managed inside the mutual fund family.

UITs are hybrids between mutual funds and closed-end funds. Like closed-end funds, they issue a fixed number of shares (*units*). The units are redeemable, like shares in mutual funds, but the UIT sponsor maintains a secondary market so that units are bought and sold between investors. A UIT buys and holds a set of assets until a preestablished termination date, when the UIT is dissolved and proceeds are paid to shareholders. Once a UIT is set up, there is typically no trading of the underlying assets. Unlike mutual and closed-end funds, UITs are so simple they do not need a board of directors or an investment advisor. But UITs are only a tiny fraction of the investment company universe (see Figure 16.2), and for this reason I do not talk about them separately in this chapter. However, the UIT category has been growing lately because some ETFs are technically classified as UITs.

ETFs trade on exchanges like closed-end funds and so offer investors immediate liquidity. Unlike closed-end funds, the number of shares is not fixed, and fund sponsors buy and sell shares to ensure that the quoted price of the ETF adheres closely to the NAV of the fund. ETFs are legally classified as mutual funds or UITs. The ETF market is growing fast. The share of assets in ETFs rose from less than 1% in 2000 to exceed 8% in 2011, and now ETFs hold over $1 trillion of assets.

2.2. MINIMIZING CONFLICTS OF INTEREST

Before the 40-Act, investors were at a huge disadvantage to managers. Simply put, managers often stole outright from investors.[13] The 40-Act stopped this and went further to "minimize conflicts of interest." It created a large class of investment vehicles that protect the common man, and it has been hugely successful in this regard.

The 40-Act mitigates agency problems by . . .

Mandating Transparency
Registered investment companies must issue a *prospectus*, which discloses the fund's investment objectives, strategies, risk, expenses, and instructions on how

---

[11] "Janus Loses a Big Client," CNNMoney, Sept 27, 2002.

[12] See Del Guercio, Reuter, and Tkac (2009).

[13] According to Farina, Freeman, and Webster (1969), an SEC report in 1940 calculated that investors lost over $1 billion in the 1920s and 1930s to investment company misconduct. The report highlighted several ways the investment managers found to steal investors' money. The variety of malfeasance makes for interesting reading.

to trade shares. The 40-Act requires that the prospectus and other reports be regularly filed to the SEC and made publicly available. Reports must be audited, fund holdings have to be reported (quarterly for mutual funds and daily in the case of ETFs), and funds must disclose how they voted their shares in proxy ballots. All this information is largely standardized, so individuals can compare it across funds; some investment advisory companies, like Morningstar, take this information, collate and distribute it, and provide fund recommendations based on the data.

Crucially, the 40-Act ensures that investors know the market value of the fund's investments through the NAV. Mutual fund investors can take comfort that they are always transacting at the fund's underlying value, less any applicable fees.

Mandating Oversight

Mutual funds have boards of directors. At least 40% of these directors must be independent from the fund management company (but whether they act independently is a different story). Since 2003, the SEC has mandated that every fund and advisor must have a chief compliance officer. Funds are monitored by the SEC to ensure compliance.

One of the most important requirements in the 40-Act is that fund assets are held separately from those of the fund's advisors. There are three ways a mutual fund company can provide segregated custody for its investments: through a bank (the most popular option), a broker (rare), or self-custody. In the latter case, there are strict requirements including that the mutual fund assets be *physically separated* from the rest of the assets of the firm.

The 40-Act also limits the types of transactions permitted between the fund, fund management, and affiliates. Before and during the Great Depression, many fund assets were sold at below market prices to the fund's advisors, the fund bought assets at inflated prices from insiders, or the fund made cheap loans to management. The 40-Act prohibits these abuses.

Fiduciary Standard

The 40-Act mandates that registered investment advisors be held to a *fiduciary standard*, which means that they must act in the best interests of their clients. Brokers are not fiduciaries and have a *suitability standard*, which means they don't have to find the best products for you, only products that are "suitable." That's right: most brokers and advisors that sell mutual funds do not have to put clients first. Even if the advisor is a registered investment advisor, the fiduciary standard does not eliminate the principal-agent problem, as chapter 15 emphasizes.

Limiting Leverage

Section 13(a) of the original 40-Act states: "No registered investment company shall, unless authorized by the vote of a majority of its outstanding Voting Securities, borrow money." Today leverage is permitted, but the SEC restricts its use. Mutual funds have a 300% maximum asset coverage (i.e., they can borrow up to 33.3%), and closed-end funds have maximum coverages of 300% for debt and 200% for preferred stock. Many funds choose themselves not to borrow at all, and also place other restrictions on their investing styles.[14]

Limiting Compensation

Mutual fund performance-based fees must be *symmetrical* around a chosen benchmark, which is referred to as a *fulcrum fee*, and fully disclosed.[15] In practice, performance-based fees also have an upper and lower limit. The law rules out *asymmetric contracts* such as contingent bonuses and option-like fees. Chapter 15 showed that using these types of contracts can increase investor welfare. (Hedge funds, which are exempt from 40-Act registration, are free to pay managers in whatever manner they wish; see chapter 17.) Most mutual funds do not employ performance fees. But for the small number of funds that do, Elton, Gruber, and Blake (2003) report that they have a slight edge over their peers without performance fees. However, funds with performance fees tend to increase risk following bad performance.

There are few restrictions on the structure of the general management fee charged by the advisor, except that the 40-Act specifies that the investment advisor of a registered investment company has a fiduciary duty to protect mutual fund shareholders from excessive fees.[16] The usual management fee is a percentage of AUM.

2.3. THERE ARE STILL AGENCY PROBLEMS

While disclosure is mandatory, the presentation can be opaque. Few people read prospectuses before investing, and they are dense and require skill to understand in full. Although fees are disclosed, few investors take the trouble to look; a survey conducted by AARP (formerly the American Association of Retired Persons) in February 2011 found that 71% of respondents thought they did not pay any fees![17]

The United States lags other countries in the disclosure of retirement asset fees. There are fees paid to the funds in the retirement plans, to the administrators

---

[14] See Almazan et al. (2004) for an analysis of self-imposed investment constraints by mutual funds.

[15] This is under the 1970 amendment of the Investment Advisers Act of 1940.

[16] Deli (2002) and Warner and Wu (2011) investigate mutual fund contracts. Coles, Suay, and Woodbury (2000) examine the compensation contracts of closed-end funds. The standard to prove mutual fund fees are "excessive" is extremely high (called the Gartenberg standard, after Gartenberg vs. Merrill Lynch Asset Management, Inc.) and many argue the law has failed; see, for example, Johnson (2009). Most suits never see trial and are dismissed because they are unable to isolate management fees from administrative costs. An important recent court case, Kasilag et al. vs. Hartford Investment Financial Services, is unresolved at the time of writing and could change this. See Braham, L., "Lawsuit Shines a Harsh Light on Subadvisory Fund Fees," Bloomberg, Feb. 21, 2013.

[17] AARP, "401(k) Participants' Awareness and Understanding of Fees," Feb. 2011.

of the plans, to the consultants, and other fees as well. Fees must be disclosed in mutual funds, but few investors saving for retirement know the fees they are paying, including the fees in the mutual funds holding their retirement monies. It was only on August 30, 2012, that the U.S. Department of Labor, which has jurisdiction over retirement savings plans, required that participants be given a breakdown of fees.[18] According to ICI, mutual funds accounted for $4.7 trillion, or 26 percent, of the $17.9 trillion U.S. retirement assets at the end of 2011. Households held 55% of their defined contribution pension plan money and 45% of their IRA money in mutual funds.

Mutual fund governance is much weaker than that of regular corporations.[19] Mutual funds are legally separate from the firms that market, sell, and run them. Having a board of directors gives a veneer of independence. But fund managers' real loyalty lies with the firm that runs the funds, rather than with the investors who are the owners of the fund. The relationship is incestuous, and investors lose. Many directors of the mutual fund—especially the board chair—are insiders of the investment advisory firm. Fund directors usually do not, and in many cases cannot, independently verify the information given by the advisor. Separating the fund's governance from its sponsor is not enough to ensure protection of the investors.

The Supreme Court has upheld this legal separation between the fund and the fund management company even though for all practical purposes mutual funds are run by mutual fund companies. *Janus Capital Group vs. First Derivative Traders* was one of the cases generated by Janus's market timing scandal in 2003.[20] In June 2011, the Supreme Court ruled that Janus's funds, not the Janus fund management company, were responsible for misleading language in their prospectuses that permitted the market timing that short-changed other investors. Legally, it was all the fault of Janus's funds. Janus the firm got a free pass, even though it sponsored, marketed, and managed the funds.[21]

2.4. SUMMARY

The advantage of being a registered investment company that is you can raise money directly from the public. To protect the little guy, the 40-Act puts restrictions on registered investment companies. The Act mandates disclosure

[18] See the GAO Report, "Defined Contribution Plans: Approaches in Other Countries Offer Beneficial Strategies in Several Areas," released in March 2012.

[19] See Radin and Stevenson (2006).

[20] See Henriques, D. B., "A Mutual Fund Ruling Remains a Head-Scratcher," *New York Times*, July 7, 2012.

[21] In 1974, John Bogle founded the Vanguard Group—which changed the investing world by making index funds available for the mass market—by exploiting the legal separation between the fund and the sponsoring company. After being fired from Wellington Management, Bogle persuaded the board of the Wellington Fund to part ways with Wellington Management to find a new investment manager. See Bernstein (2010).

and minimum levels of oversight and restricts how managers are paid. These regulations mitigate, but do not eliminate, principal-agent problems.

The 40-Act is imperfect but could be much worse—as we shall see when discussing hedge funds and private equity in chapters 17 and 18, respectively.

Exchange traded notes (ETNs) look like ETFs in that they are managed funds traded on exchanges, and they track indexes. But they are not 40-Act funds; they are regulated as fixed income securities and are technically loans to banks. They have high costs, complicated taxes, and prices that can differ significantly from their underlying market value. Unlike 40-Act funds, which must clearly disclose fees, ETNs excel in making their fees nontransparent. Jason Zweig, a financial columnist, waded through some heavy prospectuses to compute some total fees.[22] The Etracs Daily Short S&P500 VIX Futures ETN has a 1.35% "tracking fee" and fixed hedging costs of 0.077% per week, or 5.35% per annum. The Credit Suisse Long/Short ETN tries to replicate certain hedge fund strategies and charges an "annual investor fee" of 0.45%. There is also an "accrued holding rate" of 0.7% and an "accrued index adjustment factor" fee of 0.5%. The total fee is more than three times the reported fee. This level of obfuscation is not permitted for 40-Act funds.

3. Mutual Funds

Mutual funds love to advertise high past performance. While management companies rave about high returns, the truth is that the average mutual fund underperforms the market. Active mutual fund companies rarely acknowledge this, and the returns they report are biased upward.

3.1. SURVIVORSHIP BIAS

Janus Worldwide and Janus Global Research
Janus Worldwide used to be one of Janus's most popular funds. It started in the early 1990s and rode the Internet rollercoaster up into the sky in the late 1990s, and then back down after 2000. Figure 16.3, Panel A shows that the fund reached a peak of almost $45 billion in early 2000. Unlike the Janus Twenty (see Figure 16.1), Janus Worldwide's AUM never stabilized, and outflows continued over the 2000s. Janus Worldwide used to be managed by Hayes, the Janus manager who was named Morningstar Fund Manager of the Year in 1997. She retired in 2003, and her departure was partly driven by the demands of a Janus shareholder (Highfields Capital Management, a hedge fund) to reveal her salary and

---

[22] Zweig, J., "In New Funds, Old Flaws," *Wall Street Journal*, April 13, 2012.

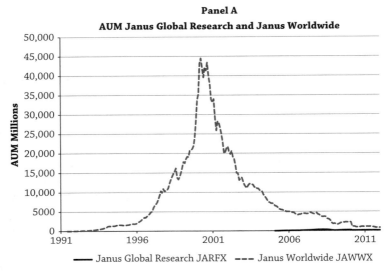

Panel A
AUM Janus Global Research and Janus Worldwide

── Janus Global Research JARFX   ─ ─ ─ Janus Worldwide JAWWX

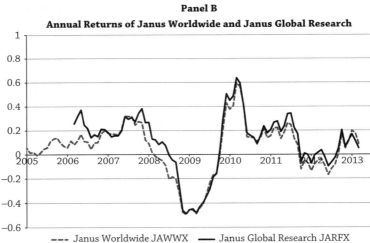

Panel B
Annual Returns of Janus Worldwide and Janus Global Research

─ ─ ─ Janus Worldwide JAWWX   ── Janus Global Research JARFX

Figure 16.3

that of other top executives.[23] As of January 31, 2013, Janus Worldwide held $2 billion in assets.

Janus Global Research's AUM is a sliver of Janus Worldwide. Starting in February 2005, it is also a much newer fund. On January 31, 2013, Janus Global Research's AUM was just $313 million. You can barely make out its AUM in Panel A of Figure 16.3.

[23] See Goldberg, S. T., "Upheaval at Janus," Kiplinger's Personal Finance Magazine, June 1, 2003, and Burton, J., "More Turmoil Shakes Janus Fund Family: Star Manager's Departure Marks End of an Era," CBSMarketWatch.com, April 21, 2003.

On March 15, 2013, the two funds merged. Janus Worldwide, the bigger fund with the longer history, ceased to exist and was absorbed by Janus Global Research, the much smaller fund with the shorter history. Why?

Panel B of Figure 16.3 plots the year-on-year returns of Janus Worldwide and Janus Global Research from February 2005 to January 2012. Janus Global Research has trounced its much bigger cousin. Over the sample, Janus Global Research averaged 9.9% while Janus Worldwide returned 5.0%. Since both funds have approximately the same standard deviation, at just under 20%, Janus Global Research's Sharpe ratio (see chapter 2) was double that of Janus Worldwide.

After the merger, the combined fund inherited only the superior performance of Janus Global Research. Janus Worldwide ceased to exist, and its inferior performance disappeared from the Janus fund family.

Killing or merging poorly performing funds is how Janus's marketing team can state with a straight face, "100 percent of Janus equity funds have beaten their benchmarks since inception."[24] *Survivorship bias* is the tendency of the worst funds, like Janus Worldwide, to vanish through mergers or dissolution. The result is that the universe of funds reporting returns presents far too rosy a picture. This is accomplished by leaving out the returns of euthanized funds.

How Large Is the Survivorship Bias?

Since all 40-Act funds are required to report their performance to the SEC, we observe the full universe of funds. We measure the effect of survivorship bias by comparing the returns of live funds, like Janus Global Research, to those that die or merge, like Janus Worldwide. The first large-scale mutual fund database without survivorship bias was put together by Mark Carhart when he was a PhD student at the University of Chicago. His data set, with updates and improvements, has been extensively used since. Carhart graduated in 1995, took a job as a finance professor at the University of Southern California, and shortly afterward was lured away to Goldman Sachs Asset Management. He ended up co-managing one of the largest quant hedge funds in the mid-2000s (which later dissolved after the financial crisis; see chapter 17).

Using only the live funds overstates mutual fund returns by 1% to 2% compared to a universe that includes both live and dead funds.[25] But the difference between live funds and the discontinued funds taken separately is about 4%.

---

[24] Cruz, H., "Don't Disregard Past Performance When Choosing a Fund: Investment Advertisements Should Still Get a Critical Look," *Chicago Tribune*, May 20, 2010.

[25] This is shown in Elton, Gruber, and Blake (1996) and Carhart's (1997) seminal paper. See also Brown et al. (1992), Carpenter and Lynch (1999), and Carhart et al. (2002). A subtle point is made by Linnainmaa (2013), who notes that while the group of mutual funds that die have lower returns than surviving funds, there can be a positive bias resulting from survivorship bias if fund-level data is used to compute mutual fund alphas, as some of the studies mentioned in Section 3.2, if the chance of a fund dying increases when a fund's alpha is low. There is no Linnainmaa survivorship bias for studies tracking all mutual funds, some of which die and some of which survive, at a point in time. Linnainmaa finds

Carhart et al. (2002) estimate that the difference in risk-adjusted returns be-tween live funds and nonsurviving funds is 3.7%. Malkiel and Saha (2005) report that the difference between the returns of live and defunct funds is 4.3%. Unfortunately for investors, mutual fund companies emphasize the returns only of existing funds. Careful academics always use databases like Carhart's, which in-clude both surviving funds and dead funds; without the dead funds, mutual fund performance is highly overstated.

3.2. (UNDER-)PERFORMANCE

The short summary of the enormous mutual fund literature is that the average ac-tive mutual fund manager underperforms after fees but slightly beats (or at best equals) the market before costs.[26] This literature originally focused just on per-formance and was started by Treynor (1965), Sharpe (1966), and Jensen (1969). Michael Jensen, now an emeritus professor at Harvard Business School, wrote the article that gets most of the citations.[27] These papers found that active mu-tual funds do not beat the market, and these results have been echoed in many follow-up papers.

Russell Wermers' (2000) study summarizes the literature nicely. Over his sam-ple, the S&P 500 returned 15.4% per year. Mutual funds beat the markets before fees, with a gross 16.9% return, but underperformed after fees, with a net return of 14.6%. This is an underperformance of 0.8%. Mutual funds with past high re-turns, however, could just have loaded up on risky stocks in rising markets. After adjusting for market and other factor risks (notably size, value-growth, and mo-mentum factors; see chapter 7), Wermers finds a return in excess of risk factors (or *alpha*; see chapter 10) of 0.8% before fees. After fees, mutual funds have a return in excess of risk of −1.2%.

Eugene Fama and Kenneth French (2010), two giants of empirical asset pricing at the University of Chicago and Dartmouth College, respectively, estimate the al-pha of equity mutual funds before fees is 0.2%, which is statistically equal to zero, and −1.1% after fees controlling for just the market factor.[28] Active mutual funds

the "reverse survivorship bias" is small: for a typical fund the Fama-French (1993) alpha is −0.44% per year while the alpha taking into account reverse survivorship bias is −0.41% per year.

[26] Other important studies not mentioned in this paragraph are Grinblatt and Titman (1989), Sharpe (1992), Malkiel (1995), Gruber (1996), and Fama and French (2010). See Ang, Goetzmann, and Schaefer (2011) for further literature review.

[27] Jensen is most famous for introducing the radical idea of paying corporate managers with op-tions. His article Jensen and Murphy (1990) led to the profusion of option payouts in the 1990s—this practice went hand-in-hand with the Internet bubble of the 1990s. Treynor (1965), Sharpe (1966), and Jensen (1969) are also notable because they were the first applications of the CAPM. Treynor and Sharpe were two of the prominent developers of this theory (see chapter 6).

[28] The average bond mutual fund also does not add value. See Blake, Elton, and Gruber (1993) and Ferson, Henry, and Kisgen (2006). Institutional funds also underperform, as shown by Busse, Goya, and Wahal (2010).

underperform by 1.3% after fees. Controlling for more sophisticated risk factors, they find that the returns of mutual funds in excess of their risk benchmarks is only 0.1% before fees, and the corresponding number after fees is −1.0%.

French (2008) goes further in his presidential address to the American Finance Association. He computes the cost of active management to all investors—including individual investors, mutual funds, pension funds and other institutional investors, and hedge funds in the U.S. equity market. He estimates that the average investor would be better off by 0.7% per year switching from active management to index funds.

Even though active managers as a group underperform, do they underperform less (or perhaps slightly add value) during bear markets or recessions? The evidence is mixed. On the one hand, Moskowitz (2000) and Kosowski (2012) find that active mutual funds significantly out-perform during recessions (as defined by the National Bureau of Economic Research). But De Souza and Lynch (2012) find the opposite.

The bottom line is that, with or without adjusting for risk, the typical active mutual fund delivers average underperformance.

Larger Mutual Funds Do Worse

Larger mutual funds do worse than smaller ones, so there are *diseconomies of scale*.[29] As a fund gets larger, it becomes harder for it to take on large positions in stocks. Many alpha opportunities are concentrated in more illiquid segments of the market. Good investment ideas thus are hard to scale. Indeed, large-fund performance is most hampered when funds hold more illiquid stocks. Larger funds also have to employ more analysts, and this makes coordination more difficult. With more employees, it is harder to pass information up the organization and to act on it. (In economics these costs are called *hierarchy costs*.[30])

More Expensive Funds Do Worse

In most industries you get what you pay for. When you shop at Saks Fifth Avenue, you pay more than at the dollar store, but you get better quality. When you eat at a three-star Michelin restaurant, you pay more than at McDonalds, but you get a more delicious meal in elegant surroundings. In so many arenas, the more you pay, the more you get. But in mutual fund land, it's the exact opposite: when you pay more, you get less.[31] Carhart (1997) finds that the more fees you pay to a mutual fund, the *lower* the return. Investors are best served by investing in funds with low expenses. Gruber (1996) finds that top performing funds charge *less* than the

---

[29] See Chen et al. (2004), Pollet and Wilson (2008), and Yan (2008).

[30] See Stein (2002).

[31] For some theoretical explanations see Christoffersen and Musto (2002) and Gil-Bazo and Ruiz-Verdu (2008). In addition, see the Berk and Green (2004) model, which is discussed in section 3.5.

worst performing funds. What's the cheapest type of fund, one that also happens to consistently outperform more than half of active funds? Index funds.

3.3. PERSISTENCE

Just like the disclaimer says, past mutual fund returns are no guarantee of future returns. Mutual fund performance just isn't very persistent. Consistency, where it exists, is of the wrong kind: underperforming funds reliably persist in underperforming, rather than from outperforming funds continuing to generate superior returns.[32]

Figure 16.4 shows mutual fund alphas controlling for the market (capital asset pricing model; CAPM) and a multifactor model with size, value-growth, and momentum factors as estimated in Carhart (1997) (see chapter 10). Funds are ranked by their return over the past year from lowest in decile 1 to highest in decile 10. The alphas are returns in excess of their risk benchmarks over the following year. Figure 16.4 shows that the average alphas, for both the CAPM and multifactor benchmarks, are negative—which means that the average mutual fund underperforms. There is some interesting persistence in CAPM alphas, but it is asymmetric. Funds with the worst returns over the last year continue to do badly and generate outperformance relative to a market benchmark of −5.4%, but funds with the best returns over the last year continue to do well and generate alphas of 2.4%.

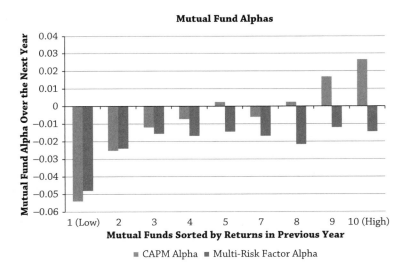

Figure 16.4

[32] See Gruber (1996) and Carhart (1997).

The performance persistence goes away once the more sophisticated factor benchmark is used. In the multifactor benchmark, all the alphas are negative over the following year. Note that the worst funds continue to do the worst, with the decile 1 multifactor alphas being much lower (–4.8%) than the decile 10 alphas (–1.4%). The multifactor benchmark controls for momentum, and this is mostly responsible for reversing the persistence.[33] Most winning funds hold momentum stocks—stocks with past high returns that continue to do well—and after adjusting for the high returns coming from a momentum factor strategy, the winning funds do not outperform.

Some Funds Do Add Value

There are mutual funds that outperform, but these are hard to find on a consistent basis. Even professors who show that it is possible to find winning mutual funds "concede that their strategy is probably more appropriate for institutions than for individual investors, because it requires the application of complex statistics to a large database of fund returns."[34]

Some of the best measures of mutual fund selection involve looking beyond past returns and at the managers and holdings of the funds. Chevalier and Ellison (1999a) find that managers who graduate from more selective colleges whose students have higher SAT scores generate higher returns. Cohen, Frazzini, and Malloy (2008) show that the people you know matters for mutual fund performance. The best connected managers place bigger bets on companies with board members who went to the same college. Managers' performance on these connected companies significantly exceeds the performance of nonconnected companies.

The holdings of funds predict performance. We should be paying active fees for managers who are actually active. Why pay high fees to managers who just mimic the S&P 500? Cremers and Petajisto's (2009) "active share" measures the deviation of a fund's holdings from the holdings of its benchmark index. Active share reflects how much active stock selection is going on.[35] Cremers and Petajisto document that funds with higher active shares have higher returns. Interestingly, tracking error—the standard deviation of the difference between the fund's returns and its benchmark—does not predict returns, indicating you need to look deep into the fund's holdings to measure the how many active bets the manager

[33] See also Daniel et al. (1997).

[34] Quoted by Hulbert, M., "The Manager Is in a Slump (Or Maybe It's Just a Phase)," *New York Times*, Nov. 20, 2005. The professors are Avramov and Wermers (2006). Baks, Metrick, and Wachter (2001) suggest that even though the average mutual fund manager underperforms, most investors would benefit from a little active management.

[35] Kacperczyk, Sialm, and Zheng (2008) develop a related measure involving the difference between the fund's return and the return implied by the fund's previously disclosed portfolio holdings. This "return gap" predicts fund performance. Amihud and Goyenko's (2013) measure is similar in spirit—funds that move most differently from their benchmarks, or are most active, have higher returns. See Kacperczyk, Sialm, and Zheng (2005) for industry concentration results.

is taking. Along these lines, managers who specialize and hold more concentrated portfolios tend to have better performance.

Even with all these measures, finding outperforming mutual fund managers is not easy.

3.4. FLOWS

Mutual fund investors, in the words of Frazzini and Lamont (2008), are "dumb money." Cash pours into mutual funds when past returns have been high, but it tends to flow into the wrong funds. Subsequent returns end up being low. Friesen and Sapp (2007) estimate that dumb money flows—investors placing money in funds with high past returns but low future returns—costs investors 1.5% per year. Mutual fund companies trumpet the past high returns of funds in their advertising. This is selective, of course, because only funds with recent good performance get star billing. Money comes in, and future returns are disappointingly low.[36]

Mutual fund money is sticky. Money flows into good performing funds, but money tends not to leave bad performing funds at the same rate.[37] In jargon: the *flow-performance relationship is convex*. Figure 16.5 shows the relationship between flows into active funds over the following year (*y*-axis) as a function of the past returns of mutual funds (*x*-axis). At the end of each year from 1980 to 2012, funds are ranked into deciles by their performance over the previous year. The flows into those funds are recorded over the following year. The figure reports the weighted average next-year flows as a function of weighted average past-year returns, in both cases using AUM weights within each decile at the end of each year. In Figure 16.5, the slope of the flow relationship is less steep for negative past returns, while high past returns induce large increases in new money. Thus, investors do not punish losses in the same way they reward success. This investor inertia saved Janus.

3.5. BERK AND GREEN (2004) MODEL

Jonathan Berk, a finance professor at Stanford University, and Richard Green, my sometime co-author and a finance professor at Carnegie Mellon University, wrote

---

[36] For an academic study on mutual fund advertising, see Jain and Wu (2000). Gruber (1996) and Zheng (1999) show that mutual fund flows predict fund returns, at least in the short run. This is consistent with the Berk and Green (2004) argument (see below) that some investors can identify skilled managers, but performance in the long run suffers as the funds grow. Lou (2012) shows that mutual fund flows predict stock returns.

[37] See Ippolito (1992), Chevalier and Ellison (1997), Goetzmann and Peles (1997), and Sirri and Tufano (1998). We observe the same convex flow-performance relationship in hedge funds (see Agarwal, Daniel, and Naik 2004 and Ding et al. 2009) and pension funds (see Del Guercio and Tkac 2002). Bergstresser and Poterba (2002) find that new money (inflows) is sensitive to past performance, while withdrawals (outflows) have no statistically significant relation to past returns.

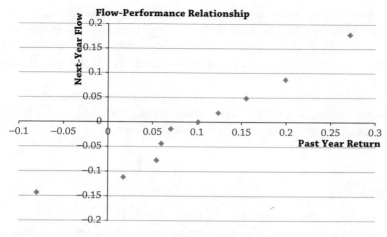

Figure 16.5

a paper in 2004 that fits the main stylized facts of mutual fund performance: (i) managers add value on a before-fee basis but underperform, on average, after fees; (ii) investors chase returns; and (iii) investors end up doing poorly when they move money into funds with the highest past returns. In the field of delegated asset management, this is the most important paper published in the past thirty years.

Berk and Green (2004) show that these facts result from a *rational equilibrium* in which fund managers have talent, on average, but some investors are talented and some are not (there is *differential ability* to generate excess returns). Investors know that some managers have talent. Fund managers, however, have *decreasing returns to scale*: as their funds become bigger, the excess returns they can generate shrink as we observe in data.

Investors know who the skilled managers are, so money flows to the best managers first. These are the managers that have generated past high returns—some of this is luck, but some of it is because they truly are talented. This explains why investors chase returns. As money flows in, the funds get bigger. But as these funds increase in size, the managers' alphas disappear. Thus there is little persistence in performance.

In allocating money, asset owners go with the best manager. The new money reduces her ability to generate high returns and drives her expected return down to the second best manager's return. At that point, asset owners put money with the second best manager. The same thing happens until the expected returns of the first two managers are forced down to equal the expected return of the third manager, and so on. This continues until all investors are indifferent between investing actively or just putting their money in a cheap, passive index fund. Although fund managers have talent, investors receive returns that are the same as the market. Tack on fees, and active mutual fund returns underperform the market.

The Berk and Green theory is remarkable because it shows that, although fund managers are talented, none of that talent filters down to asset owners in equilibrium. That is, *the managers themselves benefit from their skill*: highly skilled managers attract more money and earn more in fees but do not pass these gains to investors.

The Berk and Green story is applicable not only to mutual funds—it is also a good description of all active asset management, including hedge funds and private equity, which we cover in the next two chapters.

3.6. FEES

There are three main ways that mutual funds levy fees:

Front-end loads (or the *sales charges on purchases*) take money when you invest. For example, if you put $100 into a fund with a 5% front-end load, your balance is immediately cut to $95.

Back-end loads (or the *deferred sales charges*) take money when you leave the fund.

Operating expense fees are paid when you are in the fund and are expressed as a proportion of AUM. *Management fees* are paid to actually manage the fund. The total *expense ratio* includes management fees and other annual recurring expenses, which include marketing and distribution fees, called *"12(b)-1 fees,"* and fees for administrative expenses. *No-load funds* are funds without front-end or back-end loads, where investors only pay only annual expense fees. (Strictly no-load funds can have 12(b)-1 fees as long as they are below 0.25%.)

There are many combinations of these types of fees. Table 16.6 lists fees on Janus Global Research and Janus Worldwide in January 2013. These funds have several share classes—this is common in active mutual funds. Investors would be best off with Class N shares ("N" is usually used for no-load shares), which carry the lowest fees. But why would investors choose other shares with higher fees? Mutual fund companies tend to use different share classes for different *distribution channels*. Active funds do not sell themselves. Front-end loads and 12(b)-1 fees are paid to brokers and other agents, who steer their clients to more expensive share classes.

Class A shares have a front-end load of 5.75%. Some funds (not Janus Global Research or Janus Worldwide) have *break points*, which are levels where the front-end loads change. With break points, larger initial investments have lower fees. Front-end loads are typically paid to brokers who sell the fund and so are effectively sales commissions. Some funds still charge front loads even though they are not sold through brokers.

Class B shares have a back-end load of 1%. Some mutual funds, but not these two, have contingent back-end loads (or a *contingent deferred sales charge*). In these arrangements, the longer you stay in the fund, the lower the back-end load.

Table 16.6

Fund Expenses

Janus Global Research Fund

	Class A	Class C	Class S	Class I	Class N	Class R	Class T
Front Load	5.75%						
Back Load		1.00%					
Management Fees	0.74%	0.74%	0.74%	0.74%	0.74%		0.74%
Distribution/Service (12b-1) Fees	0.25%	1.00%	0.25%				
Other Expenses	0.23%	0.32%	0.39%	0.23%	0.13%		0.38%
Total Annual Operating Expenses	1.22%	2.06%	1.38%	0.97%	0.87%		1.12%

Janus Worldwide Fund

	Class A	Class C	Class S	Class I	Class N	Class R	Class T
Front Load	5.75%						
Back Load		1.00%					
Management Fees	0.59%	0.59%	0.59%	0.59%	0.59%	0.59%	0.59%
Distribution/Service (12b-1) Fees	0.25%	1.00%	0.25%			0.50%	
Other Expenses	0.24%	0.28%	0.33%	0.23%	0.08%	0.33%	0.33%
Total Annual Operating Expenses	1.08%	1.87%	1.17%	0.82%	0.67%	1.42%	0.92%

The **12(b)-1 fee** gets its name from the section of the 40-Act that allows mutual funds to (continually) pay distribution and marketing expenses out of the fund's assets, rather than out of (one-time) loads. 12(b)-1 fees were introduced in 1980. In 2010, investors paid $10.6 billion in 12(b)-1 fees, of which 40% went to financial advisors, brokers, and other financial professionals like retirement plan record keepers and discount brokerage firms. These financial intermediaries are involved in marketing, distribution, and administering the funds. Shareholder services account for 52% of the 12(b)-1 fees, which includes maintaining shareholder websites, call centers, and so on.[38] (One would think expenses like this would be paid out of the management fee or administration fees.) The remainder was spent on fund underwriting and advertising.

---

[38] Numbers are from ICI's 2011 Investment Company Factbook. Interestingly, ICI's 2012 version omits this information.

Classes A, C, and S shares of Janus Global Research carry 12(b)-1 fees of 0.25%, 1.00%, and 0.25%, respectively. Some investors may not realize they are paying 12(b)-1 fees because they are not loads. By setting 12(b)-1 fees on AUM, *current* shareholders pay for the fund company to increase the size of the fund (which then tends to perform poorly as the fund grows) rather than *new* shareholders.

The *other expenses* category includes custodial and legal expenses, accounting fees, and other administrative costs.

The *total operating expenses* sums up the expense ratio, 12(b)-1 fees, and other expenses. The Class C shares for Janus Global Research are very expensive, at over 2%, more than double the management fees for a typical active mutual fund. The other share classes have total annual expenses around 1%. Good passive index funds have total operating expenses well below 0.2%. In the merger of Janus Global Research and Janus Worldwide in March 2013, the fee schedules of the combined fund were the same as Janus Global Research (since Janus Worldwide disappeared). Table 16.6 shows that the fees on each separate share class are all higher for Janus Global Research. At a stroke, Janus got to collect higher fees on the much larger $2 billion in Janus Worldwide than just on the $0.3 billion in Janus Global Research by merging the two funds.

Fees Are Trending Downwards

Fees in active mutual funds have been trending downward but remain fairly high. Figure 16.7 reports mutual fund fees compiled by ICI. During the 1990s, the average mutual fund fee in equities was 1.0%. At the end of 2011, this had fallen to

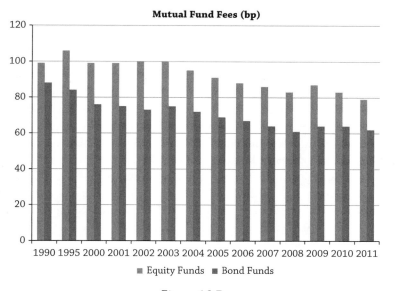

Figure 16.7

0.8%. Bond fund fees declined from 0.9% to 0.6%. Fees have been falling thanks to the rise of low-cost index funds, the shift to no-load funds, and the rise of ETFs (which we discuss below).

Hidden Fees

Despite the disclosure requirements in the 40-Act, several important costs are hidden from investors:

Trading costs are not reported by funds, nor are they included in the fund's expense ratio. Yet higher trading costs reduce returns for investors. Trading costs encompass:

1. Commissions
    Brokerage costs of buying and selling securities must be disclosed but not in the fund's prospectus.
2. Bid–ask spreads
    These are the differences between the lowest price posted by a seller and the highest price posted by a buyer.
3. Market-impact costs
    Large trades will move prices. These costs, though hidden, can exceed commissions or bid–ask spreads.

Trading costs are large. Edelen, Evans, and Kadlec (2007) estimate that trading costs are around 1.4%—exceeding even the expense ratios of active funds. Trading costs are proportional to turnover; the more you trade, the higher the transactions costs. Carhart (1997) and others following him show that the higher turnover is, the lower the fund performance. (Yet another reason to go index.)

In 2012, the turnover of Janus Worldwide was 49% versus 67% in Janus Global Research. Janus Worldwide disappeared in the merger, so its shareholders now pay the higher trading fees of Janus Global Research. Its turnover is less than the average of 80% to 90% for active equity funds. But the turnover for an index fund is usually below 5%.

Soft dollar costs are unseen by fund investors. In soft dollar arrangements, the fund directs its trades to a select few brokers who provide "free" services, research, or products so that the fund needn't buy these things separately. The problem with soft dollars is that firms can hide their true expenses. Instead of running some services through management fees, which are disclosed, they are run through soft dollar arrangements, which as transactions costs are not disclosed.

Fee Obfuscation

Also hidden are the complicated compensation arrangements brokers, marketing firms, subadvisors, consultants, and other intermediaries have with mutual fund companies: revenue sharing arrangements, rebate-based compensation schemes, and various bundled services.

Edelen, Evans, and Kadlec (2012) show that greater transparency in fee payments lowers agency costs and results in better return performance. But more opaque payments reduce fund outflows when the going gets tough, perhaps because investors can't directly see how much they're paying in fees. Barber, Odean, and Zheng (2005) show that mutual fund investors react only to in-your-face fees, like loads and commissions, rather than less obvious fees, like operating expenses. Active fund companies prefer complexity and opacity to make investor money stickier.[39]

Even if all fees were clearly marked, investors may simply not pay that much attention to them (to their detriment). Choi, Laibson, and Madrian (2010) conduct an experiment on Harvard staff, Wharton MBAs, and Harvard undergrads— among the most financially literate members of society. They find that in choosing S&P 500 *index* funds—plain vanilla products that investors should choose primarily based on fees—their subjects consistently choose funds based on past returns. The subjects continued to ignore fees even when given significant monetary incentives and help to make the best choice.[40]

Mutual Fund Company Margins Are High

Table 16.8 is the income statement for Janus in fiscal year 2011. Janus recovered nicely from its disasters in the early 2000s and enjoyed a high profit margin of 32% in the new decade. This high level of profit is typical of mutual fund companies— the mutual fund business is a great business to be in.

Table 16.8 shows that only a minority of Janus's revenue is performance-linked. In 2011, Janus lost only 1% in incentive fees for poor performance. (Remember that the 40-Act only allows symmetric performance fees, so managers lose if they underperform their benchmarks.) Most of the revenue is thus directly linked to AUM. Janus was able to maintain positive operating margins even in the early 2000s (see Figure 16.1) because a large part of its expenses also fluctuate with AUM; in particular, more than half are salaries. Janus also pays large distribution and marketing costs, which amount to 30% of its total expenses.

Gur Huberman (2010), my colleague at Columbia Business School, thinks that the high profit margins of mutual fund companies are not reflected in their share

---

[39] Carlin (2009) shows this is optimal for funds in equilibrium. Del Guercio and Tkac (2002) find that mutual fund flows do *not* respond to fees, only to past returns. See also Stoughton, Wu, and Zechner (2011), who construct an equilibrium model with kickbacks. Higher kickbacks are associated with higher portfolio management fees and reduced performance.

[40] See also Hortaçsu and Syverson (2004), who claim that some investors ignore high fees because they have high search costs.

Table 16.8

Janus Capital Corporation Income Statement 2011		
Revenue	*Millions*	*Percent*
Investment management fees	844.3	86
Performance fees	−11.7	−1
Shareowner and service fees and other	149.3	15
Total Revenue	981.9	100
Operating Expenses		
Employee compensation and benefits	294.9	44
Long-term incentive compensation	63.0	9
Marketing and advertising	28.0	4
Distribution	141.7	21
Depreciation and amortization	33.3	5
General, administrative and occupancy	109.2	16
Goodwill and intangible asset impairments		0
Total Operating Expenses	670.1	100
Operating Income	311.8	
Operating Margin	32%	

prices. He argues that the operating margins of 30% or so imply that shares should be priced at 20% to 35% of AUM. But mutual fund companies are typically priced at 1% to 4% of AUM. According to Huberman, Janus's shares are severely underpriced! Perhaps mutual fund company prices are low because investors anticipate that the active segment of the market will shrink—as it has been, albeit slowly. The ICI reports that index funds represented 7% of all equity funds in 1997, a figure that has climbed steadily to 16% in 2011. Pástor and Stambaugh (2012) claim that the size of the active mutual fund industry will decline very slowly because investors' learning about underperforming active funds is very slow. The mutual fund industry has hundreds of sponsor companies—ICI reports 713 at the end of 2011—and yet profit margins remain very high.[41]

---

[41] Whether the mutual fund industry is competitive is still an open question. The dean of my institution, Glenn Hubbard, argues it is; see Coates and Hubbard (2007). But others disagree, as in Morley and Curtis (2010).

3.7. INCUBATION BIAS

Mutual fund companies start mutual funds like Jesus' parable of the sower, where only the seed that falls on fertile ground takes root, springs up, and is harvested. Fund companies start multiple funds privately, and at the end of an evaluation period, they open them to the public. The *incubation bias* is the tendency of fund sponsors to open up and market only the successful funds. The opened funds have *selection bias*. Evans (2012) shows that funds in incubation have returns that are nearly 10% higher than nonincubated funds.[42] When these funds are open to the public, money flows in. But the success of these funds during incubation is mostly due to chance. Post-incubation, Evans finds that the outperformance disappears. There are dozens of Janus's incubated funds in Evans's database, but Janus is not alone in practicing incubation. In fact 23% of new funds are incubated.

Some fund companies engage in shady practices during incubation by *juicing* returns. Fund companies can preferentially allocate good deals to their incubated funds. For example, IPOs typically "pop" on the first day of trading and reach prices well above their issue price. Van Kampen and Dreyfus have both paid fines for unfairly allocating IPOs to their incubated funds.[43]

3.8. OTHER AGENCY ISSUES

Governance matters in mutual funds.

Funds whose directors have more skin in the game—that is, whose directors have large ownership stakes—perform better.[44] Fees are lower at mutual funds with fewer and more independent directors. At the best-governed funds, fees are charged in line with performance. Funds with more independent boards have smaller fee hikes and larger fee cuts.

Then there is the dark side mutual fund governance.[45] Fund directors and advisory firms hire each other preferentially and often not based on merit. Mutual fund families strategically favor some funds that increase the firm's profits at the expense of fund shareholders.

The Employee Retirement Income Security Act of 1974 (see chapter 1) requires trustees to be prudent in finding suitable investments for their 401(k) clients.

---

[42] See also Palmiter and Taha (2009).

[43] See SEC Release Nos. 1819 and 1870, respectively. Gaspar, Massa, and Matos (2006) study juicing. The tendency of IPO firms to increase from the offer price to the first day closing price is called *IPO underpricing*. Once IPOs list, they tend to perform poorly over two- to five-year periods compared to more seasoned companies, which is the *long-run IPO underperformance puzzle*. See Ritter and Welch (2002) for a literature summary of IPO issues.

[44] See Chen, Goldstein, and Jiang (2008) and Cremers et al. (2009) for the skin-in-the-game results. For the other results, see Tufano and Sevick (1997), Gil-Bazo and Ruiz-Verdu (2009), Adams, Mansi, and Nishikawa (2010), and Warner and Wu (2011). Dann, Del Guercio, and Partch (2003) show that closed-end funds with more independent boards also have superior performance.

[45] For these effects, see Kuhnen (2009) and Gaspar, Massa, and Matos (2006), respectively.

Trustees are typically appointed by the employer who sponsors the plan. Mutual fund families often serve as the trustees of defined contribution 401(k) plans, and they play large roles in selecting a set of funds for the participants. But mutual fund trustees have a competing interest in steering participants to their own funds. Pool, Sialm, and Stefanescu (2013) show that trustee-sponsored funds on average underperform by 3.6% compared to nontrustee funds. Trustee funds are also less likely to be removed from, and more likely to be added to, 401(k) menus. Trustee mutual fund companies tend to overweight the sponsoring company's stock—chapter 3 shows this lack of diversification hurts beneficiaries—and the way trustee funds vote in shareholder meetings depends on their sponsors' business ties.[46]

Individual investors can improve governance by piggy-backing on institutional funds, who have more resources to monitor and can chastise funds by withdrawing large sums. Evans and Fahlenbrach (2012) show that retail mutual funds with institutional offerings outperform retail funds without institutional offerings by 1.5% per year.

Why do investors stick with poorly governed, poorly performing funds? One reason is taxes—but investors are generally better off paying capital gain taxes now and moving into better funds.[47] Another reason is ignorance and slow learning; it's just hard to determine whether your fund manager is failing to deliver value.

The behavioral explanations probably resonate more with individual investors. Investors might be reluctant to realize their losses (this is called the *disposition effect*).[48] And then of course hope springs eternal—maybe the fund will come back (it won't). Gennaioli, Shleifer, and Vishny (2012) argue that the relationship between a mutual fund shareholder and its advisor is like the relationship between a patient and her doctor. Investors trust mutual fund companies, and this trust does not disappear when mutual funds stumble. Managers exploit this trust, capital is sticky, and managers can keep charging high fees even when they have no skill.

3.9. SUMMARY

Tkac (2004) calls the conflicts of interest in the mutual fund industry a "permanent morass" and pays special attention to the tension between the investor as a customer of a mutual fund sold by a mutual fund company and the legal setup of the investor as owner of the mutual fund represented by a board and procuring services from the mutual fund company. But the 40-Act has eliminated the worst

---

[46] See Cohen and Schmidt (2009) and Davis and Kim (2007), respectively.

[47] Bergstresser and Poterba (2002) report that investors take into account taxes when investing in mutual funds. See Pástor and Stambaugh (2012) for slow (rational) learning.

[48] The term is coined by Shefrin and Statman (1985).

of these principal-agent problems and has allowed the mutual fund industry to flourish.

Mutual funds have also encouraged people to save. People do indeed need to save (see chapter 5), and they would have saved far less without mutual funds. Individuals have gained access to investment skills that would be out of reach to them in running their own portfolios, and their funds are protected from the worst abuses by managers. Unfortunately, the benefit of investment skill accrues to the managers of the funds, on average, rather than to the investors in the funds. Mutual funds underperform, or at best equal, the market, and investors pile into funds with high past returns that aren't repeated going forward.

4. Closed-End Funds

Closed-end funds are ideal vehicles to hold illiquid assets because the number of shares is fixed and they are traded in the secondary market. That means there can be no redemption from the fund. So closed-end funds can harvest an illiquidity premium.[49] There is, however, a difference between the exchange price of closed-end shares and the underlying value of the fund's investments (the NAV). This difference can be large, is usually negative, and varies over time. This phenomenon is called the *closed-end fund discount puzzle*.[50]

Figure 16.9 plots the closed-end fund discount from 1934 to 2012, which is an updated series from Baker, Wurgler, and Yu (2012). The last portion of this data is the closed-end fund discount index constructed by Thomas J. Herzfeld Advisors, a firm specializing in closed-end funds. The average discount is 11%, but there is considerable time variation.

Some reasons for this negative average discount are:

1. Taxes

   The discount can arise from *tax overhang*.[51] Managers of a mutual fund can realize capital gains at a time that is inopportune for investors. (This takes away investors' tax-timing option; see chapter 12.)

2. Irrationality

   Lee, Shleifer, and Thaler (1991) argue that the closed-end fund discount is due to investor irrationality. The discount itself is used as an input into

---

[49] See Stein (2005). Note that the illiquidity premium across asset classes is small, but there are large differences between the returns of liquid and illiquid assets within asset classes; see chapter 11.

[50] See Cherkes (2012) for a summary article on closed-end funds. Some investment companies are economically similar to closed-end funds in the sense that they are listed and the number of shares is fixed. Berkshire Hathaway is a famous example. These are corporations and do not fall under the 40-Act.

[51] Originally due to Malkiel (1977). Chay, Choi, and Pontiff (2006) estimate that each dollar of distributed capital gains shrinks the discount by 7 cents.

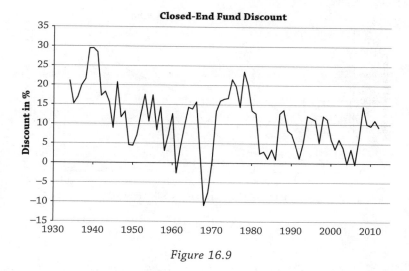

Figure 16.9

investor sentiment indices, like Baker and Wurgler (1997). Investor sentiment, however, does not explain simultaneous discounts and premiums of similar closed-end funds.

3. Agency costs

While the structure of closed-end funds offers advantages, such as the ability to harvest illiquidity premiums, there are also agency costs.[52] Managers charge fees, and when managers have no talent, there must be a discount as fees are paid out of the fund's earnings. Cherkes, Sagi, and Stanton (2009) show discounts or premiums arise as the trade-off between the benefit of transforming illiquid assets into liquid ones and managerial costs.

A number of *activist investors*, especially hedge funds, have tried to take advantage of the closed-end fund discount by *open-ending* closed-end funds.[53] Activists do this by buying enough shares to control the closed-end fund's board, and then dissolving the fund to collect the discount.

5. ETFs

There has been huge growth in both the number of ETFs and their AUM. ETFs are convenient because you can trade them instantaneously, they are cheap because they are designed for the most part to passively track indices, and there is a lot of

---

[52] This story is originally due to Boudreaux (1973). See also Ross (2005) and Berk and Stanton (2007).

[53] See Bradley et al. (2010).

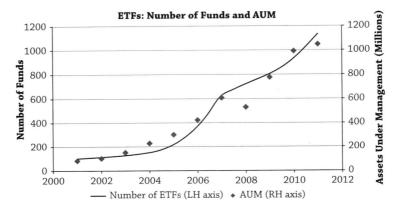

Figure 16.10

variety. There are even ETFs of ETFs. *The Economist* calls ETFs "one of the more successful financial innovations in recent decades."[54]

Figure 16.10 plots data from ICI and shows that the number of ETFs rose from about 100 in 2001 to more than 1100 at the end of 2011. While 90% of ETFs are registered investment companies and fall under the 40-Act, the remainder, which mainly invest in commodity futures, are regulated by the Commodity Futures Trading Commission (CFTC). *Synthetic ETFs* hold derivatives, mostly swaps, to engineer exposure to commodities or illiquid assets. (ETFs that physically hold commodities, like gold, are regulated by the SEC.) New synthetic ETFs have been suspended since March 2010 and are still suspended at the time of writing in 2013 (but existing ones were allowed to continue).

5.1. ETFS VERSUS MUTUAL FUNDS

ETFs have a number of advantages over mutual funds:

1. Immediate liquidity

   ETFs trade throughout the day. Investors in mutual funds, in contrast, all receive the same price at the end of the day. The disadvantage of ETFs is that the price investors pay can be different from the NAV—but the design of ETFs ensures that this discrepancy is small, at least during normal times (see below).
2. Tax efficiency

   ETFs are generally much more tax-efficient than mutual funds (see chapter 12 for tax-efficient investing). Mutual funds must sell off securities to pay off investors redeeming shares. This capital gain is passed through to investors

---

[54] *Economist*, "Exchange-Traded Funds: Twenty Years Young," Jan. 26, 2013.

no matter when an investor entered the fund. In ETFs, your tax basis depends only on when you bought the ETF.

3. More transparency

ETF holdings are published daily. Mutual funds report their holdings quarterly. The daily disclosure is actually an impediment for *actively managed ETFs*, which do not blindly track indices; why would you want to allow everyone to see what you're doing if you have a secret sauce?

4. Can be shorted

Mutual funds are long-only products. Because ETFs trade on exchanges, they can be shorted. Given the underperformance of active mutual funds, shorting actively managed ETFs might be a way to capitalize on the active management discount.

I see two major disadvantages of ETFs for individuals. First, the fact that you can easily trade means investors trade often. Odean (1999) and Barber and Odean (2000) show that individuals lose money when they trade a lot because they trade pro-cyclically: they are reluctant to sell losing stocks and are too quick to realize their winners. Second, the large assortment of ETFs can lead to some investors becoming attracted to overly narrow products that do not give them adequate diversification (see chapter 3).

5.2. FAIR PRICING

ETF prices quoted on an exchange should correspond closely with the NAV through *no-arbitrage pricing*. ETF shares are created when an *authorized participant* (brokers or institutional investors, which must be registered with the ETF) deposits a *creation basket* with the ETF. The creation basket is a portfolio of the underlying securities in the ETF, usually reflecting the index the ETF is tracking. (In some cases, small amounts of cash can be substituted for securities that are hard to obtain.) In return for depositing securities, the authorized participant receives a large block of shares, like 25,000 or even 100,000, which is the *creation unit*. The authorized participant can then break up creation units and sell the smaller blocks on the exchange. The transactions between the authorized participant and the fund are deemed *in-kind transactions* and are not subject to tax.

To do the reverse process, a creation unit can be disposed of by selling back the shares to the ETF. In return, the authorized participant receives the creation basket.

If the ETF is trading below its NAV during the day, authorized participants can buy low and sell high. They buy shares of the ETF on the market and then offer them to the ETF and receive the creation basket. As they buy ETF shares, the price of the ETF rises until the ETF price reflects the NAV. Conversely if the ETF trades above its NAV, authorized participants sell the ETF (which is expensive) and buy the creation basket (which is cheap). As they sell, the price of the ETF declines until it reaches the NAV.

How close is the NAV of the shares, at which the authorized participants trade, and the market price of the ETF, at which other investors trade? Pretty close, most of the time. Engle and Sarkar (2006) and DeFusco, Ivanov, and Karels (2011) show that ETFs are efficiently priced. The deviations from NAV are small, not persistent, and last only minutes.

Flash Crash

Except sometimes deviations are large, persistent, and last for more than just minutes.

In a mere 20 minutes starting at 2:40 pm on May 6, 2010, major futures and equities markets plummeted more than 5% before suddenly rebounding. The decline began in the equity futures market, where it was (supposedly) triggered by Waddell & Reed, an investment manager based in Kansas. Pressure from high-frequency trading algorithms soon overwhelmed available liquidity, causing an explosion of mispricing to tumble through to equities markets.[55] This was the *Flash Crash*. More than 300 securities had trades executed at prices more than 60% away from values just before the Flash Crash. Accenture, a company that has a market value in the tens of billions of dollars, traded at 1 cent. Sotheby's had been trading around $34 and then jumped to $99,999.99. This gave Sotheby's, however briefly, a market capitalization larger than the U.S. economy.

ETFs accounted for 70% of the 326 securities for which trades were canceled. Madhavan (2012) shows that ETFs experienced significantly larger drawdowns during the Flash Crash than for other securities: the average ETF drawdown was 24% versus 8% for other equities. ETFs played a special role in transmitting these shocks. Ben-David, Franzoni, and Moussawi (2011) argue that ETFs served as the conduit for shocks from the futures market (ground zero) to the equity market. It is not surprising that some regulators and others think that ETFs pose systemic risk to the financial system.[56]

There are several lessons for asset owners from the Flash Crash:

1. ETFs require liquid markets for fair pricing;
2. ETFs can exacerbate liquidity shocks; and
3. ETF no-arbitrage relationships are prone to breakdown and are very fragile during crashes.

---

[55] See U.S. Securities and Exchange Commission and the Commodity Futures Trading Commission, "Findings Regarding the Market Events of May 6, 2010," released on Sept. 30, 2010. Waddell & Reed was not named by the SEC and CFTC report. See Lash, H., and Spicer, J., "Exclusive: Waddell is Mystery Trader in Market Plunge," Reuters, May 15, 2010.

[56] See Bradley and Litan (2010).

5.3. AGENCY ISSUES

The ETF Business

ETFs have much lower margins than traditional mutual funds. While the average mutual fund has an expense ratio of 80 basis points (see Figure 16.7), the average ETF charges 20 basis points (see French (2008)). Many traditional mutual fund companies have introduced ETFs as money flowing into regular mutual funds has been slowing. They are doing this with reluctance—ETFs are generally less profitable and cannibalize higher-margin traditional funds. Janus, for example, has been late to hop on the ETF bandwagon. It filed with the SEC on September 3, 2010, to launch active ETFs, but as of the time of writing in 2013 had yet to launch an ETF.

The top three ETF sponsors at the end of 2011 were iShares, StateStreet, and Vanguard with AUMs of $448 billion, $267 billion, and $170 billion, respectively. (The rest of the players are much smaller.) The big three are engaged in a "battle of the basis points" in driving ETF costs lower.[57] Some broad-based index ETFs now carry expense ratios below 0.05%.

At the time of writing, there is only one listed pure ETF sponsor company, WisdomTree Investments. This is the only company where we can directly see the profitability of the ETF business—all the other companies that sponsor ETFs do so in divisions of larger companies and do not separately break out ETF revenue. WisdomTree's AUM was $12.2 billion at the end of December 2011, making it the seventh largest ETF sponsor in the U.S. WisdomTree launched its first ETF in June 2006 and listed on NASDAQ in July 2011. In its 2011 fiscal year, the first in which it posted a profit, WisdomTree posted an operating margin of 5%—peanuts compared with the 32% operating margin of Janus in the same year (see Table 16.8).

Low margins in the ETF business mean that you need a lot of scale. Barclays Global Investors (BGI), now part of BlackRock, launched its iShares division in 1999.[58] The plan was risky because BGI needed $100 billion of AUM to break even. When BGI jumped in, it launched an entire platform of ETFs, along with a comprehensive education campaign for investors. It was a bold, bet-the-firm kind of decision by the CEO of BGI, Blake Grossman, and the CEO of iShares, Lee Kranefuss. They made the right call—BGI's ETF business took off.

The big ETF guys need to be really big in order to make money. And they need to get even bigger as fees continue to fall.

One area that ETFs have yet to crack is the 401(k) market. Consultants and mutual fund company sponsors still dominate this arena. (Many consultants benefit from some of the 12(b)-1 fees, and consultants and plan sponsors have kickback arrangements with mutual fund companies.) ETFs account for just 0.2%

---

[57] Lydon, T., "Investors Like ETFs' Low Fees, Liquidity," ETF Trends, Dec. 27, 2012.

[58] See the Harvard Business School case, "Barclays Global Investors and Exchange Traded Funds," 2007, by Luis M. Viceira and Alison Berkeley Wagonfeld.

of retirement assets.[59] Retirement asset managers have been able to hold onto higher-fee products partly because fees on 401(k) plans were not required to be disclosed until 2012. As more investors pay attention to fees in retirement plans, money should start flowing to ETFs. The process will be slow, though, because consultants and mutual fund trustees control a lot of these funds, and fund beneficiaries have little say.

Too Much Trading?

There is another way that asset management companies can make money off ETFs, even though the margins on managing ETFs are small. John Bogle, the founder of Vanguard, says:[60] "The trick of ETFs . . . is that the costs of administration are basically thrown over to the marketplace, so people pay for them with their brokerage commissions and things of that nature."

Some asset management companies can subsidize ETFs by making money from trading costs—especially if they have their own trading platforms or work hand-in-hand with brokers. Fidelity Investments, for example, began charging high fees in March 2013 for investors who sell "commission-free" ETFs on its trading platform within short time periods.[61] Many ETF sponsors, however, do not directly benefit from their costs of trading. ETF bid–ask spreads average 0.9%, but fixed income and equity funds have bid–ask spreads below 0.25%.[62] The biggest ETFs, however, have very small trading costs and the ten largest ETFs from 2007 through 2012 have average spreads of 0.04%.[63] Nevertheless, even if you trade the biggest ETFs a lot, the expenses start to add up very quickly—and cost many times more than a traditional (buy and infrequently trade) active mutual fund. Mutual funds, in contrast, have zero bid–ask spreads.[64]

Leveraged ETFs

Retail investors must be particularly careful with leveraged ETFs. With these products, daily compounding causes returns over more than one day to differ from the underlying index. Suppose you invest $100 in a traditional fund and $100 in a hypothetical "3×Leveraged Fund" based on the same index. The index rises 10%.

[59] Computed by Cerulli Associates, as quoted by Weinberg, A. I., What ETFs' Next Act Will Look Like, *Wall Street Journal*, Oct 23, 2012.

[60] John Bogle, testimony to Senate Committee on Government Affairs Hearing on "Mutual Funds: Trading Practices and Abuses that Harm Investors, November 3, 2003.

[61] Grind, K., "Fidelity's ETF Fee Spurs a Backlash," *Wall Street Journal*, Mar 14, 2013.

[62] Numbers from IndexUniverse, quoted by Coombes, A., "Calculating the Costs of an ETF," *Wall Street Journal*, Oct. 23, 2012.

[63] Numbers computed by Paul Tetlock.

[64] In mutual funds, current shareholders absorb the liquidity costs of marginal traders, whereas the liquidity costs are borne by the traders themselves in ETFs. Because of these different liquidity profiles, Guedj and Huang (2009) show that mutual funds and ETFs will co-exist in equilibrium and attract different clienteles with different liquidity needs.

The traditional fund returns $110. The 3×Leveraged ETF adds 30% to return $130. Leveraged ETFs are "reset" daily. Now suppose on day 2, the index falls 10%. The traditional fund drops to $(1- 0.1) \times 110 = \$99$. The leveraged ETF returns $(1-0.3) \times 120 = \$84$. After two days, the index return is $99/100 - 1 = -1\%$. In comparison, the 3×Leverage Fund has returned $84/100-1 = -16\%$. This is very different from three times the index return of -1% over two days and contrary to what an ordinary investor might have expected from the fund's name. Repeat this after many days, and there can be enormous divergence between actual returns and those you expect.[65]

Figure 16.11 plots the S&P 500, the Direxion Daily S&P 500 Bear 3X, and the Direxion Daily S&P 500 Bull 3X. The latter two ETFs are designed to have triple exposure to the S&P 500 in a short and long direction, respectively. Figure 16.11 plots the cumulative return to a $1 investment in each of the three at the beginning of January 2012 until the end of December 2012. The return of the S&P 500 is –11.8%. The Bear 3X fund returned 74.6%, more than six times the S&P 500 return. The Bull 3X fund returned –31.6%, which is 2.6 times the S&P 500 return. These are very different from the expected "3" in the funds' names.

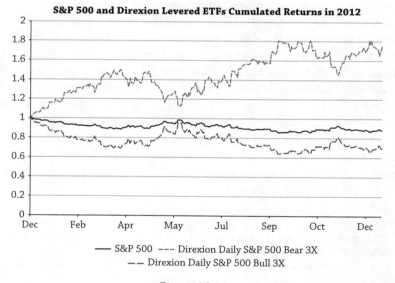

Figure 16.11

---

[65] This difference arises from arithmetic vs. geometric returns, see Cheng and Madhavan (2009), chapter 4, and the Appendix. Tang and Xu (2013), however, show that the divergence between the leveraged ETF returns and the leveraged multiple of the underlying index return cannot be explained by just compounding deviations.

6. Janus Redux

It's ironic that while Janus was the poster-child fund of the Internet investing craze of the 1990s, it was owned by an old-fashioned railroad company, Kansas City Southern Industries (KCSI). Janus Capital Corp. was founded by Thomas Bailey in 1969 in Denver. During the 1960s, creating industrial conglomerates was all the rage, and KCSI diversified into financial companies, acquiring an 82% stake in Janus in 1984.[66] Under Bailey, Janus grew fast, but its rise became meteoric after he promoted James Craig to manage the flagship Janus Fund in 1986. Janus's rise to stardom in the 1990s was due to Craig, Jack Thompson (the COO), and Tom Marisco. Marisco managed the Janus Twenty Fund and left in 1997 to found his own firm after run-ins ("philosophical disagreements") with Bailey.[67]

In 2000, KCSI spun out Stilwell Financial, which was named after one of KCSI's founders. Stilwell consisted of Janus, which had 97% of its total AUM, plus three smaller investment management businesses. Craig left the firm in August 1999, prior to the spinoff. The stated reason was to create Opportunity Capital, a management company serving his wife's charitable trust foundation, but rumors were that his resignation was prompted by the forthcoming spinoff. The creation of Stilwell was marked by bitter battles between Janus and KCSI, where Janus felt slighted that it was being lumped with lesser-known and smaller asset management companies in the holding company. Craig's timing was impeccable: he cashed in his $70 million equity stake in Janus right before the dot-com meltdown.[68]

By this time Bailey was not involved in running the firm's day-to-day operations, although he retained his large ownership stake. Bailey developed a reputation as "fun-loving," "sleazy," "was into marijuana and cocaine," and had employees cover for him with his wife (they later divorced) when he was meeting other women.[69] The terms of his sale to KCSI stipulated that Bailey had the right to sell his remaining shares at fifteen times Janus's after-tax earnings per share. Janus was also required to pay out 90% of its profits in the form of dividends. Owning 12.2% of Janus brought Bailey riches. In 1999 alone, the dividends paid by Janus gave Bailey $25 million.

---

[66] In the finance literature, diversified companies tend to have lower returns than predicted if the company were split into a portfolio of specialized firms. This is called the *diversification discount*. See Lang and Stulz (1994) and Villalonga (2004). The history of Janus is drawn from Elkind, P., 2001, "The Hidden Face of Janus," *Fortune*, Jan. 22, 2001, and Goldberg, S. T., "Upheaval at Janus," Kiplinger, June 2003.

[67] Marisco ended up selling his own asset management firm to Bank of America, which paid $150 million in 1998 for half the firm and $950 million for the other half two years later. Marisco netted half a billion for himself in the transaction. In 2007, Marisco bought back his firm from Bank of America on undisclosed terms. See Stempel, J., 2007, "Marisco Buys Itself Bank from Bank of America," Reuters, June 14, 2007.

[68] Forbes, "Stock Picking Without the Taxes," Oct. 30, 2000.

[69] See Elkind, P., 2001, "The Hidden Face of Janus," *Fortune*, Jan. 22, 2001.

Janus's assets were cut in half due to the fallout from the Internet crash in 2001; clearly the sun was setting on the Janus empire. Bailey sold his remaining Janus shares back to Stilwell. Stilwell paid $1.56 billion to acquire shares in Janus, of which approximately $1.2 billion was paid to Bailey.[70] Thus, a large portion of the fees paid by investors in Janus funds ended up in Bailey's pockets. Bailey sold out of Janus completely; he did not plough back his money into Janus funds or Stilwell stock. This is in keeping with Berk and Green's (2004) model, which says that mutual fund managers' talent, if any, accrues to the fund managers themselves and does not trickle down to the shareholders in the funds.

In 2002, Stilwell was swallowed by its more famous subsidiary and the Janus Capital Group was formed. Thanks to the stickiness of mutual fund cash flows, Janus survived the internet meltdown, market timing investigations by the SEC, and terrible performance—like all finance companies—during the 2008–2009 financial crisis.

And what of the stodgy railroad company KCSI, which previously owned Janus? At the end of 2011, it was one of the best performing stocks of the previous twenty years.[71] In the mid-1990s, Janus was earning more than KCSI's core railroad business, and KCSI's stock price rose with Janus's fortunes. In jettisoning Janus in 2000, right at the peak of the Internet bubble, KCSI's timing was perfect. KCSI got cash to pump back into its railroad operations and avoided the Internet crash that dragged down Janus's value. The proceeds reinvigorated KCSI in time for a resurgence of rail shipping in the 2000s. (The investing legend Warren Buffet bought a rail competitor of KCSI in the late 2000s.) And as an old-fashioned company, it also fared well in the financial crisis that brought down most financial firms in 2008–2009.

---

[70] Janus Capital Corp. 10-K 2002, p. 40.

[71] Sterman, D., "The Best Performing Stocks of the Last 20 Years," InvestingAnswers, May 27, 2011.

CHAPTER 17

Hedge Funds

Chapter Summary

Hedge funds (HFs) are not an asset class. HF returns have large exposure to dynamic factors—especially volatility risk. After taking these nonlinear risks into account, the average HF is unlikely to add value. HF fees are high, but, contrary to popular perception, only a minority of HF manager compensation comes from incentive fees.

1. The Quant Meltdown

In the first week of August 2007, returns of quantitative hedge funds (quant HFs) went into a tailspin.[1] From August 7 to 9, quant funds experienced huge and unprecedented losses—for no obvious reason. There was no overall market decline, and the large losses occurred only at quant funds.

Quant investing picks securities by mining data and creating quantitative signals. Its development dates to the 1960s, when the new Capital Asset Pricing Model (see chapter 6) gave fund managers a way to estimate expected returns of stocks from beta—a statistic measuring how a stock moves together with the market. High-frequency statistical arbitrage funds use highly technical strategies with very short horizons (ranging from seconds to one or two days). Longer-term *market neutral* funds have investment horizons from weeks to months and rely on economic models and lower-frequency statistical forecasting methods. Some market-neutral funds tend to use factor-based investment strategies like value-growth, size, momentum, volatility, and credit (see chapter 7). Many HFs are leveraged and take short positions.

The complex models used by quant funds amplified the funds' decline during those three grim August days. Amir Khandani, a graduate student at MIT, and his

---

[1] This is based on "The Quant Meltdown: August 2007," CaseWorks ID #080317. See also Khandali and Lo (2007) and Daniel (2009).

professor, Andrew Lo, who studies investment strategies and is an expert on HFs (he runs one himself), studied the quant meltdown. In Khandani and Lo (2007), they called it "the perfect financial storm."

Losses at some of the largest, and historically best-performing, quant funds reached 30%,[2] as they did at the Global Equity Opportunities Fund and Global Alpha fund managed by Goldman Sachs Asset Management. (Full disclosure: I was consulting for Morgan Stanley during August 2007 at a quant group that lost $500 million between the last week of July and August 9.[3])

Losses of this magnitude in the absence of direct market forces or significant news were shocking to quant HF managers. Their funds were designed to have low volatility. Losses of this size just weren't supposed to happen. David Viniar, CFO of Goldman Sachs, said:[4] "We were seeing things that were 25-standard de-viation moves, several days in a row. There have been issues in some of the other quantitative spaces. But nothing like what we saw last week."

Matthew Rothman, a quant analyst at Lehman Brothers, commented:[5] "Events that models only predicted would happen once in 10,000 years happened every day for three days."

It wasn't just the losses that were shocking. Quants combined several invest-ment strategies that were supposed to have low correlations with each other. Yet the resulting investments plummeted together. Manolis Liodakis, a strategist at Citigroup, exclaimed that "nothing seems to be working. Previously uncorrelated factors have recently been falling with the same pace, leaving investors with very few places to hide."[6]

Then, as suddenly as the losses arrived, quant returns bounced back on August 10, 2007. The storm left plenty of casualties. Many funds responded to the losses by cutting leverage. But reducing leverage meant that their exposures were much smaller when quant strategies rallied, so their gains did not make up for their losses.

Goldman's Global Equity Opportunities Fund received an injection of $3 bil-lion to stabilize the fund, of which $2 billion came from Goldman and $1 billion from investors, including Maurice "Hank" Greenberg, the former chairman of AIG (which had to be rescued during the financial crisis a year later), and billionaire Eli Broad. News of the Goldman rescue was announced on August 13, but rumors of it started spreading on August 10 and may even have triggered the rebound. The quant meltdown was the beginning of the end for the Global Equity Opportunities

[2] "The Quant Meltdown: August 2007," CaseWorks ID #080317 lists August 2007 performance for several quant HFs in Table 2, along with media sources.

[3] See Patterson, S. and A. Raghavan, "August Ambush: How Market Turmoil Waylaid the 'Quants,'" *Wall Street Journal*, Sept. 7, 2007.

[4] Larsen, P., "Goldman Pays the Price of Being Big," *Financial Times*, Aug. 13, 2007.

[5] Whitehouse, K., "One Quant Sees Shakeout for the Ages –'10,000 years,'" *Wall Street Journal*, Aug. 11, 2007.

[6] Xydias, A., "Market Turmoil is 'Perfect Storm' for Quant Funds," Bloomberg, Aug. 10, 2007.

Fund, which had commanded $7.5 billion in assets at its peak. The fund shut its doors in December 2009 after its assets had dwindled to $200 million.[7] At the end of 2011, Goldman also shut Global Alpha, once one of its biggest funds, with more than $12 billion in assets, after client redemptions shrank it to $1.6 billion.[8]

Experts have debated the surprising losses of quant funds during August 2007. Because quant fund returns were so highly correlated on the downside, several experts suggested that there were too many players in the quant HF space doing the same thing. Large common positions, common funding sources, or too many quants using the same risk models and alpha strategies could have caused losses from one strategy to spill over to all quant strategies. Some suggested a new "hedge fund beta" had come into play. According to Khandani and Lo (2007), "the fact that the entire class of long/short equity strategies moved together so tightly during August 2007 implies the existence of certain common factors within that class."

Quant funds are just one type of HF. The best description of a HF is given by Cliff Asness, a Goldman alumnus who once worked in the division that oversaw the Global Equity Opportunities and Global Alpha funds. He left Goldman in 1997 to found AQR, a HF that managed $71 billion at the end of 2012. Asness (2004) says:

> Hedge funds are investment pools that are relatively unconstrained in what they do. They are relatively unregulated (for now), charge very high fees, will not necessarily give you your money back when you want it, and will generally not tell you what they do. They are supposed to make money all the time, and when they fail at this, their investors redeem and go to someone else who has recently been making money. Every three or four years they deliver a one-in-a-hundred year flood. They are generally run for rich people in Geneva, Switzerland, by rich people in Greenwich, Connecticut.

Asness himself works and lives (in a 26,000-square-foot house) in Greenwich.[9] AQR is a quant fund, and it was not spared the harrowing experience of August 2007; AQR had losses close to 20%. "We were looking the grim reaper in the face," said Asness as he recalled his fund shrinking from $39 billion in 2007 to $17 billion by the end of 2008.[10] While Goldman's funds dissolved, everything came back for Asness, plus much more, after 2009. (Asness remains correct that, despite enactment of the Dodd-Frank Wall Street Reform and Consumer Protection Act in 2010, HFs are still relatively unregulated.)

[7] Cahill, T., "Goldman Said to Shut Global Equity Opportunities Fund," Bloomberg, Jan. 22, 2010.

[8] LaCapra, T. L., and Herbst-Bayliss, S., "Goldman to Close Global Alpha After Losses," Reuters, Sept. 16, 2011.

[9] Chung, J., "Living Very Large," *Wall Street Journal*, Feb. 10, 2012.

[10] Quote from Tully, S., "Cliff Asness: A Hedge Fund Genius Goes Retail," CNNMoney, Dec. 19, 2011.

In August 2007, quant funds didn't live up to their promise of low volatility, steady returns, or *absolute returns*—the words they used in their marketing pitches. What kind of common factors are HFs exposed to? And does their performance justify their fees?

2. Industry Characteristics

HFs are investment vehicles for rich people.[11] HFs are defined by what they are not—HFs are exempt from the Investment Company Act of 1940 and subsequent amendments and rules (or 40-Act for short; see chapter 15). The 40-Act gives strict rules on what forms 40-Act funds can take and what they can do.[12] Giving up the investor protections of the 40-Act allows HFs wide latitude in how they invest, how they pay their managers, how they disclose information, and even how (or if) investors can get their money back. Rich people don't need 40-Act protection because they can (and should) hire lawyers, accountants, financial advisors, and other professionals.

2.1. HISTORY

The first HF was created in 1949 by Alfred Winslow Jones, who had an unlikely background for a man who was to become the trailblazer of an industry now handling trillions of dollars. Before forming his "hedged fund," Jones worked as a U.S. diplomat in Germany when Nazism was on the rise, earned a PhD in sociology at my own institution, Columbia University, and for a while was a journalist at *Fortune* magazine (which published a version of his dissertation).

Jones's fund had three special features:

1. It was secretive.

    Jones went to great lengths to protect his investments from prying competitors and did not share much detail on what his funds were doing, even with clients.
2. It featured a management incentive fee.

    In fact Jones charged an incentive fee of 20% but no regular management fee, a practice modern HFs might do well to emulate (see below). At the time, managers typically charged flat fees. Jones adopted a nonlinear performance fee not because he thought it a good way to align his incentives with his clients' goals (he had not studied principal-agent theory, see chapter 15) but

---

[11] Good summaries of HFs are Stulz (2007) and Lo (2010). Do not be put off by its title: *Hedge Funds for Dummies* written by Logue (2007) is not just for dummies.

[12] While they are exempt from the 40-Act, HFs must comply with other laws and regulations, like the 1933 Securities Act and general fraud statutes. Commodity trading advisors and commodity pool operators are similar to HFs in that they have large exposure to dynamic factors: They trade futures, swaps, or options on futures or swaps and are registered with the Commodity Futures Trading Commission.

purely to minimize taxes. At the time, marginal tax rates on personal income were upward of 90%, whereas capital gains rates were just 25%. Charging only incentive fees allowed Jones to keep an extra 65 cents of every dollar earned.

3. Finally, the fund was exempt from the 40-Act.

Jones's fund was *private*, and he could not (and did not need to) solicit funds from the general public. That is, a hedge fund is not a *public* "investment company" as defined by the 40-Act. As he gained investors, he set up additional partnerships to maintain exemption. A nice feature of the funds management business is economies of scale: the fixed costs of the systems you need to manage ten funds are pretty much the same as for one. So HF managers' revenue quickly explodes with increasing assets under management. (But a larger asset base translates into less value added for investors, as I explain below.)

Modern HFs have some, if not all, of these features. It is notable that an investment vehicle now so favored by institutions was first invented to cater to individual investors. (The same is true for private equity, which I discuss in the next chapter.)

HFs can produce enormous gains. George Soros came to be called "the Man Who Broke the Bank of England" by anticipating that the United Kingdom would be forced to devalue and leave the European Exchange Rate Mechanism—which it did, on September 16, 1992. His Quantum Fund bet $10 billion by shorting sterling and buying Deutschmarks in the preceding week, earning him $1.8 billion. In 2007, John Paulson made "the greatest trade ever" in the words of Zuckerman (2009) by betting against mortgages. His HF made $15 billion on the move, of which Paulson personally took home $3.7 billion.

HFs can also lose big. In 1998, Long Term Capital Management (LTCM), a HF co-founded by Nobel Prize winners Robert Merton and Myron Scholes, collapsed when its credit bets went sour after Russia defaulted in August.[13] LTCM had begun the year with $5 billion in assets and borrowings of $125 billion (a leverage ratio of 25:1—not that far off the typical leverage of investment banks). By September 21, 1998, its assets had dropped below $1 billion and its leverage exceeded 100:1. Two days later, LTCM was bailed out by a consortium of sixteen investment firms (coordinated by the Federal Reserve Bank of New York), which provided $3.6 billion of capital. The largest loss incurred by a HF to date is Amaranth Advisors in September 2006. Amaranth lost $6 billion, or close to 65%, thanks to a lot of leverage and a wrongheaded bet on natural gas futures.[14] Investors seeking to pull out their money as soon as the losses were announced in a letter on September 29, 2006, were in for a shock—the HF imposed gates so no one could withdraw funds (see below).

---

[13] See Perold, A., 1999, Long-Term Capital Management, LP (C), Harvard Business School Case 9-200-009.

[14] See Mufson, S., "Amanrath's Losses Top 6 Billion," *Washington Post*, Sept. 22, 2006.

2.2. WHAT ARE HEDGE FUNDS?

HFs have the following features:

Limited Number of (Rich) Investors

HFs must comply with Section 3(c)(1) or 3(c)(7) of the 40-Act to be exempt from regulation by the rest of the Act. That is, HFs are *not* registered investment companies. Their investors have to be rich.[15]

The 40-Act defines rich people in two ways. First, under Section 3(c)(1), HFs are limited to 100 *accredited investors*. Accredited investors have individual or joint net worth of more than $1 million. If you don't have $1 million, then you can be counted as an accredited investor if your individual income exceeds $200,000 or your joint income exceeds $300,000 in each of the past two years. Financial institutions like banks, insurance companies, mutual funds, pension funds, trusts, and so on are accredited investors if their assets exceed $5 million.

Second, under Section 3(c)(7), HFs are limited to *qualified purchasers*. The 40-Act doesn't limit the number of qualified purchasers, but in practice HFs have no more than 499 qualified purchasers to avoid registration under the Securities Exchange Act of 1934. The bar to be a qualified purchaser is higher than an accredited investor. Qualified purchasers must have at least $5 million in investments. Qualified institutional investors own and invest at least $100 million, or they are pension funds and trusts with at least $25 million in assets.

In the United States, HFs are usually structured as limited partnerships. The *general partner* is responsible for day-to-day management of the fund. The *limited partner* is the asset owner, liable only for the sum she invests.

Minimums Are High

Because they have only a limited number of investors, HFs require high minimum investments, typically $1 million or more. *Funds-of-funds*, which are funds that invest in HFs, generally have lower minimums. A few HF firms have introduced investment company registrations, like mutual funds, where minimums may be as low as $10,000 or less, but these vehicles fall under the 40-Act.

Often Levered and Use Derivatives

This is a key feature of many HFs. Jones's first HF took short positions—unusual for funds at the time. He used the term "hedged" to describe how the fund eliminated broad market exposure. Today, HFs employ a wide range of investment strategies and, as we shall see, generate risk factor exposures not usually available in other investment vehicles.

---

[15] Prior to the Jumpstart Our Business Startups Act of 2011, HFs were banned from soliciting or advertising; they were restricted to *private offerings*. This changed under the act. At the time of writing in 2013, the SEC is still to issue final rules. Even though HFs can advertise, HF investors must be accredited investors or qualified purchases.

Limited Access to Capital

Jones imposed restrictions on capital in his first HF. As some of his investment strategies involved short positions requiring the posting of collateral, he imposed restrictions so that investors would not be withdrawing capital when he needed it to post margin. Many, but not all, modern HFs follow Jones and do not allow investors to redeem their money immediately (unlike 40-Act funds, from which investors can get their money back at least daily).

Limited Disclosure

Whereas 40-Act funds have to report what they hold (at least quarterly for mutual funds and at least daily in the case of exchange-traded funds), HFs are secretive. Most HFs provide only coarse breakdowns of their investments and fuzzy details of their investment strategies.[16] Since March 30, 2012, however, HFs with assets exceeding $150 million have been required to register and report information on assets, certain trades, their brokers, leverage, counterparty exposures, and how they value illiquid assets.[17] But they must make these disclosures only to the Securities and Exchange Commission (SEC), not to the limited partner asset owners.

Manager Fees (Are High and) Involve Significant Performance Components

Whereas mutual fund regulations do not permit nonlinear manager compensation (see chapter 15), HFs are free to do what they want. A large component of how they are paid is through nonlinear *incentive payments*.

2.3. HEDGE FUND FLOWS

At the end of 2012, investors allocated over $2.25 trillion to HFs as measured by HFR, a HF database. This is a conservative lower bound. Since HFs are not subject to the strict reporting requirements of 40-Act funds, the full size of the industry is unknown. (Remember, only large HFs must report to the SEC, and at the time of writing in 2013 the SEC had not yet released any tabulation of the information it receives.) Bear in mind that HFR is a single data vendor, and different funds report to different data vendors—if they report at all.[18]

---

[16] If a HF belongs to a HF family run by a large asset management firm with more than $100 million in assets, then the overall firm has to report security holdings every quarter (these are called 13(f) filings) but not holdings for a single HF. Short positions are not covered under 13(f) reports.

[17] This is under the Private Fund Investment Advisers Registration Act of 2010 in Title IV of the Dodd-Frank Act.

[18] The overlap of HFs reporting to even more than one of the standard databases is small. Fung and Hsieh (2006) report that fewer than 3% of HFs report to all of the five main databases used by researchers. See also Agarwal, Fos, and Jiang (2013).

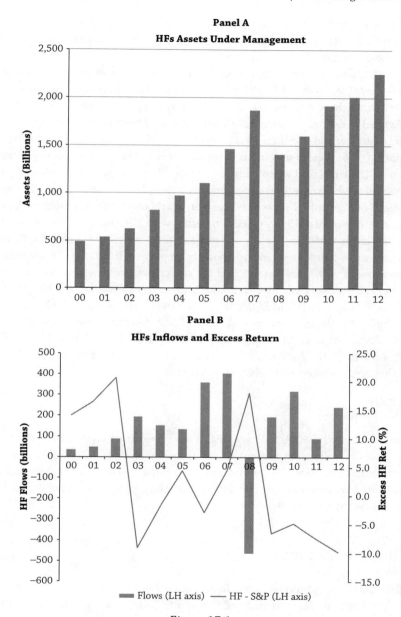

Panel A

HFs Assets Under Management

Panel B

HFs Inflows and Excess Return

■ Flows (LH axis) —— HF - S&P (LH axis)

Figure 17.1

Figure 17.1, Panel A plots assets under management in HFs since 2000 as reported by HFR.[19] From 1990 to 2012, the growth in HF assets was roughly 14% per year. It would have been even greater except for a hiatus during the financial

---

[19] HFR starts earlier, but reported data tends to be sketchy for very early years. This is true for all HF databases.

crisis year of 2008. The average HF lost 19% that year. Investors responded by yanking their money. Investors have since returned to HFs, and since 2009 HF assets have resumed their inexorable path upward.

Investors allocate money to HFs pro-cyclically, just like ordinary investors with mutual funds (see chapter 16). When HFs have done well in the past, money pours in as investors chase returns. But as assets grow, competition among HFs increase as HFs need to deploy more capital. Consequently, performance after high inflows tends to be low, and the increased competition raises the probability of the HF liquidating.[20] As Asness says in his definition of HFs, "They are supposed to make money all the time, and when they fail at this, their investors redeem and go to someone else who has recently been making money."

Panel B of Figure 17.1 plots the change in assets under management each year, or the net inflow into HFs in dollars, together with the excess HF return in that year. The latter is defined as the HF index return minus the S&P 500. Panel B shows that the two series tend to move in opposite directions: the correlation between the growth of HF assets and HF returns in excess of equities is −47%. Thus, just as investors pile into HFs, they tend to have lower excess returns.

While HFs lost 19.0% in 2008, they did better than the S&P 500, which declined by 37.0%. Yet investors pulled out of HFs at this time. They started to come back in 2009, but since then HFs have underperformed the S&P 500 by 6.5% in 2009, 4.8% in 2010, 7.4% in 2011, and 9.8% in 2012. After investors pile into HFs, they tend to offer relatively poor returns.[21]

2.4. SUMMARY

Exemption from the 40-Act allows HFs to use investment strategies that mutual funds find difficult to implement under the act's chafing limitations. The disadvantage is that since HFs are not 40-Act funds, their investors have limited protection. The advantage of HFs is that investors potentially have access to a world of new investment strategies. Do they?

3. Risk and Return

"Hedge funds are not a new asset class," states John Cochrane, a well-known finance professor at the University of Chicago.[22] "They trade in exactly the same

---

[20] See Kosowski, Naik, and Teo (2007), Fung et al. (2008), Agarwal, Daniel, and Naik (2004, 2009), Ding et al. (2009), and Getmansky (2012).

[21] Warren Buffet made a $1 million bet with a HF, Protégé Partners headed by Ted Seides and Jeffrey Tarrant, that the S&P 500 would beat HFs over a ten-year period beginning on January 1, 2008. So far, Buffet is winning. See Burton, K., 2012, "Buffet Seizes Lead in Bet on Stocks Beating Hedge Funds," Bloomberg, March 21, 2012.

[22] Quoted by Lim, T., "Institutional Investors Beware," *Private Wealth*, Jan. 4, 2013.

securities you already own." But the way they trade—dynamically churning securities, employing leverage and short positions, and trading derivatives—allows HFs to emphasize some risk factors that play minor roles in long-only, passive positions of "securities you already own." Before we measure their risk exposures (or betas), a note of caution is in order about what constitutes HF returns.

3.1. DATA BIASES

Dead men tell no tales. *Survivorship bias* arises because HFs voluntarily report to public databases. HFs don't like to report if their returns are bad—so they stop reporting when they are in distress. Therefore, we tend not to see bankrupt or liquidated funds in the databases because they remove themselves before they die. This causes an upward bias in reported HF returns. Another type of survivorship bias is caused by successful funds retroactively reporting past returns to the databases (a process called *backfilling*)—again you tend to provide this information only if the fund is doing well and past returns are good.

However, HFs report to databases to advertise themselves. (HFs can't solicit money through public offerings). If you don't need to attract investors, why report? It's better to remain secretive. As the best HFs often are not found in the databases, there is also a downward bias in reported returns.

Thus, HF databases miss the extreme left- and right-hand tails. Which effect dominates? Researchers have concluded that there are many more bad HFs that stop reporting than good HFs that never report. (Technically, the databases truncate the left-hand tail.) HF databases, therefore, reflect returns that are too good.

How large is the survivorship bias? At least 2%, and most researchers peg the bias at 3% to 4% or more.[23] Malkiel and Saha (2005) estimate the return of HFs that backfill is 14.7% compared to 7.3% for funds that do not backfill. This is a very large backfill bias of 7.3%. They estimate the survivorship bias to be 4.4%, which is the difference in the average return of live HFs compared to the returns of HFs that stop reporting or die. Fung, Xu, and Yau (2004) argue that the survivorship bias is large enough to completely wipe out any outperformance of HFs in reported data compared to boring stocks and bonds, if outperformance even exists in the first place.

Aiken, Clifford, and Ellis (2013) cleverly estimate the survivorship bias by finding a sample of HFs that do not report to the main hedge fund databases. They can see what happens to HFs that originally report and then stop. They conclude that "commercial databases are missing the worst performers in the hedge fund universe." The difference in risk-adjusted returns between reporting HFs and nonreporting HFs is 3.5% using size, value-growth, and momentum factors (see

---

[23] In addition to the references in the text, see also Fung and Hsieh (1997), Brown, Goetzmann, and Ibbotson (1999), Liang (2000), and Agarwal, Fos, and Jiang (2013).

chapters 7 and 10). The difference increases to 5.3% employing nonlinear, dynamic factors, which we consider below. These are large biases—*HFs report returns that are too good to be true.*

Asset owners should also be wary of HF indexes. The average investor cannot obtain the returns reported in these indexes because HF indexes generally are *not investable.* There is no equivalent to a S&P 500 index fund that can cheaply replicate the aggregate stock market. Nor can asset owners invest in every HF in most HF indexes—some are closed, some have minimums that are too high, and in any case there are just too many of them. And when you try to get your money out, you can't (see below), making it impossible to bail when a fund has dropped out of the index. Since investors cannot hold all the funds in a HF index, they face more idiosyncratic risk investing in HFs than is measured by the HF index, which diversifies away much more risk than an investor can.[24] I use HF index returns in this chapter, but you've been warned: they generally give too rosy a picture of returns.

Since HFs voluntarily report returns, there are other biases. Agarwal, Daniel, and Naik (2011) find that Santa Claus is kind to HFs: returns are higher in December than between January and November by 1.3%, on average. HFs do this by underreporting their returns earlier in the year and by borrowing from January returns. Why do HFs inflate their December returns? Because HFs levy fees on their December numbers. Bollen and Pool (2009) show that there are more returns just above zero than below zero at the monthly frequency. (The zero level is especially important because HFs market themselves as absolute return strategies.) This kink disappears measuring returns in two-month intervals, indicating that some monthly returns are inflated to avoid reporting losses. These overstatements are subsequently reversed when HFs have stored up a bank of good returns.

Revisions of past data by HFs are pervasive. Patton, Ramadorai, and Streatfield (2013) claim that half of the 12,128 HFs in their sample over 2007–2011 revised their previously reported returns. One-fifth of HFs modified their returns by at least 1.0%—enormous revisions compared to the average monthly HF return of 0.6%. The best way (large) asset owners can avoid data revisions is to use *separately managed accounts,* where the asset owner directly holds the assets and the HF manager trades the securities in the account.[25] This doesn't help asset owners in analyzing past, reported data to ascertain whether they should invest in a HF in the first place. For that decision, the asset owner must realize that reported HF returns are too good to be true.

---

[24] Some firms have designed *investable* HF indexes, but there is a large selection bias in the types of HFs willing to be included in such indexes. As Groucho Marx says, "I refuse to join any club that would have me as a member."

[25] Aggarwal and Jorion (2012) find no evidence that more transparency is associated with lower returns. In fact, their results suggest the opposite: the more transparent the HF, the higher the returns.

3.2. HEDGE FUND FAILURES

HFs are the fly-by-night funds of the investment world.

Each year, 10% to 15% of HFs vanish from the databases, so most HFs don't last very long.[26] Together with Nicolas Bollen, a professor of finance at Vanderbilt University, I estimate a model of HF survivorship. Figure 17.2 reports fitted durations of HFs from Ang and Bollen (2010a, 2010b) in Panel A and the probabilities of HF failure in Panel B. Figure 17.2 shows that a great many HFs fail around years 2 through 5, but some HFs last twenty years or more—so the survivorship distribution is very skewed. This is consistent with Brown, Goetzmann, and Park

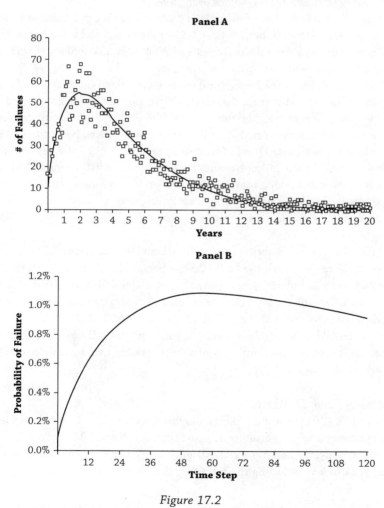

Figure 17.2

[26] See Liang (2001) and Kouwenberg (2003). HFs can delist as a result of poor performance, usually resulting in termination, or spectacular performance when they close to new investments. Jorion and Schwarz (2013) report that the latter represents only 1% of cases.

(2001), who report that 50% of HFs managers disappear within thirty months and fewer than 5% last more than ten years. Gregoriou (2002) also finds the median survival time of HFs to be around five years. Panel B of Figure 17.2 shows that the probability of a HF failing rises steeply from the fund's inception and peaks at around three years. HFR reports that 60% of the HFs that underperformed the stock market during the financial crisis in 2008 shut down.[27]

3.3. PERFORMANCE

Hedge Fund Performance Has Declined over Time
Many studies have looked at whether HFs outperform on a risk-adjusted basis.[28] The conclusions are mixed, but I believe HFs probably did add value in the 1980s, 1990s, and even possibly in the early years of 2000. But it is unlikely that HFs add value today, on average, after adjusting for risk.

In Figure 17.3, I take the hedge fund index constructed by HFR. Panel A plots the alpha of the HF index from January 1995 to December 2012, which is computed by rolling five-year regressions on the S&P 500 at the monthly frequency. (See chapter 10 for details on alpha.) During the mid-1990s, HFs returned more than 10% on a risk-adjusted basis. This dipped to 5% in 1998—the year Russia defaulted and LTCM failed. HF alphas shot back up to around 10% from 2000–2004. Since then, the value-added by HFs has been on a downward trajectory. In the post-2008 sample, HF alphas have been returning only 1% to 2% after adjusting for market risk. In the last two years of the sample, 2011 and 2012, HF alphas were negative.

Panel B of Figure 17.3 shows that while HF alphas have been falling, the correlation of HF returns with the S&P 500 has been rising. During the late 1990s, the correlation was only 50%, meaning that HFs could add large diversification benefits to an investor's portfolio (see chapter 3). Since then, the correlation has gradually increased and in 2012 and 2013 was above 85%. With such high correlations to the S&P 500, combined with negative alphas, HFs are certainly not a separate asset class; today they are probably subtracting value from investors on a risk-adjusted basis.

Larger Hedge Funds Do Worse
Dichev and Yu (2011) compute dollar-weighted returns for the whole HF industry and uncover a sorry picture of HF performance. From 1980 to 2007, the HF industry underperformed the S&P 500, with returns of 9.7% compared to 13.1% for the stock index. Including the following year, 2008, takes things from bad to

---

[27] Reported in Chung, J., "A Volatile Investor Buys Into a Softer Approach," *Wall Street Journal*, March 20, 2013.

[28] In addition to the references in the text, the "no, HFs don't add value" camp also includes Ackerman, McEnally, and Ravenscraft (1999) and Hasanhodzic and Lo (2007).

Panel A

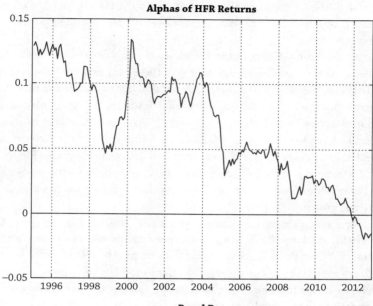

Panel B

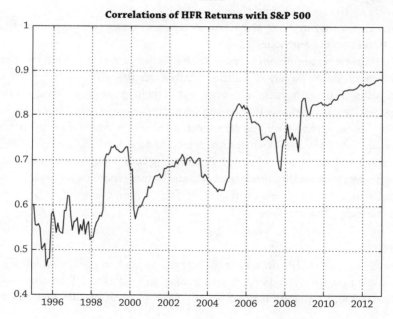

Figure 17.3

atrocious. HF returns from 1980 to 2008 were 6.0% compared to 10.9% returns for the S&P 500 over the same time period. The 6.0% HF return barely beats the T-bill return of 5.6%. Not surprisingly, Dichev and Yu title their paper "Higher Risk, Lower Returns."

Some studies find positive outperformance for HFs of around 3% to 5% compared to standard market indexes.[29] (Some of these numbers are even statistically significant, especially for the top HFs.) A notable feature of HFs is that they exhibit *decreasing returns to scale* (just like mutual funds and private equity, which are covered in chapters 16 and 18, respectively).[30] This fact means that as HFs grow, they tend to have lower returns. Many of the outperforming funds are concentrated in the early years of the HF industry when they were small (see Figure 17.3). Zhong (2008) shows that the drop in HF alphas, especially in the post-2000 period, is the result of fewer funds capable of producing large, positive alphas as the industry has grown.

When the average return is computed for the whole HF industry, as Dichev and Yu (2011) do, large funds are given larger weights commensurate with their larger assets. When these large funds underperform, the losses to the overall HF industry are much larger. The aggregate losses of the HF industry led Simon Lack (2012), an ex-hedge fund manager, to begin his book with the taunting sentence: "If all the money that's ever been invested in hedge funds had been put in treasury bills instead, the results would have been twice as good."

Lack shows that in 2008, the HF industry lost investors more money than it made them over the previous decade.

Many investors are drawn to HFs by the record of returns (sketchy as it is), which was produced largely when the industry was nascent and many HFs were small. Risks in the early years were high, but early investors prospered—they obtained high rewards ex post for bearing very large ex-ante risk. The HF industry has since matured, and true outperformers are harder to find. Often the best HFs are small. But many asset owners are reluctant to select small, unproven HFs. They gravitate instead toward large HFs with long track records, vast assets under management, high-quality infrastructure, and better reporting and risk management. Of course the returns on these large funds aren't as high, on average, as small ones: they're less risky.

Persistence

Knowing that some HFs do well is useless unless we can predict which HFs do well. Academics are divided on whether persistence exists in HF returns. Malkiel and Saha (2005) report that the fraction of the top half of HFs that end up in

---

[29] See, among others, Brown, Goetzmann and Ibbotson (1999), Ibbotson and Chen (2006), Kosowski, Naik, and Teo (2007), and Jagannathan, Malakhov, and Novikov (2010).

[30] See Agarwal, Daniel, and Naik (2009), Boyson (2008), Zhong (2008), Fung et al. (2008), Dichev and Yu (2011), Getmansky (2012), Mozes and Orchard (2012), and Ramadorai (2013).

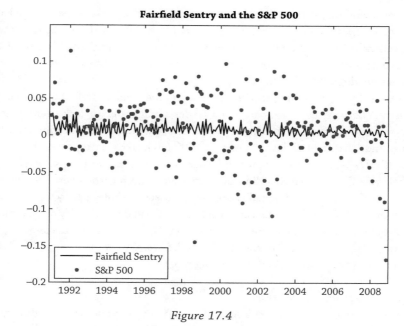

Figure 17.4

the top half a year later is 52%—essentially the same as flipping a coin. Agarwal and Naik (2000) document stronger evidence of persistence, but unfortunately it comes from losers persisting in being losers, rather than winners repeating. On the other hand, Jagannathan, Malakhov, and Novikov (2010) argue that there is significant persistence. Boyson (2008) shows that if persistence of winning HFs does exist, it is concentrated among small and young funds.

Excessive persistence is a sign that something is wrong. In fact, Getmansky, Lo, and Makarov (2004) and Bollen and Pool (2008) develop tests of HF fraud based on fund returns that are "too smooth." Figure 17.4 graphs monthly returns of one HF in the solid line and overlays S&P 500 returns. The HF in Figure 4 looks terrific, with very smooth and highly mean-reverting returns to a steady mean, especially compared to the volatility of the S&P 500. What's the fund? Fairfield Sentry, which was a feeder fund to Bernard L. Madoff Investment Securities—the largest Ponzi scheme in history.[31]

3.4. HEDGE FUND FACTORS

HFs take two main approaches to making money: (i) HFs that attempt *market timing* seek to capture market trends—directional trades—and take net long or short

---

[31] Fairfield Sentry data are from Bernard and Boyle (2009).

positions, while (ii) *nondirectional* or *market-neutral* HFs try to extract value from "arbitrage" opportunities. Although the term is widely used in industry, these funds usually do not find pure arbitrages, which are rare. Rather, this type of HF seeks to neutralize market movements and attempts to profit from securities that are misvalued relative to each other.

Within these two approaches, there are two main styles of investing: (i) *discretionary* styles rely mostly on a trader's judgment (or lack thereof), and (ii) *systematic* styles are more rules-based and rely on quantitative models. The quant funds that melted down in August 2007 fall into the latter category.

Lo (2007) suggests the quant fund losses reflect an underlying source of systematic risk. That most HFs did not deliver absolute returns over the financial crisis of 2008–2009 and instead posted large losses—whether they were market timers or nondirectional traders and whether they had discretionary or systematic styles—also suggests that all HFs, not just quant HFs, are exposed to common risk factors. In fact, *HFs are bundles of standard risk factors.*

The two most important factors are plain old. . . .

Equity Market and Volatility Risk

Table 17.5 reports partial correlations of the HF index and various HF strategies (from HFR) to the S&P 500 and a volatility factor. The latter is compiled by Merrill Lynch and is a return series from a short volatility strategy (see chapters 2 and 7). Short volatility strategies sell volatility insurance and make money during stable times but lose money when volatility spikes. I take monthly data from January 2000 to September 2012 and construct excess returns for the HF returns and the S&P 500 using U.S. T-bills as the risk-free rate. The partial correlation of the HF excess returns with the equity factor controls for the effect of the volatility factor and vice versa.

Table 17.5 shows very high correlations of all HF strategies with the market factor. The partial correlation of the HF index with respect to equity risk is a very high 0.67. HFs with emerging markets and event-driven strategies also have partial correlations above 0.6. Event-driven HFs take advantage of corporate transactions like mergers, restructurings, buybacks, security issuance, and so on. The distress, or restructuring, strategy invests in corporate bonds of companies that are in or close to bankruptcy. The partial correlation of distress with equities is 0.41. Only for the long-short equity funds, of which a large number are quant funds, is the partial correlation with equity market risk low at 0.11 and statistically insignificant. (It does seem that, on average, market-neutral HFs are market neutral.[32])

The partial correlations of HF returns with the volatility risk factor are somewhat smaller than the market, but Table 17.5 reports that they are still quite large.

---

[32] Patton (2009) argues, however, that at the individual HF level, more than a quarter of long-short HFs exhibit statistically significant and economically large exposure to the market.

Table 17.5

	Hedge Fund Partial Correlations	
	Equity	*Volatility*
HF Index	0.664	0.262
p-value	0.00	0.00
Distress	0.411	0.440
p-value	0.00	0.00
Merger Arbitrage	0.453	0.195
p-value	0.00	0.02
Equity Long/Short	0.106	0.175
p-value	0.19	0.03
Emerging Markets	0.616	0.297
p-value	0.00	0.00
Event Driven	0.624	0.384
p-value	0.00	0.00
Macro	0.399	−0.340
p-value	0.00	0.00
Relative Value	0.330	0.646
p-value	0.00	0.00
Convertible Arbitrage	0.180	0.657
p-value	0.03	0.00

The HF index has a partial correlation of 0.26 with volatility risk. Distress, event-driven, relative value, and convertible arbitrage have partial correlations with volatility of approximately 0.4 or higher. Relative value HFs take offsetting positions, often in fixed income, of securities they perceive to be mispriced relative to each other. Convertible arbitrage HFs invest in convertible fixed income securities and hedge out the equity exposure, generally by shorting common stock but also by using options. All the HF strategies have highly statistically significant exposure to volatility risk. All the volatility risk exposures are also positive with the exception of macro HFs, which trade securities in many asset classes at a global level. (This style classification includes many trend followers, which tend to be long volatility.)

Figure 17.6 graphs year-on-year HF returns with the S&P 500 and volatility risk factors for several HF strategies. Since we are interested in correlations, I have normalized all returns to have the same standard deviation, which is the

Panel A

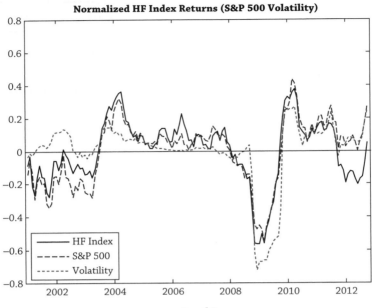

Panel B

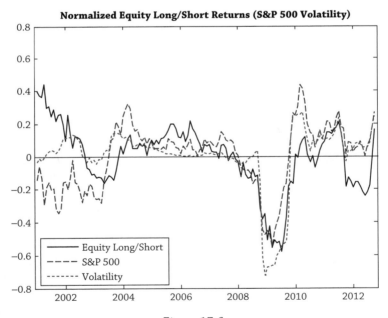

Figure 17.6

Panel C

Normalized Merger Arbitrage Returns (S&P 500 Volatility)

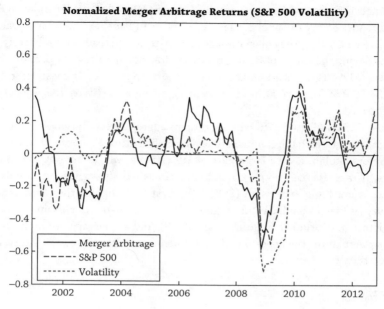

Panel D

Normalized Relative Value Returns (S&P 500 Volatility)

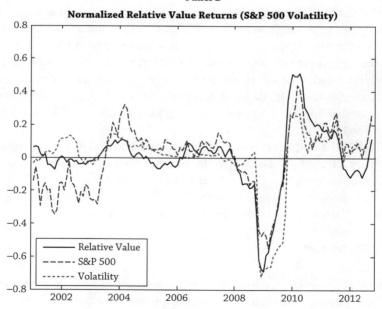

Figure 17.6 (continued)

standard deviation of the S&P 500 excess return. I have also de-meaned all series. The panels in Figure 17.6 represent very different HF styles: the HF index in Panel A, long/short equity in Panel B, merger arbitrage in Panel C, and relative value in Panel D. Remarkably, they all show a general pattern of steady and relatively high returns during the early 2000s, a substantial drawdown during 2008, and a recovery after 2009. There is an amazingly close correspondence of these HF returns with the S&P 500 and volatility factors in all the panels. *HFs repackage equity and volatility risk.*

Table 17.5 and Figure 17.6 take HF returns aggregated to the whole industry or the sector level. At the individual HF level, the literature also finds that volatility risk factors explain a very large part of HF returns. Often any outperformance of HFs, if it exists, can be partly and sometimes wholly attributed to volatility risk exposure. Fung and Hsieh (2001), the first to recognize the importance of volatility risk factors in HF returns, find no outperformance of HFs once volatility risk factors are included.[33] Fung et al. (2008) find an average HF alpha of just 6 basis points (effectively zero) with a risk benchmark that includes equity, bond and volatility risk factors.

Other Factors

There are other important factors that drive HF returns besides the equity market and volatility factors, but they tend to be sector-specific. Commodities and currency risk, for example, are reflected in macro HF returns. (Commodities and currencies themselves also reflect volatility risk.) Term spreads (the difference between long and short maturity Treasury bonds) and credit spreads (the difference between risky and safe corporate debt) are also significant risk factors for relative value strategies. Quant funds are highly exposed to value-growth and momentum risk (covered in chapter 7), and not surprisingly these factors didn't do well during August 7 to 9, 2007.

Sadka (2010) finds that many HFs are exposed to illiquidity risk. HFs with the highest illiquidity risk exposures outperform their more liquid counterparts by 6%. Interestingly, this illiquidity risk premium is not related to how easily investors can withdraw money from the HFs themselves (i.e., the illiquidity characteristics of the HFs; see below). But the most important risk factors are regular market risk and volatility risk.

In 2004, Asness foretold:

> In today's world, these strategies are not only linked by a common risk-taking/liquidity-providing element, but are also more and more pursued by the exact same investors. It is easy to imagine considerably greater potential co-movement in a crisis because of this commonality.

[33] See also Agarwal and Naik (2004), Fung and Hsieh (2004), and Lo and Hasanhodizic (2007).

This is exactly what happened in 2007 in the quant meltdown, and a year later for almost all HFs during the financial crisis.

3.5. A DEEPER LOOK AT VOLATILITY RISK

Given the myriad of HF investment styles, it might be surprising that many are economically identical in terms of selling volatility. The commonality is that many HFs choose strategies that most of the time deliver steady returns. But the cost of these steady returns during normal times is that when the bad times come, there are pronounced losses. Selling volatility is like selling hurricane insurance. You collect the premium most of the time. Then the hurricane hits and you are wiped out. The last financial hurricane occurred during 2008–2009.

A picture of a short volatility payoff is shown in Figure 17.7.

Figure 17.7 is the payoff of a short, out-of-the-money put.[34] Most of the time, the HF collects small and steady premiums equal to the price of the put. These profits look like "alpha" and HFs refer to this by various guises: "skill," "arbitrage," "mispricing," "market dislocation," "providing liquidity," "alternative beta," or just plain "short volatility." This premium does not come for free: there are occasional large losses when the assets fall sharply in price. In practice, the losses are higher than just simple put-selling because HFs use leverage. These losses do not show up

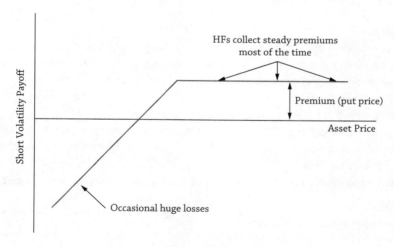

Figure 17.7

---

[34] This is actually the payoff of a rebalancing strategy as well. Any counter-cyclical investment strategy is short volatility, as chapter 4 shows. HFs just take this to the extreme. Lo (2001) creates an example of a HF that uses precisely this strategy to generate "alpha" and cheekily names the HF in his example "Capital Decimation Partners."

in standard alpha calculations (see chapter 10), so often it appears that HFs make money relative to long-only positions in plain-vanilla fixed income and equities.

Many HF strategies have short put payoffs.[35] Let's take the HF styles in Figure 17.6:

Long-Short Equity

A common quant HF strategy is short-term reversal, which takes advantage of the fact that if a stock has gone up in price today, it is likely to mean-revert back down tomorrow.[36] (This effect is observed in horizons less than a minute to one month.) The predictability of this pattern is weak (like all predictability in stock returns, see chapter 8), but quants use this strategy on thousands of stocks.[37] Lo (2007) reports that returns to this strategy have been declining over time. To maintain the overall average of their returns, quant funds juiced up this strategy with more leverage through the 2000s. This is partly what made the August 2007 losses so severe.

Nagel (2012) argues that short-term reversal strategies are a form of liquidity provision—prices decline because other market participants wish to sell, and quant HFs provide liquidity by picking up the slack. Liquidity provision is a short put—you make profits most of the time, but you take a drubbing when prices fall. The profitability of liquidity provision strategies, including short-term reversal, is highly dependent on volatility risk. As volatility jumps, liquidity evaporates merger, saddling long-short equity HFs with losses.

Merger Arb

Merger arbitrage (*merger arb* or *risk arb*) is a strategy that buys stock in companies being acquired (and shorts the acquirer). When a merger is announced, prices of the company being acquired jump, but they don't jump all the way up to the offer price. They jump on the announcement and then continue to drift upward, reaching the offer price when the merger is completed.

Mitchell and Pulvino (2001) show that merger arb is equivalent to a naked short put. In most cases, merger arb makes money because the stock of the acquired company rises to the offer price predictably. The reason prices don't jump upward immediately on announcement of the merger is that sometimes mergers

---

[35] Some HFs are put buyers, generating small losses most of the time but making a killing when markets tank. These funds lose money in the long run because you need to short volatility to earn the volatility risk premium. Nassim Taleb, the well-known pessimistic forecaster, is associated with one such fund, Universa Investments.

[36] This is different from momentum, which refers to the tendency of groups of many stocks with past high returns to exhibit high future returns compared to stocks with past low returns. See chapter 7.

[37] In terms of Grinold's (1989) "fundamental law" of active management (see chapter 10), quants take lots of small bets with positive but small chances of making money, rather than making few bets that have a relatively high chance of succeeding.

are derailed—the Justice Department blocks the merger on antitrust grounds, due diligence uncovers skeletons in the acquired company's closet, or the deal is scuttled at the last minute by an argument over who gets to be the new boss, and so on. When mergers fail, prices plummet. Thus, merger arb ekes out small returns most of the time, and then with a small probability it loses big—exactly the pattern we see in Figure 17.7. Mitchell and Pulvino also demonstrate that the rare, large losses arising when mergers fail are correlated with the market (so merger arb has *systematic risk*): in a market-wide crash, many mergers fail and merger activity dries up.

Relative Value

A comprehensive study of fixed income relative value strategies was done by Duarte, Longstaff, and Yu (2005). They examine several "arbitrages," including swap spread arbitrage, yield curve arbitrage, mortgage arbitrage, volatility arbitrage (the differential pricing of risk in different securities markets), and capital structure arbitrage (trading different securities issued by the same firm). All these strategies generate high returns most of the time and then the occasional large loss. Convertible arbitrage also falls under the relative value category as it profits from differential pricing of risk across two securities markets: convertible bonds and equities. This strategy is also vulnerable to extreme market events.[38]

Losses in relative value strategies can be nasty because fixed income HFs usually employ high leverage. Sometimes HFs are blind to the possibility of large losses—as was the case at LTCM when credit spreads widened on news of Russia's default in 1998. Most of the time housing prices are fairly stable and increase over time. But sometimes they don't, like in 2007, when mortgage spreads (over U.S. Treasuries) shot up, causing painful losses for mortgage arb strategies.

Fung and Hsieh (2002) were prescient in their study of fixed income hedge fund returns using data up to 2001. They back-tested the effects of Great Depression-scale shocks to credit spreads and forecast large potential declines saying that "there exists cyclical exposure to risk factors inherent in most Fixed-Income Arbitrage funds that may be masked by the short existence of the funds themselves." That is, a positive and significant historical alpha resulted from the risk of rare events. They were spot on as that rare event arrived toward the end of the 2000s. As Asness said in his definition of HFs, "Every three or four years they deliver a one-in-a-hundred year flood."

HF Industry

Not surprisingly, if most individual HF styles are short volatility, then the entire HF industry is just a short put as well. Jurek and Stafford (2012) show that a simple strategy of selling out-of-the-money puts accurately matches the risk profile of

---

[38] See Choi, Getmansky, and Tookes (2009) and Agarwal et al. (2011).

the HF index and actually does better. Over their sample period of 1996 to 2010, HFs returned 6.3% in excess of T-bills while the derivative strategy had excess returns of 10.2%.

Since HFs are short volatility, it is ironic that many asset owners, especially pension funds, purchase volatility protection while they own HFs that have the exact opposite exposure. They pay twice (handsomely, usually) to get back to the market portfolio.

3.6. LEVERAGE

One of the defining characteristics of HFs is that they use leverage, and, within the asset management industry, HFs make the most use of leverage. HFs use leverage to target a level of return volatility desired by investors, particularly for fixed income HFs where the underlying securities are (usually) not very volatile. HFs adjust their leverage in respond to time-varying investment opportunities. And finally, HFs lever to enhance returns (or, unfortunately, losses) on strategies that aren't sufficiently profitable on an unlevered basis.

Ang, Gorovyy, and van Inwegen (2011) examine HF leverage. When we wrote that paper, HFs did not publicly report their leverage, and ours was the first study to analyze HF leverage using actual leverage ratios. Now that the SEC gets reports on HF leverage, regulators will have a better picture of HF borrowing (even if investors might not).

We found that HF leverage is not that high—on average. There are some HFs (in fixed income) with leverage ratios above 30, but the overall HF industry has a leverage ratio around 2 or 3, as shown in Figure 17.8 (the solid line with the right-hand axis). This is because half the HF industry concentrates on equities, and leverage of equity HFs is, on average, modest. A more amazing fact is that HF leverage is counter-cyclical to the leverage of investment banks. I found this surprising because, prior to writing the paper, I thought HFs would be mini versions of investment banks in terms of leverage policies.

Figure 17.8 overlays the leverage of commercial banks, investment banks (the largest of which turned into commercial banks during the financial crisis), and the finance sector (plotted on the left-hand axis). Prior to 2007, HF leverage was around 2.3. HF leverage started to come down in 2007, a year before the financial crisis, and bottomed out below 1.5 in the last quarter of 2008 and the first quarter of 2009—the worst months of the crisis. Investment bank leverage has exactly the opposite pattern: as equity prices start to fall in 2008, leverage increases and peaks at over 40 right when HF leverage was lowest.

3.7. SUMMARY

HFs are a hodgepodge of factor risks—especially equity and volatility risk. Most HFs are short volatility and generate returns that are dependable most of the time

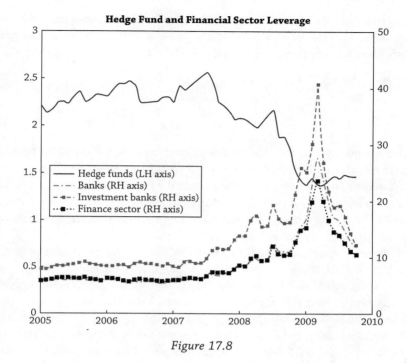

Figure 17.8

but subject to occasional terrible losses. Thus, using mean-variance optimizers to calculate allocations to HFs is dangerous—unless you are a special investor who cares only about means and variances (I've yet to meet any). If you care about occasional catastrophic losses, then you need asset allocation tools to handle strategies that "pick up nickels and dimes in front of a steamroller," as chapter 2 describes.

4. Agency Issues

Since HFs do not fall under the 40-Act, they can employ nonlinear performance contracts that can mitigate agency problems and better align the interests of agents (the HF managers) with the principals (the asset owners).

4.1. CONTRACTS

HFs charge a *management fee*, also called an *expense ratio*. A typical fee is 2%, which is levied on the (unlevered) assets in the fund, which is the *net asset value* (NAV).

HFs also charge a *performance fee*, or an *incentive fee*. The performance fee, typically 20%, is calculated net of a benchmark. Popular benchmarks are a cash benchmark, like LIBOR, the S&P 500, or some general market index, or a constant like zero.

Performance fees can get complicated. If the HF has a *high-water mark*, then performance fees are levied only when the NAV exceeds the highest NAV previously achieved. For example, suppose the NAVs of a HF are:

Time	1	2	3	4
NAV	100	120	110	145

There is no performance fee payable at time 3 because the NAV is below its high-water mark of 120. At time 4, the HF recoups its losses and has a NAV of 145. A performance fee is paid at time 4 and the fund's water-mark is now 145. If there is a *hurdle rate*, say 4%, the performance fee is paid only when returns are above 4%. With both a high-water mark and a hurdle rate, the incentive fee is paid only when both conditions are met.

While the typical combination of management and performance fees is "2 and 20" (2/20), there is some variation. The Medallion Fund of Renaissance Technologies, founded by James Simons, is one of the best performing HFs and may be the best HF in history. It charges 5/44. (No, you can't invest; it is *closed*.) The mean management and performance fees are 1.4/16.0 across all funds. Smaller firms generally have lower expense ratios and higher incentive fees (and remember, small HFs also tend to have better performance).[39]

Finally, HFs sometimes charge *withdrawal fees* when funds are redeemed.

Incentive Alignments

Do performance fees lead to better performance? Yes. Ackermann, McEnally, and Ravenscraft (1999) report that moving from a HF with no incentive fee to a HF with a 20% incentive fee increases the Sharpe ratio of a fund by 0.15, all else equal. Agarwal, Daniel, and Naik (2009) find that, consistent with agency theory, funds with better managerial incentives have better performance. In particular, the more the HF manager gets paid when the HF does well (the *performance sensitivity* of the incentive fee, in technical jargon), the better the performance of the HF. HFs with high-water marks and whose managers have larger equity stakes also tend to perform better.

On the other hand, asset owners should be wary of HFs increasing their fees due to past success. Agarwal and Ray (2012) show that HFs change their fees quite often, but fee increases are followed by *worse* performance. Agarwal and Ray find no change in (often subpar) performance when HFs lower their fees.

The lack of disclosure and the lack of control hurt investors. Lack (2012) tells colorful stories of how hedge fund returns are gamed (see Section 3.1) and how the lack of investor control encourages managers to prolong losing investments to maximize fees. Fraud thrives on opacity, and asset owners have to be careful.

---

[39] See Deuskar et al. (2011).

Many HFs suffer from operational problems, including falling afoul of legal and regulatory requirements. Brown et al. (2012) show that operational risk increases the likelihood of poor performance. Unfortunately, operational risk does not seem to influence the choices asset owners make in selecting HFs, as many investors simply chase the HFs with the best past returns.

4.2. FEES

HF fees are high.

Top-Earning Hedge Fund Managers

Table 17.9 lists the top-earning HF managers in 2011 compiled by *Alpha* magazine. The highest earning HF manager in 2011 was Ray Dalio, who heads Bridgewater Associates. He earned $3.9 billion. Dalio appeared on the top-earning HF manager list in 2010, where he earned $3.1 billion. Bridgewater also generated enormous wealth for the two men tied for number 7 on the list, Greg Jensen and Robert Prince. The number 3 manager, James Simons, earned $2.1 billion in 2011. Simons also appeared on the 2010 and 2009 lists, earning and $2.5 billion in both years.

You thought the top CEOs were well paid?[40] The right-hand side of Table 17.9 lists compensation of the top-earning CEOs in 2011 compiled by *Forbes*. There is an order of magnitude difference in the compensation of the top CEOs and the top HF managers; we need to multiply the compensation numbers of the top CEOs by at least 10 to make them comparable. Yes, the top-earning HF managers do extremely well, but before immediately rushing out to become a HF manager, remember that these managers are exceptional—the typical HF lifecycle is short, most HFs die after a few years, and you never hear of the worst-paid HF managers.

There are many ways to make the enormous amounts in Table 17.9. Bridgewater, the home of Dalio, Jensen, and Prince, is a macro fund with a quant bent. Renaissance Technologies is a quant firm, with very secretive and technical algorithms. Carl Icahn's fund fits in the event-driven style category and employs many *shareholder activist* techniques, aggressive enough that the market talks of an "Icahn Lift." Brevan Howard is a macro fund, but it runs mostly discretionary (as opposed to quant systematic) portfolios.

Oh, there are no women in Table 17.9.

Hedge Fund Compensation is a Call Option

The top-earning HF managers earn so much because of large management *and* performance fees. The performance fee is an option—the HF manager gets paid

---

[40] CEO compensation has risen significantly over the past few decades. Gabaix and Landier (2008) argue this is optimal and goes hand in hand with the large increases in market capitalization of the largest companies over this period.

Table 17.9

Top-Earning Hedge Fund Managers 2011			Top-Earning CEOs in 2011			
Source: Alpha Magazine			*Source: Forbes*			
1	Ray Dalio	3.9 billion	Bridgewater Associates	1	John Hammergren	132 million	McKesson
2	Carl Icahn	2.5 billion	Icahn Capital Management	2	Ralph Lauren	67 million	Ralph Lauren
3	James Simons	2.1 billion	Renaissance Technologies	3	Michael Fascitelli	64 million	Vornado Realty
4	Kenneth Griffin	700 million	Citadel	4	Richard Kinder	61 million	Kinder Morgan
5	Steven Cohen	585 million	SAC Capital Advisors	5	David Cote	56 million	Honeywell
6	Chase Coleman	550 million	Tiger Global Management	6	George Paz	51 million	Express Scripts
7	Greg Jensen	425 million	Bridgewater Associates	7	Jeffrey Boyd	50 million	Priceline.com
7	Robert Prince	425 million	Bridgewater Associates	8	Stephen Hemsley	48 million	UnitedHealth Group
9	Israel Englander	357 million	Millenium Management	9	Clarence Cazalot	44 million	Marathon Oil
10	Alan Howard	350 million	Brevan Howard	10	John Martin	43 million	Gilead Sciences

2% if nothing happens and then 2% plus 20% when the performance fee kicks in. This payoff is highly convex—essentially the mirror image of most HF strategies, which are concave. That is, HF compensation contracts are *long call options* and long volatility, while the strategies employed by HF managers are short put options and short volatility.

The performance fees, as a sequence of call options, encourage the HF manager to take risks.[41] If they pay off, you can hit the big leagues and sit beside Dalio and Simons. If your bet doesn't work out, you don't lose anything and still get the 2% management fee. Your investors, of course, lose. In the worst case, you perform so badly you have to close up shop. After you fail, you open up a new HF (this is a *restart option* and is a form of *implicit contract*, see chapter 15). The former partners of the failed LTCM did just that. A year after LTCM failed in 1998, Myron Scholes set up Platinum Grove Asset Management, which suffered like many other HFs during 2008 and gated its investors.[42] Scholes retired from Platinum Grove in 2011.[43] John Meriwether, another partner at LTCM, started JWM Partners with other ex-LTCM colleagues. It closed in 2009 after losses during the financial crisis.[44] Like the phoenix, new HFs also arose from the implosion of Goldman's quant funds after the quant meltdown and financial crisis. Mark Carhart, who co-headed Global Alpha, set up Kepos Capital, and Raymond Iwanowski, the other co-manager, opened Secor Asset Management.

The value of the option performance fee is roughly 3% to 4%, as first shown by Goetzmann, Ingersoll, and Ross (2003). In his PhD dissertation, my former student Sergiy Gorovyy (2012) estimated equivalent flat management fees (that gave the manager the same total compensation) for various performance structures. He found a straight 2/20 contract equivalent to a 6.4% management fee. Adding a high-water mark brought this down to 5.8%. A 2/20 contract with a high-water mark and a 4% hurdle rate was equivalent to a 5.3% management fee. The average active mutual fund fee is below 1%. These are high fees.

Asset owners shouldn't mind paying high fees but only when there is outperformance. Sadly, this is not the case in current HF contracts. Lan, Wang, and Yang (2012) build a model of HF leverage and valuation. They find that for the standard 2/20 contract, the HF manager needs to create a whopping 20% increase on

---

[41] See Goetzmann, Ingersoll, and Ross (2003), Hodder and Jackwerth (2007), and Lan, Wang, and Yang (2012). Panageas and Westerfield (2003) argue that the case when the HF has an infinite horizon, but the fund has a probability of being terminated exogenously each period, reduces these risk-taking incentives.

[42] Kishan, S., "Scholes's Platinum Grove Fund Halts Withdrawals After Losses," Bloomberg, Nov. 6, 2008.

[43] Comstock, C., 2011, "Founder Myron Scholes Retired From His Hedge Fund," Business Insider, Feb. 10, 2011.

[44] Burton, K., and S. Kishan, "Meriwether Said to Shut JWM Hedge Fund After Losses," Bloomberg, July 8, 2009.

assets under management to justify his compensation. Lan, Wang, and Yang also find that incentive fees constitute a minority—only one quarter—of the HF manager's compensation. This result doesn't change when adding other effects, like managerial ownership, new money flows, and restart options. HF management fees severely dominate incentive fees.

HF contracts are not bound by the 40-Act, so there is large scope to experiment with the best compensation structures. I would prefer to see management fees as a small fraction, 1% to 2%, of total HF manager compensation. That is, a better contract might be 0.25% in management fees and 50% or more in incentive fees. Asset owners might consider paying *fixed*, rather than *proportional*, fees to small funds to cover overheads and expenses. Any proportional cost should be very small, which reflects the fact that the opportunity cost for most investors is a low-cost index portfolio. Renaissance Medallion is right in charging high incentive fees—I believe they should be even higher than today's contracts, but the management fees should be an order of magnitude lower. The benchmark should also be changed. The most appropriate benchmark is a *factor benchmark*, especially incorporating volatility risk, since HFs are largely plays on volatility and other dynamic, or investment, factors (see below and also chapter 7).

4.3. COST OF ILLIQUIDITY

HFs restrict liquidity by a number of ways. They employ *lockups*, during which investors cannot withdraw money. Typical lockups are around three to six months but can be as long as two years or more. LTCM originally had a lock-up of three years, which explained why the fund's name included the words "long term."[45] ESL Investments, run by Edward "Eddie" Lampert, has a five-year lockup. PDT Partners, headed by Peter Mueller and spun out of Morgan Stanley in 2012, set up shop with a seven-year lockup. There are even funds with ten-year lockups. Many HFs also trade-off illiquidity and fees: they offer investors lower fees for a longer lockup and vice versa.

If the HF has a *notice period*, investors wanting to redeem have to give notice by a certain date (say the beginning of the quarter) and then wait until the end of the notice period (say the end of the quarter) before getting money. Some HFs extend this pain over multiple quarters. SAC Capital Advisors used to permit investors to withdraw only 25% of their requested funds every quarter, so it took one year to get back your money.[46] (In November 2013, SAC pled guilty to securities and

---

[45] For references behind the lockup numbers, see the Harvard Business School case, "Long-Term Capital Management, L.P.," 1999, by Andre Perold; *Economist*, "All Locked-Up," Aug. 2, 2007; FINalternatives, "Morgan Stanley Hedge Fund Spin-Off Wins $500M From Blackstone," Oct. 10, 2012.

[46] See Lattman, P., "Blackstone To Keep Bulk of Its Stake in SAC Fund," *New York Times*, Feb. 15, 2013.

wire fraud, paid $1.8 billion in fines, and stopped managing money for outside investors.[47])

Finally, HFs can impose *gates*, which allow the HFs to limit redemptions, and sometimes redemptions can be *suspended* altogether.

Lockups allow HF managers to pursue strategies that would be difficult if investors withdrew at the wrong time. That is, selling volatility will earn a long-run risk premium but only if you stick through the times when volatility spikes and prices crash. Lockups allow funds to hold more illiquid assets and earn an illiquidity risk premium (see chapter 13). Aragon (2007) shows that HFs with lockup restrictions earn 4% to 7% higher returns than HFs without lockups.

Gates and suspensions cause HFs to be like the "Hotel California" in the song by the Eagles. Investors may request their funds ("you can check out anytime you like") but HFs won't give your money back ("but you can never leave"). During the financial crisis, many investors wanted to check out of badly performing HFs, but they were stuck. This was not just a problem for 2008–2009; HFs get in trouble all the time and gate. In October 2012, the Endowment Fund, a multibillion HF run by Mark Yusko, the former chief of the endowment of the University of North Carolina at Chapel Hill, imposed gates after lousy performance over the prior two years.[48]

Illiquidity is costly to the asset owner. In Ang and Bollen (2010a, 2010b), I compute the cost of lockup and redemption restrictions using a real option approach.[49] An investor gives up an option—the right to get out of the fund when she wants, and she most wants to exercise the option when the manager is destroying value. This is precisely the time that the HF doesn't allow you to leave. I estimate the cost of a three- to six-month lockup at around 2%. The cost of a two-year lockup is 4%. The cost of illiquidity increases to 15% if the HF suspends all redemptions during bad times and rescinds the liquidity option when the investor desires it most.

4.4. THE FUTURE

HFs are not going away, and some generate sizeable returns. But most HFs are just conduits of risk factors, in opaque, illiquid, and expensive wrappers. Many of these risk factors—like volatility, credit, small-large, value-growth, and momentum—are especially attractive for long-term investors. Is there a better way of accessing these risk premiums?

The barrier to entry for many factor strategies is low. There are now mutual funds that do HF-like strategies. Some of them are HFs in everything but name—but with the protections that the 40-Act confers to investors. A few of these

---

[47] Protess, B., and P. Lattman, "After a Decade, SAC Capital Blinks," *New York Times*, Nov. 4, 2013.

[48] See Creswell, J., "After Weak Returns, the Endowment Fund Limits Withdrawals," *New York Times*, Oct. 30, 2012.

[49] See also Derman (2007).

mutual funds have even been launched by HF firms, seeking to branch out to mom-and-pop investors. (This money also tends to be more sticky than institutional HF investors.) New exchange-traded funds are specializing in some of these factor risk premiums. Many of the risk exposures that HFs bring to the table can be had more cheaply than 2/20, and many of these strategies are attracting more (and lower fee) copycats.[50] More capital piling in brings its own risks, too, as more investors may be chasing the same strategies. That could lead to more events like the August 2007 quant meltdown. As Andrew Lo says, "The whole hedge-fund industry is a series of crowded trades."[51]

There is ample room for innovation. At the time of writing in 2013, there are no large-scale, off-the-shelf factor portfolios for volatility, liquidity, or momentum that are global, diversified across asset classes, designed with low enough turnover to be very cheap (20–30 basis points), and available to ordinary investors. S&P 500, Russell 2000, and similar index funds cost 5 to 10 basis points for ordinary investors and nothing (literally, because of stock lending) for institutions, but the fees on factor portfolios will be higher because they dynamically trade. Some large investors (with tens to hundreds of billions of dollars) have created their own factor portfolios, but small asset owners can't. It is encouraging to see some asset management companies, including HF firms, pushing in this direction. Some HF firms have even introduced factor funds, but at prices much more expensive than 20 to 30 basis points. (However, the fees are generally much lower than the standard 2/20.) If factors can be commoditized, these HFs are at risk of being locked in a downward spiral of lower fees—good news for asset owners.

It's taking a while, though. Why don't we see dirt cheap factor funds now?

The First Factor Fund

We take low-cost, equity index funds for granted, but it wasn't obvious they were going to succeed when they started in the 1970s.[52] Traditional active managers, especially mutual fund families, didn't want to introduce index funds for fear of cannibalizing their higher-fee active funds, especially since active mutual funds underperform the market (see chapter 16). Offering index funds must have felt like throwing in the towel—like admitting you have no skill, and what manager wants to think that? Oldrich Vasicek, one of the early developers of the index fund said, "They thought we were crazy. . . . 'You just want to buy whatever garbage happens to be traded?' "[53]

---

[50] This includes "hedge fund replication" strategies (see Kat and Palaro 2005), but also pure factor portfolios in the spirit of chapter 14.

[51] Strasburg, J., and S. Pulliam, "Pack Mentality Grips Hedge Funds," *Wall Street Journal*, Jan. 14, 2011.

[52] The history of the index fund is outlined in Bernstein (1992) and MacKenzie (2006).

[53] Cited by MacKenzie (2006). Vasicek also wrote one of the most highly cited papers in fixed income, putting forward the Vasicek (1977) term structure model.

Clayton Christensen (1997), a guru of management at Harvard Business School, shows convincingly that it is outsiders (especially small firms) who innovate. This is true in finance too. The impertinent startup that introduced index funds was a bank—Wells Fargo—with few equity clients. Three people there led the charge: John McQuown, James Vertin, and William Fouse. "It was they who truly brought the gown to town," in Bernstein's (1992) words—appropriate because McQuown turned the asset management division into an academic powerhouse; the big guys in finance, Black, Fama, Jensen, Markowitz, Miller, and Sharpe (many going on to win Nobel Prizes), all worked for Wells Fargo at some point.

The first market index fund was a failure. In 1971, Wells Fargo created an equal-weighted index fund seeded by a pioneer, Samsonite's pension fund. It was a nightmare to trade and was eventually shut down.

In 1973, Wells Fargo launched a second attempt, this time successful. It created the modern index fund with market capitalization weights—the model for all index funds since. To seed this new fund, Wells Fargo's own pension fund put in money, along with Illinois Bell's.

Two other initial adopters of index funds were also outsiders: American National Bank, led by Rex Sinquefield, who went on to found DFA, and Batterymarch Financial Management, headed by Dean LeBaron. Neither is a household name today.

Index funds would have remained niche investments were it not for the Vanguard Group—now one of the world's largest asset managers.[54] Vanguard was started in 1975 by John Bogle with an innovative structure: the firm was owned by mutual funds, and the mutual fund shareholders paid Vanguard only what was necessary to operate the firm (which wasn't much). Vanguard is a "mutual" mutual fund company. Vanguard forsook financial advisors, sold directly to investors, and kept costs low. The firm introduced its first index fund in 1976, and index investing, thanks in large part to Vanguard's efforts, reached the lexicon of most ordinary investors in the late 1980s and attracted substantial asset flows in the mid- to late 1990s. Although Vanguard is a behemoth today, the firm was not initially successful, but it doggedly persisted: Vanguard's assets only surpassed $1 billion—a key threshold for respectability in the funds management industry—in 1998.[55]

Most of the traditional active management mutual fund companies were forced to introduce low-cost index funds. This was about thirty to forty years after the development of the theoretical Capital Asset Pricing Model by Sharpe (1964), explaining why investors should prefer market index funds, and the damning empirical work by Jensen (1968) and others showing that active mutual funds did

---

[54] This material is drawn from Hubbard et al. (2010).

[55] As reported by Bernstein (2010).

not add value. Even today, however, index funds account for less than 15% of the mutual fund market.[56]

Vanguard was a new *industrial organization* (well, financial organization, but I use the term following the branch of economics specializing in firm structures). Rose-Ackerman (1996) argues that ideologues are drawn to nontraditional corporate structures (especially nonprofits, although Vanguard is not a nonprofit) to share a vision. That vision was more than an index fund; it was a new investment philosophy—aiming for the average, doing it cheaply, and offering it directly to investors. Not for nothing are the followers of Bogle and fans of Vanguard called "Bogleheads."

The Next Generation of Factor Funds

Investors would be better off by gaining access to dynamic factor risk premiums much more cheaply. We need a new generation of factor (index) funds, which are low-cost versions of the factors in HFs. The factors can serve as benchmarks, to ensure that asset owners are getting better value and alleviating agency costs (see chapters 14 and 15). HFs will still exist, and the best HFs will deliver more than factor risk, but we will have upped the standards for HF performance. Given the large left-hand tail losses of these factor risks, greater transparency would greatly benefit investors in optimally allocating to these factor strategies.

The innovation in today's industry and the growing acceptance of factor investing makes this a prime time for new, cheap factor funds. In 2013, we don't see anything resembling a low-cost S&P 500 index fund for the dynamic factors considered in chapter 7. It took decades for cheap equity index funds to go mainstream from their academic beginnings (some findings in academia take a long time to become widely adopted in industry). Professors invented multifactor models in the late 1970s (Ross 1976), but empirical work on factors didn't permeate journals until the 1990s, so the timeline is about right for low-cost multifactor index funds to be introduced today. We can draw some lessons from the introduction of the first factor fund—the equity index fund:

1. The first versions could be failures, even if the idea is right.
   We need to experiment, and anticipate failure.
2. It will likely be introduced and popularized by an outsider.
   It takes a brave HF firm to introduce a new, cheap product that makes old, expensive ones look bad. Or it takes a HF firm that truly has the skill to do it, but those funds are giving up high-margin businesses to move into a low-margin one. Small and startup firms will likely be the pioneers. It may not, however, be the first mover that eventually makes factor portfolios go mainstream.

---

[56] See Pástor and Stambaugh (2012b).

3. Its widespread introduction might take a new organizational design.

    HFs already practice dynamic factor investing now. But they are unlikely vehicles to make factor investing low cost and widely available. Even if HFs lowered their fees, secretiveness and opacity are the antithesis of simple, well-documented factor strategies.

4. The first investors will be taking risks.

    The early investors in index funds, like the pension funds of Samsonite and Illinois Bell, took risks by investing in an unproven, nontraditional product that faced hostility from traditional management firms. This is hard for large, mainstream asset owners who like to do what everyone else is doing for "fiduciary" reasons. The giant asset owners—the sovereign wealth funds and smart pension funds with hundreds of billions—have the skills to implement, and many already trade, factor portfolios in house. The small investor may not even understand the concept of factor investing. So it will likely be large, but not huge, sophisticated institutional investors who will delegate to external factor managers. These asset owners have the capital, but not the expertise, to trade their own factor portfolios. Family offices, large endowments, and innovative pension funds are prime candidates. But they need to be brave.

5. The Quant Meltdown Redux

The quant meltdown in August 2007 showed that a set of HFs had exposures to the same risk factors. The large losses of quant funds could have been caused by one quant fund needing to liquidate immediately at fire-sale prices. Quant funds were all doing the same trades, had exposure to the same factors, and so all went down together. What caused the rebound on August 10, 2007? It could have been that the large unwind by one quant fund ended. Or it could have been that prices had moved so far from fair value, quant funds simply stopped taking their strategies off. Perhaps new capital—like the $3 billion injected into Goldman's quant funds—put the strategies back on. Whatever the reason, the quant meltdown showed that HFs are not absolute return strategies, and they are exposed to common factors.

HFs are not an asset class; they are bundles of factor risks. The most important factors are equity market risk and volatility risk. In particular, most HFs sell volatility and so generate steady returns most of the time, punctuated by the occasional frightful loss. In factor risk strategies, the regular returns during normal times compensate investors for suffering through infrequent catastrophes. HFs are at present the only large-scale organizational form to access many of these dynamic factors, but the hoped-for introduction of low-cost factor portfolios could change this.

HFs are not alternative beta. They are expensive beta.

CHAPTER 18

Private Equity

Chapter Summary

Private equity (PE) is not an asset class. Performance measurement of PE is hampered because commonly used metrics are not returns and are often manipulated. On the whole, PE does not outperform publicly traded stocks on a risk-adjusted basis, but there is large dispersion among PE funds. PE contracts are complicated and exacerbate, rather than ameliorate, agency problems.

1. South Carolina Retirement Systems

Curtis Loftis Jr., a Republican appointed state treasurer of South Carolina in January 2011, had a mess to clean up.[1]

South Carolina's public pension plan held $24.5 billion to meet its liabilities, but like many public pension funds faced a large funding shortfall (see chapter 1), in this case of $14.4 billion dollars. In an attempt to fill this hole, the pension fund started to move aggressively into PE and other alternative illiquid assets five years ago. The move was led by Robert Borden, who was appointed the pension fund's first CIO in the spring of 2006.

Before 2007, South Carolina law did not permit its pension fund to put money into investments that weren't publicly traded. Borden shook things up. His flamboyant, yellow Lamborghini brought a taste of Wall Street's excesses to Columbia, South Carolina, but the car was the least of it. He introduced exotic PE and other alternatives to the state's public employees' pension fund, which previously invested exclusively in regular bonds and public equity. PE and other alternative investments now count for $13 billion, or more than half the fund's assets.

Loftis was skeptical on whether these fancy, illiquid investments added value. The fees were high: in 2011 alone, South Carolina paid $344 million in investment

---

[1] This is based on the articles Corkery, M., "Weaning Off 'Alternative' Investments," *Wall Street Journal*, Jan. 30, 2012, and Creswell, J., "South Carolina's Pension Push into High-Octane Investments," *New York Times*, June 9, 2012.

management fees. Yet in the fiscal year ended June 30, 2012, the pension fund's return was 18.6%, which was below the average return of 21.4% among large public pension funds according to Wilshire Trust Universe Comparison Service. South Carolina's five-year performance of 4.0% also lagged other large funds, which averaged 5.1%, despite South Carolina's large exposure to sexy PE investments.

Loftis and Borden butted heads. In the summer of 2011, Loftis made a simple request to see Borden's appointment calendar; by showing how busy Borden was, Loftis hoped to bolster his case in the legislature for hiring more investment staff. But Borden, a man in charge of a $25 billion fund, had a calendar that was largely empty! (Borden claimed he did not need his calendar and planned all his meetings in his head.) Borden threatened to leave to manage Virginia's retirement funds, and the South Carolina Investment Commission voted to give him a $242,000 bonus. Loftis challenged the payment, which was later cut by $65,000. Borden resigned in December 2011 to join New England Pension Consultants, a Cambridge, Massachusetts-based investment firm that did extensive business with the South Carolina pension fund.[2]

Borden is gone, but his legacy remains.

A report by Deloitte & Touche identified several shortcomings in the fund's operations with respect to alternative assets. The fund did not have a standard process for analyzing or monitoring managers, or reviewing fees.

Loftis was fed up with years of high fees and complex terms, which are incomprehensible to the average taxpayer. "I question whether Wall Street's interests are being protected or our interests are being protected," he says. In an examination of the fees charged by one outside fund manager, he found fees were too high by $18.1 million—an amount the fund manager called "a reporting error."

Loftis did not want South Carolina to completely disinvest from complicated PE deals. But he "thinks the pension fund needs to be more mindful of its dependence on complicated deals being sold by Wall Street." Loftis has plenty of tales of what Wall Street financiers do to lure South Carolina's funds, with stories of fund manager meetings at trendy nightclubs and fund managers arranging for him to sit next to centerfold models at dinners. "This is a world where people have private jets, massive apartments overlooking Central Park, people who live exotic lives," said Loftis.

2. Industry Characteristics

2.1. WHAT IS PRIVATE EQUITY?

PE is very old. The *commenda* was a contract that arose in the tenth century to finance merchant shipping: *passive* owners put up some or all the capital, and there

---

[2] fitsnews.com, "The Real Pension 'Pay-to-Play,' " Feb. 3, 2012.

was an *active* owner who went on the voyage. Both parties shared in the profits, but the passive owners could lose only as much money as they put into the trip (their liability was *limited*). The active owner's liability, on the other hand, was *unlimited*. The commenda transformed Venice from an obscure, fog-prone marsh into La Serenissima.[3]

Today, PE investments are investments in privately held companies, which trade directly between investors instead of via organized exchanges.[4] The investments are typically made through a PE fund organized as a limited partnership. Asset owners, such as pension funds or endowments, invest in the fund and are *limited partners* (LPs). The fund is managed by a PE firm, like KKR or Kleiner Perkins, which is the *general partner* (GP). The fund itself invests in illiquid businesses (called *portfolio companies*).

The PE firm raises *commitments* of capital from LPs, who must pony up on demand at any point between the fund's start (or *vintage)* year and a predetermined date or whenever the fund is dissolved. LPs have a maximum commitment (the *committed capital*). For example, asset owners might commit to providing $100 million over the life of a PE fund. In the first year, GPs call $20 million, leaving $80 million that can be called in future years. Once committed, investors are expected to stay for the fund's duration—secondary markets for LP commitments are extremely thin and discounts are huge.

2.2. PRIVATE VERSUS PUBLIC EQUITY

Table 18.1 summarizes the differences between private and public equity. The first and obvious difference is that public equities are easily tradeable in centralized markets (that is, they are liquid), whereas private equities are traded over the

Table 18.1

	Public Equity (S&P 500)	Private Equity
Market	Centralized and liquid	Over-the-counter and illiquid
Transactions Costs	Tiny or small	Enormous
Valuation	Easy and objective in real time	Difficult and subjective and available infrequently
Horizon	Immediate	Long term (around 10 years)
Contracts	Standard	Complex

[3] See Acemoglu and Robinson (2012).

[4] Portions of Sections 2 through 4 are drawn from Ang (2011) and Ang and Sorensen (2012). Good summaries of the PE market are given by Cornelius (2011), Phalippou (2009, 2011), Robinson and Sensoy (2011a), and Harris, Jenkinson, and Kaplan (2012).

counter and only with difficulty (making them illiquid). Over the counter markets have *search frictions*, including finding a counterparty and overcoming the informational disadvantages an investor might have in evaluating the underlying value of portfolio companies. Even launching a PE fund entails search friction, since asset owners and potential GPs must find and evaluate one another. Transactions costs in secondary markets for PE are enormous: Harvard University, for example, faced discounts of 50% trying to exit from PE funds during the financial crisis (see chapter 11).[5]

The valuation of public equity is objective, happens immediately, and is easily verifiable through market pricing. PE, on the other hand, is hard to value. The valuation process is infrequent, subjective, and (unnecessarily and mysteriously) complex. Most PE funds have a stated horizon of around ten years, but many extend beyond, sometimes past fifteen. Thus, a true return on a PE fund cannot be computed for a decade or more, when liquidation finally occurs. The long horizon of PE means that investors cannot easily rebalance PE positions, which renders standard (usually mean-variance) portfolio choice models inappropriate, as discussed in chapter 13.

Finally, contracts for liquid assets are largely standardized and transparent. PE contracts are anything but, requiring far more effort and diligence from investors.

2.3. TYPES OF PRIVATE EQUITY

There are several types of PE:[6]

Leveraged buyout (or simply buyout) funds buy mature companies, often already listed, using high levels of debt. (The average leverage ratio of buyout funds is three.[7]) This subclass represents most of the money allocated to PE, and sometimes the term "PE" is used to refer to buyout funds. In this chapter, I take a broader view of PE.

Venture capital (VC) funds take stakes in companies at early stages of development using little or no leverage. *Angel investors* are special types of VC investors and typically use only their own money, rather than relying on a pool of investors as do VC funds. Angels specialize in the earliest stage of development—the proverbial startup in someone's garage. Apple, Google (both of which actually did start in garages), Amazon, and YouTube were all financed this way. That these are high-tech companies is no accident—VCs gravitate to high-growth startups, although some VC firms specialize in other areas.

PE *real estate* funds invest in property as well a real estate development. Real estate funds tend to be highly levered.

---

[5] See "Liquidating Harvard," Columbia CaseWorks ID #100312.

[6] Most academic research focuses on buyout and VC funds because of lack of data in other subclasses.

[7] See Axelson et al. (2012).

Mezzanine funds hold portfolios of loans in private companies. The debt held by these funds tends to be low on the totem pole; the term "mezzanine" implies that it is ranked below senior debt. Some mezzanine funds work hand in hand with buyout or real estate funds. This is a place to park some of the debt issued by private companies.

Infrastructure funds concentrate in capital infrastructure investments including airports, railways highways, and utilities. Typically these are leveraged.

A *distressed* fund concentrates on sick companies that are in or near bankruptcy. GPs of these funds specialize in *turnaround management*, which tries to turn sick companies into healthy ones.

Funds-of-funds are like their counterparts in hedge-fund land: they hold investments in different PE funds. Some funds-of-funds are listed.[8]

PE *secondary funds* acquire preexisting investments in PE funds from LPs. They allow existing LPs an opportunity to exit. (I discuss the secondary PE market in chapter 13.) There was a burst of secondary fund raisings during the financial crisis, as some savvy investors took advantage of distressed LPs.

LPs often invest directly in individual companies, alongside the PE funds, through *co-investments*.

2.4. PRIVATE EQUITY COMMITMENTS ARE PRO-CYCLICAL

Institutional asset owners tend to invest in PE pro-cyclically, injecting money into PE funds right at the peak of the business.[9] (These institutions have the same pro-cyclical tendencies as individuals investing in mutual funds; see chapter 16). Money piles in when current valuations are high and past distributions are large— but future expected returns are low. Paul Gompers and Joshua Lerner (2000), two prominent professors specializing in PE, call this "money chasing deals": asset owners tend to put money in PE right when it is most expensive.

Figure 18.2 shows PE fundraising over the 2000s decade as compiled by Pitchbook, a PE database. Panel A shows capital raised at around $320 billion per year peaking in 2007 and 2008, right before the financial crisis and the ensuing economic slowdown. Then in 2009 and 2010, right at the time when prices were low and expected returns were high, PE equity fundraising fell off a cliff. Panel B shows a similar picture in terms of the number of funds closed. (The correlation between the numbers in Panels A and B is approximately 90%).

---

[8] The organizational forms of listed versus unlisted private equity investment vehicles are different. Listed PE funds typically have indefinite lives and stricter reporting requirements. Jensen (2007) argues that reputational concerns give unlisted PE funds additional incentives to perform and therefore such funds should have higher returns than listed ones.

[9] See evidence documented by Gompers and Lerner (2000) and Kaplan and Lerner (2010) for VC and Kaplan and Stromberg (2009) and Axelson et al. (2012) for buyouts.

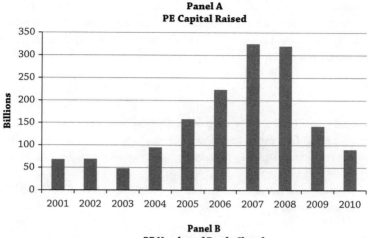

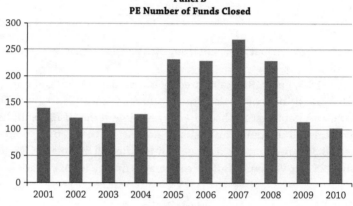

Figure 18.2

Pro-cyclicality causes the lowest returns to be earned on PE investments right when capital allocations to PE are the highest. Why do PE investors behave this way? Partly it is because PE returns are not directly observed. PE firms generally do not report returns.

3. Private Equity Risk and Return

The lack of market values and the infrequent trading of portfolio companies have led to the use of three main performance measures: (i) internal rates of returns (IRRs), (ii) *total value to paid-in capital multiples*, which are called *TVPIs* or *multiples* for short, and (iii) *public market equivalents*, or PMEs.[10] These are computed with

---

[10] While the FAS 157 rule has pushed NAVs to more reflect "market values," because there are often no market transactions, the valuations are subject to large discretion by GPs. Even when there are market transactions, there is selection bias (see chapter 13).

periodic valuations producing *net asset valuations* (NAVs), which are estimated values of portfolio companies. All three of these measures are not returns and can be highly misleading measures of performance.[11] Worse still, all of them are too often manipulated.

3.1. IRRs

Ludovic Phalippou (2011), a professor at Oxford University specializing in PE, states it bluntly: "The most frequently used performance measure IRR is uninformative and can be highly misleading; it typically exaggerates true performance."

The IRR is defined (implicitly) such that the present value (PV) of the investments is equal to zero:

$$PV = \sum \frac{Dist(t) - Call(t)}{(1 + IRR)^t} = 0, \tag{18.1}$$

where *Dist(t)* are distributions paid from the fund and *Call(t)* are capital calls paid into the fund.

In Figure 18.3, I plot IRRs calculated by Harris, Jenkinson, and Kaplan (2012). Figure 18.3 graphs IRRs of funds raised in vintage years 1984 to 2008. The Harris, Jenkinson, and Kaplan study lists the longest time series of IRRs, multiples, and PMEs available, all computed on the same data set so they can be compared.

Figure 18.3 shows that the average IRR for the full sample is 15% for buyout funds and 19% for VC funds. But these averages mask a lot of variation over time:

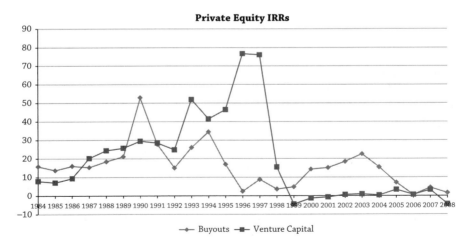

Private Equity IRRs

—◆— Buyouts   —■— Venture Capital

Figure 18.3

[11] For summaries of PE performance, see Phalippou (2009, 2011), Robinson and Sensoy (2011a), Ang and Sorensen (2012), and Harris, Jenkinson, and Kaplan (2012).

IRRs in buyout funds averaged 17% in the 1980s, peaked at 50% in 1990, and tended to decline over the 1990s. In 1996, the buyout IRR was close to zero. In the early 2000s, buyout IRRs reached 22% but since 2006 have been approximately zero. The IRRs for VC funds were stratospheric, above 70%, during the mid-1990s. Since the 2000s high-tech crash, VC IRRs have been hovering at, or just above, zero.

Any student taking an introductory MBA finance course is advised by professors not to use IRRs. One well-known problem is that the IRR assumes cash flows can be reinvested at the IRR. IRRs are also distorted by the timing of cash flows. In PE, these problems really bite. *IRRs are not returns.*

As Joshua Lerner says:[12]

> When you look at how people report performance, there's often a lot of gaming taking place in terms of how they manipulate the IRR.

Consider an investment where at time 0 an investor puts in $100 in a fund and at time 1 receives back $150:[13]

Date	0	1	2	3	4	5
	−100	150				

If the investor exits at time 1, the IRR is 50%. Now suppose there is an investment opportunity that earns 25% per year for four more years. This is a great return, and the investor would prefer to keep all her money in the fund until year 5, where it compounds to $366.

Date	0	1	2	3	4	5
	−100					366

If the GPs did this, the IRR would be 30%. Although it is better for the asset owner to remain invested until time 5, the GP prefers to exit early at time 1. Early exit happens in real life, as Gompers (1996) and Lee and Wahal (2004) show. Buyout funds have incentives to pay early dividends, which push cash flows earlier in the IRR computation. This may destroy value, but it inflates IRRs.[14]

GPs misuse IRRs in other ways. IRRs can be computed at the vintage level, which pools all funds within a given vintage, rather than computing the IRR of each fund separately. Grouping funds together hides poorly performing funds. If a

---

[12] As reported in "We Have Met the Enemy . . . And He Is Us: Lessons from Twenty Years of the Kauffman Foundation's Investments in Venture Capital Funds and the Triumph of Hope over Experience," Ewing Marion Kauffman Foundation, May 2012.

[13] This example is adapted from Phalippou (2008).

[14] See Phalippou (2009).

PE firm has some great successes in some funds early on, aggregating funds produces a high IRR and masks other bad investments. Phalippou (2008) finds that about half of buyout firms pool funds and then compute IRRs rather than first computing IRRs for each fund and then computing (weighted) averages across funds. Even some LPs use this pooling tactic to make their PE investments look better.[15]

Even a positive IRR does not mean that the asset owner is coming out ahead because of the risks entailed—the risk of the underlying portfolio companies and the risks of illiquidity, high fees, and the large agency issues between the LP and the GP (see below). Sorensen, Wang, and Yang (2012) develop a model that takes into account all these risks from the perspective of the LP. An appropriate break-even IRR is 13% to 17% for asset owners comfortable with low to moderate risk if the underlying portfolio companies have a beta of 0.5. If the portfolio companies have a beta of 1.0, the same as the market portfolio, then break-even IRRs are 17% to 19%. The average buyout fund IRR in Figure 18.3 is 16%, so moderately risk-averse investors are just breaking even. And since 2004, buyout funds have not generated value for investors.

3.2. MULTIPLES

The total value to paid-in capital multiple is calculated as the total amount of capital return to LPs (net of fees) divided by the total capital committed, or the amount invested (including fees):

$$\text{Multiple} = \frac{\sum Dist(t)}{\sum Call(t)}. \tag{18.2}$$

Multiples are less open to manipulation than IRRs. But they are just as meaningless.

Figure 18.4 graphs multiples for buy-out funds and VC funds compiled by Harris, Jenkinson, and Kaplan (2012). Like the IRR measures, multiples exhibit considerable variation over time that resembles the IRR. (The correlation of multiples with IRRs is 77% for buyout funds and 85% for VC funds.) Multiples for both buyouts and VC are generally over 2.0 in the 1980s, touch 6.5 in the mid-1990s for VC, and since the early 2000s have been fairly subdued. VC buyout multiples have hovered just above 1.0 since 1999 and buyout multiples since 2006 have been around 1.0.

If the multiple is greater than one, then an asset owner has received more money than invested. For several reasons, this doesn't mean you broke even on your PE investments:

---

[15] Phalippou (2011) documents this for CalPERS, the largest U.S. public pension fund.

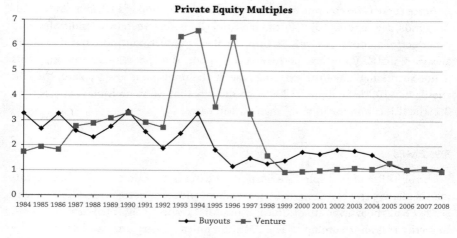

Figure 18.4

1. Time value of money

    There is no adjustment for this crucial factor. In fact, the implicit assumption is that the return on reinvested capital is zero!

2. Duration

    Multiples without duration information are pretty useless. A multiple of 2 means you've received twice as much as you put in—but is that generated over one year, which is a stunning return, or ten years, which is ho-hum? Even if you know the vintage year, you don't know if distributions have been returned early in the fund's history or toward the end. Although duration information is needed by asset owners to interpret multiples, Phalippou (2009) finds that fewer than 2% of PE prospectuses report holding period returns weighted by cash flow.[16]

3. Risk

    Multiples cannot be properly interpreted without knowing underlying leverage. Clearly a multiple of three is less impressive if the fund is levered five times than if the fund has no leverage. We also need to know the underlying risks of the portfolio companies and take into account the agency and illiquidity risks.

    After taking into account leverage and risk, Sorensen, Wang, and Yang (2012) estimate that break-even multiples range from 3 to 6. As Figure 18.4 reports, buyouts exceeded this in the 1980s and early 1990s but since then have underperformed. VC funds reached these levels in the early and mid-1990s, but since the 2000s VC underperformance has been severe.

---

[16] When multiples are below one, the IRR is negative. If IRRs are reported in those cases, prospectuses report "n.m." for not meaningful. It is meaningful: they've lost money.

Since there is no compulsory or standardized reporting of PE funds (unlike 40-Act funds, see chapter 16), GPs can pick and choose between IRRs, multiples, and other performance measures. PE buyouts always report multiples, but they don't always report IRRs. When performance is poor, the IRR is often missing. This is not surprising. Take the extreme case: if the multiple is exactly zero, the IRR should be –100%. Phalippou (2009) documents that when multiples are less than 0.1, the IRR is missing in more than 80% of cases.

3.3. PMEs

Both the IRR and multiples are absolute measures that do not calculate performance relative to a benchmark. Steven Kaplan and Antoinette Schoar (2005), who study PE at the University of Chicago and MIT, respectively, introduced the PME to rectify this shortcoming.[17] The PME computes PE performance relative to the market. Practitioners have been slow to warm to the PME, but it is widespread in academic circles.

The PME discounts LPs' inflows divided by the value of outflows using realized market returns:

$$PME = \frac{\left(\sum \dfrac{Dist(t)}{\Pi(1 + r_m(t))} \right)}{\left(\sum \dfrac{Call(t)}{\Pi(1 + r_m(t))} \right)}, \tag{18.3}$$

where $r_m(t)$ is the market return. The term $\Pi(1 + r_m(t))$ discounts the cash flows back to the start of the fund, so it takes into account the opportunity cost of being invested in the public equity market.

Figure 18.5 plots PMEs for buyouts and VC funds computed by Harris, Jenkinson, and Kaplan (2012). Taking into account market risk makes a difference. The average multiple for buyouts is 2.0 in Figure 18.4, which comes down to 1.3 in Figure 18.5 for PMEs. In particular, multiples of buyouts during the 1980s were around 3.0, but PMEs were just above 1.0. Like the multiple measures, buyout PMEs were around 1.5 in the early 2000s but since 2006 have been at or below 1.0. The story is similar for VC funds. The average VC multiple in Figure 18.4 is 2.5, and this comes down to 1.5 using PMEs. Figure 18.5 shows that although VC PMEs rose to over 4.0 in the mid-1990s, they have averaged below 1.0 since 1999.

PMEs assume capital calls and distributions have the same risk as the market. In reality, the denominator includes management fees, which are largely risk-free

---

[17] A related measure is the Profitability Index introduced by Ljungqvist and Richardson (2003), which takes a similar form to equation (18.3) except Ljungqvist and Richardson recommend discounting at a Treasury-bond rate for calls and the expected (not realized) return for distributions.

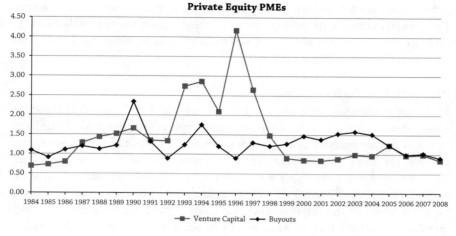

Private Equity PMEs

Figure 18.5

liabilities. Portfolio companies, which generate distributions in the numerator, are likely to have greater risk than the market portfolio. Using a higher discount rate for the numerator reduces the PME. Thus, in a careful risk treatment, the PME should exceed one before the LPs earn excess returns. Sorensen, Wang, and Yang (2012) show that an LP needs a break-even PME between 1.2 to 1.7 if the individual companies have a beta of 0.5, and break-even PMEs between 1.8 to 2.1 if the underlying individual companies have betas of 1.0. Using the latter benchmark, buyouts have only generated value for LPs briefly in the early 1990s.

3.4. RISK-ADJUSTED RETURNS

Measuring PE risk and returns is greatly hampered because returns are not directly reported, and IRRs, multiples, and PMEs are not return measures. Studies demonstrate that in the 1980s and early 1990s, PE investments beat public markets in terms of raw performance. The Harris, Jenkinson, and Kaplan (2011) study concludes, for example, that "it seems likely that buyout funds have outperformed public markets in the 1980s, 1990s, and 2000s." But once risk is taken into account, it is not clear that PE funds are generating value—especially today. In fact, PE funds have most likely underperformed public equities on a risk-adjusted basis, a fact first documented by Kaplan and Schoar (2005) approximately 30 years after institutions started making such investments.

Aggregate PE returns are strongly pro-cyclical. There are negative relations between capital invested in a given year and the return of that vintage year.[18] Phalippou (2011) finds large and negative correlations between the number of

---

[18] Kaplan and Stromberg (2009) document this effect for buyout funds and Kaplan and Lerner (2010) for VC funds. See also Gompers and Lerner (2000) and Axelson et al. (2012).

funds raised in each vintage year and IRR and multiple performance measures. This should not be a surprise: exits in buyout funds depend on hot public markets. IPOs are issued in waves, which peak at the top of markets. Merger and acquisition activity is likewise strongly pro-cyclical.[19]

Biases in Private Equity Returns

Academic studies take into account two serious biases in PE data: (i) the infrequent observations of fund or company values and (ii) selection bias.[20] The latter refers to the tendency of more successful firms and funds to be overrepresented in data, causing PE investment returns to appear better than they really are. Transactions are observed only if portfolio company values are high—only if the company is doing well will it receive the next round of financing, only if the valuation is high will the company IPO, and so on—and companies not doing well (*zombies*) are often left to linger as shells without mark-to-market valuations.

Zombie valuation is often written into PE contracts (see below), by statements like "Investments will be valued at cost unless a material change justifies a different valuation."[21] As one valuation expert says, "The manager ... has a clear incentive to hold onto investments that have poor prospects for improvement, simply to get more out of the fund in the form of management fees."[22] Zombies account for more than 5% of PE investments, according to TorreyCove Capital Partners, a consulting firm. Another survey conducted by Coller Capital, a PE investments firm, in 2011 finds that 57% of North American LPs have zombie funds in their portfolios.[23]

Academics tackling biases due to infrequent sampling and selection have used two main approaches, but both have drawbacks. First, we can examine individual portfolio company-level information. This provides more data, so there are actually returns (at irregular intervals for different companies), but selection bias is a major issue. This analysis also reflects total returns earned by a PE fund before fees and not the returns earned by an LP net of fees. Second, we can analyze PE fund-level data. The selection bias is smaller because companies that ultimately turn into zombies are eventually reflected in the fund's final closing payout. The main disadvantage of using fund-level cash flows is that these are not direct measures of returns.

---

[19] These are large literatures. See Rhodes-Kropf, Robinson, and Viswanathan (2005) for merger and acquisition waves and Ritter and Welch (2002) for IPO waves. Robinson and Sensoy (2011b) and Phalippou (2011) give overviews of buyout and VC cycles.

[20] There is also reporting and survivorship bias. Better-performing funds are more likely to report their performance. Phalippou and Zollo (2005) show that taking into account selection bias reduces IRRs by approximately 3%. Chapter 13 covers all these biases in more detail.

[21] Quoted from Phalippou (2009).

[22] The quotation and the estimate are from Pulliam, S., and J. Eaglesham, "Investor Hazard: 'Zombie Funds,'" *Wall Street Journal*, May 31, 2012.

[23] Coller Capital, Global Private Equity Barometer, Winter 2011–2012.

Company-Level Estimates

Cochrane (2005) was the first to estimate a dynamic risk-return model of PE investments taking into account selection bias. He estimates a log-return CAPM, given by

$$\ln(1 + r_i) - \ln(1 + r_f) = \alpha + \beta \left(\ln(1 + r_m) - \ln(1 + r_f) \right) + \varepsilon_i, \qquad (18.4)$$

where r_i is the return on company i, r_m is the market return, and r_f is the risk-free rate. The coefficients α and β are the log excess return (alpha) and market exposure (beta) of VC investments, respectively. Equation (18.4) is a log version of the standard CAPM regression, which is usually stated in arithmetic returns (see chapters 6 and 10).[24]

Cochrane finds the effect of selection bias is huge. Leaving aside selection bias, the (log) company alpha is 92%. Taking into account selection bias, the (log) alpha shrinks to –7%. The beta estimate is approximately 2. Portfolio company volatilities are extremely large—over 100% per year. Cochrane finds that performance of VC companies to be very similar to small- and micro-cap NASDAQ stocks. (In fact, the volatilities of comparable listed stocks are even larger than VC portfolio companies.) This reflects the lottery-like nature of starting companies and their high volatility: in PE funds, 85% of returns come from less than 10% of investments and only 13% of investments result in an IPO.[25]

Morten Sorensen, my colleague at Columbia Business School, finds in Korteweg and Sorensen (2010) that selection bias knocks off 2% to 3% (arithmetic returns) per month from the raw return estimates of VC funds. Korteweg and Sorensen estimate a higher VC beta, around 3, than does Cochrane. They find VC alphas from 1987 to 1993 were positive but modest, alphas during 1994 to 2000 were very high, but the alphas in the 2000s were negative. In particular, post-2001 arithmetic alphas for VC investments have been consistently negative at –3% per month.

Fund-Level Estimates

An advantage of fund-level estimates is that since PE funds have similar lifetimes (around 10 years) and selection issues are smaller, analysis can be carried out in more conventional arithmetic, rather than log returns. Using fund-level cash flows, Phalippou and Gottschalg (2009) find that PE funds have underperformed the S&P 500 by 3%. After taking into account additional risk factors to capture the size premium and the value-growth premium (see chapter 7), the risk-adjusted underperformance is 6%.

---

[24] The alpha in equation (18.4) is not a holding-period excess return. That is, there is a big difference between arithmetic and continuous-time (or log) returns, and that difference is due to volatility. The arithmetic alpha is approximately $\alpha + \frac{1}{2}\sigma^2$, where σ is the volatility of returns (see the Appendix).

[25] See Ewens and Rhodes-Kropf (2012).

Driessen, Lin, and Phalippou (2012) estimate betas of 1.3 for buyout funds and approximately 3 for VC funds, consistent with Korteweg and Sorensen (2010). Driessen, Lin, and Phalippou find that between 1980 and 2003—the period where the nonreturn IRR, multiple, and PME measures are highest (see Figures 18.3–18.5)—buyout funds underperform the market by 0.4% per month. The underperformance of VC funds after adjusting for market risk is 1.1% per month. This is large underperformance. After incorporating additional size and value-growth factors, the alphas for buyout and VC funds are –0.7% and –1.0% per month, respectively. These are very large underperformance numbers.

The size and value-growth exposures are important sources of risk premiums for buyout funds. Phalippou (2013) shows that any performance advantage for buyout funds, if it exists, is attributable to buying small or even tiny companies with a value bias. Both these tilts give buyout fund portfolios higher returns than the market, but you could do the same with cheap index funds. Oh, and buyout funds use lots of leverage.

Another perspective on the value added by PE is provided by Jegadeesh, Kräussl, and Pollet (2009). They examine *listed* PE funds and funds-of-funds. They report excess returns of –7% to –5% per year after controlling for risk factors in public equity markets. They also find significant exposures of listed PE to size and value factors.

Other Risk Factors

Illiquidity is an important risk factor in PE returns. Franzoni, Nowak, and Phalippou (2012) show that PE investments are exposed to the *same* illiquidity risk factor as public equity. That is, if an asset owner wants to collect an illiquidity risk premium, she might be better off collecting it in public markets rather than private markets (see also chapter 13). Franzoni, Nowak, and Phalippou find that the illiquidity risk premium accounts for approximately 3% of PE returns, which in their sample are 18%. That is, the remaining 15 percentage points of PE returns are due to other risk factors. Alphas are already modest (or even negative) before controlling for illiquidity risk and become even smaller after illiquidity risk is taken into account. Franzoni, Nowak, and Phalippou's estimate of PE alpha is zero to three decimal places after capturing illiquidity, size, and value effects.

Robinson and Sensoy (2011b) document that VC funds become "liquidity sinks" when valuations are low. Both LP capital contributions and LP distributions are pro-cyclical when liquidity is high. PE funds provide liquidity during booms, when market valuations are high, but there is no liquidity when valuations are low. This was made clear in 2007–2008 during the financial crisis as PE commitments became an albatross for many investors forced to meet capital calls at a time they most needed to conserve cash.[26]

[26] Harvard University and CalPERS were two such investors. See "Liquidating Harvard," Columbia CaseWorks ID #100312 and "California Dreamin': The Mess at CalPERS," Columbia CaseWorks, #120306.

Leverage increases exposure to systematic factor risk. Leverage accounts for a large amount of PE returns and, without taking into account leverage, asset owners overestimate the benefits of PE. Acharya et al. (2013) estimate that leverage accounts for over 50% of PE returns.

3.5. PERSISTENCE

Despite the mediocre performance of the average manager, some add value; there is large cross-sectional dispersion in PE fund returns. And those value-adding managers tend to be the same ones outperforming year after year. PE investing, therefore, is really about the cross-section rather than the average.

Since Kaplan and Schoar (2005), the academic literature has documented large persistence in PE returns. PE funds are raised in succession. If Fund ABC II raised in 2005 does well, then Fund ABC III raised in 2007 also does well. Estimates suggest that a performance increase of 1% for a fund is associated with greater performance of 0.5% for the next fund.[27] Moreover, persistence is so strong that even in skipping a fund, there is still significant predictability. That is, Fund ABC II raised in 2005 forecasts that Fund ABC IV raised in 2010 would do well.

Kaplan and Schoar (2005) find that funds in the "top quartile" outperform. If this performance is persistent, then this seems to be a way for smart LPs to pick winners who continue to win. Kaplan and Schoar's findings have led PE managers all wanting to be top quartile.

Unfortunately, in the Lake Wobegon world of PE, *everyone* is top quartile.[28] According to the consulting firm PERACS, 77% of firms claim to be in the top 25%.[29] How do they do it? There is no consistent benchmarking in PE, so managers pick the measures they want. Some funds claim top quartile status on the basis of IRRs, others on multiples. Funds can also select the benchmark they want—even after the returns have been generated. Harris, Jenkinson, and Kaplan (2012) report anecdotal evidence that VE was an easier benchmark to beat, so more GPs chose to use it. Even the vintage year is open to manipulation. Is the vintage year the year a fund begins raising funds, ends fundraising, or the year its first deal is closed?

The finding that top quartile managers outperform is also an ex-post result. That is, we know there are repeat outperformers *after* all the data are examined. In reality, it is difficult to select funds using the information at hand. Suppose Fund ABC IV was raised in 2010. In 2013 when ABC V is raised, we have at most three years of data on ABC IV. We will not know if ABC IV was indeed a top performer until it is liquidated, around 2020 or even later. Thus in 2013, there is little real-time information about ABC IV on which to base a decision on whether or not

---

[27] See Kaplan and Schoar (2005), Phalippou and Gottschalg (2009), and Hochberg, Ljungqvist, and Vissing Jørgensen (2010).

[28] The academic version of this paragraph is Harris, Jenkinson, and Stucke (2012).

[29] Quoted by Phalippou (2011).

to invest in ABC V. Using information only available at the time a fund is raised considerably weakens persistence estimates.[30]

Just knowing about the firm ABC turns out not to be enough. Relationships and talent matter considerably in PE. Many top quartile funds are not available for general entry; the funds that are open are far below top quartile. Moreover, it is not so much the firm that matters—it is the partners who comprise the firm.[31]

Finally, the PE industry exhibits the same *decreasing returns to scale* that characterize the rest of the asset management industry. Kaplan and Schoar (2005) and others document that size is strongly negatively correlated with PE performance. That is, the bigger they are, the harder they fall.

3.6. ACADEMICS VERSUS INDUSTRY

While academics hold less than sanguine, or outright negative, views on PE investing, industry professionals sing its praises. For example, the Private Equity Growth Capital Council, an industry group of PE funds, reports that at the end of 2011 PE outperformed (net of fees) the S&P for one-, five-, and ten-year horizons by 7.1%, 5.7%, and 7.6%, respectively.[32]

Why this discrepancy?

Phalippou and Gottschalg (2009) state three reasons why industry studies are misleading and overstate the benefits of PE investments:

1. Their data are too good.

   Successful funds are overrepresented. Their data comes from firms that report, and why would you report if your returns are poor?[33] (This is *selection bias*, as discussed in Section 3.4.)

2. They use multiples, IRRs, and other nonreturn performance metrics.

   I state one last time: *IRRs are not returns*. All these measures can be, and are, manipulated. None of these measures take into account risk. Even if a raw return is greater than the S&P 500, as the Private Equity Growth Capital Council claims, the number cannot be interpreted without knowing the risk taken to produce the return.

3. NAVs are subjective and judgmental.

   NAVs tend to be biased upward. Some of this happens because of the zombie effect, where old and inactive companies have high accounting values, whereas their values should be near zero. Phalippou and Gottschalg write:

---

[30] See Hochberg, Ljungqvist, and Vissing-Jørgensen (2010) and Phalippou (2010).

[31] See Ewens and Rhodes-Kropf (2012).

[32] Private Equity Growth Capital Council, Private Equity Performance Update: Returns as Reported Through December 2011.

[33] The other biases of infrequent observations and survivorship bias are discussed in chapters 13, 16, and 17.

A large part of performance [reported by industry] is driven by inflated accounting valuation of ongoing investments and we find a bias toward better performing funds in the data.

In the worst case, GPs just lie. Oppenheimer & Co. paid $2.8 million to settle charges that it inflated the value of investments in its PE fund, causing the fund's IRR to jump from 3.8% to 38.3%. The pie-in-the-sky numbers succeeded in bringing in $61 million of capital. The lack of PE market values and nontransparency make subjective valuations open to abuse, and an SEC official says the "number of cases involving PE will increase."[34]

Asset owners are warned: trusting research published by PE firms stating that PE outperforms is like believing in research conducted by cigarette companies concluding that smoking doesn't cause cancer.

3.7. PORTFOLIO COMPANY INVESTMENTS

While adding little value, on average, to LPs, PE funds do add significant value to the companies in their portfolio.[35] Kaplan and Stromberg (2009) show that profitability rises after a PE transaction. Investment in new projects also increases after a PE transaction.

PE firms create value in several ways. Of course they provide capital to up and coming firms that need it. But Chemmanur, Krishnan, and Nandy (2011) find that VC firms provide more than just financing. VCs can select higher-quality entrepreneurial firms, and they provide them with expert advice and professionalize management, as well as provide support for firms marketing their products (often using the GPs' networks). From the standpoint of principal-agent theory (see chapter 15), a buyout fund that purchases 100% of a company can reduce agency problems as there is no separation between ownership and control. Since the owners are the managers, they have more skin in the game.

The benefit of this value creation, unfortunately for asset owners, appears to be going to the PE fund managers (GPs), rather than the investors in the PE funds (LPs). This is entirely consistent with the Berk and Green (2004) model of asset management we covered in chapter 16.

3.8. SUMMARY

The lack of regular market prices and selection bias are fundamental problems in assessing the risk and returns in PE. In my reading of the literature, there is little compelling evidence to suggest that the average PE fund significantly outperforms

---

[34] SEC Administrative Proceeding File No.3-15238. Quoted by Zuckerman, G., and J. Eaglesham, "Oppenheimer & Co. to Pay Fine Over Fund," *Wall Street Journal*, March 12, 2013.

[35] See Da Rin, Hellman, and Puri (2011) for a summary.

public equity on a risk-adjusted basis. In fact, the evidence is precisely the opposite.[36] In the words of Antoinette Schoar, "This industry has had very poor performance over the last 25 years."[37]

4. Agency Issues

Most asset owners, lacking the expertise to invest in PE directly, hire outside managers to help them. PE investment is then primarily a bet on manager skill, so agency issues are extremely important.

Would you sign a contract where the investor . . .[38]

1. Has no right to examine the underlying assets?
2. Does not receive return numbers, but only complicated nonlinear functions of subjective "values" (called IRRs and multiples)?
3. Receives opaque, sometimes meaningless, status reports?
4. Can't withdraw money on demand?
5. Gives incentives to the PE manager to reduce distributions, empire-build, and make poor investments in fields outside the manager's primary expertise?
6. Is charged fees for investments the PE manager has not yet made, and in the extreme case never will make, rather than on current investments?
7. Allows managers to hold onto worthless investments so that they can milk fees from investors for as long as possible?

This is the current state of PE contracts.

4.1. PRIVATE EQUITY CONTRACTS

There are three main ways of compensating GPs:[39]

1. Regular annual fees, which are *management fees*;
2. Incentive fees, called *carried interest*; and
3. Other fees, which include fees for transactions (buying or selling companies), advisory and monitoring, specialist consulting work on the portfolio companies, director fees, and so on. These are called *portfolio company fees* (or *transactions fees*) because they are levied on the underlying private companies and are often not directly visible by LPs.

---

[36] Bond and Mitchell (2010) show a conspicuous lack of alpha, on average, for managers in the other major illiquid asset class, real estate. For a summary of active management in real estate see chapter 11 and Ang, Goetzmann, and Schaefer (2011).

[37] From a presentation made by Schoar at the World Investment Forum on May 22, 2011.

[38] Adapted from Ang (2011).

[39] LPs, not GPs, are usually responsible for *organizational fees* in forming the PE fund.

Management Fees

A typical management fee is 2% of committed capital, not invested capital. That is, even though a fund manager has found $20 million of investments in the first year, the GPs are not paid on the $20 million of assets under management. They are paid on the full $100 million of committed capital. As you can imagine, this arrangement leads to very high overall PE fees (see below). The arrangement also leads some GPs to raise the largest possible funds so they can maximize fees. Some PE funds, however, restrict access, and so deliberately refrain from raising the largest fund they can (see Kaplan and Schoar 2005).

The incentive for funds to milk management fees for as long as possible leads to zombie companies. Investors would prefer for zombies to be sold at a loss, or just wound down. Sadly, this is not a decision that the LPs can make. "Private equity is an industry with extraordinary barriers to exit," quips one PE advisory specialist.[40]

There is a rationale for levying management fees on committed, rather than invested, capital. If management fees were paid on invested capital, GPs might rush to make investments early and in inferior companies. The magnitude and break-downs of total compensation I report below, however, makes this consideration small. As always, asset owners should pay when value is actually created, not just for managers holding their funds—which could be accomplished otherwise much more cheaply (see chapters 14 and 15).

Carry

The carry is typically 20%. A common arrangement is that distributions are first paid to investors by the fund up until an IRR of 8% is obtained. (This is called the *hurdle rate*.) There are complicated rules that permit only some cash flows (capital commitments, write-downs, fees, etc.) to be counted in the IRR computation. After the 8% hurdle rate is hit, 20% of money paid out from the fund goes to the GPs, leaving investors the other 80%. (The 20% is charged from 0% not 8% at this point.) Sometimes there is a *catch-up provision*, which gives all distributions to the GPs until a certain target is received—typically when the LPs have received 80% of the money paid out. After the catch-up provision, the GPs collect their 20%. PE contracts often have a *clawback* provision. Under a clawback, the GP cannot keep distributions representing more than 20% (usually) of the fund's cumulative profits. Thus, the clawback requires that any "excess distributions" go to the LPs.

While a management fee of 2% and a carry of 20% ("2/20" in industry parlance) is a common split, there is variation. Management fees range from 1% to 2.5% and carry interest from 20% to 35%. The overall schedule of how distributions are shared between the LPs and GPs is called the *waterfall structure*. Waterfalls can be complex. Management fees, for example, could be declining over the life of a

[40] Quoted in *Economist*, "Zombies at the Gates," March 23, 2013.

fund, a (time-varying but deterministic) combination of committed and managed capital, or even just a fixed dollar amount.

Other Fees

Portfolio company fees are fees associated with the private companies managed by the GPs. They are opaque and, because they are not directly reported, asset owners usually do not know how much GPs generate through these fees.[41] These fees can be substantial. Whereas management fees are capped by the total commitment and carry is capped by the clawback, there is no limit on portfolio fees. A common transaction fee is 2%, sometimes charged both at entry and exit of a company, and monitoring fees are around 0.4%.[42]

There are many incentive problems emanating from the way industry sets management fees.[43] Management fees are typically set on the *asset value* of companies, not *equity value*. This gives an incentive for PE funds to use more debt as it increases firm assets and thus maximizes fees. GPs also prefer to spin off companies in small parts, since they earn more fees on several small pieces rather than as a whole. The fact that these fees are transactions based, and not based on value-added, drives GPs to make more changes to companies than is optimal; every change GPs make to a company's capital structure increases their fees.

The total amount of fees is poorly disclosed in PE prospectuses. Phalippou (2009) finds that only 25% of funds report past performance net of fees, and those funds are typically the ones with the highest performance.

Side Letters

Some investors receive *side letters*, which are terms in addition to the standard contract (all investors receive the standard contract). The side letters can give some investors better terms, fee offsets, and other conditions. Lucky investors receive *most preferred nation* status, which states that no other investor can have better terms. It should be no surprise that an enduring relationship with a PE firm, or a lot of committed capital, brings better terms in side letters.

4.2. FEES, FEES, AND FEES

PE fees are very high.

Table 18.6 reports management and incentive fees (it ignores transactions fees) collected by GPs. These numbers are computed by Metrick and Yasuda (2010), who develop an economic model of PE. Out of every $100 invested with a buyout fund, an average of $18 in carry and management fees is paid to

---

[41] Despite the opaqueness, of PE contracts, Litvak (2009) finds no relation between opaqueness and total compensation.

[42] See Metrick and Yasuda (2010).

[43] See Phalippou (2009).

Table 18.6

	Venture Capital			Buyout		
	25%	*Mean*	*75%*	*25%*	*Mean*	*75%*
Carry per $100	$8.09	$8.36	$8.37	$4.93	$5.28	$5.66
Management Fees per $100	$12.04	$14.80	$17.61	$8.77	$10.35	$11.65
Total Revenue per $100	$20.24	$23.16	$26.11	$15.75	$17.80	$19.60
Proportion Incentive Fees	40%	36%	32%	31%	30%	29%

the GPs. For VC funds, the mean of the carry and management fees comes to $23 per $100 invested. These are enormous fees! Table 18.6 shows that even the lower 25% distribution of fees is still large, at $16 and $20 for buyout and VC funds, respectively. The numbers in Table 18.6 are present values. Phalippou and Gottschalg (2009) compute total fees in terms of flow, which amounts to GPs collecting fees of around 6% per year. As I tell my MBA students looking at asset management careers: as a GP, PE is a wonderful business to be in.

As an LP asset owner, not so. You should be flabbergasted not by the large fees per se but by the fact that incentive fees represent only around 30 to 40% of total fees paid. Asset owners should not balk at high fees but should pay them only when value is created. Two-thirds of total revenues are paid just by virtue of being in a fund. I would prefer to see 1% or 2% of total fees paid in fixed-revenue components and the rest arising from incentive payments. GPs should work to earn their money, but this is not what the current PE contracts deliver.

Chung et al. (2012) argue that the Metrick and Yasuda (2010) analysis understates the effect of incentive fees because it ignores the GPs' ability to raise funds in the future. GPs have incentives to generate high returns for LPs, and reduce fees, in the current fund because poor performance takes away the ability to raise future funds. They find "indirect pay for performance from future fund-raising is at least as large as direct pay for performance from carried interest for first-time buyout funds." From the perspective of LPs, however, PE capital is raised pro-cyclically by GPs. More money is put into PE by LPs when PE valuations are high and future returns tend to be low. This future *performance sensitivity* of GP compensation is tied to the opportunity of LPs to invest right at the wrong time.

David Swensen (2009), master investor in PE and CIO of Yale's endowment, concisely summarizes the PE fee situation: "The large majority of buyout funds fail to add sufficient value to overcome a grossly unreasonable fee structure."

The high fees charged by GPs mean that large asset owners can achieve big savings by taking a do-it-yourself approach to PE investing, which would enable them to keep most of the fees. Many large asset owners, including pension funds such as Canada Pension Plan and Ontario Teacher's Pension Plan and sovereign wealth funds such as Abu Dhabi Investment Authority and Kuwait Investment Authority, bypass funds to invest directly in PE. Phalippou and Gottschalg (2009) estimate gross-of-fee alphas to be approximately 4%. If asset owners can keep most of these fees, PE becomes much more attractive.[44] However, it requires good governance and the ability to hire skilled teams to do in-house PE investing (see chapter 15). You also need to be big to do PE investing in-house. Once you have built the required resources there are *increasing economies of scale*; Dyck and Pomorski (2011) and Andonov et al. (2011) show that the biggest asset owners significantly outperform the small ones in PE investments.

We are seeing fees on PE gradually being nudged down. This comes about from the action of diligent leaders like Loftis, who is putting the PE fees paid by South Carolina's pension fund under a microscope. Groups of large asset owners, like the Institutional Limited Partners Association, have also issued guidelines putting pressure on fees and improving PE fund governance.[45]

There is a limit on how much fixed fees can come down given the current structure of PE contracts; the high annual management charge on committed capital should be removed entirely. A better structure would be to raise the committed capital upfront (like a hedge fund), where it is invested in (potentially levered) public equities. This public portfolio serves as the benchmark, so the equities might be tilted toward illiquid stocks, small stocks, and stocks with a value orientation. The cost for this passive portfolio should be similar to index funds—that is, low, with a little bit extra to cover firm operating expenses. As GPs find private companies to invest in, they shift money from the public equity portfolio to private investments. Incentive fees ensure that they get paid only if these companies are successful and deliver returns in excess of the public equities benchmark. (See also chapter 14 on factor investing.)

4.3. KNOCK-ON EFFECTS

The cost of PE contracts is more than just the high fees paid. The opaqueness and complexity of contracts

1. Increases the risk of blowups;
2. Makes asset-liability planning more difficult;
3. Hinders liquidity management;
4. Distorts economic value;
5. Tends to maximize, rather than minimize, information asymmetry and consequently increases agency costs;
6. Makes leverage costlier, since it is usually cheaper to do leverage in house with better risk management than in a third-party, nontransparent vehicle; and
7. Increases operational, headline, and reputation risk

---

[44] See Fang, Ivashina, and Lerner (2012).

[45] Private Equity Principles: Version 2.0, Institutional Limited Partners Association, January 2011.

All of these contract issues induce negative knock-on effects for an asset owner's larger portfolio.

4.4. SOME INVESTORS DO BETTER THAN OTHERS

There are lucky asset owners who have done extraordinarily well in PE. Conversely, many investors have done terribly.

Lerner, Schoar, and Wongsunwai (2007) call this the *limited partner performance puzzle*. They document that endowments have earned much higher returns than other investors in PE. Figure 18.7 reports IRRs in PE for different investors. (Remember, these IRRs overstate the true returns, but the return patterns will be qualitatively the same.) Endowments do the best, at 39%, and banks do the worst, at 3%. The spread between endowment and bank IRRs is a gaping 37%. Public and private pension funds have IRRs around 12%, which are toward the low end.

One reason for the vastly different investor experiences in PE is access. Some of the best PE funds are closed to new investors, and some endowments have superior access—through their networks of prominent alumni, their early entry in PE firms that have become quite successful, and their long investment horizons, which enable them to commit across several investment cycles and gain them preferential treatment. Sensoy, Wang, and Weisbach (2013) document that endowments' ability to access skilled managers has declined over time. Since 1999, they claim, endowments "no longer outperform, and neither have greater access to funds which are likely to restrict access nor make better investment selections than other types of institutional investors." This is consistent with the early-moving endowments finding success in the 1980s and 1990s when PE was a niche market. Since then, the PE industry has grown and become

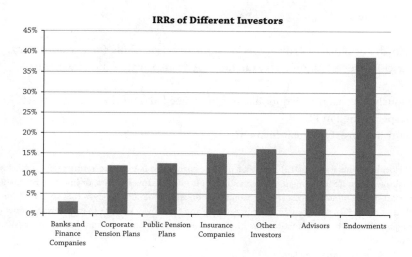

Figure 18.7

institutionalized; PE excess returns (or "alpha," see chapter 10) are now harder to find—for everyone.

Some endowments, such as those of Yale and Harvard, continue to do well in PE investments. These endowments have better ability to select good funds: they can pay (more) competitive wages and attract more qualified employees, have greater freedom, and have boards that understand and give resources to their managers to pursue PE investments. Pension plans also have more rigid investment management structures than endowments. In pension plans, salary and rank of employees often depend more on how much money they are responsible for managing, rather than on how much return they generate (see chapter 1). Some pension plan managers are enamored with PE and are essentially "captured" by their external managers—as Loftis wonders, how does the sexy model sitting next to you at dinner and the trendy nightclub atmosphere help in evaluating a PE fund? Some pension managers, like Borden, quit and go work for PE firms. Asset owners sometimes have investment aims other than maximizing return for given levels of risk. Many public pension plans and sovereign wealth funds, for example, have mandates constraining them to overweight "local" investments and lose money as a result.[46]

Banks can afford to earn low returns in PE because they earn plenty of other fees from PE firms. The division in a bank that invests in PE builds relationships and generates business for the bank's other divisions. So although banks might not make money from PE investments, they earn money from equity issuance, debt underwriting, company restructuring, merger and acquisitions, advisory work, and so on.[47]

4.5. WHY INVESTORS ARE DUPED

Swensen advises:[48]

> In the absence of truly superior fund-selection skills (or extraordinary luck), investors should stay far, far away from private equity investments.

Obviously, Swensen's wisdom has not been heeded, and the average investor has underperformed in PE.

Why are investors misinformed?

[46] Hochberg and Rauh (2013) find that public pension funds generate returns 2% to 4% lower on their own in-state investments than on similar out-of-state investments, or investments made in their state by out-of-state investors. Bernstein, Lerner, and Schoar (2013) show that sovereign wealth funds do the same thing—they invest domestically and earn lower returns than in international private equity. For both sets of institutions, the effect is more pronounced when there is more political interference.

[47] See Fang, Ivashina, and Lerner (2013).

[48] Economist, "Bain or Blessing," Jan. 28, 2012.

1. Hopes and dreams

   Maybe if we can get that one lucky investment—the next Microsoft, Apple, or Google—we can solve our funding problems today. VC investing, in particular, has an allure of changing the world and making money at the same time. It is true that portfolio company returns are highly skewed, with one or two winners subsidizing ten or more losers. But the high-flying returns of the rare success do not offset the overall damage to the average investor's portfolio. Thaler and Sunstein (2009) say that "if consumers have a less than fully rational belief, firms have more incentive to cater to that belief than to eradicate it." What is true for consumers is just as true for institutional investors.

2. Information is poor

   Contracts are opaque and contain hard-to-understand fees. Loftis is absolutely correct that PE contracts are "incomprehensible to the average taxpayer." Phalippou (2009) says that all PE information—including true returns and total fee payments—is "shrouded."

3. Selective reporting

   "Every private equity firm you talk to is first quartile," says a large pension investment manager.[49] But they're not lying. By selective reporting of IRRs, multiples, and even the vintage year, all PE firms can indeed be first quartile. Investors are fooled by dubious quality performance measures.

4. Duped by industry propaganda

   Maybe asset owners are led astray by industry claims of good PE performance. They don't know about survivorship bias, infrequent trading bias, selection bias, and all the other issues involved in measuring PE returns. Or their consultants haven't read (or understood) academic studies tackling these issues.

5. Investor myopia

   Even if investors have the ability to dig up all this information, they just ignore it.[50]

6. Inability to learn

   Or perhaps not wanting to learn? Either way, most asset owners don't have Swensen's "superior fund-selection skills." Some investors even delude themselves in thinking that current contracts are optimal. Of the prevailing 2/20 contract, CalPERS says, "When this compensation structure is used, the financial interests of the General Partner are aligned with those of the Limited Partners, including CalPERS."[51]

7. Nonpecuniary incentives

   There are reasons to invest in PE on a basis other than optimizing returns. For example, banks make lots of money by selling other services to PE firms

---

[49] Quoted in the Economist, "Bain or Blessing," Jan. 28, 2012.

[50] Preferences describing this behavior are called "myopic preferences." See Gabaix and Laibson (2006).

[51] http://www.calpers.ca.gov/index.jsp?bc=/investments/assets/equities/pe/programoverview.xml

and by this means recoup their losses on PE investments. The ordinary asset owner doesn't have this luxury.

8. Mispricing

Finally, perhaps investors pay too much for PE. There are too many LPs investing too much capital in too few PE firms. In the long run, investors may wise up and then PE prices will come down.

Some PE firms are making adjustments to a forecasted decline in business. Large buyout funds such as Blackstone, Carlyle, and KKR have diversified into hedge funds and advisory work that looks like investment banking. Magnanimously, some have even launched mutual funds, thereby enticing a new class of investors—moms and dads—to earn subpar risk-adjusted returns.[52]

4.6. KAUFFMAN FOUNDATION REPORT

The Ewing Marion Kauffman Foundation is dedicated to promoting entrepreneurship and education. It had an endowment of $1.8 billion at the end of 2011, of which 45% was invested in PE. In 2012, the foundation issued a marvelous, introspective report, *We Have Met the Enemy . . . And He Is Us: Lessons from Twenty Years of the Kauffman Foundation's Investments in Venture Capital Funds and the Triumph of Hope over Experience*. The report, which is astonishing in its honesty given that the foundation is focused on entrepreneurship, lays out the organization's failures in VC investing. It found that Kauffman's average VC investment failed to return investor capital after fees.

The report stated that the primary reason the Kauffman endowment continued to pursue the VC dream was because "investors like us succumb time and again to narrative fallacies, a well-studied finance bias. . . . The historic narrative of VC investing is a compelling story filled with entrepreneurial heroes, spectacular returns, and life-changing companies." Hopes and dreams, indeed.

The Kauffman report advocated moving away from the IRR and multiple measures to relative performance measures, using small cap stocks. This is exactly the concept of the PME, extended to size risk factors. It is also the *factor investing* concept practiced by Canada Pension Plan Investment Board (CPPIB), the fund manager of the Canada Pension Plan (see chapter 14).[53] For CPPIB, PE is not an asset class, and it is benchmarked to what the pension fund can achieve at low cost in liquid stock and bond markets. There is no set allocation to PE for CPPIB, avoiding the need to top up PE investments when they are poor investments. CPPIB can switch seamlessly between public and PE.

[52] See Suich, A., 2012, "Barbarians in a State," in Franklin, D., ed., *The World in 2013*, Economist, London.
[53] See "Factor Investing: The Reference Portfolio and Canada Pension Plan Investment Board," Columbia CaseWorks #120302.

Kauffman also recognized that current PE contracts are misaligned. The industry should change them to reduce management fees and put most of the compensation where it belongs—in the incentive fees.

4.7. SUMMARY

PE contracts today tend to exacerbate, rather than ameliorate, agency problems. Fees are exorbitant, and management fees unfortunately dominate incentive fees. Some skilled investors do well in PE, but most underperform.

Asset owners are gradually realizing that these contracts put them at a horrendous disadvantage. The Kauffman report said:

> A well-regarded GP of a perceived top-tier VC fund told us that "LPs have no leverage" to obtain firm economics. We suggested that LPs do have leverage—the same leverage that VCs have when they can't reach agreement on terms with a potential portfolio company—we can walk away. "Yes," he said, "but LPs never walk away."

Walk away.

5. South Carolina Retirement Systems Redux

While reforming South Carolina's pension fund PE investments, Loftis should keep several things in mind:

1. The standard reporting benchmarks used in the PE industry can be very misleading and invariably make PE investments look better than they truly are.
2. The average asset owner does not do well in PE investments. Academic evidence suggests that, on average, PE underperforms public equity on a risk-adjusted basis. Don't think about PE as an asset class: it is public equity made expensive and shackled by serious agency issues.
3. PE contracts are terrible for asset owners. Simplify, reduce management fees (while boosting incentive fees), and benchmark properly. Agency issues are the number-one concern in PE investing.

If you are truly skilled, like Swensen, the world of PE brings great opportunities. But if you are not like Swensen, you will be duped.

AFTERWORD

FACTOR MANAGEMENT

The first model of factor investing, the capital asset pricing model, was developed in the 1960s and suggested that one factor, the market portfolio, determined asset risk premiums. But at the time, investors had no way to invest in the market factor. The market index fund was created a decade later and gave investors a way to collect the equity market risk premium through low-cost exposure to the whole equity market. Market index funds remained niche products until the 1980s and really took off in the 1990s; now many investors invest in the market factor cheaply, in scale, and with minimal agency issues. It took twenty to thirty years, however, after the conception of the theory for investing via the market portfolio factor to become widespread.

The theory behind moving beyond just the market factor to a world of multiple factors was developed in the 1970s. Theoretical developments and substantial empirical work validating multiple sources of factor risks occurred during the 1980s and 1990s. Today we are experiencing exciting times in factor investing as industry innovates to create low-cost, scalable versions of factors that are diversified within and across asset classes and regions. A new generation of dirt-cheap factor index funds will allow investors to harvest many sources of risk premiums, including those associated with value versus growth, momentum investing, credit risk, and volatility risk. Most of the effort has been concentrated in dynamic factors that take time-varying nonmarket capitalization weighted positions, but there are also efforts to go further by linking the underlying macro factors to asset allocations.

I see three main areas where we still fall short of the theory. These are also areas where industry can help us reach the full potential of factor investing:

Identifying and Managing Bad Times
This book started with the asset owner. Her fears, desires, the riskiness of her income, her liabilities, how she perceives different sources of risk—all uniquely

define her set of bad times. Periods of low wealth are often bad times, but bad times also include times of moral indignation, jealousy when her peers and neighbors do better, and distress at how her wealth and consumption might have changed for the worse compared to what she was used to. Asset management is ultimately about building portfolios that mitigate the risk of an investor's bad times, while trading off the pain of those bad times for the potential of returns.

We have whiz-bang methods of handling bad times that arise from high volatility and low average returns (mean-variance optimization), but generally our quantitative methods of handling more general varieties of bad times leave much to be desired. This is especially true of modeling how bad times change over investors' life cycles, and dynamically handling bad times of illiquidity over long horizons, incorporating time-varying liabilities, and taking into account asymmetric treatments of losses and gains. Progress is being made, but it would be nice if we had a standard commercial optimizer that enabled us to toggle between various utility functions, especially those incorporating downside risk aversion, and see the effects on optimal portfolios. Investors need help in mapping a series of bad times and how they perceive the risk of bad times to different quantitative models of investing.

Factor Risk Premiums Are Rewards for Suffering Losses during Bad Times

The concept of factor investing compares the bad times of an investor with bad times of the typical investor—the market investor. In fact, since the market portfolio is strictly a long-only passive holding of assets, the market investor does not capture any dynamic factor risk premiums. The market also does not rebalance. We can move away from market weights to holding portfolios of securities which outperform, on average. These high returns don't come for free. Factor portfolios earn risk premiums to compensate investors for bearing losses during bad times. Bad times for the typical investor, however, may not be a bad time for you. This gives you scope to harvest a factor risk premium if you can tolerate the losses. Other investors willing to give up the factor exposure because they are too risk averse.

We are seeing many innovations that customize factor indexes with nonmarket capitalization weights, tailor the size of the risk exposures, and more cheaply create optimal factor portfolios. These are all good things. But when asset owners choose between different factor risks, and the size of the risk exposures, they rarely ask themselves: how am I different from the market? Ideally, consultants, financial advisors, and asset managers would offer guidance on how factor risk losses correspond to different bad times. We should know some economics explaining the existence of these factor risk premiums—even for the basic equity premium—before we can say whether they are appropriate for an investor. Understanding the economic theories giving rise to risk premiums, relating these stories to the realized losses and gains of various factors, and showing how the factor risks are appropriate (or not) for a particular investor is the optimal way to decide which factors an investor should collect and determine how large his factor exposures should be.

A valid criticism is that I've outlined a great many sources of factor risk and a great many investable dynamic factor premiums. How do you choose in this cornucopia? How do you make sense of all these factor risk stories? The asset owner must take a stand by identifying what he believes and what defines his specific bad times. (An investor policy statement or a statement of investment beliefs are ideal vehicles to do this.) Then we compare the investor to the market along a select number of dimensions: time horizon, capacity to bear risk or weather losses, level and nature of liabilities, reliability of labor income, and so on. Start with the market portfolio—this represents the average investor. Judge how you are different from average along these characteristics, which determine your capacity to bear risk. Investors should choose just one or two dimensions to differentiate themselves from the market, translating their comparative advantages and disadvantages into risk factor exposures. The risk exposures are not necessarily positive—it might be better for us to purchase protection when volatility spikes and pay for volatility insurance, rather than receiving small volatility insurance premiums and getting whacked with heavy losses when volatility shoots sky high.

They're Your Assets

Agency problems are front and center in asset management. We don't want to be adding bad times through dysfunctional principal–agent relationships. This is an area where both industry and academia could do more in promoting the welfare of asset owners. In industry, investment vehicles too often give asset owners a raw deal. In many hedge fund and private equity contracts, for example, asset owners have little or no control over their funds, information is terrible, and agents have little incentive to act in the best interests of asset owners. Academics could do more by making recommendations for optimal contracts and deriving optimal control and governance mechanisms for asset management organizations.

Factor investing will help. Factor benchmarks can ameliorate agency issues. They do not penalize a manager for underperformance when the losses are due to poor factor performance. From the perspective of the asset owner, factors raise the bar for active management. There is talent out there, and we want to identify those with skill and reward them handsomely. However, that talent should be producing returns in excess of factor risk exposures that can be obtained generically at low cost elsewhere.

Currently, long-only *passive* factor benchmarks predominate in industry. The creation of low-cost factor portfolios should hasten the adoption of *dynamic* factor benchmarks tailor made for each investor. If we can get factors at low cost, we can remove from expensive active returns a component that doesn't really belong there.

Asset management is not really about the management of assets. It is all about factors.

Appendix

RETURNS

1. Returns

There are several definitions of returns. This appendix shows how they are related to each other.

1.1. GROSS RETURNS

A *gross return* over one period, t to $t+1$, is defined as

$$\text{Gross return } R_{t+1} = \frac{P_{t+1} + D_{t+1}}{P_t}, \tag{A.1}$$

where P_t is the price of the asset at the beginning of the period, P_{t+1} is the price at the end of the period, and D_{t+1} is any dividend paid at time $t+1$. I denote gross returns with an upper case R. The definition in equation (A.1) assumes that we can measure prices—which is not true for some illiquid investments. For now, we assume assets are traded; I discuss illiquid asset returns in chapter 13.

As wealth cumulates over time, we compound gross returns multiplicatively. An asset earning gross returns of $R_{t+1} = 1.10$ three years in a row produces cumulated wealth at the end of three years of

$$W_{t+3} = R_{t+1}R_{t+2}R_{t+3}$$
$$= 1.10 \times 1.10 \times 1.10$$
$$= 1.3310,$$

starting with \$1 at time t.

1.2. ARITHMETIC RETURNS

We can express a gross return as an *arithmetic return*, which I denote through the book as a lower case r_{t+1}:

$$\text{Arithmetic return } r_{t+1} = R_{t+1} - 1. \qquad (A.2)$$

This is the most popular way of expressing rates of return. Arithmetic returns are also called "*simple returns*" or "*net returns*." Often we just drop any modifier and say just "returns" (as I do throughout the book).

Arithmetic returns are *not* additive over time. Assume the gross return $R_{t+1} = 1.10$. If an asset earns arithmetic returns of $r_{t+1} = (1.10) - 1 = 10\%$ for three periods, then we earn

$$W_{t+3} = (1 + r_{t+1})(1 + r_{t+2})(1 + r_{t+3})$$

$$= 1.10 \times 1.10 \times 1.10 = 1.3310$$

$$\neq 1 + r_{t+1} + r_{t+2} + r_{t+3}$$

at the end of three periods. We cannot add arithmetic returns. That is $1.3310 \neq 1 + 3 \times 0.10$, because of the compounding of wealth. Even though arithmetic returns are not additive, in some of the figures in this book, I simply cumulate arithmetic returns—to remove the effects of compounding for aesthetics.

Arithmetic returns are, however, additive across assets. Suppose that asset A has a return of 10%, $r^A_{t+1} = 0.10$ and asset B has a return of 5%, $r^B_{t+1} = 0.05$. Then, if we hold a portfolio of 50% asset A and 50% asset B, the arithmetic portfolio return is

$$r^p_{t+1} = 0.5r^A_{t+1} + 0.5r^B_{t+1} = 0.5 \times 0.10 + 0.5 \times 0.05 = 7.5\%.$$

so arithmetic returns conveniently aggregate in a portfolio.

1.3. LOG RETURNS

Log returns, or *continuously compounded returns*, are defined as the natural logarithm of gross returns and I denote them with an upper bar:

$$\text{Log return } \bar{r}_{t+1} = \ln(R_{t+1}) = \ln(1 + r_{t+1}). \qquad (A.3)$$

Or we can equivalently state everything in terms of gross returns:

$$R_{t+1} = \exp(\bar{r}_{t+1}) = 1 + r_{t+1}.$$

Log returns are also called *growth rates,* and growth occurs *exponentially.* That is, growth will eventually cause a portfolio to increase to infinity or decrease to zero in the long run.

The log return corresponding to an arithmetic return of 10% is $\bar{r}_{t+1} = \ln(1.10) = 9.53\%$. The arithmetic return of $r_{t+1} = 10\%$ and the log return of $\bar{r}_{t+1} = 9.53\%$ are both equivalent because they represent the same end-of-period wealth of \$1.10, or gross return of $R_{t+1} = 1.10$, for every \$1 invested at the beginning of the period. With the arithmetic return, the interest is returned only at the end of the period. In contrast, the log return assumes that interest is earned at every instant (hence returns are said to be "continuously compounded"). Since interest compounds on the interest at every moment in time, the continuously compounded interest rate does not need to be as high—it is only 9.53%—to reach the same end of period wealth of 1.10 at the end of the period.

Log returns aggregate over time. If we have an asset earning gross returns of $R_{t+1} = 1.10$ for three years, we can sum three years of log returns of $\bar{r}_{t+1} = 9.53\%$ to obtain the cumulated wealth at the end of three years:

$$W_{t+3} = \exp(\bar{r}_{t+1}) \exp(\bar{r}_{t+2}) \exp(\bar{r}_{t+3})$$

$$= \exp(\bar{r}_{t+1} + \bar{r}_{t+2} + \bar{r}_{t+3})$$

$$= \exp(3 \times 0.0953) = 1.3310$$

Log returns do not aggregate across assets. Suppose we take asset A with a gross return of $R_{t+1}^{A} = 1.10$ and asset B with a gross return of $R_{t+1}^{B} = 1.05$. These assets have log returns of $\bar{r}_{t+1}^{A} = \ln(1.10) = 9.53\%$ and $\bar{r}_{t+1}^{B} = \ln(1.05) = 4.88\%$, respectively. If we hold a portfolio of 50% asset A and 50% asset B, then the log return of this portfolio is

$$r_{t+1}^{p} = \ln(0.5 \exp(\bar{r}_{t+1}^{A}) + 0.5 \exp(\bar{r}_{t+1}^{B}))$$

$$= \ln(0.5 \exp(0.0953) + 0.5 \exp(0.0448)) = \ln(1.075) = 7.23\%$$

$$\neq 0.5 \times \bar{r}_{t+1}^{A} + 0.5 \times \bar{r}_{t+1}^{B}.$$

That is, the log return of the portfolio is not the weighted average of each stock's log return.

1.4. ARITHMETIC VERSUS LOG RETURNS

Many practitioners and academics have long argued about whether it is better to use arithmetic or log returns.[1] Whether you use arithmetic or log returns is like

---

[1] The debate continues today. Advocates of the arithmetic mean typically like the fact that it is unbiased. Those who prefer log returns note that they measure the actual change in wealth, and they

arguing whether you should use pounds or kilograms in your recipe to make apple pie. They represent the same thing; it is a question of which is more useful. What is crucial is the recipe itself—you need the right model for the returns; otherwise it doesn't matter whether you measure your apples in pounds or kilos.

In analyzing portfolios (e.g., as we do in chapter 7), it is easiest to use arithmetic returns because they aggregate when we form portfolios. When we analyze asset returns across time (e.g., as we do in chapters 8 and 11, which focus on long-run equity return predictability and how different assets hedge inflation in the long run, respectively), we use log returns because we can sum them across time. In both instances, we describe the same thing—returns.

This is not to say that whether you use pounds or kilos does not matter. As every dieter knows, you can't switch between calories or kilojoules without the risk of severely wrecking your waistline. Consider the following return process for a gross return:

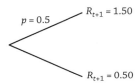

which is a 50%–50% sequence of winning or losing plus or minus 50% arithmetic returns and the probabilities are independent over time. The investor will eventually lose all her capital investing in this asset. (When you gain 50% and lose 50% you end up losing 25%!) The mean arithmetic return is zero, $E[r_{t+1}] = \frac{1}{2} \times 0.5 + \frac{1}{2} \times -0.5 = 0$ and may give a misleading picture of the long-run return of cumulated wealth. In the long run, your wealth shrinks to zero! The mean log return is

$$E[\bar{r}_{t+1}] = 0.5 \times \ln(1.5) + 0.5 \times \ln(0.5) = -14.38\%,$$

so the negative sign at least indicates that this strategy loses wealth over time. The mean log return is also called the *geometric mean*. (When returns are risky, the arithmetic mean is always greater than the geometric mean.[2]) But the better way is to look at the full distribution of returns, which is captured by the probability distribution function or density function (see chapter 2). The density function of this lottery is very simple—it provides you with risk (there is dispersion or variance) but zero return. You must have a good reason to invest in the first place,

---

automatically assume that capital is reinvested. For some references see Cooper (1996), Jacquier, Kane, and Marcus (2003), and Missiakoulis, Dimitrios, and Etriotis (2010).

[2] An approximate relation is $E[\bar{r}_{t+1}] \approx E[r_{t+1}] - \frac{1}{2}\sigma^2$, where σ^2 is the variance of arithmetic returns. This difference is a Jensen's inequality term, and it drives the rebalancing premium. See chapter 4.

right? From this point of view, the mean and variance of arithmetic returns are useful statistical measures.

Here's another example where using the arithmetic mean gets it right and using geometric means is wrong. Suppose that asset A and asset B have average gross returns of $E[R_{t+1}^A] = 1.5$ and $E[R_{t+1}^B] = 0.5$, respectively. An investor holding 50% of asset A and 50% of asset B breaks even, on average, with the arithmetic mean being zero. Taking the average of asset A and B's geometric returns would actually result in a number less than zero. Log returns do not aggregate across portfolios. In both examples, however, we are better off looking at the full distribution of returns.

ACKNOWLEDGMENTS

Factor investing is all about coping with—and exploiting—bad times. I've had the opposite experience writing this book—I've genuinely enjoyed some good times. That's because I've been fortunate to have many people in my life who have made this project a pleasure.

For their able research assistance, I thank Andrés Ayala, Bingxu Chen, Katrina Evtimova, Sergiy Gorovyy, Rudy Loo-Kung, Christy Wong, and Yu Zhang.

My work for Norway, especially my consulting for Norges Bank and the Ministry of Finance, has hugely influenced my thinking, and I am truly honored to have worked with many excellent people there. In particular I thank Sigbjørn Alte Berg, Pål Haugerud, Knut Kjær, Martin Skancke, Yngve Slyngstad, and all the members of Norges Bank, Norges Bank Investment Management, and the Ministry of Finance with whom I have worked. I also thank my fellow advisers to Norway: Antti Ilmanen, Gerlof de Vrij, and Sung Cheng Chih. I feel that I learned more from all of you than what I contributed in our meetings. I especially thank Antti, himself the author of a superb book called *Expected Returns: An Investor's Guide to Harvesting Market Rewards*, who generously provided detailed comments on the first draft of every chapter.

Most of my research focuses on asset management issues, and in my life as a scholar I've been blessed with co-authors who have taught me a great deal. It has been exciting working together—thank you. I acknowledge those whose joint research appears in this book: Geert Bekaert, Vineer Bhansali, Jean Boivin, Nick Bollen, Marie Brière, Bingxu Chen, Joe Chen, Sen Dong, Will Goetzmann, Sergiy Gorovyy, Rick Green, Bob Hodrick, Greg van Inwegen, Jun Liu, Francis Longstaff, Rudy Loo-Kung, Knut Kjær, Dennis Kristensen, Angela Maddaloni, Neil Nabar, Dimitris Papanikolaou, Monika Piazzesi, Matt Rhodes-Kropf, Stephen Schaefer, Assaf Shtauber, Ombretta Signore, Morten Sorensen, Suresh Sundaresan, Paul Tetlock, Allan Timmermann, Maxim Ulrich, Sam Wald, Min Wei, Mark Westerfield, Yuhang Xing, Xiaoyan Zhang, and Rui Zhao. Thank you to many of you for feedback, and also thank you to my co-author Ludovic Phalippou, although our research wasn't finished in time for the book.

I am privileged to have so many excellent colleagues at Columbia Business School, and I especially thank Patrick Bolton, Martin Cherkes, Kent Daniel, John Donaldson, Bob Hodrick, Gur Huberman, Wei Jiang, Lars Lochstoer, Chris Mayer, Andrea Prat, Lynne Sagalyn, Suresh Sundaresan, Paul Tetlock, Neng Wang, and Steve Zeldes for excellent comments and help in honing my analysis—especially with respect to the material outside my primary research focus.

One of the things that inspired me to write this book was the Asset Management class that I teach at Columbia. I am grateful both to Ann Kaplan and to the Program for Financial Studies at Columbia Business School for sponsoring development of the class and, of course, to my students. I especially thank Andrés Ayala, my diligent teaching assistant, for helping me develop and manage the class in the first two years.

The book is full of my case studies, and I thank Columbia CaseWorks and all my collaborators: Sarah Abbott, Jeremy Abrams, Josh Brumberger, David Denison, Elizabeth Gordon, Sterling Gunn, Brian Herscovici, Hilde Hovnanian, Bill Jacques, Ann Kaplan, Kate Permut, Valborg Lie, Gina Raimondo, Don Raymond, Jim Scott, Aslak Skancke, Rona Smith, Elizabeth Unger, and also several of the individuals I've acknowledged before. Thank you to those who also read and commented on the book draft. Jim also co-taught a class on Quantitative Investments with me, and some of the material from that class found its way into this book.

A special thank you to Peter Christoffersen and Barbara Ostdiek who adopted the book for their classes before it was even half finished. Their comments on the work in progress were very useful. I am grateful to many others for commenting on the manuscript, spotting errors, and offering helpful suggestions (some of which I ignored—it's not you, it's me): Jonathan Berk, David Chambers, James Choi, Emanuel Derman, Charles Fishkin, Ken Frier, Ken French, Francisco Gomes, Robin Greenwood (what a great suggestion of using Janus as the motivating example of chapter 16!), Henry Hansmann, David Hultstrom, Brant Maller, Olivia Mitchell, Tarun Ramadorai, Josh Rauh, Bill Sharpe, Arnie Wood, Dimitri Vayanos, Luis Viceira, and Lu Zheng. I also thank Cam Harvey and John Cochrane, who identified themselves as reviewers when I proposed the book and whose comments I took into consideration as I wrote it. Thank you, Dan Akst, for reading and commenting on the whole manuscript.

Terry Vaughn had the confidence to welcome me to Oxford University Press (OUP). Thank you to my editor Scott Paris, Cathryn Vaulman, and the rest of the OUP team for shepherding a first-timer through the book publishing process.

Most of all, I am grateful to my family. My wife and children have patiently tolerated their father's preoccupation over the last two years, and I cannot thank them enough. At the heart of this book is the role of bad times in factor investing; my family, by contrast, has brought me incredible joy and represents the greatest possible incarnation of good times.

REFERENCES

A

Aarbu, K. O., and F. Schroyen, 2009, Mapping risk aversion in Norway using hypothetical income gambles, working paper, Norwegian School of Economics and Business Administration.

Abel, A. B., 1990, Asset prices under habit formation and catching up with the Joneses, *American Economic Review*, 80, 38–42.

Abel, A. B., 2001, Will bequests attenuate the predicted meltdown in stock prices when baby boomers retire? *Review of Economics and Statistics*, 83, 589–595.

Accominotti, O., and D. Chambers, 2013, The returns to currency trading: Evidence from the Interwar period, working paper, University of Cambridge.

Acemoglu, D., and J. A. Robinson, 2012, *Why Nations Fail: The Origins of Power, Prosperity, and Poverty*, Crown Business, New York.

Acharya, V. V., O. Gottschalg, M. Hahn, and C. Kehoe, 2013, Corporate governance and value creation: Evidence from private equity, *Review of Financial Studies*, 26, 368–402.

Ackermann, C., R. McEnally, and D. Ravenscraft, 1999, The performance of hedge funds: Risk, return and incentives, *Journal of Finance*, 54, 833–874.

Adams, J. C., S. A. Mansi, and T. Nishikawa, 2010, Internal governance mechanisms and operational performance: Evidence from index mutual funds, *Review of Financial Studies*, 23, 1261–86.

Adler, M., and B. Dumas, 1983, International portfolio choice and corporation finance: A synthesis, *Journal of Finance*, 38, 925–84.

Admati, A. R., and P. Pfleiderer, 1997, Does it all add up? Benchmarks and the compensation of active portfolio managers, *Journal of Business*, 70, 323–350.

Agarwal, V., N. D. Daniel, and N. Naik, 2004, Flows, performance, and management incentives in hedge funds, working paper, London Business School.

Agarwal, V., N. D. Daniel, and N. Naik, 2009, Role of managerial incentives and discretion in hedge fund performance, *Journal of Finance*, 64, 2221–2256.

Agarwal, V., N. D. Daniel, and N. Y. Naik, 2011, Do hedge funds manage their reported returns? *Review of Financial Studies*, 24, 3281–3320.

Agarwal, V., V. Fos, and W. Jiang, 2013, Inferring reporting-related biases in hedge fund skill from hedge fund equity holdings, *Management Science*, 59, 1271–1289.

Agarwal, V., W. Fung, Y. C. Loon, and N. Y. Naik, 2011, Risk and return in convertible arbitrage: Evidence from the convertible bond market, *Journal of Empirical Finance*, 18, 175–194.

Agarwal, V., and N. Y. Naik, 2000, On taking the "alternative' route": The risks, rewards, and performance persistence of hedge funds, *Journal of Alternative Investments*, 2, 6–23.

Agarwal, V., and N. Y. Naik, 2004, Risks and portfolio decisions involving hedge funds, *Review of Financial Studies*, 17, 63–98.

Agarwal, V., and S. Ray, 2012, Determinants and implications of fee changes in the hedge fund industry, working paper, Georgia State University.

Aggarwal, R. K., and P. Jorion, 2012, Is there a cost to transparency? *Financial Analysts Journal*, 68, 108–123.

Aghion, P., and J. Tirole, 1997, Formal and real authority in organizations, *Journal of Political Economy*, 105, 1–29.

Ahearne, A. G., W. L. Griever, and F. E. Warnock, 2004, Information costs and home bias: An analysis of U.S. holdings of foreign assets, *Journal of International Economics*, 62, 313–336.

Aiken, A. L., C. P. Clifford, and J. Ellis, 2013, Out of the dark: Hedge fund reporting biases and commercial biases, *Review of Financial Studies*, 26, 208–243.

Akerlof, G. A., 1970, The market for "lemons": Quality uncertainty and the market mechanism, *Quarterly Journal of Economics*, 84, 488–500.

Allen, F., and R. Michaely, R., 1995, Dividend policy, in Jarrow, R. A., V. Maksimovic, and W. T. Ziemba, eds., *Operation Research and Management Science*, Elsevier Science, Amsterdam, pp. 793–837.

Almazan, A., K. C. Brown, M. Carlson, and D. A. Chapman, 2004, Why constrain your mutual fund manager? *Journal of Financial Economics*, 73, 289–321.

Alonso, W., 1964, *Location and Land Use*, Harvard University Press, Cambridge, MA.

Alvaredo, F., A. B. Atkinson, T. Piketty, and E. Saez, 2013, The top 1% in international and historical perspective, *Journal of Economic Perspectives*, 27, 3–20.

Amaya, D., P. Christoffersen, K. Jacobs, and A. Vasquez, 2012, Does realized skewness predict the cross-section of equity returns? Working paper, University of Toronto.

Ambrose, B. W., and P. Linneman, 2001, Organizational structure and REIT operating characteristics, *Journal of Real Estate Research*, 21, 141–162.

Ameriks, J., and S. P. Zeldes, 2004, How do household portfolio shares vary with age? working paper, Columbia Business School.

Amihud, Y., 2002, Illiquidity and stock returns: Cross-section and time-series effects, *Journal of Financial Markets*, 5, 31–56.

Amihud, Y., and R. Goyenko, 2013, Mutual fund's R^2 as a predictor of performance, *Review of Financial Studies*, 26, 667–694.

Amihud, Y., and H. Mendelson, 1991, Liquidity, maturity, and the yields on U.S. Treasury securities, *Journal of Finance*, 46, 1411–1425.

Amihud, Y., H. Mendelson, and L. H. Pedersen, 2005, Liquidity and asset prices, *Foundations and Trends in Finance*, 1, 269–364.

Amromin, G., J. Huang, and C. Sialm, 2007, The tradeoff between mortgage prepayments and tax-deferred retirement savings, *Journal of Public Economics*, 91, 2014–2040.

Andersen, T. G., T. Bollerselv, P. F. Christoffersen, and F. X. Diebold, 2006, Volatility and correlation forecasting, in Elliott, G., C. W. J. Granger, and A. Timmermann, eds., *Handbook of Economic Forecasting, Elsevier*, pp. 778–878.

Anderson, E. W., E. Ghysels, and J. L. Juergens, 2009, The impact of risk and uncertainty on expected returns, *Journal of Financial Economics*, 94, 233–263.

Anderson, S., and K. M. Nielsen, 2011, Participation constraints in the stock market: Evidence from unexpected inheritance due to sudden death, Review of Financial Studies, 24, 1667–1697.

Andonov, A., R. Bauer, and M. Cremers, 2011, Can large pension funds beat the market? Asset allocation, market timing, security selection, and the limits of liquidity, SSRN working paper.

Andonov, A., R. Bauer, and M. Cremers, 2012, Pension fund asset allocation and liability discount rates: Camouflage and reckless risk taking by U.S. public plans? SSRN working paper.

Ang, A., 2011, Illiquid assets, *CFA Institute Conference Proceedings Quarterly*, 28, 12–20.

Ang, A., 2012a, The four benchmarks of sovereign wealth funds, in Bolton, P., F. Samama, and J. Stiglitz, eds., *Sovereign Wealth Funds and Long-Term Investing*, Columbia University Press, New York, pp. 94–105.

Ang, A., 2012b, Predicting dividends in log-linear present value models, *Pacific-Basin Finance Journal*, 20, 151–171.

Ang, A., and G. Bekaert, 2002, International asset allocation with regime shifts, *Review of Financial Studies*, 15, 1137–1187.

Ang, A., and G. Bekaert, 2004, How do regimes affect asset allocation? *Financial Analysts Journal*, 60, 86–99.

Ang, A., and G. Bekaert, 2007, Stock return predictability: Is it there? *Review of Financial Studies*, 20, 651–707.

Ang, A., G. Bekaert, and J. Liu, 2005, Why stocks may disappoint, *Journal of Financial Economics*, 76, 471–508.

Ang, A., G. Bekaert, and M. Wei, 2007, Do macro variables, asset markets, or surveys forecast inflation better? *Journal of Monetary Economics*, 54, 1163–1212.

Ang, A., G. Bekaert, and M. Wei, 2008, The term structure of real rates and expected inflation, *Journal of Finance*, 63, 797–849.

Ang, A., V. Bhansali, and Y. Xing, 2010a, Build America bonds, *Journal of Fixed Income*, 20, 67–73.

Ang, A., V. Bhansali, and Y. Xing, 2010b, Taxes on tax-exempt bonds, *Journal of Finance*, 65, 565–601.

Ang, A., V. Bhansali, and Y. Xing, 2012, Decomposing municipal yield spreads: Credit, liquidity, and tax, working paper, Columbia University.

Ang, A., J. Boivin, S. Dong, and R. Loo-Kung, 2011, Monetary policy shifts and the term structure, *Review of Economic Studies*, 78, 429–457.

Ang, A., and N. Bollen, 2010a, Locked up by a lockup: Valuing liquidity as a real option, *Financial Management*, 39, 1069–1095.

Ang, A., and N. Bollen, 2010b, When hedge funds block the exits, working paper, Columbia Business School.

Ang, A., M. Brière, and O. Signore, 2012, Inflation and individual equities, *Financial Analysts Journal*, 68, 36–55.

Ang, A., B. Chen, and S. Sundaresan, 2013, Liability driven investment with downside risk, *Journal of Portfolio Management*, 40, 71–87.

Ang, A., and J. Chen, 2002, Asymmetric correlations of equity portfolios, *Journal of Financial Economics*, 63, 443–494.

Ang, A., and J. Chen, 2007, CAPM over the long run: 1926–2001, *Journal of Empirical Finance*, 14, 1–40.

Ang, A., J. Chen, and Y. Xing, 2006, Downside risk, *Review of Financial Studies*, 19, 1191–1239.

Ang, A, S. Dong, and M. Piazzesi, 2007, No-arbitrage Taylor rules, working paper, Columbia Business School.

Ang, A., W. N. Goetzmann, and S. Schaefer, 2009, Evaluation of active management of the Norwegian Government Pension Fund–Global, Report to the Norwegian Ministry of Finance.

Ang, A., W. N. Goetzmann, and S. Schaefer, 2011, Efficient market theory and evidence: Implications for active management, *Foundations and Trends*, 5, 157–242.

Ang, A., S. Gorovyy, G. B. van Inwegen, 2011, Hedge fund leverage, *Journal of Financial Economics*, 102, 102–126.

Ang, A., and R. C. Green, 2011, Lowering borrowing costs for states and municipalities through CommonMuni, The Hamilton Project Discussion Paper 2011-01, Brookings Institution.

Ang, A., R. J. Hodrick, Y. Xing, and X. Zhang, 2006, The cross section of volatility and expected returns, *Journal of Finance*, 61, 259–299.

Ang, A., R. J. Hodrick, Y. Xing, and X. Zhang, 2009, High idiosyncratic volatility and low returns: International and further U.S. evidence, *Journal of Financial Economics*, 91, 1–23.

Ang, A., and J. Liu, 2001, A general affine earnings valuation model, *Review of Accounting Studies*, 6, 397–425.

Ang, A., and J. Liu, 2007, Risk, returns, and dividends, *Journal of Financial Economics*, 85, 1–38.

Ang, A., and K. Kjær, 2011, Investing for the long run, in Franzen, T., ed., *A Decade of Challenges: A Collection of Essays on Pensions and Investments*, Andra AP-fonden, Second Swedish National Pension Fund – AP2, pp. 94–111.

Ang, A., and D. Kristensen, 2012, Testing conditional factor models, *Journal of Financial Economics*, 106, 132–156.

Ang, A., and F. A. Longstaff, 2013, Systemic sovereign credit risk: Lessons from the U.S. and Europe, *Journal of Monetary Economics*, 60, 493–510.

Ang, A., and A. Maddaloni, 2005, Do demographic changes affect risk premiums? Evidence from international data, *Journal of Business*, 78, 341–379.

Ang, A., N. Nabar, and S. Wald, 2013, Searching for a common factor in public and private real estate returns, *Journal of Portfolio Management*, 39, 120–133.

Ang, A., D. Papanikolaou, and M. M. Westerfield, 2013, Portfolio choice with illiquid assets, forthcoming *Management Science*.

Ang, A., and M. Piazzesi, 2003, A no-arbitrage vector autoregression of term structure dynamics with macroeconomic and latent variables, *Journal of Monetary Economics*, 50, 756–787.

Ang, A., M. Piazzesi, and M. Wei, 2006, What does the yield curve tell us about GDP growth? *Journal of Econometrics*, 131, 359–403.

Ang, A., M. Rhodes-Kropf, and R. Zhao, 2008, Do funds-of-funds deserve their fees-on-fees? *Journal of Investment Management*, 6, 34–58.

Ang, A., and M. Sorensen, 2012, Risks, returns, and optimal holdings of private equity: A survey of existing approaches, *Quarterly Journal of Finance*, 2, DOI: 10.1142/S2010139212500115.

Ang, A., A. Shtauber, and P. Tetlock, 2013, Asset pricing in the dark: The cross section of over-the-counter equities, forthcoming *Review of Financial Studies*.

Ang, A., and A. Timmermann, 2012, Regime changes and financial markets, *Annual Review of Financial Economics*, 4, 313–337.

Ang, A., and M. Ulrich, 2012, Nominal bonds, real bonds, and equity, working paper, Columbia University.

Ang, A., and X. Zhang, 2012, Price-to-earnings ratios: Growth and discount rates, in Hammond, B., M. Leibowitz, and L. Siegel, eds., *Rethinking the Equity Risk Premium*, Research Foundation of the CFA Institute, pp. 130–142.

Angeletos, G.-M., 2002, Fiscal policy with noncontingent debt and the optimal maturity structure, *Quarterly Journal of Economics*, 117, 1105–1131.

Aragon, G. O., 2007, Share restrictions and asset pricing: Evidence from the hedge fund industry, *Journal of Financial Economics*, 83, 33–58.

Arnold, M. B., 2011, Timor-Leste in 2010, *Asian Survey*, 51, 215–220.

Artzner, P., F. Delbaen, J.-M. Eber, and D. Heath, 1999, Coherent measures of risk, *Mathematical Finance*, 9, 203–228.

Arnott, R. D., and D. B. Chaves, 2011, Demographic changes, financial markets, and the economy, SSRN working paper.

Arnott, R. D., J. Hsu, and P. Moore, 2005, Fundamental indexation, *Financial Analysts Journal*, 61, 83–99.

Arrow, K., 1971, *Essays in the Theory of Risk-Bearing*, Markham.

Asness, C., 2004, An alternative future: Part II, *Journal of portfolio Management*, 31, 8–23.

Asness, C. S., A. Frazzini, and L. H. Pedersen, 2012, Leverage aversion and risk parity, *Financial Analysts Journal*, 68, 47–59.

Asness, C. S., R. Israelov, and J. M. Liew, 2011, International diversification works (eventually), *Financial Analysts Journal*, 67, 24–38.

Asness, C. S., T. J. Moskowitz, and L. H. Pedersen, 2013, Value and momentum everywhere, *Journal of Finance*, 68, 929–985.

Attanasio, O. P., and G. Weber, 2010, Consumption and saving: Models of intertemporal allocation and their implications for public policy, *Journal of Economic Literature*, 48, 693–751.

Auerbach, A., J. Gokhale, and L. J. Kotlikoff, 1991, Generational accounts: A meaningful alternative to deficit accounting, in Bradford, D., ed., *Tax Policy and the Economy*, vol. 5, MIT Press, pp. 55–110.

Avramov, D., and R. Wermers, 2006, Investing in mutual funds when returns are predictable, *Journal of Financial Economics*, 81, 339–377.

Avramov, D., and G. Zhou, 2010, Bayesian portfolio analysis, *Annual Reviews in Financial Economics*, 2, 25–47.

Axelson, U., T. Jenkinson, P. Strömberg, and M. S. Weisbach, 2012, Borrow cheap, buy high? The determinants of leverage and pricing in buyouts, *forthcoming Journal of Finance*.

B

Backus, D. K., and A. W. Gregory, 1993, Theoretical relations between risk premiums and conditional variances, *Journal of Business and Economic Statistics*, 11, 177–185.

Backus, D. K., A. W. Gregory, and S. E. Zin, 1989, Risk premiums in the term structure: Evidence from artificial economies, *Journal of Monetary Economics*, 24, 371–99.

Baker, M., and J. Wurgler 2007, Investor sentiment in the stock market, *Journal of Economic Perspectives*, 21, 129–157.

Baker, M., B. Bradley, and J. Wurgler, 2011, Benchmarks as limits to arbitrage: Understanding the low volatility anomaly, *Financial Analysts Journal*, 67, 1–15.

Baker, M., J. Wurgler, and Y. Yu, 2012, Global, local, and contagious investor sentiment, *Journal of Financial Economics*, 104, 272–285.

Baks, K. P., A. Metrick, and J. Wachter, 2001, Should investors avoid all actively managed mutual funds? A study in Bayesian performance evaluation, *Journal of Finance*, 56, 45–85.

Bakshi, G., and N. Kapadia, 2003, Delta hedged gains and the negative market volatility risk premium, *Review of Financial Studies*, 16, 527–566.

Bali, T., and N. Cakici, 2008, Idiosyncratic volatility and the cross section of expected returns, *Journal of Financial and Quantitative Analysis*, 43, 29–58.

Bali, T., N. Cakici, and R. F. Whitelaw, 2011, Maxing out: Stocks as lotteries and the cross section of expected returns, *Journal of Financial Economics*, 99, 427–446.

Bansal, R., 2007, Long run risks and financial markets, *Federal Reserve Bank of St. Louis Review*, July/August, 283–299.

Bansal, R., R. F. Dittmar, and C. T. Lundblad, 2005, Consumption, dividends and the cross-section of equity returns, *Journal of Finance*, 50, 1639–1672.

Bansal, R., D. Kiku, I. Shaliastovich, and A. Yaron, 2011, Volatility, the macroeconomy and asset prices, working paper, Wharton.

Bansal, R., and I. Shaliastovich, 2010, A long-run risks explanation of predictability puzzles in bond and currency markets, working paper, Duke University.

Bansal, R. and A. Yaron, 2004, Risks for the long run: A potential resolution of asset pricing puzzles, *Journal of Finance*, 59, 1481–1509.

Banz, R. W., 1981, The relationship between return and market value of common stocks, *Journal of Financial Economics*, 9, 3–18.

Bao, J., J. Pan, and J. Wang, 2011, The illiquidity of corporate bonds, *Journal of Finance*, 66, 911–946.

Barber, B. M., and T. Odean, 2000, Trading is hazardous to your wealth: The common stock investment performance of individual investors, *Journal of Finance*, 55, 773–806.

Barber, B. M., and T. Odean, 2003, Are individual investors tax savvy? Evidence from retail and discount brokerage accounts, *Journal of Public Economics*, 88, 419–442.

Barber, B. M., and T. Odean, 2011, The behavior of individual investors, SSRN working paper.

Barber, B. M., T. Odean, and L. Zheng, 2005, Out of sight, out of mind: The effects of expenses on mutual fund flows, *Journal of Business*, 78, 2095–2119.

Barberis, N., and M. Huang, 2001, Mental accounting, loss aversion, and individual stock returns, *Journal of Finance*, 56, 1247–1292.

Barberis, N., A. Shleifer, and R. Vishny, 1998, A model of investor sentiment, *Journal of Financial Economics*, 49, 307–343.

Barberis, N., and R. Thaler, 2003, A survey of behavioral finance, in Constantinides, G., R. Stulz, and M. Harris, eds., *Handbook of the Economics of Finance*, Elsevier, Boston, pp. 1051–1121.

Barkham, R., and D. Geltner, 1995, Price discovery in American and British property markets, *Real Estate Economics*, 23, 21–44.

Barro, R., 1974, Are government bonds net wealth? *Journal of Political Economy*, 82, 1095–1117.

Barro, R. J., 2009, Rare disasters, asset prices, and welfare costs, *American Economic Review*, 99, 243–264.

Barro, R. J., and J. F. Ursua, 2011, Rare macroeconomic disasters, NBER working paper, 17328.

Basu, S., 1977, Investment performance of common stocks in relation to their price–earnings ratios: a test of the efficient market hypothesis, *Journal of Finance*, 32, 663–682.

Basu, S., J. G. Fernald, and M. S. Kimball, 2006, Are technology improvements contractionary? *American Economic Review*, 96, 1418–1448.

Bauer, R. M. M. J., K. J. M. Cremers, and R. G. P. Frehen, 2009, Pension fund performance and costs: Small is beautiful, SSRN working paper.

Baxter, M., and U. J. Jermann, 1997, The international diversification puzzle is worse than you think, *American Economic Review*, 87, 170–180.

Bebchuk, L. A., A. Cohen, and C. C. Y. Wang, 2013, Learning and the disappearing association between governance and returns, *Journal of Financial Economics*, 108, 323–348.

Bebchuk, L. A., and M. S. Weisbach, 2010, The state of corporate governance research, *Review of Financial Studies*, 25, 341–376.

Becker, G. S., 1964, *Human Capital: A Theoretical and Empirical Analysis, with Special Reference to Education*, University of Chicago Press, Chicago.

Bekaert, G., and X. Wang, 2010, Inflation risk, *Economic Policy*, October, 755–806.

Bekaert, G., and G. Wu, 2000, Asymmetric volatility and risk in equity markets, *Review of Financial Studies*, 13, 1–42.

Benartzi, S., 2001, Excessive extrapolation and the allocation of 401(k) accounts to company stock, *Journal of Finance*, 56, 1747–1764.

Benartzi, S., A. Previtero, and R. H. Thaler, 2011, Annuity puzzles, *Journal of Public Economics*, 82, 29–62.

Ben-David, I., F. Franzoni, and R. Moussawi, 2011, ETFs, Arbitrage, and Contagion, Working Paper 2011–20, Dice Center, Ohio State University.

Bengen, W., 1994, Determining withdrawal rates using historical data, *Journal of Financial Planning*, 7, 171–180.

Benhabib, J., S. Schmitt-Grohe, and M. Uribe, 2001, Monetary policy and multiple equilibria, *American Economic Review*, 91, 167–186.

Bennedsen, M., K. M. Nielsen, F. Pérez-González, and D. Wolfenzon, 2007, Inside the family firm: The role of families in succession decisions and performance, *Quarterly Journal of Economics*, 122, 647–691.

Bennedsen, M., F. Pérez-González, and D. Wolfenzon, D., 2010, The governance of family firms, in Baker, H. K., and R. Anderson, eds., *Corporate Governance: A Synthesis of Theory, Research, and Practice*, Wiley, Hoboken, N.J., doi: 10.1002/9781118258439.ch19.

Ben-Rephael, A., O. Kadan, and A. Wohl, 2008, The diminishing liquidity premium, working paper, Tel Aviv University.

Benzoni, L., P. Collin-Dufresne, and R. S. Goldstein, 2007, Portfolio choice over the life cycle when the stock and labor markets are cointegrated, *Journal of Finance*, 62, 2123–2167.

Bergstresser, D., J. M. R. Chalmers, and P. Tufano, 2009, Assessing the costs and benefits of brokers in the mutual fund industry, *Review of Financial Studies*, 22, 4129–4156.

Bergstresser, D., and J. Pontiff, 2009, Investment taxation and portfolio performance, forthcoming *Journal of Public Economics*.

Bergstresser, D., and J. Poterba, 2002, Do after-tax returns affect mutual fund inflows? *Journal of Financial Economics*, 63, 381–414.

Bergstresser, D., and J. Poterba, 2004, Asset allocation and asset location: Household evidence from the survey of consumer finances, *Journal of Public Economics*, 88, 1893–1915.

Berk, J. B., and R. C. Green, 2004, Mutual fund flows and performance in rational markets, *Journal of Political Economy*, 112, 1269–1295.

Berk, J., R. Green, and V. Naik, 1999, Optimal investment, growth options, and security returns, *Journal of Finance*, 54, 1553–1607.

Berk, J. B., and R. Stanton, 2007, Managerial ability, compensation, and the closed-end fund discount, *Journal of Finance*, 62, 529–556.

Bernanke, B., and A. Blinder, 1988, Credit, money, and aggregate demand, *American Economic Review Papers and Proceedings*, 78, 435–439.

Bernard, C., and P. P. Boyle, 2009, Mr. Madoff's amazing returns: An analysis of the split strike conversion strategy, *Journal of Derivatives*, 17, 62–76.

Bernstein, P. L., 1989, *Against the Gods: The Remarkable Story of Risk*, Wiley, New York.

Bernstein, P. L., 1992, *Capital Ideas: The Improbable Origins of Modern Wall Street*, Free Press, New York.

Bernstein, S., J. Lerner, and A. Schoar, 2013, The investment strategies of sovereign wealth funds, *Journal of Economic Perspectives*, 27, 219–238.

Bernstein, W. J., 2010, *The Four Pillars of Investing: Lessons for Building a Winning Portfolio*, McGraw Hill, New York.

Beshears, J., J. J. Choi, D. Laibson, B. C. Madrian, and S. P. Zeldes, 2012, What makes annuitization more appealing? NBER Working Paper 18575.

Bessembinder, H., 1992, Systematic risk, hedging pressure, and risk premiums in futures markets, *Review of Financial Studies*, 5, 637–667.

Bessembinder, H., A. Carrion, L. Tuttle, and K. Venkataraman, 2012, Predatory or sunshine trading? Evidence from crude oil ETF rolls, working paper, University of Utah.

Betermier, S., T. Jansson, C. Parlour, and J. Walden, 2012, Hedging labor income risk, *Journal of Financial Economics*, 105, 622–639.

Bewley, T. F., 1977, The permanent income hypothesis: A theoretical formulation, *Journal of Economic Theory*, 16, 262–292.

Bhansali, V., 2007, Volatility and the carry trade, *Journal of Fixed Income*, 17, Winter, 72–84.

Bhattacharya, S., and P. Pfleiderer, 1985, Delegated portfolio management, *Journal of Economic Theory*, 36, 1–25.

Bhattacharya, S., A. Dasgupta, A. Guembel, and A. Prat, 2008, Incentives in funds management: A literature overview, in Boot, A., and A. Thakor, *The Handbook of Financial Intermediation and Banking*, Elsevier, Boston, pp. 285–308.

Biais, B., and R. C. Green, 2005, The microstructure of the bond market in the 20th century, working paper, Carnegie Mellon University.

van Binsbergen, J. H., M. W. Brandt, and R. S. J. Koijen, 2008, Optimal decentralized investment management, *Journal of Finance*, 63, 1849–1895.

Black, F., 1972, Capital market equilibrium with restricted borrowing, *Journal of Business*, 45, 444–455.

Black, F., 1976, Studies of stock price volatility changes, *Proceedings of the 1976 Meetings of the American Statistical Association, Business and Economical Statistics Section*, American Statistical Association, pp. 117–181.

Black, F., 1980, The tax consequences of long-run pension policy, *Financial Analysts Journal*, 36, 1–28.

Black, F., 1993, Beta and return, *Journal of Portfolio Management*, 20, 8–18.

Black, F., 1989, Should you use stocks to hedge your pension liability? *Financial Analysts Journal*, 45, 10–12.

Black, F., M. C. Jensen, and M. S. Scholes, 1972, The capital asset pricing model: Some empirical tests, in Jensen, M. C., ed., *Studies in the Theory of Capital Markets*, Praeger, New York.

Black, F., and R. Litterman, 1991, Asset allocation: Combining investor views with market equilibrium, *Journal of Fixed Income*, 1, September, 7–18.

Black, F., and M. S. Scholes, 1973, The pricing of options and corporate Liabilities, *Journal of Political Economy*, 81, 637–654.

Blake, D., 2006, *Pension Economics*, Wiley, Hoboken, N.J.

Blake, C. R., E. J. Elton, and M. J. Gruber, 1993, The performance of bond mutual funds, *Journal of Business*, 66, 371–403.

Blitz, D. C., and W. de Groot, 2013, Strategic allocation to commodity factor premiums, working paper, Robeco Asset Management.

Blitz, D. C., and P. Van Vliet, 2008, Global tactical cross-asset allocation: Applying value and momentum across asset classes, *Journal of Portfolio Management*, 35, 23–38.

Blume, M. E., 1975, Betas and their regression tendencies, *Journal of Finance*, 30, 785–95.

Blume, M. E., J. Crockett, and I. Friend, 1974, Ownership in the United States: Characteristics and trends, *Survey of Current Business*, 54, 16–40.

Bodie, Z., 1983, Commodity futures as a hedge against inflation, *Journal of Portfolio Management*, 9, 12–17.

Bodie, Z., 1990a, The ABO, the PBO and pension investment policy, *Financial Analysts Journal*, 46, 27–34.

Bodie, Z., 1990b, Inflation, index-linked bonds, and asset allocation, *Journal of Portfolio Management*, 16, 48–53.

Bodie, Z., 1995, On the risk of stocks in the long run, *Financial Analysts Journal*, 51, 18–22.

Bodie, Z., and M. Brière, 2013, Sovereign wealth and risk management: A new framework for optimal asset allocation of sovereign wealth, SSRN working paper.

Bodie, Z., J. B. Detemple, and M. Rindisbacher, 2009, Life cycle finance and the design of pension plans, *Annual Review of Financial Economics*, 1, 249–286.

Bodie, Z., A. Kane, and A. J. Marcus, 2011, *Investments*, 9th ed., McGraw-Hill, Boston.

Bodie, Z., R. C. Merton, and W. F. Samuelson, 1992, Labor supply flexibility and portfolio choice in a life cycle model, *Journal of Economic Dynamics and Control*, 16, 427–449.

Bodie, Z., and R. Taqqu, 2012, *Risk Less and Prosper*, Wiley, Hoboken, N.J.

Bohn, H., 2011, Should public retirement plans be fully funded? *Journal of Pension Economics and Finance*, 10, 195–219.

Bollen, J., H. Mao, and X. Zeng, 2011, Twitter mood predicts the stock market, *Journal of Computational Science*, 2, 1–8.

Bollen, N., and V. Pool, 2008, Conditional return smoothing in the hedge fund industry, *Journal of Financial and Quantitative Analysis*, 43, 267–98.

Bollen, N., and V. Pool, 2009, Hedge fund risk dynamics: Implications for performance appraisal, *Journal of Finance*, 64, 987–1037.

Bollerslev, T., 1986, Generalized autoregressive conditional heteroskedasticity, *Journal of Econometrics*, 31, 307–327.

Bolton, P, and M. Dewatripont, 2005, *Contract Theory*, MIT Press, Cambridge, Mass.

Bonaparte, Y., and A. Kumar, 2013, Political activism, information costs, and stock market participation, *Journal of Financial Economics*, 107, 760–786.

Bond, S. A., and P. Mitchell, 2010, Alpha and persistence in real estate fund performance, *Journal of Real Estate Finance and Economics*, 41, 35–79.

Booth, D. G., and E. F. Fama, 1992, Diversification returns and asset contributions, *Financial Analysts Journal*, 48, 26–32.

Bossaerts, P., P. Ghirardato, S. Guarnaschelli, and W. Zame, 2010, Ambiguity in asset markets: Theory and experiment, *Review of Financial Studies*, 23, 1325–1359.

Boudoukh, J., M. Richardson, and R. F. Whitelaw, 2008, The myth of long–horizon predictability, *Review of Financial Studies*, 21, 1577–1605.

Boudreaux, K. J., 1973, Discounts and premiums on closed-end funds: a study in valuation, *Journal of Finance*, 28, 515–22.

Boyer, B., 2012, Stock related comovement: Fundamentals or labels? forthcoming *Journal of Finance*.

Boyer, B., T. Mitton, and K. Vorkink, 2010, Expected idiosyncratic skewness, *Review of Financial Studies*, 23, 169–202.

Boyson, N. M., 2008, Hedge fund performance persistence: A new approach, *Financial Analysts Journal*, 64, 27–44.

Bradley, H., and R. E. Litan, 2010, Choking the recovery: Why new growth companies aren't going public and unrecognized risks of future market disruptions, research report, Ewing Marion Kauffman Foundation.

Bradley, M., A. Brav, I. Goldstein, and W. Jiang, 2010, Activist arbitrage: A study of open-ending attempts of closed-end funds, *Journal of Financial Economics*, 95, 1–19.

Brandon, D. L., 1998, Federal taxation of real estate investment trusts, in Garrigan, R. T., and J. F. C. Parsons, eds., *Real Estate Investment Trusts*, McGraw-Hill, New York, pp. 83–130.

Brandt, M. W., 1999, Estimating portfolio and consumption choice: A conditional Euler equations approach, *Journal of Finance*, 54, 1609–1645.

Brandt, M. W., 2009, Portfolio choice problems, in Aït-Sahalia, Y., and L. P. Hansen, eds., *Handbook of Financial Econometrics*. Vol. 1, *Tools and Techniques*, Elsevier, Boston, pp. 269–336.

Brandt, M. W., A. Goyal, P. Santa-Clara, and J. Stroud, 2005, A simulation approach to dynamic portfolio choice with an application to learning about return predictability, *Review of Financial Studies*, 18, 831–873.

Brav, A, W. Jiang, F. Partnoy, and R. Thomas, 2008, Hedge fund activism, corporate governance, and firm performance, *Journal of Finance*, 63, 1729–1775.

Brennan, M. J., 1970, Taxes, Market valuation and corporate financial policy, *National Tax Journal*, 23, 417–27.

Brennan, M. J., 1993, Agency and asset prices, working paper, UCLA.

Brennan, M. J., E. S. Schwartz, and R. Lagnado, 1997, Strategic asset allocation, *Journal of Economic Dynamics and Control*, 21, 1377–1403.

Brennan, M. J., and Y. Xia, 2005, Tay's as good as cay, *Finance Research Letters*, 2, 1–14.

Brinson, G. P., L. R. Hood, and G. L. Beebower, 1986, Determinants of portfolio performance, *Financial Analysts Journal*, 42, 39–44.

Broadie, M., M. Chernov, and S. Sundaresan, 2007, Optimal debt and equity values in the presence of Chapter 7 and Chapter 11, *Journal of Finance*, 62, 1341–1376.

Brooks, R. J., 2002, Asset market effects of the baby boom and social security reforms, *American Economic Review Papers and Proceedings*, 92, 402–406.

Brown, D. T., G. Ozik, and D. Sholz, 2007, Rebalancing revisited: The role of derivatives, *Financial Analysts Journal*, 63, 32–44.

Brown, J. R., 2008, Guaranteed trouble: The economic effects of the Pension Benefit Guaranty Corporation, *Journal of Economic Perspectives*, 22, 177–198.

Brown, J. R., 2009, Understanding the role of annuities in retirement planning, in Lusardi, A., ed., *Overcoming the Saving Slump*, University of Chicago Press, Chicago, pp. 178–206.

Brown, J. R., S. G. Dimmock, J.-K. Kang, and S. Weisbenner, 2013, How university endowments respond to financial market shocks: Evidence and implications, forthcoming *American Economic Review*.

Brown, J. R., and A. Finkelstein, 2007, Why is the market for long-term care insurance so small? *Journal of Public Economics*, 91, 1967–1991.

Brown, J. R., and A. Finkelstein, 2011, Insuring long-term care in the United States, *Journal of Economic Perspectives*, 25, 119–142.

Brown, J. R., O. S. Mitchell, and J. M. Poterba, 2002, Mortality risk, and annuity products, in Mitchell, O., Z. Bodie, P. B. Hammond, and S. P. Zeldes, eds., *Innovations in Retirement Financing*, University of Pennsylvania Press, Philadelphia, pp. 175–197.

Brown, K. C., L. Garlappi, and C. Tiu, 2010, The troves of academe: Asset allocation, risk budgeting and the investment performance of university endowment funds, *Journal of Financial Markets*, 13, 268–294.

Brown, S. J., W. N. Goetzmann, and R. G. Ibbotson, 1999, Offshore hedge funds: Survival and performance 1989–95, *Journal of Business*, 72, 91–117.

Brown, S. J., W. N. Goetzmann, R. G. Ibbotson, and S. A. Ross, 1992, Survivorship bias in performance studies, *Review of Financial Studies*, 5, 553–580.

Brown, S. J., W. N. Goetzmann, B. Liang, and C. Schwarz, 2012, Trust and delegation, *Journal of Financial Economics*, 103, 221–234.

Brown, S. J., W. N. Goetzmann, and J. Park, 2001, Careers and survival: Competition and risk in the hedge fund and CTA industry, *Journal of Finance*, 56, 1869–1886.

Brunnermeier, M. K., 2009, Deciphering the liquidity and credit crunch 2007–2008, *Journal of Economic Perspectives*, 23, 77–100.

Brunnermeier, M. K., and S. Nagel, 2008, Do wealth fluctuations generate time-varying risk aversion? Micro-evidence on individuals' asset allocation, *American Economic Review*, 98, 713–736.

Buckle, D., 2004, How to calculate breadth: An evolution of the fundamental law of active portfolio management, *Journal of Asset Management*, 4, 393–405.

Bulow, J. I., and M. S. Scholes, 1983, Who owns the assets in a defined-benefit pension plan? in Bodie, Z., and J. Shoven, eds., *Financial Aspects of the United States Pension System*, University of Chicago Press, Chicago, pp. 17–36.

Burnside, C., M. Eichenbaum, I. Kleshchelski, and S. Rebelo, 2010, Do peso problems explain the returns to the carry trade? *Review of Financial Studies*, 24, 853–891.

Busse, J. A., A. Goyal, and S. Wahal, 2010, Performance and persistence in institutional active management, *Journal of Finance*, 65, 765–790.

Buss, A., R. Uppal, and G. Vilkov, 2012, Asset prices in general equilibrium with transactions costs and recursive utility, working paper, EDHEC.

Buss, A., and G. Vilkov, 2012, Measuring equity risk with option-implied correlations, *Review of Financial Studies*, 25, 3113–3140.

C

Caballero, R. J., and E. Farhi, 2013, A model of the safe asset mechanism (SAM): Safety traps and economic policy, NBER Working Paper 18737.

Cagetti, M., and M. De Nardi, 2008, Wealth inequality: Data and models, *Macroeconomic Dynamics*, 12, 285–313.

Cai, Y., K. L. Judd, and R. Xu, 2013, Numerical solution of dynamic portfolio optimization with transaction costs, NBER Working Paper 18709.

Calvet, L. F., J. Y. Campbell, and P. Sodini, 2009, *Fight or flight: Portfolio rebalancing by individual investors*, Quarterly Journal of Economics, 124, 301–348.

Campbell, J. Y., 1991, A variance decomposition for stock returns, *Economic Journal*, 101, 157–179.

Campbell, J. Y., and J. H. Cochrane, 1999, By force of habit: A consumption-based explanation of aggregate stock market behavior, *Journal of Political Economy*, 107, 205–251.

Campbell, J. Y., J. Cocco, F. J. Gomes, and P. J. Maenhout, 2001, Investing retirement wealth: A life-cycle model, in Campbell, J. Y., and M. Feldstein, eds., *Risk Aspects of Investment-Based Social Security Reform*, University of Chicago Press, Chicago, pp. 439–482.

Campbell, J. Y., and S. Thompson, 2008, Predicting excess returns out of sample: Can anything beat the historical average? *Review of Financial Studies*, 21, 1509–1531.

Campbell, J. Y., and L. M. Viceira, 1999, Consumption and portfolio decisions when expected returns are time varying, *Quarterly Journal of Economics*, 114, 433–495.

Campbell, J. Y., and L. M. Viceira, 2001, Who should buy long-term bonds? *American Economic Review*, 91, 99–127.

Campbell, J. Y., and L. M. Viceira, 2002, *Strategic Asset Allocation*, Oxford University Press, New York.

Campbell, R. A. J., 2008, Art as a financial investment, *Journal of Alternative Investments*, 10, 64–81.

Cannon, V. T., 2007, Secondary markets in private equity and the future of U.S. capital markets, working paper, Harvard University, Cambridge, Mass.

Cao, J., and B. Han, 2013, Cross section of option returns and idiosyncratic volatility, *Journal of Financial Economics*, 108, 231–249.

Carhart, M. M., 1997, On persistence in mutual fund returns, *Journal of Finance*, 52, 57–82.

Carhart, M. M., J. N. Carpenter, A. W. Lynch, and D. K. Musto, 2002, Mutual fund survivorship, *Review of Financial Studies*, 15, 1439–1463.

Carlin, B. I., 2009, Strategic price complexity in retail financial markets, *Journal of Financial Economics*, 91, 278–287.

Carlin, B. I., and G. Manso, 2011, Obfuscation, learning, and the evolution of investor sophistication, *Review of Financial Studies*, 24, 754–785.

Carlson, M., S. Titman, and C. Tiu, 2010, The returns of private and public real estate, working paper, UBC.

Carpenter, J. N., and A. W. Lynch, 1999, Survivorship bias and attrition effects in measures of performance persistence, *Journal of Financial Economics*, 54, 337–374.

Carlson, M., Z. Khokher, and S. Titman, 2007, Equilibrium Exhaustible Resource Price Dynamics, *Journal of Finance*, 62, 1663–1703.

Carroll, C. D., 2001, Theoretical foundations of buffer stock savings, working paper, John Hopkins University.

Casassus, J., P. Liu, and K. Tang, 2013, Economic linkages, relative scarcity, and commodity futures returns, *Review of Financial Studies*, 26, 1324–1362.

Case, B., and S. M. Wachter, 2011, Inflation and real estate investments, SSRN working paper.

Chai, J., W. Horneff, R. Maurer, and O. S. Mitchell, 2011, Optimal portfolio choice over the life cycle with flexible work, endogenous retirement, and lifetime payouts, *Review of Finance*, 15, 875–907.

Chalmers, J., and J. Reuter, 2012a, How do retirees value life annuities? Evidence from public employees, *Review of Financial Studies*, 25, 2601–2634.

Chalmers, J., and J. Reuter, 2012b, What is the impact of financial advisors on retirement portfolio choices and outcomes? NBER Working Paper 18158.

Chambers, D., and E. Dimson, 2012, Keynes the stock market investor, SSRN working paper.

Chambers, D., E. Dimson, and A. Ilmanen, 2012, The Norway model, *Journal of Portfolio Management*, 38, 67–81.

Chan, K. C., P. H. Hendershott, and A. B. Sanders, 1990, Risk and return on real estate: Evidence from equity REITs, *Real Estate Economics*, 18, 431–452.

Chang, B. Y., P. Christoffersen, and K. Jacobs, 2013, Market skewness risk and the cross section of stock returns, *Journal of Financial Economics*, 107, 46–68.

Chaves, D. B., 2012, Eureka! A momentum strategy that also works in Japan, working paper, Research Affiliates.

Chay, J. B., D. Choi, and J. Pontiff, 2006, Market valuation of tax-timing options: Evidence from capital gains distributions, *Journal of Finance*, 61, 837–865.

Chemmanur, T. J., K. Krishnan, and D. K. Nandy, 2011, How does venture capital financing improve efficiency in private firms? A look beneath the surface, *Review of Financial Studies*, 24, 4037–4090.

Chen, H., 2010, Macroeconomic conditions and the puzzles of credit spreads and capital structure, *Journal of Finance*, 65, 2171–2212.

Chen, N.-F., R. Roll, and S. A. Ross, 1986, Economic forces and the stock market, *Journal of Business*, 59, 383–403.

Chen, Q., I. Goldstein, and W. Jiang, 2008, Directors' ownership in the U.S. mutual fund industry, *Journal of Finance*, 63, 2629–2677.

Chen, Q., I. Goldstein, and W. Jiang, 2010, Payoff complementarities and financial fragility: Evidence from mutual fund outflows, *Journal of Financial Economics*, 97, 239–262.

Chen, J., H. Hong, M. Huang, and J. Kubik, 2004, Does fund size erode performance? Liquidity, organizational diseconomies, and active money management, *American Economic Review*, 94, 1276–1302.

Chen, J., H. Hong, and J. Kubik, 2010, Outsourcing mutual fund management: firm boundaries, incentives, and performance, working paper, UC Davis.

Chen, J., H. Hong, and J. Stein, 2002, Breadth of ownership and stock returns, *Journal of Financial Economics*, 66, 171–205.

Chen, L., P. Collin-Dufresne, and R. S. Goldstein, 2009, On the relation between the credit spread puzzle and the equity premium puzzle, *Review of Financial Studies*, 22, 3367–3409.

Chen, L. H., G. J. Jiang, D. D. Xu, and T. Yao, 2012, Dissecting the idiosyncratic volatility anomaly, SSRN working paper.

Chen, L., D. A. Lesmond, and J. Wei, 2007, Corporate yield spreads and bond liquidity, *Journal of Finance*, 62, 119–149.

Chen, Q., I. Goldstein, and W. Jiang, 2008, Directors' ownership in the U.S. mutual fund industry, *Journal of Finance*, 63, 2629–2677.

Chen, Y.-C., K. S. Rogoff, and B. Rossi, 2010, Can exchange rates forecast commodity prices? *Quarterly Journal of Economics*, 125, 1145–1194.

Cheng, M., and A. Madhavan, 2009, The dynamics of leveraged and inverse exchange-traded funds, *Journal of Investment Management*, 7, 43–62.

Cherkes, M., 2012, Closed-end funds: A survey, *Annual Review of Financial Economics*, 4, 431–45.

Cherkes, M., J. Sagi, and R. Stanton, 2009, A liquidity-based theory of closed-end funds, *Review of Financial Studies*, 22, 257–297.

Chevalier, J., and G. Ellison, 1997, Risk taking by mutual funds as a response to incentives, *Journal of Political Economy*, 105, 1167–1200.

Chevalier, J., and G. Ellison, 1999a, Are some mutual fund managers better than others? Cross-sectional patterns in behavior and performance, *Journal of Finance*, 54, 875–899.

Chevalier, J., and G. Ellison, 1999b, Career concerns of mutual fund managers, *Quarterly Journal of Economics*, 114, 389–432.

Chhabra, A. B., 2005, Beyond Markowitz: A comprehensive wealth allocation framework for individual investors, *Journal of Wealth Management*, 7, 8–34.

Chien, Y., H. Cole, and H. Lustig, 2012, Is the volatility of the market price of risk due to intermittent portfolio rebalancing? *American Economic Review*, 102, 2859–2896.

Choi, D., M. Getmansky, and H. Tookes, 2009, Convertible bond arbitrage, liquid externalities, and stock prices, *Journal of Financial Economics*, 91, 227–251.

Choi, J. J., D. Laibson, and B. C. Madrian, 2010, Why does the law of one price fail? An experiment on index mutual funds, *Review of Financial Studies*, 23, 1405–1432.

Chordia, T., and L. Shivakumar, 2006, Earnings and price momentum, *Journal of Financial Economics*, 80, 627–656.

Choueifaty, Y., and Y. Coignard, 2008, Towards maximum diversification, *Journal of Portfolio Management*, 34, 40–51.

Christensen, C. M., 1997, *The Innovator's Dilemma: When New Technologies Cause Great Firms to Fail*, Harvard Business Review Press, Boston.

Christiansen, C., J. Joensen, and H. Nielsen, 2007, The risk–return trade-off in human capital investment, *Labour Economics*, 14, 971–986.

Christoffersen, P., V. Errunza, K. Jacobs, and H. Langlois, 2013, Is the potential for international diversification disappearing? A dynamic copula approach, *Review of Financial Studies*, 25, 3712–3751.

Christoffersen, S. E. K., and D. K. Musto, 2002, Demand curves and the pricing of money management, *Review of Financial Studies*, 15, 1499–1524.

Chua, C. T., S. Lai, and K. K. Lewis, 2010, Is the international diversification potential diminishing for foreign equity inside the U.S.? working paper, Wharton.

Chua, D. B., M. Kritzman, and S. Page, 2009, The myth of diversification, *Journal of Portfolio Management*, 36, 26–35.

Chung, J.-W., B. A. Sensoy, L. Stern, and M. S. Weisbach, 2012, Pay for performance from future fund flows: The case of private equity, *Review of Financial Studies*, 25, 3259–3304.

Clarida, R., J. Galí, and M. Gertler, 2000, Monetary policy rules and macroeconomic stability: Evidence and some theory, *Quarterly Journal of Economics*, 115, 147–180.

Clarke, R., H. de Silva, and S. Thorley, 2006, Minimum-variance portfolios in the U.S. equity market *Journal of Portfolio Management*, 33, 10–24.

Coates, J. C. IV, and R. G. Hubbard, 2007, Competition in the mutual fund industry: Evidence and implications for policy, *Journal of Corporation Law*, 33, 151–222.

Cocco, J. F., F. J. Gomes, and P. J. Maenhout, 2005, Consumption and portfolio choice over the life cycle, *Review of Financial Studies*, 18, 491–533.

Cochrane, J. H., 1991, Production-based asset pricing and the link between stock returns and economic fluctuations, *Journal of Finance*, 46, 209–237.

Cochrane, J. H., 1992, Explaining the variance of price–dividend ratios, *Review of Financial Studies*, 5, 243–280.

Cochrane, J. H., 1996, A cross-sectional test of an investment-based asset pricing model, *Journal of Political Economy*, 104, 572–621.

Cochrane, J. H., 1999, Portfolio advice for a multifactor world, Economic *Perspectives Federal Reserve Bank of Chicago*, 23, Quarter 3, 59–78.

Cochrane, J. H., 2001, *Asset Pricing*, Princeton University Press, Princeton, N.J.

Cochrane, J. H., 2005, The risk and return of venture capital, *Journal of Financial Economics*, 75, 3–52.

Cochrane, J. H., 2007, *Portfolio Theory, Lecture Notes*, University of Chicago.

Cochrane, J. H., 2011, Presidential address: Discount rates, *Journal of Finance*, 66, 1047–1108.

Cochrane, J. H., 2013a, A mean-variance benchmark for intertemporal portfolio theory, NBER Working Paper 18768.

Cochrane, J. H., 2013b, Finance: Function matters, not size, *Journal of Economic Perspectives*, 27, 29–50.

Cohen, L., A. Frazzini, and C. Malloy, 2008, The small world of investing: Board connections and mutual fund returns, *Journal of Political Economy*, 116, 951–979.

Cohen, L., and B. Schmidt, 2009, Attracting flows by attracting big clients, *Journal of Finance*, 64, 2125–2151.

Coles, J. L., J. Suay, and D. Woodbury, 2000, Fund advisory compensation in closed-end funds, *Journal of Finance*, 55, 1385–1414.

Collier, P., F. van der Ploeg, M. Spence, and A. J. Venables, 2010, Managing resource revenues in developing economies, *IMF Staff Papers*, 58, 84–118.

Collin-Dufresne, P., R. S. Goldstein, and J. S. Martin, 2001, The determinants of credit spread changes, *Journal of Finance*, 56, 2177–2207.

Connor, G., and R. A. Korajczyk, 1986, Performance measurement with the arbitrage pricing theory, *Journal of Financial Economics*, 15, 373–394.

Connor, G., and R. A. Korajczyk, 1993, A test for the number of factors in an approximate factor model, *Journal of Finance*, 48, 1263–1291.

Constantinides, G. M., 1979, Multiperiod consumption and investment behavior with convex transactions costs, *Management Science*, 25, 1127–1137.

Constantinides, G. M., 1983, Optimal stock trading with personal taxes, *Econometrica*, 51, 611–636.

Constantinides, G. M., 1986, Capital market equilibrium with transactions costs, *Journal of Political Economy*, 94, 842–862.

Constantinides, G. M., 1990, Habit formation: A resolution of the equity premium puzzle, *Journal of Political Economy*, 98, 519–43.

Constantinides, G. M., J. B. Donaldson, and R. Mehra, 2002, Junior can't borrow: A new perspective on the equity premium puzzle, *Quarterly Journal of Economics*, 118, 269–296.

Constantinides, G. M., and D. Duffie, 1996, Asset pricing with heterogeneous consumers, *Journal of Political Economy*, 104, 219–240.

Conti-Brown, P., 2010, Finance, and culture of elite university endowments in financial crisis, *Stanford Law Review*, 63, 699–749.

Cook, T., 1989, Determinants of the Federal Funds Rate: 1979–1982, *Federal Reserve Bank of Richmond Economic Review*, January/February, 3–19.

Cooper, I., 1996, Arithmetic versus geometric mean estimators: Setting discount rates for capital budgeting, *European Financial Management*, 2, 157–167.

Cooper, I., and E. Kaplanis, 1994, Home bias in equity portfolios, inflation hedging, and international capital market equilibrium, *Review of Financial Studies*, 7, 45–60.

Cooper, M., O. Dimitrov, and P. R. Rau, 2001, A rose.com by any other name, *Journal of Finance*, 56, 2371–2388.

Cooper, M. J., R. C. Gutierrez, and A. Hameed, 2004, Market states and momentum, *Journal of Finance*, 59, 1345–1365.

Cornelius, P., 2011, *International Investments in Private Equity: Asset Allocation, Markets and Industry Structure*, Academic Press, Burlington, Mass.

Cosemans, M., R. Frehen, P. C. Schotman, R. Bauer, 2012, Estimating security betas using prior information based on firm fundamentals, SSRN working paper.

Coval, J., and T. Moskowitz, 2001, The geography of investment: Informed trading and asset prices, *Journal of Political Economy*, 109, 811–841.

Coval, J., and E. Stafford, 2007, Asset fire sales (and purchases) in equity markets, *Journal of Financial Economics*, 86, 479–512.

Cowan, M. J., 2008, Taxing and regulating college and university endowment income: The literature's perspective, *Journal of College and University Law*, 34, 507–553.

Cox, J., 2009, The money pit: An analysis of Nauru's phosphate mining policy, *Pacific Economic Bulletin*, 24, 174–186.

Cox, J. C., J. E. Ingersoll, and S. A. Ross, 1985, A theory of the term structure of interest rates, *Econometrica*, 53, 385–407.

Cremers, M., J. Driessen, P. Maenhout, and D. Weinbaum, 2009, Does skin in the game matter? Director incentives and governance in the mutual fund industry, *Journal of Financial and Quantitative Analysis*, 44, 1345–1373.

Cremers, M., and A. Ferrell, 2012, Thirty years of shareholder rights and stock returns: Beta, not alpha? Working paper, Harvard Law School.

Cremers, M., and A. Petajisto, 2009, How active is your fund manager? A new measure that predicts performance, *Review of Financial Studies*, 22, 3329–3365.

Cremers, M., A. Petajisto, and E. Zitzewitz, 2012, Should benchmark indices have alpha? Revisiting performance evaluation, *Critical Finance Review*, 2, 1–48.

Cruces, J. J., and C. Trebesch, 2013, Sovereign defaults: The price of haircuts, *American Economic Journal: Macroeconomics*, 5, 85–117.

Culbertson, J., 1957, The term structure of interest rates, *Quarterly Journal of Economics*, 71, 485–517.

Culver, C., and B. Gert, 1981, The morality of involuntary hospitalization, in Spicker, S. F., J. M. Healy Jr., and H. T. Engelhardt Jr., eds., *The Law Medicine Relation: A Philosophical Exploration*, Reidel, pp. 159–175.

Cuoco, D., and R. Kaniel, 2010, Equilibrium prices in the presence of delegated portfolio management, working paper, Wharton.

Curcuru, S., J. Heaton, D. Lucas, and D. Moore, 2004, Heterogeneity and portfolio choice: Theory and evidence, in Aït-Sahalia, Y., and L. P. Hansen, eds., *Handbook of Financial Econometrics: Tools and Techniques*, Elsevier, pp. 337–382.

Cvitanić, J., and F. Zapatero, 2004, *Introduction to the Economics and Mathematics of Financial Markets*, MIT Press, Boston.

D

Dai, Q., and K. J. Singleton, 2000, Specification analysis of affine term structure models, *Journal of Finance*, 55, 1943–1978.

Dai, Q., and K. J. Singleton, 2002, Expectation puzzles, time-varying risk premia, and affine models of the term structure, *Journal of Financial Economics*, 63, 415–441.

D'Amico, S., D. H. Kim, and M. Wei, 2009, Tips from TIPS: The information content of Treasury Inflation-Protected Securities, Working Paper 2010–19, Federal Reserve Board.

Dammon, R. M., C. S. Spatt, and H. H. Zhang, 2004, Optimal asset allocation and allocation with taxable and tax-deferred investing, *Journal of Finance*, 59, 999–1037.

Dangl, T., and M. Halling 2012, Predictive regressions with time-varying coefficients, *Journal of Financial Economics*, 106, 157–181.

Daniel, K., 2009, Anatomy of a crisis, *CFA Institute Conference Proceedings Quarterly*, 26, 11–21.

Daniel, K., M. Grinblatt, S. Titman, and R. Wermers, 1997, Measuring mutual fund performance with characteristic-based benchmarks, *Journal of Finance*, 52, 1035–1058.

Daniel, K., D. Hirshleifer, and A, Subrahmanyam, 1998, Investor psychology and security market under- and over-reaction, *Journal of Finance*, 53, 1839–1886.

Dann, L., D. Del Guercio, and M. Partch, 2003, Governance and boards of directors in closed-end investment companies, *Journal of Financial Economics*, 69, 111–152.

Da Rin, M., T. F. Hellmann, and M. Puri, 2011, A survey of venture capital research, forthcoming Constantinides, G., M. Harris, and R. Stulz, eds., *Handbook of the Economics of Finance*, vol 2., Elsevier, Boston.

Dasgupta, A., A. Prat, and M. Verardo, 2010, The price impact of institutional herding, working paper, LSE.

David, A., 2008, Heterogeneous beliefs, speculation, and the equity premium, *Journal of Finance*, 63, 41–83.

Davidoff, T., J. R. Brown, and P. A. Diamond, 2005, Annuities and individual welfare, *American Economic Review*, 95, 1573–1590.

Davis, G. F., and E. H. Kim, 2007, Business ties and proxy voting by mutual funds, *Journal of Financial Economics*, 85, 552–570.

Davis, J., R. Ossowski, J. Daniel, and S. Barnett, 2001, Stabilization and savings funds for nonrenewable resources, IMF Occasional Paper 205.

DeAngelo, H., L. DeAngelo, and D. J. Skinner, 2004, Are dividends disappearing? Dividend concentration and the consolidation of earnings, *Journal of Financial Economics*, 72, 425–456.

Deaton, A., 1991, Saving and liquidity constraints, *Econometrica*, 59, 1221–1248.

Deaton, A., 2005, Franco Modigliani and the life cycle theory of consumption, working paper, Princeton University.

Deaton, A., and G. Laroque, 1992, On the Behavior of Commodity Prices, *Review of Economic Studies*, 59, 1–23.

Decker, M. O., 1998, The modern real estate investment trust industry: An overview, in Garrigan, R. T., and J. F. C. Parsons, eds., *Real Estate Investment Trusts*, McGraw-Hill, New York, pp. 3–8.

Deep, A., and P. Frumkin, 2006, Sooner or later? The foundation payout puzzle, in Damon, W., and S. Verducci, *Taking Philanthropy Seriously: Beyond Good Intentions*, Indiana University Press, Bloomington, pp. 189–204.

DeFusco, R. A., S. I. Ivanov, and G. V. Karels, 2011, The exchange traded funds' pricing deviation: Analysis and forecasts, *Journal of Economics and Finance*, 35, 181–197.

Del Guerico, D., and P. A. Tkac, 2002, The determinants of the flow of funds of managed portfolios: Mutual funds vs. pension funds, *Journal of Financial and Quantitative Analysis*, 37, 523–557.

Del Guercio, D., J. Reuter, and P. A. Tkac, 2009, Unbundling the value of portfolio management and distribution in retail mutual funds: Evidence from subadvisory contracts, working paper, University of Oregon.

Deli, D., 2002, Mutual fund advisory contracts: An empirical investigation, *Journal of Finance*, 57, 109–133.

DeLong, J. B., and L. H. Summers, 1988, How does macroeconomic policy affect output? *Brookings Papers on Economic Activity*, 2, 433–494.

DeLong, J. B., 1997, America's peacetime inflation: The 1970s, in Romer, C. D. and D. H. Romer, eds., *Reducing Inflation: Motivation and Strategy*, University of Chicago Press, Chicago, pp. 247–280.

DeLong, J. B., A. Shleifer, L. H. Summers, and R. J. Waldmann, 1990, Positive feedback investment strategies and destabilizing rational speculation, *Journal of Finance*, 45, 379–395.

DeMarzo, P. M., R. Kaniel, and I. Kremer, 2005, Diversification as a public good: Community effects in portfolio choice, *Journal of Finance*, 59, 1677–1716.

DeMiguel, V., L. Garlappi, and R. Uppal, 2009, Optimal versus naïve diversification: How inefficient is the 1/N portfolio strategy? *Review of Financial Studies*, 25, 1915–1953.

DeMiguel, V., and R. Uppal, 2005, Portfolio investment with the exact tax basis via nonlinear programming, *Management Science*, 51, 277–290.

Dempster, M. A. H., I. V. Evstigneev, and K. R. Schenk-Hoppé, 2009, Volatility-induced financial growth, in Dempster, M. A. H., G. Mitra, and G. Pflug, eds., *Quantitative Fund Management*, Chapman & Hall, Boca Raton, Fla., pp. 67–84.

Demsetz, H., 1968, The cost of transacting, *Quarterly Journal of Economics*, 82, 33–53.

De Nardi, M., E. French, and J. B. Jones, 2010, Why do the elderly save? The role of medical expenses, *Journal of Political Economy*, 118, 39–75.

den Haan, W. J., 1995, The term structure of interest rates in real and monetary economies, *Journal of Economic Dynamics and Control*, 19, 909–940.

Derman, E., 2007. A simple model for the expected premium for hedge fund lockups, *Journal of Investment Management*, 5, 5–15.

de Souza, A., and A. W. Lynch, 2012, Does mutual fund performance vary over the business cycle? NBER working paper 18137.

Deuskar, P., Q. H. Nguyen, Z. J. Wang, and Y. Wu, 2011, The dynamics of hedge fund fees, working paper, University of Illinois at Urbana–Champaign.

Diamond, P. A., 1965, National debt in a neoclassical growth model, *American Economic Review*, 55, 1126–1150.

Diamond, P. A., 1982, Aggregate demand management in search equilibrium, *Journal of Political Economy*, 90, 891–894.

DiBartolomeo, D., and E. Witkowski, 1997, Mutual fund misclassification: Evidence based on style analysis, *Financial Analysts Journal*, 53, 32–43.

Dichev, I. D., and G. Yu, 2011, Higher risk, lower returns: What hedge fund investors really earn, *Journal of Financial Economics*, 100, 248–263.

Dick-Nielsen, J., P. Feldhutter, and D. Lando, 2012, Corporate bond liquidity before and after the onset of the subprime crisis, *Journal of Financial Economics*, 103, 471–492.

Dimmock, S. G., 2012, Background risk and university endowment funds, *Review of Economics and Statistics*, 94, 789–799.

Dimmock. S. G., R. Kouwenberg, O. S. Mitchell, and K. Peijnenburg, 2013, Ambiguity attitudes and economic behavior, NBER Working Paper 18743.

Dimson, E., O. Karakas, and X. Li, 2012, Active ownership, working paper, Cambridge University, Cambridge.

Dimson, E., P. Marsh, and M. Staunton, 2011, Credit Suisse Global Investment Returns Sourcebook, Credit Suisse Research Institute.

Dimson, E., and C. Spænjers, 2011, Ex post: The investment performance of collectible stamps, *Journal of Financial Economics*, 100, 443–458.

Ding, B., M. Getmansky, B. Liang, and R. Wermers, 2010, Share restrictions and investor flows in the hedge fund industry, working paper, University of Massachusetts Amherst.

Dittmar, R. F., 2002, Nonlinear pricing kernels, kurtosis preference, and evidence from the cross section of equity returns, *Journal of Finance*, 57, 369–403.

Driessen, J., T.-C. Lin, and L. Phalippou, 2012, A new method to estimate risk and return of non-traded assets from cash flows: The case of private equity funds, *Journal of Financial and Quantitative Analysis*, 47, 511–535.

Driessen, J., P. Maenhout, and G. Vilkov, 2009, The price of correlation risk: Evidence from equity options, *Journal of Finance*, 64, 1377–1406.

Dooley, M. P., D. Folkerts-Landau, and P. Garber, 2004, The revived Bretton Woods system: The effects of periphery intervention and reserve management on interest rates and exchange rates in center countries, NBER Working Paper 10332.

Dow, C. H., 1920, *Scientific Stock Speculation*, The Magazine of Wall Street, New York.

Dow, J., and S. R. C. Werlang, 1992, Uncertainty aversion, risk aversion and the optimal choice of portfolio, *Econometrica*, 60, 197–204.

Duarte, J., F. A. Longstaff, and F. Yu, 2005, Risk and return in fixed-income arbitrage: Nickels in front of a steamroller? *Review of Financial Studies*, 20, 769–811.

Duchin, R., and H. Levy, 2009, Markowitz versus the Talmudic portfolio diversification strategies, *Journal of Portfolio Management*, 35, 71–74.

Duffie, D., 1996, Special repo rates, *Journal of Finance*, 51, 493–526.

Duffie, D., 2001, *Dynamic Asset Pricing Theory*, 3d ed., Princeton University Press, Princeton, N.J.

Duffie, D., 2010, Asset price dynamics with slow-moving capital, *Journal of Finance*, 65, 1237–1267.

Duffie, D., W. Fleming, M. Soner, and T. Zairphopoulou, 1997, Hedging in incomplete markets with HARA utility, *Journal of Economic Dynamics and Control*, 21, 753–782.

Duffie, D., and R. Kan, 1996, A yield-factor model of interest rates, *Mathematical Finance*, 6, 379–406.

Duffie, D., and B. Strulovici, 2012, Capital mobility and asset pricing, *Econometrica*, 80, 2469–2509.

Dumas, B., 1989, Two-person dynamic equilibrium in the capital market, *Review of Financial Studies*, 2, 157–188.

Dunn, K. B., and K. J. Singleton, 1987, Modeling the term structure of interest rates under non-separable utility and durability of goods, *Journal of Financial Economics*, 17, 27–55.

Dusenberry, J. S., 1952, *Income, Saving, and the Theory of Consumer Behavior*, Harvard University Press, Cambridge, Mass.

Dybvig, P. H., 1995, Dusenberry's ratcheting of consumption: Optimal dynamic consumption and investment given intolerance for any decline in standard of living, *Review of Economic Studies*, 62, 287–313.

Dybvig, P. H., 1999, Using asset allocation to protect spending, *Financial Analysts Journal*, 55, 49–62.

Dybvig, P. H., H. K. Farnsworth, and J. N. Carpenter, 2010, Portfolio performance and agency, *Review of Financial Studies*, 25, 1–23.

Dybvig, P. H., Ingersoll, J. E., 1982, Mean-variance theory in complete markets, *Journal of Business*, 55, 233–251.

Dyck, A., and L. Pomorski, 2011, Is bigger better? Size and performance in pension plan management, working paper, University of Toronto.

E

Easterlin, R. A., 1974, Does economic growth improve the human lot? Some empirical evidence, in David, P. A., and M. W. Reder, eds., *Nations and Households in Economic Growth: Essays in Honor of Moses Abramovitz*, Academic Press, New York, pp. 89–125.

Edelen, R. M., 1999, Investor flows and the assess performance of open-ended fund managers, *Journal of Financial Economics*, 53, 439–466.

Edelen, R. M., R. B. Evans, G. B. Kadlec, 2007, Scale effects in mutual fund performance: The role of trading costs, SSRN working paper.

Edelen, R. M., R. B. Evans, G. B. Kadlec, 2012, Disclosure and agency conflict: Evidence from mutual fund commission building, *Journal of Financial Economics*, 103, 308–326.

Eichengreen, B., and P. M. Garber 1991, Before the Accord: U.S. monetary-financial policy, 1945–51, in Hubbard, R. G., *Financial Markets and Financial Crisis*, University of Chicago Press, Chicago, pp. 175–206.

Eiling, E., 2013, Industry-specific human capital, idiosyncratic risk, and the cross-section of expected stock returns, *Journal of Finance*, 63, 43–84.

Ellis, C. D., 1975, The loser's game, *Financial Analysts Journal*, 31, 19–26.

Ellis, C. D., 1987, *Investment Policy*, McGraw-Hill, New York.

Ellis, C. D., 2012, Investment management fees are (much) higher than you think, *Financial Analysts Journal*, 68, 4–6.

Ellis, C. D., 2013, *Winning the Loser's Game: Timeless Strategies for Successful Investing*, 6th ed., McGraw-Hill, New York.

Elton, E. J., M. J. Gruber, and C. R. Blake, 1996, Survivorship bias and mutual fund performance, *Review of Financial Studies*, 9, 1097–1120.

Elton, E. J., M. J. Gruber, and C. R. Blake, 2003, Incentive fees and mutual funds, *Journal of Finance*, 58, 779–804.

Engel, R. F., 1982, Autoregressive conditional heteroskedasticity with estimates of the variance of United Kingdom inflation, *Econometrica*, 50, 987–1008.

Engle, R., and D. Sarkar, 2006, Premiums-discounts and exchange traded funds, *Journal of Derivatives*, 13, 27–45.

Epple, D., R. Romano, and H. Seig, 2006, Admission, tuition, and financial aid policies in the market for higher education, *Econometrica*, 74, 885–928.

Epstein, L. G., and S. E. Zin, 1989, Substitution, risk aversion, and the temporal behavior of consumption and asset returns: A theoretical framework, *Econometrica*, 57, 937–969.

Erb, C. B., and C. R. Harvey, 2006, The strategic and tactical value of commodity futures, *Financial Analysts Journal*, 62, 69–97.

Erb, C. B., and C. R. Harvey, 2013, The golden dilemma, *Financial Analysts Journal*, 69, 10–42.

Erb, C. B., C. R. Harvey, and T. E. Viskanta, 1997, Demographics and international investments, *Financial Analysts Journal*, 53, 14–28.

Errunza, V., K. Hogan, and M-W. Hung, 1999, Can the gains from international diversification be achieved without trading abroad? *Journal of Finance*, 54, 2075–2107.

Estrella, A., and F. S. Mishkin, 1998, Predicting U.S. recessions: Financial variables as leading indicators, *Review of Economics and Statistics*, 1, 45–61.

Evans, R. B., 2010, Mutual fund incubation, *Journal of Finance*, 65, 1581–1611.

Evans, R. B., and R. Fahlenbrach, 2012, Institutional investors and mutual fund governance: Evidence from retail-institutional fund twins, *Review of Financial Studies*, 3530–3571.

Evstigneev, I. V., and K. R. Schenk-Hoppé, 2002, From rags to riches: on constant proportions investment strategies, *International Journal of Theoretical and Applied Finance*, 5, 563–573.

Ewens, M., and M. Rhodes-Kropf, 2012, Is a VC partnership greater than the sum of its partners? Working paper, Harvard University.

F

Falkenstein, E. G., 2012, *The Missing Risk Premium: Why Low Volatility Investing Works*, Author.

Fama, E. F., 1970, Efficient capital markets: A review of theory and empirical work, *Journal of Finance*, 25, 383–417.

Fama, E. F., 1975, Short-term interest rates as predictors of inflation, *American Economic Review*, 65, 269–282.

Fama, E. F., 1981, Stock returns, real activity, inflation, and money, *American Economic Review*, 71, 545–565.

Fama, E. F., and R. R. Bliss, 1987, The information in long-maturity forward rates, *American Economic Review*, 77, 680–692.

Fama, E. F., and K. R. French, 1992, The cross-section of expected stock returns, *Journal of Finance*, 47, 427–465.

Fama, E. F., and K. R. French, 1993, Common risk factors in the returns on stocks and bonds, *Journal of Financial Economics*, 33, 3–56.

Fama, E. F., and K. R. French, 2001, Disappearing dividends: changing firm characteristics or lower propensity to pay? *Journal of Financial Economics*, 60, 3–43.

Fama, E. F., and K. R. French, 2010, Luck versus skill in the cross section of mutual fund returns, *Journal of Finance*, 65, 1915–1947.

Fama, E. F., and K. R. French, 2012, Size, value, and momentum in international stock returns, *Journal of Financial Economics*, 105, 457–472.

Fama, E. F., and M. C. Jensen, 1983, Separation of ownership and control, *Journal of Law and Economics*, 26, 301–325.

Fama, E. F., and J. D. MacBeth, 1973, Risk, return, and equilibrium: Empirical tests, *Journal of Political Economy*, 81, 607–636.

Fama, E. F., and G. W. Schwert, 1977, Asset returns and inflation, *Journal of Finanfial Economics*, 5, 115–146.

Fang, L. H., V. Ivashina, and J. Lerner, 2012, The disintermediation of financial markets: Direct investing in private equity, SSRN working paper.

Fang, L. H., V. Ivashina, and J. Lerner, 2013, Combining banking with private equity investing, *Review of Financial Studies*, 26, 2139–2173.

Farhi, E., and S. Panageas, 2007, Saving and investing for early retirement: A theoretical analysis, *Journal of Financial Economics*, 83, 87–121.

Farina, R. H., J. P. Freeman, and J. Webster, 1969, The mutual fund industry: A legal survey, *Notre Dame Lawyer*, 44, 732–983.

Feldstein, M., 1999, A self-help guide for emerging markets, *Foreign Affairs*, 78, 93–109.

Fernald, J., 2009, A quarterly, utilization-adjusted series on total factor productivity, working paper, Federal Reserve Bank of San Francisco.

Fernholz, R., R. Garvy, and J. Hannon, 1998, Diversity-weighted indexing, *Journal of Portfolio Management*, 24, 74–82.

Ferson, W., T. R. Henry, and D. J. Kisgen, 2006, Evaluating government bond funds using stochastic discount factors, *Review of Financial Studies*, 19, 423–455.

Fidora, M., M. Fratzscher, and C. Thimann, 2007, Home bias in global bond and equity markets: The role of real exchange rate volatility, *Journal of International Money and Finance*, 26, 631–655.

Fischer, M., and M. Z. Stamos, 2013, Optimal life cycle portfolio choice with housing market cycles, *Review of Financial Studies*, 26, 2311–2352.

Fisher, I., 1896, Appreciation and interest, *Publications of the American Economic Association*, 11, 1–198.

Fisher, I., 1930, *The Theory of Interest: As Determined by Impatience to Spend Income and Opportunity to Invest It*, MacMillan, New York.

Fisher, J. D., D. Gatzlaff, D. Geltner, and D. Haurin, 2003, Controlling for the impact of variable liquidity in commercial real estate price indices, *Real Estate Economics*, 31, 269–303.

Fisher, J. D., D. Geltner, and H. Pollakowski, 2007, A quarterly transactions-based index of institutional real estate investment performance and movements in supply and demand, *Journal of Real Estate Financial Economics*, 34, 5–33.

Fisher, J. D., and M. S. Young, 2000, Institutional property tenure: Evidence from the NCREIF Database, *Journal of Real Estate Portfolio Management*, 6, 327–338.

Fleckenstein, M., F. A. Longstaff, and H. Lustig, 2010, Why does the Treasury issue TIPS? The TIPS-Treasury bond puzzle, working paper, UCLA.

Fleming, J., C. Kirby, and B. Ostdiek, 2001, The economic value of volatility timing, *Journal of Finance*, 56, 329–352.

Florance, A. C., N. G. Miller, J. Spivey, and R. Peng, 2010, Slicing, dicing, and scoping the size of the U.S. commercial real estate market, working paper, CoStar Group.

Foster, D. P., and H. P. Young, 2010, Gaming performance fees by portfolio managers, *Quarterly Journal of Economics*, 4, 1435–1458.

Frank, M., 2002, The impact of taxes on corporate defined benefit plan asset allocation, *Journal of Accounting Research*, 40, 1163–1190.

Franzoni, F., E. Nowak, and L. Phalippou, 2012, Private equity performance and liquidity risk, *Journal of Finance*, 67, 2341–2373.

Frazzini, A., D. Kabiller, and L. H. Pedersen, 2012, Buffet's alpha, working paper, NYU.

Frazzini, A., and O. Lamont, 2008, Dumb money: Mutual fund flows and the cross-section of stock returns, *Journal of Financial Economics*, 88, 299–322.

Frazzini, A., and L. H. Pedersen, 2011, Betting against Beta, NYU working paper.

French, K. R., 2008, The cost of active investing, *Journal of Finance*, 63, 1537–1573.

Friedman, M., 1957, *A Theory of the Consumption Function*, Princeton University Press, Princeton, N.J.

Friend, I., and M. Blume, 1970, Measurement of portfolio performance under uncertainty, *American Economic Review*, 60, 561–575.

Friend, I., and M. Blume, 1975, The demand for risky assets, *American Economic Review*, 65, 900–922.

Friesen, G. C., and T. R. A. Sapp, 2007, Mutual fund flows and investor returns: An empirical examination of fund investor timing ability, *Journal of Banking and Finance*, 31, 2796–2816.

Friewald, N., R. Jankowitsch, and M. G. Subrahmanyam, 2012, Illiquidity or credit deterioration: A study of liquidity in the U.S. corporate bond market during financial crises, *Journal of Financial Economics*, 105, 18–36.

Fuhrer, J. C., 2000, Habit formation in consumption and its implications for monetary-policy models, *American Economic Review*, 90, 367–390.

Fung, H., X. Xu, and J. Yau, 2004, Do hedge fund managers display skill? *Journal of Alternative Investments*, 6, 22–31.

Fung, W., and D. A. Hsieh, 1997, Survivorship bias and investment style in the returns of CTAs, *Journal of Portfolio Management*, 24, 30–42.

Fung, W., and D. A. Hsieh, 2001, The risk in hedge fund strategies: Theory and evidence from trend followers, *Review of Financial Studies*, 14, 313–341.

Fung, W., and D. A. Hsieh, 2002, Risk in fixed-income hedge fund styles, *Journal of Fixed Income*, 12, 6–27.

Fung, W., and D. A. Hsieh, 2004, Hedge fund benchmarks: A risk based approach, *Financial Analysts Journal*, 60, 65–80.

Fung, W., and D. A. Hsieh, 2006, Hedge funds: An industry in its adolescence, *Federal Reserve Bank of Atlanta Economic Review*, 4, 1–34.

Fung, W., D. A. Hsieh, N. Y. Naik, and T. Ramadorai, 2008, Hedge funds: Performance, risk, and capital formation, *Journal of Finance*, 63, 1777–1803.

G

Gabaix, X., and D. Laibson, 2006, Shrouded attributes, consumer myopia, and information suppression in competitive markets, *Quarterly Journal of Economics*, 121, 505–540.

Gabaix, X., and A. Landier, 2008, Why has CEO pay increased so much? *Quarterly Journal of Economics*, 123, 49–100.

Galí, J., 1994, Keeping up with the Joneses: Consumption externalities, portfolio choice, and asset prices, *Journal of Money, Credit and Banking*, 26, 1–8.

Gallmeyer, M., and S. Srivastava, 2011, Arbitrage and the tax code, *Mathematics and Financial Economics*, 4, 183–221.

Gans, J. S., and A. Leigh, 2006, Did the death of Australian inheritance taxes affect deaths? B. E. *Journal of Economic Analysis & Policy*, 6, Article 23.

Garlappi, L., R. Uppal, and T. Wang, 2007, Portfolio selection with parameter and model uncertainty: A multi-prior approach, *Review of Financial Studies*, 20, 42–81.

Gârleanu, N., 2009, Portfolio choice and pricing in illiquid markets, *Journal of Economic Theory*, 144, 532–564.

Gârleanu, N., and L. H. Pedersen, 2012, Dynamic trading with predictable returns and transactions costs, forthcoming *Journal of Finance*.

Gaspar, J-M., M. Massa, and P. Matos, 2006, Favoritism in mutual fund families? Evidence on strategic cross-fund subsidization, *Journal of Finance*, 61, 73–104.

Gatev, E., W. N. Goetzmann, and K. G. Rouwenhorst, 2006, Pairs trading: Performance of a relative-value arbitrage rule, *Review of Financial Studies*, 19, 797–827.

Gatzlaff, D., and D. Geltner, 1998, A transaction-based index of commercial property and its comparison to the NCREIF index, *Real Estate Finance*, 15, 7–22.

Geanakoplos, J., M. Magill, and M. Quinzii, 2004, Demography and the long-run predictability of the stock market, *Brookings Papers on Economic Activity*, 1, 241–307.

Geanakoplos, J., and S. P. Zeldes, 2011, The market value of Social Security, working paper, Columbia Business School.

Geczy, C. C., R. F. Stambaugh, and D. Levin, 2004, Investing in socially responsible mutual funds, working paper, Wharton.

Gehrig, T., 1993, An information-based explanation of the domestic bias in international equity investment, *Scandinavian Journal of Economics*, 95, 97–109.

Gelpern, A., 2011, Sovereignty, accountability, and the sovereign wealth fund conundrum, *Asian Journal of International Law*, 1, 289–320.

Geltner, D., 1991, Smoothing in appraisal-based returns, *Journal of Real Estate Finance and Economics*, 4, 327–345.

Geltner, D., 1993, Temporal aggregation in real estate return indices, *Journal of the American Real Estate and Urban Economics Association*, 21, 141–166.

Gennaioli, N., A. Shleifer, and R. W. Vishny, 2012, Money doctors, NBER Working Paper 18174.

Gerdesmeier, D., F. P. Mongelli, and B. Roffia, 2007, The Eurosystem, the U.S. Federal Reserve, and the Bank of Japan: Similarities and differences, *Journal of Money, Credit and Banking*, 39, 1785–1819.

Gervais, S., R. Kaniel, and D. H. Mingelgrin, 2001, The high volume-return premium, *Journal of Finance*, 56, 877–919.

Getmansky, M., 2012, The life cycle of hedge funds: Flow flows, size, and performance, *Quarterly Journal of Finance*, 2, DOI: 10.1142/S2010139212500036.

Getmansky, M., A. W. Lo, and I. Makarov, 2004, An econometric model of serial correlation and illiquidity in hedge fund returns, *Journal of Financial Economics*, 74, 529–609.

Ghilarducci, T., 2008, *When I'm Sixty-Four: The Plot against Pensions and the Plan to Save Them*, Princeton University Press, Princeton, N.J.

Giannone, D., L. Reichlin, and D. Small, 2008, Nowcasting: The real-time information content of macroeconomic data, *Journal of Monetary Economics*, 55, 665–676.

Giesecke, K., F. A. Longstaff, S. Schaefer, and I. Strebulaev, 2011, Corporate bond default risk: A 150-year perspective, *Journal of Financial Economics*, 102, 233–250.

Gil-Bazo, J., and P. Ruiz-Verdu, 2008, When cheaper is better: Fee determination in the market for equity mutual funds, *Journal of Economic Behavior and Organization*, 67, 871–885.

Gil-Bazo, J., and P. Ruiz-Verdu, 2009, The relation between price and performance in the mutual fund industry, *Journal of Finance*, 64, 2153–2183.

Gilbert, T., and C. M. Hrdlicka, 2012, Why do university endowments invest so much in risky assets? working paper, University of Washington.

Gilboa, I., and D. Schmeidler, 1989, Maxmin expected utility with nonunique prior, *Journal of Mathematical Economics*, 18, 141–153.

Gillan, S., and L. Starks, 2007, The evaluation of shareholder activism in the United States, *Journal of Applied Corporate Finance*, 19, 55–73.

Glaeser, E. L., 2008, *Cities, Agglomeration and Spatial Equilibrium*, Oxford University Press, Oxford.

Glaeser, E. L., and G. A. M. Ponzetto, 2013, Shrouded costs of government: The political economy of state and local public pensions, NBER Working Paper 18976.

Glaeser, E. L., and B. A. Ward, 2009, The causes and consequences of land use regulation: Evidence from greater Boston, *Journal of Urban Economics*, 65, 265–278.

Glascock, J. L., C. Lu, and R. W. So, 2002, REIT returns and inflation: Perverse or reverse causality effects? *Journal of Real Estate Finance and Economics*, 24, 301–317.

Glassman, D. A., and L. A. Riddick, 2001, What causes home asset bias and how should it be measured? *Journal of Empirical Finance*, 8, 35–54.

Glosten, L. R., and R. Jagannathan, 1994, A contingent claim approach to performance evaluation, *Journal of Empirical Finance*, 1, 133–160.

Glosten, L. R., R. Jagannathan, and D. E. Runkle, 1993, On the relation between the expected value and the volatility of the nominal excess return on stocks, *Journal of Finance*, 48, 1779–1801.

Glosten, L., and P. Milgrom, 1985, Bid, ask, and transaction prices in a specialist market with heterogeneously informed traders, *Journal of Financial Economics*, 14, 71–100.

Goetzmann, W. N., 1992, The accuracy of real estate indices: Repeat sales estimators, *Journal of Real Estate Finance and Economics*, 51, 5–54.

Goetzmann, W. N., 1993, Accounting for taste: Art and financial markets over three centuries, *American Economic Review*, 83, 1370–1376.

Goetzmann, W. N., J. Griswold, and W.-F. Tseng, 2010, Educational endowments in crises, *Journal of Portfolio Management*, 36, 112–123.

Goetzmann, W. N., J. E. Ingersoll, Jr., and S. A. Ross, 2003, High-water marks and hedge fund management contracts, *Journal of Finance*, 58, 1685–1718.

Goetzmann, W. N., and S. Oster, 2012, Competition among endowments, NBER Working Paper 18173.

Goetzmann, W. N., and N. Peles, 1997, Cognitive dissonance and mutual fund investors, *Journal of Financial Research*, 20, 145–158.

Goetzmann, W. N., and E. Valaitis, 2006, Simulating real estate in the investment portfolio: Model uncertainty and inflation hedging, working paper, Yale University, New Haven, Conn.

Goetzmann, W., J. Ingersoll, M. Spiegel, and I. Welch, 2007, Portfolio performance manipulation and manipulation-proof performance measures, *Review of Financial Studies*, 1503–1546.

Goetzmann, W. N., and P. Jorion, 1993, Testing the predictive power of dividend yields, *Journal of Finance*, 48, 663–679.

Gold, J., 2005, Accounting/actuarial bias enables equity investment by defined benefit pension plans, *North American Actuarial Journal*, 9, 1–21.

Goltz, F., and C. H. Campani, 2011, A review of corporate bond indices: Construction principles, return heterogeneity, and fluctuations in risk exposures, working paper, EDHEC-Risk.

Gomes, F., L. Kotlikoff, and L. M. Viceira, 2008, Optimal life-cycle investing with flexible labor supply: A welfare analysis of life-cycle funds, *American Economic Review: Papers & Proceedings*, 98, 297–303.

Gomes, F., and A. Michaelides, 2005, Optimal life-cycle asset allocation: Understanding the empirical evidence, *Journal of Finance*, 60, 869–904.

Gompers, P. A., 1996, Grandstanding in the venture capital industry, *Journal of Financial Economics*, 42, 133–156.

Gompers, P. A., J. L. Ishii, and A. Metrick, 2003, Corporate governance and equity prices, *Quarterly Journal of Economics*, 118, 107–155.

Gompers, P. A., and J. Lerner, 2000, Money chasing deals? The impact of fund inflows on private equity valuation, *Journal of Financial Economics*, 55, 281–325.

Gompers, P. A., and A. Metrick, 2001, Institutional investors and equity prices, *Quarterly Journal of Economics*, 116, 229–259.

Gong, G., and A. Webb, 2010, Evaluating the advanced life deferred annuity: An annuity people might actually buy, *Insurance: Mathematics and Economics*, 46, 210–221.

Goodfriend, M., 1999, The role of a regional bank in a system of central banks, *Carnegie Rochester Conference Series on Public Policy*, 51, 51–71.

Goodfriend, M., 2000, Overcoming the zero bound on interest rate policy, *Journal of Money, Credit and Banking*, 32, 1007–1035.

Goodman, J., and D. N. Ostrov, 2010, Balancing small transaction costs with loss of optimal allocation in dynamic stock trading strategies. *SIAM Journal of Applied Mathematics*, 70, 1977–1998.

Gordon, M. J., 1963, Optimal investment and financing policy, *Journal of Finance*, 18, 264–272.

Gordon, J. N., 2007, The rise of independent directors in the United States, 1950–2005: Of shareholder value and stock market prices, *Stanford Law Review*, 59, 1465–1568.

Gorovyy, S., 2012, Hedge fund compensation, working paper, Columbia University.

Gorton, G. B., 2010, *Slapped in the Face by the Invisible Hand: The Panic of 2007*, Oxford University Press, Oxford.

Gorton, G. B., and G. Ordonez, 2013, The supply and demand for safe assets, NBER Working Paper 18732.

Gorton, G. B., and K. G. Rouwenhorst, 2006a, Facts and fantasies about commodity futures, *Financial Analysts Journal*, 62, 47–68.

Gourinchas, P.-O., and J. A. Parker, 2002, Consumption over the life cycle, *Econometrica*, 70, 47–89.

Gourinchas, P.-O., and H. Rey, 2007, International financial adjustment, *Journal of Political Economy*, 115, 665–703.

Goyenko, R., A. Subrahmanyam, and A. Ukhov, 2011, The term structure of bond market liquidity and its implications for expected bond returns, *Journal of Financial and Quantitative Analysis*, 46, 111–139.

Grable, J., and R. H. Lytton, 1999, Financial risk tolerance revisited: The development of a risk assessment instrument, *Financial Services Review*, 8, 163–181.

Graff, R. A., 2001, Economic analysis suggests that REIT investment characteristics are not as advertised, *Journal of Real Estate Portfolio Management*, 7, 99–124.

Graff, R. A., and M. S. Young, 1996, Real estate return correlations: Real-world limitations on relationships inferred from NCREIF data, *Journal of Real Estate Finance and Economics*, 13, 121–142.

Graham, B., and D. Dodd, 1934, *Security Analysis*, McGraw-Hill, New York.

Graham, J. R., and C. Harvey, 2001, The theory and practice of corporate finance: Evidence from the field, *Journal of Financial Economics*, 60, 187–243.

Graham, J. R., and A. Kumar, 2006, Do dividend clienteles exist? Evidence on dividend preferences of retail investors, *Journal of Finance*, 65, 1305–1336.

Green, R. C., 1993, A simple model of the taxable and tax-exempt yield curves, *Review of Financial Studies*, 6, 233–264.

Green, R. C., and B. Hollifield, 1992, When will mean-variance efficient portfolios be well diversified? *Journal of Finance*, 47, 1785–1809.

Green, R. C., and B. Hollifield, and N. Schürhoff, 2007, Dealer intermediation and price behavior in the aftermarket for new bond issues, *Journal of Financial Economics*, 86, 643–682.

Greenwood, R., and D. Vayanos, 2010, Bond supply and excess bond returns, working paper, LSE.

Greenwood, R., L. Viceira, A. Ang, M. Eysenbach, and W. Jacques, 2010, Report on the risk anomaly, Martingale Asset Management.

Gregoriou, G. N., 2002, Hedge fund survival lifetimes, *Journal of Asset Management*, 3, 237–252.

Grinblatt, M., and M. Keloharju, 2000, The investment behavior and performance of various investor-types: A study of Finland's unique data set, *Journal of Financial Economics*, 55, 43–67.

Grinblatt, M., M. Keloharju, and J. Linnainmaa, 2011, IQ and stock market participation, *Journal of Finance*, 66, 2121–2164.

Grinblatt, M., and S. Titman, 1989, Mutual fund performance: An analysis of quarterly portfolio holdings, *Journal of Business*, 62, 393–416.

Grinold, R.C., 1989, The fundamental law of active management, *Journal of Portfolio Management*, 15, 30–37.

Grinold, R.C., and R. N. Kahn, 1999, *Active Portfolio Management: A Quantitative Approach for Producing Superior Returns and Controlling Risk*, McGraw-Hill, New York.

Grossman, S. J., and J. E. Stiglitz, 1980, On the impossibility of efficient markets, *American Economic Review*, 70, 393–498.

Gruber, M. J., 1996, Another puzzle: The growth in actively managed mutual funds, *Journal of Finance*, 52, 783–810.

Guasoni, P., G. Huberman, and Z. Wang, 2011, Performance maximization of actively managed funds, *Journal of Financial Economics*, 101, 574–595.

Guedj, I., and J. Huang, 2009, Are ETFs replacing index mutual funds? SSRN working paper.

Guidolin, M., and F. Rinaldi, 2010, Ambiguity in asset pricing and portfolio choice: A review of the literature, 2010, Federal Reserve Bank of St Louis Working Paper 2010–028A.

Guiso, L., T. Jappelli, and D. Terlizzese, 1996, Income risk, borrowing constraints, and portfolio choice, *American Economic Review*, 86, 158–172.

Guiso, L., P. Sapienza, and L. Zingales, 2008, Trusting the stock market, *Journal of Finance*, 63, 2557–2600.

Gul, F., 1991, A theory of disappointment aversion, *Econometrica*, 59, 667–686.

Guo, H., and R. F. Whitelaw, 2006, Uncovering the risk-return relation in the stock market, *Journal of Finance*, 61, 1433–1463.

Gürkaynak, R., B. Sack, and E. Swanson, 2005, The excess sensitivity of long-term interest rates: Evidence and implications for macroeconomic models, *American Economic Review*, 95, 425–436.

Gürkaynak, R., B. Sack, and J. H. Wright, 2010, The TIPS yield curve and inflation compensation, *American Economic Journal: Macroeconomics*, 2, 70–92.

Guvenen, F., S. Ozkan, and J. Song, 2012, The nature of countercyclical income risk, NBER Working Paper 18035.

Gyourko, J., and D. Keim, 1992, What does the stock market tell us about real estate returns? *Journal of the American Real Estate and Urban Economics Association*, 20, 457–485.

Gyourko, J., and P. Linneman, 1988, Owner-occupied homes, income-producing properties, and REITs as inflation hedges: empirical findings, *Journal of Real Estate Finance and Economics*, 1, 347–372.

Gyourko, J., C. Mayer, and T. Sinai, 2012, Superstar cities, working paper, Wharton.

H

Hall, R. E., 1978, Stochastic implications of the life cycle-permanent income hypothesis: Theory and evidence, *Journal of Political Economy*, 86, 687–712.

Hallerbach, W. G., 2011, On the expected performance of market timing strategies, SSRN working paper.

Hamilton, J. D., 1989, A new approach to the economic analysis of nonstationary time series and the business cycle, *Econometrica*, 57, 357–384.

Hamilton, J. D., 2013, Off-balance-sheet federal liabilities, NBER Working Paper 19253.

Hamilton, J. D., and J. C. Wu, 2012, The effectiveness of alternative monetary policy tools in a zero lower bound environment, *Journal of Money, Credit and Banking*, 44, 3–46.

Han, B., and A. Kumar, 2013, Speculative retail trading and asset prices, *Journal of Financial and Quantitative Analysis*, 48, 377–404.

Han, Y., and D. Lesmond, 2011, Liquidity biases and the pricing of cross-sectional idiosyncratic volatility, *Review of Financial Studies*, 24, 1590–1629.

Hansen, L. P., and R. Jagannathan, 1991, Implications of security market data for models of dynamic economies, *Journal of Political Economy*, 99, 225–262.

Hansen, L. P., and R. Jagannathan, 1997, Assessing specification errors in stochastic discount models, *Journal of Finance*, 52, 557–590.

Hansen, L. P., and R. Hodrick, 1980, Forward exchange rates as optimal predictors of future spot rates: An econometric analysis, *Journal of Political Economy*, 88, 829–853.

Hansen, L. P., and T. J. Sargent, 2008, *Robustness*, Princeton University Press, Princeton, N.J.

Hansen, L. P., and K. J. Singleton, 1983, Stochastic consumption, risk aversion, and the temporal behavior of asset returns, *Journal of Political Economy*, 9, 249–265.

Hansmann, H., 1990, Why do universities have endowments, *Journal of Legal Studies*, 19, 3–42.

Harris, L., and E. Gurel, 1986, Price and volume effects associated with changes in the S&P 500 list: New evidence for the existence of price pressures, *Journal of Finance*, 41, 815–829.

Harris, R. S., T. Jenkinson, and S. N. Kaplan, 2012, Private equity performance: What do we know? NBER Working Paper 17874.

Harris, R. S., T. Jenkinson, and R. Stucke, 2012, Are too many private equity funds top quartile? *Journal of Applied Corporate Finance*, 24, 77–89.

Harrison, J. M., and D. M. Kreps, 1979, Martingales and arbitrage in multiperiod securities markets, *Journal of Economic Theory*, 20, 381–408.

Hartzell, D., and A. Mengden, 1986, Real estate investment trusts: Are they stocks or real estate? *Salomon Brothers Real Estate Research*, August 27.

Harvey, C. R., 1998, The real term structure and consumption growth, *Journal of Financial Economics*, 22, 305–333.

Harvey, C. R., 2004, Country risk components, the cost of capital, and returns in emerging markets, in Wilkin, S., ed., *Country and Political Risk: Practical Insights for Global Finance*, Risk Books, London, pp. 71–102.

Harvey, C. R., Y. Liu, and H. Zhu, 2013, . . . and the cross-section of expected returns, working paper, Duke University.

Harvey, C. R., and A. Siddique, 2000, Conditional skewness in asset pricing tests, *Journal of Finance*, 55, 1263–1295.

Hasanhodzic, J., and A. W. Lo, 2007, Can hedge fund returns be replicated? The linear case, *Journal of Investment Management*, 5, 5–45.

Hasbrouck, J., 2007, *Empirical Market Microstructure: The Institutions, Economics and Econometrics of Securities Trading*, Oxford University Press, Oxford.

Haugen, R. A., N. L. Baker, 1991, The efficient market inefficiency of capitalization-weighted stock portfolios, *Journal of Portfolio Management*, 17, 35–40.

Haugen, R. A., and A. J. Heins, 1975, Risk and the rate of return on financial assets: Some old wine in new bottles, *Journal of Financial and Quantitative Analysis*, 10, 775–784.

He, Z., and W. Xiong, 2011, Delegated asset management and investment mandates, working paper, Princeton University, Princeton, N.J.

Heaton, J., and D. Lucas, 1997, Market frictions, savings behavior, and portfolio choice, *Macroeconomic Dynamics*, 1, 76–101.

Heaton, J., and D. Lucas, 2000, Portfolio choice and asset prices: The importance of entrepreneurial risk, *Journal of Finance*, 55, 1163–1198.

Heckman, J., 1979, Sample selection bias as a specification error, *Econometrica*, 47, 153–162.

Heffetz, O., and R. H. Frank, 2011, Preferences for status: Evidence and economic implications, in Benhabib, J., M. O. Jackson, and A. Bisin, eds., *Handbook of Social Economics*, vol 1A, Elsevier, Boston, pp. 69–91.

Heller, R. H., 1966, Optimal international reserves, *Economic Journal*, 76, 296–311.

Hempel, G. H. H., 1971, *The Postwar Quality of State and Local Debt*, National Bureau of Economic Research.

Henkel, S. J., J. S. Martin, and F. Nardari, 2011, Time-varying short-horizon predictability, *Journal of Financial Economics*, 99, 560–580.

Henriksson, R., D. and R. C. Merton, 1981, On market timing and evaluating performance II: Statistical procedures for evaluating forecasting skills, *Journal of Business*, 54, 513–533.

Hensel, C. R., D. D. Ezra, and J. H. Ilkiw 1991, The importance of the asset allocation decision, *Financial Analysts Journal*, 47, 65–72.

Hermalin, B., and M. S. Weisbach, 1991, The effects of board composition and direct incentives on firm performance, *Financial Management*, 20, 101–112.

Hermalin, B., and M. S. Weisbach, 2003, Board of directors as an endogenously determined institution: A survey of the economic literature, *Federal Reserve Bank of New York Economic Policy Review*, 9, 7–26.

Hertwig, R., G. Barron, E. U. Weber, and I. Erev, 2004, Decision from experience and the effect of rare events in risky choice, *Psychological Science*, 15, 534–539.

Heston, S. L., 1993, A closed-form solution for options with stochastic volatility with applications to bond and currency options, *Review of Financial Studies*, 6, 327–343.

Hicks, J. R., 1939, *Value and Capital: An Inquiry into Some Fundamental Principles of Economic Theory*, Claredon Press, Oxford.

Hochberg, Y., A. Ljungqvist, and A. Vissing-Jørgensen, 2010, Information hold-up and performance persistence in venture capital, working paper, Northwestern University.

Hochberg, Y., and J. D. Rauh, 2013, Local overweighting and underperformance: Evidence from limited partner private equity investments, *Review of Financial Studies*, 26, 403–451.

Hodder, J. E., and J. C. Jackwerth, 2007, Incentive contracts and hedge fund management, *Journal of Financial and Quantitative Analysis*, 42, 811–826.

Hodrick, R., 1992, Dividend yields and expected stock returns: Alternative procedures for inference and measurement, *Review of Financial Studies*, 5, 357–386.

Holmstrom, B., and P. Milgrom, 1991, Multitask principal–agent analyses: Incentive contracts, asset ownership, and job design, *Journal of Law, Economics, and Organizations*, 7, 24–52.

Holmstrom, B., and J. Tirole, 1998, Private and public supply of liquidity, *Journal of Political Economy*, 106, 1–40.

Hong, H., and M. Kacperczyk, 2009, The price of sin: The effects of social norms on markets, *Journal of Financial Economics*, 93, 15–36.

Hong, H., J. D. Kubik, and J. A. Scheinkman, 2012, Financial constraints on corporate goodness, working paper, Princeton University.

Hong, H., J. D. Kubik, and J. Stein, 2004, Social interaction and stock market participation, *Journal of Finance*, 59, 137–163.

Hong, H., and D. Sraer, 2012, Speculative betas, working paper, Princeton University.

Hong, H., and M. Yogo, 2012, What does futures market interest tell us about the macroeconomy and asset prices? *Journal of Financial Economics*, 105, 473–490.

Hortaçsu, A., and C. Syverson, 2004, Product differentiation, search costs, and competition in the mutual fund industry: A case study of S&P 500 index funds, *Quarterly Journal of Economics*, 119, 403–456.

Hotelling, H., 1931, The economics of exhaustible resources, *Journal of Political Economy*, 39, 137–175.

Hou, K., and R. K. Loh, 2012, Have we solved the idiosyncratic volatility puzzle?, working paper, Ohio State University.

Hu, Y-W., 2010, Management of China's foreign exchange reserves: A case study on the State Administration of Foreign Exchange (SAFE), Economic Papers 421, Economic and Financial Affairs Directorate-General, European Commission.

Hu, X., J. Pan, and J. Wang, 2012, Noise as information for illiquidity, working paper, MIT.

Huang, J., 2008, Taxable and tax-deferred investing: A tax-arbitrage approach, *Review of Financial Studies*, 21, 2173–2207.

Huang, J.-Z., and M. Huang, 2012, How much of the corporate-treasury yield spread is due to credit risk? *Review of Asset Pricing Studies*, 2, 153–202.

Huang, H., and S. Hudson-Wilson, 2007, Private commercial real estate equity returns and inflation, *Journal of Portfolio Management*, 33, 63–73.

Hubbard, R. G., M. F. Koehn, S. I. Ornstein, M. Van Audenrode, and J. Royer, 2010, *The Mutual Fund Industry*, Columbia University Press, New York.

Hubbard, R. G., J. Skinner, and S. P. Zeldes, 1995, Precautionary saving and social insurance, *Journal of Political Economy*, 103, 360–399.

Huberman, G., 2001, Familiarity breeds investment, *Review of Financial Studies*, 14, 659–680.

Huberman, G., 2010, Is the price of money managers too low? *Rivista Bancaria–Minerva Bancaria*, 1, 7–37.

Humphrey, T. M., 1974, The concept of indexation in the history of economic thought, *Federal Reserve Bank of Richmond Economic Review*, 60, November/December, 3–16.

Hurd, M., 1989, Mortality risk and bequest, *Econometrica*, 57, 779–813.

I

Ibbotson, R. G., and P. D. Kaplan, 2000, Does asset allocation policy explain 40, 90, or 100 percent of performance?, *Financial Analysts Journal*, 56, 26–33.

Ibbotson, R. G., and P. Chen, 2006, The A, B, Cs of hedge funds: Alphas, betas, and costs, working paper, Yale University.

Idzorek, T. M., and M. Kowara, 2013, Factor-based asset allocation vs. asset-class-based asset allocation, *Financial Analysts Journal*, 69, 19–29.

Ilmanen, A., 2011, *Expected Returns: An Investor's Guide to Harvesting Market Rewards*, Wiley, Chichester, U.K.

Ilmanen, A., 2012, Do financial markets reward buying or selling insurance and lottery tickets? *Financial Analysts Journal*, 68, 26–36.

Inkmann, J., P. Lopes, and A. Michaelides, 2010, How deep is the annuity participation puzzle? *Review of Financial Studies*, 24, 279–319.

Ippolito, R. A., 1992. Consumer reaction to measures of poor quality: evidence from the mutual fund industry, *Journal of Law and Economics*, 35, 45–70.

Israel, R., and T. J. Moskowitz, 2011, How tax efficient are equity styles? working paper, University of Chicago, Chicago.

Israel, R., and T. J. Moskowitz, 2013, The role of shorting, firm size, and time on market anomalies, *Journal of Financial Economics*, 108, 275–301.

Iyengar, S., 2010, *The Art of Choosing*, Twelve, New York.

J

Jacobs, H., S. Müller, and M. Weber, 2010, How should investors private diversify? An empirical evaluation of alternative allocation policies to construct a world market portfolio, SSRN working paper.

Jacoby, G., and I. Shiller, 2008, Duration and pricing of TIPS, *Journal of Fixed Income*, 18, 71–85.

Jagannathan, R., K. Kubota, and H. Takehara, 1998, Relationship between labor income risk and average return: Empirical evidence from the Japanese stock market, *Journal of Business*, 71, 319–347.

Jagannathan, R., and T. Ma, 2003, Risk reduction in large portfolios: Why imposing the wrong constraint helps, *Journal of Finance*, 58, 1651–1683.

Jagannathan, R., A. Malakhov, and D. Novikov, 2010, Do hot hands persist among hedge fund managers? An empirical evaluation, *Journal of Finance*, 65, 217–255.

Jagannathan, R., and Z. Wang, 1996, The conditional CAPM and the cross-section of expected returns, *Journal of Finance*, 51, 3–53.

Jacquier, E., A. Kane, and A. J. Marcus, 2003, Geometric or arithmetic mean: A reconsideration, *Financial Analysts Journal*, 59, 46–53.

Jain, P. C., and J. S. Wu, 2000, Truth in mutual fund advertising; Evidence on future performance and fund flows, *Journal of Finance*, 55, 937–958.

James, W., and C. Stein, 1961, Estimation with quadratic loss, in *Proceedings of the Fourth Berkeley Symposium on Mathematics and Statistics*, University of California Press, Berkeley, pp. 361–379.

Jarrell, G. A., and F. C. Dorkey, 1993, University of Rochester's Endowment Fund Review, working paper, University of Rochester.

Jeanne, O., and R. Rancière, 2006, The optimal level of international reserves for emerging market countries: formulas and applications, IMF Working Paper 06/229.

Jegadeesh, N., R. Kräussl, and J. Pollet, 2009, Risk and expected returns of private equity investments: Evidence based on market prices, working paper, Emory University.

Jegadeesh, N., and S. Titman, 1993, Returns to buying winners and selling losers: implications for stock market efficiency, *Journal of Finance*, 48, 65–91.

Jegadeesh, N., and S. Titman, 2001, Profitability of momentum strategies: An evaluation of alternative explanations, *Journal of Finance*, 56, 699–720.

Jensen, M. C., 1968, The performance of mutual funds in the period 1945–1964, *Journal of Finance*, 23, 389–416.

Jensen, M. C., 2007, The economic case for private equity, Harvard NOM Research Paper 07–02.

Jensen, M. C., and K. J. Murphy, 1990, Performance pay and top management incentives, *Journal of Political Economy*, 98, 225–265.

Jerison, M., 1984, Social welfare and the unrepresentative representative consumer, working paper, SUNY Albany.

Jermann, U. J., 1988, Asset pricing in production economies, *Journal of Monetary Economics*, 41, 257–275.

Jiang, G. J., D. Xu, and T. Yao, 2009, The information content of idiosyncratic volatility, *Journal of Financial and Quantitative Analysis*, 44, 1–28.

Johannes, M., A. Korteweg, and N. Polson, 2011, Sequential learning, predictive regressions, and optimal portfolio returns, working paper, Columbia University.

Johnson, E. D., 2009, The fiduciary duty in mutual fund excessive fee cases: Ripe for reexamination, *Duke Law Journal*, 59, 145–181.

Johnson, W. B., R. P. Magee, N. J. Nagarajan, and H. A. Newman, 1985, An analysis of the stock price reaction to sudden executive deaths, *Journal of Accounting and Economics*, 7, 151–174.

Jones, C. S., 2001, Extracting factors from heteroskedastic asset returns, *Journal of Financial Economics*, 62, 293–325.

Jorion, P., and W. N. Goetzmann, 1999, Global stock markets in the twentieth century, *Journal of Finance*, 54, 953–980.

Jorion, P., and C. Schwarz, 2013, The delisting bias in hedge fund databases, working paper, UC Irvine.

Jostova, G., S. Nikolova, A. Philipov, and C. W. Stahel, 2013, Momentum in corporate bond returns, *Review of Financial Studies*, 26, 1649–1693.

Jotikasthira, P. A., A. Le, and C. T. Lundblad, 2010, Why do term structures in different countries comove? Working paper, UNC.

Jun, D., and B. Malkiel 2008, New paradigms in stock market investing, *European Financial Management*, 14, 118–126.

Jurek, J. W., and E. Stafford, 2012, The cost of capital for alternative investments, working paper, Princeton.

K

Kacperczyk, M. T., C. Sialm, and L. Zheng, 2005, On industry concentration of actively managed equity mutual funds, *Journal of Finance*, 60, 1983–2011.

Kacperczyk, M. T., C. Sialm, and L. Zheng, 2008, Unobserved actions of mutual funds, *Review of Financial Studies*, 21, 2379–2416.

Kahneman, D., 2011, *Thinking Fast and Slow*, Farrar, Straus and Giroux, New York.

Kahneman, D., and A. Tversky, 1979, Prospect theory: An analysis of decision under risk, *Econometrica*, 47, 263–292.

Kaltenbrunner, G., and L. A. Lochstoer, 2010, Long-run risk through consumption smoothing, *Review of Financial Studies*, 23, 3190–3224.

Kapadia, N., and X. Pu, 2012, Limited arbitrage between equity and credit markets, *Journal of Financial Economics*, 106, 542–564.

Kaplan, H. R., 1987, Lottery winners: The myth and reality, *Journal of Gambling Behavior*, 3, 168–178.

Kaplan, S. N., and J. Lerner, 2010, It ain't broke: The past, present, and future of venture capital, *Journal of Applied Corporate Finance*, 22, 36–47.

Kaplan, S. N., and A. Schoar, 2005, Private equity performance: Returns, persistence, and capital flows, *Journal of Finance*, 60, 1791–1823.

Kaplan, S. N., and P. Strömberg, 2009, Leveraged buyouts and private equity, *Journal of Economic Perspectives*, 23, 121–46.

Karabulut, Y., 2010, Financial advice: An improvement for the worse? working paper, Goethe University Frankfurt.

Karabulut, Y., 2011, Can Facebook predict stock market activity? working paper, Goethe University Frankfurt.

Karnosky, D. S., and B. D. Singer, 1994, Global Asset Management and Performance Attribution, Research Foundation of the Institute of Chartered Financial Analysts.

Karolyi, G. A., 2002, Did the Asian financial crisis scare foreign investors out of Japan? *Pacific Basin Finance Journal*, 10, 411–442.

Karolyi, G. A., and R. M. Stulz, 2003, Are financial assets priced locally or globally? in Constantinides, G. M., M. Harris, and R. M. Stulz, eds., *Handbook of the Economics of Finance*, Elsevier, Boston, pp. 975–1020.

Kat, H. M., and H. P. Palaro, 2005, Who needs hedge funds? A copula-based approach to hedge fund return replication, working paper, City University London.

Kaya, H., W. Lee, and Y. Wan, 2011, Risk budgeting with asset class and risk class, June, Neuberger Berman.

Keim, D. B., 1999, An analysis of mutual fund design: The case of investing in small-cap stocks, *Journal of Financial Economics*, 51, 173–194.

Kelly, J. L., 1956, A new interpretation of information rate, *Bell System Technical Journal*, 35, 917–926.

Kempf, A., and P. Osthoff, 2007, The effect of socially responsible investing on portfolio performance, *European Financial Management*, 13, 908–922.

Kennickell, A. B., 2011, Tossed and turned: Wealth dynamics of U.S. Households 2007–2009, working paper, Federal Reserve Board.

Keynes, J. M. 1923, Some aspects of commodity markets, *Manchester Guardian Commercial*, 13, 784–786.

Keynes, J. M., 1936, *The General Theory of Employment, Interest and Money*, Palgrave Macmillan.

Khandani, A., and A. W. Lo, 2007, What happened to the quants in August 2007? *Journal of Investment Management*, 5, 5–54.

Kimball, M. S., 1990, Precautionary savings in the small and in the large, *Econometrica*, 58, 53–73.

Kimball, M. S., C. R. Sahm, and M. D. Shapiro, 2008, Imputing risk tolerance from survey responses, *Journal of the American Statistical Association*, 103, 1028–1038.

Kimball, M. S., M. D. Shapiro, T. Shumway, and J. Zhang, 2011, Portfolio rebalancing in general equilibrium, working paper, University of Michigan.

Kirby, C., and B. Ostdiek, 2012, It's all in the timing: Simple active portfolio strategies that outperform naïve diversification, *Journal of Financial and Quantitative Analysis*, 47, 437–467.

Kirman, A. P., 1992, Whom or what does the representative individual represent? *Journal of Economic Perspectives*, 6, 117–136.

Klein, P., 2001, The capital gain lock-in effect and long-horizon return reversal, *Journal of Financial Economics*, 59, 33–62.

Kleymenova, A., E. Talmor, and F. P. Vasvari, 2012, Liquidity in the secondaries private equity market, working paper, London Business School.

Knight, F. H., 1921, *Risk, Uncertainty and Profit*, Houghton Mifflin, Boston.

Koijen, R., T. Moskowitz, L. Pedersen, and E. Vrugt, 2012, Carry, working paper, University of Chicago.

Koo, H. K., 1998, Consumption and portfolio selection with labor income: A continuous-time approach, *Mathematical Finance*, 8, 49–65.

Konchitchki, Y., 2011, Inflation and nominal financial reporting: Implications for performance and stock prices, *Accounting Review*, 86, 1045–1085.

Kopczuk, W., and J. Slemrod, 2003, Dying to save taxes: Evidence from estate-tax returns on the death elasticity, *Review of Economics and Statistics*, 85, 256–265.

Kopczuk, W., E. Saez, and J. Song, 2010, Earnings inequality and mobility in the United States: Evidence from Social Security data since 1937, *Quarterly Journal of Economics*, 125, 91–128.

Korteweg, A., and M. Sorensen, 2010, Risk and return characteristics of venture capital-backed entrepreneurial companies, *Review of Financial Studies*, 23, 3738–3772.

Korteweg, A., R. Kräussl, and P. Verwijmeren, 2012, Does it pay to invest in art? A selection-corrected returns perspective, working paper, Stanford University.

Kose, M. A., C. Otrok, and H. Whiteman, 2003, International business cycles: World, region, and country-specific factors, *American Economic Review*, 93, 1216–1239.

Kosowski, R., N. Y. Naik, and M. Teo, 2007, Do hedge funds deliver alpha? A Bayesian and bootstrap analysis, *Journal of Financial Economics*, 84, 229–264.

Kosowski, R., 2011, Do mutual funds perform when it matters most to investors? U.S. mutual fund performance and risk in recessions and expansions, *Quarterly Journal of Finance*, 1, 607–664.

Kotlikoff, L. J., 1988, Intergenerational transfers and savings, *Journal of Economic Perspectives*, 2, 41–58.

Kourtis, A., G. Dotsis, and R. N. Markellos, 2009, Parameter uncertainty in portfolio selection: Shrinking the inverse covariance matrix, SSRN working paper.

Kouwenberg, R., 2003, Do hedge funds add value to a passive portfolio? Correcting for non-normal returns and disappearing funds, *Journal of Asset Management*, 3, 361–382.

Krasker, W. S., 1979, The rate of return to storing wines, *Journal of Political Economy*, 87, 1363–1367.

Krasker, W. S., 1980, The peso problem in testing the efficiency of the forward exchange markets, *Journal of Monetary Economics*, 6, 269–276.

Kritzman, M. P., 2000, *Puzzles of Finance: Six Practical Problems and Their Remarkable Solutions*, Wiley, Hoboken, N.J.

Krishnamurthy, A., 2002, The new bond/old bond spread, *Journal of Financial Economics*, 66, 463–506.

Krishnamurthy, A., and A. Vissing-Jørgensen, 2012, The aggregate demand for Treasury debt, *Journal of Political Economy*, 120, 233–267.

Kuhnen, C. M., 2009, Business networks, corporate governance, and contracting in the mutual fund industry, *Journal of Finance*, 64, 2185–2220.

Kydland, F., and E. C. Prescott, 1977, Rules rather than discretion: The inconsistency of optimal plans, *Journal of Political Economy*, 85, 473–492.

Kydland, F. E., and E. C. Prescott, 1982, Time to build and aggregate fluctuations, *Econometrica*, 50, 1345–1370.

Kyle, A., 1985, Continuous auctions and insider trading, *Econometrica*, 53, 1315–1336.

L

Laakso, E., 2010, Stock market participation and household characteristics in Europe, Masters thesis, Alto University.

Labonte, M., 2012, Changing the Federal Reserve's mandate: An economic analysis, Congressional Research Service Report 7-5700.

Lack, S., 2012, *The Hedge Fund Mirage: The Illusion of Big Money and Why It's Too Good to Be True*, Wiley, Hoboken, N.J.

Laibson, D., 1997, Golden eggs and hyperbolic discounting, *Quarterly Journal of Economics*, 112, 443–477.

Laibson, D., A. Repetto, and J. Tobacman, 2012, Estimating discount functions with consumption choices over the lifecycle, forthcoming *American Economic Review*.

Lakonishok, J., A. Shleifer, R. W. Vishny, 1992, The structure and performance of the money management industry, *Brookings Papers on Economic Activity: Microeconomics*, 229–229.

Lakonishok, J., A. Shleifer, R. W. Vishny, 1994, Contrarian investment, extrapolation, and risk, *Journal of Finance*, 49, 1541–1578.

Lan, Y., N. Wang, and J. Yang, 2012, The economics of hedge funds: Alpha, fees, leverage, and valuation, working paper, Columbia University.

Lang, L. H. P., and R. M. Stulz, 1994, Tobin's q, corporate diversification, and firm performance, *Journal of Political Economy*, 102, 1248–1280.

Larsson, B., 2011, Becoming a winner but staying the same: Identities and consumption of lottery winners, *American Journal of Economics and Sociology*, 70, 187–209.

Latané, H., 1959, Criteria for choice among risky ventures, *Journal of Political Economy*, 67, 144–155.

Ledoit, O., and M. Wolf, 2003, Improved estimation of the covariance matrix of stock returns with an application to portfolio selection, *Journal of Empirical Finance*, 10, 603–621.

Lee, J., 2004, Insurance value of international reserves: An option pricing approach, IMF Working Paper WP/04/175.

Lee, C. M. C., A. Shleifer, and R. H. Thaler, 1991, Investor sentiment and the closed-end fund puzzle, *Journal of Finance*, 46, 76–110.

Lee, P. M., and S. Wahal, 2004, Grandstanding, certification, and the underpricing of venture capital backed IPOs, *Journal of Financial Economics*, 73, 375–407.

Leippold, M., and P. Rohner, 2009, Equilibrium implications of delegated asset management under benchmarking, working paper, University of Zurich.

Leland, H., 1994, Corporate debt value, bond covenants, and optimal capital structure, *Journal of Finance*, 49, 1213–1252.

Lerner, J., A. Schoar, and J. Wang, 2008, Secrets of the academy: The drivers of university endowment success, *Journal of Economic Perspectives*, 22, 207–222.

Lerner, J., A. Schoar, and W. Wongsonwai, 2007, Smart institutions, foolish choices? The limited partner performance puzzle, *Journal of Finance*, 62, 731–764.

Lettau, M., and S. Van Nieuwerburgh, 2008, Reconciling the return predictability evidence, *Review of Financial Studies*, 21, 1607–1652.

Lettau, M., and S. Ludvigson, 2001a, Consumption, aggregate wealth, and expected stock returns, *Journal of Finance*, 56, 815–849.

Lettau, M., and S. Ludvigson, 2001b, Resurrection the (C)CAPM: a cross-sectional test when risk premia are time varying, *Journal of Political Economy*, 109, 1238–1287.

Levit, D., 2012, Expertise, structure, and reputation of corporate boards, working paper, Wharton.

Levy. H., 1994, Absolute and relative risk aversion: An experimental study, *Journal of Risk and Uncertainty*, 8, 289–307.

Levy, H., and H. M. Markowitz, 1979, Approximating expected utility by a function of mean and variance, *American Economic Review*, 69, 308–317.

Levy, R. A., 1967, Relative strength as a criterion for investment selection, *Journal of Finance*, 22, 595–610.

Lewellen, J., and S. Nagel, 2006, The conditional CAPM does not explain asset pricing anomalies, *Journal of Financial Economics*, 82, 2464–2491.

Lewis, K. K., 2011, Global asset pricing, *Annual Review of Financial Economics*, 3, 435–466.

Lewis, M., 1989, *Liar's Poker*, Norton, New York.

Lhabitant, F. S., 2000, Derivatives in portfolio management: Why beating the market is easy, *Derivatives Quarterly*, 6, 39–43.

Li, G., 2009, Information sharing and stock market participation: Evidence from extended families, working paper, Federal Reserve Board.

Li, C. W., and A. Tiwari, 2009, Incentive contracts in delegated management, *Review of Financial Studies*, 22, 4681–4714.

Liang, B., 2000, Hedge funds: The living and the dead, *Journal of Financial and Quantitative Analysis*, 35, 309–326.

Liang, B., 2001, Hedge fund performance: 1990–1999, *Financial Analysts Journal*, 57, 11–18.

Lin, H., J. Wang, and C. Wu, 2011, Liquidity risk and expected corporate bond returns, *Journal of Financial Economics*, 99, 628–650.

Lin, Z., and K. D. Vandell, 2012, Illiquidity and pricing biases in the real estate market, working paper, Fannie Mae.

Ling, D. C., and A. Naranjo, 1997, Economic risk factors and commercial real estate returns, *Journal of Real Estate Finance and Economics*, 14, 283–307.

Ling, D. C., and A. Naranjo, 1999, The integration of commercial real estate markets and stock markets, *Real Estate Economics*, 27, 483–515.

Linnainmaa, J. T., 2013, Reverse survivorship bias, *Journal of Finance*, 68, 789–813.

Lintner, J., 1965, The valuation of risk assets and the selection of risky investments in stock portfolios and capital budgets, *Review of Economics and Statistics*, 47, 13–37.

Lintner, J., 1975, Inflation and security returns, *Journal of Finance*, 30, 259–280.

Litterman, R., and J. Scheinkman, 1991, Common factors affecting bond returns, *Journal of Fixed Income*, 1, 54–61.

Litvak, K., 2009, Venture capital partnership agreements: Understanding compensation agreements, *University of Chicago Law Review*, 76, 161–218.

Liu, J., 2007, Portfolio selection in stochastic environments, *Review of Financial Studies*, 20, 1–39.

Liu, P., and W. Qian, 2012, Does (and what) illiquidity matter for real estate prices? Measure and evidence, SSRN working paper.

Ljungqvist, A., and M. Richardson, 2003, The cash flow, return and risk characteristics of private equity, working paper, NYU.

Lo, A. W., 2001, Risk management for hedge funds: Introduction and overview, *Financial Analysts Journal*, 57, 16–33.

Lo, A. W., 2002, The statistics of Sharpe ratios, *Financial Analysts Journal*, 58, 36–52.

Lo, A. W., 2008, Where do alphas come from? A measure of the value of active management, *Journal of Investment Management*, 6, 1–29.

Lo, A. W., 2010, *Hedge Funds: An Analytical Perspective*, Princeton University Press, Princeton, N.J.

Lo, A., and J. Hasanhodzic, 2007, Can hedge fund returns be replicated? The linear case, *Journal of Investment Management*, 5, 5–45.

Lo, A. W., H. Mamaysky, and J. Wang, 2004, Asset prices and trading volume under fixed transactions costs, *Journal of Political Economy*, 112, 1054–1090.

Logue, A. C., 2007, *Hedge Funds for Dummies*, Wiley.

Longstaff, F. A., 2009, Portfolio claustrophobia: Asset pricing in markets with illiquid assets, *American Economic Review*, 99, 1119–1144.

Longstaff, F. A., 2011, Municipal debt and marginal tax rates: is there a tax premium in asset prices? *Journal of Finance*, 66, 721–751.

Longstaff, F. A., S. Mithal, and E. Neis, 2005, Corporate yield spreads: Default risk or liquidity? New evidence from the credit default swap market, *Journal of Finance*, 60, 2213–2253.

Lou, D., 2012, A flow-based explanation for return predictability, *Review of Financial Studies*, 25, 3457–3489.

Loughran, T., 1997, Book-to-market across firm size, exchange, and seasonality: Is there an effect? *Journal of Financial and Quantitative Analysis*, 32, 249–268.

Love, D. A., P. A. Smith, and D. W. Wilcox, 2011, The effect of regulation non optimal corporate pension risk, *Journal of Financial Economics*, 101, 18–35.

Low, B., and S. Zhang, 2005, The volatility risk premium embedded in currency options, *Journal of Financial and Quantitative Analysis*, 40, 803–832.

Lucas, R. E., 1978, Asset prices in an exchange economy, *Econometrica*, 46, 1429–1445.

Lucas, R. E., and N. Stokey, 1983, Optimal fiscal and monetary policy in an economy without capital, *Journal of Monetary Economics*, 12, 55–93.

Luenberger, D. G., 1997, *Investment Science*, Oxford University Press, New York.

Lusardi, A., P.-C. Michaud, and O. S. Mitchell, 2013, Optimal financial knowledge and wealth inequality, NBER Working Paper 18669.

Lusardi, A., and O. S. Mitchell, 2006, Financial literacy and planning: Implications for retirement wellbeing, working paper, Dartmouth. Lustig, H. N., and S. Van Nieuwerburgh, 2005, Housing collateral, consumption insurance and risk premia: an empirical perspective, *Journal of Finance*, 60, 1167–1219.

Lustig, H., and S. Van Nieuwerburgh, S., 2008, The returns on human capital: Good news on Wall Street is bad news on Main Street, *Review of Financial Studies*, 21, 2097–2137.

Lustig, H. N., N. Roussanov, and A. Verdelhan, 2011, Common risk factors in currency markets, *Review of Financial Studies*, 24, 3732–3777.

Luytens, C., 2008, The Private Equity Secondaries Market: A Complete Guide to Its Structure, Operation, and Performance, PEI Media.

Lynch, A. W., and S. Tan, 2011, Labor income dynamics at business cycle frequencies: Implications for portfolio choice, *Journal of Financial Economics*, 101, 333–359.

M

Madhavan, A., 2012, Exchange-traded funds, market structure, and the flash crash, *Financial Analysts Journal*, 68, 20–35.

MacLean, L. C., E. O. Thorp, and W. T. Ziemba, eds., 2011, *The Kelly Capital Growth Investment Criterion: Theory and Practice*, World Scientific Publishing, Singapore.

MacKenzie, D., 2006, *An Engine, Not a Camera: How Financial Models Shape Markets*, MIT Press, Cambridge, Mass.

Maenhout, P. J., 2004, Robust portfolio rules and asset pricing, *Review of Financial Studies*, 17, 951–983.

Maillard, S., T. Roncalli, and J. Teiletche, 2010, On the properties of equally-weighted risk contributions portfolios, *Journal of Portfolio Management*, 36, 60–70.

Malkiel, B. G., 1977, The valuation of closed-end investment-company shares, *Journal of Finance*, 32, 847–58.

Malkiel, B. G., 1990, *A Random Walk Down Wall Street*, Norton, New York.

Malkiel, B. G., 1995, Returns from investing in equity mutual funds 1971 to 1991, *Journal of Finance*, 50, 549–572.

Malkiel, B. G., and A. Saha, 2005, Hedge funds: Risk and return, *Financial Analysts Journal*, 61, 80–88.

Malmendier, U., and S. Nagel, 2011, Depression babies: Do macroeconomic experiences affect risk taking? *Quarterly Journal of Economics*, 126, 373–416.

Makarov, I., and G. Plantin, 2012, Rewarding trading skills without inducing gambling, working paper, London Business School.

Mankiw, N. G., and S. P. Zeldes, 1991, The consumption of stockholders and non-stockholders, *Journal of Financial Economics*, 29, 97–112.

Manski, C., 1988, Ordinal utility models of decision making under uncertainty, *Theory and Decision*, 25, 79–104.

Marcato, G., and T. Key, 2005, Direct investment in real estate, *Journal of Portfolio Management*, 31, 55–69.

Marekwica, M., 2012, Optimal tax-timing and asset allocation when tax rebates on capital losses are limited, *Journal of Banking and Finance*, 36, 2048–2063.

Markowitz, H., 1952, Portfolio selection, *Journal of Finance*, 7, 77–91.

Marks, H., 2011, *The Most Important Thing: Uncommon Sense for Thoughtful Investors*, Columbia University Press, New York.

Marshall, S., K. M. McGarry, and J. S. Skinner, 2010, The risk of out-of-pocket health care expenditure at end of life, NBER working paper 16170.

Martin, I., 2012, On the valuation of long-dated assets, *Journal of Political Economy*, 120, 346–358.

Martinelli, L., 2008, Toward the design of better equity benchmarks, *Journal of Portoflio Management*, 34, 1–8.

Masset, P., and J.-P. Weisskopf, 2010, Raise your glass: Wine investment and the financial crisis, SSRN working paper.

Maurer, R., O. S. Mitchell, R. Rogalla, and V. Kartashov, 2013, Lifecycle portfolio choice with systematic longevity risk and variable investment-linked deferred annuities, forthcoming *Journal of Risk and Insurance*.

Mayers, D., 1973, Nonmarketable assets and the determination of capital asset prices in the absence of a riskless asset, *Journal of Business*, 46, 258–267.

Maymin, P. Z., and G. S. Fisher, 2011, Preventing emotional investing: An added value of an investment advisor, *Journal of Wealth Management*, 13, 34–43.

McDonald, R. I., and D. Siegel, 1985, Investment and the valuation of firms when there is an option to shut down, *International Economic Review*, 26, 331–349.

Meghir, C., and L. Pistaferri, 2011, Earnings, consumption, and lifecycle choices, in Ashenfelter, O., and D. Card, eds, *Handbook of Labor Economics*, vol. 4B, Elsevier, Boston, pp. 774–854,

Mehra, R., 2006, The equity premium puzzle: A review, *Foundations and Trends in Finance*, 2, 1–81.

Mehra, R., and E. C. Prescott, 1985, The equity premium: A puzzle, *Journal of Monetary Economics*, 15, 145–61.

Mehra, R., and E. C. Prescott, 1988, The equity risk premium: A solution, *Journal of Monetary Economics*, 22, 133–136.

Mei, J., and A. Lee, 1994, Is there a real estate factor premium? *Journal of Real Estate Finance and Economics*, 9, 113–126.

Mei, J., and M. Moses, 2002, Art as an investment and the underperformance of masterpieces, *American Economic Review*, 92, 1656–1668.

Meltzer, A. H., 2003, *A History of the Federal Reserve*. Vol. 1, *1913–1951*, University of Chicago Press, Chicago.

Meltzer, A. H., 2005, Origins of the great inflation, *Federal Reserve Bank of St. Louis Review*, 87, March/April, 145–175.

Menkhoff, L., L. Sarno, M. Schmeling, and A. Schrimpf, 2012a, Carry trades and global foreign exchange volatility, *Journal of Finance*, 57, 681–718.

Menkhoff, L., L. Sarno, M. Schmeling, and A. Schrimpf, 2012b, Currency momentum strategies, *Journal of Financial Econmoics*, 106, 660–684.

Merton, R. C., 1969, Lifetime portfolio selection under uncertainty: The continuous-time case, *Review of Economics and Statistics*, 51, 247–257.

Merton, R. C., 1971, Optimal consumption and portfolio rules in a continuous-time model, *Journal of Economic Theory*, 3, 373–413.

Merton, R. C., 1973, An intertemporal capital asset pricing model, *Econometrica*, 41, 867–887.

Merton, R. C., 1974, On the pricing of corporate debt: The risk structure of interest rates, *Journal of Finance*, 29, 449–470.

Merton, R. C., 1980, On estimating the expected return of the market: An exploratory investigation, *Journal of Financial Economics*, 8, 323–361.

Merton, R. C., 1987. A simple model of capital market equilibrium with incomplete information. *Journal of Finance*, 42, 483–510.

Merton, R. C., 1990, Optimal investment strategies for university endowment funds, in *Continuous-Time Finance*, Blackwell, Malden, Mass.

Merton, R. C., 1993, Optimal investment strategies for university endowment funds, in Clotfelter, C. T., and M. Rothschild, eds., *Studies of Supply and Demand in Higher Education*, University of Chicago Press, Chicago, pp. 211–242.

Merton, R. C., and P.A. Samuelson, 1973, Fallacy of the log-normal approximation to optimal portfolio decision-making over many periods, *Journal of Financial Economics*, 1, 67–94.

Messmore, T., 1995, Variance drain, *Journal of Portfolio Management*, 21, 104–111.

Metrick, A., 1995, A natural experiment in Jeopardy, *American Economic Review*, 85, 240–253.

Metrick, A., and A. Yasuda, 2010, The economics of private equity funds, *Review of Financial Studies*, 23, 2303–2341.

Michaelides, A., 2002, Buffer stock saving and habit formation, working paper, London School of Economics.

Michaud, R. O., 1989, The Markowitz optimization enigma: Is "optimized" optimal? *Financial Analysts Journal*, 45, 31–42.

Milevsky, M. A. 2005, Real longevity insurance with a deductible: Introduction to advanced-life delayed annuities (ALDA), *North American Actuarial Journal*, 9, 109–122.

Milevsky, M. A., 2009, *Are You a Stock or a Bond? Create Your Own Pension Plan for a Secure Financial Future*, Pearson Education, Upper Saddle River, N.J.

Milevsky, M. A., 2012, *The 7 Most Important Equations for Your Retirement: The Fascinating People and Ideas behind Planning Your Retirement Income*, Wiley, Hoboken, N.J.

Milevsky, M. A., and H. Huang, 2011, Spending retirement on Planet Vulcan: The impact of longevity risk aversion on optimal withdrawal rates, *Financial Analysts Journal*, 67, 45–58.

Milevsky, M. A., and S. E. Posner, 2001, The Titanic option: Valuation of the guaranteed minimum death benefit in variable annuities and mutual funds, *Journal of Risk and Insurance*, 68, 93–128.

Miller, E. M., 1977, Risk, uncertainty and divergence of opinion, *Journal of Finance*, 32, 1151–68.

Miller, M. H., 1977, Debt and taxes, *Journal of Finance*, 32, 261–275.

Miller, M. H., and F. Modigliani, 1958, The cost of capital, corporate finance and the theory of investment, *American Economic Review*, 48, 261–297.

Miller, M. H., and F. Modigliani, 1961, Dividend policy, growth and the valuation of shares, *Journal of Business*, 34, 411–433.

Miller, M. H., and M. S. Scholes, 1978, Dividends and taxes, *Journal of Financial Economics*, 6, 333–364.

Mills, E. S., 1967, An aggregative model of resource allocation in a metropolitan area, *American Economic Review*, 57, 197–210.

Missiakoulis, S., V. Dimitrios, and N. Etriotis, 2010, Arithmetic mean: A bellwether for unbiased forecasting of portfolio performance, *Managerial Finance*, 36, 958–968.

Mitchell, M., and T. Pulvino, 2001, Characteristics of risk and return in risk arbitrage, *Journal of Finance*, 56, 2135–2175.

Mitchell, O. S., 2012, Public pension pressures, in Conti-Brown, P., ed., *When States Go Broke: The Origins, Context, and Solutions for the American States in Fiscal Crisis*, Cambridge University Press, Cambridge, pp. 57–76.

Mitchell, O. S., J. M. Poterba, M. J. Warshawsky, and J. R. Brown, 1999, New evidence on the money's worth of individual annuities, *American Economic Review*, 89, 1299–1318.

Mitton, T., and K. Vorkink, 2007, Equilibrium underdiversification and the preference for skewness, *Review of Financial Studies*, 20, 1255–1288.

Modigliani, F., 1986, Life cycle, individual thrift, and the wealth of nations, *American Economic Review*, 76, 297–313.

Modigliani, F., and R. H. Brumberg, 1954, Utility analysis and the consumption function: An interpretation of cross-section data, in Kurihara, K. K., ed., *Post-Keynesian Economics*, Rutgers University Press, New Brunswick, N.J., pp. 388–436.

Modigliani, F., and R. H. Brumberg, 1980, Utility analysis and aggregate consumption functions: An attempt at integration, in Abel, A., ed., *The Collected Papers of Franco Modigliani*. Vol. 2, *The Life Cycle Hypothesis of Saving*, MIT Press, Cambridge, Mass., pp. 128–197.

Modigliani, F. and R. Cohn, 1979, Inflation, rational valuation, and the market, *Financial Analysts Journal*, 35, 24–44.

Modigliani, F., and R. Sutch, 1966a, Debt management and the term structure of interest rates: An empirical analysis of recent experience, *Journal of Political Economy*, 75, 569–589.

Modigliani, F., and R. Sutch, 1966b, Innovations in interest rate policy, *American Economic Review*, 56, 178–197.

Morley, J. D., and Q. Curtis, 2010, Taking exit rights seriously: Why governance and fee litigation don't work in mutual funds, *Yale Law Journal*, 120, 84–142.

Morse, A., and S. Shive, 2011, Patriotism in your portfolio, *Journal of Financial Markets*, 14, 411–440.

Moskowitz, T. J., 2000, Discussion: Mutual fund performance: An empirical decomposition into stock-picking talent, style, transaction costs, and expenses, *Journal of Finance*, 55, 1655–1703.

Moskowitz, T., and K. Daniel, 2012, Momentum crashes, working paper, Columbia Business School.

Mossin, J., 1966, Wages, profits and the dynamics of growth, *Quarterly Journal of Economics*, 80, 376–399.

Mouakhar, T., and M. Roberge, 2010, The optimal approach to futures contract roll in commodity portfolios, *Journal of Alternative Investments*, 12, 51–60.

Mozes, H. A., and J. Orchard, 2012, The relation between hedge fund size and risk, *Journal of Derivatives and Hedge Funds*, 18, 85–109.

Mueller, P., A. Vedolin, and Y. Yen, 2012, Bond variance risk premia, working paper, London School of Economics.

Mullinathan, S., M. Noth and A. Schoar, 2012, The market for financial advice: An audit study, NBER Working Paper 17929.

Munneke, H., and B. Slade, 2000, An empirical study of sample-selection bias in indices of commercial real estate, *Journal of Real Estate Finance and Economics*, 21, 45–64.

Munnell, A. H., and M. Soto, 2007, Why are companies freezing their pensions? Working Paper 2007-22, Center for Retirement Research at Boston College.

Munnell, A., M. Soto, A. Webb, F. Golub-Sass, and D. Muldoon, 2008, Health care costs drive up the national retirement risk index, Issue in Brief 8-3, Center for Retirement Research at Boston College.

Musto, D., G. Nini, and K. Schwarz, 2011, Notes on bonds: Liquidity at all costs in the great recession, working paper, Wharton.

Muth, R., 1969, *Cities and Housing*, University of Chicago Press, Chicago.

N

Nagel, S., 2012, Evaporating liquidity, *Review of Financial Studies*, 25, 2005–2039.

Nakajima, M., and I. A. Telyukova, 2012, Home equity in retirement, working paper, UC San Diego.

Nakamura, E., and J. Steinsson, 2008, Five facts about prices: A reevaluation of menu cost models, *Quarterly Journal of Economics*, 123, 1415–1464.

Negishi, T., 1960, Welfare economics and existence of an equilibrium for a competitive economy, *Metroeconomica*, 12, 92–97.

Nelson, E., 2005, The great inflation of the seventies: What really happened? *B. E. Journal of Macroeconomics: Advances in Macroeconomics*, 5, 1–48.

Newey, W., and K. West, 1987, A simple, positive semi-definite, heteroskedasticity and autocorrelation consistent covariance matrix, *Econometrica*, 55, 703–708.

Novy-Marx, R., and J. D. Rauh, 2009, The liabilities and risks of state-sponsored pension plans, *Journal of Economic Perspectives*, 23, 191–210.

Novy-Marx, R., and J. D. Rauh, 2011a, The crisis in local government pensions in the U.S., in Fuchita, Y., R. J. Litan, and R. E. Herring, eds., *Growing Old: Paying for Retirement and Institutional Money Management after the Financial Crisis*, Brookings Institution Press, Washington, D.C., pp. 47–76.

Novy-Marx, R., and J. D. Rauh, 2011b, Public pension promises: How big are they and what are they worth? *Journal of Finance*, 66, 1207–1245.

O

Obstfeld, M., 2011, International liquidity: The fiscal dimension, *Monetary and Economic Studies*, 29, 38–48.

Odean, T., 1999, Do investors trade too much? *American Economic Review*, 89, 1279–1298.

O'Hara, M., 1995, *Market Microstructure Theory*, Blackwell, Malden, Mass.

Oikarinen, E., M. Hoesli, and C. Serrano, 2011, The long-run dynamics between direct and securitized real estate, *Journal of Real Estate Research*, 33, 73–103.

Okunev, J., and D. White, 2003, Hedge fund risk factors and value at risk of credit trading strategies, SSRN working paper.

Olen, H., 2012, *Pound Foolish: Exposing the Dark Side of the Personal Finance Industry*, Penguin Books, New York.

Ott, D. J., and A. H. Meltzer, 1963, *Federal Tax Treatment of State and Local Securities*, Brookings Institution, Washington, D.C.

Ou-Yang, H., 2003, Optimal contracts in a continuous-time delegated portfolio management problem, *Review of Financial Studies*, 16, 173–208.

P

Pagel, M., 2012, Expectations-based reference-dependent life-cycle consumption, working paper, UC Berkeley.

Pagliari, J., K. Scherer, and R. Monopoli, 2005, Public versus private real estate equities: A more refined, long-term comparison, *Real Estate Economics*, 33, 147–187.

Palacios-Huerta, I., 2003, Risk properties of human capital returns, *American Economic Review*, 93, 293–316.

Palmiter, A. R., and A. E. Taha, 2009, Star creation: The incubation of mutual funds, *Vanderbilt Law Review*, 62, 1483–2009.

Palumbo, M., 1999, Uncertain medical expenses and precautionary saving near the end of the life cycle, *Review of Economic Studies*, 66, 395–421.

Pan, J., 2002, The jump-risk premia implicit in options: Evidence from an integrated time-series study, *Journal of Financial Economics*, 63, 3–50.

Panageas, S., and M. M. Westerfield, 2009, High-water marks: High risk appetites? Convex compensation, long horizons, and portfolio choice, *Journal of Finance*, 64, 1–36.

Pang, G., and M. J. Warshawsky, 2010, Optimizing the equity-bond-annuity portfolio in retirement: The impact of uncertain health expenses, *Insurance: Mathematics and Economics*, 46, 198–209.

Paravisini, D., V. Rappoport, and E. Ravina, 2010, Risk aversion and wealth: Evidence from person-to-person lending portfolios, working paper, Columbia University.

Parker, J. A., and C. Julliard, 2005, Consumption risk and the cross section of expected returns, *Journal of Political Economy*, 113, 185–222.

Pástor, Ľ., and R. F. Stambaugh, 2003, Liquidity risk and expected stock returns, *Journal of Political Economy*, 111, 642–685.

Pástor, Ľ., and R. F. Stambaugh, 2009, Predictive systems: Living with imperfect predictors, *Journal of Finance*, 64, 1583–1628.

Pástor, Ľ., and R. F. Stambaugh, 2012a, Are stocks really less volatile in the long run? *Journal of Finance*, 68, 431–477.

Pástor, Ľ., and R. F. Stambaugh, 2012b, On the size of the active management industry, *Journal of Political Economy*, 120, 740–871.

Pástor, Ľ., and P. Veronesi, 2012, Political uncertainty and risk premia, working paper, University of Chicago.

Patton, A., 2009, Are "market neutral" hedge funds really market neutral? *Review of Financial Studies*, 22, 2495–2530.

Patton, A., T. Ramadorai, and M. Streatfield, 2013, Change you can believe in? Hedge fund data revisions, working paper, Duke University.

Paulsen, D. J., M. L. Platt, S. A. Huettel, and E. M. Brannon, 2012, From risk-seeking to risk-averse: The development of economic risk preference from childhood to adulthood, *Frontiers in Psychology*, 3, 1–6.

Pauly, M., 1990, The rational nonpurchase of long-term care insurance, *Journal of Political Economy*, 98, 153–168.

Paye, B. S., 2012, 'Deja vol': Predictive regressions for aggregate stock market volatility using macroeconomic variables, *Journal of Financial Economics*, 106, 527–546.

Paye, B. S., and A. Timmermann, 2006, Instability of return prediction models, *Journal of Empirical Finance*, 13, 274–315.

Peijnenburg, K., 2011, Life-cycle asset allocation with ambiguity aversion and learning, working paper, Bocconi University.

Pennacchi, G. G., and C. M. Lewis, 1994, The value of Pension Benefit Guaranty Corporation insurance, *Journal of Money, Credit and Banking*, 26, 735–753.

Pérez-González, F., 2006, Inherited control and firm performance, *American Economic Review*, 96, 1559–1588.

Perold, A. F., 2007, Fundamentally flawed indexing, *Financial Analysts Journal*, 63, 31–37.

Perold, A. F., and W. F. Sharpe, 1988, Dynamic strategies for asset allocation, *Financial Analysts Journal*, 44, 16–27.

Petkova, R., and L. Zhang, 2005, Is value riskier than growth? *Journal of Financial Economics*, 78, 187–202.

Pettenuzzo, D., A. G. Timmermann, and R. Valkanov, 2012, Forecasting stock returns under economic constraints, SSRN working paper.

Pflueger, C., and L. M. Viceira, 2011, An empirical decomposition of risk and liquidity in nominal and inflation-indexed government bonds, Harvard Business School Working Paper 11-094.

Phalippou, L., 2008, The hazards of using IRR to measure performance: The case of private equity, *Journal of Performance Measurement*, 12, 55–66.

Phalippou, L., 2009, Beware of venturing into private equity, *Journal of Economic Perspectives*, 23, 147–166.

Phalippou, L., 2010, Private equity funds performance: risk and selection, in Athanassiou, P., ed., *Research Handbook on Hedge Funds, Private Equity and Alternative Investments*, Edward Elgar, Northampton, Mass., pp. 113–139.

Phalippou, L., 2011, An evaluation of the potential for GPFG to achieve above average returns from investments in private equity and recommendations regarding benchmarking, Report to the Norwegian Ministry of Finance.

Phalippou, L., 2013, Performance of buyout funds revisited? forthcoming *Review of Finance*.

Phalippou, L., and O. Gottschlag, 2009, The performance of private equity funds, *Review of Financial Studies*, 22, 1747–1776.

Phalippou, L., and M. Zollo, 2005, The performance of private equity funds, working paper, Oxford University.

Phillips, A. W., 1958, The Relationship between unemployment and the rate of change of money wages in the United Kingdom 1861–1957, *Economica*, 25, 283–299.

Piazzesi, M., 2010, Affine Term Structure Models, in Aït-Sahalia, Y., and L. P. Hansen, eds., *Handbook of Financial Econometrics*. Vol. 1, Elsevier, pp. 691–766.

Piazzesi, M., and M. Schneider, 2006, Equilibrium Yield Curves, in Acemoglu, D., K. Rogoff, and M. Woodford, eds., *NBER Macroeconomics Annual*, MIT Press, Cambridge, Mass., pp. 389–442.

Pindyck, R. S., 1980, Uncertainty and exhaustible resource markets, *Journal of Political Economy*, 88, 1203–1225.

Pliska, S. R., and K. Suzuki, 2004, Optimal tracking for asset allocation with fixed and proportional transactions costs, *Quantitative Finance*, 4, 233–243.

Pollet, J., and M. Wilson, 2008, How does size affect mutual fund behavior? *Journal of Finance*, 63, 2941–2969.

Polkovnichenko, V., 2007, Life-cycle portfolio choice with additive habit formation preferences and uninsurable labor income risk, *Review of Financial Studies*, 20, 83–124.

Pool, V. K., C. Sialm, and I. Stefanescu, 2013, It pays to set the menu: Mutual fund investment options in 401(k) plans, NBER Working Paper 18764.

Poterba, J. M., 2003, Employer stock and 401(k) plans, *American Economic Review*, 93, 398–404.

Poterba, J. M., and A. A. Samwick, 2002, Taxation and household portfolio composition: U.S. evidence from the 1980s and 1990s, *Journal of Public Economics*, 87, 5–38.

Poterba, J., S. Venti, and D. Wise, 2011a, The composition and drawdown of wealth in retirement, *Journal of Economic Perspectives*, 25, 95–118.

Poterba, J., S. Venti, and D. Wise, 2011b, The drawdown of personal retirement assets, NBER Working Paper 16675.

Pratt, S. P., 1971, Relationship between variability of past returns and levels of future returns for common stocks, 1926–1960, in Fredrickson, E. B., ed., *Frontiers of Investment Analysis*, Intext Textbook, Scranton, Pa.

Pratt, J. W., 1964, Risk aversion in the small and in the large, *Econometrica*, 32, 122–136.

Prokopczuk, M., and C. Wese, 2012, Variance risk premia in commodity markets, SSRN working paper.

Q

Qian, E., 2006, On the financial interpretation of risk contribution: Risk budgets do add up, *Journal of Investment Management*, 4, 1–11.

R

Radin, R. F., and W. B. Stevenson, 2006, Comparing mutual fund governance and corporate governance, *Corporate Governance: An International Review*, 14, 367–376.

Ramadorai, T., 2012, The secondary market for hedge funds and the closed hedge fund premium, *Journal of Finance*, 67, 479–512.

Ramadorai, T., 2013, Capacity constraints, investor information, and hedge fund returns, *Journal of Financial Economics*, 107, 401–416.

Rampini, A., and S. Viswanathan, 2013, Household risk management, working paper, Duke University.

Ramsey, F. P., 1928, A mathematical theory of saving, *Economic Journal*, 38, 543–559.

Ranish, B., 2012, Why do households with risky labor income take greater financial risks? working paper, Harvard University.

Rapach, D. E., and G. Zhou, 2011, Forecasting stock returns, forthcoming *Handbook of Economic Forecasting*.

Rappaport, A., 2011, *Saving Capitalism from Short-Termism: How to Build Long-Term Value and Take Back our Financial Future*, McGraw Hill, New York.

Rauh, J. D., 2006, Investment and financing constraints: Evidence from the funding of corporate pension plans, *Journal of Finance*, 61, 33–71.

Rauh, J. D., I. Stefanescu, and S. P. Zeldes, 2012, Cost shifting and the freezing of corporate pension plans, working paper, Columbia Business School.

Reichling, F., and K. Smetters, 2013, Optimal annuitization with stochastic mortality probabilities, NBER Working Paper 19211.

Reinganum, M. R., 1981, Misspecification of asset pricing: Empirical anomalies based on earnings yields and market values, *Journal of Financial Economics*, 9, 19–46.

Reinhart, C. M., and K. S. Rogoff, 2008, The forgotten history of domestic debt, NBER Working Paper 13946.

Reinhart, C. M., and K. S. Rogoff, 2011, *This Time Is Different: Eight Centuries of Financial Folly*, Princeton University Press, Princeton, N.J.

Reinhart, C. M., and M. B. Sbrancia, 2011, The liquidation of government debt, NBER Working Paper 16893.

Rhodes-Kropf, M., D. T. Robinson, and S. Viswanathan, 2005, Valuation waves and merger activity: The empirical evidence, *Journal of Financial Economics*, 77, 561–603.

Riedel, F., 2009, Optimal consumption choice with intolerance for declining standard of living, *Journal of Mathematical Economics*, 45, 449–464.

Ricciuti, R., 2003, Assessing Ricardian equivalence, *Journal of Economic Surveys*, 17, 55–78.

Rietz, T. A., 1988, The equity risk premium: A solution, *Journal of Monetary Economics*, 22, 117–131.

Ritter, J., and I. Welch, 2002, A review of IPO activity, pricing and allocations, *Journal of Finance*, 57, 1795–1828.

Roback, J., 1982, Wages, rents, and the quality of life, *Journal of Political Economy*, 90, 1257–1278.

Robinson, D., and B. Sensoy, 2011a, Private equity in the 21st century: Liquidity, cash flows, and performance from 1984–2010, working paper, Duke University.

Robinson, D., and B. Sensoy, 2011b, Cyclicality, performance measurement, and cash flow liquidity in private equity, working paper, Duke University.

Roll, R., 1992, A mean-variance analysis of the tracking error, *Journal of Portfolio Management*, 8, 13–22.

Romer, C. D., and D. H. Romer, 2000, Federal Reserve information and the behavior of interest rates, *American Economic Review*, 90, 429–457.

Rosen, S., 1979, Wage-based indexes of urban quality of life, in Mieszkowski, P., and M. Straszheim, eds., *Current Issues in Urban Economics*, John Hopkins University Press, Baltimore, pp. 74–104.

Rose-Ackerman, S., 1996, Altruism, nonprofits, and economic theory, *Journal of Economic Literature*, 34, 701–728.

Rosen, H. S. and S. Wu, 2004, Portfolio choice and health status, *Journal of Financial Economics*, 72, 457–484.

Rosenthal, R., 1979, The "file drawer problem" and tolerance for null results, *Psychological Bulletin*, 86, 638–641.

Ross, S. A., 1976, The arbitrage theory of capital asset pricing, *Journal of Economic Theory*, 13, 341–360.

Ross, S. A., 2005, *Neoclassical Finance*, Princeton University Press, Princeton, N.J.

Ross, S. A., 2011, The recovery theorem, NBER working paper 17323.

Ross, S., and R. Zisler, 1991, Risk and return in real estate, *Journal of Real Estate Finance and Economics*, 4, 175–190.

Rostek, M., 2010, Quantile maximization in decision theory, *Review of Economic Studies*, 77, 339–371.

Routledge, B. R, and S. E. Zin, 2010, Generalized disappointment aversion and asset prices, *Journal of Finance*, 65, 1303–1332.

Roy, A. D., 1952, Safety first and the holding of assets, *Econometrica*, 20, 431–49.

Rozanov, A., 2005, Who holds the wealth of nations? *Central Banking Journal*, 15, 52–57.

Rubinstein, M., 1994, Implied binomial trees, *Journal of Finance*, 49, 771–818.

Rubinstein, M., and H. Leland, 1981, Replicating options with positions in stocks and cash, *Financial Analysts Journal*, 37, 63–72.

Rudebusch, G. D., and E. T. Swanson, 2012, The bond premium in a DSGE model with long-run real and nominal risks, *American Economic Journal: Macroeconomics*, 4, 105–143.

S

Sack, B., and R. Elasser, 2004, Treasury inflation-indexed debt: A review of the U.S. experience, *Federal Reserve Bank of New York Economic Policy Review*, 10, 47–63.

Sadka, R., 2010, Liquidity risk and the cross section of hedge fund returns, *Journal of Financial Economics*, 98, 54–71.

Sagalyn, L. B., 1996, Conflicts of interest in the structure of REITs, *Real Estate Finance*, 9, 34–51.

Sala-i-Martin, X., and A. Subramanian, 2003, Addressing the natural resource curse: an illustration from Nigeria, NBER Working Paper 9804.

Salanie, P., 1997, *The Economics of Contracts: A Primer*, MIT Press, Cambridge, Mass.

Samuelson, P. A., 1958, An exact consumption-loan model of interest with or without the social contrivance of money, *Journal of Political Economy*, 55, 467–482.

Samuelson, P. A., 1969, Lifetime portfolio selection by dynamic stochastic programming, *Review of Economics and Statistics*, 51, 239–246.

Samuelson, P. A., 1971, The "fallacy" of maximizing the geometric mean in long sequences of investing or gambling, *Proceedings of the National Academy of Sciences*, 68, 2493–2496.

Samuelson, P. A., 1979, Why we should not make mean log of wealth big though years to act are long, *Journal of Banking and Finance*, 3, 305–307.

Santos, T., and P. Veronesi, 2006, Labor income and predictable stock returns, *Review of Financial Studies*, 19, 1–44.

Sanzillo, T., 2012, The New York State comptroller's office, in Benjamin, G., *The Oxford Handbook of New York State Government and Politics*, Oxford University Press, New York, pp. 287–356.

Sargent, T. J., 1999, *The Conquest of American Inflation*, Princeton University Press, Princeton, N.J.

Savage, L. J., 1954, *The Foundations of Statistics*, Wiley, Hoboken, N.J.

Scherer, B., 2005, *Liability Hedging and Portfolio Choice*, Risk Books, London.

Scherer, B., 2011, Portfolio choice for oil-based sovereign wealth funds, *Journal of Alternative Investments*, 13, 24–34.

Schieber, S. J., 2012, *The Predictable Surprise: The Unraveling of the U.S. Retirement System*, Oxford University Press, New York.

Schoemaker, P. J. H., 1982, The expected utility model: Its variants, purposes, evidence and limitations, *Journal of Economic Literature*, 20, 529–563.

Scholz, J. K., and A. Seshadri, 2009, What replacement rates should households use? Working Paper 2009–214, Michigan Retirement Research Center, University of Michigan.

Scholz, J. K., A. Seshadri, and S. Khitatrakun, 2006, Are Americans saving 'optimally' for retirement? *Journal of Political Economy*, 116, 607–43.

Schwager, J. D., 1992, *The New Market Wizards: Conversations with America's Top Traders*, Wiley, Hoboken, N.J.

Schwed, F., Jr., 1940, *Where Are the Customers' Yachts?* Simon & Schuster, New York.

Schwert, G. W., 2003, Anomalies and market efficiency, in Constantinides, G.M., M. Harris, and R. M. Stulz, eds., *Handbook of the Economics of Finance*, Elsevier, Boston, pp. 939–974.

Scholes, M. S., M. A. Wolfson, M. Erickson, E. Maydew, and T. Shevlin, 2005, *Taxes and Business Strategy: A Planning Approach*, Pearson Prentice Hall, Upper Saddle River, N.J.

Scott, J. H., 2012, Managing institutional equity, working paper, GM Asset Management.

Scott, J. S., J. G. Watson, and W. Y. Hu, 2011, What makes a better annuity? *Journal of Risk and Insurance*, 78, 213–244.

Seascholes, M. S., 2000, Smart foreign traders in emerging markets, working paper, UC Berkeley.

Sensoy, B. A., Y. Wang, and M. S. Weisbach, 2013, Limited partner performance and the maturing of the private equity industry, NBER Working Paper 18793.

Sharpe, W. F., 1964, Capital asset prices: A theory of market equilibrium under conditions of risk, *Journal of Finance*, 19, 425–442.

Sharpe, W. F., 1966, Mutual fund performance, *Journal of Business*, 39, 119–138.

Sharpe, W. F., 1976, Corporate Pension Funding Policy, *Journal of Financial Economics*, 3, 183–193.

Sharpe, W. F., 1981, Decentralized investment management, *Journal of Finance*, 36, 217–234.

Sharpe, W. F., 1992, Asset allocation: Management style and performance measurement, *Journal of Portfolio Management*, 18, 7–19.

Sharpe, W. F., 2010, Adaptive asset allocation policies, *Financial Analysts Journal*, 66, 45–59.

Sharpe, W. F., and L. G. Tint, 1990, Liabilities—A New Approach, *Journal of Portfolio Management*, 16, 5–10.

Scharfstein, D. S., and J. C. Stein, 1990, Herd behavior and investment, *American Economic Review*, 465–479.

Shefrin, H., and M. Statman, 1985, The disposition to sell winners too early and ride losers too long: Theory and evidence, *Journal of Finance*, 40, 777–790.

Shiller, R. J., 1979, The volatility of long-term interest rates and expectations models of the term structure, *Journal of Political Economy*, 87, 1190–1219.

Shiller, R. J., 1981, Do stock prices move too much to be justified by subsequent changes in dividends? *American Economic Review*, 71, 421–436.

Shiller, R. J., 1993, The invention of inflation-indexed bonds in early America, NBER Working Paper 10183.

Shiller, R. J., 1995, Aggregate income risks and hedging mechanisms, *Quarterly Review of Economics and Finance*, 35, 119–152.

Shiller, R. J., 2000, *Irrational Exuberance*, Princeton University Press, Princeton, N.J.

Shiller, R. J., 2005, The life-cycle personal counts proposal for Social Security: An evaluation, NBER Working Paper 11300.

Shleifer, A., 1986, Do demand curves for stocks slope down? *Journal of Finance*, 41, 579–590.

Shleifer, A., and R. W. Vishny, 1997, The limits of arbitrage, *Journal of Finance*, 52, 35–55.

Shukla, R., and G. van Inwegen, 1995, Do locals perform better than foreigners? An analysis of UK and U.S. mutual fund managers, *Journal of Economics and Business*, 47, 241–254.

Sialm, C., 2009, Tax changes and asset pricing, *American Economic Review*, 99, 1356–1383.

Sidrauski, M., 1967, Rational choice and patterns of growth in a monetary economy, *American Economic Review*, 57, 534–544.

Siegel, J. J., 1994, *Stocks for the Long Run*, McGraw-Hill, New York.

Simon, D., 2010, Examination of long-term bond iShare option selling strategies, *Journal of Futures Markets*, 30, 465–489.

Sinclair, S., and K. Smetters, 2004, Health shocks and the demand for annuities, Congressional Budget Office Technical Paper 2004–09.

Sirri, E., and P. Tufano, 1998, Costly search and mutual fund flows, *Journal of Finance*, 41, 1589–1622.

Skinner, J., 2007, Are you sure you're saving enough for retirement? *Journal of Economic Perspectives*, 21, 59–80.

Smets, F., and R. Wouters, 2007, Shocks and frictions in US business cycles: A Bayesian dynamic stochastic general equilibrium approach, *American Economic Review*, 97, 586–606.

Sodolfsky, R. M., and R. L. Miller, 1969, Risk premium curve for different classes of long-term securities, 1950–1966, *Journal of Finance*, 24, 429–446.

Solow, R. M., 1957, Technological change and the aggregate production function, *Review of Economics and Statistics*, 39, 312–320.

Sorensen, M., N. Wang, and J. Yang, 2012, Valuing private equity, working paper, Columbia University.

Stambaugh, R. F., 1999, Predictive regressions, *Journal of Financial Economics*, 54, 375–421.

Stein, J. C., 1989, Efficient capital markets, inefficient firms: A model of myopic corporate behavior, *Quarterly Journal of Economics*, 104, 655–669.

Stein, J. C., 2002, Information production and capital allocation: Decentralized versus hierarchical firms, *Journal of Finance*, 57, 1891–921.

Stein, J. C., 2005, Why are most funds open-ended? Competition and the limits of arbitrage, *Quarterly Journal of Economics*, 120, 247–72.

Stevens, A. H., D. L. Miller, M. Page, and M. Filipski, 2012, Why do more people die during economic expansions? Center for Retirement Research at Boston College, Working Paper 12–8.

Stock, J. H., and M. W. Watson, 2002, Has the business cycle changed? Evidence and explanations, in Gertler, M., and K. Rogoff, eds., *NBER Macroeconomics Annual*, 17, 159–218.

Storesletten, K., C. I. Telmer, and A. Yaron, 2007, Asset pricing with idiosyncratic risk and overlapping generations, *Review of Economic Dynamics*, 10, 519–548.

Stoughton, N., M., 1993, Moral hazard and the portfolio management problem, *Journal of Finance*, 48, 2009–2028.

Stoughton, N. M., Y. Wu, and J. Zechner, 2011, Intermediated investment management, *Journal of Finance*, 66, 947–980.

Stracca, L., 2006, Delegated portfolio management: A survey of the theoretical literature, *Journal of Economic Perspectives*, 20, 823–848.

Stevenson, B., and J. Wolfers, 2008, Economic growth and subjective well-being: Reassessing the Easterlin paradox, *Brookings Papers on Economic Activity*, Spring, 1–87.

Stulz, R. M., 2007, Hedge funds; Past, present, and future, *Journal of Economic Perspectives*, 21, 175–194.

Sturzenegger, F., and J. Zettelmeyer, 2008, Haircuts: Estimating investor losses in sovereign debt restructurings, 1998–2005, *Journal of International Money and Finance*, 27, 780–805.

Sundaresan, S. M., 1989, Intertemporally dependent preferences and the volatility of consumption and wealth, *Review of Financial Studies*, 2, 73–89.

Swanson, E. T., 2012, Risk aversion and the labor margin in dynamic equilibrium models, *American Economic Review*, 102, 1663–1691.

Swensen, D. F., 2009, *Pioneering Portfolio Management: An Unconventional Approach to Institutional Investment*, Free Press, New York.

T

Taleb, N. N., 2004, *Fooled by Randomness*, Random House, New York.

Tang, H., and X. E. Xu, 2013, Solving the return deviation conundrum of leveraged exchange-traded funds, *Journal of Financial and Quantitative Analysis*, 48, 309–342.

Taylor, A. M., and M. P. Taylor, 2004, The purchasing power parity debate, *Journal of Economic Perspectives*, 18, 135–158.

Taylor, J. B., 1993, Discretion versus policy rules in practice, *Carnegie-Rochester Conference Series on Public Policy*, 39, 195–214.

Taylor, J. B., 1999, An historical analysis of monetary policy rules, in Taylor, J. B., ed., *Monetary Policy Rules*, University of Chicago Press, Chicago, pp. 319–341.

Tepper, I., 1981, Taxation and corporate pension policy, *Journal of Finance*, 1–14.

ter Horst, J. R., T. E. Nijman, and F. A. de Roon, 2004, Evaluating style analysis, *Journal of Empirical Finance*, 11, 29–53.

Thaler, R. H., and S. Benartzi, 2004, Save more tomorrow: Using behavioral economics to increase employee savings, *Journal of Political Economy*, 112, 164–187.

Thaler, R. H., and C. R. Sunstein, 2009, *Nudge: Improving Decisions About Health, Wealth, and Happiness*, Penguin, New York.

Timmermann, A., 2006, Forecast combinations, in Elliott, G., C. W. J. Granger, and A. Timmermann, eds., *Handbook of Economic Forecasting*, vol. 1, Elsevier, Boston, pp. 135–196.

Tkac, P. A., 2004, Mutual funds: Temporary problem or permanent morass, *Federal Reserve Bank of Atlanta Economic Review*, Quarter 4, 1–21.

Tobin, J., 1958, Liquidity preferences as behavior towards risk, *Review of Economic Studies*, 25, 65–86.

Tobin, J., 1969, A general equilibrium approach to monetary theory, *Journal of Money, Credit, and Banking*, 1, 15–29.

Tomz, M., and M. L. J. Wright, 2013, Empirical research on sovereign debt and default, NBER Working Paper 18855.

Treynor, J., 1961, Market value, time, and risk, unpublished manuscript.

Treynor, J., 1965, How to rate management of investment funds, *Harvard Business Review*, 43, January/February, 63–75.

Treynor, J., 1977. The principles of corporate pension finance, *Journal of Finance*, 32, 627–638.

Treynor, J. and K. Mazuy, 1966, Can mutual funds outguess the market? *Harvard Business Review*, 44, 131–136.

Trojani, F., and P. Vanini, 2004, Robustness and ambiguity aversion in general equilibrium, *Review of Finance*, 8, 279–324.

Troyer, T. A., 2000, The 1969 Private Foundation Law: Historical perspective on its origins and underpinnings, *Exemption Organization Tax Review*, 27, 52–65.

Truman, E. M., 2010, *Sovereign Wealth Funds: Threat or Salvation?* Peterson Institute for International Economics.

Tu, J., and G. Zhou, 2011, Markowitz meets Talmud: A combination of sophisticated and naïve diversification strategies, *Journal of Financial Economics*, 99, 204–215.

Tufano, P., and M. Sevick, 1997, Board structure and fee-setting in the U.S. mutual fund industry, *Journal of Financial Economics*, 46, 321–355.

Tversky, A., and D. Kahneman, 1992, Advances in prospect theory: Cumulative representation of uncertainty, *Journal of Risk and Uncertainty*, 5, 297–323.

U

Ulrich, M., 2011, Observable long-run ambiguity and long-run risk, working paper, Columbia University.

V

Valkanov, R., 2003, Long-horizon regressions: Theoretical results and applications, *Journal of Financial Economics*, 68, 201–232.

Vanderbilt, A. T., II, 1989, *Fortune's Children: The Fall of the House of Vanderbilt*, Morrow, New York.

van der Ploeg, F., 2011, Natural resources: curse or blessing? *Journal of Economic Literature*, 49, 366–420.

Van Nieuwerburgh, S., and L. Veldkamp, 2009, Information immobility and the home bias puzzle, *Journal of Finance*, 64, 1187–1215.

Vasicek, O., 1977, An equilibrium characterization of the term structure, *Journal of Financial Economics*, 5, 177–188.

Vayanos, D., 1998, Transactions costs and asset prices: A dynamic equilibrium model, *Review of Financial Studies*, 11, 1–58.

Vayanos, D., and J. L. Vila, 2009, A preferred-habitat model of the term structure of interest rates, working paper, LSE.

Vayanos, D., and J. Wang, 2012, Market liquidity: Theory and empirical evidence, forthcoming Constantinides, G., M. Harris, and R. Stulz, eds., *Handbook of the Economics of Finance*, Elsevier.

Vayanos, D., and P. Woolley, 2013, An institutional theory of momentum and reversal, *Review of Financial Studies*, 26, 1087–1145.

Vasicek, O., 1977, An equilibrium characterization of the term structure, *Journal of Financial Economics*, 5, 177–188.

Veldkamp, L., 2011, *Information Choice in Macroeconomics and Finance*, Princeton University Press, Princeton, N.J.

Venti, S. F., and D. A. Wise, 2002, Aging and housing equity, in Mitchell, O. S., O. B. Hammond, and S. Zeldes, eds., *Innovations in Retirement Financing*, University of Pennsylvania Press, Philadelphia, pp. 254–281.

Viceira, L. M., 2001, Optimal portfolio choice for long-horizon investors with nontradeable labor income, *Journal of Finance*, 56, 433–470.

Viceira, L. M., 2008, Life-cycle funds, in Lusardi, A., ed., *Overcoming the Savings Slump: How to Increase the Effectiveness of Financial Education and Savings Programs*, University of Chicago Press, Chicago, pp. 140–177.

Villalonga, B., 2004, Diversification discount or premium? New evidence from the business information tracking series, *Journal of Finance*, 59, 479–506.

Vissing-Jørgensen, A., 2002, Towards an explanation of household portfolio choice heterogeneity: Nonfinancial income and participation cost structures, working paper, Northwestern University.

Vogel, E. F., 1979, *Japan as Number One: Lessons for America*, Harvard University Press, Cambridge, Mass.

von Neumann, J., and O. Morgenstern, 1944, *Theory of Games and Economic Behavior*, Princeton University Press, Princeton, N.J.

W

Wachter, J., 2006, A consumption-based model of the term structure of interest rates, *Journal of Financial Economics*, 79, 365–399.

Wachter, J., 2010, Asset allocation, *Annual Review of Financial Economics*, 2, 175–206.

Wang, J., 1996, The term structure of interest rates in a pure exchange economy with heterogeneous investors, *Journal of Financial Economics*, 41, 75–110.

Wang, Z., 2005, A shrinkage approach to model uncertainty and asset allocation, *Review of Financial Studies*, 18, 673–705.

Wang, Z., and X. Zhang, 2012, Empirical evaluation of asset pricing models: Arbitrage and pricing errors in contingent claims, *Journal of Empirical Finance*, 19, 65–78.

Warner, J. B., and J. S. Wu, 2011, Why do mutual fund advisory contracts change? Performance, growth, and spillover effects, *Journal of Finance*, 66, 271–306.

Webb, A., and N. Zhivan, 2010, How much is enough? The distribution of lifetime health care costs, Center for Retirement Research at Boston College Working Paper, 2010–1.

Weil, P., 1989, The equity premium and the risk-free rate puzzle, *Journal of Monetary Economics*, 24, 401–421.

Weinstein, M. C., and R. J. Zeckhauser, 1975, The optimal consumption of depletable natural resources, *Quarterly Journal of Economics*, 92, 371–392.

Weise, C. L., 2012, Political pressures on monetary policy during the US Great Inflation, *American Economic Journal: Macroeconomics*, 4, 33–64.

Welch, I., 2008, The consensus estimate for the equity premium by academic financial economists in 2007, working paper.

Welch, I., and A. Goyal, 2008, A comprehensive look at the empirical performance of equity premium prediction, *Review of Financial Studies*, 21, 1455–1508.

Wermers, R., 2000, Mutual fund performance: An empirical decomposition into stock-picking talent, style, transactions costs, and expenses, *Journal of Finance*, 55, 1655–1695.

West, J., 2010, The style roulette and RAFI strategy, working paper, Research Affiliates.

Whitelaw, R. F., 2000, Stock market risk and return: An equilibrium approach. *Review of Financial Studies*, 13, 521–548.

Willenbrock, S., 2011, Diversification return, portfolio rebalancing, and the commodity return puzzle, *Financial Analysts Journal*, 67, 42–49.

Williams, J., 1977, Capital asset prices with heterogeneous beliefs, *Journal of Financial Economics*, 5, 219–239.

Winston, M., S. Winston, P. Appelbaum, and N. Rhoden, 1982, Can a subject consent to a "Ulysses contract"? *Hasting Center Report*, 12, 26–28.

Wolf, A. M., 2011, The problems with payouts: Assessing the proposal for a mandatory distribution requirement for university endowments, *Harvard Journal on Legislation*, 48, 591–622.

Wolff, E. N., 2010, Recent trends in household wealth in the United States: Rising debt and the middle-class squeeze—an update to 2007, Working Paper No. 589, Levy Economics Institute of Bard College.

Wood, J. H., 1983, Do yield curves normally slope up? The term structure of interest rates, 1862–1982, *Federal Reserve Bank of Chicago Economic Perspectives*, 7, 17–23.

Woodford, M., 1990, Public debt as private liquidity, *American Economic Review Papers and Proceedings*, 80, 382–388.

Y

Yaari, M., 1965, Uncertain lifetime, life insurance, and the theory of the consumer, *Review of Economic Studies*, 32, 137–150.

Yan, X. S., 2008, Liquidity, investment style, and the relation between fund size and performance, *Journal of Financial and Quantitative Analysis*, 43, 741–768.

Ye, J., 2008, How variation in signal quality affects performance, *Financial Analysts Journal*, 64, 48–61.

Yogo, M., 2011, Portfolio choice in retirement: Health risk and the demand for annuities, housing and risky assets, SSRN working paper.

Z

Zeldes, S., 1989, Optimal consumption with stochastic income: Deviations from certainty equivalence, *Quarterly Journal of Economics*, 104, 275–298.

Zhang, F., 2010, High-frequency trading, stock volatility, and price discovery, working paper, Yale University.

Zhang, L., 2005, The value premium, *Journal of Finance*, 60, 67–103.

Zheng, L., 1999, Is money smart? A study of mutual fund investors' fund selection ability, *Journal of Finance*, 43, 901–933.

Zhong, Z., 2008, Why does hedge fund alpha decrease over time? Evidence from individual hedge funds, SSRN working paper.

Zhou, G., 2010, How much stock return predictability can we expect from an asset pricing model? *Economics Letters*, 108, 184–186.

Zietzewitz, E., 2006, How widespread was late trading in mutual funds? *American Economic Review Papers and Proceedings*, 96, 284–289.

Zivney, T. L., and R. D. Marcus, 1989, The day the United States defaulted on Treasury bills, *Financial Review*, 24, 475–489.

Zhou, G., 2008, On the fundamental law of active portfolio management: What happens if our estimates are wrong? *Financial Analysts Journal*, 34, 26–33.

Zuckerman, G., 2009, *The Greatest Trade Ever: The Behind-the-Scenes Story of How John Paulson Defied Wall Street and Made Financial History*, Random House, New York.

AUTHOR INDEX

SUBJECT INDEX

Canada Pension Plan, 13, 22–23, 321, 508, 613
Canada Pension Plan Investment Board (CPPIB),
    459–63, 508–10, 514, 618
  Reference Portfolio, 456, 460–63, 510–12
capital allocation line (CAL), 58–59, 91–93, 198
capital asset market pricing model (CAPM), 18, 77,
    85, 98–99, 108–9, 196–202, 204–6, 214,
    225–29, 231, 305, 309, 313–15, 329, 332,
    333, 341–44, 466–67, 589, 621
  capital allocation line (CAL), 58–59, 91–93, 198
  capital market line (CML), 200
  conditional CAPM, 467
  failures of, 207–9. See also factor investing
capital market line (CML), 200
CAPM. See Capital asset market pricing model
    (CAPM)
career concerns, 503
carried interest (carry), private equity contracts,
    610–12
carry (foreign exchange), 234, 458
Carter, Jimmy, 349
cash flow effect
  inflation and returns, 256
  predictability, 257–59, 266
cash flow matching, liability hedging, 142
cash return, commodities, 368–69
catastrophes, equity premium, 246
catching up with the Joneses utility, 27–28, 67–69,
    96, 206
catch-up provisions, private equity contracts, 611
certainty equivalent, 44, 53–54, 65–66, 83,
    93–94, 140, 331, 435, 437–38
Chile, Copper Stabilization Fund, 10
China, bond clientele, 293–94
China Investment Corporation (CIC), 5
Citigroup, 274
Clinton, Bill, 520
closed-end funds, 523–24, 546–47
closed-end fund discount puzzle, 546
CML. See capital market line (CML)
cointegration, 172
COLAs. See cost-of-living adjustments (COLAs)
collateral, safe assets, 478
Columbia University, 26, 230, 233, 559
commenda, 593
commissions, 504, 538, 541–42, 552. See also
    compensation, asset managers
commitment, private equity, 594
commodities, 364–74
  factors in, 365–67
  risk and return, 367–70
  spot, cash, and roll returns, 367–71
Commodity Futures Trading Commission (CFTC),
    365, 548
Commodity Trading Advisers (CTAs), 365
compensation, asset managers
  financial advisors, 503–6
  hedge funds, 583, 585–86
  limiting, 40-Act, 527

mutual funds, 538–43
private equity, 610–14
concavity of utility functions, 42–43
conflicts of interest, minimizing through 40-Act,
    522–23, 525–27. See also agency issues and
    problems
ConocoPhillips, 4
conservatism bias, 238
constant relative risk aversion (CRRA) utility,
    40–41, 43, 50, 61, 64, 66, 116–17, 331
constraints, use of in mean-variance investing,
    81–83, 97
Consumer Price Index (CPI), 347, 350
consumption, 8, 31, 67–68, 350, 360, 406–7,
    437
  as factor, 206, 215–17, 231, 240, 242–47, 249,
    260, 262–63, 467, 622
  over life cycle, 162, 171–72, 177, 179–80, 188
contango, commodities, 369. See also roll return,
    commodities
contemporaneous beta and returns, 337–38
contemporaneous volatility and returns, 334–35,
    337
contracts
  explicit vs. implicit contract, 495
  hedge funds, agency issues, 581–83
  mutual funds, agency issues, 538–43
  optimal, in delegated portfolio management,
    501–3
  private equity, agency issues, 610–19
contribution holiday, 18
convenience yield, commodities, 370
corporate bonds (credit spread) 295–304, 429. See
    also bonds
correlations varying over time, 85–86
cost-of-living adjustments (COLAs), 186, 188
cost push inflation, 348
counter-cyclical
  counter-cyclical strategy is short volatility,
    135–41, 577
  hedge fund leverage, 580
  investing, 123–29, 133–34, 265, 433–34, 473,
    577
  rebalancing, 123, 125–27, 133, 433, 265
  risk premiums, 263–64, 291–92
CPI. See Consumer Price Index (CPI)
CPPIB. See Canada Pension Plan Investment Board
    (CPPIB)
credit risk, 182–83, 397–99, 478. See also
    corporate bonds (credit spread); sovereign
    (risk-free) bonds
credit spread puzzle, 300–3
cross-sectional strategy, 236
Currency Composition of Official Foreign Exchange
    Reserves (COFER), 6, 480–82
curvature, utility function, 40–42, 67, 245. See
    also risk aversion
curvature factor, bonds, 276
customized factor benchmark, 471–72